MENTAL HEALTH IN CHILDREN

VOLUME III

VOLUME III

DIAGNOSTIC, PSYCHIATRIC, BIOLOGIC, THERAPEUTIC AND LANGUAGE STUDIES. LONGITUDINAL, AND PROGRAM STUDIES ETC.

Any opinions, feelings or recommendations expressed in this volume belong to the particular author(s) and do not constitute those of others including the publishers.

Library of Congress Catalog Card No. 74-27252
International Standard Book No. 0-9600290-9-5

This Volume Constitutes Volume III in the Series on

MENTAL HEALTH IN CHILDREN

MENTAL HEALTH IN CHILDREN

EDITED BY

D. V. SIVA SANKAR

VOLUME III

CONTRIBUTING AUTHORS

Harvey R. Alderton, Robert W. Amidon, Lauretta Bender, Laure Branchey, Jean Braun, Marie Brittin, Peter Bruggen, L. A. Buck, Frances Cheek, R. Chuda, J. Clausen, Kevin Connolly, Cynthia Contessa, T. J. Crow, Joseph Currier, Solomon Cytrynbaum, Richard Epstein, Richard K. Eyman, N. Freshley, Arnold J. Friedhoff, Judy L. Genshaft, Phillip B. Goldblatt, Louis A. Gottschalk, Henry G. Hansberg, Ann Harrison, Margaret E. Hertzig, H. E. Himwich, Michael Hirt, Anna Kline, Valerie Klinge, Michael Koch, Herbert Kohn, Ulrich Langenbeck, J. K. Y. Lee, Kathleen Lennox, A. Lidsky, Alexander Lucas, Paul Manowitz, A. Marinow, Frank Menolascino, N. Narasimhachari, Jon Neiditch, Johannes Nielsen, Don A. Olson, Elizabeth V. Phillips, Leonard R. Piggott, David Pipher, Patricia O. Quinn, Judith L. Rapoport, Cintra C. Sander, R. L. Schiefelbusch, E. A. Sersen, L. Shapiro, Ingelise Sillesen, Gerald Silverman, Clyde B. Simson, David L. Snow, Gary L. Tischler, Habib Vaziri, Walter Vom Saal, Harriet Wadeson, Leonard White, Charles D. Windle and Arthur Wolpert.

PJD PUBLICATIONS LIMITED

WESTBURY, N.Y. 11590

PREFACE

Mental Health is a peculiar problem to mankind. Originating from the corporeal, mentative and extracorporeal aspects of human life, it is now fast becoming an object of Systems Analyses and the Politics of Delivery of Health Care Services. The professionals and the politics have contributed to what Maurice Greenhill questions as the "Self-Destruction of Psychiatry".

In this kind of turmoil, editing this series of books on Mental Health in Children has been particularly enjoyable and yet tumultuous to me. Mental health in children is more complicated than in adults. The problems of development, learning, exercise of mentative faculties, conditioning, behavior and many more facets of human life come into the focus. With the advent of nuclear families and the heterogeniety of American Community life, there is ample provision for the "American" child not to develop into a full blossom. A quote from DeTocqueville is perhaps illuminating-"The inhabitant of the United States learns from birth that he must rely on himself to combat the ills and trials of life". This could be a heavy burden on a child. Yet it is the very plasticity of life processes that gives the child ability to overcome these and other developmental processes of life. Adjustment, compensation and both the will and the joy of living are fundamental psychobiologic facilities. This series of books examines these diverse aspects. Taken as a total set of four volumes, including the one on *Psychopharmacology of Childhood*, a total spectrum from cultural, genetic and community aspects is presented. Typical of our technological advances, systems analyses are also part of this work.

It has been a long and intellectually satisfying work. However, no man stands alone, and in this work I had many excellent people helping me. The most note-worthy are my wife, Barbara Sankar, and the about two hundred authors of the numerous chapters and papers in this series. They have been patient and cooperative, helpful and understanding. What more can an editor ask for in these days of possible "Self-Destruction of Psychiatry"?. Thanks to one and thanks to all.

D. V. Siva Sankar

TABLE OF CONTENTS

This Volume on Psychiatric and Related Problems of Childhood is the Third Volume in a Three Volume Publication on **MENTAL HEALTH IN CHILDREN**. The other Two Volumes deal with **Genetics, Community, Family and Transcultural Studies** (VOLUME I) and **Neurophysiological, EEG, MBD, Sleep, Developmental and Psychological Studies, Autism Etc.** (VOLUME II). A Companion Volume on **PSYCHOPHARMACOLOGY OF CHILDHOOD** has been also published in 1976. The four monographs together occupy about 2400 pages and constitute the **most important** series of studies on **MENTAL HEALTH IN CHILDREN**.

These three volumes and the companion volume on "Psychopharmacology of Childhood" are based on a Conference held under the auspices of the Eastern Psychiatric Research Association.

MENTAL HEALTH IN CHILDREN, Volume III
Edited By D. V. Siva Sankar

A CLINICAL APPROACH TO EMOTIONAL DISTURBANCES IN THE MENTALLY RETARDED

Frank Menolascino

University of Nebraska Medical Center, Omaha

In recent years there has been a more enlightened medical approach concerning ways of contributing to the welfare and overall adjustment of the mentally retarded. To help the retarded individual fully use his potentials, he should be fitted into the world of respectability, productivity, and social ability. But, what is expected from him as to his behavioral characteristics? Unfortunately, an attempt is usually made to make the retarded person into a nice, quiet, and obedient individual who always does what he is told and continually shows his appreciation. This is no longer the expected behavior of retarded individuals. Without increasing recognition of the wide behavioral dimensions in the general population, the mentally retarded person's physical differences, mental limitations, and social infractions are more readily overlooked as manifestations of developmental delay rather than "differentness and danger."

What the retarded individual will be programmed for depends primarily on his parents' expectations from him.

Parents depend heavily on their physicians for guidelines for themselves and their children; therefore, the physician is in an ideal position to help sketch out the expectancy for and from the young mentally retarded member of any family he serves.

Mental retardation directly affects about 3 per cent of our population. Thus, it indirectly affects 1 in 15 of our population (close relatives of the retarded), and the physician will frequently be requested to diagnose and treat mentally retarded and emotionally disturbed. This chapter deals with the dual problem--emotional disturbances in the mentally retarded and their diagnosis, treatment, and management.

A Comprehensive Treatment Approach

Principles for comprehensive treatment of mentally retarded children with emotional disturbances are summaried in Table 1. Discussion of the individual points follow.

Table I

Comprehensive Treatment Principles

1. Keep an open-minded approach in diagnosis and treatment; reevaluate with the same inquiring attitude.
2. Engage the family through active participation.
3. Early descriptive diagnosis followed by early treatment is essential.
4. Begin with acceptance of each child as he is in all aspects of behavior; equal acceptance for his family is needed.
5. Focus on what the child *can* do, lead him step-by-step toward maximal development.
6. Coordinate the services needed for the child; clarity and continuity of communication are of prime importance.

1. *Open Minded Approach*

The diagnosis and treatment of children who are both mentally retarded and emotionally disturbed underscores the necessity of an open-minded approach. Not only is this the first basic principle for the clinician who plans treatment for these youngsters, and it is important to maintain this approach throughout treatment. Periodic reevaluation often reveals developmental surprises which underscore the need for a flexible diagnostic-prognostic attitude.

2. *Active Participation by Family*

The second principle in treatment planning for children with both mental retardation and emotional disturbance is to engage the family through active participation as early as possible. The family is the key to any effective treatment program. The clinician's attitudes and level of interest are frequently the key to success in this endeavor; thus, future cooperation (or lack of it) may reflect the unspoken, as well as the spoken, attitudes at the time of first contact. The therapist needs to convey to the family his willingness to share with its members the facts he learns, not at as an end in itself but as part of the first step in treatment. Treatment plans become a cooperative process which parents and clinician work out over the course of time. It is valuable in an early contact to indicate that treatment planning rarely results in a single recommendation; but, it is something which may shift in focus and alter its course as the child grows and develops. Early implementation of this idea helps develop the concept of the clinician who views the total child, referring to other special sources of help as indicated. This forestalls the "doctor-shopping" which may occur secondary to a referral concerning some special, allied problem.

Much has been written about the grief reactions of families with handicapped children. Such a reaction frequently occurs in parents of children with mental retardation as they become aware that their child is handicapped. Alertness to this dimension must be retained by clinicians evaluating these children, and it must not be forgotten at the time of interpretation to parents or in subsequent interviews. Assessment of family interaction and strengths is a necessary part of the total evaluation, since these assets are essential to plan a comprehensive treatment program. Some of the psychopathology encountered in these families serves to reactivate their difficulties with the child in question. Several interviews may be necessary to determine the nature of the family's involvement with the handicapped child.

3. *Early Diagnosis and Treatment*

A third principle of the comprehensive treatment approach is early, descriptive diagnosis and early treatment. This includes clarification, not only of what needs treatment but also of what can and what cannot be actively treated. Full discussion of these considerations can assist families in establishing realistic expectations so mutual frustration is reduced and fewer secondary psychiatric problems are encountered. In this sense, prevention becomes a cohesive part of the ongoing work with the child and his family. This total approach requires continued follow-up of a patient. Periodic reevaluations must be done, with appropriate shifts in treatment carried out as they are needed.

The advent of a wide range of psychopharmacologic agents to modify overt behavioral manifestations of cerebral dysfunction has materially increased the range of active treatment for many youngsters. The level of arousal and motor activity, convulsive thresholds, and emotional status may be increased, decreased, or altered. Since the reaction to psychopharmacologic agents is unpredictable, the physician must be prepared to use several drugs sequentially or in combination on any one patient.

4. *Initial Contact*

The fourth principle is to accept each child as he is at the time of initial contact. He needs acceptance for what he is, not what he might have been without his problem or what he might have been if therapy had been undertaken sooner. A corollary of this awareness of the family's feelings and acceptance of them as they are at this time. Increasing the parent's guilt feelings is rarely, if ever, desirable in attempting to motivate them toward therapy.

5. *Developmental Potential*

The fifth principle involves focusing, in each instance, on the maximation of developmental potential. It involves a different type of goal setting from the usual treatment expectation, since the focus must often be on what the child can do rather than anticipation of a "cure." The goal then becomes how to go about providing the child with necessary opportunity and support to develop maximally with a minimum of obstacles.

Some crisis situations will be encountered, but a majority can be anticipated and either avoided or minimized. Knowing the child's developmental and emotional needs and what crises are most likely to occur, the physician can help the parents aniticipate and handle emerging adjustment difficulties. After the initial contacts, when rapport with the family has been established, much of the work involves preventative psychiatry. This approach is consistent with the life-planning approach for other chronically handicapped children.

6. *Coordination of Services*

The sixth principle is to coordinate the services needed for the child. This requires awareness of the various services available in a given community and an attitude which permits collaboration. It necessitates sharing of the overall treatment plan with the child (when appropriate), the family, and community resources, with special emphasis on the child's teacher. Close attention to the clarity and continuity of communication is essential.

Services which emotionally disturbed-retarded children may need range from psychotherapy in selected instances, through many types of specialized medical care, to special education. Psychopharmacologic adjuncts to modify overt behavioral manifestations may be useful in some instances and will be discussed shortly.

Emotionally disturbed-retarded children are different from other retarded children. Some of these differences are subtle and perplexing to parents. Parental reaction frequently causes the child to realize he is different, but not in what way or what he can do about it. A feeling of estrangement may ensue. If the child already percieves the world in a somewhat distorted way, this weakens his anchor to reality so normal avenues of learning and reality testing undergo interference or even destruction. Increased disorganization of behavior to the point of psychosis may occur.

Psychopharmacologic Agents

Many psychopharmacologic agents have been employed as treatment adjuncts in emotionally disturbed-mentally retarded children. However, most reported studies have been in inpatient settings, and there is an apparent reluctance to combine psychopharmacologic agents with ambulatory treatment programs. There has been apprehension about the use of drugs because some clinicians feel that drugs will dull perception, stifle learning, or disrupt the therapeutic relationship. There is no proof to support these fears. In some patients drugs may increase the effectiveness of the treatment program. The newer drugs were developed to improve symptoms, increase the child's function, aid his maturation, and enable him to participate in educational programs. However, heavy sedation is not desirable. In attempting to briefly review the use of pharmacologic agents in emotionally disturbed-retarded children, the number of agents recommended and the conflicting claims of their efficacy is confusing. Further complicating the picture is the placebo effect. Some reports indicate that beneficial response is not only engendered by the patient's enthusiasm for the medication, but it is also induced by the attitude of the physician.

Psychopharmacologic agents are frequently employed as treatment adjuncts in the following types of emotional problems: (1) mild to moderate behavioral reactions, (2) severe behavioral reactions, and (3) psychotic reactions in the mentally retarded.

The Adolescent Retardate: A Clinical Challenge

Adolescence for the mentally retarded is more than a transitional period of testing and separating from authority figures on the road to relative self-sufficiency. The search for sexual identity and group acceptance, moving away from the family group, preparation for personal and financial independence, and similar dimensions challenge the flexibility and adaptive capacity of the best endowed youngster. However, in the mentally retarded, adolescence may represent only the beginning of a concerted move toward less dependent relationships with his parents. Heterosexual experiences are at times outside of the mentally retarded child's interest or capacity, and social experiences with persons outside of his family are often only emerging on a limited scale. Such considerations suggest that his concept of self as distinctly different from other people may only be beginning to develop. The forced dependency of a mentally retarded individual early in life and the subsequent limitations of mobility and range of personal-social experiences mean that he has not had sufficient opportunities to test interpersonal experiences which permit the full development of self-identity.

Thus, the mentally retarded adolescent is frequently handicapped by both actual mental limitations of performance and the psychosocial equipment that is essential to engaging in activities independent of his parents or in the kind of interpersonal exchanges involved in relationships with the opposite sex. This particular type of difficulty tends to set up a vicious cycle so psychologic defects seem to place further barriers in the kind of life experiences which may, in turn, increase readiness in subsequent opportunities. As a result of these particular limitations, the mentally retarded adolescent lacks a constructive set of past social experiences. He has usually been served and protected since infancy, and he has been cast in a passive and accepting role, seldom in an active and contributing one. Early in life he is frequently raised in an atmosphere of parental anxiety, and he is not really treated as a useful member of the family. As he passes out of childhood, the sympathy and tolerance which he has received change to more demanding and less accepting attitudes in those around him. In some instances he becomes acutely aware, because of the preoccupation of his parents, that he has failed despite their hopes for him. Thus, the mentally retarded adolescent is frequently an isolated person, and his parents' overconcern with his limitations often result in social immobilization. The lack of ordinary social relations and his inability to relate to others, except as they serve him, tend to prevent satisfying social interaction; therefore, such activity becomes minimal.

In the treatment of retarded adolescents, there is a need for some innovative approaches which stress the programs that permit mentally retarded adolescents to have life experiences designed to provide as much protection and assistance as he requires to engage in work, play, and education--all of which are necessary for his psychosocial growth. Realistic therapeutic planning can make possible these experiences, and the mentally retarded adolescent can achieve an altered view of himself and his potentialities.

Group therapy has numerous advantages for adolescents who are usually denied the opportunity of belonging to meaningful social groups. Similarly, group activities such as music, dance, and crafts are used to establish an atmosphere in which the adolescent can begin to more closely recognize his problems and act or verbalize his feelings. Group therapy is valuable to the mildly retarded because they are better able to articulate their feelings, their problems can be discussed and shared, and they can understand their deep reaction to continuing failure. Group therapy sessions can substitute, in many ways, for the supportive peer group that is often unavailable to them. The sessions may represent the first time it is possible for them to help someone else, and they also experience the feeling of belonging. The goal of the group is to help the mentally retarded adolescent through a difficult phase of growing up, with an improved and more realistic self-image.

Any program of treatment for the mentally retarded assumes the involvement of families. The mentally retarded adolescent remains dependent on his parents and continues to react on a primitive level to the attitudes and feelings within the home. His overall progress cannot be permanently achieved without simultaneous improvement of the parents.

Discussion

Behavioral differences reflecting the overlay of emotional problems that often complicate the lives of mentally retarded individuals are increasingly being appreciated. However, equally important in our current thinking is the knowledge that mentally retarded individuals no longer represent a homogeneous group in characteristics: intellectual, physical, social, or cultural. In brief, the mentally retarded individual is a thinking and feeling individual who, like any other person, is prone to similar emotional problems and social difficulties. Like the more normal child, the mentally retarded child may avoid facing his problems and may become anxious, agressive, hostile, and antisocial. Similarly, he may be responsive, friendly, passive, and cooperative like other children.

It has become increasingly clear that there is no natural line of separation between adequate intellectual functioning and abnormal intellectual function. The major differentiation between the retarded individual and his normal peer appears to be his overt and socially judged, adaptive behavior. These intellectual limitations can seriously interfere with both his capacity to obtain satisfaction for his own efforts in regard to how he understands the world around him and his capacity to meet environmental demands and expectations. Since he has social adaptive difficulties, the mentally retarded individual tends to need ongoing help from others. Thus, the extent to which he is surrounded by supportive adults becomes the major difference in whether or not he makes a satisfactory emotional adjustment. However, when adults are inconsistent in their attitudes or support and are only demanding, undependable, and generally nonsupportive of the mentally retarded individual's efforts--his needs emerge with greater urgency. Thus, when he finds that the demands made on him are confusing or impossible to meet or his necessarily limited accomplishments are unappreciated or ridiculed, his symptomatic behavior may become increasingly intensified. Such situations may develop in the home or in school, and become chronic even though parents and teachers are aware of the child's retardation. Intellectually, parents may accept the problem the child has, but they may have strong emotional reasons that stand in the way of their accepting the child for what he is. This problem is frequently noted in parents who place a major premium on the achievements of their children. Parents may see, in their mentally retarded child, that their collective hopes for personal and social achievements will go unfulfilled. They become increasingly disenchanted with the child's inability to perform at the expected level for his chronological age. Some parents may react to the child with anger and withdrawal of love, and they may consider their child stubborn, ill-tempered, or lazy--parental attitudes which increasingly push them to view their child with nonacceptance or nonrecognition of his capabilities. The child's withdrawal or retaliation against people and events in his immediate world may teach him to increasingly view the world as more threatening. This vicious cycle can literally force him to experience failure, which leads to lack of responsiveness and diminished efforts. His personality may appear to have strong emotional reasons that stand in the way of their accepting the child for what he is. Consequently, his personality may appear to be a paradox of severe, passive dependency with much flee-floating anxiety, interspersed with periodic episodes of acting-out behavior. The overall result is an individual who has to cope with both his intellectual limitations and the psychosocial or emotional handicaps produced by the negative reoccuring interactions with his outside support systems (both in the family and in the general world outside).

As previously noted, the mentally retarded child is frequently susceptible to environmental stress and needs a strong support system. He has difficulty in adapting to sudden changes in his interpersonal environment (e.g., meeting new or strange people), and this difficulty presents greater demands on both the retarded individual and his family. Thus, lack of flexibility and unavailability of a strong family support system may eventuate in chronic maladaptive emotional responses on the part of the child. Since all behavior is aimed at finding the safest position in the ongoing social-interpersonal system, the child may also react by avoidance via withdrawal, timidity, or apathy. An illustration of this dynamic balance between the retarded child's needs and the nature of his support system is the situation wherein a timid child is unable to focus his attention and assimilate what the teacher is attemping to present. However, with a less domineering teacher, a timid child is more relaxed and may be able to mobilize his attention toward ongoing pursuits. Accordingly, relief from stresses and similar tensions can dispel behavioral symptoms, such as feeding problems, masturbation, and enuresis.

In a disturbed family setting wherein failure is answered with rejection, the child is continually subjected to increasing insecurity, and he may develop chronic anxiety with fixed pathologic dimensions (i.e., a psychoneurosis). He may become neurotically frightened and diffusely anxious in many areas, and he may develop phobic phenomena and compulsiveness as a defensive response to the severe, free-floating anxiety. Alternately, such a child may remain passive and dependent, with particular focus on staying with the "old and safe" approaches to interpersonal relationships; such a neurotic defense can drastically interfere with ongoing learning opportunities. These particular types of emotional disturbances, which are neurotic in their way of structuring the inside world of the retarded individual, are less likely to yield to environmental manipulation. Here the psychological exploration of the child-parent interactional unit must deal with more formal treatment approaches, such as psychosexual adjustment.

Summary

In the overview of the most common behavioral reactions noted in mentally retarded individuals, an attempt was made to delineate some of the behavioral reaction patterns secondary to cerebral insults, the role of superimposed interpersonal conflicts and their residuals, and those instances wherein all of these factors are operative. It was stressed that treatment approaches must first focus on the global nature of the child's interactional problems, and only secondarily focus on specific handicaps such as a seizure disorder, motor dysfunction, or speech and language delay. Many of the behavioral disorders in the mentally retarded can be helped by widely differing treatment methods and approaches because of the multifactorial complex of forces which are usually present.

No treatment approach is successful unless a continuous working relationship with the family has been established. Initial, tactful interviews can provide the "foothold" for the establishment of such a mutual contract of help with the family, and the multidimensional treatment needs can be delineated, augmented, and followed through. In comprehensive treatment planning, it is helpful to focus not on what the child presently is, but on what he can become!

References

Chess, S. Emotional problems in mentally retarded children. In F.J. Menolascino (Ed.), *Psychiatric Approaches to Mental Retardation.* Basic Books, New York, 55-57, (1970).

Freeman, R.D. Psycho pharmacology and the retarded child. In F.J. Menolascino (Ed.), *Psychiatric Approaches to*

Mental Retardation. Basic Books, New York, 294-367, (1970).

Menolascino, F.J. *Ment. Retardation. 10,* 3, (1972).

Menolascino, F.J. *Amer. J. Psychiat. 124,* 459, (1967).

Webster, T.G. Unique aspects of emotional development in mentally retarded children. In F.J. Menolascino (Ed.), *Psychiatric Approaches to Mental Retardation.* Basic Books, New York, 3, (1970).

Wolfensberger, W. Counseling parents of the retarded. In A.A. Baumuster (Ed.), *Mental Retardation Appraisal, Education and Rehabilitation.* Aldine, Chicago, 329, (1970).

MENTAL HEALTH IN CHILDREN, Volume III
Edited By D. V. Siva Sankar

STUDIES IN DIFFERENTIATING SUBGROUPS IN MENTAL RETARDATION

J. Clausen, A. Lidsky and E.A. Sersen

N.Y.S. Institute for Research in Mental Retardation
Staten Island, N.Y. 10314

For over a century, since Edouard Seguin presented a definition of idiocy and distinguished between simple and complex idiocy (1), definition and classification in mental retardation have remained unsatisfactory and controversial. Reflecting the fact that mental retardation is the end product of a wide variety of causes, the classification system of the American Association on Mental Deficiency is primarily based on etiology. Despite considerable research activity in the area of mental retardation in the last 15 years, little systematic effort has been made in assessing the functional characteristics of the clinical categories.

The current article is a review of a series of studies, conducted at the Training School at Vineland and at the Institute for Research in Mental Retardation, focussing on functional characteristics of subgroups of retardates.

In 1957 the Ability Structure Project (2) was started in Vineland. The main purpose of this project was to establish homogeneous subgroups of mental retardation on the basis of functional similarities, i.e. constellations of impaired and intact functions. A battery of 33 tests, yielding 50 scores and requiring a total testing time of 8-10 hours, included measures of sensory, motor, perceptual, and cognitive tasks in addition to neurological and EEG examinations. The study included 276 retarded subjects in three age groups: 8-10, 12-15, and 20-24, and 112 normal controls in the 8-10 year age range. The IQ range for the retardates was 30-70, and for the normals 90-140. Etiological selection of the retarded population was unsystematic but patients were subsequently assigned to etiological subcategories (3), which essentially is a systematic attempt at determining the presence of organic impairment.

Multivariate analysis (traditional and inverse factor analysis, and Saunder's Syndrome Analysis) applied to the data, did not result in easily interpretable clusters, and comparison of etiological groups did not yield significant differences. For all practical purposes "functional" subgroups had not been defined. But inspection of the data provided some interesting suggestions. While pure tone audiometry indicated severe hearing loss for both ears in all three retarded groups, thresholds for speech detection were close to normal. Apparently the hearing was nearly normal, but the testing methods affected the result. Similarly, when motor tests were arranged according to presumed increase in degree of complexity, with the expectation of a growing disparity between patients and normals, the opposite turned out to be the case. That is, the simplest motor tasks were executed extremely poorly.

The study concluded that while the retarded groups exhibit more variability than the normal, these subjects constitute a semi-homogeneous mass, where the individuals differ from each other in so many little ways, that attempts at subgrouping are defied. They exhibit a somewhat fuzzy kind of similarity, regardless of etiology and age. This may suggest impairment of some central function which permeates all tasks, but in a differential manner. The retardates seem to lack the normal person's readiness to respond to outside stimuli, and are not able to focus attention on a sustained task, particularly tasks without high intrinsic interest, such as pure tone audiometry and simple motor tasks. In interpreting the data, we were impressed by Lindsley's *en passant* remark (4), that in retardation the ascending reticular activating system may be impaired. Through the relationship of the reticular formation to the arousal mechanism the possibility existed that impairment of the ARAS provided a neurophysiological substrate for the behavior of the retardates. Thus, we postulated that the central mechanism which permeated all activities was arousal, that the retardates have a generally low arousal level, and are more dependent on the arousal characteristics of stimuli than are normals. In the present context, arousal refers to the general response or response readiness of an individual, modifiable by stimulation, and measurable in terms of performance level or physiological activity.

In the classical report (5) on the effect of ablation and stimulation of the reticular formation in the cat, changes in brain wave synchronization and in autonomic activity were observed. This suggested that recordings of psychophysiological functions in the retardates may produce further evidence for arousal impairment in retarded populations.

The first autonomic study. In collaboration with Karrer (6) a comparison was made between 27 so-called organic retardates and 22 normals in the age range from 10 to 17 years for skin resistance, heart rate, heart rate variability, systolic blood pressure, finger volume, and respiration. These variables were recorded during rest, in response to auditory stimulation, during habituation to repeated stimulation, and in addition, the amount of spontaneous activity during rest was measured. During rest, lower skin resistance and higher blood pressure (only the former significant) were found in the retardates, suggesting increased sympathetic activity. In response to stimulation, the retardates showed generally less reactivity, with heart rate and heart rate variability differing significantly. In addition, more non-responders, particularly for skin resistance, were found among retardates, who also showed a tendency to response increment rather than habituation to repeated stimulation. If sympathetic activity is considered an index of arousal, this would indicate an increased arousal level during rest, but reduced arousal increment resulting from stimulation.

The second autonomic study. This study was replicated a few years later again in collaboration with Karrer, but with some modifications in design (7). To the former variables, blood volume change of the forehead was added. The population was 10 non-organic retardates, 10 organic retardates, and 10 normals, all of the same age, and the two retarded groups were matched for IQ and MA. The subjects were recorded twice, one week apart. Following the recording during rest, reactivity to a series of sound and a series of light stimuli was measured.

Both retarded groups had higher blood pressure, faster heart rate, and lower skin resistance during rest, although only the first two measures reached significance. In essence, the higher sympathetic activity during rest among retardates was confirmed, although the level of significance for the different variables was inconsistent.

The reactivity data to the series of sound and light stimulation were analyzed with respect to the occurrence and habituation of the orienting response (OR) (8), which Russian investigators have claimed are deficient in oligophrenic subjects. According to their suggestion, simultaneous vaso-dilation in the head and vaso-constriction in the periphery was used as an index for OR. The normal subjects had significantly more OR's than the two retarded groups, particularly on the first day. Skin resistance changes practically always accompanied OR in normals and non-organics, but less often in organics. Blood pressure changes, on the other hand, were considerably more independent of OR. The groups showed no differences with respect to habituation, and a novel stimulus (light) failed to recover the OR's. While the data support earlier reports of impaired OR's in retardates, some reservation is attached to this conclusion, because of the difficulties encountered in determining *bona fide* blood volume changes from a tracing which also reflects pulse beat and respiration.

The response data were also analyzed with respect to group differences in temporal factors such as latency, time-to-peak, and recovery for changes in skin resistance and the two blood volume measures (9). It was found that these temporal factors do not discriminate between normal and mentally retarded subjects.

In the two autonomic studies inter-correlations between the amount of reactivity in the different variables were determined. Correlations were consistently low, suggesting that sympathetic action is not as unitary as physiology textbooks would lead us to believe. This type of independence represents a severe obstacle for the use of autonomic variables as an index of arousal.

The third autonomic project. This project was carried out at the Institute for Research in Mental Retardation (10). The same autonomic variables as in the second project were included: skin resistance, heart period, systolic blood pressure, respiration amplitude and period, and blood volume changes of the forehead and finger. To assess the reliability of the data, recordings during Rest and Auditory Stimulation were obtained for four sessions, followed by a fifth session, where autonomic activity was obtained during a Vigilance test. The patient population this time consisted of four clinical groups: 29 Familials, 30 Down's cases, 25 PKU's, and 31 Encephalopathies, plus 30 Normals, all ranging in age from 10 to 30 years.

Some of the results are presented in Fig. 1. This figure presents four of the variables for the patient groups, expressed as standard scores with reference to normal data, and arranged so that positive values on the ordinate represent sympathetic-like activity. Two of the variables, heart period and skin resistance, are on the sympathetic side of the reference line, consistent with previous findings. All patient groups, however, have lower blood pressure than the normals. This might be compensatory for increased heart rate but there are also technical difficulties in recording this variable. High respiration amplitude has been regarded as a sympathetic index, but amplitude could be reduced as compensation for fast breathing, so the interpretation here is uncertain. But taken at face value, the autonomic variables are not uniform in their direction of deviation from the Normals.

The figure also shows differences between the retarded groups. The Familials are consistently on the parasympathetic side, the PKU's have low skin resistance and particularly high respiration amplitude, and the Down's and Encephalopathic groups have essentially the same patterns, except that Down's cases have greater deviations from the Normals. Skin resistance response to the auditory stimulation over the four sessions is presented in Fig. 2. Skin resistance is chosen since it is the only variable which shows significant group differences in all four sessions. The figure shows consistently less reactivity for the Familial, Down's, and Encephalopathy groups than for the Normals. The PKU's, while generally less reactive than Normals, tend to be more reactive than the other patient groups, and show greater intersession variability.

The vigilance test involved pressing a response key every time a moderately soft tone was presented at intervals of 15 to 240 seconds. A verbal "ready" signal followed by tones was used at the beginning of the session, to serve as a reference for vigilance RT's. The Normals and Familials had shorter baseline RT's than the Down's, PKU, and Encephalopathy groups, and the commonly faster RT for males were confirmed. Vigilance RT data, adjusted for differences in baseline RT's, showed neither Group nor Sex differences. At the longest stimulus intervals, however, the RT's of the Down's, PKU, and Encephalopathy groups increased, suggesting difficulty in maintaining arousal or attention.

In an attempt to integrate data for autonomic resting level, reactivity, and RT as an index of performance, a set of hypothetical curves was proposed. Skin resistance was selected to represent autonomic activity, since it is the only variable which gave consistent differences between the groups, and since the sweat glands provide the purest index of sympathetic activity, with no para-sympathetic innervation. It was hypothesized that skin resistance as a function of arousal describes an ogival relationship. For RT, optimal performance at a moderate level of arousal was assumed, with reduced performance at either increased or decreased degrees of arousal. This relationship is illustrated in Fig. 3. The clinical groups are placed on the abscissa according to their resting skin

Fig. 1. Z-scores for four variables with significant group differences during rest (10).

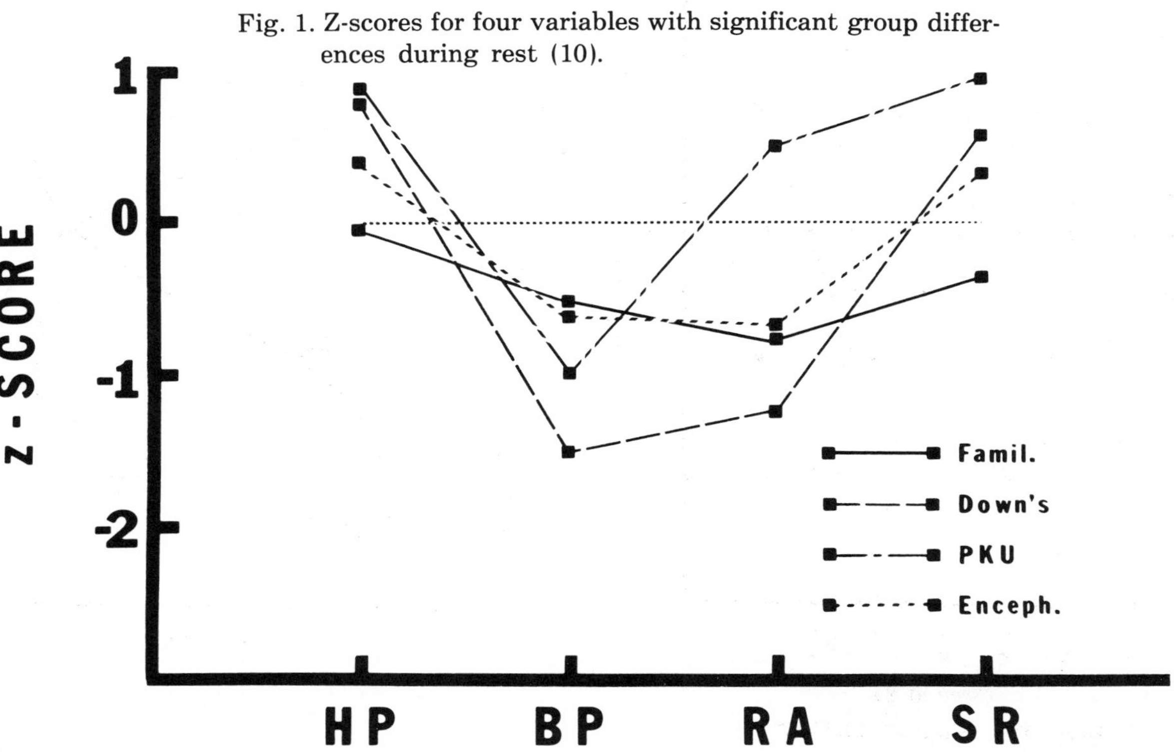

Figure 2

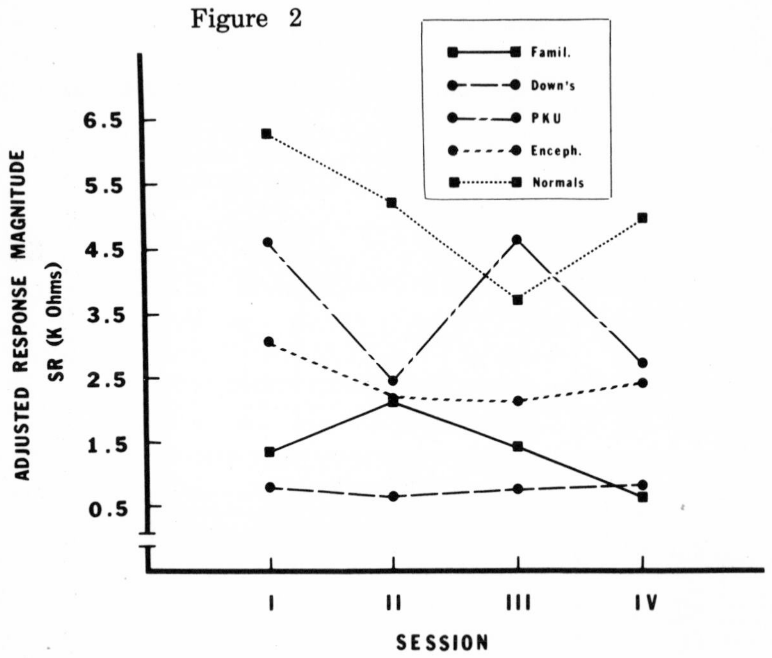

Figure 3

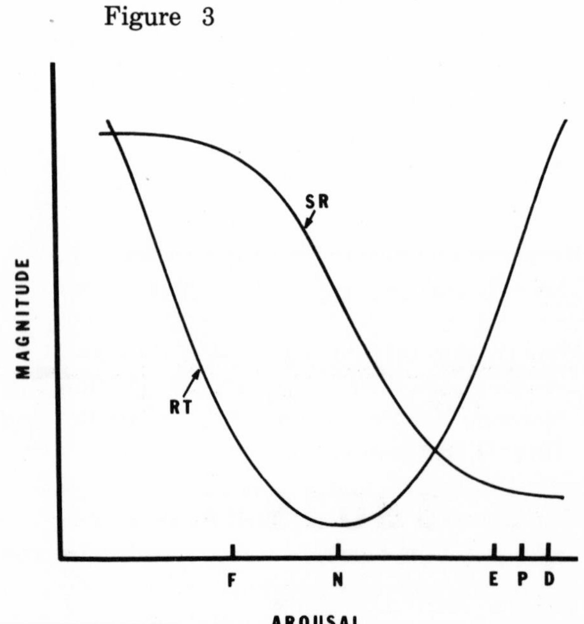

Figure 4

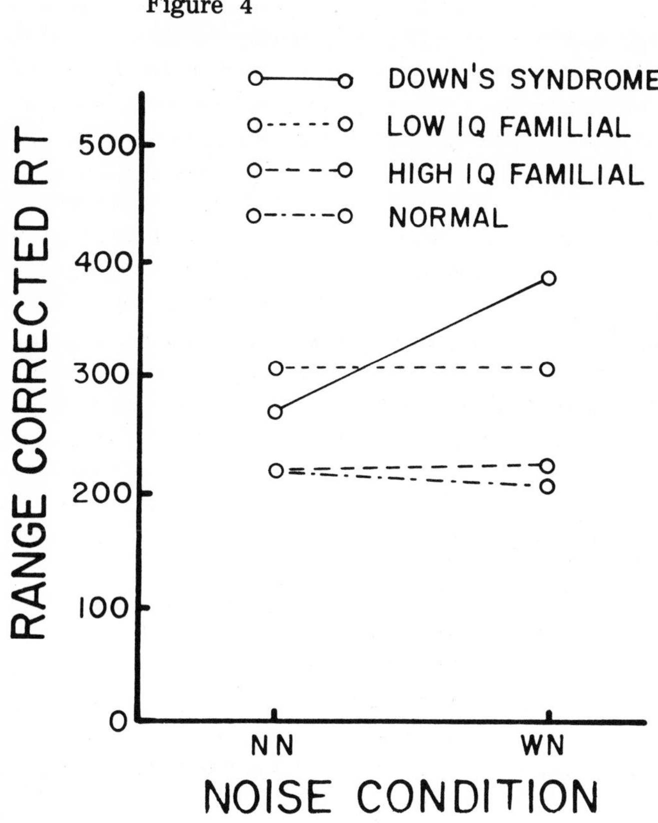

Fig. 2. Response magnitude for skin resistance during Auditory Stimulation adjusted for prestimulus level (10).

Fig. 3. Hypothetical relationship of skin resistance (SR) and reaction time (RT) to arousal. (F=Familial, N=Normal, E=Encephalopathy, P=PKU, and D=Down's Syndrome) (10).

Fig. 4. Mean reaction time (corrected for differences in range) as a function of subject group and noise condition (12).

resistance level and their reaction time. An external stimulus - such as an auditory signal - which would increase the level of arousal, would have different consequences for the various groups. The Normals, on the steepest slope of the curve, would have a much greater decrease in skin resistance than any of the patient groups, located on the flatter portions of the curve.

In relation to the model, two subsequent studies in our laboratories have provided some additional information and partial confirmation. Recording pupillary responses to light stimulation, Lidsky found smaller initial pupil diameters in Familials than in Normals (11), confirming the previous observation of reduced sympathetic activity during rest. In response to stimulation, at least for the lower light intensities, he obtained smaller pupillary contractions for the Familials, suggesting in addition attenuated para-sympathetic reactivity. Data for a few Down's cases, on the other hand, showed smaller initial diameter and greater than normal contractions, which tentatively suggest a consistent pattern of elevated parasympathetic level and responsiveness.

The model also predicts changes in RT with increased arousal. The RT changes should be small for Normals, in the direction of shorter RT for Familials, and in the direction of longer RT for the other retarded groups. Miezejeski (12) recorded RT under conditions of no noise and white noise, with white noise assumed to produce arousal increase. His subjects included two Familial groups (high and low IQ), a Down's group, and a Normal group. His data are shown in Fig. 4. Consistent with prediction, the Normals did not change under the white noise condition, and the Down's group showed a significant increase in RT. The high IQ Familials did not change, but as their no-noise RT was exactly like the Normals, no change should be expected. The low IQ Familials had the highest no-noise RT, which was not changed during white noise. One could, however, question the diagnostic purity of a low IQ Familial group.

Current projects. Several other psychophysiological projects relative to the arousal concept are currently in progress in our laboratories, including recordings of sleep stages, evoked cortical potentials, and contingent negative variation. Prominent among these projects is the recording of sleep stages, since sleep represents minimum arousal, and since emphasis was given to the close anatomical relationship between cortical centers for sleep and for arousal (13, 14). We are currently in the process of analyzing sleep records for a group of 20 Down's cases and 20 Normals. In the near future we intend to record sleep for other etiological categories.

Sersen is recording cortical potentials evoked by different sensory stimuli, with particular concern with cross modality and laterality effects for the purpose of assessing hemispheric interactions. Evoked cortical potentials have been related to mental retardation in two types of studies. Reports are made of prolonged latencies for evoked potentials in retardates (15, 16, 17) and related amplitudes of the late evoked potential components to level of attention (18). The latter authors observed that the late components derive from extra-lemniscal pathways passing through the reticular formation.

Our interest in the contingent negative variation has been stimulated by findings (19) of differences in topography and timing of steady potential changes between normals and retardates, which are interpreted as impairment of attentional set in the retardates.

We are currently preparing a project where a variety of psychophysiological variables will be recorded for selected etiological groups with the dual purpose of group comparison and of determining the relationships between the variables. Included will be autonomic measures during rest and stimulation, patterns of sleep stages, evoked cortical potentials, contingent negative variation, and motor performance under various conditions of arousal.

Summary

In summarizing these findings, three points may be made:

1. Subgroups of retardates seem to be better characterized by psychophysiological variables than by sensory, motor, perceptual, or complex mental functions. It is particularly

impressive that for some autonomic variables, Familials fall on one side of the normals, while Down's cases, PKU's and Encephalopathies fall on the other.

2. Autonomic activity does not constitute a uniform response pattern, as some variables indicate increased and others decreased sympathetic tonus, and correlations between responsivity in the different variables are low. This may be a result of dual sympathetic and para-sympathetic innervation of so many of the autonomic organs. Perhaps more consistent results would be obtained if single innervation systems are used, such as sweat gland activity and pupillary contraction. Alternatively, one may have to consider several different "arousals."

3. In most retarded groups, except the Familials, there seems to be a dissociation between resting level, which indicates increased sympathetic activity, and response level which indicates reduction in sympathetic activity.

Application of a concept of arousal to mental retardation requires caution. Not all the data that have been reviewed are consistent with arousal deficiency. In addition, the concept lacks specificity, and various authors have applied it to all types of psychopathology. Despite its limitations, however, the concept of arousal continues to provide a working hypothesis for integrating a considerable amount of available data.

References

1. Seguin, E. In *Idiocy and its treatment by the physiological method.* William Wood and Co., 1866 New York, Reprinted: New York: Agustus M. Kelley, (1971).

2. Clausen, J. In *Ability structure and subgroups in mental retardation.* Spartan Books, Washington, D.C., (1966).

3. Riggs, M.M. and Rain, M.E. *Training Sch. Bull. 49,* 75, (1952).

4. Lindsley, D.B. Psychophysiology and motivation. In *Nebraska symposium on motivation.* Edited by Jones, M.R. University of Nebraska Press, Lincoln, p. 44, (1957).

5. Moruzzi, G. and Magoun, H.W. *Electoencephalogr. Clin. Neurophysiol. 1,* 455, (1949).

6. Karrer, R. and Clausen, J. *J. Ment. Defic. Res. 8,* 149, (1964).

7. Clausen, J. and Karrer, R. *Amer. J. Ment. Defic. 75,* 361, (1970).

8. Clausen, J. and Karrer, R. *Amer. J. Ment. Defic. 73,* 455, (1968).

9. Clausen, J. and Karrer, R. *Amer. J. Ment. Defic. 74,* 80, (1969).

10. Clausen, J., Lidsky, A., and Sersen, E.A. Measurements of autonomic functions in mental deficiency. In *The developmental psychophysiology of mental retardation.* Edited by Karrer, R. Charles C. Thomas, Springfield, Ill., in press.

11. Lidsky, A. and Richman, S. Pupil size and responses to light in retardates and Normals. Paper presented at *8th Colloguium on the Pupil.* Wayne State University, Detroit, (1973).

12. Miezejeski, C.M. *Amer. J. Ment. Defic. 79,* 39, (1974).

13. Hernández-Péon, R. Central neuro-humoral transmission in sleep and wakefulness. In *Sleep mechanisms.* Edited by Akert, K., Bally, C., and Schade, J.P. Elsevier, New York, p. 96, (1965).

14. Akert, K. The anatomical substrate of sleep. In *Sleep mechanisms.* Edited by Akert, K., Bally, C., and Schade, J.P. Elsevier, New York, p. 9, (1965).

15. Ellingson, R.J. Neurophysiology. In *Mental retardation-an annual review. Vol. 1.* Edited by Wortis, J. Grune and Stratton, New York, p. 164, (1970).

16. Galbraith, G.C., Gliddon, J.B. and Busk, J. *Amer. J. Ment. Defic. 75,* 341, (1970).

17. Hernández-Péon, R. Physiologic mechanisms in attention. In *Frontiers in physiological psychology.* Edited by Russel, R.W. Academic Press, New York, p. 121, (1966).

18. Rhodes, L.E., Dustman, R.E., and Beck, E.C. *Electroencephalogr. Clin. Neurophysiol. 27,* 364, (1969).

19. Karrer, R. and Ivins, J. Steady potentials accompanying perception and response in mental retardates. In *The developmental psychophysiology of mental retardation.* Edited by Karrer, R. Charles C. Thomas, Springfield, Ill., in press.

Figures 1, 2 and 3 have been reproduced with permission from "*The Developmental Psychophysiology of Mental Retardation*" Edited by R. Karrer. Courtesy of Charles C. Thomas, Publisher, Springfield, Illinois.
Figure 4 has been reproduced with permission from American Association on Mental Deficiency from the *American Journal of Mental Deficiency* from the paper by Dr. C. M. Miezejeski, in 1974.

MENTAL HEALTH IN CHILDREN, Volume III
Edited By D. V. Siva Sankar

INTRAPSYCHIC EFFECT OF AMPHETAMINE IN HYPERKINESIS AS REVEALED THROUGH ART PRODUCTIONS

Harriet Wadeson * and Richard Epstein

National Institute of Mental Health
Bethesda, Maryland 20014

ABSTRACT

Although dexedrine (amphetamine) has been widely employed as a useful medication for hyperkinetic children for many years, most studies have either advanced physiological theories for the mechanism of its beneficial effect or have documented changes in external behavior. We believe the interface between pharmocologic intervention and intrapsychic effects to be an important area of investigation often neglected because of methodologic difficulties in assessment. The present study conducted at the National Institute of Mental Health attempts to assess intrapsychic phenomena through changes in art productions produced on varying doses of dexedrine and placebo.

---

*Research Psychologist and Psychiatric Art Therapist, Psychiatric Assessment Section, Adult Psychiatry Branch, National Institute of Mental Health, Building 10, Room 4N214, Bethesda, Maryland 20014.

For this purpose, a minimally brain-damaged child, typical in many characteristics of those for whom dexedrine is frequently prescribed, was selected to participate in a series of semi-structured art therapy sessions. During the course of the sessions and evaluation and comparison of the pictures, the art therapist remained blind to drug dosage. Observations were then made by her in regard to pictorial content, style, the child's associations to the pictures, and his behavior during the sessions.

The results, as evidenced in the pictures, indicated major changes in handling of aggression, self-concept, and related mood on the various doses of amphetamine and placebo. On a low dose of dexedrine (10 mg.) or placebo, there was much expressiveness and play of fantasy, particularly around conflicts between hostile feelings and the need to please, accompanied by positive relatedness, physical restlessness, flight of ideas and perseveration. On a high dose (30 mg.), there was self-contempt and self-punitiveness, depression, less play of fantasy, and much frustration and lack of warm relatedness. On 20 mg., there was self-satisfaction, less expressiveness and play of fantasy, remote interpersonal relatedness, greater concentration, and a less troubled condition.

INTRODUCTION

The use of dexedrine for school age children on a massive scale in recent years has evoked criticism that our children are being drugged to submissive conformity to ineffectual schools and pathologic families. Many years of clinical study purports that amphetamine is a useful medication for hyperkinetic behavior in children (1, 2, 3, 4, 5), and a number of physiological theories on the mechanism by which amphetamine exerts its beneficial effect have been advanced (6). There has been little investigation known to the authors, however, on the child's inner experience, and not merely his external behavior.

The interface between physiological intervention and intrapsychic result is a most difficult terrain to explore. Whereas physiological parameters and behavioral manifestations are readily observable, psychic state is usually assessed through implication, occasionally with corroboration from the subject. Most likely, it is for these reasons that there is a dearth of solid information in this area. Although these difficulties apply to other populations as well, obtaining corroboration for speculations on intrapsychic states of children is particularly difficult. Children are not apt to be sufficiently reflective or to give information directly in an interview or to respond to questionnaires.

The present study is reported in order to suggest a direction for research in this area and to illustrate a research tool for investigating the physiological-psychological interface. For this purpose we have chosen a case study of a child typical in many respects of those for whom amphetamine is perscribed.

Although picture making is an established mode of clinical work with children, it has been used very little as a research modality for tapping subjective experience. We will attempt to assess intrapsychic phenomena through changes in art productions produced on varying doses of dexedrine and placebo.

The only other study with a similar focus on subjective psychic actions of amphetamine, of which we are aware, was published by Bender in 1942 (7). Also using art productions, she compared reactions to amphetamine in children having varying diagnoses. (See discussion, below.)

METHOD

Since a significant proportion of children who are hyperkinetic or have specific learning disorders for whom dexedrine is recommended show signs of neurologic deficiency the term Minimal Brain Disorder (MBD) has been used for all children with the syndrome, whether brain injury can be documented or not. From a series of such children being studied for biochemical changes associated with the MBD Syndrome, we selected one who seemed typical for study of intrapsychic phenomena utilizing picture making.

HISTORY: Clark is a seven-year old Caucasin boy referred for treatment because of maladaptive behavior at home and at school. His mother described him a "high strung", distractable, impatient, short of temper, and given to raging when frustrated, though not prone to remain angry for an extended period of time. His school teacher stated that although intelligent, he was disruptive in class, disobedient, had a poor attention span, was unable to sit in his chair, and became angry when reprimanded. The above picture is typical of the behavior for which dexedrine is given.

Also typical is a lack of hard physiological symptoms or negative history, a presence of emotionally pathologic family factors, and a favorable response to amphetamine medication in terms of decrease of the presenting symptoms.

There was no history of perinatal trauma or illness, and the developmental history was normal. His only serious illness occurred at age six months when he developed bronchial asthma.

Physical examination revealed no abnormalitites except mild wheezes. EEG, skull and chest X-rays, CBC, urinanalysis, and neurologic responses were all normal.

Clark has two sisters, age eight and four, who showed no evidence of behavior disorder. The paternal grandmother, however, was hospitalized for chronic psychosis for twenty years with onset after Clark's father's birth.

In family evaluation, Clark's father appeared to be an anxious, tense individual whom his wife felt "couldn't handle the burdens of family life." It was observed that he had a competitive relationship with Clark and felt considerable guilt and anger in relation to the mother. She seemed overprotective both toward Clark and her husband whom she still had hopes of "changing." She noted the onset of Clark's disruptive behavior at age four when her husband separated from the family to live for a year with another woman. She blamed Clark's illness on the father's irresponsiblity, and the father accepted this.

ART SESSIONS: Clark was seen by the art therapist (H.W.) in five individual art therapy sessions lasting for approximately 1 - 1-1/2 hours each. The sessions were scheduled in accordance with his drug dosage and covered a period of several months. Throughout the period of the art sessions and during subsequent evaluation of the pictures the art therapist remained blind to the medication dosage in order that her observations be unbiased by expectations of drug effects. Clark and his family were also blind to drug dosage.

Materials used in the sessions were: thick pastels which offer the possibility of using vivid color, are easy to control, and provide the opportunity for both hard lines and smearing; and water paints which are runny. Work was done at both an easel and a table, the latter providing a surface on which the paint would not run. White 18" x 24 " paper was used.

The sessions were structured as follows: picture 1, a pastel drawing at the easel; picture 2, a painting at the easel; picture 3, a painting at the table; picture 4, a self-portrait with the medium of his choice; several more pictures of his choice, the number depending on his interest. There was some variation in the procedure at times of frustration in which the art therapist did not insist on his using a medium he didn't want. During one session when Clark was extremely frustrated and self-punative, the art therapist made some suggestions as to how he might better manage dripping paint and unwanted pastel smudges; otherwise no art instruction was given. After each painting or drawing, Clark was encouraged to talk about his picture.

During all the sessions Clark was fully cooperative and evidenced none of the disruptive or angry behavior of which his mother and teacher complained. It should be emphasized, however, that the art sessions involved a one-to-one relationship for a short period of time and an activity which Clark enjoyed.

RESULTS

The most significant changes in the pictures were related to the handling of aggression and self-concept. Behavior varied also from session to session particularly in regard to physical activity, relationship to the art therapist, handling of frustration, perseveration, and affect. In order to give an overview of the tone of each session, behavior will be discussed first.

BEHAVIOR: Clark was receiving 10 mg. of dexedrine on the day of his first session. He evidenced no hyperactivity, was pleasant, cooperative, somewhat shy, and seemed to enjoy the session. Initially he produced no associations to his pictures and replied, "I don't know" to questions. As the session progressed, however, he became more free, expressing fantasies and drawing a picture of a dream. When the paint ran, he was able to blend in the drips.

Although still receiving 10 mg. of dexedrine at the second session, Clark's behavior was quite different. He was physically restless and more talkative with words running together and showing evidence of confusion and flight of ideas. He came in smiling, and there was much positive affect expressed toward the art therapist, which took pictorial form, as well, in a smiling portrait of "a friend" who was the art therapist, a painting of himself and the art therapist at his house, and a drawing of Santa Claus who would give his first gift to the art therapist. He associated freely to his pictures, and his associations were richer than before. There was some perseveration in his selecting for his first three pictures the same subjects as his first three pictures from the last session, but this time there was elaboration in the direction of greater expressiveness.

On a 30 mg. dose at the third session, Clark showed marked changes. He was withdrawn, soft spoken, spoke little, and turned away when questioned. He appeared sad, depressed, and angry. There was a decided lack of the warm positive feelings he was expressing toward the art therapist at the previous session. There was no perseveration. He had so much difficulty with the paint smearing that he had to be given technical assistance (at the previous sessions he was able to integrate the drips into the picture). For the first time he was upset about getting chalk on his hands and cleaned them elaborately. In making the next picture he wrapped tissue around each pastel he used in order to keep his hands clean and took quite a bit of time to put the pastels neatly back in the box in their proper order. He was not pleased with his work, asking that his picture be thrown away, and seemed very disgusted with himself. At one point he berated himself for breaking a pastel, saying dejectedly, "I always break things." He experienced the session as "not fun" which was very much in contrast with his positive reactions of the previous sessions. It was only with his final picture that he was able to leave off smearing, not be disturbed by some accidental smudges, incorporate a technical suggestion and fantasize in relation to the picture. (This change during the session is discussed under Aggression below).

At session four on 20 mg. of dexedrine, Clark once again seemed to enjoy the session and was engrossed in his work. There was not the depression or self-contempt of the previous session. He was shy, soft-spoken, less troubled, less expressive and more remote. He did not express the warmth toward the art therapist he had shown at earlier sessions. There was no perseveration. He had fewer problems with running paint. Although there was some smearing, it was not accompanied by the self-digust of the previous session.

At the final session, Clark was on placebo. He was wiggly, distracted, evidenced silly, inappropriate smiling and wrinkling of the face. He was initially full of smiles but seemed less happy at the end of the session. His affect was more enthusiastic than in the previous two sessions and his response to the art therapist more warm and personal. He was more expressive and there was greater play of fantasy. Although there was expression of some self-contempt, there was not the totally self-contemptuous affect expressed on the high dose. The thematic perseveration returned: the first three pictures were of the same subjects as in the first two sessions on the low dose of dexedrine. In one picture he was able to control the paint; in another he was not and ended up smearing it and feeling disappointed.

Table I summarizes Clark's behavior in the five sessions on the varying doses of dexedrine.

THE PICTURES: It is significant that the major affective changes which impressed the art therapist in the pictures and associated fantasies was the patient's manner of handling aggressive, sometimes hostile, urges. This area posed a major problem for Clark. On varying doses of amphetamine he appeared to experience and deal with the conflicts differently. These changes were directly associated with changes in his self concept as well.

Low Dexedrine Dose and Placebo: On low doses (10 mg.) and placebo there was much aggressive fantasy in the pictures

TABLE I: BEHAVIOR

SESSION	DEXEDRINE DOSE	AFFECT	PHYSICAL & MENTAL ACTIVITY	TRANSFERENCE	FRUSTRATION	ASSOCIATIONS	PERSEVERATION
1	10 mg.	Cooperative Pleasant Shy	Normal	Positive	None	Initially few but became richer	
2	10 mg.	Cooperative Warm Smiling	Restless Words ran together Flight of ideas	Very Positive	None	Very rich	Yes
3	30 mg.	Cooperative Withdrawn Sad Depressed Angry self-contemptuous	Spoke little Spoke softly	Lack of positive expression Turned away when questioned	Much	Few	None

4	20 mg.	Cooperative Shy Less troubled Less expressive	Soft spoken Normal	More remote	A little, but well handled	Less expressive	None
5	Placebo	Initially full of smiles, but less happy later Enthusiastic	Wiggly Distracted Inappropriate smiling & wrinkling of face Some flight of ideas	Warm Personal	Some	More expressive	Yes

Figure 1: Low Amphetamine dose - ambivalent identification with bear in colorful cave - attacker, victim, friend.

Figure 2: Placebo - larger bear in murky cave - conflict over attacking nature of bear.

Figure 3: Low Amphetamine dose - dream of self and mother (small figures) about to jump into hole (center) to hide from trees which have turned into monsters.

Figure 4: Placebo - "ugly" monster which is himself.

Figure 5: High Amphetamine dose - self-portrait which he smeared over many times.

Figure 6: High Amphetamine dose - emergence of aggressive fantasy of harpooning an angry whale.

Figure 7: Medium Amphetamine dose - Apollo rocket launch, conventionally channeled aggression.

Figure 8: Medium Amphetamine dose - "Happy dog who is going home to eat." Compare with bear and whale, figures 2 and 6.

Figure 9: Medium Amphetamine dose - self-portrait which he saw as "happy." Compare with figure 4 and 5.

Figure 1

Figure 2

Figure 3

Figure 4

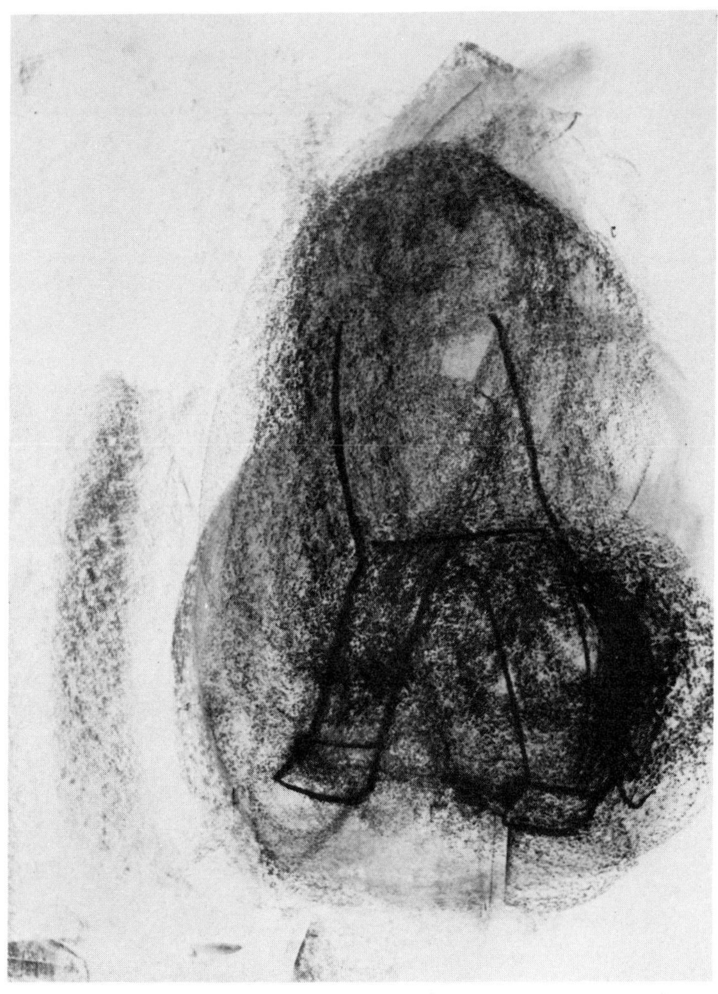

Figure 5

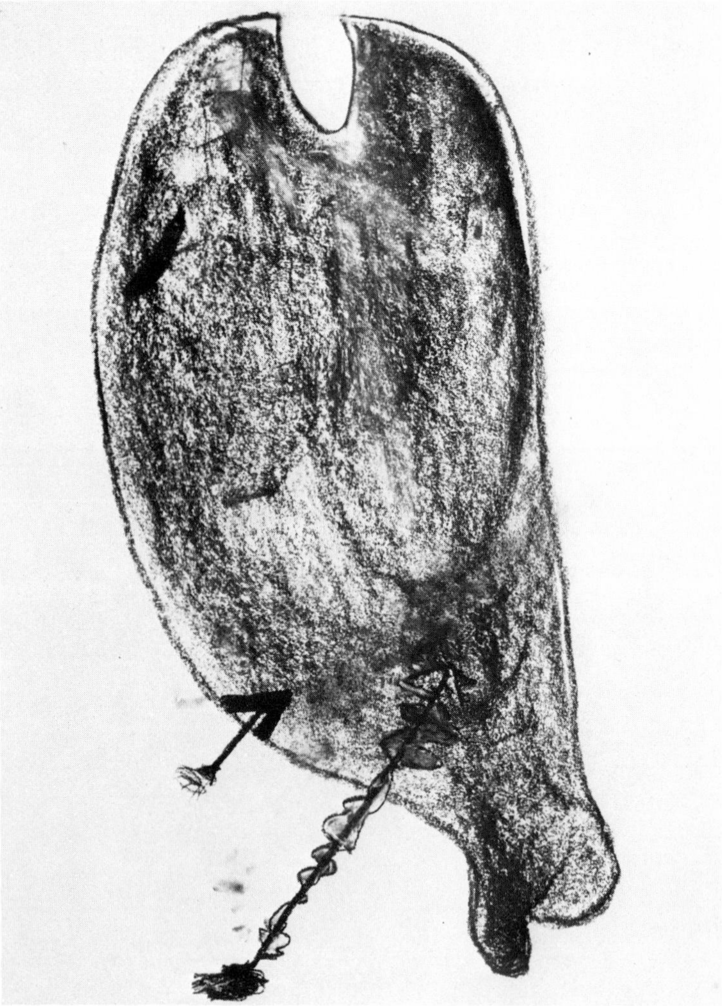

Figure 6

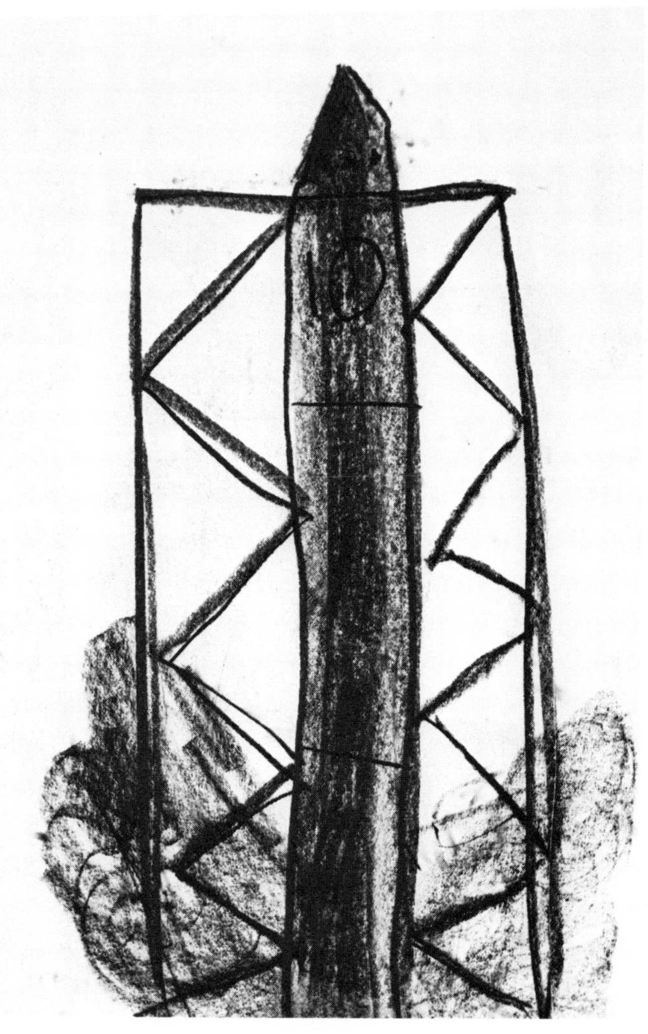

Figure 7

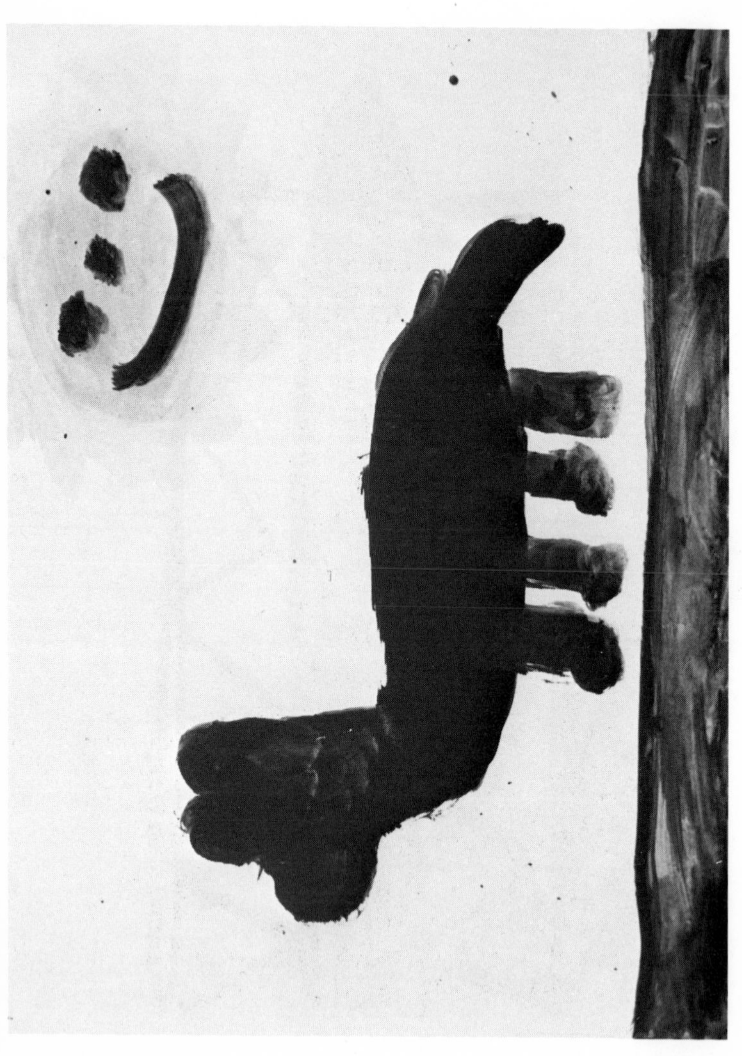

Figure 8

Figure 9

accompanied by ambivalence of identification. For example, the third picture of sessions one, two, and five (perseveration) was of a bear hiding in a cave. At the first session he didn't draw the bear because it was "hiding" or a cat that he said was hiding in the trees being attacked by birds. He spoke of wishing to hide from his mother and fantasized her looking for him. He was identifying with the bear. At the second session he drew the bear in the cave (figure 1) saying it growled at the birds and would eat up himself, his mother, the art therapist, a number of friends he named, but not his father because Daddy would shoot the bear with a gun. He then said that he didn't want to be that bear -- he would like to be a friendly bear. There seemed to be ambivalence about identifying with the aggressor or victim. His third picture of this theme was painted at the final session when he was on placebo. The bright colors of the previous bear pictures have become murky, and the bear is larger (figure 2). Clark said the bear's "smiling because it's going to eat me." He then retracted and said that it was smiling because it liked him and wouldn't eat him but then vacillated again and said when he got in the cave the bear would eat him. Here he was victim. On the small (10 mg.) dose, the aggressive fears seemed a little less blatant than when on placebo.

During the low dose and placebo sessions there were other hostile subjects as well -- his father's submarine torpedoing Grandpa's navy ship, and "monsters" including those appearing in a dream the previous night (figure 3) as well as one which he identified as himself (figure 4).

At the first session on the 10 mg. dose, he drew himself as Santa Claus giving his first present to the art therapist -- a record player which was what Clark wanted for Christmas. It seems that Clark may handle some of his fears by trying to deny his aggressive urges and pleasing others. There is much ambivalence here, however, as seen by his varying identifications with the bear -- attacker, victim, friendly bear. At the final session when on placebo, he drew a "monster" whom he saw as "ugly" and "getting ready to eat me" (figure 4). He then decided the monster was himself, and he was going to kill a friend he doesn't like. He wrote his name on the picture because, "it's me and I'm ugly."

It seems, then, that the friendly, placating self is acceptable to Clark, whereas the attacking self is "ugly" and a "monster". In addition, there were a number of fantasies of hiding in connection with the attacking bears and monsters (in his dream, for example, he and his mother are depicted as about to jump in a hole to hide from the monsters, [figure 3]).

High Dexedrine Dose: On higher doses of amphetamine, on the other hand, the situation is quite different. On 30 mg., aggression took the form of self-punitiveness. He worked very angrily on his self-portrait, covering the mouth and teeth with brown, then smearing the face with blue, angrily enlarging the mouth and eyes with brown, and finally covering the whole face with brown. He said, "my face is messy," and that it's bad to have a messy face. He seemed quite disgusted with himself and asked the art therapist to throw away the picture.

Since the experience had been so frustrating for him, the art therapist suggested that he try another picture of himself, this time working with pastels at the easel where he would be less likely to smudge the pastels with his hands than he had at the table, which had seemed to disturb him. It was at this time that he carefully put Kleenex around each pastel he used (he had never done this before). Nevertheless, this picture developed similarly to the previous one. He made the facial features three times, at first smiling, then sad looking, then jack-o-lantern type features, each time smearing them over. Finally, he smeared the background and extended the smearing to cover the whole figure. Rather angrily and hostilely he said that it pleased him to smear it, but that it was not fun. He drew over the figure in brown, had a problem with the side of the leg, made sort of a brown mess there which appeared quite fecal, then picked up several chalks at once and smeared over the whole thing (figure 5). At this point one of the pastels fell on the floor and broke, and he berated himself saying, "I always break things." Despite reassurances about breaking the pastel, he seemed very despondent.

During this session, there was much frustration in handling the materials, which was not the case at other times. At other sessions he encountered the same difficulties of runny paint and smudgy pastels, but was able either to integrate the mistakes into his pictures, or disregard them. At this session, however, there was a combination of regressive smearing, careful neatness and very little play of fantasy.

Interestingly, these conditions changed in the final picture of this session. He drew a whale with harpoons in it, fantasized about it, and desisted from both the smearing and the concern about neatness (figure 6). Although the picture had some smudges, they did not seem to bother Clark, and he was able to make use of one of the art therapist's suggestions when he was having difficulty changing a line he wished to eliminate in order to draw the whale's mouth opened. He said that the whale had been shot with a flaming arrow by a nice fisherman. He then smiled for the first time in the session and said that he had shot the whale and that it was going to be stuffed for a museum. He retracted this, however, and said he was just pretending he shot it. He thought the whale looked angry.

It seemed that when he was able to express some of his aggressive feelings and tolerate aggressive fantasies, Clark was able to desist from smearing, concern with neatness, and self punishment and find satisfaction in expressing himself rather than being disgusted with his difficulties in expressing himself. Even so, he still needed to retract the statement that it was he who shot the whale.

On low doses of dexedrine and placebo, the aggressive urges seemed much more available to Clark than on the 30 mg. dose, at which time the aggression appeared to be directed toward himself and his resultant affect was quite depressed.

Twenty Mg. Dexedrine Dose: With 20 mg. Clark's intrapsychic condition seemed quite different from either the low or high dose. Neither fearful fantasies nor self contempt were expressed. The most aggressive picture was one of a rocket (he was very interested in a recent Apollo launch) (figure 7). It was well drawn and seemed appropriate for a boy his age, although the rocket's restraining super-structure was perhaps a bit overemphasized. (The rocket's phallic nature is obvious.) There was some smearing in other pictures, but without either regressive preoccupation or self disgust. The monsters and bears of other sessions were replaced by a "happy" dog who is going home to eat (figure 8). He said that the face in the sun, which often served as a barometer for the mood of his pictures, was happy because it was a nice day. Clark worked a long time on this picture, silently engrossed.

He made two pictures of himself at this session. The first he smeared over with black paint and said it was "messy" but that he did not feel that way. The second self portrait, however, drawn with pastels, was more complete and mature than any other (figure 9). He thought it looked "nice" and was himself "standing here drawing" and was "happy." He said he is happy most of the time now.

The pictures at this session were less expressive than at other times, and it seemed that on the 20 mg. dose there was an abatement of the fearful aggressive fantasies but that the aggression did not turn against himself as on the high dose. There appeared to be greater equilibrium with aggression channeled toward less fearful boyish interests such as the rocket and a substantial looking friendly animal, the dog. On the other hand, his interpersonal remoteness was probably related to the decrease in fantasy material.

In sum, then, on a low dose of dexedrine (10 mg.) or placebo, there was much expressiveness and play of fantasy, particularly around conflicts between hostile feelings and the need to please, accompanied by positive relatedness, physical restlessness, flight of ideas and perseveration. On a high dose (30 mg.), there was self-contempt and self-punitiveness, depression, less play of fantasy, and much frustration and lack of warm relatedness. On 20 mg., there was self-satisfaction, less expressiveness and play of fantasy, remote interpersonal relatedness, greater concentration, and a less troubled condition.

DISCUSSION

Because we have presented only a single case, it is necessary to emphasize the tentativeness of the directions we are suggesting.

The findings suggest that MBD children of Clark's type have a defect in coping with aggressive affect, perhaps of a specific nature. This defect can be altered by pharmacologic agents in positive and negative ways which are dose related.

The change in Clark's pictures through the various dosages of dexedrine offer a theroretical formulation for the dynamics of the changes, both negative and positive, produced by stimulant medication. The lower dose and placebo drawings reveal a child who subjectively cannot find, or identify with, a "good" force among the confusing array of aggressive elements he experiences. These are perceived as overwhelming and threatening. This subjective experience is reflected in the clinical observation of a child who cannot benefit from his parents' efforts to change maladaptive behavior. It certainly can be argued, however, that much of the problem is learned and acquired as the result of parental psychopathology and shortcomings. In many cases such as Clark's, there is ample evidence to support this possibility. Nevertheless, the dramatic behavioral changes brought about by stimulative drugs such as dexedrine, with resulting improvement in the child's ability to benefit from his albeit imperfect social and familial environment, suggest a basic defect in the child's ability to identify with a parental figure who brings on frustration or discomfort. (For example, the shifting identifications of aggressor or victim in relation to the bear pictures).

Besides anecdotal accounts, to our knowledge the only other report of specific alteration in the means of dealing with aggressive affect in children receiving amphetamine has been described by Bender (7). In studying the art productions of emotionally disturbed children, before and after medication with amphetamine, she found that those diagnosed as neurotic became less involved in conflict-laden themes in their art work and showed an elevation in mood after being placed on amphetamine. Children diagnosed as hyperkinetic showed a release of tension and a greater ability to identify with neutral, conflict-free subjects. Also of interest in light of our case was her finding with children diagnosed as psychopathic. She found that children who were previously aggressive and insensitive to others became depressed, withdrawn and fearful if criticized. This phenomenon is similar to our observation of Clark on high dosage. We observed this self-punitiveness and excessive sensitivity to criticism in some of our other cases, as well as those reported to us anecdotally by colleagues. This alteration in reaction suggests that in addition to the well-documented action of stimulant medications in enabling MBD children to become more accessible to new cognitive experiences in the classroom, they also render the child more accessible to emotional and affective experiences as well. For some children, it appears that a sudden removal of insensitivity to criticism, discipline, and other forms of environmental pressure is overwhelming. Fortunately in Clark's case, the "over-effect" of dexedrine was related to over-dosage. On the more moderate dose of 20 mg., this difficulty was minimal.

CONCLUSION

Certainly the area of intrapsychic phenomenology in a drug as widely used for children as amphetamine is of utmost importance. The paucity of investigation in this area is impressive and suggests a lack of suitable instruments or inadequate ones. It has been surprising to us that only Bender (7) has made use of picture-making for study in this area. Certainly art activity has been a long-recognized instrument for clinical work with children.

We feel that the demonstration of stimulant drug effect on the relationship between aggressive urges, self-concept, and affect is a significant one. It is our hope that future studies of more subjects will illuminate the terrain between physical intervention and overt behavior: the intrapsychic experience.

Furthermore, studies of other pharmocologic agents for other populations often relate psychobiological conditions to behavioral manifestations. We believe it is necessary to find methods to explore the intervening area of intrapsychic state. In addition to increasing understanding of the whole person, such investigation might enhance resolution between clinical polarities of advocacy of the use of medication only, on the one hand, and psychotherapy without drugs, on the other.

REFERENCES

1. Bradley, C. *Amer. J. Psychiat. 94,* 577, (1937).

2. Eisenberg, L., *et al. Amer. J. Orthopsychiat. 33,* 431, (1963).

3. Ginn, S. and Hohman, L. *Southern Med. J. 46,* 1124, (1953).

4. Knobel, M. *Arch. Gen. Psychiat. 6,* 198, (1962).

5. Zrull, J., *et al. Amer. J. Psychiat. 120,* 590, (1963).

6. Bradley, C. and Bowen, M. *Amer. J. Psychiat. 11,* 92, (1941).

7. Bender, L. and Cottington, F. *Amer. J. Psychiat. 99,* 116, (1942).

MENTAL HEALTH IN CHILDREN, Volume III
Edited By D. V. Siva Sankar

CHILDREN'S DRAWING AND SCHIZOPHRENIC ART PRODUCTION

A. Marinow

Psychiatric Hospital
Bela, Bulgaria

Drawing means to compose signs and to communicate by means of signs. From this arises a direct connection between thinking, observation and action. In this way the reciprocal correlation between perception and communication is perfected. In this sense drawing may be considered as pictorial writing, which has not lost its value from its most distant origins until today.

Pictorial expression is a special mode of non-verbal communication, whereby psychic experiences become accessible to other human beings. Children endeavor particularly to express graphically the external world by trying to realise a true representation of their environment, although their ideas and concepts are not yet sufficiently developed. At the base of the simple character of children's drawings lie a defective knowledge of reality and the undeveloped thought processes. When drawing children stress details, which they consider to be important for the figures they have drawn, or they neglect certain principal elements, which they feel to be less significant. The details are, however, illustrated more through the thought-connections than through an analysis of the perceptions.

All children, even when they are able to represent skillful and natural pictures do not express in their drawings their perceptions and feelings, but the drawings themselves serve as an antenna. Children draw according to an "inner model" (the "modèle interne" of Luquet). In other words they represent mostly what they know and experience - "intellectual realism" (réalisme intellectuel), but not what they contemplate and see - "visual realism" (réalisme visuel) or as Herbert Reed (1) says: "The child draws what it knows, not what it sees". The same phenomena are explained away as morbid determination in schizophrenic patients. They are directly related to the particular psychopathological syndromes and especially to hallucinations and delusions.

In children and schizophrenics not logical, but primitive modes of thought are to be found. The development of abstract thinking, from object to the simple symbols and abstract signs, may be traced through the phylo- and ontogenetic evolution of the writing: first pictorial writing developes, after that various symbols (hieroglyphs) take shape and only later a fuller abstract writing will be reached (alphabet).

Kretschmer (2) distinguishes two groups of pictorial expressions: a subjective group - representing the Ego as well as the imagination and an objective group - representing the external world as well as perception. These mechanisms of graphic expression are not yet developed in children, while in schizophrenics they are disturbed by the psychosis. Schizophrenic patients are very often unable to separate the Ego from the external world. Their imaginations are not clearly enough separated from their perceptions and they are confused within large and fluctuating limits. The dividing-line between infancy (imagination) and reality (perception) remains unclear and vague.

In children's and schizophrenic drawings we find very similar graphic phenomena. The impulse in children to scribble can be found both in their spontaneous rhythmic motion and in their delight in imitating gestures (Figures 1 and 2). These first scribbles (thing - formed) may have various meaning for the child - a man, a house or an animal, because the optic-identical evaluation is in the final analysis of secondary importance. As it grows up, the child becomes able to draw consciously a form representing an object and this begins to work purposefully. By scribbling and drawing the child takes possession of the world. As it draws, the child explains the objects to itself and "comprehends" the world of things.

Dracoulides (3) describes scribbling as a graphic automatism (automatisme graphique) in neurotic children and considers it as a symbolic expression of liberating tendencies with a therapeutic value. Prinzhorn (4) has given numerous illustrations of schizophrenics' disorderly scribbles. Rennert (5) finds the formless scribblings in incoherent patients and considers this phenomenon not so characteristic of schizophrenics (Figures 3 and 4). The incoherent confused thinking may be expressed in schizophrenic drawings by means of scribbles and conglomerations of peculiar form elements and entirely different motives, which Rennert (5) describes as "picture - salad" (Figures 5 and 6). While "head - foot" forms, both "X-ray drawings" and the side view of the figures are a simple and typical representation of children for the human figure (Figure 7 - 11), these phenomena are considered as regressive motives in schizophrenics (5) (Figures 12 and 13). In profile head-representation a "mixed-profile" is often produced by means of the fusion of both profile and side view (Figures 14 and 15). Machover's (6) drawing test profile drawing is considered as introversion, whereas the "en-face" representation is considered as extraversion in the person under experiment.

Navratil (7) considers the profile as a higher formation model, which the child acquires in later stages of its psychic development. The mixed-profile is based on a discrepency between volition and ability. Because of this disproportion the dividing-line between the Self and the external world becomes confused, from which arises the experience of dissolution of the personality and the doubt in one's identity. The mixed-profile is one of the most impressive symbols of the schizophrenic dissociation, which we have described in 1963 in the terminal stages of schizophrenia (8). The mixed-profile marks a traditional stage in pictorial development of the child. The same phenomenon is a characteristic element of style for a schizophrenic formation, as well as a motive of the mannerism of many modern painters such as Picasso, Klee and Miro.

The graphic representation of movement is necessary as a

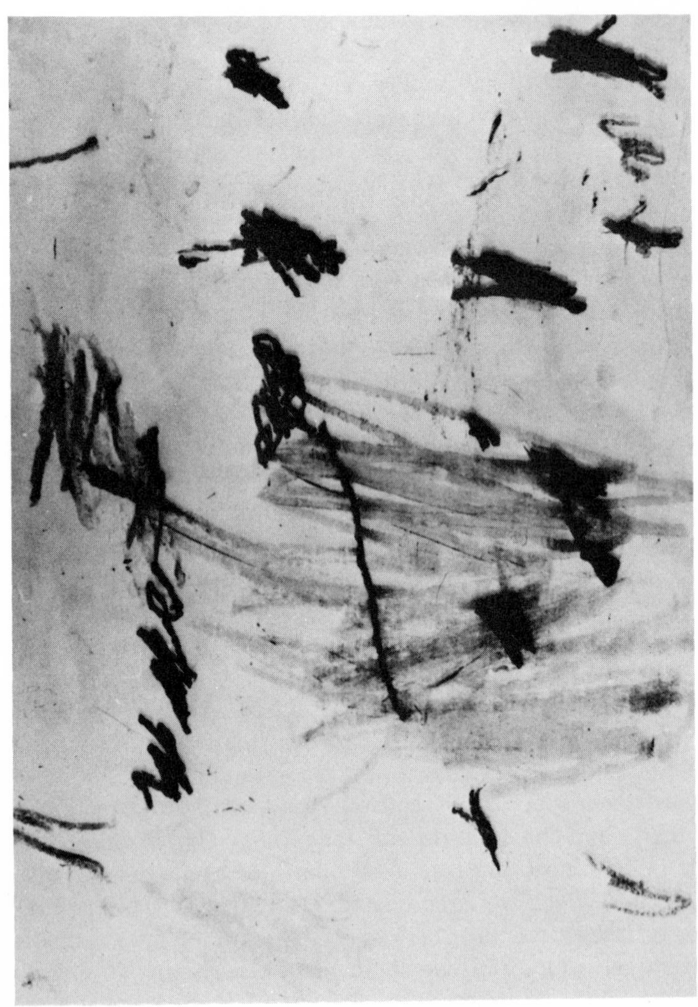

Fig. 1: Monkeys. Scribble, age $3\frac{1}{2}$, girl.

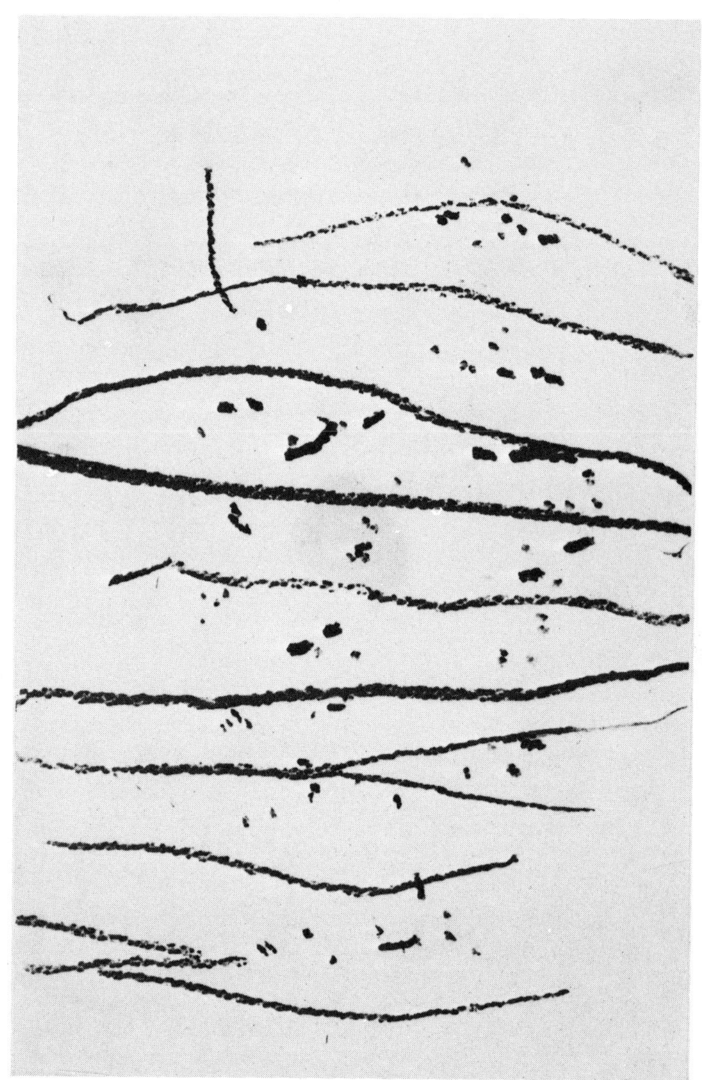

Fig. 2: High hauses and people. Scribble, age 3½, girl.

Fig. 3: My enemy. Scribble, age 28, Chronic paranoid schizophrenia, male.

Fig. 4: My persecutors. Age 28, Chronic paranoid schizophrenia, male.

Fig. 5: Picture salad. Age 28, Chronic paranoid schizophrenia, male.

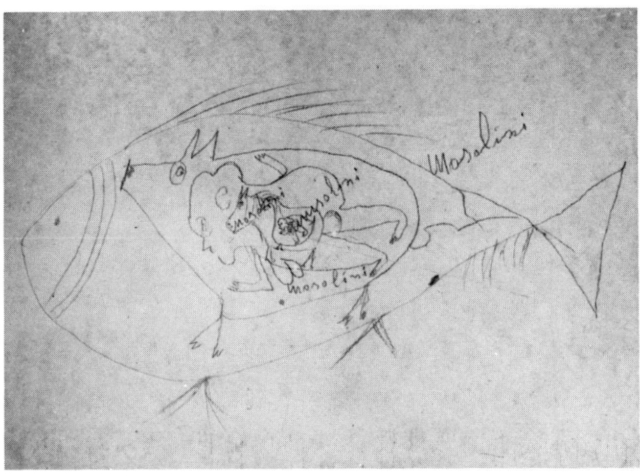

Fig. 6: Conglomerations and Transparency, age 52, paraphrenia, male.

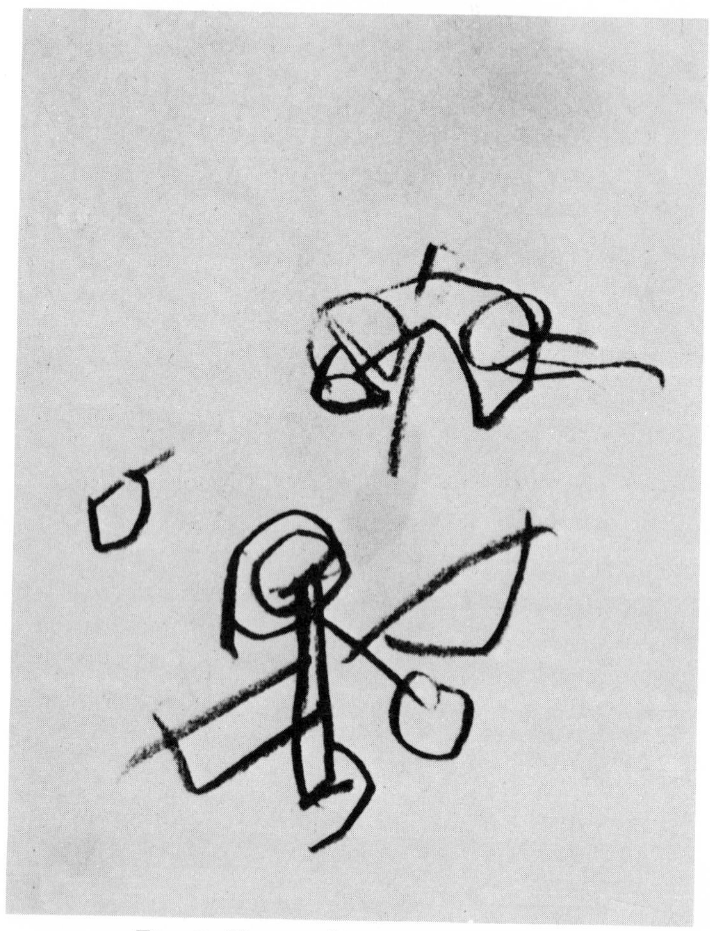

Fig. 7: Human figures. age 3½, girl.

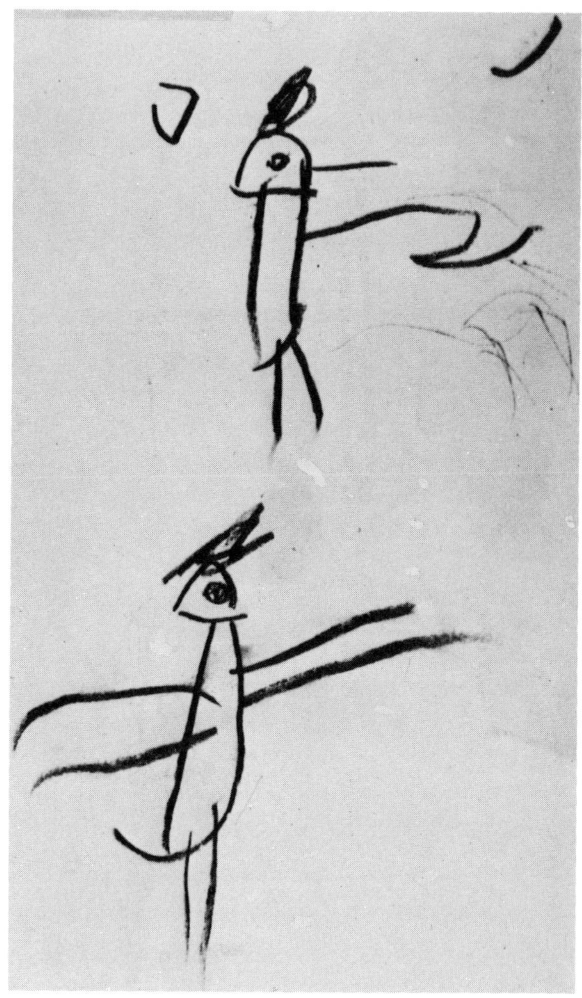

Fig. 8: Human figures, Age 4, girl.

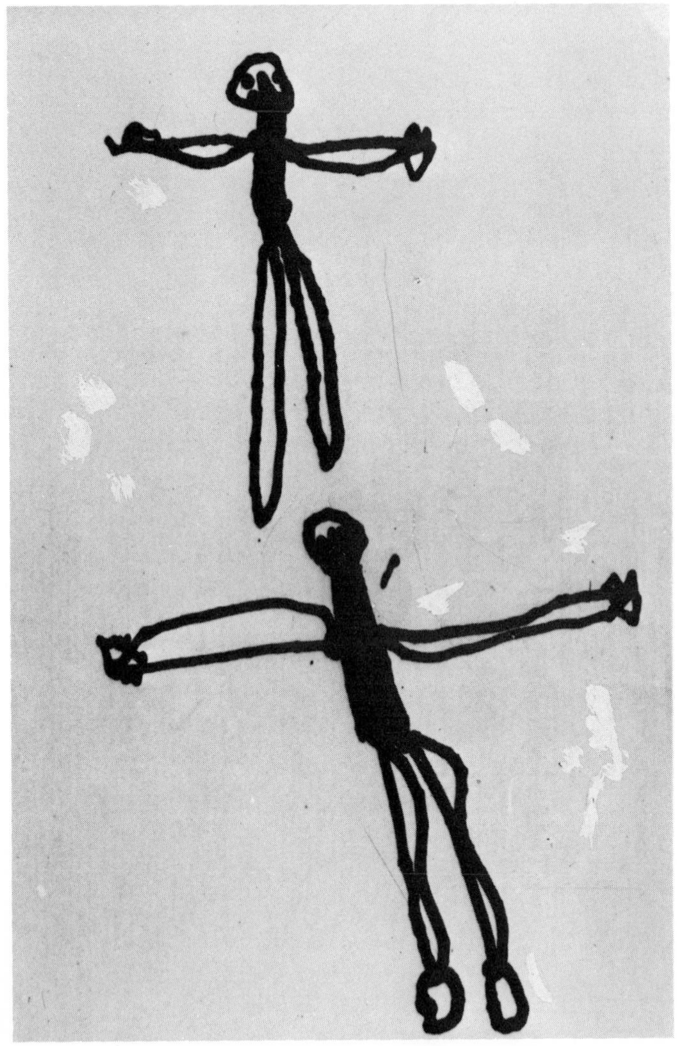

Fig. 9: Human figures. Age 5, girl.

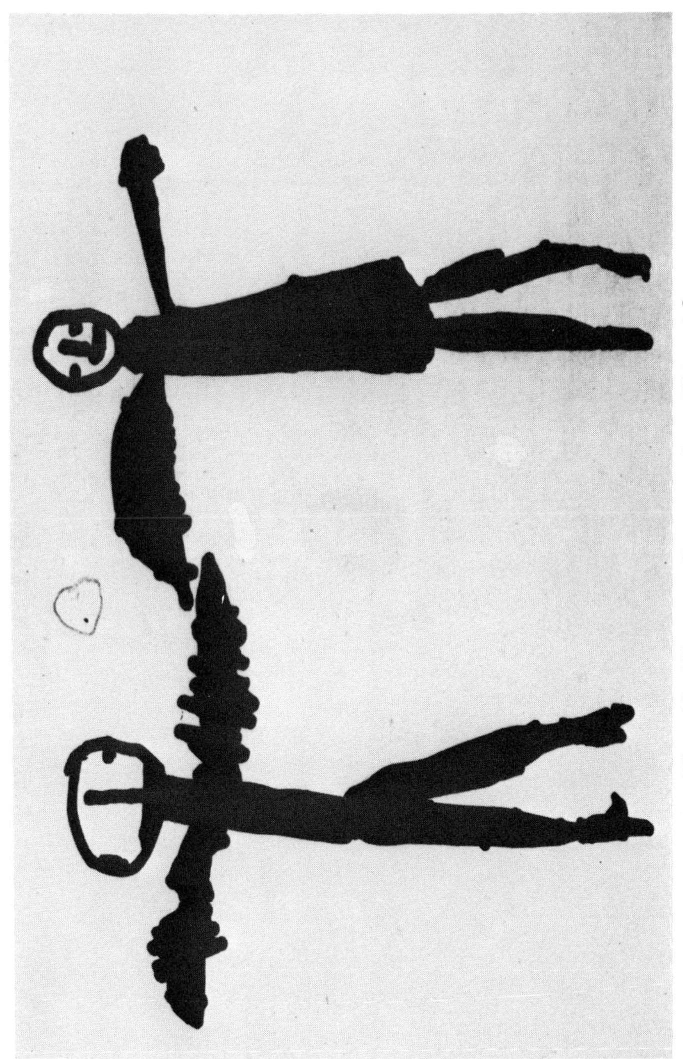

Fig. 10: Human figures. Age 5½, girl.

Fig. 11: My mother walking. Age 6, school girl.

Fig. 12: Deformation and transparency. Age 52, Paraphrenia, male.

Fig. 13: Deformation, disproportion and mixing side view with en-face position. Sexual aggressiveness. Age 28, Chronic paranoid. Sch., male.

Fig. 14: Deformation, disproportion, mutilation, symbolization. Mixing profile and en-face position. Regression. Acute paranoid Sch. , male, age 32.

Fig. 15: Mixing profile and en-face position. Schematization and disproportion. Age 28, male, Chronic paranoid schizophrenia.

Fig. 16: The eyes of my enemy. Symbolization. Age 42, painter, male. Chronic paranoid schizophrenia.

Fig. 17: The face of my enemy. Symbolization with geometrization. Dissolution of the image. Age 42, male, painter. Chronic paranoid schizophrenia.

degree of the development of thinking and expressive potential. Movement always depends on activity and brings several people into contact. In children's and schizophrenics' drawings, movement is very often represented defectively, so that the pictures are stiff and rigid and they appear petrified.

In time children overcome the initial primitive stages of their expressive potential, while schizophrenic patients show a hopeless deformation of the pictorial expression, to which Navratil (7) pays special attention. The graphic symbols of children's drawings may be explained by their poverty of ideas and an insufficiently developed thinking - intellectual rationalism. These graphic phenomena are in schizophrenics morbidly conditioned - morbid rationalism - and they are connected with the hallucinations and the delusions. Therefore, we can consider them as "Picto - grapho - syndromes" (9) (Figures 16 and 17). The morphological deformation and the disproportion space of the figures drawn, with addition of details, leads to pictorial conglomerations in children's drawings (3). The same graphic phenomena are described in schizophrenics by Bobon and Maccagnani (10) as para- and neomorphisms.

Summary:

Drawings of *children and schizophrenics* are a particular mode of expression, and non-verbal communication, whereby psychic experiences become accessible to other human beings. In both of these plastic works we find very similar graphic phenomena.

The style of *children's pictorial works* is related to their psychological development and it ameliorates gradually as the child grows up. In *schizophrenics*, and especially in chronic and terminal stages of the psychosis, the style of the patients' works is determined by the psychopathological syndromes, whereby very often a "Stilwandel" (change of style) may appear.

The similarities between drawings of children and schizophrenics is only superficial and seeming.

References:

1. Reed, H.: *Erziehung durch Kunst.* Knaur, Munchen, (1962).
2. Kretschmer, E.: *Medizinische Psychologie.* Thieme, Stuttgart, (1956).
3. Dracoulides, N.N.: *Psychanalyse de l'artiste et de son oeuvre.* Mont-Blanc S.A., Geneve, (1952).
4. Prinzhorn, H.: *Bildnerei der Geisteskranken.* Springer, Berlin, (1922).
5. Rennert, H.: *Merkmale schizophrener Bildnerei.* Fischer, Jena, (1962).
6. Machover, K.: *Personality Projection in the Drawing of the Human Figure.* Thomas, Springfield, Ill., (1948).
7. Navratil, L.: *Schizophrenie und Kunst.* dtv, Munchen, (1965).
8. Marinow, A.: *Conf. Psychiat. 6,* 102, (1963).
9. Marinow, A.: *Diagnostische und phanomenologische Bewertung der bildnerischen Tatigkeit Geisteskranker. III.* Coll. Internat. SIPE, Freudenstadt, (1965).
10. Bobon, J.: *Psychopathologie de l'expression.* Masson, Paris, (1962).

Additional References:

1. Abraham, A.: Le dessin d'une personne. Le test de Machover. Delachaux-Nestle, Neuchatel, (1963).
2. Jakab, I.: Zeichnungen und Gemalde der Geisteskranken. Budapest, (1956).
3. Müller, R.: Vorschulkinder malen und zeichnen. Volk u. Wissen Verlag, Berlin, (1969).
4. Pfennig, R.: Zeichnen als Vorgang und als kurzester Weg. Kunst u. Unterricht, H. 5, Sept. 1969, S. 12, Friedrich Verlag, Vellor b. Hannover.
5. Volmat, R.: La schizophrenie par l'image. Paris, (1956).

MENTAL HEALTH IN CHILDREN, Volume III
Edited By D. V. Siva Sankar

RELATIONSHIP BETWEEN SYMPTOMATOLOGY AND DIAGNOSIS IN CHILD CLINICAL PRACTICE

Jean S. Braun

Oakland University
Rochester, Michigan 48063

For most practitioners it is a truism that the symptom should not be confused with the "disease," i.e. a diagnosis cannot be made on the basis of the presenting problem, especially in child practice. Nevertheless since, in clinical training, we are accustomed to teach probabilities, there are temptations to assume that, if a given presenting symptomatology appears, it will be accompanied by a certain dynamic and behavioral picture which in turn implies a specific diagnosis.

The principal aim of this study was to determine empirically whether or not it is possible to make such probability statements on the basis of one practitioner's experience with 600 cases. No theoretical formulation was made, nor any predictions or hypotheses. This was an attempt to see whether or not certain diagnoses did in fact flow out of the evaluation procedure when specific symptomatology presented itself. The evaluation included an interview with one or both parents and a psychological examination. In some cases, depending upon the source of the referral, there was a history from the school or a complete psychiatric evaluation. Children, in this instance, were defined as individuals from pre-school age through 17 years.

Clearly, from a methodological point of view, there are criticisms to be made of this study and these may explain in part why no similar studies were to be found in the literature. There are statistics regarding the incidence or prevalence of a given psychiatric diagnostic group in the general population, but these do not take into account the original presenting problem. A study of this type is unavoidably subjective: it was necessary to group together certain kinds of symptoms and there could be quarrels as to whether the groupings are homogeneous. In addition, there were often multiple presenting problems, and it was necessary to decide which was the major one, for purposes of the study. Finally, the diagnostic categories employed are not always those described in the Psychiatric Handbook and are also open to question, if not argument. To help the reader identify possible biases in the author's judgment, we should add that the present writer tends to formulate dynamics in a Freudian or Eriksonian fashion, but has done a good deal of research into learning disabilities and so holds the view that deficits in cognitive-perceptual-motor areas are more often implicated in such disabilities than are dynamic conflicts.

With the awareness of these *caveats*, let us proceed to the method and analysis. The following information was recorded on all 600 cases: presenting problem, age, IQ level, sex of subject and diagnosis. Despite efforts to combine presenting problems, there were 25 final categories under this heading: school problem (behavioral or academic); depression and withdrawal; acting out (which could include tantrums in an older child); sexual deviation or question of it; question of hysterical basis of somatic complaints; hyperactivity; sibling had problem; question of retardation; bizarre behavior; conflicts with parents; question of degree of functional loss through injury or known neurological condition; speech problems; compulsions; question of suitability for adoption; tics; drug use; school refusal; social immaturity; pregnancy; question of school or vocational planning; developmental immaturity;

somatic complaints; enuresis; elective mutism and custody question in divorce.

Age levels were: below five years; five years; six to seven; eight to 10; 11 to 12; 13 to 15; and 16 to 17. IQ level divisions were: retarded; borderline; dull normal; average; bright normal; superior; very superior; significant discrepancy between WISC or WAIS verbal and performance scales with verbal higher; significant discrepancy between verbal and performance scales with performance higher. A significant discrepancy in this case was at least 15 points.

Diagnostic categories totalled 18 and are largely self explanatory. They include: normal child (in personality functioning, although IQ might be below average); character disorder (on the psychopathic continuum); neurotic; depressed; prepsychotic; adjustment reaction (in a child with sound history when symptoms seemed a result of the child's interaction between child's developmental stage and parental reactions); cognitive-perceptual-motor deficits with intact personality development (but usually with academic learning problem); psychotic; definite indications of brain damage or other neurological dysfunction; hyperkinesis; immature personality (developmentally defined, of course); unpatterned because of poor parenting (primitive in personality); cognitive-perceptual-motor deficits and characterological problems; characterological problems, not crystallized; homosexual identification; hysterical personality; cognitive-perceptual-motor deficits with neurotic problems (usually in child whose emotional difficulties stem from factors independent of those often implicated in C-P-M children); and aphasic.

Appendix A lists all of the diagnoses accompanying each presenting problem and indicates the percentage of children manifesting the presenting problem that received each diagnosis. Appendix B shows the percentage of cases (of the total of 600) that came with each presenting problem. It should be noted that some presenting problems occurred infrequently, e.g. question of custody in a divorce case (N=1), when 100% of the total is still only one.

The presenting problem that occurred most frequently was a school problem. This may be a function of the special interests of the present writer. However, a count of the referral sources to the Lafayette Clinic (Detroit, Michigan) over a year's time some years ago showed that 55% of the cases came from schools, so that it seems likely that children's problems manifest themselves particularly clearly in the schools. Part of the reason is that parents have few other children with whom to compare their offspring, while the schools have a readily-available norm group, and, additionally, parents are often less threatened by bringing their child to a professional person with a concern about his school performance rather than about some interpersonal difficulty. This latter point seems corroborated to some degree by the fact that the presenting problem of school difficulties is the only one which is associated with every one of the possible diagnostic categories. As would be predicted, however, more than half of the children with this presenting problem were found to have C-P-M- deficits or to have quite definite indications of neurological dysfunction--all of these diagnoses being on the "organic" continuum. The only other sizeable groups within this presenting problem were neurotics (10.7%) and immature personality (6.8%).

The striking factor in the diagnoses associated with the symptoms of depression and withdrawal is that one third of this group were found to be either psychotic or prepsychotic (a total of 30.8%). Neurotics and hysterical personalities were equally represented (17.9% each), but only 15.4% of this group were diagnosed as depressed. Of course, some of the neurotics and hysterics showed depressive features, but this diagnosis was not used unless depression was the predominant feature of the personality functioning.

As might be expected, more that 40% of the acting out patients received diagnoses on the characterological continuum, i.e. character disorder, character problems not crystallized and immature personality. However, 11.3% of this group proved to be neurotic, indicating the danger of concluding from an acting out symptom that anxiety is not present.

Neurotic children made up a sizeable fraction of the group with hyperactivity (15.4%), while almost half of this group were seen as hyperkinetic or having C-P-M- deficits. This corroborates the clinical impression that some children are hyperactive because of dynamic difficulties, not because of organicity.

The variety of possible diagnoses associated with a similar presenting problem is illustrated by both the school refusal and the social immaturity groups. Although there are traditional dynamic formulations suggested by school refusals, this group proved to be one-third psychotic, with neurotic and depressed representing only another third. The most sizeable diagnostic categories associated with social immaturity were psychosis, character disorder and prepsychotic, perhaps the child version of the adult inadequate personality.

As is the case with virtually every aspect of child psychological problems studied, boys in this study population outnumbered the girls, 386 boys to 214 girls. Appendix C gives the breakdown by sex of the presenting problem groups. The percentages in parentheses indicate what percentage of the total number of boys and girls, respectively, manifested the specific presenting problem. The three presenting problems seen most often in boys were school difficulties (39.8%), acting out (15.1%) and question of school or vocational planning (7.6%.) Girls also were reported as experiencing school difficulties, but less frequently than boys (25%) and the percentage of girls acting out (22.6%) was also much higher. The third most frequent category for girls was conflict with parents (19.3½), which may, of course, reflect differing expectations for girls' behavior. When the diagnostic categories were broken down by sex, because of the differences in the size of the groups, the largest percentage of cases seen was male, in all except three diagnostic categories--adjustment reaction, hyperkinesis and hysterical personality (even though the present writer is a woman and presumably free from the stereotyped expectations!) Appendix D gives the complete list of percentages by diagnostic category and sex. In the analysis of percentage of total male or female group assigned each diagnosis, it can be seen that both sexes were represented in all diagnostic categories. The three most frequent among boys were neurotic (12%), C-P-M- with neurotic features (11%) and, tied at 10% each, C-P-M- with intact personality and C-P-M- with characterological features. Among girls the largest diagnostic category was neurotic (14%), followed by hysterical personality (11%) and immature personality (10%). Since in both sex groups the most common diagnosis was neurosis, it would appear that the anxious, conflicted child is still very much with us, despite the diversification of diagnostic categories and the possible effects of changes in childrearing practices.

When this population is broken down by age group, several factors are notable. Two peaks occur in referrals, the group from eight to 10 years of age, long enough in school and peer group activities for problems to be defined, and the group from 13 to 15, or the beginnings of adolescence. Acting out, vocational and school planning, and conflict with parents are the only presenting problem found at every age level, with school difficulties found at every age in which children are in school. Question of retardation is the presenting problem only in the three youngest age groups and this is largely true of developmental immaturity also. Bizarre behavior was reported as young as six to seven. Other problems, such as suspected sexual deviation, are found at the age levels at which they might be predicted, i.e. principally in adolescence.

In relating diagnosis to age, one perhaps unexpected factor emerges. The unpatterned child, the individual whose difficulties appear to stem from the failure of parents to make expectations clear and to set appropriate standards, is found at every age level except the oldest, 16 to 17. It might have been expected that this is a picture to be seen principally at younger ages. Hyperkinetic children were not so diagnosed above the age of 10. C-P-M- with characterological problems tend to be older than C-P-M- children with intact personalities and this may be a function of the effect repeated stress has had upon the child's personality development, as would be predicted. Normal children were seen at all ages, except preschool.

Analysis of results by IQ level does not present many surprises. In nearly all categories with sizeable numbers, the largest percentage of children were found to be average. This was not true among those where the question was degree of functional loss stemming from injury or known neurological condition. Similarly, those children diagnosed as manifesting definite neurological signs were found to cluster at the lower end of the IQ scale. Normal children were found at all IQ levels, as were C-P-M- children with intact personality development, except that the latter included none in the borderline IQ range. Crystallized character disorders were seen only at dull normal levels and above, as were children with character problems not yet crystallized. The same was true of prepsychotic children. Despite the usual belief that the presence of thought disorder will result in retarded obtained IQs, none of the psychotic group scored at the retarded level, 7.7% were borderline, but all others were average or above.

While we have seen that some generalizations can be made regarding the probably diagnosis in the face of a given presenting problem the data on these 600 cases suggest that, at most, these generalizations can provide the most tentative of hypotheses. The age and IQ distributions show that, except for a few situations, which might also be determined by "common sense," there is little correlation between these variables and presenting problem or diagnosis. Sixty per cent of children referred because of developmental immaturity, for example, showed indication of brain damage or definite neurological dysfunction and 40% were retarded, but 10% were, respectively, C-P-M- normal, C-P-M- with characterological problems, aphasic--all on the "organic" continuum--and immature personality, while 20% were average in IQ and 10% were superior. In individual cases, therefore, the clinician will still have to proceed with his usual caution to ascertain that he is not dealing with the case who contradicts the possible generalization.

DIAGNOSES ASSOCIATED WITH SPECIFIC PRESENTING PROBLEMS
APPENDIX A

(Percentages represent frequency of diagnosis within group presenting specific problem)

Presenting Problem	Diagnosis	Percent of Problem Group
School	C-P-M- Normal	19.4
	C-P-M Character Probs.	17.0
	Neurotic	10.7
	C-P-M Neurotic	9.7
	Brain damaged	10.2
	Immature personality	6.8

	Normal	4.4
	Character disorder	4.4
	Prepsychotic	2.9
	Depressed	2.4
	Aphasic	2.4
	Character Probs., not crystallized	2.4
	Unpatterned, poor parenting	1.9
	Hysterical personality	1.5
	Hyperkinetic	1.5
	Adjustment reaction	1.0
	Psychotic	1.0
	Homosexual identification	.5
Depression and withdrawal	Prepsychotic	23.1
	Neurotic	17.9
	Hysterical personality	17.9
	Depressed	15.4
	Adjustment reaction	12.8
	Psychotic	7.7
	C-P-M Normal	2.6
	Immature personality	2.6
Sexual deviation or question of	Neurotic	33.3
	Immature personality	22.2
	Character problems not crystallized	22.2
	Character disorder	11.1
	Brain damaged	11.1
Question of hysterical somatic complaints	Hysterical personality	50.0
	Neurotic	25.0
	Brain damaged	25.0
Hyperactivity	Hyperkinetic	23.1
	C-P-M normal	15.4
	Neurotic	15.4
	Character disorder	7.7
	Depressed	7.7
	Prepsychotic	7.7

	Immature personality	7.7
	C-P-M character problems	7.7
	C-P-M neurotic	7.7
Sibling had problem	Normal	55.6
	C-P-M neurotic	22.2
	Adjustment reaction	11.1
	C-P-M normal	11.1
Acting out	Character disorder	18.9
	Character probs., not crystallized	13.2
	Immature personality	12.3
	Neurotic	11.3
	Adjustment reaction	7.5
	C-P-M character problems	5.7
	C-P-M neurotic	4.7
	Depression	4.7
	Unpatterned	4.7
	Psychotic	3.8
	Brain damaged	3.8
	Hysterical personality	3.8
	Prepsychotic	3.8
	Normal	.9
	Hyperkinetic	.9
Question of retardation	Brain damaged	57.1
	C-P-M normal	14.3
	Unpatterned	14.3
	Aphasic	
Bizarre behavior	Immature personality	25.0
	Hysterical personality	25.0
	Neurotic	12.5
	Adjustment reaction	12.5
	Psychotic	12.5
	Brain damaged	12.5
Conflicts with parents	Neurotic	21.5
	Adjustment reaction	12.3
	Immature personality	10.8

	Character probs., not crystallized	18.08
	Normal	9.2
	C-P-M character probs.	7.7
	Hysterical personality	7.7
	Unpatterned	4.6
	Depressed	3.1
	C-P-M normal	3.1
	C-P-M neurotic	1.5
	Homosexual identification	1.5
	Hyperkinetic	1.5
	Brain damaged	1.5
Question of functional loss from injury or known neuro-logical condition	Brain damaged	47.1
	Normal	23.5
	Character disorder	5.9
	Immature personality	5.9
	Unpatterned	5.9
	Aphasic	5.9
	Character problems not crystallized	5.9
Speech problems	Neurotic	100.0
Compulsions	Psychotic	100.0
Question of adoption	Character problems, not crystallized	40.0
	C-P-M character probs.	20.0
	Normal	20.0
	Brain damaged	20.0
Tics	Character disorder	50.0
	Neurotic	50.0
Drug use	Character disorder	21.1
	Depressed	21.1
	Prepsychotic	15.8
	Adjustment reactions	10.5
	Immature personality	10.5
	Character probs., not crystallized	10.5
	Neurotic	5.3
	C-P-M character problems	5.3

School refusal	Psychotic	33.3
	Character disorder	16.7
	Neurotic	16.7
	Depressed	16.7
	Immature personality	16.7
Social immaturity	Immature personality	24.1
	Neurotic	20.7
	Prepsychotic	13.8
	Character disorder	6.9
	C-P-M character problems	6.9
	Normal	3.4
	Depressed	3.4
	C-P-M- Normal	3.4
	Brain damaged	3.4
	Unpatterned	3.4
	Character probs., not cryst.	3.4
	Hysterical personality	3.4
	Aphasic	3.4
Pregnancy	Depressed	66.7
	Immature personality	33.3
Question of school or vocational planning	Brain damaged	21.2
	Normal	18.2
	Unpatterned	12.1
	Hyperkinetic	9.1
	Immature personality	9.1
	Neurotic	6.1
	C-P-M- neurotic	6.1
	Aphasic	6.1
	Character disorder	3.0
	Depressed	3.0
	Adjustment reaction	3.0
	C-P-M- normal	3.0
Developmental immaturity	Brain damaged	60.0
	C-P-M- normal	10.0
	Immature personality	10.0
	C-P-M character probs.	10.0
	Aphasic	10.0
Somatic complaints	Normal	33.3
	Hysterical personality	33.3
	C-P-M- neurotic	33.3

Enuresis	Adjustment reaction	100.0
Elective mutism	Neurotic	100.0
Question of custody in divorce case	Normal	100.0

APPENDIX B

PERCENTAGE OF CASES REPRESENTED BY EACH PRESENTING PROBLEM
N=600

Presenting Problem	Percentage of Total
School difficulties--behavior and/or learning	34.4
Acting out	17.7
Conflicts with parents	10.9
Depression and withdrawal	6.5
School or vocational planning	5.5
Social immaturity	4.8
Drug use	3.2
Question of functional loss through injury or known neurological condition	2.8
Hyperactivity	2.2
Developmental immaturity	1.7
Sexual deviation or question of	1.5
Sibling had problem	1.5
Bizarre behavior	1.3
Question of retardation	1.2
School refusal	1.0
Question of adoption	.8
Question of hysterical somatic complaints	.7
Somatic complaints	.5
Pregnancy	.5
Tics	.3
Speech problems	.2
Compulsions	.2
Enuresis	.2
Elective mutism	.2
Question of custody in divorce case	.2

APPENDIX C

Presenting Problem by Sex of Patient

Presenting Problem	% Male	% Total Males	% Female	% Total Females
School	74.3	39.8	25.7	25.0
Depression	61.5	6.3	38.5	7.1
Acting out	54.7	15.1	45.3	22.6
Sex deviation	100.0	2.3	--	--
Hysterical somatic	50.0	.5	50	.9
Hyperactivity	69.2	2.3	30.8	1.9
Sibling problem	75.0	1.6	25.0	.9
Question--retard.	85.7	1.6	14.3	.5
Bizarre behavior	--	--	100.0	3.8
Conflict with parents	35.9	6.0	64.1	19.3
Functional loss?	76.5	3.4	23.5	1.9
Speech problems	--	--	100.0	.5
Compulsions	100.0	.3	--	--

Adoption ?	60.0	.8	40.0	.9
Tics	100.0	.5	--	--
Drug use	78.9	3.9	21.1	1.9
School refusal	50.0	.8	50.0	1.4
Social immaturity	60.7	4.4	29.3	5.2
Pregnancy	--	--	100.0	1.4
Vocational planning	87.9	7.6	12.1	1.9
Developmental immat.	60.0	1.6	40.0	1.9
Somatic complaints	75.0	.8	25.0	.5
Enuresis	100.0	.3	--	--
Elective mutism	100.0	.3	--	--
Divorce custody	--	--	100.0	.5

APPENDIX D

Diagnosis by Sex of Patient

Diagnosis	N	% Male	% Total Males	% Female	% Total Females
Normal	34	61.8	5.0	38.2	5.0

Character Disorder	43	83.3	9.0	16.7	3.0
Neurotic	76	61.3	12.0	38.7	14.0
Depressed	28	67.9	5.0	32.1	4.0
Prepsychotic	28	71.4	5.0	28.6	4.0
Adjustment reaction	30	31.0	2.0	69.0	9.0
C-P-M- Intact	51	78.0	10.0	2.0	5.0
Psychotic	13	69.2	2.0	30.8	2.0
Neurological	57	71.4	11.0	28.6	7.0
Hyperkinetic	11	45.5	1.0	54.5	3.0
Immature personality	55	60.0	9.0	40.0	10.0
Unpatterned	18	61.1	3.0	38.9	3.0
C-P-M Character	52	71.2	10.0	28.8	7.0
Character Problems	34	61.8	5.0	38.2	6.0
Homosexual	2	50.0	.03	50.0	.05
Hysterical Personality	25	4.0	.03	96.0	11.0
C-P-M- Neurotic	32	84.4	7.0	15.6	2.0
Aphasic	11	81.8	2.0	18.2	1.0

N= 386 males, 214 females

APPENDIX E

Age Groups by Presenting Problem
Diagnosis

Presenting Problem	% Below 5 N=16	% 5 years N=24	% 6-7 yrs. N=108	% 8-10 N=131	% 11-12 N=83	% 13-15 N=128	% 16-17 N=100
School	--	1.0	24.3	36.4	18.4	15.5	4.4
Depression	--	--	5.1	2.6	7.1	35.9	48.7
Acting out	2.8	1.9	7.5	12.3	14.2	38.7	22.6
Sexual deviation	--	--	--	22.2	--	44.4	33.3
Hysterical somatic	--	--	--	--	--	100.0	--
Hyperactivity	--	--	61.5	38.5	--	--	--
Sibling problem	--	--	66.7	22.2	11.1	--	--
of retarded	42.9	28.6	14.3	--	--	--	--
Bizarre behavior	--	--	12.5	12.5	25.0	25.0	25.0
Conflict with parents	3.1	4.6	10.8	13.8	15.4	29.2	23.1
Functional loss ?	--	11.8	47.1	23.5	5.9	11.8	--
Speech problems	--	--	--	--	100.0	--	--
Compulsions	--	--	--	--	--	100.0	--
Adoption ?	20.0	--	20.0	60.0	--	--	--
Tics	--	--	--	50.0	--	--	50.0

Drug use	--	--	--	--	--	42.1	57.9
School refusal	--	--	--	16.7	16.7	33.3	33.3
Social immaturity	--	3.4	13.8	24.1	31.0	13.8	13.8
Pregnancy	--	--	--	--	---	33.3	66.7
School, Vocational Planning	12.1	30.3	15.2	9.1	6.1	6.1	21.2
Developmental Immaturity	30.0	10.0	50.0	10.0	--	--	--
Somatic Complaints	--	--	25.0	--	--	50.0	25.0
Enuresis	--	--	--	100.0	--	--	--
Elective mutism	--	--	100.0	--	--	--	--
Custody ?	--	100.0	--	--	--	--	--
Diagnosis							
Normal	--	17.1	28.6	22.9	5.7	14.3	11.4
Character Disorder	--	--	2.4	11.9	23.8	33.3	28.6
Neurotic	--	--	10.7	30.7	17.3	18.7	22.7
Depression	--	--	14.3	7.1	10.7	35.7	32.1
Prepsychotic	--	3.6	10.7	14.3	21.4	28.6	21.4
Adjustment reaction	3.4	--	10.3	3.4	--	48.3	34.5
C-P-M- Intact	--	2.0	42.0	44.0	6.0	4.0	2.0
Psychotic	--	--	--	7.7	7.7	53.8	30.8

Neurological	10.7	10.7	25.0	23.2	14.3	14.3	1.8
Hyperkinetic	9.1	18.2	54.5	18.2	--	--	--
Immature Personality	--	--	7.1	26.8	7.1	33.9	25.0
Unpatterned	36.8	26.3	21.1	5.3	5.3	5.3	--
C-P-M Characterological	--	1.9	21.2	23.1	30.8	17.3	5.8
Character Problems	2.9	--	14.7	17.6	23.5	32.4	8.8
Homosexuality	--	--	--	--	--	--	100.0
Hysterical Personality	--	--	--	4.0	12.0	44.0	40.0
C-P-M- Neurotic	--	3.1	37.5	25.0	15.6	12.5	6.3
Aphasic	--	9.1	18.2	54.5	--	--	18.2

APPENDIX F

Pres. Prob.	% Retard.	% Bord.	D.	% Norm.	% Ave.	% B.N.	% Sup.	% V.Sup.	% Hi V
School	1.5	3.9	9.2	38.8	9.2	6.3	1.9	9.7	19.4
Depressed	--	2.6	5.1	41.0	20.5	10.3	--	15.4	5.1
Acting Out	--	5.7	9.4	39.6	12.3	11.3	3.8	8.5	9.4
Sexual Deviation	--	--	11.1	33.3	22.2	--	11.1	11.1	11.1
Hysterical Somatic	--	--	--	75.5	25.0	--	--	--	--
Hyperactivity	--	--	--	53.8	15.4	15.4	--	--	--
Sibling Problem	--	--	11.1	22.2	22.2	11.1	11.1	11.1	11.1
?Retarded	14.3	14.3	14.3	28.6	14.3	--	--	--	--
Bizarre	12.5	--	--	25.0	--	50.0	12.5	--	--
Conflict with Parents	--	--	3.1	29.2	29.2	12.3	9.2	10.8	6.2
Functional Loss?	29.4	--	23.5	17.6	5.9	5.9	--	--	--
Speech Problems	--	--	--	--	--	--	100.0	--	--
Compulsions	--	--	--	--	100.0	--	--	--	--
Adoption?	--	--	--	40.0	40.0	--	--	--	20.0
Tics	--	--	--	--	50.0	--	50.0	--	--
Drug Use	--	--	5.3	52.6	15.8	5.3	--	5.3	15.8
School Refusal	--	16.7	--	50.0	16.7	16.7	--	--	--

Social Immaturity	--	--	3.4	31.0	13.8	10.3	3.4	17.2	20.7
Pregnancy	--	--	33.3	33.3	--	--	--	--	33.3
Vocational Planning	6.1	3.0	6.1	39.4	12.1	15.2	12.1	3.0	3.0
Developmental Immaturity	40.0	10.0	20.0	20.0	--	10.0	--	--	--
Somatic Compulsions	--	--	--	25.0	--	50.0	--	--	25.0
Enuresis	--	--	--	--	--	100.0	--	--	--
Elective mutism	--	--	--	--	--	100.0	--	--	--
Custody	--	--	--	100.0	--	--	--	--	--
Diagnosis									
Normal	2.9	2.9	17.1	28.6	14.3	17.1	14.3	2.9	--
Character Disorder	--	--	16.7	38.1	14.3	7.1	4.8	9.5	9.5
Neurotic	--	1.3	--	38.7	30.7	17.3	6.7	1.3	4.0
Depressed	--	--	7.1	42.9	21.4	3.6	--	14.3	10.7
Prepsychotic	--	--	7.1	39.3	10.7	10.7	3.6	21.4	7.1
Adjustment reaction	--	--	17.2	20.7	20.7	27.6	3.4	6.9	3.4
C-P-M- Intact	2.0	--	2.0	44.0	4.0	10.0	2.0	12.0	24.0
Psychotic	--	7.7	--	30.8	7.7	30.8	--	7.7	15.4
Neurological	25.0	17.9	23.2	17.9	1.8	--	1.8	3.6	8.9
Hyperactive	--	--	--	45.5	27.3	9.1	--	9.1	9.1

Immature Personality	--	10.7	12.5	50.0	12.5	1.8	1.8	1.8	8.9
Unpatterned	--	--	--	47.4	21.1	10.5	15.8	--	5.3
C-P-M- Character	--	--	1.9	44.2	7.7	1.9	--	11.5	32.7
Char. Probs.	--	--	5.9	38.2	11.8	14.7	11.8	8.8	8.8
Homosex.	--	--	--	--	100.0	--	--	--	--
Hyst. Pers.	--	--	--	40.0	20.5	16.0	--	16.0	8.0
CPM-Neurot.	--	--	--	21.9	12.5	6.3	3.1	28.1	28.1
Aphasic	--	--	9.1	54.5	--	--	--	--	36.4

MENTAL HEALTH IN CHILDREN, Volume III
Edited By D. V. Siva Sankar

PERSONALITY ASSESSMENT AND TESTS FOR CHILDREN

Michael Hirt
Kent State University

Judy L. Genshaft
Canton, Ohio, Public Schools

Historical Perspectives

When primitive man had to determine the intent of a stranger with a club approaching him, he practiced some form of personality assessment. The subsequent reliance upon such techniques as palmistry and phrenology were major advances in the development of assessment practices. The use of psychological tests represented another major step in the evolution of assessment.

The use of psychological tests for purposes of personality assessment constitutes one effort to apply scientific methodology to the understanding of man. Its development was involved with critical aspects of nineteenth century philosophical thought. The development of various psychometric techniques between 1850 and 1900 occurred within the philosophical framework of Descartes' doctrine of dualism. As the materialistic determinism of physics became dominant in the biological and physiological sciences, there was an increased endeavor on the part of the dualists to safeguard the scientific status of the mind. There was a need to demonstrate that psychological processes could be examined within the same general scientific framework as that advocated by physics. The development of the mathematics of mental dynamics by Herbart in 1850 and the psychophysical measurement procedures by Fechner in 1860 were among the many attempts along these general lines. The impetus for mental measurement produced the first laboratory of psychology, established by Wundt in Germany in 1876. In England, Galton adapted the recently formulated probability theory to the measurement of the mind and further increased the respectability of the new science of mental measurement. Within the same background of dualistic theory, Binet, in France, developed the first standardized test of intelligence for children. The movement then spread to America by way of Wundt's students, Titchener and Cattell.

In the rich soil of Yankee pragmatism, and especially sanctioned by the philosophy of usefulness espoused by William James and John Dewey, psychological testing took firm root. The testing movement lost much of its philosophical fervor and adapted itself to practical realities. With this focus on the applied, the tests were turned toward measuring units of outward or observable behavior, rather than toward European mentalistic concerns of sensation, perception or consciousness. The matching of grade level of work to school children's measured ability and the screening of Army inductees were immediate applications.

These early mental testers, interested in measuring overt behavioral characteristics, focused primarily on cognitive processes, i.e., memory, problem solving, etc. While Wundt had directed some attention to the measurement of affect, the new testers found the classical efforts to examine emotion to be of little use in their work. Emotion, used in the sense of visible reaction or self-report of one's feelings, was quite different from the concepts of motivation that were later to become incorporated into the framework of psychodynamics.

Testing in the area of "depth" or motivational understanding of the individual was influened from an entirely separate stream of thinking. In view of the forces in scientific psychology up to the 1920's and 30's, it is not strange to find that testing ideas related to motivation entered the field from foreign sources, that is, outside of America and outside of psychology. Jung integrated the developing dynamic orientation of psychoanalysis with scientific methodology through the use of the word association technique to study personality.

In American universities the behavioristic rebellion rejected the European mentalistic orientation. Behaviorism was marked by a sharp rejection of the "mind" and even of consciousness as appropriate objects of psychological study. Clinical assessment of the "whole man" was scorned by academic psychology, which focused on S-R units. Later developments in clinical testing in America gave rise to and were influenced by various theoretical conflicts (i.e., nomothetic vs. idiographic; clinical vs. actuarial prediction; molar vs. molecular). In retrospect, such conflicts represented the lack of integration between academic and clinical psychology. While these conflicts were never adequately resolved, they became overshadowed by new influences and ideas. The development of ego psychology with its emphasis upon character, defenses, and more specific relationships between specific treatments and various types of pathology. Within academic psychology emphasis changed from the study of basic drives and basic principles of learning to culturally relevant variables in behavior acquisition and change. The work of such psychologists as Hebb, Harlow, Hunt, and Piaget stimulated interest in the role of stylistic variables in the processing and organizing of environmental data.

Concurrent with the growth of interest in cognitive development, there has developed acceptance of direct attacks on problems of concern to society, such as those involved in the mental health and the anti-poverty programs. Earlier government support of psychological research had been widely accepted but had, in most instances, dealt with problems which were easily amenable to rigorous experimental design e.g., human factors, engineering, brain physiology). Currently, psychological research in educational methods, in teacher training, and in modes of rehabilitation of disturbed or delinquent children are surprisingly accepted, considering the attitudes prevalent a few years ago.

The impact of these developments has considerably changed test usage. Among these changes is an emphasis upon the following in personality assessment (1):

A. *The Adaptive Orientation*

Corresponding to the change from "id" - oriented to an "ego"-oriented framework is the emphasis on defensive and adaptive potential. This orientation is more concerned with the patient's current adjustive equilibrium and his resources for coping with stress. A psychologist influenced by this framework is less likely to be concerned with genetic or unconscious forces in a patient or to emphasize early infantile fixations or current conflicts related to sexual or aggressive drives. He is more likely to find data in the test responses which are relevant to the patient's ability to integrate thought and affect, to delay and control expression, and to relate these to the demands currently made upon the patient by his environment.

B. *Cognitive Styles*

The work on cognitive styles has had multiple effects on clinical assessment. One effect has been the finer discrimination of relationships between reactions to environmental stimuli and modes of coping. This is in contradistinction to formulations that previously were couched in terms of symbolism and unconscious motivation. Symbolic interpretation, closely related to "id" psychology, rested heavily on "cookbook" formulas of underlying drives and required an extended series of inferences in order to move from test responses to predictions of behavior. In a more direct manner the analysis of cognitive styles focuses on the ways in which the ego perceives, organizes, and relates affect and ideation to the environment.

A second influence of the cognitive approach on testing has been an emphasis on the interrelationships of various aspects of functioning. The work of Klein (2) and that of Witkin (3) have demonstrated that tests merely tap immediate facets of broad organizing forces. Perceptual styles, kinds of fantasy, use of memory, nature of thought association, and integration of affect and thought or any other aspect of mental life are all assumed to operate within a framework of patterned organization. By the same token, aspects of functioning which had earlier been dealt with as though they were independent traits are now encompassed within a more unitary framework. An outstanding example of this change is the concept of intelligence. Intelligence has been considered as a discrete function, but intelligence is better considered as the area of functioning where the ego's resources in perception, memory, and organization are brought to bear on certain types of problem-solving situations. Thus intelligence is an area of application of basic personality resources.

The work of cognitive styles has also broadened the range and depth of concepts useful in understanding test data. For example, the concept of "tolerance for ambiguity" has enriched the understanding of borderline or acute states of ego disorganization. Similarly, the concept of "field dependence" can be translated directly into behavioral terms that give added meaning to analyses of personality. Bt tracing the viscissitudes of cognitive functioning, the diagnostician is in a relatively better position to delineate the patient's interactions with his environment.

C. *Relationship to Therapeutic Variables*

There has been a shift in perspective in the use of psychological tests, with the focus now upon the use of tests to assess behavioral tendencies which are directly relevant to therapeutic intervention. The range of available therapeutic interventions is now much broader than the model of attempting to resolve intrapsychic conflicts by transforming them into conscious material. A considerable range of personality disturbances are currently seen as resulting from ego defects or interactional combinations of ego difficulties and intrapsychic conflict. Treatment methods are available that involve specific environmental conditions which are designed to interact with ego resources. Certainly, the view of pathology as a dysfunction of the adaptive apparatus, rather than solely as intrapsychic conflict, has provided a rationale for the newer sociopsychological treatment orientations.

The psychologist, in this context, shifts away from the variables that had previously been his sole concern -- that is, symbolic interpretation of content and stylistic variables related to early infantile impulses and genetic material. He is now more concerned with patient variables that emerge from examination of the test data as samples of contemporary functioning and he is more concerned with the meaningfulness of his information for therapeutic change. Thus, the psychologist is more concerned with understanding data which bear on the patient's tolerance for anxiety, his capacity to express affect, and his ability to channel behavior in adaptive directions.

Personality Theory and Assessment

Considerable ambiguity has resulted from the confusion between the terms personality and behavior. While they have often been used interchangeably, the term behavior is better limited to observable events, while personality is an abstraction or a hypothetical construct derived from or descriptive of behavior (4). Traditionally, statements about personality have hypothesized internal states and behavioral observations have been used as signs of such inferred attributes.

The two major systems of personality theory construction have been trait and psychodynamic theories. These approaches assume an internal, structural dynamic hierarchy. Within this hierarchy are hypothesized characteristics which have a superordinate-subordinate relationship. The dynamic interaction between these characteristics determine the observable behavior (4).

Both trait and psychodynamic theories minimize the role of the environment, emphasizing instead underlying traits or psychodynamic processes. Assessment thus consists of a description of the hypothesized attributes, which are inferred from test responses and other behaviors.

The term "trait" is confusing because it has been used in many different ways. At the simplest level, trait refers to directly observable behavior or characteristics of two or more people on a defined dimension. It is a summary term of observable and stable individual differences. At another level, trait is a personality construct which accounts for enduring behavioral consistencies and differences. At this level trait is used only as an explanatory concept, without being conceptualized as a process or state within the individual. Another conceptualization of trait has been in terms of underlying characteristics, qualities or processes that exist within individuals (5). In essence, traits can be seen as constructs or as real processes within the individual. These constructs are the examiner's inferences about the individual's underlying processes which are inferred from his test responses.

Traits are seen as having an active role in determining behavior. The major aim of those using the trait approach is to infer the underlying personality structure and to compare individuals and groups on these established trait dimensions. Underlying traits are inferred from observable behavior and are invoked to account for the observed behavioral consistencies. For the trait theorist, assessment consists of delineating these stable enduring characteristics and using their occurrence to predict future behavior.

In psychodynamic theories, the first few years of life provide the basis for personality development. During this time there are a series of dynamically differentiated stages and the child learns impulse control and socially acceptable ways of gratifying his instinctual wishes by coping with the developmental demands of these stages.

The major determinants of behavior are considered unconscious and often irrational. The persistent demands from within the individual are aggressive and/or sexual and demand immmediate gratification. When these demands conflict with external reality or with internalized values, the individual becomes anxious. In order to deal with this anxiety, elaborate defenses, often involving distortion and displacement, are developed. The subsequent behavior is often a symbolic expression of the underlying motives.

The role of personality theory in assessment might be expressed as follows:

Information from assessment procedures	→	Personality description	→	Personality theory	→	Decisions about the patient

In addition to different theories of personality, our decision are also influenced by different methods of data collection. A brief description of the major approaches to assessment should be useful.

Sample vs. Sign Approaches

After the development of Binet's intelligence scales, similar procedures for the classification of individuals into personality groupings were developed. Social and emotional characteristics were inferred on the basis of one's classification and behavior in specific future situations was predicted.

This approach led to the development of numerous procedures for the study of personality differences. These procedures were such objective methods as direct observation, standardized rating scales, questionnaires, check lists, preference ratings, and personality inventories. These sampling methods assumed the sample was adequate and unbiased, and the sample represented all essential features of the universe in their proper relationships and proportions.

The use of sampling methods to assess personality presents a number of difficulties. With this method, the test sample situation has to be specified; otherwise, the universe which is being sampled is undetermined. Thus, in measuring personality traits, the behavioral universe must be defined. To define a behavioral universe, the stimuli eliciting the response must be known.

In sampling approaches, the choice of stimuli used to measure complex performance depends on one's concept of the universe being measured. Agreement on the nature of the universe and its organization is seldom reached. Furthermore, since the level of subject motivation is often unknown, the level of the response cannot be interpreted.

An alternative to sampling methods has been the sign approach. The basic assumption of this approach is that there are different innate tendencies which become further differentitated through experience. Since perceptions differ, behavior, including test responses, are indirect manifestations of some underlying personality characteristic. The sign approach does not consider test behavior as a subtest of the actual behaviors of interest. Projective techniques and other traditional personality tests have typically taken the sign approach to interpretation; behavioral procedures have relied more upon a sample orientation.

Ego Development Approach

Assessment within this context is based upon two familiar principles about development. First, that a child's functioning develops from concrete, gross reactions to increasingly coordinated and finely developed functions. The second principle is that behavior develops from wholes to parts at an irregular pace.

Ego development proceeds similarly to physical development. By the age of six the child is assumed to have acquired most of the major techniques of ego functioning. However, the child's rate of ego development is variable. The functions involved in ego development might be summarized as: (a) cognitive; (b) social; (c) conative; (d) perceptual; (e) motoric; and (f) affective (6). These functions are interrelated and inferences about ego development are made from measurement of these functions.

While each of the approaches discussed has a different orientation and focus, influencing how clinical problems are perceived and evaluated, there is considerable overlap. Trait and psychodynamic theories are similar to the sample and sign approaches. Ego development theories, while stressing the role of learning, also assume stages of psychosexual development which are similar to the dynamic theories. While there are some assessment techniques which are relatively specific to certain theoretical positions, there is sufficient similarity among all these theories to permit considerable overlap of assessment techniques.

Before considering the many tests available for the assessment of children, some general observations about the nature of testing may be useful (7).

The Nature of Testing

One difference between psychological testing and other methods of clinical assessment is the increased distance between the examiner and the patient inherent in psychological testing. In less structured assessment procedures, such as most interviews, it is often desirable to develop and evaluate hypotheses about the patient which are based upon the immediate interaction. These hypotheses guide the direction of the interview. The psychologist is relatively bound to data-collecting operations guided by the structure of the tests rather than by his own immediate hypotheses about the patient.

Psychological testing is based on a composite of operating assumptions, of which empiricism is but one. Psychological testing, particularly in its application to clinical problems, must encompass a broader theoretical approach which includes understanding the nature of the testing situation (and its perception by the patient), the nature of the test materials and the demands these impose upon the patient, and a theoretical framework which permits the psychologist to integrate data from these different origins.

Psychological testing, to be most meaningful for clinical purposes, necessitates a battery of tests covering a wide spectrum of functioning. In gathering data about the spectrum or range of behavior, the psychologist usually assumes that: (a) he is not being consulted to administer a specific test to answer a partial, pre-existing hypothesis, such as "what is the patient's I.Q.?"; (b) he will need to have a broad conceptual and theoretical orientation in order to integrate successfully the different types and levels of behavior elicited by various tests; and (c) he will arrive at a description of the patient which will permit conceptualization of the patient's total personality organization and functioning. The spectrum concept of assessment necessitates that the psychologist be able to conceptualize personality as a unitary function of the organism. His task is to arrive at a formulation which will integrate the complex and often seemingly disparate test behavior of the patient, and which will have relevance to clinical questions.

Before considering the possible meaning of the patient's behavior in response to the various tests, the psychologist must make judgements about the background or field against which these responses are occurring. Schachtel (8), for example, has discussed the influence of the patient's subjective definition of a test situation upon test performance. It is quite probable that the patient who defines the test situation as a competitive one, for example, will be influenced differently than were he to have an authoritarian definition. The nature of such judgments by the psychologist, as well as his reactions to the patient, and his relationship to those seeking his consultation are relevant factors in the psychologist's appraisal of the patient before him.

What Tests Test

It is important to understand that while tests cover a range of functions, there is no direct correspondence between scores on given tests and certain patient characteristics in which one might be interested. Thus, there is no test that measures "organicity" nor any that measure "depression" or "homosexuality." Tests are only samples of behavior obtained under well-defined conditions. Test interpretation theory assumes that the behavior being sampled represents the patient's efforts at adaptive functioning and therefore has generalizability to other aspects of patient behavior. Adaptive functioning is assumed to be a derivative of basic personality organization. It is the basic personality organization that the psychologist formulates from the test data which permit him to generalize to non-test contexts.

The large number of tests available may be categorized on the basis of the different demands they make upon the patient. One aspect of the validity of the judgments made about a patient's functioning is contingent upon having provided him with sufficient opportunity to meet a wide range of demands.

Inference and Formulation

The psychologist transforms test data into clinically useful information on the basis of his understanding of what functions are sampled in testing and how these functions relate to personality organization. One of the basic postulates of the examiner is that his data are an end product of a complex system of functioning. This means that taking a portion of his data as the bases from which to make inferences about non-test behavior is a procedure of limited usefulness. A number of psychologists do interpret tests in this piece-meal fashion. They transpose portions of data into clinical inferences until all the portions are used up. The difficulty with this procedure is that it assumes a special congruence between specific test situations and specific extra-test situations. In order to arrive at the most valid formulation of patient functioning, the psychologist must reconstruct several steps that mediate between test data and the formulations which can be made about the more general functioning of a person. The test data must be brought into a schema or patterning that has a hierarchical organization in which the inferences from the data are linked together and converge on more basic concepts. Table 1 is a representation of this process.

In Column A of Table 1 the first level of inferences are given. We note that the focus at this point is on attempting to get some "handle" on the qualities of responses and their fluctuations. The first level of inferences deal with such as-

Table 1

Representation of Stages in Formulating and Translating Data From Test Responses to Clinical Judgments

Test Responses					
A	B	C	D	E	F
Symbolic content; relationship of responses to stimuli; coherence and organization of responses; reaction to changes in stimuli; complexity of responses.	Differential patterns of functioning; range of reactions; level of intensity; indications of delay or control capacity.	Relationship of content and structure; cognitive or perceptual patterns; energy deployment; coordination of processes; degree of ego stability.	Formulation of personality dynamics, personality structure and current level of functioning.	Capacity for relationships, capacity for change, points of amenability.	Specific extrapolate of anticipated course of behavior.

pects as the complexity of responses, their internal coherence, the quality of their "fit" with stimulus situations, the nature of variations in quality, and how all these relate to the range of test situations. This information is not taken from one or another test but represents the psychologist's inferences from the wide range of test data.

At B, the psychologist moves a step away from the response-based observations and begins to formulate concepts of the patient's personality functioning. He looks for convergence of inferences that relate to level of anxiety, patterns of reaction to anxiety and stress, evidence of how the patient reacts to regression-inducing stimuli, and indications of delay and control capacity. In step C, the psychologist generally makes several decisions of differentiating diagnosis and attempts to refine his formulations. This permits him to begin approximating the patient's personality structure in terms of basic modes in organization, energy deployment, and styles of cognitive and defensive functioning.

Step D, in a sense, completes the bridge between test data and clinical inferences. The psychologist's conception of how the personality functions is the mediating construct that leads toward extrapolations to non-test behavior in steps E and F.

In the final two steps, the psychologist may go back and check fine points of his formulation as he addresses himself to the clinical questions. These steps are mainly concerned with extrapolation. How does such a person function with the kind of personality organization that has been formulated? How does he experience himself and his world? What molds his behavior? How do we understand his current life situation? What is the locus of concern or fear? How malleable (or entrenched) are his behavior patterns? At this stage, the psychologist is no longer interpreting from his tests; the extrapolation at this point is based on the construction of the patient's personality that the psychologist has developed. To illustrate this point, we may have a patient where the personality structure that has been inferred is one of infantile ego development with poorly organized coping devices and regressive patterns of thought and behavior. While specific analysis of test information may suggest erotically charged oedipal conflicts, more total knowledge of the patient from the test data and the inferred formulations suggest that rather than suffering from problems of the oedipal stage, the patient relates to people in a more "immediate need" and helpless, clinging, demanding manner.

In the final step, the psychologist has the task of coming to grips with the clinical questions that have generated the test referral. Before discussing some of the considerations involved in dealing adequately with the test referral, a brief review of many of the tests available for children will be presented. While this review is not completely exhaustive, it is sufficiently comprehensive to indicate adequately the large number of children's tests available and their limited psychometric properties.

Global Personality Assessment

The techniques included in this category emphasize the individual's overall personality functioning. The majority of these techniques are projectives which consider behavior as a manisfestation of underlying processes. Trait theories, psychodynamic theories, as well as sample and sign approaches generally share this particular point of view.

Braverman-Chevigny Auditory Projective Test:

Suitable for ages four and over, this technique is similar to the TAT except it is auditory. The individual listens to a tape which consists of four parts, a series of 20 utterances, a series of 8 sound affects, a series of 11 interpersonal interactions enacted by professional actors and the same 11 situations spoken in nonsense language. The instructions are to listen to the conversation as a whole, give a general impression of what is going on, what led up to the story and the outcome. No reliability or validity data are available.

Columbia Sentence Completion:

A personality projective test for preschoolers. The test consists of words which elicit meaningful material, such as I would like to, at home, my mother, etc. No norms are available.

Despert Fables:

Ranges from three year olds to upper elementary ages. The test measures psychodynamics by having the children respond to questions after they have heard the fable. The Despert Fables are not suitable for differential diagnosis. Reliability and validity have not been shown to be satisfactory.

Early School Personality Questionnaire:

An orally administered questionnaire suitable for six to eight year olds. The ESPQ is a downward extension of Cattell's 16-PF. The questionnaire consists of thirteen scales purporting to describe personality dimensions which extend into adult life. Because of the absence of both normative and validity data this test should be used only as a research tool.

Kent-Rosanoff Free Association Test:

Can be used with children as young as four years of age. The test attempts differential diagnosis on the basis of word association. It may be useful in generating clinical hypotheses.

Hand Test:

Suitable for children six and over. The technique consists of 10 cards, nine of which contain India ink drawings of hands in different positions and one blank card. The individual is instructed to tell what the hand might be doing. Four major response classes have been developed. While a limited number of reliability and validity studies have been published, more developmental work is required before this test can be used effectively as a diagnostic tool.

Koppitz Human Figure Drawings:

Suitable for children five through 12 years of age. This test has an objective scoring system which evaluates human figure drawings for emotional indicators. Although it is assumed that a child "projects" through his drawings, this has not been well documented. There are no studies which have shown reliable differences between drawings of normal and emotionally disturbed children.

Holtzman Inkblot Techniques:

It is suggested this instrument can be used with children as young as five years of age. This technique is the application of the Rorschach to a new set of variables. Psychometrically, this technique is considerably superior to the Rorschach. It has not been used as extensively in clinical settings; either because it does not yield clinical data as useful as the Rorschach or possibly because of the better established tradition of the Rorschach.

Lowenfeld Kaleidoblocs:

Suitable for children as young as three years. The child is given a set of blocks; first he is allowed to construct what he wants then he is given problems. The test supposedly assesses his imaginative and spontaneous behavior. This test is basically still in the developmental stages.

Minnesota Personality Profile:

For pre-school through elementary age children. This is a Likert type instrument which supposedly yields an overall picture of the child's personality structure. Neither normative nor validity data are available currently.

School Observation Schedule:

Suitable for kindergarten and elementary age children. This schedule is a rating scale to be completed by the teacher, designed primarily to identify the child's problem areas. It is a relatively subjective instrument without norms or validity information.

Wishes and Fears Inventory:

Used with four to eight year olds. This self-report inventory is used primarily to structure individual interviews with the child. Areas scored are wishes, positive indentification, negative identification, desired activities, undesired activities, fears, and earliest recollections. While normative information is availabe, neither validity nor reliability data have been published.

Mooseheart Wishes and Fears Inventory:

This is a personality inventory suitable for children four to 16 years of age. It attempts to assess the wishes, sources of identification, and fears of children through a series of direct questions. Neither normative nor validity data have been reported.

Toy World Test:

Suitable for children as young as two years of age. This test consists of a kit of reuseable toys. The child is allowed to play with any of the approximately 150 to 300 wooden items. His play activity is recorded with particular emphasis on variables such as aggression, distortion, symbolic arrangements, empty worlds, etc. While some normative data are available, the reliability and validity of this instrument have not been established.

Personality Dynamics:

This category is concerned primarily with the specification of the dynamics underlying a child's emotional development and personality structure. There is emphasis on determining whether the child has mastered the appropriate developmental stages. Both psychodynamic theories and some aspects of the ego development theories provide the theoretical rationale for these techniques.

Bender-Gestalt Test for Young Children:

Suitable for children five to 10 years of age, this test purports to measure a child's emotional developmental level. The child is given nine geometric figures which are presented one at a time and he is asked to copy these. Most children are capable of copying all nine figures by the time they are nine years of age. The test has limited use with children under five years of age. There are rather extensive norms available for school children with this test and reliability information is available for the developmental scoring system. Some validity data are also available particularly for differentiating between levels of normal development; the test does not seem to discriminate between normal and clinical samples.

The Blacky Pictures:

Suitable for children as young as five years of age, this is the only test designed specifically to assess a child's progress through various stages of psychosexual development. The test consists of 10 cards depicting a dog who experiences some of the classic problems associated with various stages of psychosexual development. The child is instructed to tell a spontaneous story about each picture and subsequently is required to answer a series of standardized questions about each picture. There is an experimental scoring system available and there are some norms for young children. The evidence concerning the validity of this test is somewhat conflicting and inconclusive.

CAT:

Suitable for children three to 10 years of age. A test modeled after the TAT but using animals engaging in human behaviors. The range of human situations presented permits expression of fantasies relating to various problems. Available research suggests that animals are not necessarily easier for children to identify with. Evidence does not warrant use of the CAT in preference to the TAT.

The IES Test:

Suitable for children ten years and older. The purpose of this test is to measure the relative strength of impulses, ego and superego and the complex interaction of these functions. IES is composed of several sub-tests which provide controlled stimulus situations in which it is assumed impulses, ego and superego will manifest themselves in distinct and measureable ways. Limited normative data based upon small stratified samples is available. Reliability data are quite low.

Kahn Test of Symbol Arrangement:

Suitable for children six years and older. The KTSA is an omnibus performance projective technique consisting of several subtests. While standardization data for adults exist modification of norms is necessary to include both women and children. Reliability data are available and indicate adequate stability for KTSA performance. Scoring criteria need clarification and additional validity evidence is needed.

Lowenfeld Mosaic Test:

Supposedly suitable for children as young as two years of age. The child is given blocks in different shapes and colors and is instructed to build pictures of whatever he wants. The major limitation of this test is the absence of an objective scoring system. The examiner is required to evaluate the child's responses at a highly arbitrary level. Both validity and reliability data are lacking.

Machover Draw-A-Person Test:

Suitable for children as young as two years of age, measures psychosexual development through assessment of the child's drawings of human figures. Normative data are available for children five to 12 years. Published validity studies have reported conflicting results and additional research is needed to identify specific clinical uses of the test.

Make A Picture Story Test:

Suitable for chidlren six and older. This is essentially a variation of the TAT principle in which the background and figures are separated and the individual has the opportunity to select one or more figures to populate the background of his choosing. Published normative data are available for various clinical populations. Validation data are relatively inconclusive. This appears to be a promising technique for subjective evaluation of playroom types of activities.

The Michigan Picture Test:

Measures emotional development of children ages eight

through 14. Modeled after the TAT, the child responds to 15 cards and one blank card. Standardized normative data are available and interjudge scoring reliability has been relatively high. While the validity data have not been reported, the instrument seems useful as a screening device.

The Picture Story Test:

This is another modification of the TAT procedure for children six years of age and older. The PST can be analyzed for both content and formal characteristics. No particular method of interpretation is suggested by the author. Normative data are negligible and little reliability or validity data are reported.

Rorschach Inkblots:

Suitable for children as young as three years of age. This test attempts to assess personality structure through responses to 10 standardized inkblots. Responses are scored for location, determinants, and content. Reliability and validity data have been contradictory.

South African Picture Analysis Test:

This test is intended for elementary school children and is presumed to gap the TAT and CAT. The child creates a story from 10 pictures and his responses are scored into eight interpretive categories of which four relate to content and four relate to formal characteristics of the story. Neither normative data nor validity information are available.

Specimen Record Method:

An instrument for Psychosocial Description: Not limited to any particular age, this is a detailed sequential narration of everything occurring in the child's life at the moment. Specimen descriptions are then coded according to a detailed psychosocial category system that describes aspects of the child's environment as well as his behavior in various social interactions. While reliability data are adequate, neither norms nor validity is reported.

Szondi Test:

Suitable for children five years and older. The child is presented with six sets of eight facial pictures of psychiatric patients. The child selects the two pictures he likes best and the two he likes least. Normative data and reliability data are not available. The available validity data failed to support underlying hypotheses claimed for the test.

TAT:

Used with children as young as four years of age. The examiner may select from 20 stimulus cards. The child is asked to make up a story about each stimulus picture including what led up to the story, how the characters in the stories are feeling, and how the story will end. While a formal scoring system is available, most clinicians prefer to use the test at an impressionistic level. Much like the Rorschach, the validity reports are contradictory.

Personality Trait

This category considers techniques which attempt to evaluate personality structure and organization by studying the individual underlying attributes or characteristics. It is assumed that these underlying traits determine how the individual behaves with little regard for the environment in which the individual resides. Trait theories and sampling approaches support this point of view.

Adjective Checklist:

Can be used with children as young as 15 years of age. The individual is presented with a list of adjectives from which he selects those he feels are self-descriptive. The instrument can be scored for 24 variables which include 15 needs, measures of personal adjustment, etc. The absence of validity and reliability information limits the adjective checklist to research purposes.

Affectional and Aggressive Observational Checklists:

Suitable for preschool children. Using time sampling and a list of predetermined categories, each child's behavior during a self-directed activity is observed and simultaneously coded into 11 affectional categories (6 for physical behaviors, 5 for verbal behaviors) and 18 aggressive categories (8 for physical and 10 for verbal behavior). The child's score is the number of times that such behaviors were observed during a specified period. Neither norms nor validity have been established.

Affective Situations Empathy List:

For four to seven year old children. This test measures empathy expressed by a young child. The examiner presents 8 situations, illustrated in sequences of 3 pictures and the child tells how he feels after the situation is described. There are 2 sets of sequences for each of 4 different affective situations--happiness, sadness, fear and anger. The child's response is recorded verbatim and scored by giving 1 point for each empathy acknowledged by the child. While interrater reliability is high, norms and validity information are not available.

Affectivity Interview Blank:

For five to 12 year old children. The scale attempts to assess children's feelings with a structured interview consisting of 69 items such as "How are you getting along this year?" Norms, validity, and reliability data are not available.

Aggression Rating Scale:

Suitable for children four to seven years of age. The scale measures a child's aggression as assessed by the teacher on nine 5-point items that are concerned with manifest instances of overt physical and verbal acts. Neither norms nor validity have been established; test-retest reliability is adequate.

Beller's Child Dependency on Adults Scale; *and Beller's Scale of Independency or Autonomy Among Children*:

Suitable for preschool children. The scale measures the dependency of the child on the teacher. The scale consists of 5 subscales, including measures of dependency striving and the frequency with which the child seeks recognition, physical contacts, attention and proximity to teachers or peers. Each scale has 7 points and 2 criteria of frequency and persistence. Neither norms nor validity information is avialable.

Borke Empathy Test:

Suitable for preschool children. The test consists of a two-part procedure. In part one the child is familiarized with drawings of happy, sad, afraid, and angry faces. Next the child is read stories and he selects the faces to go with the emotions expressed in the stories. In part two, the child is read eight stories and selects a face to represent how he perceives theother child feels. Research regarding the validity, norms, and reliability are not available.

California Personality Inventory:

May be used with children thirteen years and older. CPI consists of 480 items presented in a true-false format. The goal of the CPI is to measure those character traits which arise directly and necessarily from interpersonal life. This test yields scores of 18 scales. While descriptions of the scale construction procedure is rather limited, the test shows much promise on the basis of validity information published.

Child's Risk Taking Scale:

Suitable for children five to 13 years of age. The child is seated before a panel with a set of 10 toggle switches which can be connected to a buzzer. The child is told to show how many toggle switches he can flick before he touches the one connected to the buzzer. The score is the number of switches he flips before stopping. Research evidence on validity, reliability, and norms is not available.

Color Pyramid Test:

May be used with children as young as six years. The individual is asked to make consecutively and in 2 dimensions, 3 pyramids of 15 squares culled from a large assortment of available colors and hues. After the completion of 3 pretty pyramids, he then has to make 3 ugly pyramids. Pretty pyramids reveal manifest emotional structure while uglies represent latent modes of affective responses. Although it is considered a projective technique, there appears to be little rationale for the interpretation of the test. Reliability and validity data are lacking.

Depression Adjective Checklist:

Suitable for adults and children as young as 14. There are seven different forms of the depression adjective checklist. Each of the first four forms consist of 32 self-descriptive adjectives and the last three forms include 34 such items. The person checks each adjective which is descriptive of "how you feel now--today". The score consists of the total number of depressive adjectives checked added to the total number of positive adjectives not checked. Norms are provided in terms of means and standard deviations. Impressive cross validation data have been provided and internal consistence is good. It appears that the DACL provides a brief, reliable, and valid self-report measure of depression.

The Eysenck Personality Inventory; the Junior Eysenck Personality Inventory; and the New Junior Maudsley Inventory:

All attempt to measure neuroticism at different age levels. These are all self-report inventories with extensive norms, but inadequate validity and reliability.

Fels Child Behavior Scale:

Suitable for preschool age children. The scale consists of 30 rating scales measuring 30 personality traits. The manual advises that the scale be used only after a minimum 2-week period of observation of the child in his preschool setting. The child's manifestation of each trait is established by locating the child's behavior on a rating line described by 5 behavior descriptions for each trait. Reliability and validity data are not available.

The Firo Scales:

Suitable for ages 15-21. The scales are self-report questionnaires designed to assess one's needs for inclusion, control and affection. There are 6 scales: FIRO-B (behaviors one directs toward others, FIRO-F (feelings he holds toward others), LIPHE (feelings and behavior he remembers having desired from his parents), MATE (feelings and behavior he desires of his spouse), VALE D (feelings and behavior he desires the teachers and school administrators should hold), and COPE (questionnaire to assess an individual's performance among 5 defense mechanisms). In each of the questionnaires, separate subscales are constructed to assess each of the 3 needs. Norms have been established but reliability and validity data are lacking.

Generosity Test:

Suitable for preschool children. Each child is placed in a situation where he can either assign candy to his peers or keep it. The amount of candy given away is an index of generosity. Research evidence is not available.

Gottschalk-Gleser Content Analysis Scales:

For children 14 and older. The scales are concerned with the measurement of transitory feeling states and with relatively small fluctuations of feelings. Affects are defined as a class of feeling states that have attributes of quality and quantity, with subjective, purely psychological components as well as psychological, biochemical and behavior concomitants. Affects are defined as being different from mood and emotion. Content analysis are done with 2 or more scores of 5 minute verbal samples. Normative data are available. Reliability evidence on certain scales is impressive. Validation studies are highly promising, but reflect the authors' commitment of the view that psychological states have biological roots.

Hartup-Keller Nurturance and Dependency:

Suitable for preschool children. During 2-minute intervals, a child's behavior is observed in a preschool setting and simultaneously coded into 4 nurturance categories and 6 dependency categories. The score in a particular category is the number of occurrences of that behavior for a certain time period. Norms are not available. Reliability has not been established and the validity studies are confusing and inconclusive.

Heathers Emotional Dependence and Independence Measure:

Suitable for preschool children. During 3-minute intervals, an observer interviews or observes a child in a preschool setting and makes a running account of the child's behavior. The child is observed for a total of 30 three-minute periods. Protocols are coded into 4 emotional dependency categories, six emotional independence categories and 4 play categories. Norms are not available and validity evidence has not been presented.

ITAT - Children's Personality Questionnaire:

Suitable for children eight through 12 years of age. This inventory samples 14 traits. There are two forms available each consisting of 140 true-false items. Norms are recorded by age and sex. Reliability and validity data are relatively low suggesting that the ITAT is most appropriate for research purposes only.

Lerner Murphy Frustration Test:

Suitable for preschool children. The test consists of two blocking techniques in which the experimenter starts from one end of a road, made up of large play blocks, while the subject starts from the other end. The experimenter meets the subject in an area of conflict. There are eight repetitions of such situations. The situation is characterized as being one of mild, repeated frustration. Neither norms nor evidence of validity are available. Reliability is adequate.

Merrill Palmer Scales:

Suitable for children two to five years of age. There are nine scales, such as response to authority, independence of adult affection, socialability, etc. Each scale contains items representing both the positive and negative end of the scale contiuum. Information is available with regard to validity and reliability of the scales and considerable normative data have been published.

Multiple Affect Adjective Checklist:

Suitable for ages eight through 16. The MAACL is a downward extension of the Affective Adjective Check List. It contains 132 adjectives which the individual checks if the adjective describes how he generally feels and how he feels today. The MAACL is a relatively crude psychometric test. Although reliabilities are high, the scores clearly are susceptible to response sets. It is unique in that it allows the assessment of transient levels of negative affect. Norms are available and validity research has been reported.

Object Relations Test:

Can be used with children as young as six years of age. The ORT consists of three series of 4 cards each, on which is found either one person, 2 people, 3 people or a large group of people. In addition, a blank card is used. Series A cards are characterized by light charcoal shadings. Interpretation is similar to the Rorschach. B cards have heavier shading and series C are drawn with clear lines. The individual is to imagine what the picture represents and tell a story. No specific interpretation scheme is given. Normative data are provided, but validity and reliability studies are not available.

Observer Rating Scale:

Suitable for preschool children, these scales measure such traits as masculinity-femininity, aggression, attention seeking, etc. While norms are not available for these scales, the rater reliability is adequate and the scales correlate highly with other similar rating techniques.

Palmer Sweat Prints:

Can be used with children as young as four years of age. The measurement procedure is in three steps. Measurement is done with a densitometer, which measures the relative amount of light passing through the print. Density is directly proportional to the amount of sweating. Norms are not available. The results of validation studies are inconclusive; reliability coefficients are low.

Parent-Child Need Assessment:

Suitable for children two to five years of age. Child needs are inferred through parent interviews and child observation protocols. Data are scored on several variables thought to reflect the child's needs. Available evidence suggests unacceptable reliability and inadequate validity for this procedure.

Partner Leadership Measure:

Suitable for preschool children. A child is observed during free play and simultaneously coded. Each child is observed for 20 to 60+ minute periods randomly selected. A leadership score is given which is the sum of products computed by multiplying the number of times a child is classified in a category by the assigned weight of the category. Norms in the form of percent frequency scores for each category are available.

Peterson Problem Checklist:

Suitable for kindergarten to elementary school age children. The checklist, to be completed by the teacher, is designed to identify personality behavioral problems. All items are rated on three levels of severity. Efforts at establishing the validity of this checklist have not been too successful; the reliability data suggest inadequate reliability for this instrument.

Picture Story Measure of Kindness Concept:

Can be used with children five to 15 years of age. The child is presented with 10 pairs of stories, accompanied by illustrative pictures. Next he selects the picture in which he thinks the child is kinder and explains why. Explanations are classified as articulate explanations of choice, articulate explanations of predicted choice and non-discriminating explanations. Research evidence supporting the test are not available.

Primary Academic Sentiment Scales:

For children four to six years of age. This is a group administered timed test requiring 2 sessions. Items which request information on a child's preferred activities and behavior as well as his parents' activities and behaviors are read aloud to the children. Norms in the form of age quotients are available. Validity is fair, overall reliability is poor.

Resistance to Temptation Measure:

Suitable for preschool children. Materials include a box and a panel wired with lights and chimes. The child is told to throw 5 bean bags from a certain marker over a board, so as to hit a string on the other side. Each time the string is hit a light comes on and chimes ring. The child selects toys that he would like to win. A set of standard instructions is read to the child. The examiner leaves the room for 30 minutes, giving the child the opportunity to cheat. Behavior is scored on a 7 point resistance measure scale. Normative data are not available. Validity and reliability evidence appear to be inconclusive.

Risk Taking 2:

Suitable for preschool children. Without prior knowledge of outcome, a child is presented with a choice between a certainty, represented by a toy placed in front of him and an uncertainty represented by a paper bag which may contain 5 or more toys. The percent of children choosing the uncertain outcome on each trial is available, and presented at 3-month intervals. Validity and reliability are not reported.

Rosenzweig-Picture Frustration Study:

Can be used with children as young as four years. The test allows for the study of typical reaction patterns in potentially frustrating situations. The individual is shown cartoon-like drawings of frustrating situations. Each form consists of 24 situations involving two people in which one figure says something which frustrates the other. The subject is to give the verbal reaction to the other person. There are 9 possible classification categories. Norms are available. In all normative studies, developmental changes in the expression of aggression were found. Test-retest reliability is available; validity studies have reported contradictory results.

Story Completion Test:

Suitable for preschool to sixth grade children. A child is read 10 short stories that depict a hero who is looking forward to a desirable event. In each story, the hope of achieving the goal of the main character is threatened. The examiner reads three possible alternative endings which represent wish fulfillment, pessimism and compromise. The child selects the ending he believes actually happened. A child receives a score in each category based on the number of times he chose that ending. Mean scores are available for each category. In all three samples, the tendency to select a compromising solution when faced with a frustrating situation increases with age. Reliability information is not available.

Thompson-McCandless Femininity Scale:
Suitable for preschool children, this rating scale consists of 16 items which supposedly measure 10 feminine traits, such as passivity and timidity and masculine traits. Each child is rated on a 5 point scale. Norms are not available. The validity data presented are very minimal.

Behavioral Correlates and Antecedents of Identification

The techniques in this area are concerned with documenting the behavioral correlates and antecedents of identification. Most such techniques are rating scales. Both behavior theorists and ego development theorists would find these techniques useful for describing the child's behavior, his abilities, his environment, his achievements, and his potential for coping.

Behavior Checklist:
Suitable for children five to 10 years of age. The teacher rates the child on 39 items, most of which have been developed by other screening techniques. The teacher has the opportunity to indicate the frequency of the behavior. Norms are not available. The validity of some of the symptomatic behavior clusters seems adequate, but the majority of correlations were quite low. The techniques can be used as a research tool.

Behavior Scale and Screening Questionnaire:
Can be used with children as young as three years. In a structured interview, a child's parent is asked 60 questions referring to current health, development and behavior of the child. Each question is rated on a 3-point scale. Twelve items are used to form a behavior scale score that has a maximum of 24 points. Norms are not available. Validity studies have shown that the overall assessment was much more reliable and valid than that of a particular behavior sign.

Behavior Unit Observations:
Suitable for nursery school children. The scale consists of a number of subscales, including 5 measures of dependency,

12 of aggression and 10 of adult roles. The rater records the main behavioral category exhibited by the child during each 30 second observational unit. The score is a percentage of the behaviors in the total number of 30 second intervals. Neither normative data nor validity data are available.

Devereaux Child Behavior Rating Scales:
Suitable for 5 to 12 year old children. The scales are designed to assess behavioral symptoms in atypical children. It is a 97-item rating scale designed to assess behavior as the child relates to his world of things and people. The scale is useful but limited in application.

Devereaux Adolescent Behavior Rating Scale:
Suitable for adolescents. The scale's purpose is to describe and communicate the overt behaviors which define the total clinical picture. The scale isn't intended to provide a measure of personality traits; it is most useful for gross identification of disturbed adolescents.

Missouri Children's Behavior Checklist:
Can be used with children five to 16 years of age. The checklist consists of 70 descriptive phrases describing these areas of behavior: aggression, inhibition, hyperactivity, sleep disturbance, somatization, and sociability. The checklist requires someone who knows the child well, and checks the items which are reasonably accurate descriptions of his behavior. No research evidence is available.

Missouri Children's Picture Series:
Can be used with children five to 16 years of age. The test is made up of 238 stimulus items which are line drawings of children engaged in various activities. Each item is responded to by placing it in a fun or not fun category. Raw scores on a particular scale are the number of instances checked. No research evidence is available.

Permissive Doll Play:
Suitable for nursery school children, the scale samples manipulative fantasy behavior from children. Assessment includes two 20-minute sessions in which the child is presented

with 5 standard doll figures in a doll house. The child is asked to show what the family did in the house. Behavior is recorded in terms of successive behavior units. No research evidence is available.

Preschool Behavior Q-sort:
Suitable for preschool children. Each child is rated on 72 items devised to measure two supposedly unrelated dimensions of competence, social responsibility vs. irresponsibility and independent vs. suggestible behavior. Items are sorted into nine categories from most characteristic to least characteristic. Norms are not available. All studies regarding validity support the existence of a circumplex model of social behavior. Reliability has been adequate.

Structured Doll Play Test:
Suitable for preschool children. Using a doll house, the child is presented with six incomplete stories about the same sex doll and is asked to complete the stories. Completions are scored on 19 categories. Norms are not available. Validity and reliability data are marginal.

Personality and Socio-emotional Adjustment

In this category the major emphasis is the socio-emotional adjustment which the child has attained. The concern is not with personality structure or the organization of the underlying processes which determined the behavior, but how the child has adjusted. No one theory is embodied in this category.

Bristol Social Adjustment Guides:
Suitable for children five to 15 years of age. The guides allow a general statement to be made about the social adjustment of the child. The guides consist of a series of four different checklists of statements describing items of behavior significantly related to the emotional adjustment of the child. The child is examined in school, in the family situation, and in a residential treatment center. The child is classified as stable, unsettled, or maladjusted. Norms aren't available. Validity is fair and reliability is poor.

California Test of Personality:

Suitable for children five to eight years of age. The test is designed to test personal and social adjustment of the child. Personal adjustment is divided into 6 subtests. Social adjustment is divided into social standards, antisocial tendencies, and family relations. Items are presented in question form. The child answeres yes-no questions about how he would feel and act in a variety of situations. Percentage norms on total score, main scales and subscores are available. Validity and reliability are poor, which limits its clinical use.

Buttons: A Projective Test for Pre-Adolescent and Adolescent Boys and Girls:

The test is in cartoon format, with eleven animal cartoon sequences. Each of these sets up a school situation or problem which requires resolution. Scoring is accomplished by coding the child's responses as acceptable or unacceptable. The scoring scheme assumes how a well adjusted adolescent behaves in a manner acceptable to society and satisfying to himself. There are no normative data regarding initial, content and total scores or about the relationship between the three. As a psychometric instrument, Buttons falls short of acceptable evidence of reliability and validity criteria.

Case Study Method:

Suitable for preschool children. This method focuses on a single child interacting with its environment and attempts to assess socioemotional adjustment. Observations of the child are made throughout the year in the school setting. Neither norms, validity or reliability studies are available.

The Child Behavior Rating Scales:

Can be used with children five to 10 years of age. The scales consist of several behavior ratings to be completed by teachers or parents. The Scales are still in the research stage.

Draw-A-Person:

Can be used with children as young as five years of age. The test is based on the H-T-P test and Machover's Draw-A-Person Test. The child draws a figure which is analyzed according to five themes. It is used as a clinical diagnostic tool, but norms, reliability and validity evidence is not available.

The Driscoll Play Kit:

Suitable for children two to 10 years of age. The play kit consists of a plywood apartment composed of six rooms, 27 pieces of furniture and five figure dolls. No scoring or interpretive procedure is available with the kit. Norms, validity or reliability studies are not available.

Gesell Development Schedules: *Personal Social Behavior*:

Suitable for children from one month to six years of age. The rating scale is administered by a physician who rates the child's personal reactions to other persons and his adjustment to domestic life property, social groups and community conventions. The score is the child's developmental quotient. Developmental norms are available, but both validity and reliability estimates are poor.

The Graphoscopic Scale: *A Projective Psychodiagnostic Method*:

Suitable for children five to 16 years of age. The scale contains 10 drawing plates; 8 having semistructured perceptual cues, one which is fairly structured and one which asks for a free drawing. Little information is available with which to determine the clinical usefulness of this technique.

Horn-Hellersburg Test:

Can be used with children as young as three years. The test looks at the capacity to function or adapt in a given surrounding. The test is based on drawings adapted from the Horn Art Aptitude test. The child is presented with 12 small rectangles. Each rectangle contains portions of lines taken from well known pictures and a blank rectangle. The child is told to complete the pictures. After this is done, the child is interviewed to determine the significance of each drawing to him. No validity or reliability data are presented.

House-Tree-Person Test:

Can be used with children as young as three years. The test is used to help obtain information concerning the sensitivity, maturity, flexibility and degree of personality integration of the child. Norms for children do not exist. Studies indicate that the test can be used for differential diagnosis. Reliability is questionable. The test can be used in conjunction with other tests for diagnostic purposes.

The Jeness Inventory:

Can be used with children as young as eight years. It is a self report inventory designed to: (a) distinguish delinquents from non-delinquents, b) provide a basis for personality description, and c) provide a measure sensitive to change. The inventory consists of 155 true-false items, yielding 11 scale scores. Although some research has been reported, the inventory is of limited use.

Miniature Situation Test:

Can be used with children as young as five years. The test measures functioning by assessing covert coping responses. The child chooses between two options in 41 pairs of tasks. Options require the child to physically act on, manipulate or avoid objects presented to him. There are no norms available. Validity and reliability studies are lacking.

Pickford Projective Pictures:

Suitable for children five to 15 years old. The PPP attempts to provide both therapeutic and diagnostic insights. Materials include 120 pictures which are shown to the child, 6 at a time over 20 sessions. The child creates stories about the line drawings which represent a wide variety of situations encountered by children. The technique has not been standardized.

Preprimary Profile:

Suitable for preschool children. Parents rate children in the following areas: self care, social behavior, skill development, language development and previous experience. An attainment age and attainment quotients are computed. No research has been provided.

Rock-A-Bye Baby: *A Group Projective Test for Children*:

Can be used with children five to 10 years old. Children are shown a 35 minute filmed puppet show. After the film, the group suggests endings for the story and each child is interviewed individually about his reactions. While this test may be useful with older children, no data are available with which to evaluate its clinical usefulness.

School Apperception Method:
Suitable for children five to 14 years old. The SAM is modelled after the TAT, consisting of 30 drawings of children and adults in every-day school situations. The child is asked to construct a story about the school oriented pictures. Little evidence has been presented that the stimuli sample is typical of school problems. Norms, reliability and validity data are lacking.

Teachers Rating Scales of Adjustment:
Suitable for children five to eight years of age. The teacher rates the child on 79 separate scales which represent many different behaviors. No norms are available and the existing validation studies have failed to support the usefulness of this test as a diagnostic instrument.

Perception of Environment and Social Behavior

Rather than being concerned with the characteristics of the child, these tests are directed at the child's perceptions of his environment and his behavior toward peers and adults. Some of these techniques attempt to assess how realistic the child's perceptions are. These techniques are favored by behaviorists and ego developmental theorists, who emphasize the child's environment as a determinant of his behavior.

A. Attitudes Toward Adults

Childs Self-Social Construct Test:
Suitable for preschool age children. The test measures identification with and preference for mother, father, teachers and friends. It is a self report, non-verbal, semi-projective technique. The child responds by pointing or by pasting a circle representing himself next to other symbols in a picture presented to him. To assess identification with another person, the child is presented a row of circles, with a figure represent-

ing either mother, father, teacher or friends occupying the circle on the extreme left. The score consists of the number of circles between self and other, with a closer placement of self to other interpreted as greater identification. Normative, validity and reliability studies are not available.

Child Nurturance Control Scale:

Suitable for children three to five years old. The scale is an attempt to gain an identification index. The measure is a structured doll play interview that is conducted individually. The dolls used represent a mother, a father, a baby, and the child himself. There are 8 standard situations. Norms have not been established, although validity and reliability data seem adequate.

Family Relations Test:

Can be used with children as young as three years. The test is an objective technique for exploring emotional attitudes. The list consists of figures which represent members of the family and a "nobody" figure. There are 40 cards containing statements which reflect feelings of like, dislike, hate and love. The child places each item behind the figure for which the statement is appropriate. The test is unique because of its play nature and the fact that no verbalization is required. At present, research is limited. Norms have not been established and validity and reliability studies are promising, but limited.

Imitation Schedule:

Can be used with children three to eight years old. The schedule measures like-sexed parent identification through a structured doll play interview. The schedule is composed of 18 items, 15 of which are designed to measure like sexed parent identification, and 3 are used for relief purposes. The items are presented to the subject in a cyclical order, with the order of presentation being balanced. The score is the number of times the subject used the child-doll to imitate the like-sex parent. Norms for the schedule have not been established. Validity and reliability data indicate that the schedule can be useful in determining sex identification.

IT Scale for Children:

Suitable for use with preschool children. Presumably this is a sexless stick figure with whom the child can identify. The child makes a choice between pairs of stimuli that "IT" would prefer to have or be. The stimuli are ambiguous and are presented on 36 picture cards. Normative data are available. Validity studies have found that the IT figure is seen as masculine by both girls and boys. All studies indicate that reliability is poor.

Perception of Parents:

Can be used with children three to 10 years old. The interview is devised to elicit children's attitudes toward their parents. The interview uses three measures to assess the child's perception of parents with respect to nurturance, punitiveness, and source of fear. The procedures involved are indirect questions, picture methods and direct questions. No research evidence is available with respect to validity, reliability or norms.

Structured Doll Play Test:

Suitable for use with preschool children. The technique provides a projective screen for eliciting fantasy material and conflict areas. The test consists of two series. Series I consists of 12 figures and four background cards and covers most aspects of daily living for a typical child. Series II consists of 10 figures and three background cards and takes the child to school, doctors, etc. and introduces more symbolic fantasy. In every scene, the child makes a choice between a more and a less mature object or between parents. The child is encouraged by more open questions to extend his fantasy. The test is counter balanced so as not to limit fantasy to the chosen parent. Standardization data and validity data have been established. Reliability information is more limited.

Sechrist's Structured Interview Schedule:

Suitable for children four to eight years of age. The schedule is designed to assess the child's attitude toward his classroom teacher. The child is asked 10 structured questions about school situations and 10 objective questions relating to specific motivational techniques used by children. Norms are not available, validity and reliability data are lacking.

Role Distribution-Children's Series:

Suitable for children five to 11 years of age. This test is an experimental technique used to assess identification. The stimulus material consists of pictures of objects, locales, scenes with sample aspects of the child's experiences in play, peer contacts, parental activities, chores, intrafamilial relationships and cultural activities. The child is asked to tell whether the stimulus picture is more closely related to girls' or boys' activities or both. This instrument is in the experimental stages.

B. Attitudes toward Peers

Birthday Test: *Junior Form*:

Can be used with preschool children. The child names 3 adults and 3 children whom he would invite to his birthday party. The child then picks three from this group as associates in each of six structured situations at the party. Scores are given for attachment to adults or children, preferences for each of the six people chosen and preference in dependent and independent situations. Normative, validity, and reliability evidence are not available.

Social Discrimination Questionnaire:

Can be used with children five to 12 years of age. This is a sociometric questionnaire, designed to investigate the hypothesis that the presence of amputation represents a threat of bodily integrity for the non-amputee. The threat is reflected in attitudes of rejection. The scale consists of 17 questionnaires. No information is available which substantiate any claims for this questionnaire.

C. Racial Attitudes and Preferences

Clark Doll Test - Revised:

Suitable for preschool children. This is a structured doll play interview which is individually administered. The test has been adapted from another test consisting of two seventeen inch dolls differing only in pigment color. The child is questioned about the dolls. No information exists on reliability, validity or norms.

Color Meaning Picture Series - Revised:

Suitable for preschool children. This self-report series attempts to determine racial attitudes by assessing the connatative meanings of "black" and "white". The materials include 12 pictures of animals. The child is told a story about each picture after which he is asked to select the animal in thepicture that depicts the adjective described. Norms have been established and construct validity has been shown. More information is necessary before the series can be recommended for use.

Doll Play Interview:

Suitable for preschool children. This is a doll play situation used to assess the child's racial preference. The materials consist of a miniature playground and two dolls, one black and one white. The child's attention is called to the dolls and then the child is presented with 15 projective questions, such as "Here are two little boys who would like to play on this playground. Do they look the same? Are they Different?" There is no supporting evidence to indicate this is a reliable or valid instrument for assessing preferences.

Social Episodes Test:

Can be used with children five to eight years of age. A semi-projective interview method which attempts to assess racial and ethnic attitudes. The child responds to a series of ambiguous pictures consisting of children of different races and sexes in simple social situations. There are four categories of social episodes; race or religious, race or non-religious barrier, religious symbols, and cultural observance techniques. This instrument is still in the experimental stages and evidence regarding norms, validity and reliability data are not available.

Social Schemata:

Suitable for children four to nine years old. This self-report technique considers interpersonal racial attitudes. The child places a gummed label (on which is drawn a picture of a child of similar age, sex and race) on another page, near another figure such as mother, teacher, etc. Before the test questions begin, the child picks the figure most like himself from three color shades. The linear distance between the chosen figure and the self figure relative to the vertical axis of the page is the child's score. The lack of supportive information limits the use of this test for research purposes.

Stevenson and Stewart Racial Awareness Battery:
Suitable for preschool children. This is a situational structured doll play interview with incomplete stories. The battery includes four individually administered tests that measure the ability to discriminate among races and racial attitudes and preferences. There is neither reliability nor validity evidence.

D. Social Behavior

Children's Behavior Scale:
Suitable for children three to 12 years. The items on the behavioral rating scale are those most likely to provide pertinent personality data. The items represent 13 distinct underlying behavioral factors or traits. The raw score is the number of items that agree with the key for each factor. Norms have not been established. Validity studies indicate that none of the 13 traits correlate significantly with any other test; reliability coefficients are adequate.

California Preschool Social Competency Scale:
Suitable for preschool children. This is a measure of children's interpersonal behavior and assumption of social responsibility. The scale is adapted from the Cain-Levine Social Competency Scale. A teacher rates the child on 30 items covering a wide range of behavior. Each item contains four descriptive statements representing varying degrees of competency. These are Guttman scales and the child is assumed to be able to perform the sum of all the ratings for the 30 items. Normative data based on 800 children are reported. The scale does not appear to be a valid instrument.

Emmerich Classroom Observation Rating Scale:
Suitable for preschool children. Each child is rated on 127 unipolar scales and 21 bipolar scales. The child is observed

in free play for 25 to 30 minutes, after which the child is rated by two paraprofessional raters. The ratings are compared and combined into one rating which is considered a basic unit of measurement for the child. The scales have four rating steps. No supportive evidence is available.

ETS Locus of Control Scale:
Can be used with children five to eight years old. A measure to determine the extent to which the child perceives that his behavior determines what happens to him. The test consists of 22 cards with cartoon-style drawings of children in a school or social situation. The child is asked to pick an explanation for the character's success or failure from a pair of forced choice responses. The child's score is the sum of all internalized choices. The test is counter-balanced for race. Norms have not been established and its validity hasn't been demonstrated.

Forced Choice Sociometric Interview:
Suitable for preschool children. An individually administered interview which requires the child to state both positive and negative play preferences to a fixed set of questions. The child names the peer in his class whom he considers the most preferable playmate. This is done 3 times. The same 3-choice procedure is followed in securing negative choices. The final step is asking the child whether he wants to play with each of the other children. Each choice is given a weighted score. The total score is the algebraic sum of the numerical weights. Although normative data aren't available, both validity and reliability studies have been very promising.

Helping Behavior Observational System:
Can be used with three to nine year-old children. Each child is observed by two observers during several free play periods for a total of one hour. Behavior is coded as task oriented or psychologically oriented. Six categories are used for each child's actions with respect to the opportunity given him. Norms are not available. Validity has not been high and only inter-observer reliabiltiy has been demonstrated.

McCandless-Marshall Sociometric Status Test:

Suitable for preschool children. A measure of social acceptance which includes a board with pictures of each child in the class. The child is asked to name three children with whom he likes to play best in three different situations. Additional choices given by the child are also recorded and scored. A child's score is the sum of appropriate weightings given to choices for that child by all children for all proposed situations. Norms have not been established. Validity studies have shown that the measure correlates significantly and positively with the child's choices on the Play Interaction Measure. Reliability has been demonstrated to some degree.

McCandless-Marshall Play Interaction Measure:

Suitable for preschool children. The child's social interactions are observed in free play situations for two-minute intervals and simultaneously classified into four categories. Each child is observed for a total of 100 minutes. The score for each category is based on the average number of interactions with different children per minute. The total score is the average number of all interactions per minute. Both validity and reliability seem to be adequate; normative data have not been provided.

Moreland Picture Interview:

Suitable for preschool children. A partially structured interview, this technique was developed to assess four aspects of social awareness, racial acceptance, racial preference, racial self identification and racial cognition ability. The child is asked a series of questions about pictures that portray black and white children and adults of both sexes in different preschool situations. Normative data and reliability evidence are not available. It has been shown that children differ in racial awareness, but no further information is available.

Open Field Test:

Can be used with children three to eight years old. Measures quality of play and the ability to cope in unfamiliar settings. The child is brought into a testing room and told he can do anything he wants to with the 10 standard toys placed in the room. The observer initiates no interaction and responds minimally to any advances the child makes. Every 30 seconds the child is observed and his behavior is coded into a set of predetermined categories which describe every play activity with each object and all non-play behavior. Mean and standard deviation scores are available. No validity or reliability data have been reported.

SRI Classroom Observation Instrument:

Can be used with children four to 12 years old. Measures the child's interactive social learning behaviors in the classroom. The instrument has three major parts, a section for describing the physical environment, a classroom checklist and a 5-minute observation form. The classroom checklist is used to give a snapshot picture of the classroom. The 5-minute observation form is filled out immediately following the completion of the checklist and records who does the action, to whom it is done, what is done and how it is done. The observers are trained to make observations of each child in the classroom or of a classroom activity. No research evidence is available.

E. Social Skills

Columbus Picture Analyses of Growth Toward Maturity:

Can be used with preschool children and young adults. This is a projective technique which is similar to the TAT. Materials include 24 TAT type pictures of common, every day scenes from a child's life. The child is asked to describe and analyze each scene from different points of view. No general scheme for scoring is proposed. Details about the technique are sparse and statistical analyses have not been reported.

Detroit Adjustment Inventory:

Delta Form: Suitable for children five to eight years. A teacher rating scale which uses 64 scales to assess a child's habits, social adjustment and emotional and ethnic adjustment in the areas of self, school, community and home environment. No research evidence is available.

Draw-A-Classroom Test:

Can be used with children four to 10 years old. A projective technique in which the children is given paper, crayons and the standard instructions to look all around the room and draw his classroom. After the child is done, he talks with the teacher about his drawing. Drawings and responses are coded according to 83 categories dealing with space, people and objects, but the scoring system is not explicitly detailed. As with most drawing techniques, the information gained is dependent primarily on the examiner using the instrument rather than the test itself.

Koch Sociometric Status Test:

Suitable for preschool age children. A paired comparison sociometric technique used over a period of four months. Each child is presented with all pairs of children in the group and he selects his preferred peer in each group. Norms are not available. Correlations with teacher rankings, observational findings and children's tests are available and are quite high.

F. Social Status

Minnesota Sociometric Status Test:

Suitable for preschool children. This test combines Dunnington's verbal interview with the McCandless and Marshall's picture board presentation. The child is asked to indicate recognition of his peers after which he is asked several times to select someone he especially likes. The same procedure is used for those children he dislikes. Each of the remaining unselected children are gone through and the child indicates whether he likes or dislikes them. Each child's score is the algebraic sum of the points given him by others in his class. The test lacks supportive evidence.

Mummery Scale of Ascendent Behavior:

Suitable for preschool children. A rating scale which attempts to assess behavior by which a child attains or maintains the mastery of a social situation. There are 79 categories of childrens' behavior classifiable under six headings. The procedure is to pair children for playing games, recording their behavior for five minutes in a controlled play situation and complete the record by totalling the sum in each category. Norms are not available and correlations of teachers' ratings with the Mummery scores are not significant.

Parlen Social Participation Measure:

Suitable for preschool age children. A measure of socialization, the child's behavior is observed and recorded into a predetermined set of categories for describing six social participation categories during free play. Each child is observed for 20 to 60 one-minute intervals. Correlations between teachers' ratings and the scales tend to be low and not significant.

Play Report:

Can be used with children five to 10 years of age. Each child given two responses to five questions such as "What do you like to play most?" The child qualifies each response with whether he is usually engaged in such play "by myself, with grownups, with friends or on a team". Each child's responses are classified as individual, adult oriented, informative social, individual competitive and cooperative-competitive. Mean scores are available but validity information is inadequate.

Preschool Attainment Record:

Can be used from infancy up to seven years of age. A rating scale and checklist which attempt to measure a child's physical, social and intellectual development. The record includes eight categories of development: ambulation, manipulation, rapport, communication, responsibility, information, ideation and creativity. The record is very much like the Vineland Social Maturity Scale. Validity has not been established and the record is lacking reliability and normative studies.

Social Behavior Checklist:

Can be used from infancy to six years of age. A measure of social competency, the child's behavior is observed in a natural setting and coded into 10 categories of interaction with adults, 13 interaction categories with peers, 4 categories of a child's individual activities that may not involve interaction with adults or peers. The checklist attempts to include all social behaviors. Norms are not available. Construct validity was established in the development of the checklist and the overall reliability coefficients reported is high.

Social Perception Interview:

Suitable for preschool children. A measure of social perception, the SPI is a three phase interview based on a series of 14 life situation pictures with three basic social backgrounds: rural and urban differences, upper and lower class differences, and child-adult differences. In the three phases, the child is asked what the pictures say, which figures belong to each picture and which pictures he likes most and least. The child's responses are recorded and coded into the following dimensions of social perception: recognition, spatial setting, temporal setting, attitude, picture preference and figure selection. Validity data are confusing and reliability is low.

Social Value Acquisition Battery:

Suitable for preschool children. The cultural value experiences and the child's conformity to these is measured with this self report inventory. To measure the child's perceptions, his responses to 12 animal pictures depicting and identification figure for the child in different behavior situations are coded according to cultural expectations. To measure the child's conformity, the mother rates the child on several weighted scales. No research evidence is available.

Socialization Scale:

Can be used with preschool children. This is a behavior rating instrument that directs the items to the behavior of specific children in the classroom. There are 45 items on the scale slanted in an undesirable direction, with the child's score being the total number of items checked. The scale focuses on patterns of aggression, social maladjustment, educational maladjustment and behavior suggesting internal unhappiness. Since the scale is part of an unpublished doctoral dissertation, research evidence regarding validity, reliability and normative data are lacking. The scale may be useful as a research tool.

Starkweather Social Conformity Test:

Suitable for preschool children. This is a self report inventory which focuses on color preference. The child selects pages for a booklet of a color the same or different from those of his parents and his peers. This test accompanies the Starkweather Form Board Test, which assesses conformity in a non-social situation. Norms, validity and reliability data are not available.

Stevenson's Behavioral Unit Observational Procedure:

Suitable for preschool children. This procedure consists of 3 components: behavioral units, definition of variables, and procedures for simultaneous observation and ratings. The core is the behavioral unit, which may be rated for any number of behavior categories. There is a checklist of categories and levels, as well as predetermined time units of observation and a recording method. Evidence regarding validity, reliability, and norms is ambiguous.

Uses Test:

Can be used with children five to 11 years old. This test purportedly is an index of activities, interests, and values prevailing in society. The test can be administered either as a structured individual interview or as a group questionnaire. The universal question is "What is ------ for?" No research evidence is available.

The Vineland Social Maturity Scale:

Can be used with young infants. The scale offers information of the child's maturational interaction with the social milieu. The scale requires information from an individual intimately knowledgeable with the child. The final score is the total number of items successfully performed. The scale has demonstrated its ability to differentiate between true mental defectives, those who are socially inadequate, and people who are of sub-normal intelligence. Age norms of social quotients are available for the scale's original standardization sample.

Reliability and validity are adequate, particularly for preschool children.

Young Children's Social Desirability Scale:

Suitable for preschool children. A self report inventory of social desirability. The child is presented 26 questions requiring a choice between a behavior that is culturally approved and behavior that is culturally disapproved. The 26 items are then rated by judges for degree of social desirability. Although research data is available, the scale does not appear to be clinically useful.

G. Isolated Social Behavior

Classroom Behavior Inventory:

Can be used with children four to 11 years old. Uses teacher ratings for task orientation, extroversion and hostility. The teacher rates the child on 15 seven-point scales. Validity information is meager and suggests the inventory is not a valid instrument.

Hyperactivity and Withdrawal Rating Scales:

Suitable for preschool children. Children are rated on nine 11-point scales representing six aspects of hyperactivity and three aspects of withdrawal. Intermediate points as well as end points on the scale are defined. A child's factor score is the sum of the appropriate factor weights. Research evidence is not available.

Mischel Technique:

Can be used with children five to 12 years old. A measure of the child's ability to delay gratification. The test is given by trained paraprofessionals. The child chooses between an immediate small reward and a delayed larger reward. From the research evidence available, it is questionable how useful the technique is.

Playfulness Scale:

Can be used with children through elementary school age. The measure is composed of 12 items, 5 two-part items and 2 single items. Part A measures the frequency of playfulness and Part B measures the quality of playfulness. Both reliability and validity evidence are quite low.

Sociodramatic Play Index:

Suitable for preschool children. A child's play is categorized as dramatic or sociodramatic upon the following criteria: themes and roles used, utilization of toys and dogs, functions of verbalizations, the functions of a group leader and the handling of tense situations. Conclusive evidence is not available.

Children's Play Behavior Measure:

Suitable for preschool children. Characteristics of a child's play are observed by placing the child in an experimental play situation with a standard set of toys in a standard arrangement. The child is told he can play with any toy in the room. The session lasts 75 minutes. Behavior is recorded by an observer through a one-way mirror, and a record of the child's verbal comments and examples of imaginative play is kept. The child's play is scored in several categories. Conclusive data are not available, but the technique appears to be potentially useful.

Observational Record of Discipline:

Suitable for children three to nine years old. This is a self administered instrument designed to obtain consistent observations from and about parents. The sole concern is objective description of parental child-rearing practices. Behavior is recorded in terms of the following variables: time of occurrence, place of occurrence, duration of the disciplinary incident, difficulties that arose, the child-rearing practices used, the persons using control, the issues involved, the outcome of the incident, the reactions of the child and the duration of the reaction. No research evidence is available, although the record seems to have potential use.

Self Concept

Animal Picture Q-Sort:

Suitable for children four to nine years old. A measure of the child's self concept and adequacy of sex role. The child is asked to sort 36 animal pictures into a forced normal distribution of 7 categories ranging from like me to unlike me. No other information is available.

Brown IDS Self Concept Referents Test:

Can be used with preschool children. A polaroid full length picture of the child is taken at the beginning of the test situation. The child verifies the picture is of him and he is asked 14 to 21 questions in an either/or format. Some questions ask "Is the child happy or sad?" Others ask the child if he does or doesn't possess a certain characteristic. Norms are available for two samples, but validity coefficients are low.

Children Projective Pictures of Self Concept:

Can be used with children of preschool age. The test measures the development of self-concept in young children. In 10 pictures of children interacting with each other or adults, a child picks the child in the picture acting as he would. Forms are available for girls and for boys. Research evidence concerning norms and validity are not available.

Faces Scales:

Suitable for children five to 10 years old. The test measures self-concept with respect to school, social relationships, physical development and home situations. The teacher asks a question to which the child responds by checking a happy or sad face. Norms are not available. The Faces Scales have low correlations and their reliability is low.

Inferred Self Concept Judgment Scale:

Can be used with children four to nine years of age. Adult judges rate a child's view of himself on 30 five-point scales. Experienced raters are necessary. Validity has not been established and norms aren't available.

Learner Self Concept Test:

Suitable for preschool children. A child's self concept as a learner in relation to teachers, peers and classroom materials is assessed. In several drawings depicting classroom situations, the child selects the child most like himself. Forms are available for males, females, non-whites and whites. Norms and reliability have not been established. Validity is low, but the test correlated significantly with teacher ratings of self concept.

Perception Score Sheet:

Can be used with children five to eight years old. The child is rated on 39 items with a five-point scale. The items represent 10 areas: self generally, self as instrument, self with peers, self with adults, self with teachers and perception of schools. Trained raters are necessary. Norms are not available. Validity evidence is limited.

Pictorial Self Concept Scale:

Can be used with children five to nine years old. The PSCS is a non-verbal test. Materials include 50 cartoon style pictures of stick figures in various situations. The cards are sorted into 3 piles: like me, sometimes like me and not like me. Male and female forms are available. The score is the weighted values of each card as determined by a panel of eight psychologists and child development specialists. Norms are not available although validity and reliability seem to be adequate.

The Piers Harris Children's Self Concept Scale:

Can be used with children eight to 18 years old. The CSCS consists of 80 first person declarative statements to which the child responds yes or no. Almost half of the statements indicate a positive self concept and slightly more than half indicate a negative self concept. The scale has been standardized. Internal consistency ranges from .78 to .93 and retest reliability ranged from .71 to .77. The scale correlates with similar instruments and shows much potential.

Preschool Self Concept Picture Test:

Can be used with preschool children. This is a pictorial, non-verbal self concept test. The test consists of 10 plates with paired pictures on each plate. The pictures represent personal characteristics inherent in the environment of most preschoolers. Children choose the picture they like best from each pair. The test is lacking in normative and validity data, but it's reliability has been established.

Self Concept Interview:

Can be used with preschool children. The measure assesses self concept with respect to school and to peers. After a child first talks freely about a picture of himself, he is asked 20 structured questions. His score is obtained from both parts of the interview. Validity studies indicate low correlations of test results with teacher ratings; norms are not available.

Self Concept and Motivation Inventory:

Suitable for preschool children. A semi-projective inventory which attempts to measure self concept with respect to school. The child responds to questions by marking faces with happy or sad expressions. Although reliability norms have been established, no validity data are available.

Structured Doll Play Interview:

Suitable for preschool children. The child responds to five social and non-social situations portrayed by dolls. Teachers respond to the same questions as they think the child would. Each child is given a competence index. The research available suggests this technique has potential for clinical use.

It is apparent, from the large number of assessment techniques reviewed, that the "state of the art" has been improved only moderately since primitive man had to decide upon the intent of a stranger with a club. While such findings might add credence to the argument that personality assessment should be discontinued and abandoned until better procedures are available, the pragmatics of the situation mitigate against such a position. Indeed, psychological testing continues to represent a large portion of the time expenditure of psychologists involved in various professional settings. It therefore seems more realistic and useful to discuss those issues which will make assessment more utilitarian.

Base Rates

Stated most simply, the term *base rate* is the relative frequency with which an event, such as a symptom or a specified behavior, occurs in a particular population. Knowledge and consideration of base rates are invaluable in determining the overall usefulness of a test. Suppose, for example, we wished to determine how many of the children who had been identified as behavior problems in a given grade would continue to be behavior problems the following year (or would change their behavior because of some therapeutic intervention). If we know that children of this age in this particular school have a 20% base rate of behavior problems, the prediction that none of these children will continue to be behavior problems would be correct in 80% of the cases and incorrect in the remaining 20%. Assessment procedures, to be useful, would have to improve the accuracy of our prediction beyond the 80% predicted from knowledge of the base rate.

While the importance of base rates was identified 20 years ago (9), psychologists continue to avoid incorporating such information in their clinical work.

Sources of Information

It is probably true that most clinicians, regardless of the nature of the assessment question referred to them, administer essentially the same battery of tests. This approach disregards the unique differences between individuals and fails to consider which unique combination of assessment procedures is optimal for the task at hand.

While the available research evidence is based upon psychiatric patient populations, the results are probably applicable to most assessment situations. From this evidence it appears that the most valid judgments about psychiatric patients are made with data provided by a thorough social case history plus any one additional test. It does indeed appear as if the specific additional test selected is relatively unimportant and that the addition of several tests does not add significantly to either predictions or personality description (10,11,12,13).

The issue of test selection is complicated by findings which challenge the accuracy of judgments made by clinical "experts". The data suggest that often the experienced clinician is no better able than the inexperienced clinician to make valid judgments (14).

These results require some caution, however. Not only are they based upon psychiatric patients, but these studies were concerned with very general personality descriptions, rather than the prediction of specific traits and behaviors. These cautions not withstanding, it is abundantly clear that test instruments with greater specificity need to be developed and clinicians need to be aware of which specific signs are related to which specific behavioral predictions.

Criticisms of Personality Assessment

No discussion of personality assessment should be concluded without examining the criticisms which have been levelled toward his endeavor. While tests have been criticized for many years, the issues were brought into sharp focus by the congressional hearings of 1965. These hearings identified the proper use of tests and the morality of test usage as major concerns.

More specifically, valid tests have often been applied to tasks for which their validity has not been demonstrated. The use of personality tests such as the MMPI and the Rorschach (whose use is intended primarily in psychiatric settings), in school settings or for personnel decisions or by individuals without adequate academic training is illustrative of the misuse of relatively valid instruments. An equally damaging criticism has been directed at the use of tests without clearly demonstrated validity. One need only review the many tests described previously to appreciate the extent of this problem.

While better trained and/or more responsible clinicians might not misuse valid tests or apply tests with inadequate (or unknown) validity, there are some problems which are more directly related to the tests themselves, rather than their users. For example, many tests purport to measure behaviors for which no clear-cut criteria exist or where the accepted criterion is highly unreliable (i.e. psychiatric diagnosis). Additionally, many tests are interpreted on the basis of accumulated clinical lore and common sense, but without empirical evidence. Such "illusory correlations" (15) undoubtedly contribute to the enthusiasm and frequency with which tests of unproven validity continue to be used.

The morality of test usage, much like any moral issue, is very difficult to identify clearly and to resolve. The major issue involved is the invasion of privacy through tests. Dahlstrom (16) has further delineated this issue by referring to confidentially, the right to withhold information not clearly relevant to the assessment goals (i.e. questions about sexual behavior not related to job suitability) and inviolacy, the right not to have one's privacy intruded upon.

While not part of the congressional hearings, the use of assessment procedures also pose threats to personal freedom, as may occur when childrens' academic placement and opportunities are determined by test performance. Along a similar vein, the extent to which practically all tests currently available discriminate against minority group members is a serious concern.

It should be abundantly clear that, to the extent to which those who are called upon to provide personality assessment are willing and capable of dealing with these criticisms, the practice of assessment will remain (or become) a viable part in making decisions about people.

References

1. Kaplan, M. L., Hirt, M. L., and Kurtz, R. M. *Comprehensive Psychiat. 8*, 299, (1967).
2. Klein, G. S. The personal world through perception. In *An approach to personality*. Edited by Blake, R. R. and Ramsey, G. V. Ronald Press, New York, (1951).
3. Witkin, H. A., Lewis, H. B., Hertzman, M., Machover, K., Meissner, P. B., and Wapner, S. *Personaltiy through perception: An experimental and clinical study*. Harper and Row, New York, (1954).
4. Mischel, W. *Introduction to personality*. Holt, Rinehart and Winston, New York, (1971).

5. Allport, B. W. *Pattern and growth in personality.* Holt, Rinehart and Winston, New York, (1961).
6. Palmer, J. O. *The psychological assessment of children.* John Wiley, New York, (1970).
7. Hirt, M. L., and Kaplan, M. L. *Comprehensive Psychiat. 8,* 310, (1967).
8. Schachtel, E. B. *Psychiatry, 6,* 393, (1943).
9. Meehl, P. E., and Rosen, A. *Psychol. Bull. 52,* 194, (1955).
10. Golden, M. *J. Consult. Psychol. 28,* 440, (1964).
11. Little, K. B., and Schneidman, E. S. *Psychol. Monographs 73,* 6, (1959).
12. Kostlan, A. *J. Consult. Psychol. 18,* 83, (1954).
13. Sines, L. K. *J. Consult. Psychol. 23,* 483, (1959).
14. Goldberg, L. R. *Amer. Psychol. 23,* 483, (1968).
15. Chapman, L. J., and Chapman, J. P. *J. Abnormal Psychol. 72,* 193, (1967).
16. Dahlstrom, W. G. Invasion of privacy: How legitimate is the current concern over this issue? In *MMPI: Research developments and clinical applications.* Edited by Butcher, J. N. McGraw-Hill, New York, (1969).

MENTAL HEALTH IN CHILDREN, Volume III
Edited by D. V. Siva Sankar

THE USE OF THE SEPARATION ANXIETY TEST IN THE DETECTION OF SELF-DESTRUCTIVE TENDENCIES IN EARLY ADOLESCENCE

Henry G. Hansburg
Psychiatric Clinic
Jewish Child Care Association, New York, N. Y.

I. *INTRODUCTION*

Self-destructive feelings and behavior have long been linked with unfortunate, seriously disturbing or tragic separation experiences. The suicide of young frustrated and rejected lovers has been memorialized in many stories and plays, the most famous among them being Romeo and Juliet. The self-destructive behavior of many youngsters who are abandoned by their parents is a common occurrence. More devastating is the slow erosion of the inner security by the constant inaccessibility of parental figures, who although physically available, are either emotionally insensitive or unresponsive or constantly misunderstanding of the child's needs. At the same time it is a truism that the capacity to separate from parental or other closely significant persons for necessary periods and for personal explorations of the social and physical environment is essential for individuation and ego development.

Bowlby's concept known as attachment theory (1) provides us with a significant base of operations for understanding the pathology of self-destructiveness. Psychoanalytic concepts more traditionally employed the attack on the introjected love object. Bowlby, instead, gives more attention to attachment frustration with its acompanying emotional turmoil which intrudes on the capacity to cope with environmental demands. Actual or threatened abandonment is seen as an experience which disrupts functioning capacity. Bowlby states, "----there is extensive support for the view that anxious attachment is a common consequence of a child having experienced actual separation, threats of abandonment or combinations of the two" (2). Additionally, anger is conceived as a normal, healthy component of attachment deprivation and as an effort toward regaining the association with the love object (1) (Bowlby, 73) 9 (Hansburg, 72). The fact that anger can become pathological is then pointed out as a serious consequence of continued frustration of attachment need. Although Bowlby does not deal with the potential self-destructiveness derived from this, there is considerable body of evidence that this is so.

Thus, the failure to achieve dependability from an attachment figure may lead to attacks against the self under certain conditions. These conditions have been described by many workers who have studied suicide or suicidal equivalents in children and adolescents. It is the thesis of this paper that youngsters who experience the intense conflict of strong attachment need and equally strong frustration and instability in the gratification of this need, suffer from severe separation ambivalence. Further, this ambivalence is coupled with severe emotional turmoil, which even if temporarily assuaged, continues as a sub-surface phenomenon which will re-appear sometimes without warning if abandonment or threats of abandonment develop or are anticipated. This will be accompanied by a great sense of helplessness, pain, hostility, intense denial, difficulties in maintaining self-love (feelings of rejection and intra-punitiveness) and inability to face the normal identity stresses of adolescence. This pattern is likely to lead to self-destructive reactivity or to a psychotic break during the increasing demands of adolescent adjustment. The derivation of this thesis comes from the literature on child and adolescent suicide, and from my own studies in the use of the Separation Anxiety Test (9) (Hansburg 1972).

Note:

Mahler's (3) theory of three stages of object relations-autistic, symbiotic and separation-individuation, despite differences in terminology, closely resembles Bowlby (1, 2) and Ainsworth's (5) concept of the development of proximity-seeking as contrasted with exploratory behavior with the awareness of accesibility of an attachment figure. The gradual development of self-reliance as confidence in the accessibility of the attachment figure increases is similar in both theories based upon their varied observations with different populations. The anxiety and other attendant emotional reactions such as anger, aggression and loss of concentration on activities are described in both theoretical formulations. The differences relate to the intrapsychic tactics which are adapted to deal with separation. Mahler prefers the concepts of the introjection of love objects and object constancy while Bowlby is more partial to the feeling of self-reliance (also see White's concept of competence and effectance) and the ability to find needed attachment figures in the environment when dependency needs require it. Bowlby (1) eschews the use of the term "symbiosis" which is considered phase specific (also see N. Friedman (6)) but psychoanalysts like Mahler consider the symbiotic quality as a phenomenon which attains internalized psychological significance. Regardless of the differences it seems likely that we can use the term "symbiotic" as representing more severe degrees of attachment need even when the symbiotic object no longer derives either unconscious or conscious gratifications from the relationship.

In our cases in this study it is conceivable that failures in the gratification of the symbiotic needs at early stages of development (before 18 months) made it difficult for the child to negotiate the separation-individuation phase with any degree of confidence. Thus, an intensified state of vulnerability to emotional turmoil during separation experiences in later life becomes a relatively fixed characteristic of separation behavior. Defensive character manoevers must then ensue in order to offer protection against the internally felt stress.

The incidence of suicide and suicide attempts among children and adolescents has markedly increased in recent years according to United States Vital Statistics (7). This increase has been largely in the 15-19 year age group although there have been some increases in the ages from infancy to 14. Males generally show a larger percentage of such acts than females. I am told that during the year 1972 (personal communication) twenty-two cases of children aged 4 to 12 were hospitalized at Mt. Sinai Hospital (New York) for attempted suicide. Actually the incidence of self-destructive behavior is difficult to measure and is far greater than suicide attempts (8) depending on the population studied and the methods and interpretations utilized in the studies.

At the Jewish Child Care Association there have been many reports from group residences concerning self-destructive behavior and threats of suicide. Recent literature on the suicide attempts have proliferated in an attempt to locate the risk population and to develop methods of prevention and treatment (see reference list). It has become especially urgent to develop techniques of prediction which would be of value in determining the degree of childhood and adolescent potential self-destructive risks. In the course of work in diagnosing separation problems in early adolescence, I have developed the method known as the Separation Anxiety Test. Using this method I have been able to identify a pattern of response which shows a marked similarity to the description of the child who is vulnerable to self-destructive and/or suicidal tendencies (9-12). The descriptions of such children have appeared in the literature with increasing frequency.

Tobbachnick and Farberow (14) stated the following:

> "The important dynamics (suicide) are as follows: depression, particularly when accompanied by anxiety, tension and agitation, hostility and guilt (these seem to lead to acting out motor impulses that may be directed upon the self), and dependency needs, particularly if they have been frustrated or threatened to any considerable degree."

In my study I have used the word "attachment" rather than dependency as I believe with Bowlby that this concept is more appropriately differentiated from generalized dependency by its more specific and demanding nature in children.

Schecter in a work by Schneidman and Farberow (15) indicated:

> "Dynamics of depression have been well described. In general in adults these descriptions have stated that when an individual's hostility cannot be expressed outwardly, it is turned against the introjected objects which-because they are part of the self-results in the attempted or actual destruction of the self. Depressions in children have also been described clinically. While the same dynamics of hostility directed against the formerly loved, but now hated, introjected objects we hypothesized, these descriptions have also stressed the factor of the extreme dependence of the child on the parents, his love object. Thus, whenever children feel the threat of the loss of a love object, they not only develop feelings of rage towards the frustrating object, but feelings of helplessness and of worthlessness as well. This results in and is equivalent to, a depression.----It is when the degree of tension is extremely high and the defense mechanisms break down or become ineffective, that suicide or suicidal equivalents may appear."

The author felt that children, rather than attempting suicide simply expressed their self-destructive feelings in other ways. These may be called "suicidal equivalents", that is:

> "an attentuated attack on the introjected object which results in depressions, accidental injuries, anti-social acts and the like-all of which have the potentiality for ending in the destruction of the individual. They are desperate efforts at regaining contact with the lost gratifying object."

Wolff (18) described the pattern of suicide among adolescents as –

> "those associated with depression, with social withdrawal, loss of initiative and self-esteem, sadness crying spells, and sleep disturbances being major manifestations of depression.---the pattern usually emerging in the adolescent attempting suicide is that of an unhappy, lonely, often sensitive person----the syndrome which has high rates of suicide share a common feature, reduced ego capacity. Persons with lower threshholds for tension might habitually use chemical agents to reduce the tension load and inadvertently program themselves to use suicidal means to control continued overloads of anxiety."

In the same edited work Cantor(18)urged the following:

> "I am certain that serious research can be conducted to determine whether a suicidal personality exists. It should also be possible to some day predict who in a group of individuals would more likely commit suicide."

Studies of animals, particularly non-human primates, have also demonstrated how self-destructive they can be if separation experiences are prolonged or tragic. An interesting example of the latter was provided by Jane Goodall in her work with chimpanzees in an African setting. The following example is drawn from her book "In the Shadow of Man" and quoted elsewhere (17). The incident is derived from a family of chimpanzees in which the mother is Flo, the daughter is Fifi and the son is Flint. Goodall states:

> "I would strongly suspect that the kind of affection between a chimp mother and her offspring and a human mother and her children is very, very similar. The motivation to protect, to nurture and to suckle is very close in both species. Flint's grief at his mother's (Flo) death, for example, underscores this point. Flint had been with his mother when she died while crossing a stream. For three days after her death Flint returned to her body and tried to extricate maggots from the corpse. Within a week following the death of his mother Flint became so lethargic and depressed that he lossed

a third of his weight. He exhibited all the signs associated with severe depression; he refused to eat and would sit huddled up in a ball. On the fifth day Flint met his sister Fifi, and it seemed as if her presence helped him relax. When she moved away, we were sure that Flint would follow. Although Fifi waited patiently, Flint lay down under a bush. During the last two weeks of his life, he hardly moved at all. The day before he died, he returned to the place in the stream where his mother had been. He spent a long time looking at the rock on which she had been before he moved away".

Such severe attachment and its tragic consequences when death separates a child from its mother strongly suggest the possibility of a pathological condition in which a sense of helplessness (4) related to a severe separation results in obvious self-destruction.

It appears logical, therefore, that we should be concerned with the identification and treatment of human children who show such pathological attachment without adequate attendant defenses. The Separation Anxiety Test seems particularly adapted for such identification. Working together in the Psychiatric Clinic of the Jewish Child Care Association, Miss Christine Duplak and I have tentatively been able to elicit patterns of response easily diagnosable as the suicidal equivalent or self-destructive reactivity. These patterns have been examined in an empirical, clinical manner and collated later with pscho-social histories obtained from the records in five cases. While there are no two patterns exactly alike, there are certain similarities which suggest a diagnosis of weakened ego strength, strong ungratified attachment need, depressive and withdrawal defenses and considerable losses of self-love and self-esteem. In addition, powerful pain reactions are often evoked without the necessary defenses to deal with the pain. In all of these cases the suspicion of self-destructive reactions to separation is strongly justified.

For those who have some familiarity with the Separation Anxiety Test Method, I present below the specific patterns which are diagnosable as self-destructive. 1) A strong attachment need in the presence of a low-separation-individuation level; 2) a strong attachment and a weak separation-individuation level on mild pictures, a reversal of the normative condition and an almost ambi-equal individuation on mild and strong pictures - a representation of a serious deficiency in the attachment-individuation relationship; 3) the presence of intense separation pain, intense separation hostility or both, with pain generally somewhat stronger, but the total of these representing a form of separation turmoil of more than one third of the total responses; 4) evidence that self-love loss is stronger than self-esteem loss in every case with the self-love loss being especially strong in relation to the normative picture obtained in other cases; 5) an abnormal denial pattern with a definitly heightened separation denial percentage; and 6) a weak identity stress reaction, a phenomenon suggesting a general lag in the maturational level especially in the psychosexual area.

II. *CASE REPORTS OF SELF-DESTRUCTIVE PATTERNS*

The cases described below were encountered during the normal course of clinical practice in the psychiatric clinic at Jewish Child Care Association. I began to recognize the patterns involved after the first rather dramatic case came to my attention. The delineation of this pattern became clearer with each new case and with startling clarity. I did not believe that this was the only pattern to be found in cases of self-destructive intentions or acts, but up to his time I have failed to find any other pattern associated with this behavior although I am certain that it will emerge with increasing contact with such patients.

CASE 1. N.G.-Age 12-8

N.G. was referred by the Far Rockaway Group Residence and given the Separation Anxiety Test on 11/22/71 by Miss Christine Duplak. She consulted me with the resultant protocol and I was told nothing of the circumstances of the referral. The resultant protocol of 94 responses appears in Appendix I exactly as it was produced and it is accompanied by the summary chart obtained from it.

In addition to the patterns revealed there were a number of interesting reactions to the pictures which bear comment. For example, on the mild separation picture (# 9) which presents a sleeping child and a mother leaving the room, he selected the following responses: rejection, loneliness, withdrawal and empathy - a combination which indicates an unusual reaction to such a mild stimulus-especially when one considers his age. The picture of the child leaving the mother to go to school produced six responses: impaired concentration, phobic feeling, generalized anxiety, withdrawal, somatic reaction and anger - obviously a strong emotional disturbance to a mild separation stimulus. There were other mild pictures producing strong reactions. Reality testing was poor (eight absurd responses). In addition, there were five projection responses-an indication that separation stress was producing a paranoid reaction which could certainly be interpreted as an ominous development.

While the patterns of response indicated a normal total attachment percentage, an overly strong attachment reaction appeared on mild pictures. The most significant item was an extreme drop in the individuation level, that is, the acceptance of separation experiences (3%). This must be considered to be a serious development, an indication that he felt completely helpless in the face of separating experiences. The separation pain level was so strong as to exceed the attachment level, a pathognomic indicator of the danger of decompensation in the presence of intolerable pain. Strong affect hunger with attendant inner turmoil was indicated. The hostility level was also overpowering (19%) suggesting that he was being inundated by severe, unalleviated separation disturbance. Separation denial approached high levels (17%) and since the fantasy level was low and withdrawal and evasion strong, the probability of acting out was strengthened. In line with this, the self-love loss was very high (14%) and overshadowed self-esteem loss - a demonstration of deep feelings of rejection. The attachment-individuation balance had moved to the unstable side, a manifestation of unstable reactions to separation.

It seemed likely from this protocol that N.G. was in a serious condition and was ready to act out in the direction of self-destruction. No other sensible interpretation was possible. All of the attributes previously discussed were present - a strong, ungratified attachment need, a very low separation acceptance (individuation), strong separation hostility and separation pain, very high self-love loss involving deep feelings of rejection, intense separation denial, weak identity stress and serious weakness of the attachment-individuation relationship. In addition, there were two serious indicators of illness - a large number of absurd responses (poor reality testing) and a paranoid reaction to separation.

The prediction that this boy would do something to destroy himself was partially fulfilled within two weeks on 12/7/71. Precipitating factors included break-up with a girl friend and an argument with students on a school bus. He had been complaining of a desire to leave the residence and to live with a brother. He began to talk seriously of suicide, "by jumping off the roof, putting his head through the window or taking pills". He was then hospitalized at Elmhurst General for a period of six weeks. He was discharged with a diagnosis of schizophrenic reaction, shizoid affective type, placed on medication and recommended for long term placement and residential treatment. Subsequently, he was placed at the Pleasantville Cottage School. Many difficulties appeared and in July, 1972, he ran away but was later returned. At this writing he is still at Pleasantville.

The history indicated that N.G. was the youngest of three brothers and had always been considered to be the most sensitive. He was very tall and heavy so that he appeared far older than his years. His relationship with his parents had always been poor and he apparently did not miss his mother when she died at the time N.G. was four years old. When the boy was 11, the father was hospitalized for acute depression and suicidal thinking and subsequently died of a heart attack in the hospital. In May 1970 the caseworker had described N.G. as a "verbal, sensitive, pre-adolescent who presented a superficially well functioning picture. However, he has a tremendous craving for emotional and financial security and maternal attention." Apparently, it was the placement and separation from the family and the father's death which precipitated the serious depression and paranoid ideation. Despite this, he had been found to be intelligent and quite successful in school. A fluctuatiing adjustment appeared in the group residence during the year and a half prior to the onset of serious disturbance.

It is interesting to note that in earlier psychiatric and psychological studies, this boy had simply been described as an intelligent, sensitive boy who was showing an "adjustment reaction of childhood". It is obvious that the true nature of his disorder went unrecognized because of a failure to study his reactions to separation experiences. The evidence in this case suggested a strong correlation between the patterns of the Separation Anxiety Test and the historical progression of events in this boy's life. The test indicated that self-destructive potential was very strong and likely to ensue. It seems likely that the hospitalization and subsequent placement in a residential treatment center was essential to save him from self-destruction. There is also a suggestion that this boy is highly vulnerable to intense disturbance when his attachment needs are not met or when even mild separations occur. Surveillance is essential to prevent future breakdowns of this kind.

CASE 2. *M.G. AGE*-12½

This boy first came to my attention in February,1972. He had been seen for psychological examination by Mrs. Patricia Horn and during the course of this was given the Separation Anxiety Test. Mrs. Horn brought this material to me in consultation and I was not apprized of any details nor did I see the boy. The test protocol appears in Appendix I.

He gave a total of 62 responses with only 19 to the mild and 43 to the strong pictures, the percentage difference between these two figures being excessive (38%) - an abnormal sign. Very strong qualitative as well as quantitative reactions to the strong pictures were shown - especially to the grandmother, judge and runaway pictures - and strong enough reactions to the hospitalization and death of the mother pictures. There were also strong reactions to a few mild pictures, school and camp, indicating intense emotional feelings with regard to separation from the maternal figure.

The pattern of responses indicated without doubt a serious emotional disturbance, especially strong in the area of self-destructiveness. His attachment percentage was quite strong (29%) and when compared to the very low individuation percentage of 8, represented a serious failure in the separation-individuation process. It was also observable that there were practically no individuation responses on the strong pictures - a very unusual result - while the difference between the individuation on the mild and strong pictures is negligible. This highly sensitive separation index was accompanied by severe self-love loss (4 rejection and 4 intrapunitive responses) all on the strong pictures. Such severe self-deprecation in addition to the failure in the separation-individuation process is an ominous sign.

Accompanying the above were strong pain and hostility, an index of considerable separation turmoil. At the same time, intense separation denial involving 7 withdrawal, 3 fantasy and 3 evasion responses, - a 21% level. This intensive denial must be considered as both delusional and asocial. Lastly, the identity stress level was below the norms. All of these factors were theoretically and clinically pathognomic of a self-destructive personality. In this case, the evidence suggested that he was capable of reality breaks, even though the number of absurd responses was within normal limits.

The pattern in this case strongly resembles that of N.G. Subsequently what I learned about M.G. was confirmatory of the depth of the attachment need and his self-destructive tendencies. The psychologist was impressed by the corroboration of other interpretive material obtained from drawings, Rorschach and T.A.T. She said in her report:

> "because of his anticipation of being rejected and/or hurt in interpersonal relations, M.G. often tries to withdraw from and/or avoid becoming involved with others-----there are indications that his deep needs for motherance and affection are on a more immature, that is, symbiotic, level -----there are indications of M.G.'s concern about his own sanity. The depth of his despair and his inability to control his life in conjunction with the possibility of impulsive outbursts, the relative ineffectuality of his defenses and his turning anger against himself, indicate the possibility of serious self-destructive tendencies."

It was later reported to me that M.G. was seen wandering around both at the residence and school in a daze. On several occasions it was observed by the teacher that he was attempting to injure himself by jabbing the point of a pencil compass into his arms several times. A camp report (summer 1970) indicated this boy's disturbed social relationships and his tendency to depressed states. In a check list, it was noted that destructiveness was checked in the "very much" column, in addition to attention seeking, head banging, temper outbursts and withdrawal. His overall self-confidence was double checked as "very poor" as was his ability to develop friendships. School report (1970) also checked "withdrawn" and "depressed" and it was recorded that he habitually ripped up his own papers in the class. A camp report in 1972 stated:

> "moody, withdrawn and involved with self and family problems. Very negative about himself and the world at large."

M.G. had improved a good deal after removal from the home and placed at the Mt. Vernon group residence. Several diagnoses had indicated a very intelligent youngster of variable functioning and probably basically schizophrenic. His worker at the residence indicated that while he has improved a great deal:

> "Life is a daily struggle for him and it is only within an accepting, understanding and supportive atmosphere that----M.G. has a chance----He still occasionally lapses into bizarre behavior.----it is only through continued living in a therapeutic milieu that M.G. may develop a coping mechanism to make it possible for him to withstand the demands of a society which seems too difficult for him to bear at present."

The corroboration of historical and diagnostic material from other sources with the pattern of the Separation Anxiety Test is striking. On the basis of the test, it was recommended that treatment be initiated immediately. It was later learned that M.G. was put into more intensive casework therapy individually and in group and has done much better since. Nevertheless, it should be pointed out that he is a highly vulnerable youngster who under stress of any significant separation has strong potential for self-destructive acting out.

CASE 3. *J.C.* -*AGE* 11½

This boy was tested with the Separation Anxiety Test at the request of the psychiatrist and was administered by Miss Christine Duplak who also saw his twin sister, M.C. Of the five cases described in this report, J.C.'s record showed the greatest strength and the mildest self-destructive patterning.

He gave a normal number of responses (62) with some lowering of the percent difference between the mild and strong pictures. There was some suggestion of overreaction to the mild pictures which included such reactions as phobic feelings, generalized anxiety, loneliness, fantasy and anger, a sure sign of acute emotional distress at that time. The lack of well-being responses (0) was noteworthy and was pathognomic of serious difficulty in accepting separation. It was interesting that the sleep picture caused an intrapunitive reaction - the mother was leaving the room because he had not been a good boy.

The most important factors in the patterns obtained included a general lowering of the individuation pattern to 11%, a severe intensification of reality avoidance (21%), intense separation pain (19%), higher than hostility and a self-love loss stronger than self-esteem-loss. Identity stress was weak (7%). This pattern is consistent with the self-destructive potential described previously. Yet this patterning must be considered as mild in comparison to the two more serious cases described above.

The psychologist's remarks referred largely to the intense distress and vulnerability to anxiety generated by separation. It was her feeling that the resultant disturbance due to separation would be neurotic rather than psychotic in nature. Further discussion with the psychologist indicated that an acute state rather than a symbiotic condition was present and that a current situation had stimulated the present pattern on the test.

Both J.C. and his twin sister M.C. had resided in a foster home for at least ten years. They had been quite happy there and did not want to return to live with their own psychotic mother. On a week-end home visit and at the time they were supposed to return to the foster home, the natural mother suddenly decided not to permit them to return. This sudden decision threw them into a panic. Shortly thereafter, they were seen by a staff psychiatrist who felt that serious damage to the mental health of both children would result from retention by their natural mother. It was after a case conference that recommendation was made for referral for a Separation Anxiety Test.

J.C.'s behavioral, emotional and intellectual history had generally been satisfactory. Several examinations given at earlier ages and psycho-social evaluations had shown him to be a healthy, happy youngster, although with some tendency toward constiction and withdrawal in critical situations. In early childhood he was considered to be more dependent than his sister. After two years in one foster home, the children were replaced in their more recent one. At that time, social work notes indicated that J.C. was more sensitive than M.C. There were also indications of compulsivity and perfectionism which eased somewhat with latency. He was highly sensitive to slight criticism, a pattern which correlated highly with the sensitivity and vulnerability seen in the Separation Anxiety Test.

Since May 1972, both J.C. and M.C. have been back in their own mother's home with all their other siblings. They went through some stormy periods and then in October, 1972, the mother began to have more trouble managing the children and by November, 1972, J.C. was having continual behavior problems at home. J.C. became more defiant, more involved in angry altercations with the mother and had severe temper tantrums. The mother's psychotic need to use the oldest male child in the home as a scapegoat soon became apparent and the boy's struggle for acceptance and love from the mother was constantly frustrated. As a result of a conference with the case worker, J.C. was referred for psychiatric evaluation and the psychiatrist reported that he was both "depressed and impulsive". On March 23, 1973, I received a note from the social worker that subsequent to the psychiatric examination J.C. had become very angry in an argument with his mother, gone to his room and on the way kicked a wall so hard with his tennis shoes, that a hole appeared in the wall. During the argument he said, "I want to kill myself, I am no damn good." It was later learned that at one time one of J.C.'s older brothers had attempted suicide through excessive drug intake and had been hospitalized.

Recommendations for psychotherapeutic treatment on an out-patient basis were made by the psychiatrist and by myself in consultation with the case worker. There is evidence in this case that an increasing intra-psychic stress was developing between this boy and his mother. It appeared to be based in large part on an intense need for maternal approval and contact. It strongly suggested that an intra-psychic disturbance was developing as this boy moved into adolescence and that the separation-individuation process was beginning to give him more serious trouble. It is likely that this trouble was being exacerbated by the psychotic reactivity of the mother.

CASE 4 *L.W. AGE* 13

This early adolescent black girl was referred to me for a Separation Anxiety Test in October, 1972 by an intake social worker from the Joint Planning Division of Jewish Child Care Association. At the time the only information available to me was that the Angel Guardian Home in Brooklyn, a Catholic foster care agency, was seeking placement for the girl in one of J.C.C.A.'s facilities. The protocol of 54 responses and the summary chart is presented in Appendix I.

Responses numbered 24 on mild and 30 on strong pictures. Loneliness was the most frequently recorded response (10), a result which indicates intensity of inner emptiness under even mild separation conditions, and of secondary but strong intensity, phobic, anxiety, and withdrawal responses. This indicated the extent of intense pain. Intense feelings of considerable frequency were stirred by the mild pictures, resulting in only a 12% differential between mild and strong pictures. Thus, on the class transfer picture, responses included feelings of rejection, impaired concentration, phobic feeling, anxiety, loneliness and withdrawal. Anxiety and loneliness were reported on the sleep picture as well.

Important pattern disturbances were demonstrated. Attachment responses were 30% of the total indicating a strong symbiotic undercurrent. This is emphasized by the 15% separation-individuation reactions which is a severe disturbance of the balance. Significant aspects of the balance are seen by the excess of attachment to individuation reactions on mild pictures - which is unusual and typically found in basic symbiotic problems. Further, the separation-individuation reactions to the mild pictures were equal to those on the strong pictures - a phenomenon indicating the serious problem of the earlier separation-individuation process. Severe inner separation pain is demonstrated (31%), a finding of considerable significance. At the same time there is an unusual suppression of separation hostility reactions (5.6%). When the latter is coupled with the high level pain and the severe symbiotic and poor separation-individuation reactions, we are left with evidence of severe unconscious super-ego problems. The 13% withdrawal response suggests a strong tendency to a loner status and a sullen withdrawal accompanied by panic. It is also noted that self-love loss was stronger than self-esteem loss, a phenomenon when accompanied by the above patterns indicates that she falls back on narcissistic involvement.

We would therefore expect that threats of geographic or intra-psychic separation from significant attachments, would lead to alternation between withdrawal, inhibition and depression or outbursts of panic. Such a condition could, no doubt lead to self-destructive reactions. It is further noted that the identity stress level is low - a poor prognosticator for self-image development in adolescence, and at the least, the likelihood of immature psycho-sexual development. In my report on this girl, I stated: "She has deep, ungratified attachment needs and her immaturity and emotional development make it difficult for her to express these needs in a normal way." It was recommended that residential treatment be avoided for a time and efforts made to treat the foster family.

Subsequent to the examination, I consulted the case worker on the history and read the record. The life experiences of this girl provided considerable reasons for the condition noted above but there were some differences between what the test showed and psychiatric opinion. She had been referred for treatment to a child guidance clinic because in the past year she had become sullen, resentful and withdrawn. She refused to eat and often complained of being "picked on" by the foster mother. Her behavior and her words became quite threatening and the foster mother became fearful that L.W. would do something quite drastic. She began talking about killing herself and the foster mother; as a result the entire family came under great strain.

L.W., a second child, was born prematurely to a mother who had been a delinquent girl, a runaway, incorrigible, ungovernable and sexually permissive and promiscuous. She had been in institutions and had lived alternately with maternal grandmother and mother. The mother abandoned L.W. as a baby in the hospital and her whereabouts were unknown until October, 1966 when L.W. was seven years of age. Seen for a short time, the mother disappeared again in December, 1966 and was never seen or heard from again. The father was unknown. L.W. lived in a nursery as an infant and was then placed in the present foster home in November, 1961 at the age of two. She has had many ups and downs in this home, being obedient, polite and well behaved for periods of time and at times bursting out with hostility and defiance. Some of this was related to the discovery of the existence of her own mother.

In May 1970, she was reported by the school to be inattentive; indifferent but shy and polite. A counselor noted that L.W. seemed to have a depressed personality and described her as a loner. She appeared to relate to her peers but tended to be withdrawn and unresponsive. Previous to this report, in February, 1970, the school telephoned the case worker stating that L.W. had informed the teacher that she wished to die and might kill herself. She also complained that no one loved her. Various physical complaints including stomach and knee pains were made but physical findings were negative. She was then referred (May 1970) for study at a mental hygiene clinic. Psychological testing at the time revealed that she was of slow intelligence, bland and overtly unemotional. Jealousy and hostility toward a foster sibling were reported. Projective tests at the time yielded little of value because of constriction.

After a school change and some medication. L.W. did better but periods of quiet were at times interrupted by severe outbursts of stubborness, manipulativeness and hostility toward the foster mother and the foster sibling. In March 1971, she refused to attend school. In addition, whenever the foster mother denied her anything, she broke out into a rage. Continuous ambivalence by foster parents with regard to handling and placement continued while the psychiatrist and case worker made efforts at residential placement. Shortly thereafter, the foster parents appeared to have alleviated the problems and decided to keep her home.

Things ran smoothly with no recurrence of disturbance and sessions at agency's clinic were discontinued. Then by the summer of 1972, a resurgence took place. L.W. was felt to be threatening to the happiness of the entire family and placement was again requested. The agency worker said: "It is felt that the foster family never incorporated this child as a true member of its household." However, and despite this, on 9/25/72, the foster mother decided that placement request was percipitant and based mainly on the father's impulsiveness. The family again wanted to keep her. The psychiatrist then found L.W. to be almost mute, unresponsive and with an intense distaste for the foster home. She was referred back for further psychotherapy but in October, 1972, another disturbance with further study and referral occurred. The ambivalent home status continued with increasing disturbance and resentment in L.W. By February 1973, she was beginning to request placement out of the home and the Angel Guardian psychiatrist referred her for further psychological testing.

The Ferer Structured Completion Test was administered and on this test marked suicidal as well as homocidal reactions were laid bare. The psychiatrist said: "In my opinion L.W. will not make a suicidal attempt of any severity so long as she believes that there are people interested in her and attempting to plan meaningfully and constructively for her. However, should she be forced to remain in a living situation she percieves as inimical to her interest and one in which she is subjected to constant, unwarranted criticism, it is my feeling that her capacity for acting out in this fashion would be increased."

At this writing the Joint Planning Division is recommending hospitalization prior to consideration of residential treatment. The one interesting difference between the Separation Anxiety Test protocol and the background material is the suppressed hostility on the former and the overt hostility on the latter. It appears that the turmoil in this girl was expressed largely through need (30%) and separation pain (31%), a total of 61% of the responses. Since the test material reported reactions to separation, whether mild or severe, it seems likely that this girl was emphasizing her attachment need and severe pain at separation and the lack of restitution, whereas, in the environment this girl was overtly clamoring for restitution of the lost love object. The latter appeared to have been stimulated by the short appearance of the natural mother, although it became obvious that the ambivalence of the foster parents in the handling of this girl was a seriously contributing factor. Constant threats of abandonment were seriously exacerbating her condition. The inability of this girl to psychologically gratify her attachment need in this family setting and the extraordinary emotional pain she was experiencing in the process resulted in an intense clamoring for maternal attention which was not forthcoming in a meaningful way.

Since the time of the above events, L.W. attempted suicide by slashing her wrists when the foster father attempted to take her back to the agency for placement. This dramatic occurrence is a startling corroboration of the signficance of the self-destructive pattern being discussed here.

CASE 5 - *E.B. AGE* 15

This girl was given the Separation Anxiety Test on November 10, 1972. She resided at the Pleasantville Cottage School and was tested by Dr. George Sackheim who had had no previous experience with the test. Dr.Sackheim brought the test protocol to a seminar meeting of the psychologist division of the psychiatric clinic of Jewish Child Care for evaluation. Nothing in this girl's background was known to me at the time of presentation but was known to one member of the seminar group. The obtained protocol is presented in Appendix I.

It should be pointed out that during the administration of the Separation Anxiety Test there are mental set questions which procedé the request for responses to the pictures. E.B. reported an unusual number of separation experiences (10 out of 12 pictures). Such severe disruption of life relationships represents an abnormal experience when compared to the average number of "yes's" obtained on the mental set questions. There were a total of 62 responses with 26 on the mild and 36 on the strong pictures. This gave a percentage difference of 16% which is somewhat low and indicates an increased sensitivity to the mild pictures. This was especially noteworthy on the school transfer picture in which she had 7 responses - rejection, fear, loneliness, withdrawal, projection, intrapunitiveness and identity stress - an unusual patterning for a girl of this age. Of further significance was the selection of the loneliness response on each of the 12 pictures. Additionally, there were strong emphases on the phobic and withdrawal responses. There was no evidence of inadequate reality testing.

Nevertheless, a very serious patterning of disturbance was revealed. As noted on the pattern chart, 29% of the responses were in the attachment area. Such strong need for closeness was accompanied by only 3 responses (5%) on the separation-individuation pattern. There was a strong attachment need pattern on the mild pictures, exceeding the individuation pattern while the individuation patterns on both mild and strong pictures were practically equal. This serious weakness was accompanied by intense separation hostility-largely intrapunitive - a turning inward of strong hostile feeling. Separation pain was very severe reaching 22% of the total. The evidence of severe emotional turmoil in the presence of separation phenomena is obvious. Strong self-love loss (13%) seriously exceeded self-esteem loss, indicating a serious breakdown in self-confidence and a regression to narcissism. Separation denial was strong (16%) with considerable emphasis on withdrawal and fantasy.

The above pattern describes a deeply needful individual beset by serious weaknesses in the separation-individuation process resulting in severe emotional turmoil and self-destructive potential. She is thus a highly sensitive and vulnerable girl constantly open to serious emotional disturbance at the slightest threat of separation from the source of love and security. The resulting instability indicates the need for a carefully protected environment in which care is taken to avoid precipitant ego frustrations or deprivations of supportive relationships.

The history of this girl is tragic in many aspects as attested by the long case record of the J.C.C.A. Born in Greece, this girl was abandoned by her mother when the father died and placed in the care of an older woman. Very little is known of her early development. At age 4 and along with another Greek orphan girl, she was adopted by an elderly couple who had lost all of their three children in adolescence by tragic illness and accident. These adoptive parents were themselves very shaky in their physical and emotional well being, the mother being a depressed and bitter woman. As it turned out E.B. was disliked by the adoptive mother and favored by the adoptive father. By the time she was nine, the adoptive mother was so seriously ill, that it was necessary to place E.B. in a foster home. The adoptive mother died shortly thereafter and E.B. was blamed for this by the adoptive father. In the foster home, she was very difficult and unable to relate adequately and was replaced in another home where she remained until age 12. During this three year period she related better but was difficult and destructive. The foster father became seriously ill when E.B. was approaching adolescence and she was transferred to the J.C.C.A.'s Mt. Vernon Group Residence. The foster father then died suddenly of a heart attack.

When E.B.'s adjustment at Mt. Vernon proved very precarious, she was placed at Grasslands Hospital for a short time and then returned to J.C.C.A. and placed at Pleasantville Cottage School. She was now 13 years old. Earlier when she was 11, she had been described by a psychiatrist as deeply troubled, depressed and anxiety ridden with feelings of loneliness and insecurity and embittered, suspicious and lacking in basic trust of people. Her dependence on parental assurance for feelings of worth and significance was still very strong. Her sense of self and her ego development were very shaky. Two years later the psychiatrist said that she was not psychotic but that she easily regressed in a crisis. She was considered impulsive with a low frustration tolerance, prone to depressive episodes because of her extreme sensivity, feelings of rejection and deep seated guilt feelings.

During the past several years she had shown wide mood swings between hysteria and depression during psychotherapeutic treatment. It was most interesting that with her beautiful singing voice she sang melancholy songs and talked about needing someone to love her (note the high attachment need on the Separation Anxiety Test). Recent psychiatric and psychological studies of this girl have emphasized her problems in object relations, her unconscious need for reunion with her lost mother, her inability to form really close and satisfying human relations because of the intense need for the basic maternal figure. Her present psychiatrist suggested that "It is probably not far-fetched to assume that this girl will avoid at all costs the possibility of another disappointment or rejection as has occurred in her short life-time." Another psychiatrist and her recent examining psychologist characterized her as having "a Marilyn Monroe syndrome." The psychologist found evidence of suicidal potential in the TAT and in addition he noted that heterosexual relationships would be likely to be casual, superficial and unsatisfactory. The psychologist found further that this girl suffered from severe unconscious guilt and that her acting out and defiance was in response to great inner emotional suffering. E.B. was considered to be of bright normal intelligence with considerable variability in functioning.

The corroborative material in this case is quite extensive and especially noteworthy in a number of areas. The Separation Anxiety Test indicated the intensity of the loneliness and affect hunger which was described in various terms by the case worker, psychiatrist and psychologist. The depressive trend as well as inner emotional turmoil were emphasized by both psychiatrist and psychologist. Weak identity formation was seen by the psychologist in the Rorschach and her identity stress index in the Separation Anxiety Test. Especially significant is the corroboration of self-destructive potential in the TAT material and in the implications of the history of the frequency of illness and death in adoptive and foster families resulting in strong inner depression. While all those who have had contact with her describe her as a very personable, intelligent and capable adolescent with positive potential and a strong drive to prove herself, there lurks within her a trend which if permitted to surface as a result of a keen disaapointment and a separation experience, a suicide attempt could result.

The five cases presented above are summarized in Table I in Appendix II. The similarity of patterns is unmistakeable, and should be considered as a basis for further research on self-destructive vulnerability to separation experiences.

III. *A COMPARATIVE STATISTICAL STUDY OF THREE GROUPS OF CASES RELATIVE TO SEPARATION DETERMINED SELF-DESTRUCTIVE VULNERABILITY*

In this section of the report I shall make comparisons between the group of five cases presented above and two other groups of cases. These latter two groups consist of one group of fourteen unselected clinic cases and thirty cases selected from the records of unselected populations from my original study of adolescent separation stress. The purpose of this comparison is to note the relative presence of the self-destructive patterns in these groups which were diagnosed in the group of five cases. This also provides an opportunity to rate the extent of self-destructive vulnerability in other cases. In order to make this comparison, I should like to re-iterate and then elaborate on, the six factors which appear in the records of the five cases with self-destructive tendencies and which are summarized in Table I, Appendix II.

FACTOR 1: This deals with attachment in relation to separation and individuation. There is a normal or very strong attachment percentage which is based upon the responses of loneliness, feelings of rejection and empathy which is the index adopted originally for the test. At the same time there is a severe lowering of the separation acceptance or indivduation index. This percentage is based upon the responses of adaptation, well being and sublimation. The comparison of these two indices indicates such a severe lowering of the individuation percentage in relation to the attachment percentage based on the original norms for the test as to suggest a serious disorder of the separation-individuation process.

FACTOR 2. This refers to the relationship between the attachment individuation construction and the strength of the separation stimulus. On the six mild pictures the five children referred to above showed a stronger attachment reaction than individuation reaction, a serious reversal of a normal reaction. This suggested an overly strong reaction and a severe sensitivity to slight separation experiences, a phenomenon suggesting an anxious attachment as defined by Bowlby. Such a sensitivity would have to be considered as a strong vulnerability to separation experiences and environmental changes from familiar to unfamiliar settings. Included in this factor was a general equality between the individuation reactions on the mild and strong pictures. Both of these conditions indicated an abnormal deficite in the reactions to the separation stimulus.

FACTOR 3. We deal here with the strength of the reported emotional turmoil which results from the separation experiences. These affect reactions include six responses grouped under separation hostility and separation pain; the former including anger, projection and intrapunitiveness, and the latter, fear, anxiety, and somatic reactions. In our five cases the combination of these affect areas was very high encompassing between one-third and two-fifths of the responses (Table I, Appendix II). In all five cases separation pain exceeded separation hostility and in four out of the five cases, hostility was quite strong. This indicates that in combination with the disturbance in the separation-individuation process there is a considerable affect upheaval of great inner significance.

FACTOR 4. This aspect is concerned with the strength of separation denial, an index consisting of withdrawal, evasion and fantasy. When this is strong, especially if fantasy dominates, it signifies a delusional trend. In our five cases it can be seen from the data that this factor was definitely stronger than the norms (17%). Such a factor would represent a danger to the self when it is combined with the other indexes, and could add to the danger of suicidal reactions in the presence of separation.

FACTOR 5. This factor refers to the severe loss of self-love in relationship to the self-esteem pattern. The self-love loss index consists of rejection and intrapunitive responses. A higher than normal percentage here is an indicator of an abnormal self-rejection; the normative population generally shows a higher self-esteem loss than self-love loss. Our five cases showed factor 5 present in each case.

FACTOR 6. Here we are concerned with the identity stress response. In each of the five cases the identity stress percentage was low or very low. This suggested difficulty in handling the normal regressive tendency of early adolescence; therefore a hindrance to psycho-sexual maturation. This difficulty strongly indicates a fear of going to pieces during a separation experience and therefore an unwillingness to accept any personality change at this stage of life.

The data in these five cases which are summarized in Table I, Appendix II, suggest that when all six factors are present, the combination has lethal or destructive potential toward the self. This theoretical formulation coincides with the clinical data as well as with material drawn from the literature. We see a severe, almost unquenchable affect hunger for being wanted and loved by an attachment figure, a tremendous difficulty in accepting even mild separations, a severe inner emotional turmoil which is unneutralized, a trend toward withdrawal and possibly delusional reactions, a severe sense of self-castigation and denegration and a lack of ability to handle identity stress. Lacking an adequate defense in the face of these weaknesses, these children may be prone to depressions and/or delusional episodes.

Now let us consider a random sampling of 14 cases drawn from our clinic records of youngsters who were given the Separation Anxiety Test. These cases showed a median age of 12½ which is the same as our five cases listed above. From Table II, Appendix II, we will note that each of the 14 cases have been checked for each of the six factors. The presence of a factor in a given case is noted by a / sign while the absence is noted by an X. We will note that no case showed all six factors, one case showed five factors and one case, four factors. Eight cases showed zero to two factors and four cases showed three factors. The median percentage of factors was 33%. The last column would suggest that potential of self-destructive behavior; six cases show a 50% potential or more.

An examination was made of the records of these 14 children and in the six cases noted above there was much stronger evidence than in the other eight cases of considerable sensitivity to separation. These children seemed more threatened by object loss and their defenses were strongly masochistic. It is also important to note that we are dealing with gradations of capacity for defense against self-destructiveness. In the Table it may be seen that factors 3 and 6 were not as differentiating as factors 1,2,4, and 5. From this data it seemed that attachment need with poor balance between this and individuation as well as separation denial and identity responses were most differentiating between our five cases and the unselected clinic cases.

Table III Appendix II presents an evaluation of self-destructive patterns (referrable to the five cases) in an unselected group of 30 cases from a school population of non-placed children. Striking differences appear. Only 20% of this group showed indexes from the six factors of 50% or more. Only one child showed a really strong potential for self-destructiveness as measured by this scale. Factors most differentiating between this population and our five cases were numbers 1, 2, and 6.

Table IV Appendix II indicates that the more we move from the strongly self-destructive population through clinic cases and then, more normative population, we see a gradual decrease in the degree of the presence of the six factors. Noteworthy, is the finding that factors 1 and 2 were least present in both the clinic and normative population. Such a finding suggests that the attachment level in relation to the individuation level on both mild and strong pictures is a very sensitive indicator for self-destructive potential. While these two factors are the most sensitive, it seems obvious that when the other four factors are combined with these two, the potential is far greater. For example, intense emotional reactions as seen in factor 3 (separation hostility and separation pain) occurred in our five cases (Table I) while in our unselected clinic cases, 57% of the children showed this intensity and in our unselected normative population, only 13% showed this. There is some suggestion from this material, if one is permitted a bit of theorizing, that many children may have counteracting defenses which prevent separation turmoil from disrupting the ego - a kind of immunization probably related to a stronger separation-individuation achievement.

IV. SUMMARY AND CONCLUSIONS

This paper has been concerned with the relationship between self-destructive potential in early adolescence and a specific pattern of responses on the Separation Anxiety Test. Theoretical and clinical material from the literature indicated that there is a strong relationship between intense separation experiences from significant love objects and self-destructive or suicidal trends in humans as well as animals. At least there is evidence that fears of abandonment as well as actual loss of love objects can be precipitating factors in suicidal behavior. Locating children whose sensitivity and vulnerabiliy to separation is intense and whose patterns are self-destructively responsive to actual or threatened separation from significant attachment figures has been considered an important task for mental health workers.

The Separation Anxiety Test is so designed as to reveal internal feeling reaction to intensity gradations of separation experiences. During the course of my work with this instrument at the Jewish Child Care Association I have uncovered what appears to be a special group of highly sensitive youngsters who are prone to self-destructive reactions under separation stress whether threatened or actual. The five youngsters described in this report are certainly not diagnostically similar; they range from psychotic propensity to neurotic problems and character difficulties. Yet, they all show a Separation Anxiety Test pattern markedly similar and with evidence from other data of self-destructive trends.

The milieus in which these children have lived varied from foster homes to group residences to institutional settings. Their histories are considerably different in many respects but in all cases fears of abandonment and actual abandonment had been experienced with great intensity. While patterns of defense and ego potential vary, their sensitivity to attachment deprivation appears to be expressed in severe overt distress of a magnitude likely to result in a self-destructive or suicide attempt.

The evolvement of the recognition of this test pattern came to me slowly as each case was presented. It certainly cannot be considered as final in any sense. Further, it is likely that other patterns exist in which a trend toward self harm will be discerned. To uncover such patterns might necessitate several types of studies; some might be post hoc (subsequent to suicide or self-destructive efforts) and others, follow-up studies of large populations over long periods of time to determine the degree and extent of such behavior among test-determined potential cases as differentiated from controls.

In the present study it was possible to make comparisons of three groups of youngsters for the presence and extent of the six factors (described on pages 184-186). It was seen that unselected clinic cases showed a considerably lessened number of cases with the six-factor pattern and unselected normative populations, still far less. This data provides some, but not by any means, final confirmation of the signficance and prevalence of the pattern.

I should not like to leave this paper without considering the clinical significance of this data. The material suggests that in the presence of strong attachment need, some children are unable to accept even mild separation experiences and show a definite disturbance in the separation-individuation process. This results in severe emotional turmoil - an effort to retrieve the lost love object - but at the same time a severe lowering of self-love. This corroborates Bowlby's concept of protest and despair. The strong feeling of abandonment which ensues and the inability to handle the normal identity stress and regressive pulls of early adolescence, produces an unusual combination of depression and impulsiveness which endangers the welfare of the youngster. When this is combined with a pull toward denial, temporary delusional reaction is possible.

From this material it follows that these children require special care by child care agencies. The most signficant safeguard is likely to lie in the provision of long-term attachment figures. In addition it seems likely that these youngsters will need to be carried in psychotherapeutic treatment as a bulwark against suicide attempts. From the experience with these five cases reported herein there is some suggestion that when active intervention by mental health workers is made available, there is a likelihood that successful suicide attempts will not ensue.

TABLE I

SEPARATION ANXIETY TEST PROTOCOL SUMMARIES OF FIVE CASES OF YOUNGSTERS WITH SELF DESTRUCTIVE TENDENCIES

FACTOR PATTERN	CASES AND AGES‘						
	I-12½	II-12½	III-11½	IV-13	V-15	Median	Comp. Norms
1 A. Attachment	21%	29%	22%	30%	29%	29%	Very High
B. Individuation	3%	5%	11%	15%	5%	5%	Very Low
2 A. Attach-Ind.	Mild	Mild	Mild A-I	Mild A-I	Mild A-I	Mild A-I	Serious
B. Balance Deficits	A-I	A-I	Ind.Bal	Ind.Bal	Ind.Bal	Ind.Bal	Weakness
3 A. Separation Hostility	19%	16%	13%	5½%	16%	16%	Strong
B. Separation Pain	22%	17½%	19%	31%	21%	21%	Very Strong

4	A. Conc.-Sub. Ratio	5%	6%	8%	5½%	1½%	5½%	A weaker than
	B. Self-Love Loss	14%	13%	9%	7½%	13%	13%	B
5	Separation Denial	17%	21%	21%	13%	16%	17%	Very High
6	Separation Identity Stress	6%	4½%	7%	3½%	10%	6%	Weak
	Attach.-Indiv. Balance	47%	82%	40%	22%	34%	40%	Strong but not diff.
	Absurd Responses	8	2	1	1	3	2	Generally Normal
	Mild-Strong Diff.	20%	38%	22%	12%	18%	20%	Generally Normal

TABLE II

DEGREE OF SELF DESTRUCTIVE SEPARATION ANXIETY TEST PATTERNS ON FOURTEEN UNSELECTED CLINIC CASES

Case	Age	Pattern Significant Factors						Total	Index
		1	2	3	4	5	6		
1	10	X	X	X	X	X	/	1	17%
2	12	X	X	X	X	X	/	1	17%
3	13½	X	X	X	X	X	X	0	0%
4	14½	X	X	/	X	X	X	1	17%
5	14	/	/	/	/	/	X	5	83%
6	14½	X	/	/	X	/	/	4	67%
7	12½	/	X	/	X	X	/	3	50%
8	13	/	/	/	X	X	X	3	50%
9	12	X	X	/	/	X	/	3	50%
10	12½	X	X	/	X	X	X	1	17%
11	12	X	X	/	X	X	/	2	33%
12	11	X	X	X	/	/	/	3	50%
13	12	X	X	X	/	X	/	2	33%
14	13	X	X	X	X	X	X	0	0%

Median 12½ Range of Points 0 - 5 Median 2 Median Index % 33% Number of Cases Showing Significant % (above or at 50) 6 43% Points of strong significance 3 (emotional turmoil) and 6 (identity stress)

Factors most differentiating between self-destructives and the unselected clinic cases: 1, 2, 4, 5.

TABLE III

DEGREE OF SELF DESTRUCTIVE SEPARATION ANXIETY TEST PATTERNS OF THIRTY NON-PLACED CHILDREN IN A RANDOM POPULATION SAMPLING

Case	Age	Pattern Significant Factors 1	2	3	4	5	6	Total	Index
1	12½	X	X	X	X	X	X	0	0%
2	13	/	X	/	/	/	/	5	83%
3	13	X	/	/	X	/	X	3	50%
4	12½	X	X	X	X	/	/	2	33%
5	13	X	X	/	/	X	X	2	33%
6	13	/	X	/	/	X	X	3	50%
7	13	X	X	X	X	X	X	0	0%
8	13½	X	X	/	X	/	/	3	50%
9	13	/	X	/	X	X	X	2	33%
10	12½	X	X	/	X	/	X	2	33%
11	12½	X	X	X	X	X	X	0	0%
12	13	X	X	X	X	/	X	1	17%
13	12½	X	X	X	/	/	X	2	33%
14	14	X	X	X	X	X	X	0	0%
15	14	/	X	X	X	/	X	2	33%
16	13½	X	X	/	/	X	X	2	33%
17	12½	X	X	X	/	/	/	3	50%
18	14½	X	X	/	/	X	X	2	33%
19	14	X	X	X	/	X	X	1	17%
20	14½	X	X	X	/	X	X	1	17%
21	12	X	X	/	/	X	X	2	33%
22	14	X	X	X	/	X	X	1	17%
23	14½	X	X	X	/	X	X	1	17%
24	13	X	X	X	/	X	X	1	17%
25	13½	X	X	X	/	X	X	1	17%
26	13	X	X	X	X	/	X	1	17%
27	13½	X	X	X	/	X	X	1	17%
28	15½	X	X	X	/	/	X	2	33%
29	12½	X	X	X	X	X	X	0	0%
30	12	/	X	/	/	X	X	3	50%

Table III

Median 13½ Range of Points 0 - 5 Median 2 Median Index % 33% Number of Cases Showing Significant % (above or at 50) 6 20% Points of Strong Significance 3 (emotional turmoil), 4 intensity of self love loss, and 5, separation denial

Factors most differentiating between self-destructiveness and the unselected normal population, 1, 2 and 6.

The recording form for the Separation Anxiety Test is depicted in the original work (9). Copies of the form may be obtained from the author at the Jewish Child Care Association at 345 Madison Avenue, New York, N.Y. 10017.

TABLE IV

Summary of Self-Destructive Tendencies for Three Groups Depicted in Tables I, II and III

Group	No. of Cases	Age Range	Median Age	% Cases at 50% or Above Self-Dest.	Differentiating Factors
A. Self-destructive Cases	5	11½-15	12½	100%	1, 2, 3, 4, 5,6
B. Unselected Clinic Cases	14	10-14½	12½	43%	1, 2, 4, 5
C. Unselected Normal Population	30	12-15½	13	20%	1, 2, 6

Factors which are most differentiating are 1 (severe lowering of total individuation in relation to attachment need) and 2 (attachment-individuation balance deficits -high level of attachment response to mild stimuli and fairly equivalent individuation response to mild and strong stimuli).

INDEX TO THE FIVE CASE PROTOCOLS PRESENTED IN SECTION II

A summary of the five protocols is presented below. The original text (9) may be referred to for additional details. A short description of the test and its method is also given here for the reader's assistance in understanding the procedure involved.

The test consists of 12 pictures of separation situations, six mild and six strong separation experiences. These pictures are accompanied by several mental set questions and seventeen phrases which the subject is required to select from as many as he wishes which indicate how the child in the picture feels. These responses are recorded on a record blank by encircling the number of the phrases selected. Each of the seventeen phrases represent the following: rejection, impaired concentration, phobic feeling,anxiety, loneliness, withdrawal, somatic reaction, adaptive reaction, anger, projection, empathy, evasion, fantasy, well-being, sublimation, intrapunitive reaction and identity stress. These are later arranged in patterns which include: attachment, individuation, hostility, painful tension, reality avoidance, self-love loss, concnetration impairment versus sublimation and identity stress. A set of absurd responses are also included for purposes of reality testing. A balance is obtained between attachment and individuation which is considered to be a basic core personality phenomenon.

CASE 1 (N. G. Age 12-8)

Rejection -8 (Mild 2, strong 6), Imp. conc. -4 (M 2, S 2), Phobic -8 (3,5); Anxiety -9 (5,4); Loneliness -10 (4,6); Withdrawal -9 (5,4); somatic 4 (1,3); Adaptive -1 (1,0); Anger -8 (4,4); Projection 5 (1,4); Empathy -8 (3,5); Evasion -6 (2,4); Fantasy 1 (0,1); Well-being -1 (1,0); Sublimation -1 (1,0); Intrapunitive -5 (0,5); and Identity Stress -6 (2,4). Total: 94, (Mild 37, Strong 57).

Patterns:

Attachment -26 (Mild 9, Strong 17) 21%; Individuation -3 (M 3, S 0) 3%; Hostility -18 (5, 13) 19%; Painful Tension -21, (9, 12) 22%; Reality Avoidance 16 (7, 9) 17%; Conc. Imp. vs. Sub. 3:2 5%; Self-Love Loss 13 -(2, 11) 14%; Identity Stress 6 (2,4) 6%; Absurd Responses 8 (2,6).

CASE 2 (M.G. Age 12-5)

Rejection - 4 (Mild 0, Strong 4); Imp. Conc. 2 (M 1, S 1); Phobic - 3 (2, 1); Anxiety - 5 (3, 2); Loneliness - 8 (2, 6); Withdrawal - 7 (2, 5); Somatic - 3 (1, 2); Adaptive - 1 (1, 0); Anger - 5 (1, 4); Projection - 1 (0, 1); Empathy - 6 (1, 5); Evasion - 3 (1, 2); Fantasy - 3 (0, 3); Well Being - 2 (1, 1); Sublimation - 2 (2, 0); Intrapunitive - 4 (0, 4); and Identity Stress - 3 (1, 2). Total - 62 (Mild 19, Strong 43).

Patterns

Attachment - 18 (Mild 3, Strong 15) 29% ; Individuation - 5 (M 4, S 1) 8% ; Hostility - 10 (1, 9) 16% ; Painful Tension - 11 (6, 5) 17½% ; Reality Avoidance - 13 (3, 10) 21% ; Imp. *vs*. Sub. 2:2, 6% ; Self - Love Loss - 8 (0, 8) 13% ; Identity Stress - 3 (2, 1) 5% ; Absurd Responses 2 (0, 2).

CASE 3 (J. C. Age 11-8)

Rejection - 2 (Mild 0, Strong 2); Imp. Conc. - 4 (M 1, S 3); Phobic - 6 (5, 1); Anxiety - 6 (2, 4); Loneliness - 8 (3, 5); Withdrawal - 7 (3, 4); Somatic - 0 (0, 0); Adaptive - 6 (3, 3); Anger - 4 (2, 2); Projection - 0 (0, 0); Empathy - 4 (0, 4); Evasion - 0 (0, 0); Fantasy - 6 (2, 4); Well - Being - 0 (0, 0); Sublimation - 1 (1, 0); Intrapunitive - 4 (1, 3); Identity Stress - 4 (1, 3); Total - 62 Mild 24, Strong 38).

Patterns

Attachment - 14 (Mild 3, Strong 11) 22% ; Individuation - 7 (M 4, S 3) 11% ; Hostility - 8 (3, 5) 13% ; Painful Tension - 12 (7, 5) 19% ; Reality Avoidance - 13 (5, 8) 21% ; Conc. Imp. 4:1, 8% ; Self - Love Loss - 6 (1, 5) 9% ; Identity Stress - 4 (1, 3) 7% ; Absurd Responses - 1 (0, 1).

CASE 4 (L. W. Age 12-11)

Rejection - 3 (Mild 1, Strong 2); Imp. Conc. - 1 (1, 0); Phobic - 7 (4, 3); Anxiety - 7 (3, 4); Loneliness - 10 (5, 5); Withdrawal - 7 (4, 3); Somatic - 3 (0, 3); Adaptive - 4 (1, 3); Anger - 2 (1, 1); Projection - 0 (0, 0); Empathy - 3 (1, 2); Evasion - 0 (0, 0); Fantasy - 0 (0, 0); Well - Being -2 (1, 1); Sublimation - 2 (2, 0); Intrapunitive - 1 (0, 1); Identity Stress - 2 (0, 2); Total - 54 (Mild 24, Strong 30).

Patterns

Attachment - 16 (Mild 7, Strong 9) 30% ; Individuation - 8 (4, 4) 15% ; Hostility - 3 (1, 2) 5½% ; Painful Tension - 17 (7,

10) 31%; Reality Avoidance 7 (4, 3) 13%; Conc. Imp. *vs.* Sublimation 1:2, 5½%; Self - Love Loss - 4 (1, 3) 7½%; Identity Stress - 2 (0, 2) 3½%; Absurd Responses - 1 z)1, 0).

CASE 5 (E. B. Age 15-3)

Rejection - 3 (Mild 1, Strong 2); Imp. Conc. - 1 (M1, S0); Phobic - 7 (3, 4); Anxiety - 6 (2, 4); Loneliness - 12 (6, 6); Withdrawal - 7 (5, 2); Somatic - 1 (0, 1); Adaptive - 3 (1, 2); Anger - 4 (1, 3); Projection - 1 (1, 0); Empathy - 3 (0, 3); Evasion - 0 (0, 0); Fantasy - 3 (0, 3); Well - Being - 0 (0, 0); Sublimation - 0 (0, 0); Intrapunitive - 5 (2, 3); Identity Stress - 6 (3, 3); Total: 62 (Mild 26, Strong 36).

Patterns

Attachment - 18 (Mild 7, Strong 11) 29%; Individuation - 3 (M 1, S 2) 5%; Hostility - 10 (4, 6) 16%; Painful Tension - 14 (5, 9) 22%; Reality Avoidance - 10 (5, 5) 16%; Conc. Imp. *vs.* Sub. 1:0, 1½%; Self - Love Loss - 8 (3, 5) 13%; Identity Stress - 6 (3, 3) 10% Absurd Responses - 3 (0, 3).

BIBLIOGRAPHY

1. Bowlby, J. *Separation: Anxiety and Anger. Vol. 2, Attachment and Loss.* Hogarth Press, London, (1973).
2. Bowlby, J. Attachment Theory, Separation Anxiety and Mourning. In *American Handbook of Psychiatry. Vol. VI. New Psychiatric Frontiers.* Edited by Hamburg, D.A. and Brodie, H.K., (1974).
3. Mahler, M.D. *On Human Symbiosis and the Vicissitudes of Individuation. Vol. 1 Infantile Psychosis.* N.Y. International Universities Press, New York, (1968).
4. Seligman, M. *Psychol. To-Day* 7, 43, (1973).
5. Ainsworth, M.D.S. and Wittig, B.A. Attachment and Exploratory Behavior of One Year Olds in a Strange Situation. In *Determinants of Infant Behavior.* Vol. 4 Edited by Foss, B.M. Methuen, London, (1969).
6. Friedman, N. Varieties of Symbiotic Manifestations. Inst Psychoanal Res Train, N.Y., 1967.
7. Vital Statistics of the United States. Vol. II. Mortality. *U.S. Health and Education Welfare Services,* (1970).
8. Whitehead, P.C., Johnson, F.G. and Ferrence, R. *Amer. J. Orthopsychiat. 43,* (1973).

9. Hansburg, H.G. *Adolescent Separation Anxiety.* C.C. Thomas, Springfield, Ill., (1972).
10. Hansburg, H.G. Separation problems of displaced children. In *The Emotional Stress of War, Violence and Peace.* Edited by Parker, R. Stanwyx House, Pittsburg, Pa., (1972).
11. Hansburg, H.G. Adolescent Separation Hostility: A Prelude to Violence. Proceedings XX International Congress of Psychology, Tokyo, Japan. p. 599, (1972).
12. Hansburg, H.G. *Clin. Issues Psychol. 4,* 30, (1972).
13. Hansburg, H. G. *Amer. J. Orthopsychiat. 42,* 330, (1972).
14. Farberow, N.L. and Schneidman, E.S. *Clues to Suicide.* McGraw Hill, N.Y., (1957).
15. Farberow, N.L. and Schneidman, E.S. *Cry For Help.* McGraw Hill, N.Y., (1961).
16. May, Rollo. *Power and Innocence.* W. W. Norton and Co., N. Y. (1972).
17. Begers, C. *Beauty and Her Beasts.* Saturday Review, The Sciences, Vol. 1, No. 1, Jan. 27, 1973. Interview with Jane Goodall at Stanford University, pp. 34-37.
18. Wolff, K. *Patterns of Self Destruction.* C.C. Thomas. Springfield, Ill., (1972).

MENTAL HEALTH IN CHILDREN, Volume III
Edited By D. V. Siva Sankar

DEFECTIVE INFORMATION PROCESSING IN CHILDREN - IMPLICATIONS FOR PSYCHIATRIC SERVICE PLANNING

Margaret E. Hertzig

Rockland Children's Psychiatric Hospital
Orangeburg, New York 10962

Everyone who has been concerned with planning of or the evaluation of comprehensive psychiatric service has, at one time or another, had to address himself to the following kinds of questions: who requires services? for what purpose? and how should they be organized? In relation to children, the answer to the question "who" had tended to take the form of a description of age-groups, i.e. infants, pre-schoolers, latency age children, adolescents, or diagnostic entitties, i.e. emotionally disturbed, mentally retarded, brain-injured children or sub-groups within a population, defined ethnically or socio-economically, i.e. the disadvantaged. The question "what for" had traditionally been approached in terms of the concepts of primary, secondary or tertiary prevention, while the question of "how" has most usually involved discussions of diagnostic evaluation, outpatient care, various forms of partial hospitalization programs, residential treatment, or inpatient care. Confronted with the necessity of formulating programs designed to meet a multiplicity of needs on a number of different levels, the service planner must exert considerable effort in order to avoid being overwhelmed by the wide range of demands on his skill and ingenuity.

The achievement of increased sharpness and clarity of focus in the face of such complexity may be facilitated by organizing and integrating an approach to problems and issues in terms of model systems. The developmental model has frequently been suggested as providing one such conceptual frame, but it too is broadly encompassing. Therefore, I wish to direct attention to a particular aspect of development - intersensory organization. I wish to review briefly the developmental course of intersensory organization in normal children and to discuss the relation of disturbances in the orderly emergence of the ability to integrate multimodal information to abnormalities of behavior. Finally, I would like to consider some of the problems surrounding the provision of services from this vantage point.

Numerous workers have focused upon the importance of an understanding of afferent organization to an understanding of the central nervous system and of behavior. In particular Sherrington (1) suggested that the evolution of the nervous system was characterized by the establishment of better liaison between sense systems through the development of a "central clearing house of sense." Birch and Lefford (2, 3) examined the developmental course of the establishment of relations between the different sense systems. Through the utilization of a method of equivalence, in which subjects were asked to judge if a stimulus presented in one sense modality was the same or different from that presented in another, these workers were able to demonstrate that few, if any, normal children below the age of five years are able to accurately determine the equivalence of multimodal sensory inputs at better than a chance level. However, with increasing age, competence with respect to the processing of intermodal information also increases, exhibiting a developmental course of improvement which is as regular as that of physical growth. These workers have demonstrated too that the development of competence in the judgment of equivalence appears to underly the normal development of perceptual analysis and synthesis, as well as of perceptually guided action.

Disturbances in patterns of intersensory integration have been found in the course of studies of a number of different groups of aberrently functioning children including schizophrenic children (4, 5), psychiatrically disturbed adolescents (6, 7), children and adolescents with cerebral palsy and so-called minimal brain-damage (8), children retarded in reading (9), children of low birthweight (10), as well as children with histories of both acute and chronic protein-calorie malnutrition during infancy and early childhood (11).

Thus, abnormalities in the ability to integrate information presented in the different sense modalities has tended to be a ubiquitous finding among children who have developed, or who are at significant risk of developing one or another of a wide range of handicapping conditions. However, the specific patterns of intersensory disturbance appears to be quite different in the different groups of children studied. For example, the ability of children with significant growth retardation from areas such as the highlands of Guatamala where subnutrition among infants and young children is endemic, to integrate intersensory information, does improve with age but at a rate much slower than that of taller and heavier children from the same geographic area. However, schizophrenic children between the ages of 8 and 11 years tend to function at the level of normal six year olds and show little or no improvement in the level of intersensory competence with increasing age. Furthermore, among children with actual or presumptive evidence of damage to the brain, disturbances in intersensory integrative ability appear to be accompanied by abnormalities in intrasensory organization as well.

What could be the consequences for the organization of behavior, and the development of cognitive skills, in a child who fails to develop an ability to see the world as others see it at a time of life when others do so? An organism with an inability to integrate multimodal sensory inputs is an organism in whom the different sense systems provide conflictful information with respect to the nature of the environment.

This source of conflict is most probably not related to the emergence of behavioral disturbance in very young children because in general the form and content of environmental demands does not include an expectation of intersensory competence. However, when the nature of environmental demand changes, based upon experiences with the capacities of normal, older children, those who are handicapped may well begin to experience conflict between different bodies of sensory information and/or between the perceptions, experiences and expectations of themselves and others.

Experimental studies of animals (12, 13) exposed to demands for impossible discriminations provide some clues as to what a possible range of behavioral response to informational conflict might be, particularly if such conflict is severe. These may well include inhibition of responsiveness to some of the sense systems and a selective attention to information deriving from only one sensory source, sterotyped and repetitive activities, withdrawal and social isolation, as well as a failure to develop more organized patterns of behavior or thought.

The appearance of behavioral symptoms as well as their severity could be viewed as an expression of the discrepancy between the nature of the objective situation in which a child finds himself and his perception of it. The magnitude of this discrepancy, in turn, could be considered to be determined by the specific nature of the underlying handicap, as well as by the variations in the level of adaptation to it. Thus, in the first instance, children who are developmentally "out of phase" with respect to the organization of relations between sense systems, are clearly different from those in whom such abilities fail to develop at all. Among the latter, improvement in clinical state may be a consequence of the development of more effective ways to overcome or to bypass a primary defect in information processing. Perhaps as a result of medication, education, therapy, or simply experience over time, a new and more effective level of adaptation to experience may be achieved. Such consolidation may persist unchanged for a time, or may break down because of an inability to sustain a tenuously established although more effective pattern of response to the environment. More likely however, is that the re-appearance of clinical symptoms occurs as a consequence of changes in the nature of the environmental situation. Increased complexity may require more rapid shifts in response patterns which an individual with an integrative handicap is unable to execute. Thus, one would expect that such individuals would exhibit a diminution of overt symptomalogy in situations of reduced environmental demand, and an increase in symptomology when the demands of the environmental situation become more numerous or more intricate.

In addition to these possible behavioral consequences of disturbances in intersensory organization, a considerable body of evidence suggests that the ability to equate information, most particularly in the auditory and visual modalities may well underly the acquisition of reading skills in many children (9). Furthermore, because of the relation of intersensory abilities to more general perceptual and motor functions such as perceptually guided action, other phases of academic learning are also undoubtedly adversely affected. Primary learning disabilities, as a consequence of disturbance in the development of patterns of intersensory organization, are not only of importance in their own right, but also because of the increased likelihood of the development of behavioral disturbance secondary to school failure.

Thus far I have sketched roughly and much too quickly some of what is known about the development of intersensory organization in children and have considered what the impact of such disturbance might be on behavior and cognition. I have tried to underscore the view that a defect in the ability to integrate intersensory information represents an underlying handicap which in affected children may erupt symptomatically in the face of the discrepancy between the objective characteristics of the environment and the child's perceptions of his surroundings beyond the level of his adaptive capacities. Symptoms may appear and disappear, but the underlying handicap remains, and in and of itself, is of importance in relation to the degree of success with which the child copes with one of the primary tasks of childhood, i.e. the acquisition of academic skills.

Can we utilize these considerations about intersensory organization, in and of itself an integrating function, to integrate our thinking about levels of psychiatric care? It is, of course, not new to call attention to the need to develop techniques for preventing the development of handicap, to manage symptomatic disorders, to minimize consequences of underlying handicap, and to prevent further decompensation (14). As disturbances in the ability to integrate intersensory information are most probably a reflection of a disturbance in CNS organization more generally, the usually described control measures such as adequate general medical, prenatal and well baby care, as well as nutrition, are appropriate measures of primary prevention. The problem here is not so much with identification but with implementation.

Of more direct psychiatric relevance, however, are questions relating to the total management of children with an underlying handicap such as the ability to integrate intersensory information. Children with such a disorder require a system of care which can respond appropriately to their needs at given points in time - including the early identification of children at risk, the recognition of defect, the provision of appropriate treatment of acute behavioral disturbance in the child and his family, the availability of special educational intervention and the meeting of rehabilitative requirements with the full recognition that these needs vary over time. Symptomatic recovery does not mean the disappearance of underlying handicap, which may still be manifest in school learning situations and which may reappear clinically as well.

The concept of an underlying handicap with variable clinical expression at different points in time suggests that the same child may require different inputs at different points in time. What is an appropriate method of care at one time may not be appropriate at another. The provision of services must be sufficiently integrated so that each new event is not treated in isolation. Too often the developmental model has focused upon the problem of the provision of appropriate services for children within a defined age or mental-age range. This look at the behavioral consequences of defective information processing in children has served to underscore the requirement that comprehensive service planning must include not only provisions for different kinds of treatment, education and care, but coordinative efforts whereby the differing requirements of the same child over time can be provided without fragmentation and the efforts of the different individuals who intervene in the life of the child be consolidated.

References

1. Sherrington, C. C. *Man on His Nature.* Cambridge University Press. Cambridge, England, (1951).
2. Birch, H. G. and Lefford, A. *Monogr. Soc. Res. Child Develop. 28,* (1963).
3. Birch, H. G. and Lefford, A. *Monogr. Soc. Res. Child Develop. 28,* (1967).
4. Walker, H. A. and Birch, H. G. *J. Nerv. Ment. Dis. 151,* 104, (1970).
5. Walker, H. A. and Birch, H. G. Intersensory organization of schizophrenic children. *Develop. Med. Child Neurol., Monograph* (accepted for publication), (1974).
6. Hertzig, M. E. and Birch, H. G. *Arch Gen. Psychiat. 15,* 590, (1966).
7. Hertzig, M. E. and Birch, H. G. *Arch. Gen. Psychiat. 19,* 528, (1968).
8. Birch, H. G. *Brain Damage in Children: Biological and Social Aspects.* Williams and Wilkins, Baltimore, (1964).
9. Birch, H. G. and Belmont, L. *Percept Mot. Skills 20,* 295, (1965).
10. Hertzig, M. E. Unpublished data, (1974).
11. Cravioto, J., DeLicardie, E. R. and Birch, H. G. Supplement to *Pediatrics, J. Amer. Acad. Pediatrics 38,* 319, (1966).
12. Pavlov, I. P. Relation between excitation and inhibition, delineation between excitation and inhibition, experimental neuroses in dogs. In *Selected Works.* Foreign Language Publ. House, Moscow, (1955).
13. Maier, W. R. F. *Studies of Abnormal Behavior in the Rat; The Neurotic Pattern and Analysis of the Situation which Produces it.* Edited by Murphy, G. Harper, New York, (1939).
14. Eisenberg, L. and Gruenberg, E. M. *Amer. J. Orthopsychiat., 31,* 355, (1961).

MENTAL HEALTH IN CHILDREN, Volume III
Edited By D. V. Siva Sankar

PJD Publications Ltd., Westbury, N. Y.

TRANSPLACENTAL EFFECTS OF PSYCHOTROPIC DRUGS ON POST-NATAL BRAIN CHEMISTRY

Laure Branchey and Arnold J. Friedhoff

New York University School of Medicine
New York, N.Y. 10016

During the neonatal period the CNS of the rat undergoes rapid developmental changes and is subject to permanent modifications after brief exposure to various substances. Long lasting disturbances in emotionality, activity levels and learning ability, as well as in body weight and mortality, have been reported in animals exposed prenatally to a number of psychotropic drugs. Werboff and Dembicki found that the offspring of rats treated with meprobamate, chlorpromazine or reserpine during the gestation period had a higher mortality rate and a lower body weight (1). Werboff and Kesner gave pregnant rats meprobamate, chlorpromazine and reserpine and studied the maze learning ability of their progeny which were tested at 82 days of age (2). The meprobamate treated animals displayed an impairment in learning ability. The authors suggest that the absence of effects resulting from exposure of the young to reserpine and chlorpromazine is due to differences in the sites of action of the different drugs, meprobamate being more active on the cerebral cortex. The authors suggest also that the changes observed could result not only from a direct effect of meprobamate on the fetal cortex but also from changes in the metabolism of the gravid animals which in turn caused alterations in the fetal CNS.

Hoffeld and Webster administered chlorpormazine, reserpine and meprobamate to female rats for 4 successive days in early, mid and late pregnancy and studied maze learning ability and conditioned avoidance responses of the offspring in adulthood (3). Unlike Werboff and Kesner they found that chlorpromazine impaired the maze learning ability. They attributed to methodological differences between the 2 experiments, the differences between their findings and those of Werboff and Kesner. They also showed that the period of administration of the drugs was important. The young of females treated in early and mid pregnancy showed an effect while those of females treated in late pregnancy showed no effect due to the treatment. In a similar experiment the authors studied activity levels (4). They found that animals exposed in utero to chlorpromazine and reserpine were significantly more active than controls when tested in activity wheels.

Morphine administered to gravid females can also induce lasting changes in the offspring. Morphine crosses the placental barrier (5). In addition, from recent studies it appears that the blood brain barrier does not exist in the fetal rat and is fully effective only a few weeks after birth (5,6,7). Tolerance to the analgesic effects of morphine has been demonstrated 2 weeks after birth in rats treated prenatally (8). The same phenomenon has been demonstrated in mice 2.5 months after birth. Tolerance thus appears to be independent of the full development of animals as well as of the maturation of their CNS.

These findings are consistent with the hypothesis that permanent neurochemical changes may be produced by early exposure to psychotropic drugs. However, only a few experiments have been carried out on the effects of prenatal drug administration on biochemical alterations in the brain of developing animals. Studies of the influence of chemical agents on glucose metabolism, protein synthesis and immunoglobins in the developing fetus can be found in a volume reviewing the influence of drugs on fetal development (9). Although these factors would be expected to influence brain function, none of the studies cited involve direct examination of brain tissue, nor has the influence of psychotropic agents been studied.

Several studies of the influence of psychotropic drugs on brain chemistry have been carried out, however. Tongue gave rats solutions of methylamphetamine, chlorpromazine, phenlycyclidine and imipramine for 6 weeks before mating and during pregnancy (10). Male offspring were killed at 3, 6 and 9 months and norepinephrine (NE) and dopamine (DA) measured in their brains. NE was found to be increased in rats which had received methylamphetamine or chlorpromazine while an increase in dopamine was found in rats exposed to phenylcyclidine. There were also differences in the rate at which monoamines were depleted after synthesis blockade. Vernadakis and Clark investigated the effects of prenatal treatment with amphetamine and chlorpromazine on the activity of butyrylcholinesterase (BUCHE) and actylcholinesterase (ACHE) in various brain areas (11). Pregnant rats were injected on the 12th, 13th and 14th day of gestation. Both drugs decreased BUCHE activity measured at birth in the diencephalon and cerebral hemispheres, the least mature of the CNS structures studied, but had no effect on ACHE. It should be noted that in the two studies mentioned above amphetamine and chlorpromazine which usually have different pharmacological effects, affected the developing brain in a similar fashion. At present, there is no explanation for this phenomenon.

Changes in behavioral and biochemical parameters are not limited to exposure of developing animals to drugs during the prenatal period. Administration of various substances to nursing mothers have also resulted in long lasting changes in their young. Lundborg gave nursing rabbits haloperidol during the first postnatal week (12). He observed gross behavioral abnormalities in the offspring. Engel and Lundborg treated nursing rats with the neuroleptic penfluridol during the week following delivery (13). They found that the acquisition of a conditioned avoidance response was impaired in the offspring 4 weeks after birth.

Most experiments investigate either behavioral or biochemical changes resulting from early exposure to drugs. The relevance of changes in brain metabolism to behavioral modifications is thus difficult to determine. In an attempt to investigate the existence of a correlation between behavioral and biochemical parameters Engel and Lundborg replicated the experiment described above and studied catecholamine metabolism in the progeny of mothers given penfluridol during the lactation period (14). They observed a decrease in activity of brain tyrosine hydroxylase in the pups at 4 weeks of age.

Ethanol is known to cross the placenta. Fetal levels of ethanol rapidly equilibrate with maternal levels. There is evidence that ethanol given during the gestation period can have an effect on the performance of pups. Vincent found that when pregnant rats were subjected to small amounts of ethanol the offspring were less emotional than controls while the offspring of mothers treated with larger doses were more emotional and inferior in learning ability (15). Anroux and Dehaupas found that rats exposed to ethanol during the gestation period performed better in a conditioned avoidance test (16). Little is known however, about the biochemical modifications underlying these changes.

Ethanol has been shown to induce changes in motor coordination, arousal and affective state and catecholamines are believed to play a role in the regulation of these functions. In addition, ethanol has been shown to induce changes in NE and DA in animals. Truitt and Duritz found that injections of ethanol lowered rat brain NE (18). Reichle *et al.* observed a decrease in brain dopamine in rats given ethanol for three days (18). A decrease in tyrosine hydroxyalse after prolonged ethanol treatment has been reported in adult rats by Friedhoff and Miller (19) and Branchey and Friedhoff (20,21), Branchey and Friedhoff gave three month old rats ethanol for a period of fifty days and measured TH in their caudate nuclei and hypothalami. They observed a significant reduction in TH activity in these two regions (see table 1).

Catecholamines as well as the enzymes involved in their biosynthesis, tyrosine hydroxylase (TH), dopa decarboxylase (DCO) and dopamine B-hydroxylase (DBH) have been found in the rat brain as early as on the 15th day of gestation (22,23,24). There is evidence that by the 18th day of pregnancy NE and DA levels are under controls similar to those known to occur in adults (25). During the last week of gestation and during the first few weeks of life enzymes and amines rise quickly. NE and DA for example increase fifteen fold during the last week of gestation (25,26). The enzymes and their products reach adult values several weeks postnatally (22,23,27). A drug interfering with catecholamine metabolism during the pre- and early postnatal periods might have an effect on postnatal catecholaminergic functions. For this reason, it was felt that the activity of TH should be evaluated in the offspring of rats treated with ethanol during gestation.

Effect of Ethanol on TH of Offspring

Twenty pregnant rats were assigned to a control or an ethanol group. Prior to the 10th day of pregnancy all rats received regular lab chow. Beginning with the 10th day and until delivery the experimental group received a liquid diet made of ethanol and liquid metrecal while the control group received metrecal and a replacement of sucrose for ethanol. The metrecal mixtures offered were reduced to amounts that were completly consumed by rats in both groups. Rats had continual access to the diets in order to encourage intake throughout each 24 h period. Each experimental rat took daily 12 g of ethanol/kg body weight. After delivery all mothers were offered only lab chow. At birth each litter was culled to 4 male pups. Pups were killed at 8, 15 and 22 days of age. Their caudate were assayed for TH according to the method of Nagatsu *et al.* which is based on the observation that tritiated water is formed quantitatively during the enzymatic hydroxylation of tritiated tyrosine. Enzyme activity was found to be significantly increased over controls in the experimental pups at 8, 15 and 22 days of age (20,21), (see table 2).

This study shows a long lasting alteration in one of the enzymes involved in catecholamine biosynthesis following prenatal exposure to ethanol. These data do not permit definitive conclusions about the permanence of change in brain catecholamines. However, no trend toward normal levels appeared in the pups of ethanol treated mothers, even after 22 days.

With the limited data at hand it is only possible to speculate about the mechanisms involved in the production and maintenance of elevated TH. This effect may have been mediated by a nutritional impairment produced in the rat through ethanol ingestion. Alternatively the pup, nursing post-partum from mothers treated with ethanol pre-partum, may have suffered a deficit from inadequate milk, either in value or quality. This question can be resolved by cross fostering

TABLE I

Tyrosine Hydroxylase in Rat Caudate and Hypothalamus

	No. of rats	Controls	Experimental	P
Caudate Mean Values	6	31.1 ± 6.6	21.9 ± 3.4	< .025
% of control			70.4	
Hypothalamus Mean Values	6	5.2 ± 3.4	3.4 ± .5	< .025
% of control			65.2	

Each value is the mean for all assays in each group ± SD. It is expressed in mμmoles of DOPA formed hr/mg protein.

TABLE II

Tyrosine Hydroxylase Activity in Rat Caudate

Age days	No. of rats control	No. of rats experimental	Tyrosine Hydroxylase Control	Tyrosine Hydroxylase Experimental	Percent of control	P (Students t-test)
8	18	18	6.34 ± 1.48	7.86 ± 1.98	124	< 0.025
15	12	12	11.14 ± 0.62	13.18 ± 0.26	119	< 0.025
22	8	8	14.24 ± 1.76	17.12 ± 3.10	120	< 0.05

Each value is the mean for all assays in each group ± SD. It is expressed in mμmoles of DOPA formed/h/mg protein.

studies. Another possibility is that the pups may be showing withdrawal effects from their ethanol exposure *in utero*. Studies in which nursing mothers are maintained on ethanol would help to clarify this issue. Finally, the ethanol may have a direct effect on the prenatal synthesis of TH or may effect TH synthesis indirectly through feedback effects from some step in transmitter release or inactivation.

The maintenance of high levels post partum may also be mediated through several means. It is possible that rats born with higher levels of TH are different behaviorally and that this different behavior in turn maintains the higher TH levels; or it may be that ethanol directly affects the enzyme regulating mechanism in the fetus, resulting in long lasting post partum changes in enzyme activity, although this has not been reported.

The relevance of these findings to human development is not known. There has been great concern about the possible effects of drug taking on fetal development, particularly since the well known thalidomide tragedy. Ethanol has been reported to have adverse effects and has been reported to produce a syndrome of developmental abnormalities including the brain (28,29,30), although the evidence is sparse. Even smoking has been suspect, but not implicated, as a factor in fetal malformation (31). However, very few studies have been concerned with abnormalities at the biochemical rather than the anatomical level. As a result, there have been almost no studies of abnormal function which might result from aberrations in central nervous system chemistry. Evidence reviewed here points up the necessity for further studies of the effects of pre-natal influences on brain chemistry.

REFERENCES

1. Werboff, J. and Dembicki, E. *J. Neuropsychiat.* *4*, 87, (1962).
2. Werboff, J. and Kesner, R. *Nature* *197,* 106, (1963).
3. Hoffeld, D.R. and Webster, R.L. *Nature 13,* 1070, (1965).
4. Hoffeld, D. R., McNew, J. and Webster, R. L. *Nature 218,* 357, (1968).
5. Johannesson, T., Steele, W. and Becker, B. A. *Acta Pharmacol. Toxicol.* *31,* 353, (1972).
6. Huidobro, J. P. and Huidobro, F. *Psychopharmacologia* *28,* 27, (1973).

7. Kupfenberg, H.J. and Way, E.L. *J. Pharmacol. Exp. Therap.* *141,* 105, (1963).
8. Johannesson, T. and Becker, B. *Acta Pharmacol. Toxicol.* *31,* 305, (1972).
9. Klingberg, M., Abramovici, A. and Chemke, J. *Advan. Exp. Med. Biol.* *27,* (1972).
10. Tongue, S. *J. Pharm. Pharmacol. Suppl.* *24,* 149, (1972).
11. Vernadakis, A. and Clark, C. V. *Brain Res.* *21,* 460, (1970).
12. Lundborg, P. *Brain Res.* *44,* 684, (1972).
13. Engel, J. and Lundborg, P. *Naunyn-Schmied. Arch. Pharmacol.* *282,* 327, (1974).
14. Ahlenius, S., Brown, R., Engel, J. and Lundborg, P. *Naunyn-Schmied. Arch. Pharmacol.* *279,* 31, (1973).
15. Vincent, N. M. *Amer. Psychol.* *13,* 401, (1958).
16. Auroux, M., Dehaupas, M. *C. R. Soc. Biol.* *164,* 1432, (1970).
17. Truitt, E. and Duritz, G. *Biochemical Factors in Alcoholism.* Edited by Maickel, R. Pergamon Press, Oxford-New York, (1967).
18. Reichle, F., Goodman, P., Reichle, R. M., Labinsky, L. and Rosemond, G. *Fed. Proc.* *30,* 382, (1971).
19. Friedhoff, A. J. and Miller, J. Effect of ethanol on biosynthesis of dopamine. In *Proceedings of National Council of Alcoholism.* Edited by Seixas, F. A. Symposia Specialists 1972, Miami (in press, 1973).
20. Branchey, L. and Friedhoff, A.J. *Res. Comm. Chem. Pathol. Pharm.* *6,* 787, (1973).
21. Branchey, L. and Friedhoff, A. J. *Psychopharmacologia* *32,* 151, (1973).
22. Coyle, J. T. and Axelrod, J. *J. Neurochem.* *19,* 449 (1972).
23. Coyle, J. T. and Axelrod, J. *J. Neurochem.* *19,* 1117, (1972).
24. Coyle, J. T. and Henry, D. *J. Neurochem.* *21,* 61, (1973).
25. missing, but in reading.
26. Loizou, B. *J. Anat.* *104,* 588, (1969).
27. Karki, N., Kuntzman, R. and Brodie, B. B. *J. Neurochem.* *9,* 53, (1962).
28. Palmer, H., Ouelette, E., Warner, L. and Leichtman, S. *Pediatrics* *53,* 490, (1974).

29. Jones, K., Smith, D., Ulleland, C. and Streissguth, P. *Lancet,* 1267-1271 (1973).
30. Ulleland, C. *Ann. N. Y. Acad. Sci. 197,* 167, (1972).
31. Hardy, J. B. and Mellits, F. D. *Lancet 2,* 1332, (1972).

MENTAL HEALTH IN CHILDREN, Volume III
Edited by D. V. Siva Sankar

SCHIZOPHRENIA(S): INBORN ERROR(S) OF METABOLISM

Paul Manowitz

Rutgers Medical School
Piscataway, New Jersey 08854

Various disorders, including certain forms of mental retardation, have been shown to be due to a lack of particular enzymatic activities. This paper will review some of the evidence suggesting that schizophrenia is caused by abnormally low levels of enzymatic activities or variations in physical parameters of specific enzymes.

It has been said that there are two types of scientists, the gee-whiz scientist and the so-what scientist (1). If the gee-whiz scientist is told about a recent observation, he exclaims, "Gee Whiz!" On the other hand, if the same observation is told to the so-what scientist, he replies with a challenging, "So what?" Needless to say, the gee-whiz scientist is very well liked by other scientists. The first part of this paper will be addressed to the gee-whiz scientist and the second part to the so-what scientist.

In the behavioral sciences, there is a wide variety of natural phenomena. Human behavior in particular is composed of a rich array of phenomena which are difficult to catalog no less to quantify. Even if the discussion is restricted to the less frequently occurring, abnormal behaviors, there is still a wide assortment of "types" as is indicated in the American Psychiatric Association's (APA) *Diagnostic and Statistical Manual of Mental Disorders* (2), which attempts to classify all mental illnesses. The APA's classification system for schizophrenia is as follows:

295 Schizophrenia
.0 simple
.1 hebephrenic
.2 catatonic
.3 paranoid
.4 acute episode
.5 latent
.6 residual
.7 schizo-affective
.8 childhood
.9 chronic undifferentiated
.99 other (and unspecified)

General, catch-all categories are included in the APA system such as "mental retardation with other (and unspecified) condition" or "schizophrenia, chronic undifferentiated type". Furthermore, within this classification system, there are people who are classified in more than one category. For example, there are people who are both schizophrenic and mentally retarded, and, thus, are given two classifications, such as "mental retardation following major psychiatric disorder" and "schizophrenia, childhood type."

If variation in biological rather than behavioral phenomena is examined, again much diversity is evident except that here it can be more easily categorized and quantified. At one extreme of this diversity are people having very low levels of enzymatic activities. For example, some people have very low levels of phenylalanine hydroxylase activity. This enzyme catalyzes the conversion of the amino acid phenylalanine to tyrosine.

Biological diversity can also be studied by measuring the variation in physical properties of enzymes. Harris and co-workers studied this form of biological variation by measuring the relative migration speeds of enzymes in an electric field (3). These investigators found that enzymes which catalyze the same reaction from different people often migrates at different rates. For example, the majority of people have type 1 peptidase A which migrates primarily as a single band (Figure 1). However, in about 1% of a Negro population a second form of the enzyme, type 2, is found which is identified by its faster migration rate in an electric field as compared with type 1. In addition, peptidase A from people who are heterozygous for types 1 and 2 appears primarily as three bands (type 2-1). Hence, there is variation in migration rate depending upon the enzyme's source.

An enzyme is said to be polymorphic if it exists in more than one form among groups of people. The genes which code for a polymorphic enzyme are said to be alleles, i.e., alternative forms of the same gene locus. Table 1 shows a summary of Harris and co-workers' study with twenty arbitrarily chosen enzymes (4). Only commonly occurring alleles with frequencies greater than 0.01 are included in Table 1. Although thirteen of the enzymes did not show electrophoretic polymorphism, the other seven enzymes are polymorphic.

For example, in an European population, 36 percent of the genes coding for red cell acid phosphatase were of one form, 60 percent were of a second form, and 4 percent were of a third form. In the Negro population, only the first two alleles for red cell acid phosphatase were found. To take another example, only one form of the enzyme peptidase A was found in the European population. As is shown in Figure 1, in a Negro population there are at least two alleles for peptidase A.

All of this diversity, both biological and behavioral, provide much glee to the gee-whiz scientist. This abundance of diversity, however, may leave the so-what scientist somewhat indifferent. After all, it can be argued that this additional knowledge only confirms the old adage that no two people are alike. So what?

Behavior in Metabolic Diseases

I would like to postulate that, in humans, behavioral variation is related to biological variation, that many, various kinds of behavior are expressions of biological determinants. If this is so, then it is likely that much abnormal behavior observed in psychopathology is the result of biological abnormalities.

For certain inherited metabolic disease states, this hypothesis has much supporting evidence. For example, the disease, phenylketonuria, which is caused by the lack of phenylalanine hydroxylase activity, is characterized, in part, by behavioral abnormalities. In 1957, Wright and Tarjan (5) studied 21 patients who were hospitalized in an institution for the mentally retarded and had positive urine tests for phenylketonuria. They found the following in these 21 phenylketonurics:

"The general behavior in several of our patients showed a marked deviation from that of other defective children. None could be described as friendly, placid, or happy...Some patients were completely inaccessible to the examiner. Severe fright reactions were common. Digital mannerisms were frequent; they were slow, methodical, and stereotyped, or rapid and purposeless...Most of the patients came (to the institution) because their hyperactive behavior, irritability, episodes of screaming, noisiness, uncontrollable temper tantrums, and general untidiness placed a heavy physical and emotional burden upon the parents and siblings."

Thus, in this disease, phenylketonuria,which is of known biological origin, there are well documented instances of behavior abnormalities.

In addition, there are a number of diseases of known biological origin whose first, primary manifestations are behavioral or psychological. One example of this is the disease adult metachromatic leukodystrophy (6). The word "metachromatic" indicates that certain tissues from these patients stain histochemically in an abnormal fashion. For example, they appear pink after being stained with toluidine blue. The word "leukodystrophy" refers to abnormal nourishment of the white matter of the nervous system. In this disease there are abnormally low levels of the enzyme arylsulphatase A (7) which plays a key role in the degradation of cerebroside sulphate to cerebroside plus sulphate. Cerebroside sulphate is a lipid found in nervous tissue, particularly in brain white matter.

The first symptoms of adult metachromatic leukodystrophy are the presence of schizophrenic-like or organic dementia-like behavior patterns in the patients. Neurological symptoms do develop eventually which may include seizures, tremors, or choreic movements. However, the significant feature of this disease, which has particular relevance to this discussion, is that the schizophrenic-like or dementia-like state can last decades without any neurological manifestations. By definition the adult form of metachromatic leukodystrophy occurs only in people older than 21 years of age. However, this may be a formalism since similar symptoms have been found to occur in adolescents between the ages of 13 and 21, who subsequently are diagnosed as having the adult form of metachromatic leukodystrophy.

In addition, there is another form of the disease called late infantile metachromatic leukodystrophy, which is much more severe than the adult form. In the late infantile form, there is a general degeneration of the nervous system. Although development during approximately the first year of life is normal, thereafter, there is a progressive deterioration eventually leading to death within a few years. In both the infantile and adult forms of metachromatic leukodystrophy, the enzyme arylsulphatase A appears to be deficient. It is not known why two different forms of the disease are caused by the same enzymatic deficiency.

Enzymatic Defects in Schizophrenia

In purely behavioral disorders which are devoid of physical symptoms, genetic studies have begun to prove that

TABLE 1

*Gene Frequencies for Enzymes from an European and a Negro Population**

Enzymes	*Negroes* Alleles 1	2	3	*Europeans* Alleles 1	2	3
Acid phosphatase	0.17	0.83	-	0.36	0.60	0.04
Phosphoglucomutase						
Locus PGM_1	0.79	0.21	-	0.77	0.23	-
Locus PGM_3	0.37	0.63	-	0.74	0.26	-
Adenylate kinase	1.00	-	-	0.95	0.05	-
Peptidase A	0.90	0.10	-	1.00	-	-
Peptidase D	0.95	0.03	0.02	0.99	0.01	-
Adenosine deaminase	0.97	0.03	-	0.94	0.06	-

*Modified from Harris (4)

the abnormal behaviors are related to biological phenomena. In particular, there are a large number of studies which link one class of abnormal behavior, schizophrenia, with genetic factors (8). The results of these studies provide a preponderance of evidence that schizophrenia is caused, at least partially, by genetic factors, although the exact nature of the abnormality is not known.

Various attempts have been made to detect an enzymatic defect in schizophrenia, but, although there have been many reports from various laboratories, as yet no such defect has been clearly established. This problem is complicated by the fact that most schizophrenics receive drug therapy. Furthermore, many chronic schizophrenics are hospitalized for long periods of time. Therefore, how do we know that any abnormal biochemical finding in schizophrenics is not the result of the disease process rather than a cause of it?

One recent approach to this problem, which shows promise, is a study of monozygotic twins who are discordant for schizophrenia, i.e., one member of the twin pair is schizophrenic

TABLE 2

*Monoamine Oxidase Activity in Platelets of Monozygotic Twins Discordant for Schizophrenia**

	*N***	*Platelet Monoamine Oxidase Activity****
Schizophrenic twins	13	3.9 ± 2.3
Non-schizophrenic twins	13	4.7 ± 2.9
Non-twin controls	23	6.4 ± 2.7

*Modified from Wyatt, Murphy, Belmaker *et al.* (9)
**Number in each group
***Mean ± standard deviation

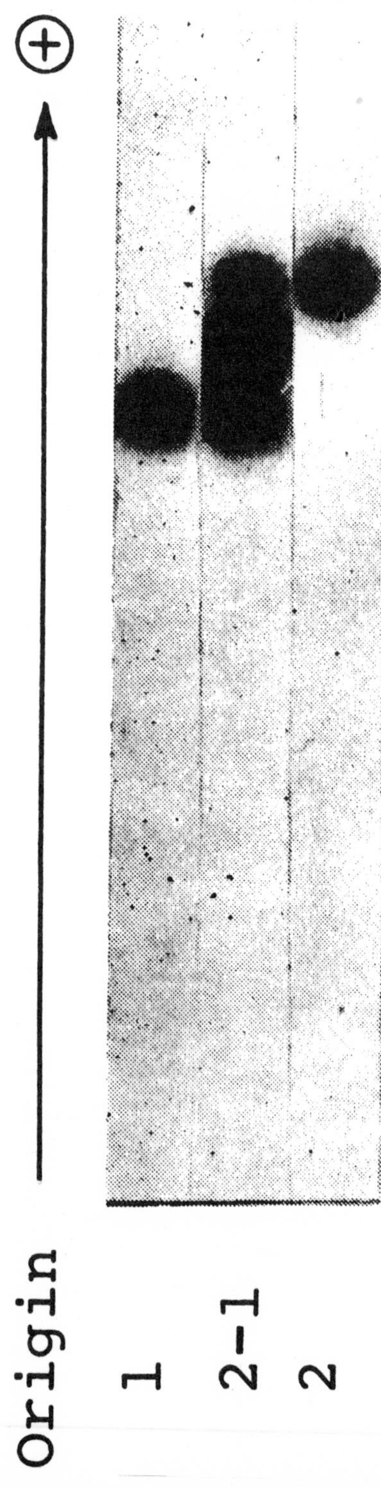
+
Origin
1
2-1
2

and the other member is not. Monozygotic twins are twins who develop from the same fertilized egg and, therefore, are genetically identical. If one member of the monozygotic twins has genetic predisposition for schizophrenia, then the other twin must have this same genetic predisposition also. The normal, non-schizophrenic twin, of course, will neither be hospitalized nor be receiving psychotherapeutic medication.

The experimental approach is to measure biochemical parameters in both members of monozygotic twins discordant for schizophrenia. If an abnormality is found in only the schizophrenic twin but not in the non-schizophrenic twin, then, the abnormality is presumably a result or part of the disease process rather than a cause of the disease. If it is found in both twins, then this is an indication that the defect may be a predisposing factor in the etiology of schizophrenia.

Wyatt and co-workers studied the levels of monoamine oxidase activity in blood platelets of monozygotic twins discordant for schizophrenia (9). The values for the schizophrenic twins and their sibs, the non-schizophrenic twins, are shown in Table 2. The monoamine oxidase levels of both the schizophrenic and non-schizophrenic twins do no differ significantly from each other but each group is significantly less than that of the non-twin controls ($p < 0.005$ and 0.05 respectively). Further work needs to be done to establish that low levels of monoamine oxidase do indeed predispose a person to schizophrenia. The approach of using monozygotic twins discordant for schizophrenia promises to be a very useful one in the biochemical investigation of this disease.

It seems likely that abnormal biological factors, presumably abnormal enzymes, cause certain types of schizophrenia, types which may be classified presently in catch-all classifications such as chronic, undifferentiated schizophrenia or in multiple classifications. Hopefully, as our knowledge expands we will be able to determine which enzymatic defects are associated with schizophrenia. Of course, if we do, there will still be some scientists who will say, "Gee whiz!" and others who will say, "So what?"

REFERENCES

1. Grossman L, personal communication

2. Diagnostic and Statistical Manual of Mental Disorders. *Amer. Psychiat. Assocn.*, Washington, D.C., (1968).

3. Lewis, W.H.P. and Harris, H. *Nature 215,* 351, (1967).

4. Harris, H., *The Principles of Human Biochemical Genetics.* American Elsevier Pub, N.Y., p. 227, (1970).

5. Wright, S.W. and Tarjan, G. *Amer. J. Dis. Child. 93,* 405, (1957).

6. Moser, H.W. Sulfatide lipidosis: Metachromatic Leukodystrophy. In *The Metabolic basis of Inherited Disease.* Edited by Stanbury, J.B., Wyngaarden, J.B. and Fredrickson, D.S. McGraw-Hill, New York, p. 688, (1972).

7. Percy, A.K., Farrell, D.F., and Kaback, M.M. *J. Neurochem. 19,* 233, (1972).

8. Wender, P.H. *Ann. Rev. Med. 23,* 355, (1972).

9. Wyatt, R.J., Murphy, D.L., Belmaker, R. *et al. Science 179,* 916, (1973).

MENTAL HEALTH IN CHILDREN, Volume III
Edited by D. V. Siva Sankar

A COMPARISON BETWEEN BOYS WITH ENLARGED Y AND BOYS WITH NORMAL Y IN A CHILD PSYCHIATRIC HOSPITAL

Ingelise Sillesen and Johannes Nielsen

The Cytogenetic Laboratory and the
Child Psychiatric Hospital
Risskov, Denmark

SUMMARY

We have made a psychiatric study of boys with large Y (Y/F index $\geqslant$ 1.00) found in a child psychiatric hospital and compared them with boys from the same hospital with normal Y (Y/F index between 0.80 and 0.90). The incidence study, in which these boys were found, has previously been described by Christensen and Nielsen (1).

The present study has been made in order to test previously found differences in behaviour and personality between boys with normal Y and boys with enlarged Y. Nordland and Nielsen (3) found indications of a correlation between a high level of activity and enlarged Y. Nordland (2) further found that a group of boys with enlarged Y from milieus with conflicts seemed to be more active, extrovert, and gay than boys with shorter Y chromosome. Such boys were more dominating and carefree, they often came into conflicts and became unpopular. They had a poor concentration ability, they easily gave up work they disliked, and problems would often arise before school age. The mothers of the boys with enlarged Y chromosome were often nervous and despairing (3).

MATERIAL AND METHODS

The probands comprise all boys with Y/F $\geqslant$ 1.00 found in the incidence study as well as 3 boys with Y/F $\geqslant$ 1.00 found in the same hospital before the incidence study, giving a total number of 18 boys. These boys are compared with 18 boys randomly selected from the same hospital, but with Y/F index between 0.80 and 0.90 matched for age and parental social class with the 18 probands. The distribution of the Y/F index of all 162 boys from the incidence study and of a control group is shown in Fig. 1.

The distribution of the Y/F index in the controls as well as in the boys from the Child Psychiatric Hospital was a normal Gaussian distriubtion as shown by the Kolmogorov-Smirnov test of goodness of fit.

The normal range of the Y/F index estimated from the control sample as described by Nielsen and Friedrich (10) was 0.70 to 0.99; thus if the Y/F index is below 0.70, the karyotype is written 46, XYq-, and if the index is $\geqslant$ 1.00, the karyotype is written 46, XYq+.

Chromosome analysis was made on leucocytes cultured for 48 hours. The Y and F chromosomes were measured in five well-spread metaphases, in which the Y chromosome could easily be distinguished. The Y chromosome can usually be identified in cells of good technical quality, some of the characteristics being the unseparated chromatids of the long arms, the fuzzy outlines of the long arms which often exhibit several constricted bands, the heteropyknosis, and the peripheral localization in the cell. Pictures of the metaphases were taken in a Zeiss photomicroscope with magnification x 600, and the measurements of the chromosomes were made with a slide gauge on projections of approximately x 6,000. The F chromosomes were measured diagonally from the end of one chromatid to the end of the opposite chromatid, and the Y from the end of the short arms to the end of the long arms. Measurement of the Y chromosome in the same individual by the same or different observers never varied more than 5% and usually much less. We found, as did other authors, that the length of the Y chromosome is constant within an individual (4,5,6,7).

The psychiatric study was made by one of the authors (IS) who did not know the Y/F index in any of the boys at the time of the examination.

All the data of the children were obtained from the case books which mostly contained information given by the parents and the school together with a psychiatric-psychological observation of the child. We made a score system from 1 to 5 for the clinical data mentioned by Nordland and Nielsen (3), as shown in Table 1.

RESULTS

As seen in Table 1, we did not find any significant difference between the two groups of boys from the hospital for any of the clinical data. Nordland found a high activity level to be especially characteristic for boys with enlarged Y. We found no significant difference between activity level between the two groups of boys in the study. The 18 boys with Y/F 0.80 - 0.90 had a mean score for activity = 3.5. The 9 boys with Y/F 1.00 - 1.05 had a mean score = 3.3, and the 9 boys with Y/F $\geqslant$ 1.05 had a mean score = 2.9. The differences are not significant.

The range of the total score varied from 28 to 47 with a mean of 35.4. There was an equal number of boys with enlarged Y and normal Y who scored over the average. Three of the six boys with the highest scores had enlarged Y, and three had a Y of normal length.

We further compared the two groups of boys with regard to bed-wetting, involuntary defecation, pilfering, theft, and wanton destruction, arson, aggressivity, and impulsiveness, but we did not find any significant difference between the two groups. We also compared birth weight and birth length, as well as weight and length at the time of the examination, EEG, IQ, and psychiatric diagnoses, and did not find any significant difference between the two groups.

TABLE I

A comparison between 18 boys with enlarged Y and 18 boys with normal Y on basis of mean scores for some clinical data

Clinical data	Mean scores	
	Y/F $\geqq$ 1.00	Y/F 0.80-0.90
Active	3.1	3.5
Extrovert	2.4	2.8
Carefree	2.8	2.6
Gay	2.8	2.4
Dominating	3.1	3.3
Often in conflict	3.6	3.8
Giving up work which he dislikes	3.5	3.5
Unpopular	3.5	3.7
Poor concentration ability	3.6	3.7
Problems before school age	3.2	3.3
Nervous and dispairing mother	3.4	3.4

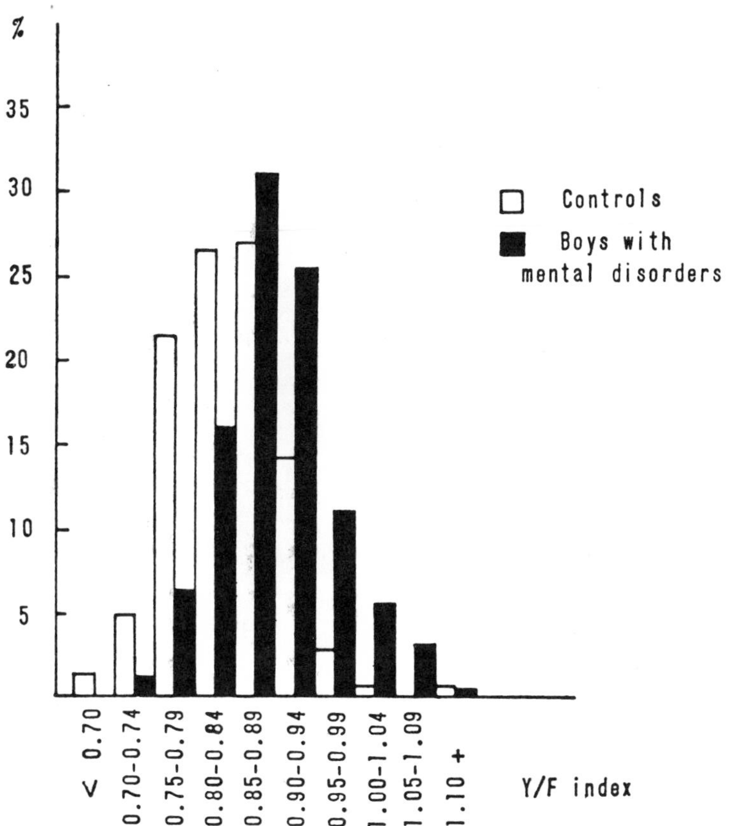

Fig. 1

Controls (a 10 % sample of 1,400 newborn boys), mean Y/F index 0.84, SD 0.07 and 162 boys with mental disorders, mean Y/F index 0.89, SD 0.07 ($t = 7.010$, $P < 0.001$)

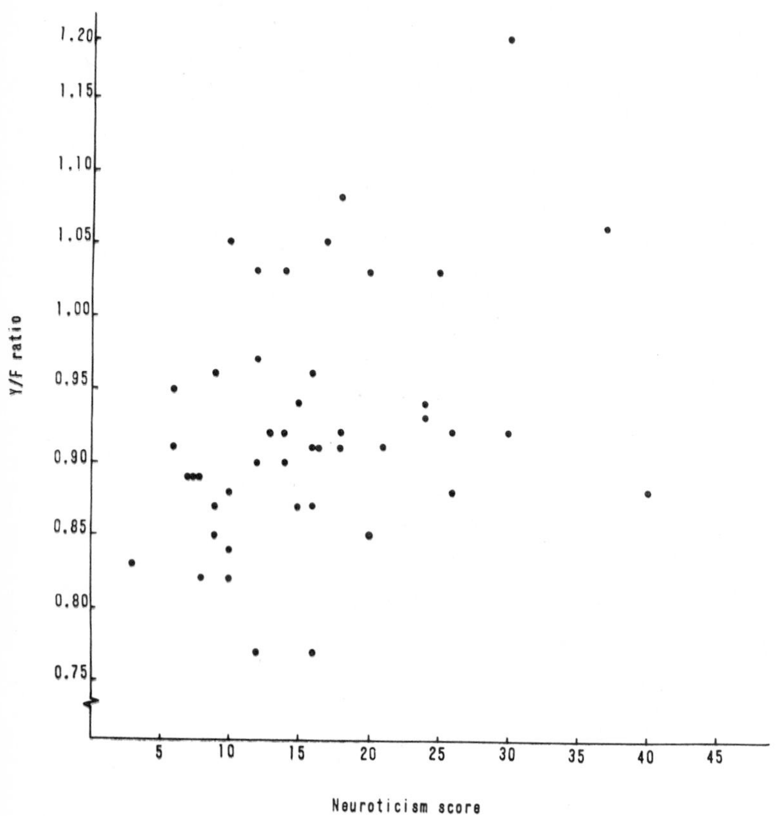

Fig. 2

Neuroticism and Y/F ratio

(ρ, 0.40; t = 2.65, $P < 0.01$)

DISCUSSION

In the majority of cases increase of the Y chromosome above a certain length is most probably due to duplication of part of the brilliant fluorescent material of the distal part of the long arms Y as indicated in previous studies (8, 9, 10, 11).

There are strong indications that genes concerning the male gonadal development are located in the short arms of the Y chromosome (12,13,14). Genes in the brilliant fluorescent part of the long arms of the Y may have influence on mental function.

Nielsen (15), Kahn *et al.* (16), Nielsen and Friedrich (17), and Soudek and Laraya (18) have found an increase of males with comparatively large Y among males with criminality.

A study of Baekgaard and Nielsen (21) of 52 medical students showed a significant correlation between neuroticism and length of the Y chromosome when the students were tested with the Maudsley Personality Inventory Test (Fig. 2) (20). Neuroticism refers to the general emotional instability of a person, his emotional overresponsiveness and his liability to neurotic breakdown under stress.

In the incidence study of 162 boys in a child psychiatric hospital from which the present group was taken (1), a significantly increased frequency of boys with comparatively large Y chromosome (Y/F index $\geqq$ 1.00) was found, 9.3% compared with a frequency of 1.0% found in a control group of 140 randomly selected newborn boys, and the mean Y/F for the 162 boys in the psychiatric hospital was 0.89, SD 0.07, compared with 0.84, SD 0.07 for the controls ($t=7.010, P< 0.001$) (Fig. 1).

The results of Nordland (2), Nielsen and Nordland (1975) (19) also indicated an association between length of the Y chromosome and some behaviour and personality disorders, and our study was made in order to test some of these associations.

If studies like those of Nordland (2,3) Nielsen and Nordland (1975) and Baekgaard and Nielsen (21) were confirmed, it would have very interesting implications for the study of genetic and environmental factors in the development of personality.

The present study did not, however, confirm the studies of Nordland and Nielsen, and we did not find any significant difference between boys with enlarged Y and boys with normal Y in any of the clinical data which we examined.

Nordland and Nielsen especially stressed the finding of a higher activity for boys with enlarged Y, but our findings did not reveal any significant difference in activity between boys with enlarged Y and boys with normal Y.

In the studies by Nordland and Nielsen, as well as in the present study, the groups of boys examined were, however, small and selected.

Studies of boys from institutions most probably can not solve the question of a possible association between behaviour and personality disorder on the one side and length of the Y chromosome on the other. In order to reach a conclusion concerning the question of such an association it would be necessary to make psychiatric studies of large unselected groups of boys from the general population, and such studies are needed.

ACKNOWLEDGMENT: We are very thankful to Birte Høeg Brask, chief of service at the Child Psychiatric Hospital for encouragement and assistance.

REFERENCES

1. Christensen, K.R., and Nielsen, J. *Clin. Genet. 5,* 205, (1974).

2. Nordland, E. *Nordisk Tidsskrift for Kriminalvidenskab 57,* 74, (1969).

3. Nordland, E. and J. Nielsen. *Triselog Arv,* Nordisk Forlag A/S, Copenhagen, (1975).

4. Bishop, A., Blank, C.E. and Hunter, H. *Lancet ii,* 18, (1962).

5. de la Chapelle, A., Hortling, H., Edgren, J. and Kaa Riainen, L. R. *Hereditas 50,* 351 (1963).

6. Cohen, M.M., Shaw, M.W. and Mac Cluer, J.W. *Cytogenetics 5,* 34, (1966).

7. Unnerus. V., Fellman, J., and de la Chapelle, A. *Cytogenetics 6,* 213, (1967).

8. Sperling, K., and Lackmann, I. *Clin. Genet. 2,* 352, (1971).

9. Whalström, J. *Hereditas 69,* 125, (1971).

10. Knuutila, S., and Gripenberg, U. *Hereditas 70,* 307 (1972).

11. Tishler, P.V., Lamborot-Manzur, M. and Atkins, L. *Clin. Genet. 3,* 116, (1972).

12. Fraccaro, M., Lindsten. J., Klinger, H.P. Tiepolo, L., Bergstrand. C.G., Herrlin, K.M., Livaditis, A., Pehrson, M. and Tillinger, K.G. *Ann. Hum. Genet. 29, 281,[1966*].

13. Jacobs, P.A., and Ross, A. *Nature* [*Lond.*] *210,* (1966).

14. Nielsen, J., and Friedrich, U. *Clin. Genet. 3,* 281, (1972).

15. Nielsen, J. *Brit. J. Psychiat. 114,*1589, (1968).

16. Kalm, J., Carter, W.I., Dernley, N., and Slater, E.T.O. *In Criminological Implications of Chromosome abnormalities,* West, D.J. (ed.), Cambridge, (1969).

17. Nielsen, J. and Friedrich, U. *Clin. Genet. 3,* 52, (1972).

18. Soudek, D. and Laraya, P. *Clin. Genet. 6,* 225, (1974).

19. Nielsen, J. and E. Nordland. (1975) *Clin. Genet. 8,* 152, 1975.

20. Eysenck, H.J. The Maudsley Personality Inventory. San Diego: Educational and Industrial Testing Service, (1962).

21. Baekgaard, W. and Nielsen, J. *Brit. J. Soc. Clin. Psychol. 14,* 197, (1975).

Summary of a study by Nielsen and Nordland 1975

In a cytogenetic-psychological study of 47 school boys in special classes and 48 controls in normal classes in a Danish city no significant difference was found between the mean Y length. There were, however, four boys with enlarged Y among the 47 in special classes, compared with one of the 48 in the normal classes.

We found a significant correlation between length of Y and level of activity with increase of level of activity correlated with increase of length of Y when both groups were taken together ($P < 0.005$). The mean activity score was 6.5 for the boys with Y/F $\leq$ 0.83, compared with 8.1 for those with Y/F $\geq$ 0.95 ($P < 0.005$).

If the milieu is restrictive with poor understanding and support for the need of a boy, a comparatively large Y with associated high level of activity might intensify the problems of such a boy. If the milieu is positive, understanding, permissive and with possibilities of channeling activity, the large Y associated with a high level of activity might be a positive factor in personality development and social adjustment. The present study shows certain tendencies to confirm this.

MENTAL HEALTH IN CHILDREN, Volume III
Edited by D. V. Siva Sankar

PJD Publications Ltd., Westbury, N. Y.

A SYNOPSIS OF SECONDARY DEFECTS IN PHENYLKETONURIA

Ulrich Langenbeck

University of Goettingen
Goettingen, Germany

Summary

A multiplicity of secondary defects due to substances accumulated in tissues and body fluids of patients with phenylketonuria (PKU) has been detected *in vivo* and *in vitro*. In the following review it is attempted to present most of the respective data in a coherent way.

The thought is expressed that a multitude of small deviations from the normal state may lead by summation and interaction to the abnormal phenotype in PKU patients.

Introduction

Phenylketonuria (PKU) is a "molecular disease" (1) due to a hereditary defect of the enzyme phenylalanine hydroxylase (2) which converts phenylalanine to tyrosine. Since the discovery in 1934 by the Norwegian physician Foelling (3) a large number of papers on this disease has been written because of the fascinating association of a single Mendelian factor with overwhelming mental deficiency. (Bibliography in 4; see also reviews 5,6).

From the beginning attempts were made to find the link between the primary metabolic abnormality and the terminal reaction - mental deficiency. A failure of oxidative metabolism in patients with PKU was already suggested in 1940 (7) from *in vivo* studies on O and glucose utilization of brains of PKU patients. Yet, the about 20% reduction in uptake from blood of O_2 and glucose found later to correspond quite well to a 20% reduction in brain weight of PKU patients (8).

Thus it became obvious that analyzing the causal relationship of enzyme defect and impairment of mental function would be an exceedingly difficult task.

The question was and still is whether a single major secondary derangement or a complex chain (or net) of events leads to brain dysfunction of PKU. Whole groups of hypotheses emerged emphasizing either amino acid transport, protein synthesis, glucose metabolism, biogenic amines, gamma-amino butyric acid or lipid metabolism.

Facing so many excellent reports on possible secondary defects in patients with PKU one can but wonder whether these authors are right all together. The view will be presented in this article that by interaction and summation of a multitude of major and minor disturbances due to phenylalanine and its metabolites (phenylpyruvic acid, phenethylamine and phenylacetic acid) the fine regulations of cerebral function are broken down in PKU.

The lines of research up to 1962 are well presented by Armstrong (9) and Jervis (10). A recent monograph (11) sums up newer developments.

The research on PKU has always been hampered by the impossibility of obtaining direct information on the *in vivo* chemical state of the phenylketonuric brain. An animal disease homologue would resolve the dilemma. Yet, none has been found: It is now generally agreed that the "dilute lethal" syndrome of mice has no connection to human PKU (12-15).

Feeding or injecting rats with high doses of phenylalanine leads to an increase of tyrosine also - in sharp contrast to the human condition. To the use of inhibitors of phenylalanine hydroxylase like p-chlorophenylalanine (16) objections may also be raised as specificity of inhibition is not guaranteed (17) and excretion into urine of phenylpyruvic acid is not observed (18). Nevertheless, the combination of both afore mentioned procedures in rats has resulted in the best *in vivo* animal model presently available: The excretion of organic acids in urine closely resembles the human situation and tyrosine levels are no longer elevated (19).

In vitro systems (brain slices, brain homogenates, purified brain enzymes) are disadvantageous in that pre-existing metabolic equilibria are disrupted and rarely can be taken into account. The relevance of inhibitor constants thus obtained is therefore difficult to ascertain.

Metabolic studies on PKU patients mainly rely on urine, blood and cerebrospinal fluid (CSF). Urine and blood hardly reflect the situation prevailing in brain. The physiology let alone the pathology of CSF is only partly understood (20). Studies of lumbar and occipital CSF yield different results.

Despite such a lack of optimal experimental conditions a large body of data has been accumulated over the years which will be discussed in part in the following paragraphs.

In discussions on brain dysfunction in PKU two general phenomena should be distinguished: first, the irreversible change in brain structure (defect of myelination) and second, reversible abnormalities like misbehaviour and ataxia (6). The first may be due to decreased synthesis of macro-molecules whereas the second could be the consequence of dysregulation of endogenous levels of biogenic amines and neuro-transmitters or of the synthesis of neurotoxic compounds.

It is commonly assumed in interpretations based on *in vitro* data that brain and CSF contain the organic acids found to exert inhibitory effects.

Presence of phenyllactic acid in phenylalanine treated rats was demonstrated already in 1961 (21). This compound may cross the blood-brain-barrier freely (19). Phenylacetic acid on the other hand is formed from phenylalanine in brain through phenethylamine (19,22).

Brain phenylpyruvic acid has not been measured yet in experimental PKU. It ought to be present there because of the existence in brain of phenylalanine transaminase (23,24) and it has been detected of course qualitatively even in normal rat brain (25).

Phenylpyruvic concentration in CSF of a patient with PKU was measured once to be 1/8 of the concentration in plasma (26). Thus a level of 5uM seems to be a reasonable assumption for this keto acid. (Based on data in 27 and 21).

Defects in Synthesis of Macromolecules

The integrity of protein synthesis may be attacked in PKU from different sites.

The uptake of amino acids from bowel to blood (28) as well as from blood to brain (29,30) is impaired. As a consequence imbalance of amino acids in blood (28) and CSF (31,32) is found.

The amino acid imbalance in CSF may be age dependent because conflicting results have been reported especially for glycine (31,32). Moreover, not all the model data are in accordance with the CSF data in man. For example, blood brain barrier transport of histidine as well as its uptake by brain slices was found in rat to be inhibited by phenylalanine. Yet, in CSF of PKU patients its concentration was reported to be increased (31,32). A possible explanation could be the ability of man - in contrast to rat - to synthesize histidine (33, 34).

In addition to gross amino acid imbalance, protein synthesis is inhibited through disaggregation of brain ribosomes which has been demonstrated biochemically and morphologically in rats and mice (35-39). This disaggregation may be an indirect result of inhibition of protein synthesis (36) thus creating a vicious circle. Depletion of tryptophan has been implicated in the causation of polyribosome disaggregation (37). Tryptophan however is increased in CSF of human PKU patients (32). This may be taken as another indication that intracellular metabolite levels in human PKU are badly needed.

Inhibition of RNA synthesis from uridine *in vivo* after injection of phenylalanine has been found in mice (36). The time course was different from inhibition of protein synthesis. Phenylpyruvic acid was found to inhibit *in vitro* RNA synthesis from glucose in fetal rat brain (40).

Finally, inhibition of lipid synthesis from glucose and

acetate has been amply demonstrated in experimental PKU (41-43). Cholesterol synthesis is inhibited by phenylpyruvic acid in sub-millimolar concentration at the stage of decarboxylation of mevalonic acid pyrophosphate (44). Inhibition of brain fatty acid synthetase by phenylpyruvic acid (45) seems to be a second important factor leading to dysmyelination. From a normal cholesterol: galactolipid: phospholipid ratio in purified myelin a simple arrest of myelination was called for in experimental (46) as well as in human PKU (47). Yet, recent data on fatty acid composition of myelin of hyper-phenylalaninemic rats (48) indicate that myelin may not be entirely normal also in human PKU. A reduced proportion of long chain and unsaturated fatty acids as observed in rats could alter the normal characteristics of myelin. Thus, an important difference to hypomyelination due to undernourishment is demonstrated (48).

A most recent review which was not yet available to me summarizes the problems of myelination and amino acid imbalance in the developing brain (49).

Defects in Metabolism of Small Molecules

The following discussions are mainly concerned with inhibitory action of phenylalanine and its metabolites on glycolysis, Krebs cycle, gluconeogenesis, 5-OH-indole metabolism, catecholamine synthesis, gamma-amino butyric acid formation, and synthesis of possible neurotoxic compounds.

It may be the sum of all these derangements that lead to deterioration of behavior (50) and EEG (51) after phenylalanine loads given to dietetically treated PKU patients.

Dysregulation of glycolysis and adjacent pathways is also of direct consequence to the synthesis of macromolecules (40) as described above.

Utilization of glucose is inhibited by phenylpyruvic acid at the stage of hexokinase (52) and 6-phosphogluconate dehydrogenase reaction (53) and by phenylalanine at the stage of pyruvate kinase reaction (52-54). Inhibition of pyruvate kinase can be reverted by alanine (54). Yet, this amino acid seems to be diminished in the CSF of PKU patients (31,32). A high glucose diet should be beneficial in overcoming this inhibition (40,54).

The inhibitor constants reported for hexokinase and pyruvate kinase are rather high (3-6 m M). However, absolute activities of both enzymes in fetal brain are very low in comparison to the adult (52). That the mechanism proposed by Weber (52) may be of relevance *in vivo* has been shown recently through measurement of glycolytic metabolites in rat brain after injection of phenylalanine (55). Still, it remains to be established whether a diminished flux through glycolysis really takes place under these conditions.

Pyruvate metabolism is disturbed by phenylpyruvic acid in different ways. The oxidation of pyruvate is inhibited in intact mitochondria without uncoupling of phosphorylation (56). Oxidative decarboxylation of pyruvate is inhibited by 5 to 10 mM phenylpyruvic acid (57-59). These rather high concentrations needed to inhibit decarboxylation of pyruvate suggest that this effect is not of prime importance in pathogenesis of PKU (59). In contrast, inhibitor constants of phenylpyruvic acid in the submillimolar range have been found for pyruvate carboxylation in rat and human brain (60,61), as well as for citrate synthetase in rat brain (45). Thus, the Krebs cycle is depleted of intermediates by decreased synthesis of citrate and oxaloacetate. Diminished synthesis of aspartate from glucose (62) through oxaloacetate is a further consequence.

Substrate depletion of Krebs cycle by transamination between phenylalanine and pyruvate or ketoglutarate has been envisioned many years ago (63). To my knowledge this interesting hypothesis has not been tested in long term experiments. One hour after a single injection of phenylalanine (10 m Moles/kg) both keto acids had about normal levels in rat brain (55).

An early finding in attempts to explain mental deficiency in PKU was the demonstration of inhibition of brain glutamic acid decarboxylase by phenylpyruvic acid and phenylacetic acid as well as by the respective p-OH- derivatives (64-66). The inhibitor constants in guinea pig brains were found to be rather low (0.03-0.05 mM) (65). Thus depletion of gamma-amino butyric acid should be occurring *in vivo.* In addition, depletion of ketoglutaric acid (see above) could enhance the effect. Deficiency of this inhibitory transmitter (67) may then lead to neurologic deficits.

The problems related to mental deficiency in PKU and to metabolism of 5-hydroxyindoles have been discussed in a review by Pare (68). The reader is referred to this article for the original literature. Depression of serotonin levels in human and experimental PKU is thought to result from inhibition of tryptophan hydroxylation and of decarboxylation of 5-hydroxytryptophan as well as from defects in transport of tryptophan and its 5-hydroxy derivative (68). Increased amino transfer from tryptophan to aromatic ketoacids could well result in depletion of the precursor of serotonin (69). However, tryptophan levels in CSF were found increased in PKU (32).

How depression of serotonin formation could lead to mental deficiency is not at all understood. Patients with Down's syndrome and PKU both have low levels of total 5-hydroxyindoles (70), but surely, the aspect of mental dysfunction is quite different in both groups. In addition, severely retarded patients may show up with hyperserotoninemia (70). In considerable contrast to the data obtained in blood 5-hydroxytryptophan and serotonin were found increased in CSF of untreated patients with PKU (32,71). The assay system of the authors (72) seems to be more specific and more sensitive than the fluorimetric assay used by other authors. Studies with labeled precursors (see below) should be done in order to shed more light on the interesting behavior of 5-hydroxyindoles in CSF.

Blood levels of the neurotransmitter adrenaline are depressed in PKU (73). Inhibition of catecholamine synthesis may be due to inhibition of tyrosine hydroxylase by phenylalanine (74), or by inhibition of DOPA decarboxylase by aromatic acids (see ref. 9). Increased aminotransfer from DOPA to aromatic ketoacids could also result in diminished catecholamine synthesis (69). How low levels of catecholamines could result in mental deficiency is just as little understood as the relation of disturbed serotinin metabolism with mental defect.

The increased turnover of phenethylamines in experimental and human PKU (22) could deplete tissues of vitamine B_6 through formation of a Schiff base. However, such a depletion of B_6 vitamers could not be demonstrated in experimental PKU (75).

A good candidate for an agent causing hyperexcitability and convulsions in PKU is homocarnosine (76). The concentration of this compound is increased in CSF of patients with PKU (31,32,77) and carnosinemia (78). Patients with carnosinemia also show convulsions and severe mental impairment. Therefore a central neurotoxic action of homocarnosine (76) should be seriously considered furthermore (79).

Promising New Developments

The development of combined gas chromatography-mass spectrometry and the recently improved availability of compounds labeled with stabile isotopes (^{13}C, ^{15}N, ^{18}O) both have opened up a whole new area of research. Metabolic pathways may now be studied in man without harm due to radioactive isotopes and without need anymore to dissect molecules chemically in order to track synthetic pathways (80).

The effects of *in vivo* inhibitory actions as well as of metabolic defects can easily be documented as shown by Curtius *et al.* (81,82) and Sedvall *et al.* (83). From the studies of Curtius *et al.* (82) it can be deduced that the main inhibitory action in the catecholamine pathways is exerted on tyrosine hydroxylase: specific labeling of final metabolites is identical to that of dopamine itself. (See discussion above).

Conclusions

Seven years ago Menkes wrote with respect to pathogenesis of PKU: "It is likely that no single answer will be found but rather that cerebral malfunction is the outcome of a number of chemical abnormalties occurring within the brain as a consequence of deranged internal milieu present during a critical phase of its development'' (84). I hope I have been able to show in the preceding paragraphs that this prediction endured the times (85).

The study of pathogenesis of mental retardation in maple syrup urine disease, another inborn error of amino acid metabolism, has yielded results largely homologous to those reported in the present article. Possibly, the study of mental retardation due to specific enzyme defects will help to identify mechanisms which operate also in the causation of ''nonspecific'' mental retardation. One of those mechanisms, justification or optimal balance of metabolites (86) is prerequisite to normal mental function. Pauling has coined the term ''Orthomolecular Psychiatry'' (87) for disturbance of this most intricate achievement of evolution.

The author's own work is supported by grants from the Deutsche Forschungsgemeinschaft, Bad Godesberg, Federal Republic of Germany (SFB33).

References

1. Pauling, L., Itano, H. A., Singer, S. J. *et al. Science 110,* 543, (1949).
2. Jervis, G. A. *Proc. Soc. Exp. Biol. Med. 82,* 514, (1953).
3. Folling, A. *Zschr. Physiol. Chemie 227,* 169, (1934).
4. Lyman, F. L. *Phenylketonuria.* Charles C. Thomas, Springfield, Ill., (1963).
5. Blaskovics, M. E. and Nelson, T. L. *Calif. Med. 115,* 42, (1971).
6. Knox, W. E. Phenylketonuria. In *The Metabolic Basis of Inherited Disease.* Third edition. Edited by Stanbury, J. B., Wyngaarden, J. B. and Fredrickson, D. S. McGraw-Hill, New York, p. 266, (1972).
7. Himwich, H. E. and Fazekas, J. F. *Arch. Neurol. Psychiat. 44,* 1213, (1940).
8. Jervis, G. A. Pathology. In ref. 4, pp 96-100.
9. Armstrong, M. D. Biochemistry. In ref. 4, pp 62-95.
10. Jervis, G. A. Pathogenesis of the mental defect. In ref. 4, pp 101-113.
11. Bickel, H., Hudson, F. P. and Woolf, L. I. Phenylketonuria and some other inborn errors of amino acid metabolism. *Biochemistry, Genetics, Diagnosis, Therapy.* Georg Thieme Verlag, Stuttgart, (1974).
12. Zannoni, V. G. and Moraru, E. *FEBS Symp. 19,* 347, (1969).
13. Woolf, L. I., Jakubovic, A., Woolf, F. *et al. Biochem. J. 119,* 895, (1970).
14. Seller, M. J. *Clin. Genet. 3,* 495, (1972).
15. Treiman, D. M. and Tourian, A. *Biochim. Biophys. Acta 313,* 163, (1973).
16. Lipton, M. A., Gordon, R., Guroff, G. *et al. Science 156,* 248, (1967).
17. Koe, B. K. and Weissman, A. *Advan. Pharmacol. 6B,* 29, (1968).
18. Hole, K. *Develop. Psychobiol. 5,* 157, (1972).
19. Edwards, D. J. and Blau, K. *Biochem. J. 130,* 495, (1972).
20. Davson, H. *Physiology of the Cerebrospinal Fluid.* J. and A. Churchill, London, (1967).

21. Goldstein, F. B. *J. Biol. Chem. 236,* 2656, (1961).
22. Edwards, D. J. and Blau, K. *Biochem. J. 132,* 95, (1973).
23. Tangen, O., Fonnum, F. and Haavaldsen, R. *Biochim. Biophys. Acta 96,* 82, (1965).
24. Benuck, M., Stern, F. and Lajtha, A. *J. Neurochem. 19,* 949, (1972).
25. Haavaldsen, R. *Biochem. J. 92,* 23 P, (1964).
26. Jervis, G. A. Personal communication to the present author. August 14, (1972).
27. Jervis, G. A. *Proc. Soc. Exp. Biol. Med. 81,* 715, (1952).
28. Linneweh, F., Ehrlich, M., Graul, E. H. *et al. Klin. Wochenschr. 41,* 253, (1963).
29. Neame, K. D. *Nature 192,* 173, (1961).
30. Oldendorf, W. H. *Arch. Neurol. 28,* 45, (1973).
31. van Sande, M., Mardens, Y., Adriaenssens, K. *et al. J. Neurochem. 17,* 125, (1970).
32. Quentin, C-D, Behbehani, A. W., Schulte, F. J. *et al. Neuropädiatrie 5,* 138, (1974).
33. Mahler, H. R. and Cordes, E. H. *Biological Chemistry.* Harper and Row, New York, p. 666, (1966).
34. Oldendorf, W. H. *Amer. J. Physiol. 221,* 1629, (1971).
35. Aoki, K. and Siegel, F. L. *Science 168,* 129, (1970).
36. MacInnes, J. W. and Schlesinger, K. *Brain Res. 29,* 101, (1971).
37. Gerritsen, T. and Siegel, F. L. *Monogr. Human Genet. 6,* 22, (1972).
38. Copenhaver, J. H., Vacanti, J. P., and Carver, M. J. *J. Neurochem. 21,* 273, (1973).
39. Pasquier, D. A., Coca, M. C., and Bosque, P. G. *et al. Experientia 29,* 63, (1973).
40. Glazer, R. I. and Weber, G. *J. Neurochem. 18,* 2371, (1971).
41. Barbato, L. M. and Barbato, I. M. *Brain Res. 13,* 569, (1969).
42. Barbato, L., Barbato, I. W. M. and Hamanaka, A. *Brain Res. 7,* 399, (1968).
43. Shah, S. N., Peterson, N. A. and McKean, C. M. *J. Neuro-*

chem. 17, 279, (1970).

44. Shah, S. N., Peterson, N. A. and McKean, C. M. *Biochim. Biophys. Acta 187,* 236, (1969).
45. Land, J. M. and Clark, J. B. *Biochem. J. 134,* 545, (1973).
46. Shah, S. N., Peterson, N. A. and McKean, C. M. *J. Neurochem. 19,* 479, (1972).
47. Shah, S. N., Peterson, N. A. and McKean, C. M. *J. Neurochem. 19,* 2369, (1972).
48. Johnson, R. C. and Shah, S. N. *J. Neurochem. 21,* 1225, (1973).
49. Agrawal, H. C. and Davison, A. N. Myelination and amino acid imbalance in the developing brain. In *Biochemistry of the Developing Brain.* Vol. 1. Edited by Himwich, W. Marcel Dekker, New York, p. 143, (1973).
50. Bickel, H., Boscott, R. J. and Gerrard, J. Observations on the biochemical error in plenylketonuria and its dietary control. In *Biochemistry of the Developing Nervous System.* Edited by Waelsch, H. Academic Press, New York, p. 417, (1955).
51. Clayton, B. E. Moncrieff, A. A., Pampiglione, G. *et al. Arch. Dis. Child. 41,* 267, (1966).
52. Weber, G. *Proc. Nat. Acad. Sci. US 63,* 1365, (1969).
53. Weber, G., Glazer, R. I. and Ross, R. A. Regulation of human and rat brain metabolism: Inhibitory action of phenylalanine and phenlypyruvate on glycolysis, protein, lipid, DNA and RNA metabolism. In *Advances in Enzyme Regulation.* Vol. 8. Edited by Weber, G. Pergamon, Oxford, p. 13, (1970).
54. Schwark, W. S., Singhal, R. L. and Ling, G. M. *J. Neurochem. 18,* 123, (1971).
55. Miller, A. L., Hawkins, R. A. and Veech, R. L. *Science 173,* 904, (1973).
56. Gallagher, B. B. *J. Neurochem. 16,* 1071, (1969).
57. Kini, M. M. 1965, cited in ref. 56.
58. Bowden, J. A. and McArthur, III, C. L. *Nature 235,* 230, (1972).
59. Land, J. M. and Clark, J. B. *Biochem. J. 134,* 539, (1973).
60. Patel, M. S. *Biochem. J. 128,* 677, (1972).
61. Patel, M. S., Grover, W. D. and Auerbach, V. H. *J. Neuro-*

chem. 20, 289, (1973).
62. Itoh, T. *Can. J. Biochem. 43,* 835, (1965).
63. Korey, S. R. A possible mechanism in phenylpyruvic oligophrenia. Report of 23rd Ross Pediatric Research Conference, Columbus, Ohio, p. 34, (1957).
64. Hanson, A. *Naturwissenschaften 45,* 423, (1958).
65. Hanson, A. *Acta Chem. Scand. 13,* 1366, (1959).
66. Tashian, R. E. *Metabolism 10,* 393, (1961).
67. Krnjevic, K. *Nature 228,* 119, (1970).
68. Pare, C. M. B. *Advan. Pharmacol. 6B,* 159, (1968).
69. Lees, G. J. and Weiner, N. *J. Neurochem. 20,* 389, (1973).
70. Tu, J. and Partington, M. W. *Develop. Med. Child. Neurol. 14,* 457, (1972).
71. Behbehani, A. W., Quentin, C-D, Schulte, F. J. *et al. Neuropädiatrie 5,* 258, (1974).
72. Neuhoff, V. Microdetermination of amino acids and related compounds with dansyl chloride. In *Micromethods in Molecular Biology.* Edited by Neuhoff, V. Springer, p. 85, (1973).
73. Weil-Malherbe, H. Blood adrenaline and intelligence. In *Biochemistry of the Developing Nervous System.* Edited by Waelsch, H. Academic Press, New York, p. 458, (1955).
74. Nagatsu, T., Levitt, M. and Udenfriend, S. *J. Biol. Chem. 239,* 2910, (1964).
75. Loo, Y. H. and Mack, K. *J. Neurochem. 19,* 2377, (1972).
76. Turnbull, M. J., Slater, P. and Briggs, J. *Arch. Int. Pharmacodyn. 196,* 127, (1972).
77. Quentin, C-D, Behbehani, A. W., Schulte, F. J. *et al. Neuropädiatrie 5,* 274, (1974).
78. Perry, T. L., Hansen, S., Tischler, B. *et al. N. Engl. J. Med. 277,* 1219, (1967).
79. Allen, R. J., Tourtellotte. W. W., Adriaenssens, K. *et al. Lancet 1,* 1249, (1968).
80. Langenbeck, U. and Seegmiller, J. E. *Anal. Biochem. 56,* 34, (1973).
81. Curtius, H-C, Vollmin, J. A. and Baerlöcher, K. *Clin. Chim. Acta 37,* 277, (1972).
82. Curtius, H-C, Baerlöcher, K. and Vollmin, J. A. *Clin. Chim. Acta 42,* 235, (1972).

83. Sedvall, G., Mayevsky, A., Fri, C. G. *et al.* The use of stable oxygen isotopes for labeling of homovanillic acid in rat brain. In *Gas Chromatography-Mass Spectrometry in Neurobiology* (Adv Biochem Psychopharmacol 7). Edited by Costa, E. and Holmstedt, B. Raven Press, New York, p. 57, (1973).
84. Menkes, J. H. *Pediatrics 39,* 297, (1967).
85. Langenbeck, U. *Lancet 1,* 785, (1973).
86. Bessmann, S. P. *J. Pediat. 81,* 834, (1972).
87. Pauling, L. *Science 160,* 265, (1968).
88. Arinze, I.J. and Patel, M.S. *Biochemistry 12,* 4473, (1973).
89. Nordyke, E.L. and Roach, M.K. *Brain Res. 67,* 479, (1974).
90. Gimenez, C., Valdivieso, F. and Mayor, F. *Biochem. Med. 11,* 81, (1974).
91. Valdivieso, F., Gimenez, C. and Mayor, F. *Biochem. Med. 12,* 72, (1975).
92. Rowe, V.D., Fales, H.M., Pisano, J.J. *et al. Biochem. Med. 12,* 123, (1975).
93. Langenbeck, U. and Dieckmann, K-P. Unpublished results.
94. Partington, M.W. and Vickery, S.K. *Neuropadiatrie 2,* 125, (1974).

Addendum

Phenylpyruvic acid inhibits gluconeogenesis in isolated perfused rat liver, perhaps mainly by inhibittion of decarboxylation of ketoglutaric acid. This inhibitory effect on the tricarboxylic acid cycle activity may account for the reduction of glucose production from malate, alanine and other compounds (88).

Treatment of neonatal rats with p-chlorophenylalanine and phenylalanine up to 21 days of age leads to reduced body and brain weight as well as to decreased brain levels of glutamate and glutamine. Amino acid compartmentation develops more slowly than in controls indicating inhibition of neuronal process growth (89).

In confirmation of the results of Miller *et al.* (55), Gimenez *et al.* (90) found impairment of glycolysis in brain and liver of rats treated with p-chlorophenylalanine and esculin (91). In brain pyruvate was greatly diminished, whereas dihydroxyacetone phosphate, glyceraldehyde phosphate and phosphoenolpyruvate were increased in concentration (90).

Guroff's group (92) analyzed the urine of F344 rat pups treated with p-chlorophenylalanine and phenylalanine. They, like Edwards and Blau (19), found the classical acidic products of phenylalanine when high doses of phenylalanine (4g/kg) were given.

In the CSF of an untreated 16 year old girl with PKU we found only traces (ca. 1 μM) of phenylpyruvic acid by gas chromatography - mass spectrometry (single ion detection) of the quinoxalinole-TMSi derivative (93). In the CSF of one of 11 PKU patients Partington and Vickery (94) found ca. 10 μM phenylpyruvic acid. They found none in the CSF of the other 10 patients. It is difficult to conclude from these CSF data that phenylpyruvic acid is of no relevance in the pathogenesis of PKU: A brain - CSF barrier may obscure to the observer's eyes the true metabolic state of the brain.

MENTAL HEALTH IN CHILDREN, Volume III
Edited By D. V. Siva Sankar

CATECHOLAMINE-CONTAINING NEURONES AND THE MECHANISMS OF REWARD

T.J. Crow

Northwick Park Hospital
London, HA1, 3UJ, England

That behaviour is regulated by reward and punishment is a truism. Natural selection ensured at an early stage that there are mechanisms whereby biologically-advantageous actions are, where possible, continued, and actions whose consequences are, or may become, harmful to the organism cease. Perhaps much later in phylogeny organisms evolved which had the capacity to benefit from their previous experience of favourable and unfavourable circumstances and thereby acquired the ability to maximise their biological advantage in a wider range of environmental situations. Seen in this light it is easy to envisage a mechanism of reward without a mechanism for learning, but hardly the reverse. In order to learn the organism must have a means of detecting what to learn.

Amongst psychological theorists Thorndike (1) in particular has emphasised the role of reward in learning. Spence (2) and Sheffield (3), on the other hand, have drawn attention to the "incentive" or "drive inducing" aspects of rewarding stimuli. Thus it appears that rewarding stimuli may have two quite separate effects upon behavior: 1. to elicit increased motor activity and approach, and 2. to increase the probability that a particular rewarded behaviour will occur in the future.

Investigation of the neurological basis of the mechanisms of reward was opened up by the discovery of intracranial self-stimulation by Olds and Milner (4). That animals will press a lever to deliver trains of stimuli through electrodes implanted in certain lateral hypothalamic sites, and that, in some cases, they persist in this behaviour for long periods of time against the interests of homeostasis, testifies to the existence of powerful motivational mechanisms which in normal circumstances mediate some of the effects of rewarding environmental stimuli on the organism's behaviour.

The Neurological Basis of Reward

What are the neural pathways which must be activated to obtain self-stimulation behaviour? The most extensive investigations in the rat (5), cat (6) and rabbit (7) agree in finding self-stimulation to be most easily obtained from areas in lateral hypothalamus which extend forwards to the olfactory bulbs and backwards as far as the ventral tegmental area. These regions correspond approximately in extent with the rather ill-defined medial forebrain bundle, which nevertheless includes amongst its various components a large number of mono-amine containing fibres which pass through the lateral hypothalmic region in their course from cell-body groups in the brain stem to terminal distributions in various prosencephalic areas (8).

While the anatomical identity of the pathways underlying electrical self-stimulation remained obscure, various studies suggested that these pathways might have specific chemical characteristics. Stein (9) drew attention to the remarkable enhancement of self-stimulation responding which follows administration of small doses of the amphetamines, and Poschel and Ninteman (10) observed that responding can be inhibited by the catecholamine synthesis inhibitor α-methyl-p-tyrosine. Both authors' suggested that a catecholamine, perhaps noradrenaline, might be the neurohumour released by a central reward mechanism.

A direct prediction from this hypothesis is that self-stimulation sites should be closely related to at least one of the known systems of ascending catecholamine-containing neurones in the brain. Such systems arise from the brainstem where anatomical studies of self-stimulation have been relatively neglected. At the level of the cell-bodies, however, monoamine systems can be distinguished from each other, although at a more rostral level in the lateral hypothalamus their fibres are closely inter-related.

According to Ungerstedt (11) there are three major systems of ascending catecholamine-containing neurones (figure 1): dopamine neurones arising from cell body groups A8, 9 and 10 in the ventral mesencephalon, the "dorsal bundle" of noradrenaline neurones arising mainly from the A6 (the locus coeruleus) group, and the "ventral bundle" of noradrenaline neurones arising from cell body groups A1 and A2 in the caudal brainstem.

In a series of studies my colleagues and I have investigated the relationship of self-stimulation sites in the brainstem to the location of catecholamine-containing cell-body groups. These studies have been conducted at the level of origin of each of the three systems and the results are summarised in figures 2 to 4. In an investigation at the level of the mesencephalon (figure 2) twenty-seven positive sites were located either in the region directly around the interpeduncular nucleus, corresponding closely to the distribution of the A9 and A10 dopamine-containing cell bodies, or in the interpeduncular nucleus itself (12,13). A second group of five positive sites were located in the region immediately lateral to the central grey matter at a point corresponding approximately to that at which the ascending fibres of the dorsal bundle of noradrenaline-containing neurones passes through the mesencephalon (11).

If these latter electrodes had supported self-stimulation because they activated the dorsal bundle one might predict that self-stimulation would be possible with electrodes in the cell-bodies of origin of this system, the nucleus locus coeruleus (A6 area), in the floor of the fourth ventricle. This prediction was confirmed, (14,15): figure 3, which includes the earlier findings, shows the sites of twenty-five electrode tips which had supported electrical self-stimulation, all of which were situated either within or directly beside the locus coeruleus, together with the sites of thirty-eight electrode tips from which self-stimulation could not be obtained (16).

Figure 1

Schematic representation of the three main ascending systems of catecholamine-containing neurones in the rat brain (adapted from Ungerstedt (11)). The dopamine neurones (----------) arising from areas A8, 9 and 10 in the central mesencephalon innervate the corpus striatum and some more medially placed nuclei (the nucleus accumbens and tuberculum olfactorium). The dorsal bundle of noradrenaline neurones (———) arising from the A6 area (locus coeruleus) in the floor of the fourth ventricle innervates the cerebral cortex, and the ventral bundle of noradrenaline neurones from the A1 and A2 areas, innervates various hypothalamic nuclei.

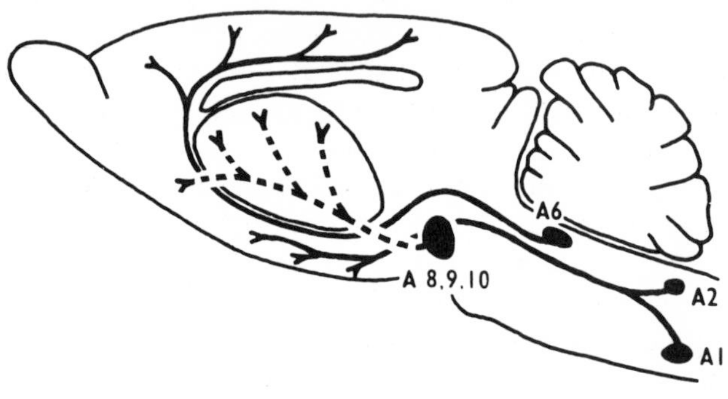

Figure 2

A series of eighty-two electrodes implanted on a grid of sites across the mesencephalon. Sites positive for intra-cranial self-stimulation (I.C.S.S.) fall into two groups - a ventral group (25 sites) which corresponds approximately to the A9 and A10 dopamine-containing cell body-groups, and includes also the interpeduncular nucleus, and a dorsal group (5 sites) lateral to the central gray matter and close to the point at which the fibres of the dorsal noradrenaline bundle pass through the mesencephalon.

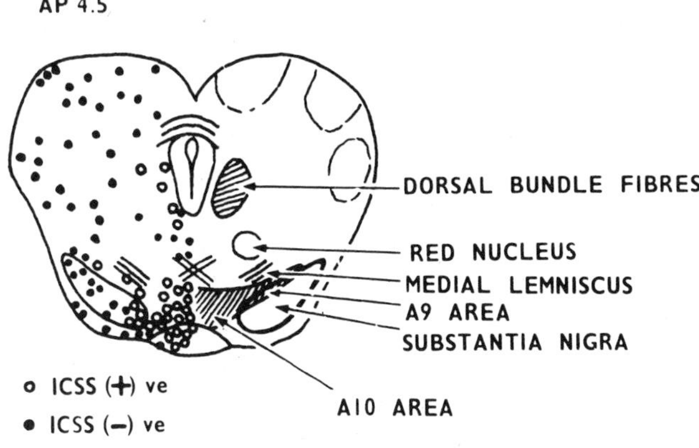

Figure 4 shows the results of an investigation into the question of whether self-stimulation can be obtained from electrodes implanted in the cell-bodies of origin of the ventral noradrenaline bundle, the A1 and A2 areas (16). On histological examination it was found that four electrode tips had been within the A2 area and six within A1. However, none of these electrodes, nor any of those located at other sites within this plane of the caudal brainstem, had supported self-stimulation.

These findings have been interpreted (17,18) as consistent with the hypothesis that electrical self-stimulation results from activation of either of two catecholamine-containing systems - the dopamine-containing neurones arising from areas A9 and A10 (and possibly also A8 since these three areas form a continuous sheet of cells), and the dorsal bundle of noradrenaline-containing neurones arising from the locus coeruleus (A6 area). The data do not support the hypothesis (19) that the ventral noradrenaline bundle is involved, but are consistent with the findings of a more recent investigation aimed at answering these same questions (20).

Various more recent findings support this analysis of the relationship between self-stimulation and catecholamine-containing neurones. Self-stimulation through electrodes in the locus coeruleus is accompanied by increased turnover of noradrenaline, as assessed by accumulation of the metabolite H. M. P. G., in the ipsilateral cerebral cortex (21), self-stimulation through electrodes implanted in the lateral hypothalamus close to the course followed by the nigrostriatal dopamine neurones can be abolished by intra-cerebral injections of 6-OH dopamine which induce maximal denervation of the ipsilateral corpus striatum (22), and Phillips and Fibiger (23) have shown that the relative potencies of (+) and (-) amphetamine in enhancing self-stimulation in different hypothalamic sites vary in a manner which suggests that sometimes dopamine- and sometimes noradrenaline-containing neurones are involved.

The Functions of Rewarding Stimuli

If, indeed, both these systems function as reward pathways the question arises as to why there should be two such systems, and as to what their separate functions may be. It is very striking that the motor behaviours which accompany self-stimulation in the two sites are quite different. With electrodes in the vicinity of the interpeduncular nucleus there are marked increases in locomotor activity together with elements of the sniffing, licking and gnawing syndrome which has been attributed to central dopamine release (12,13). With electrodes in the region of the locus coeruleus there are no such obvious behavioural concomitants, and self-stimulation responding usually takes longer to establish (15).

These differences may reflect on the different physiological functions of these two catecholamine-containing reward systems. Since rewarding stimuli have been held to exert both "incentive motivational" (2) and "reinforcing" (1, 24) effects on behaviour (for discussions see 25, 26, 27) it seems possible that these two effects are separated in the nervous system and mediated by discrete neural pathways. According to this analysis (18, 28) the "incentive motivational" or "drive inducing" effects are mediated by dopamine neurones, and the "reinforcing effects" by way of the coerulo-cortical noradrenaline system. This hypothesis explains why increases in locomotor activity are seen with stimulation of dopamine neurones, but do not occur with electrical activation of the locus coeruleus system. It is also relevant that the distribution of the former system is to the corpus striatum and related structures, which most likely have a function in relation to control of the motor apparatus, while the distribution of the latter is to the cerebral cortex, where the neural changes which underly learning presumably take place.

Further evidence on the function of these two systems is available from ablation studies. Ungerstedt (29) observed that lesions of the dopamine system, whether induced electrolytically or by intra-cerebral injection of 6-OH-dopamine, result in a syndrome of profound akinesia, aphagia and adipsia, and has argued that interruption of the nigrostriatal dopamine system is the critical element in the development of the "lateral hypothalamic syndrome" (30,31). By contrast animals with complete bilateral ablations of the locus coeruleus show little impairment of motor or motivational behaviour, but may have lost the capacity to adapt their behaviour to new environmental circumstances (32).

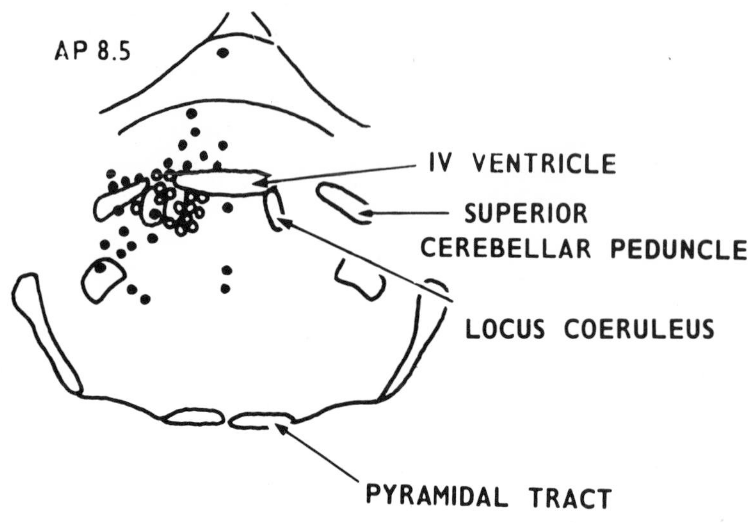

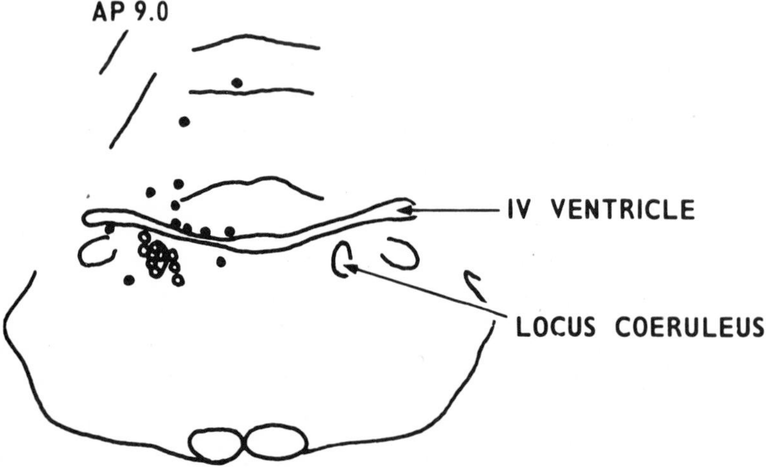

Figure 3

The sites of twenty-five electrode tips which had supported electrical self-stimulation (open circles) which were found to be located either within or in direct proximity to the nucleus locus coeruleus in the floor of the fourth ventricle. Thirty-eight electrode tips which had not supported self-stimulation (filled circles) were located dorsally (in the cerebellum), laterally, medially or ventrally to this nucleus.

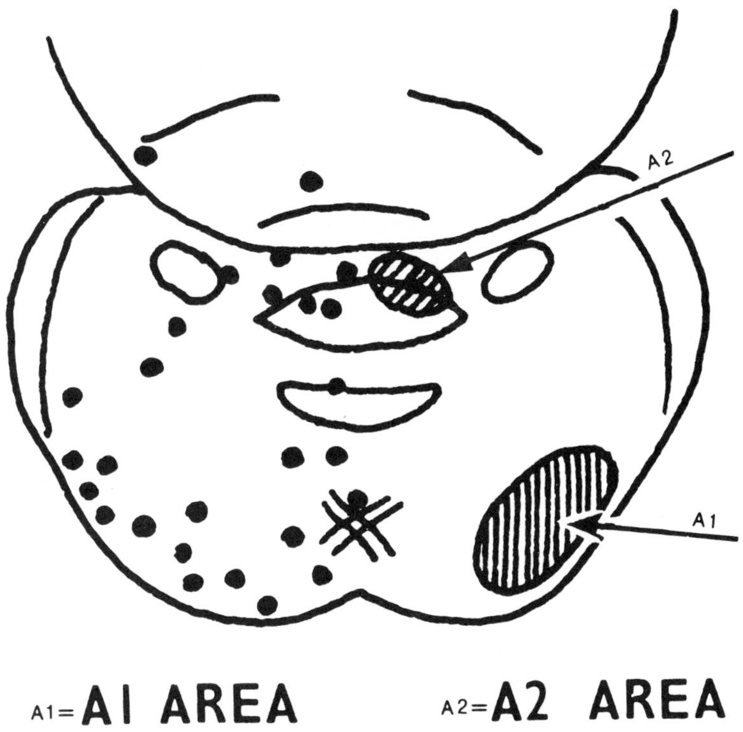

Figure 4

The sites of twenty-seven electrodes implanted in a plane (AP 14.0) through the caudal brainstem which includes the cell body groups A1 and A2, the cells of origin of the ventral bundle of noradrenaline neurones. Four tips were found to be located within the A2 area and at least six within A1, but none of these electrodes had supported self-stimulation.

These observations are consistent with the hypothesis that the organism's motor response to biologically significant environmental stimuli is mediated via the dopamine neurones while the adaptational changes which result from interaction with such stimuli are dependent upon coerulo-cortical noradrenaline neurones.

One may speculate concerning the phylogenetic origin of these apparently powerful and widely-distributed systems. Although these catecholamine neurones ascend from the brainstem and are distributed to various prosencephalic structures they are apparently unrelated to classical afferent pathways such as the medial lemniscus, but may have a relationship with visceral afferent connexions. Crow and Arbuthnott (18) have drawn attention to the fact that the locus coeruleus lies at the head of the visceral afferent column of the brainstem, whose main component is the nucleus of the tractus solitarius, the central relay for gustatory afferents, while the cell bodies of the dopamine neurones which comprise the A9 and A10 areas enclose the interpeduncular nucleus, which, according to Herrick (33) is a relay station for transmitting the effects of olfactory stimulation to the motor apparatus. This analysis corresponds quite closely to behavioural observations. The primary function of olfaction is to mobilise the organism towards potential rewards in the environment (34,35). Gustatory stimuli elicit responses in the visceral, rather than the somatic, musculature, and at the successful completion of a behavioural chain, at the point at which the "reinforcement" or "results of action" signal (36) may be expected to occur. One can therefore discern behavioural and anatomical reasons for postulating a connexion between olfaction, "incentive motivation", and dopamine neurones, and between gustation, "reinforcement", and the noradrenaline neurones of the locus coeruleus (28). One may speculate that systems whose function was originally tied to stimulation in one modality, have developed in the course of evolution to the point where they may be activated by diverse influences acting on the organism through a variety of modalities.

Little has been said concerning the function of the third major ascending catecholamine system, the ventral bundle of noradrenaline neurones, except to note that activation of this system probably does not support self-stimulation. Recently Kapatos and Gold (37) and Ahlskog and Hoebel (38) have presented evidence that ablations of this system lead to increased food intake and weight gain, and have put forward the hypothesis that this system functions as a component of a "satiety mechanism". The interest of this suggestion in the present context lies in the opportunity which it may provide for formulating an overall generalisation concerning the functions of these three major catecholamine systems. For although the ventral bundle does not seem to function as a "reward system" in the same way as the dopamine neurones and dorsal noradrenaline bundle, it seems possible that this system also may be concerned with mediating some aspects of rewarding stimuli, particularly those which lead to termination of consummatory behaviour. Thus the sequence of activity of the three systems may be as follows:

1. Activation of dopamine neurones by potentially-rewarding stimuli in the environment, resulting in increased motor activity which mobilises the organism towards the stimulus (the "incentive motivation" or "drive induction" effect).
2. Activation of coerulo-cortical noradrenaline neurones by primarily rewarding gustatory stimulation. The effect of this stimulation is to facilitate the acquisition of stored traces of the immediately preceding motor behaviours (the "reinforcement" effect).
3. Activation of the ventral bundle of noradrenaline neurones by stimuli, presumably gastric, which result from continued ingestational behaviour and lead to its termination (the "satiety" mechanism).

According to this analysis (Table I) all three catecholamine systems play a part in mediating the effects of rewarding stimuli on the organism's behaviour although the outcome in each case is quite different and is exerted through different structures in the prosencephalon. Although the separate functions are most easily worked out in relation to "simple" ingestational behaviours one may assume that in the course of evolution, and particularly in the case of human behaviour, they have acquired much more general significance. Therefore the consequences of a disturbance of one or more of these systems, whether innate or acquired, may be expected to be profound.

TABLE 1

ASCENDING SYSTEMS OF CATECHOLAMINE-CONTAINING NEURONES - EFFECTS OF STIMULATION AND ABLATION AND A HYPOTHESIS CONCERNING THEIR PHYLOGENETIC ORIGIN AND BEHAVIOURAL FUNCTIONS

CATECHOLAMINE SYSTEM	*STIMULATION*	*ABLATION*	*ASSOCIATED AFFERENT MECHANISM*	*BEHAVIOURAL FUNCTION*
dopamine neurones (from cell-body groups A8, 9 & 10)	electrical self-stimulation; in--creased activity; sniffing and gnaw-ing	akinesia, aphagia, adipsia	olfaction	"incentive motiva-tion" or "drive induction"
dorsal bundle of noradrenaline neurones (mainly from group A6)	electrical self-stimulation	impaired learning	gustation	"reinforcement" or results of action signal
ventral bundle of noradrenaline neurones (mainly from groups A1 and A2)	----	increased food intake	?gastric afferent activity	satiety signal

Summary

Several lines of evidence suggest a relationship between central catecholamine-containing neurones and the mechanisms of reward. Electrical self-stimulation behaviour is a technique for investigating these mechanisms, and some anatomical evidence is reviewed which suggests that this behaviour results from activation of either of two catecholamine systems - the dopamine neurones arising from the ventral mesencephalon, and the noradrenaline neurones arising from the locus coeruleus. The motor behaviours associated with activation of these two systems, and the effects of ablation of each system separately, are quite different. Activation of the dopamine neurones leads to marked increases in motor activity, and ablation results in aphagia, adipsia and akinesia. Ablation of the coerulo-cortical noradrenaline system causes no significant change in motor or motivational behaviour, but impairs the organism's ability to learn.

These results, together with recent evidence that the ventral bundle of noradrenaline neurones may form part of a satiety mechanism, support a concept that the three major ascending catecholamine systems mediate different aspects of the effects of rewarding stimuli on behaviour. According to this hypothesis the dopamine neurones activate and energise the organism's motor behaviour towards potential environmental rewards, the dorsal bundle of noradrenaline neurones signals the results of action, and thereby ensures that successful behaviours are learned, and the ventral bundle of noradrenaline neurones terminates the sequence of consummatory activity by delivering a satiety signal. Although in higher mammals these systems are probably activated by a variety of different types of sensory input, the possibility is suggested that they may have evolved in close relationship with afferent pathways for olfaction, gustation, and gastric sensation respectively.

REFERENCES

1. Thorndike, E. L. *Psychol. Rev. 40,* 434, (1933).
2. Spence, K. W. In *Behavior Therapy and Conditioning.* Yale University Press, New Haven, (1956).
3. Sheffield, F. D. A drive-induction theory of reinforcement. In *Current Research in Motivation.* Edited by Haber, R. N. Holt, Rhinehart, and Winston, New York, p. 98, (1966).
4. Olds, J. and Milner, P. *J. Comp. Physiol. Psychol. 47,* 419, (1954).
5. Olds, J. and Olds, M. E. *J. Comp. Neurol. 120,* 259, (1963).
6. Wilkinson, H. A. and Peele, T. L. *J. Comp. Neurol. 121,* 425, (1963).
7. Bruner, A. *J. Comp. Neurol. 131,* 615, (1967).
8. Anden, N. E., Dahlstrom, A., Fuxe, K., Larsson, K., Olson, L., and Ungerstedt, U. *Acta Physiol. Scand. Suppl. 67,* 313, (1966).
9. Stein, L. *Fed. Proc. 23,* 836, (1964).
10. Poschel, B. P. H. and Ninteman, F. W. *Life Sci. 5,* 11, (1966).
11. Ungerstedt, U. *Acta Physiol. Scand. Suppl. 367,* 95, (1971).
12. Anlezark, G. M., Arbuthnott, G. W., Christie, J. E. and Crow, T. J. *J. Physiol. 234,* 103 P, (1974).
13. Crow, T. J. *Brain Res. 36,* 265, (1972).
14. Arbuthnott, G. W., Crow, T. J. and Spear, P. J. *J. Physiol. 211,* 28 P, (1970).
15. Crow, T. J., Spear, P. J. and Arbuthnott, G. W. *Brain Res. 36,* 275, (1972).
16. Anlezark, G. M., Arbuthnott, G. W., Christie, J. E., Crow, T. J. and Spear P. J. *J. Physiol. 237,* 31 P, (1974).
17. Crow, T. J. *Psychol. Med. 2,* 414, (1972).
18. Crow, T. J. and Arbuthnott, G. W. *Nature New Biol. 238,* 245, (1972).
19. Arbuthnott, G. W., Fuxe, K., and Ungerstedt, U. *Brain Res. 27,* 406, (1971).
20. Clavier, R. and Routtenberg, A. *Anat. Rec. 175,* 293, (1973).
21. Anlezark, G. M., Arbuthnott, G. W., Crow, T. J., Eccleston, D. and Walter, D. S. *Brit. J. Pharmacol. 47,* 645 P, (1973).
22. Christie, J. E., Ungerstedt, U. and Ljungberg, T. *J. Physiol.*

234, 80 P, (1973).

23. Phillips, A. G. and Fibiger, H. C. *Science, 179,* 575, (1973).
24. Skinner, B. F. *The Behavior of Organisms; an Experimental Analysis.* Appleton, New York, (1938).
25. Bindra, D. *Psychol. Rev. 75,* 1, (1968).
26. Bolles, R. C. *Theory of Motivation.* Harper, New York, (1967).
27. Wilcoxon, H. C. Historical introduction of the problem of reinforcement. In *Reinforcement and Behavior.* Edited by Tapp, J. T. Academic Press, New York, p 1, (1969).
28. Crow, T. J. *Psychol. Med. 3,* 66, (1973).
29. Ungerstedt, U. *Acta Physiol. Scand. Suppl. 367,* 95, (1971).
30. Anand, B. K. and Brobeck, J. R. *Yale J. Biol. Med. 24,* 123, (1951).
31. Teitelbaum, P. and Epstein, A. N. *Psychol. Rev. 69,* 74, (1962).
32. Anlezark, G.M., Crow, T.J. and Greenway, A.P. *Science 181,* 682, (1973).
33. Herrick, C.J. In *The Brain of the Tiger Salamander, Ambystoma Tigrinum.* University of Chicago Press, Chicago, (1948).
34. Herrick, C.J. *J. Comp. Neurol. 18,* 157, (1908).
35. Sherrington, C.S. In *The Integrative Action of the Nervous System.* Yale University Press, New Haven, (1906).
36. Young, J.Z. In *A Model of the Brain.* Oxford University Press, Oxford, (1964).
37. Kapatos, G., and Gold, R.M. *Pharmacol. Biochem. Behav. 1,* 81, (1973).
38. Ahlskog, J.E. and Hoebel, B.G. *Science 182,* 166, (1973).

MENTAL HEALTH IN CHILDREN, Volume III
Edited By D. V. Siva Sankar

MINOR PHYSICAL ANOMALIES (STIGMATA) AND EARLY DEVELOPMENTAL DEVIATION: A MAJOR BIOLOGIC SUBGROUP OF "HYPERACTIVE CHILDREN"

Judith L. Rapoport and Patricia O. Quinn

Georgetown University Hospital
Washington, D.C. 20007

Minimal Brain Dysfunction (MBD) is an omnibus term referring to a poorly defined population of children presenting a variety of symptoms including developmental delay, clumsiness, impulsivity and behavior problems, learning difficulties, and distractibility, who appear before pediatricians, psychologists, neurologists, psychiatrists and education specialists. The label 'MBD' is likely to be applied when these symptoms are found in children with normal intelligence, without known neurologic disease or major psychiatric illness. Estimates on the incidence of these difficulties vary from 5% to 15% of grade school children (1), and there is growing awareness that this group of patients accounts for a large fraction of child guidance clinic populations, and that some children in this group have persisting pathology past the years when motor restlessness is manifest (2,3).

Because of the obvious heterogeneity of this patient mass, several attempts at subgrouping have been made. The familial clustering of MBD symptoms has been noted, and possible genetic subgroups discussed (1,4,5,6). The frequent dramatic response to stimulant medication, known to affect central monoamine metabolism, has led to the proposal that there is a subgroup suffering from a disorder of amine metabolism, which may be genetically transmitted (1,7).

The work of Pasamanick and co-workers (8,9,10), has demonstrated a higher rate of pregnancy complications for cases of behavior disorder compared with controls. Some replications of these findings have supported their postulate of a 'continuum of reproductive casualty', in which disability varies with the extent of the damage. However, recent studies of behavior disorders have not found a clear relation between perinatal difficulties and cognitive abnormalities or behavior problems (11). In a careful study, Wolff (12) found a higher incidence of miscarriages in other pregnancies, verified by hospital records, for a behavior-disordered group compared with controls, although there was not a higher incidence of complications for the index pregnancy.

A common difficulty in these studies is the grouping of all behavior-disordered children without further subdivision. Because of this lack of classification, the results have been inconclusive and a conceptual model of hyperactive children as 'biologic variants' (11) has been proposed, as an alternative to viewing these patients as brain damaged.

Other recent investigations have examined the incidence of congenital, anatomical deviations in populations with abnormal behavioral and intellectual development. These minor physical anomalies, it is reasoned, may be used as markers for fetal maldevelopment. Minor anomalies are so termed to distinguish them from major anomalies which are of cosmetic or medical concern to the afflicted individual.

In an unpublished study, Goldfarb and Botstein (13) compared 29 schizophrenic children, 76 controls and 11 children with behavior disorders, for the occurrence of minor anomalies following the terminology of Swiss physicians originating the research. They found the highest incidence of these stigmata was in the schizophrenic group, the lowest in the controls, while incidence in the behavior disordered group was between the two. Smith and Bostian (14) showed that children with idiopathic mental retardation were more likely to have three or more minor anomalies than a control group or children with a single major anomaly. Forty-two per cent of those with idiopathic mental retardation, but only ten per cent and eighteen per cent of children with cleft lip and palate or ventricular septal defect, respectively, had three or more anomalies. None of the control group had more than two anomalies. Smith, therefore, concluded that minor anomalies may parallel central nervous system developmental deviation.

Teeth, which embryologically originate from the same germinal layer as the central nervous system would also be subject to insult during the early differentiation phase. Goodwin and Erickson (15) found a higher incidence of abnormal primary teeth in children with behavior problems, and a significant correlation with mild (but not profound) retardation. In 1968 Waldrop, Pedersen and Bell (16), in a normal preschool population, reported a higher incidence of minor physical anomalies in children who had difficulty with impulse control. Their list of anomalies was taken from Goldfarb's study. They used Goldfarb's data to add scoring weights for some of the items.

Since the original study, Waldrop and co-workers have completed five additional studies of over 500 children, replicating their original work, and also finding an increased incidence of anomalies in children with speech disturbances. Interrater reliability correlations for weighted stigmata scores have been between 0.73 and 0.90. The stability of anomalies scores from birth to 7 years, and age norms from birth to age 12 have been established (17).

The anomalies and scoring weights used by Waldrop are given in Table 1.

Rosenberg and Weller (18) screened 99 first grade students for the presence of minor anomalies, using the Waldrop scoring system. They found that the weighted stigmata score could predict first grade failure to a highly significant degree ($p < .001$). When the teachers rated the children for personal attractiveness, weighted stigmata scores did not correlate significantly with the teachers' 'attractiveness' rating of the children. In a recent study, Halverson and Victor (19) found a significant correlation between anomaly scores and teacher and peer rated problem behaviors in a sample of 100 randomly selected grade school children.

The anomalies listed in Table 1 are formed in the first trimester of fetal development (20). While they are most commonly seen in children with Down's syndrome, these anomalies also occur in other conditions such as trisomy 13 and Seckel's syndrome. One of the three anomalies can be found in large portions of non-clinical populations. Of particular interest is the occurrence of some of these anomalies (epicanthal folds, small head size, hypertelorism, auricular abnormalities and cleft palate) in children born in women who had tried unsuccessfully to abort themselves with the folic acid antagonist aminopterin (Aminopterin Induced Syndrome). The history of ingestion of this drug between the fourth and tenth week of gestation permits the approximate dating of the formation of some of the anomalies (20).

This paper will summarize a series of ongoing studies at the Hyperactivity Clinic, Department of Pediatrics, Georgetown University Hospital, in which a large outpatient population of hyperactive boys and their siblings were surveyed for anomalies. We have become increasingly impressed with the importance of this measure in young hyperactive children. In addition to defining a sizeable subgroup of our clinical population, the association of anomalies with behavior disorders provides compelling evidence for the contribution of congenital factors to behavior.

Stigmata Score and Clinical Characteristics of a Hyperactive Child Population

As part of an outpatient drug study comparing imipramine and methylphenidate treatments of grade school, hyperactive boys (21,22) a weighted stigmata score was obtained at the first clinic visit. While the waiting of the anomalies and even the decision about their presence or absence seemed somewhat subjective to the novice, interrater reliabilities for the clinic staff were between 0.74 and 0.87.

Full face color photographs were taken for 73 of the children; these were rated for 'attractiveness' on a 4 point bipolar scale by a nurse and a special education teacher*, who were unaware of the purpose of the study. There was surprisingly good agreement ($r = 0.72$) between the two raters as to which children are considered attractive; however, there was *no*

* We would like to thank Mrs. Judy Fish and Mrs. Doris Garrett for their help.

Table 1

Anomalies and scoring weights for obtaining the 'stigmata' scores.

ANOMALY	SCORING WEIGHTS
Head	
Head circumference	
1.5 S.D.	2
1 to 1.5 S.D.	1
'Electric' hair	
very fine hair that won't comb down	2
fine hair that is soon awry after combing	1
Two or more whorls	0
Eyes	
Epicanthus	
where upper and lower lids join at the nose,	
point of union is: deeply covered	2
partly covered	1
Hypertelorism	
approximate distance between tear ducts:	
1.5 S.D.	2
1.25 to 1.5 S.D.	1
Ears	
Low-set	
bottom of ears in line with:	
mouth (or lower)	2
area between mouth and nose	1
Adherent lobes	
Lower edges of ears extend:	
upward and back toward crown of head	2
straight back toward rear of neck	1
Malformed	1
Asymmetrical	1
Soft and pliable	0
Mouth	
High palate	
roof of mouth steepled	2
roof of mouth moderately high	1
Furrowed tongue	1
Smooth-rough spots on tongue	0
Hands	
Fifth finger	
markedly curved inward toward other fingers	2
slightly curved inward toward other fingers	1
Single transverse palmar crease	1
Index finger longer than middle finger	0
Feet	
Third toe	
definitely longer than second toe	2
appears equally in length to second toe	1
Partial syndactyly of two middle toes	1
Gap between first and second toe (approximately ¼ inch)	1

significant correlation between the weighted stigmata score and the attractiveness ratings (product moment r = 0.01). This agrees with our clinical impression that the children with higher anomaly scores were not 'funny looking' or unattractive when compared with the rest of the sample. Evidently, their appearance would not lead to negative social stereotypes.

While stigmata were being scored, the parents completed a medical history form and a teacher rating scale (23) was requested. Thus stigmata scoring was carried out without previous knowledge of classroom behavior or developmental history. As has been described elsewhere (22), the stigmata score had a significant positive correlation with the 'hyperactivity' and 'conduct problem' factors on the teacher rating scale (r = 0.28 and 0.31 respectively). As shown in Figure 1, the presence of 'soft neurologic signs' (SS) and abnormal EEG were independent of weighted stigmata score.

Children with stigmata scores of 5 or more were characterized by an earlier onset of difficulties. As shown in Table 2 the child seen as 'a problem' by his parents before the age of 3 was more likely to be in the high anomaly group (chi square = 16.50 $p < .001$).

Also of interest was the association of higher scores with a history of head banging in infancy. Ten of 81 children (12%) were reported to have been head bangers; 8 of these 10 had stigmata scores of 5 or more (chi square = 12.93 $p < .001$. Head banging occurs in 16% of an unselected pediatric outpatient population (24), which is similar to the incidence in our sample, but the relation of head banging to stigmata score suggests that this subgroup represents those with early developmental deviation.

The weighted stigmatia score was also associated with obstetrical complications in the index pregnancy (22). Of the 73 patients of whom obstetrical data was available (8 children were adopted), 23 mothers reported obstetrical complications; 11 of these pregnancies resulted in children whose stigmata scores were 5 or more (chi square = 14.33 $p < .001$). As part of a longitudinal study, Dr. M. Waldrop examined data obtained by Dr. Howard Moss of the Child Research Branch, National Institutes of Mental Health, from 130 women in their eighth month of pregnancy; of 22 reporting first trimester bleeding, 17 gave birth to high stigmata offspring (M. Waldrop, personal communication).

A strong positive relationship was also found between the index child's stigmata score and mother's report of miscarriages or stillbirths in other pregnancies. As shown in Table 3, of 82 hyperactive boys for whom obstetrical data and stigmata score were available, 73 from the drug study and 9 from a previous pilot study (25), 19 (23%) of the mothers reported one or more miscarriages or stillbirths in other pregnancies. Fourteen of these mothers had produced boys with weighted stigmata scores of 5 or more ($X^2 = 15.88$ $p < .001$). The incidence of miscarriages in this group of mothers as a whole does not differ significantly from that of the control group examined by Wolff in the study mentioned earlier in this paper. A significant relation to obstetrical history is only obtained for the high stigmata subgroup.

As our *entire sample* was restricted to mothers of hyperactive boys being evaluated for medical treatment of their behavior, differential reporting of obstetrical data seems unlikely for the 'low' and 'high' stigmata groups. However, this finding remains to be confirmed by a prospective study.

Pathology in the Father

Stigmata score also had a significant positive relation to a report of paternal hyperactivity (22). Eighteen fathers reported a childhood history of hyperactivity; 9 were fathers of children with stigmata scores of 5 or more ($X^2 = 4.78$ $p < .05$).

Norms were obtained for headsize and intercanthal distance in adult white males from a population of 50 male medical students. Stigmata scores were then obtained, using deviations from the norms, on 39 of the fathers from the drug study. Fathers' weighted scores correlated significantly with sons' stigmata scores ($r = 0.50$ $p<.01$). The fathers (of high stigmata boys) who themselves had had childhood hyperactivity ($n = 7$) did not have higher stigmata scores than did the fathers (of high stigmata boys) whose wives had obstetrical difficulties ($n = 5$). Thus, a clear 'genetic' group has not emerged in this parent study. However, the 18 fathers with a positive (retrospective) history for childhood hyperactivity did

	Seen as Problems	
	Before age 3	After age 3
Stigmata score 5 or more	21	3
Stigmata score less than 5	20	37

(N = 81)

$X^2 = 16.50$

$p < .001$

Table 2. Weighted stigmata score and age of onset for low and high stigmata patients.

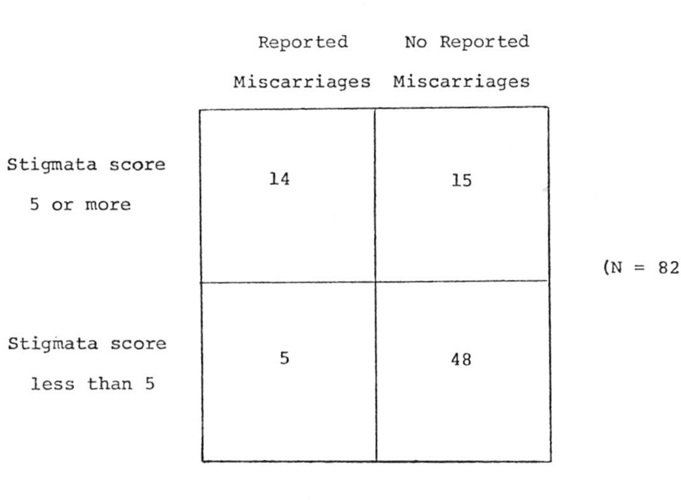

	Reported Miscarriages	No Reported Miscarriages	
Stigmata score 5 or more	14	15	(N = 82)
Stigmata score less than 5	5	48	

$X^2 = 15.88$

$p < .001$

Table 3. Index child stigmata score and reported miscarriages (or stillbirths) in other pregnancies.

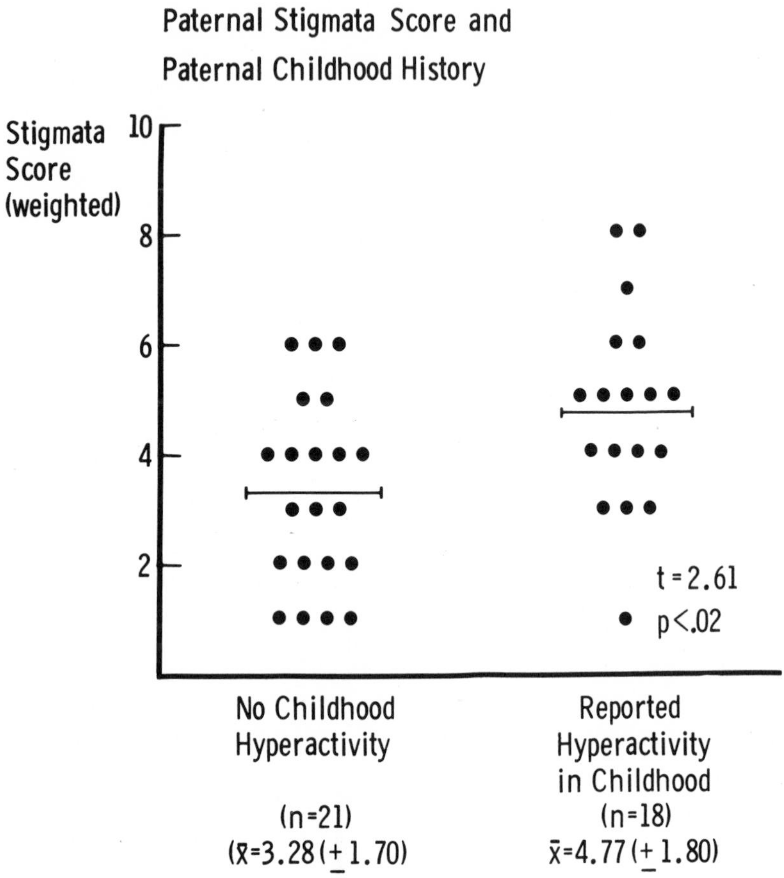

have a higher mean stigmata score than did the 21 fathers without such a history. This is shown in Figure 2. These pilot findings in an adult population are difficult to interpret, however, as a stability of stigmata scores has not been demonstrated after age 12. The familial patterns of hyperactivity in high stigmata children and their families are being examined currently in a pedigree study.

Stigmata and Plasma Dopamine beta Hydroxylase Activity

Dopamine-beta-hydroxylase is the final enzyme in the biosynthesis of norepinephrine. It is released stochiometrically by the peripheral nerves (26).

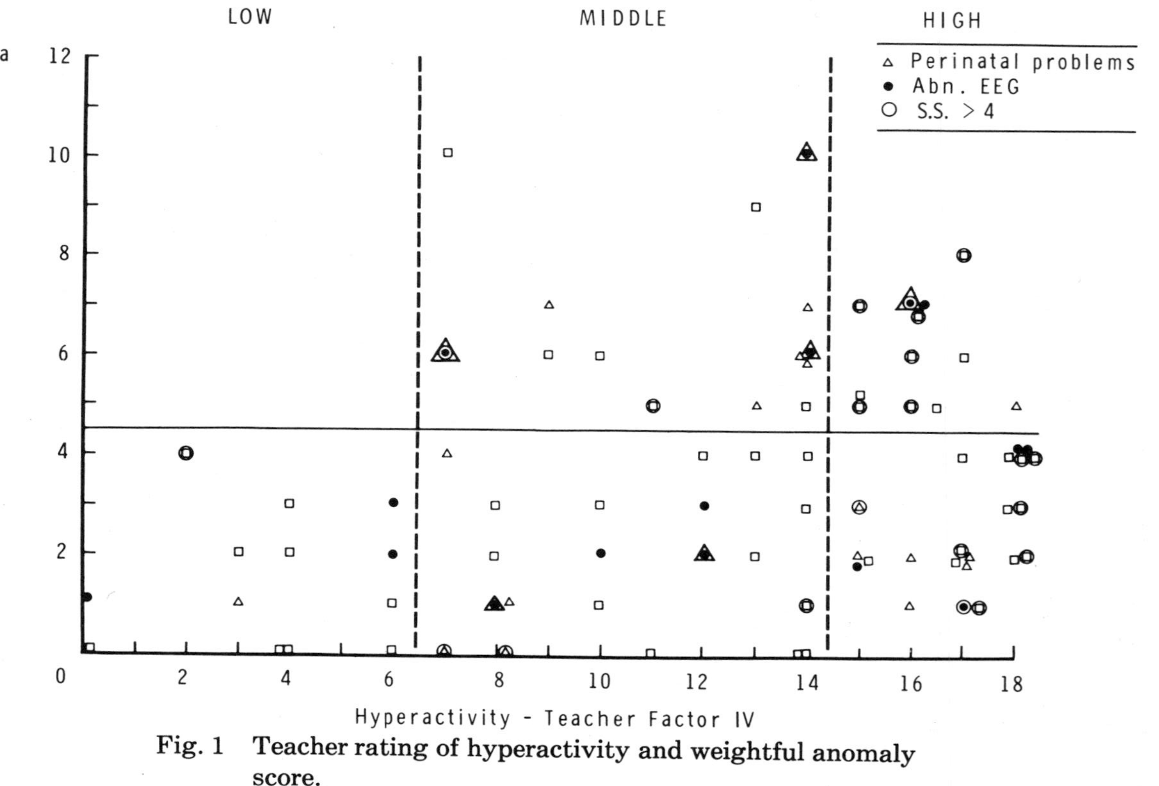

Fig. 1 Teacher rating of hyperactivity and weightful anomaly score.

Plasma DBH had a low but significant correlation ($r = 0.38$ $p < .01$) with weighted stigmata score. This has been reported in detail elsewhere (27). It should be stressed, however, that since the correlation is so low, little of the variance in plasma DBH is accounted for by the stigmata score. This finding remains to be replicated. Both methylphenidate and imipramine increased plasma DBH (27); however, this increase did not parallel clinical response.

Identification of a Clinical Subgroup

It appears then, that there is a distinct subgroup within the population of children attending a hyperactivity clinic, characterized by an early onset of difficulties including fussiness, or head banging in infancy, and having either a paternal history of hyperactivity or a maternal history of obstetrical difficulties.

A stepwise linear discriminate function analysis (28) was able to distinquish 40 low stigmata children (weighted scores from 0 to 4) from 18 high stigmata children (scores from 6 to 10) with a highly significant degree of confidence, as shown in Table 4.

Utilizing the four variables discussed above (age of onset, plasma dopamine-beta-hydroxylase, paternal history of hyperactivity and obstetrical history) the computer sorting agreed with the division of high and low stigmata groups (chi square = 32.98 $p<.001$). This suggests a genetic disorder which may be, and frequently is, phenocopied by trauma early in fetal development.

Stigmata Score and Clinical Status at One Year Follow-Up

A one year follow-up comparing imipramine and methylphenidate treatments has been completed in the clinic. Seventy-four of the 77 patients in the original drug study were seen. From this sample, we compared 19 high stigmata (weighted score 6 or more) with 20 low stigmata (weighted score 0 to 3) children matched for initial severity of hyperactivity on the Conners rating scale. Four children in the 'low' and five children in the 'high' group were receiving imipramine; the rest were being treated with methylphenidate.

	"Computer Low"	"Computer High"
High stigmata (6-10) n = 18	5	13
Low stigmata (0-3) n = 40	39	1

$X^2 = 32.98$

$p < .001$

Table 4. Classification outcome table
Stepwise linear discriminate function: based on age of onset, plasma DBH, paternal history and obstetrical history

Clinical change, as measured by the follow-up teacher rating scale, WRAT achievement scores, or global ratings of clinical status did not differ significantly between the groups, although there was a tendency for the high stigmata group to do less well on all these measures. The follow-up was carried out without control for knowledge of the experimenters for which children were in each group, but the failure to find a difference between the groups renders this limitation in research design irrelevant.

Sibling Study

We were able to examine 30 siblings (7 female; 23 male) of 21 high stigmata hyperactive boys during the past year at a mean age of 7.25 years (±3.28). The examination was carried out by the pediatrician (P.Q.) while the clinic history was obtained independently. A guest worker at our clinical independently examined 21 children; her ratings agreed well with our own ($r = 0.74$)**. Siblings were considered behavior problems only if the parents had had independent professional consultation for the child's learning or behavioral difficulties. A total of ten siblings were considered hyperactive or as showing behavior disorder by these criteria (three were currently receiving Ritalin for hyperactivity). The parents also completed a Parent Symptom Questionnaire for the sibling group (29). The mean anomalies score for the sibling group was 5.17 ± 2.01).

The correlation between weighted stigmata score and Factor III on the Parent Symptom Questionnaire was .30 ($p<.05$), on the sample of 30 siblings. Seven of the ten hyperactive sibs had stigmata scores of 6 or above (chi square = 10.68 $p<.01$). Three of the high stigmata hyperactive sibs were female; they did not differ clinically from their male sibs. There were 3 siblings with high scores (all had weighted scores of 8) who had never, at any time, been seen as problems by their schools or families. Three siblings who were considered hyperactive did *not* have high stigmata scores. This indicates that the presence of anomalies represents only one of the several factors which must interact in a complex way to influence personality and behavioral development. Only a large whole-population screening study would establish the diagnostic usefulness of stigmata scoring.

** We would like to thank Dr. Benda Herzberg, Dundee Royal Infirmary, Scotland, for her help with this Reliability Study.

During the past year, we have evaluated several young children referred for behavior problems and hyperactivity. All had high stigmata scores and deviant infant histories. Brief clinical descriptions of some patients are provided below. All were from white middle-class homes; all have responded to specific remedial programs and to stimulant medication.

Case Illustrations

#1. Martin was seen at 4 years, 11 months of age, for hyperactive and distractible behavior. The father, a college graduate, reports that he had been considered a behavior problem while he was in grade school, frequently running out of the classroom. Two of four step-brothers from father's previous marriage have behavior and learning problems. The patient had been evaluated at age 3 for delayed speech, but his participation in speech therapy class was prevented by his hyperactive, restless behavior.

Playroom interview indicated a friendly, but very active boy. Psychological testing showed low normal intelligence (WPPSI IQ 86) with prominent perceptual motor difficulties. An EEG was normal. Physical examination showed a stigmata score of 13. Chromosomal karyotyping was normal. He has responded well to dextroamphetamine (5 mg daily) and is gaining language skills with the help of a special speech program.

Two step-brothers were also examined. One, age 13, with history of repeated school failure and expulsion for negativistic classroom behavior, had a stigmata score of 11. He is responding well to Ritalin. The other step-brother, age 19, with no history of difficulties, had a stigmata score of 4.

#2. Mark was first seen at 5 years, 10 months, because of hyperactivity 'since infancy.' Mark had shown a moderate response to dextroamphetamine, and the consultation was for adjustment of dosage. The patient was the second born of fraternal twins. The twin brother had never been considered a problem.

Mark was described as having had 'temper tantrums in early infancy', and was considered temperamentally different from his twin and four older brothers. Playroom behavior was extremely distractible, although he was not destructive. Psychological testing was not carried out, but he was able to read on a second grade level. Pysical examination revealed a weighted stigmata score of 11.

Mark's twin brother was also examined; his stigmata score was 8.

#3. John was seen at 3 years, 6 months for agressive, overactive, and nervous behavior which included biting his arms when angry and making excessive demands for attention. There was no history of hyperactivity in any family member. Pregnancy was normal but delivery was by caesarian section because of failure of labor. Playroom interview indicated an extremely distractible but evidently intelligent child. Full scale IQ (WPPSI) was 126. Neurologic examination was normal. The patient's stigmata score was 9.

He has responded well to dexedrine, and the parents feel that they have benefited from counseling sessions, helping them set limits on their son's demands. A brother, 10 months younger, considered temperamentally quiet and easy-going, had a stigmata score of 3.

All of these patients were considered fussy, unsatisfying infants to raise.

Our examinations have consistently found low stigmata scores for those children whose difficulties commenced in first grade, or later. The low stigmata 'late onset' group, however, does not differ from that of our high stigmata group with regard to family, background, the presence of specific learning disability or psychological test profiles.

Discussion

The symptoms of hyperactivity and impulsivity are most probably a final common path through which a variety of congenital, toxic, and environmental influences may be expressed. The present findings, in agreement with those of Goldfarb, Smith, Waldrop, and co-workers, support the idea that minor anatomical anomalies are a useful measure in populations of children who are behaviorally deviant, particularly for younger pediatric groups. These anomalies may reflect minor developmental defects of the central nervous system.

The possibility is raised by this finding that screening for those anomalies in infancy or the newborn period may alert the pediatrician to a patient's susceptibility to a spectrum of developmental disorders. A child so identified would be a possible candidate for special educational efforts, or possible pharmacologic treatment that might lessen or prevent difficulties by school age.

A possible application of these findings to other clinical populations may be the identification of a 'high stigmata' subgroup of delinquent adolescents. Since follow-up studies have suggested that some adolescent offenders may have had restless, distractible symptoms suggestive of MBD in early grade school (3) we hypothesize that stigmata scores may be elevated in a group of juvenile offenders with a supportive, middle-class social background, compared with a group of offenders from adverse childhood environments. The former group would be expected to have a greater preponderance of biological factors contributing to the development of behavior disorder.

Similarly, a review of studies of children at 'high risk' for schizophrenia, suggests that some subgroup of these children may have symptoms resembling the impulsive behavior disorder spectrum seen in 'Minimal Brain Dysfunction' (30). It is possible, therefore, that some adult psychotic populations might contain a 'high stigmata' subgroup.

Finally, with one subgroup of hyperactive children tentatively recognized, it is hoped that other groups will be more easily identified, and that our ability to identify high risk groups for speech, learning and behavior disorder will be further increased.

References

1. Wender, P. In *Minimal brain dysfunction in children.* John Wiley, New York, (1971).

2. Weiss, G., Minde, K., Werry, J. S., Douglas, V., and Nemeth, E. *Arch. Gen. Psychiat. 24*, 409 (1971).

3. Robbins, L. N. *Deviant children grown up.* Williams and Williams, Baltimore, (1966).

4. Cantwell, D. P. Genetic studies of hyperactive children: Psychiatric illness in biologic and adopting parents. Presented at American Psychiatric Association Meeting, Detroit, Michigan, (1974).

5. Morrison, J. R. and Stewart, M. A. *Biol. Psychiat. 3,* 189 (1973).

6. Morrison, J. R. and Stewart, M. A. *J. Nerv. Ment. Dis. 158,* 226 (1974).

7. Kornetsky, C. *Psychopharmacologia 17,* 105, (1970).

8. Pasamanick, B., Rogers, M., and Lilienfield, A. *Amer. J. Psychiat. 112,* 613 (1956).

9. Knobloch, H. and Pasamanic, B. *Child Dev. 33,* 181 (1962).

10. Pasamanick, B. and Knobloch, H. *Amer. J. Orthopsychiat. 30,* 298 (1960).

11. Werry J. S. Organic factors in childhood psychopathology. In *Psychopathological disorders of childhood.* Edited by Quay, H. C. and Werry, J. S. John Wiley and Sons, New York. 83 (1972).

12. Wolff, S. *J. Child Psychol. Psychiat., 8,* 57 (1967).

13. Goldfarb, W. and Botstein, A. Physical stigmata in schizophrenic children. Unpublished ms. Henry Ittleson Center, New York, (1956).

14. Smith, D. and Bostian, K. *J. Pediat. 65,* 189 (1964).

15. Goodwin, W. and Erickson, M. *Amer. J. Ment. Defic. 78,* 199 (1973).

16. Waldrop, M., Pedersen, F., and Bell, R. *Child Dev. 39,* 391 (1968).

17. Waldrop, M. and Halverson, C. Minor physical anomalies and hyperactive behavior in young children. In *The exceptional infant, Vol. 2.* Edited by Hellmuth, J. Mazel, New York, 343 (1971).

18. Rosenberg, J. B. and Weller, G. M. *Dev. Med. Child Neurol. 15,* 131 (1973).

19. Halverson, C. F. and Victor, J. P. Minor physical anomalies and problem behavior in elementary school children. Child Development in Press, (1976).

20. Smith D. In *Recognizable patterns of human malformation.* W. B. Saunders. Philadelphia, (1970).

21. Rapoport, J. L., Quinn, P. O., Bradbard, G., Riddle, K. D., and Brooks, E. *Arch Gen. Psychiat., 30,* 789 (1974).

22. Quinn, P. O. and Rapoport, J. L. *Pediatrics 53,* 742 (1974).

23. Conners, C. K. *Amer. J. Psychiat. 126,* 884 (1969).

24. Lourie, R. S. *Amer. J. Psychiat. 105,* 653 (1949).

25. Weinshilboum, R. M., Thoa, N. B., Johnson, D. G., Kopin, I., and Axelrod, J. *Science, 174,* 1349 (1971).

27. Rapoport, J. L., Quinn, P. O., and Lamprecht, F. *Amer. J. Psychiat., 131,* 386 (1974).

28. Dixon, W. J. (Ed.) Health Sciences Computing Facility Department of Biometrics, School of Medicine UCLA BMD - Biomedical Computer Program. University of California Press, Berkely, California, 233-252. Program BMD 07M Stepwise Discriminate Analysis.

29. Conners, C. K. *Child Dev., 41,* 667 (1970).

30. Rieder, R. O. *J. Nerv. Ment. Dis., 157,* 179 (1973).

Acknowledgement

This work was supported by grant # MH 20802, Psychopharmacology Branch, National Institute of Mental Health.

MENTAL HEALTH IN CHILDREN, Volume III
Edited By D. V. Siva Sankar

EARLY INFANTILE AUTISM: BIOCHEMICAL STUDIES

N. Narasimhachari and H.E. Himwich

Galesburg State Research Hospital
Galesburg, Illinois 61401

INTRODUCTION

In 1943 Kanner described "early infantile autism," a specific syndrome beginning in infancy. These children are extremely withdrawn, self-absorbed and introverted. They are unable to form affectionate human relationships, manifest excessive aloneness and obsessively insist on the preservation of sameness. They have language difficulties which include mutism, echolalia, pronominal reversal, affirmation by repetition and part-whole confusion.

Bender (1,2) made a longitudinal study of the life course of 30 patients who met the criteria of infantile autism described by Kanner. All of these children, who had shown a clinical picture of autism before the age of 2 years, were as adults diagnosed as having schizophrenia with mental retardation.

Ornitz (3) concluded that since the disturbed modulations of sensory input which occur in children with early infantile autism are also found in the prodromal and early stages of adult schizophrenia, the clinical differences between early infantile autism and its variants and adult schizophrenia need not be fundamental but may reflect the influence of maturational levels on the overt expression of a single disease process.

Thus, although different clinical methods were used, there is agreement between the observations of Bender and Ornitz. Among those disagreeing are Rutter (16), Wing (18) and Rimland (15), who have noted that the two disorders differ in sexual distribution, social background, family history of schizophrenia, intellectual level, cognitive pattern, presence of delusions and hallucinations, etc. Parental, particularly maternal, pathology has been indicated in the etiology of the disorder. Parental responsibility for the illness has been so frequently cited in the popular press that a great deal of education has been required to remove the burden of guilt from the parents of these psychotic children without obvious physical stigmata.

We had previously demonstrated that, in contrast to normal controls, chronic schizophrenics excrete psychotogenic *N*, *N*-dimethyltryptamines, dimethyltryptamine (DMT), 5-methoxy-*N*,*N*-dimethyltryptamine (5-MeODMT) and bufotenin, in their urine (Narasimhachari *et al.* 8, 11, 12). In the hope of establishing whether a biologic process is implicated in the etiology of early infantile autism and, if so, of providing objective criteria, we undertook a series of studies to determine whether such children might also excrete *N*,*N*-dimethyltryptamines.

In the first investigation, random 24-hour urinary collections were made while the twelve subjects of the study were on different diets in their respective homes (Himwich *et al.* (3)). When the coded urine samples were analyzed by two-dimensional thin-layer chromatography (TLC), four of the subjects were found positive for bufotenin from 1 to 6 times and eight were never positive. Later it was revealed that of the 12 subjects six were normals and six had been diagnosed as possible early infantile autism. In the second investigation the six who had been diagnosed as autistic were patients at our hospital for two weeks. Twentyfour hour urine collections were made every day during this period. A blood sample (10 ml) was also collected from each of the subjects.

Subsequently we extended our investigations to a larger population. In this, our third study, 24-hour urine samples from 23 children with a possible diagnosis of autism and from 13 normals, mostly college students and some adults, were collected at their homes, coded at a receiving center and sent to our laboratory by Mrs. Marylou Ebersole of the Warren Achievement School.

We then decided to conduct an in-hospital study under strictly controlled conditions of 10 children with a diagnosis of infantile autism and of 10 normal controls matched for age, sex, and height. We sought the children with a diagnosis of autism by approaching associations for the parents of autistic children and schools for retarded children with requests for volunteers. In this, and in the third study described in the preceding paragraph, the diagnosis of early infantile autism was based solely on reports from family physicians or, in a few cases, from psychiatrists, on case histories and on information provided by the parents. Urine samples from 18 children with a diagnosis of early infantile autism were obtained from various parts of the country. The urine was frozen, packed in dry ice and sent to the laboratory at Galesburg.

A fifth group from whom 24-hour urine samples were obtained was comprised of parents and grandparents of autistic children found positive for bufotenin in previous investigations.

Typical examples of case histories of autistic children -- one by a parent, the other by a physician are given below.

Information from the mother of a child ten years of age in 1973

The baby's behavior took us by surprise. Our plans for an evening stroll with our new baby in her buggy ended because she seemed frantic from the moment my husband and I took her outside until we got her back in her crib. She resisted any change of routine, would stiffen when she was held, refused her bottle unless it was propped in her bed, resisted any change in her diet and made it unpleasant for us to take her out at all. It seemed at the time as if she had a willful, fiery personality. We even took pride in the fact that our infant was not going to be a placid little thing, but before she was nine months old, I began to feel a hint of suspicion that all was not right with my baby. My next door neighbor had a baby almost exactly her age. The comparison I made between the two babies was not very flattering to our child. The neighbor's baby was beginning to hold out his arms to his mamma to be picked up and followed her around with his eyes. Our daughter seemed to need no company outside of her own wrist which waved constantly in front of her face and which to this day is a constant mannerism.

She fretted constantly when she was out of her crib - hated to be on a blanket on the floor - and it occurred to me that stimulation, which is so important for an infant, was what upset her so much. She was perfectly happy in bed by herself, loved certain rattles, fanned the pages of a magazine for hours, but never looked at me or even turned her head to watch me as I entered her room.

I still kept my fears to myself, feeling that since her physical coordination was so much better than average (she sat easily at five months, jumped in her crib at eight months and walked at a year), she couldn't be retarded. I knew her hearing was normal as loud sounds would bother her and during nap time the slightest noise would wake her. I took her to my eye doctor and nearsightedness was eliminated.

My pediatrician was not concerned about her. He did prescribe a light tranquilizer for her when she was three months old which he thought might get her over her crying spells. He felt she was having discomfort with teeth and colic. Her first teeth came through when she was five months old.

When she was nine months old, I picked up an article about an autistic child named Amy. The child was so strikingly like our daughter that I went home and told my husband I knew she was autistic. He was rather stuffy about my diagnosis I thought, and said I should know better than to diagnose my own child out of a magazine article. But this started our ten-year search for help for her and it was not particularly satisfying to be able to say,"I told you so" when the first of many doctors, a psychologist, confirmed my diagnosis.

From the time she was two we really began to have trouble with her. Her tantrums got worse and she was very much like a wild baby animal, pulling hair, throwing anything she could pick up, refusing to eat unless it was fixed exactly the way she wanted food - and speech did not come. We found a psychiatrist who consented to work with her if we would bring her four times a week - and so she saw this doctor until she was four and until we had convinced ourselves she was no better.

Information from the physician of a patient ten years of age in 1973

Since infancy, this child was noted to be different in his behavior. He had sleep problems as a young infant and was not cuddly and affectionate. He crawled at nine months, did not walk until 20 months seemingly because he was afraid of letting go. He did not develop any speech until after three years of age. He communicates chiefly by echolalic phrases, but at times will emerge with complete well-enunciated sentences.

Other than his abnormal behavior, the formal neurological examination has not revealed any definite abnormalities. His head circumference is large, 57.5 cm. His father's head is 60 cm in circumference. He has had several EEGs, the latest one on January 31, 1973, and all of these have been normal.

He was examined by an audiologist who found that he had good peripheral auditory function but stated that his central auditory functions showed clear signs of the perceptual inconsistency described by Ornitz and Ritvo (14). The audiologist felt there was a basic problem in cortical auditory integration which was, in his opinion, compatible with autism.

Additional medical data are that skull X-rays have been normal except for demonstrating the enlargement of the head. There is a family history of gout and, in addition, an uncle, his mother's brother, has been institutionalized with what has been described as chronic schizophrenia. His mother, who is a very good observer, feels that the child resembles her brother in many ways.

The boy can ride a bicycle with training wheels and can draw a square. He has always had good tactile and motor function. He loves to play with gadgets. In school, they have observed that he often appears lethargic, that he seems to know what is going on, but cannot put it all together and express himself.

BIOCHEMICAL METHODS

Because the biochemical methods used in the qualitative identification and quantitation of the *N*, *N*-dimethyltryptamines have been described in detail in earlier publicaions (Narasimhachari *et al.* 10; Narasimhachari and Himwich, G, 7, only a brief outline will be presented here (6, 7).

The tertiary amine fraction obtained by concentrating 80% of a 24-hour urine collection (Narasimhachari *et al.* 10)) was dissolved in 100 µl of ethyl acetate. Ten-µl aliquots were spotted on Silica gel G and cellulose thin-layer plates for two-dimensional TLC. Reference compounds of bufotenin and 5-methoxy-*N,N*-dimethyltryptamine (5-MeODMT) (0.5 µg) were spotted on the Silica gel G plates and DMT, bufotenin and 5-MeODMT) (0.1 µg) on the cellulose plates. *O*-Phthaladehyde (OPT) and *p*-dimethylaminocinnamaldehyde (DACA) were used as spray reagents for the Silica gel G and cellulose plates, respectively. In a few cases where spray with OPT did not yield a fluorescence maxima and a spectrofluorometric reading, a modified OPT method (Narasimhachari and Himwich (11)) was used in which a 20-µl aliquot of the tertiary amine fraction was combined with OPT reagent, heated and then spotted on Silica gel G plates. The two spots corresponding to bufotenin were scraped, extracted with 1.5 ml 6 N HCL and read on an Aminco Bowman spectrofluorometer.

Gas Chromatographic Mass Spectrometry (*GC-MS*)

The tertiary amine fraction remaining (60-80 ul) was evaporated to dryness and heated with 20 ul of Regisil [bis(trimethylsilyl)trifluoroacetamide plus 1% trimethylchlorosilane) in a sealed tube for 1 hr. Two ul of this mixture were used for analysis and for quantitation by monitoring the ion at *m/e* 58 during GC-MS as described in an earlier paper (Narasimhachari *et al.* 12) (Fig. 1). At least one sample from each subject was used to obtain the mass spectrum of the GC peaks corresponding to the trimethylsilyl derivatives of DMT and bufotenin.

Samples were considered positive for DMT only if cellulose TLC and selected ion monitoring during GC-MS gave positive results. Similar criteria were used for the positive identification of bufotenin: TLC on Silica gel G with OPT spray and selected ion monitoring during GC-MS.

Assays of Indolethylamine N-methyltransferase Activity in Serum

Assays of indolethylamine N-methyltransferase activity in serum samples were performed by the specific GC-MS method previously described by Narasimhachari *et al.* (9). A mixture of 50 mg of lyophilized serum, 1 mM NMT, 25 µg *S*-adenosylmethionine and phosphate buffer pH 7.9 in a total volume of 0.5 ml was incubated for 90 min. The blank contained no NMT. After the addition of 4 drops of 2 N NaOH, the incubation mixture was extracted with 10 ml of ethyl acetate (nanograde). The ethyl acetate was dried over sodium sulfate and evaporated to dryness under vacuum. The residue was dissolved in 20 µl of ethyl acetate and a 2-µl aliquot was injected into the GC-MS system. DMT was quantitated by monitoring a selected ion, the base peak at *m/e* 58 (Narasimhachari and Himwich, (12)) (Fig. 2).

RESULTS

The results of the four studies of autistic children and of a single study of the parents and grandparents of some of the autistic children who had been the subjects of our investigations are presented in Table 1. In Study 1, analyses of the samples collected at home showed that four of six children with a possible diagnosis of infantile autism were positive for bufotenin, whereas the six normal children excreted no bufotenin. In Study 2 with the six autistic children of Study 1 in the hospital, five of the six were positive for bufotenin. The patient negative for bufotenin was the one who had been diagnosed by the child psychiatrist who examined the subjects of the study (Himwich *et al.* (3)) as having mild mental retardation associated with prematurity. At 21 years of age she was constantly extroverted and insistent upon her mother's attention.

No significant differences were observed in the levels of enzyme activity with the serum of children with a diagnosis of

TABLE I

Summary of Findings of Bufotenin in Urine Samples of Children with a Diagnosis of Infantile Autism and of Normal Subjects

Study	I*		II	III		IV	V
	N	A	A	N	A	A	N
	6	6	6	13	23	18	27
Positive for bufotenin	0	4	5	1	9	6	13
Positive for DMT			3		4	3	0

*N: normal; A: autistic.

Study I: double-blind study; urines collected at home. Study II: the six children previously diagnosed as autistic who were the subjects of Study I hospitalized and on a controlled diet. Study III: double-blind study; urines collected at home. Study IV: children who had been previously diagnosed as autistic; urines collected at home. Study V: parents and grandparents of some of the autistic children who were the subjects of previous studies; samples positive for bufotenin were negative for DMT by GC-MS.

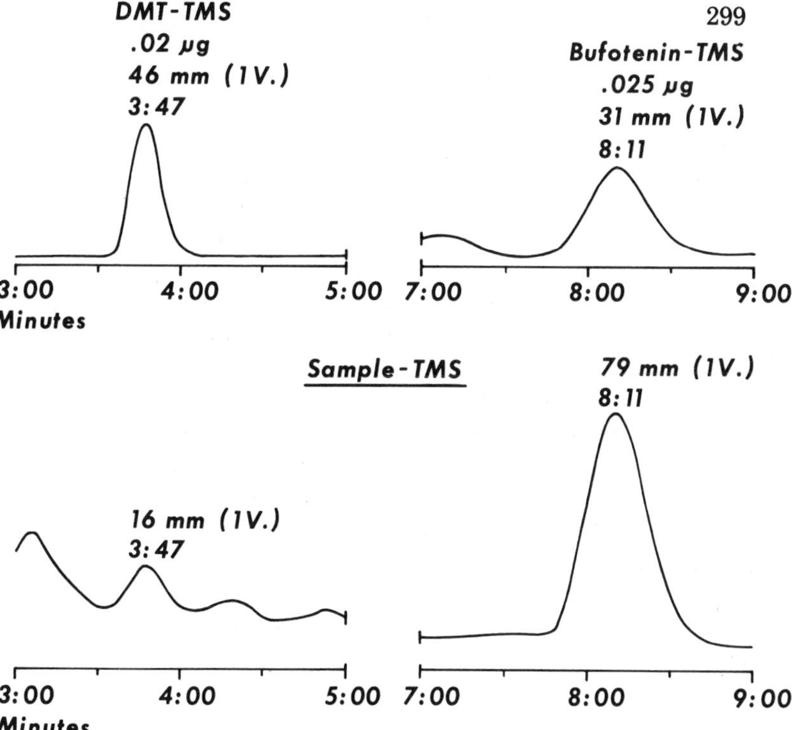

Figure 1 Single ion monitor (*m/e* 58) of the TMS derivatives of a standard solution of DMT and bufotenin (upper tracing) and of the tertiary amine fraction of a urine sample from a drug-free chronic schizophrenic patient (lower tracing). The sensitivity scale, quantity injected and peak height are shown for the standard and the sensitivity scale and peak height for the sample. By calculations based on a comparison of peak heights the sample contained 2.4 ng of DMT and 20 ng of bufotenin.

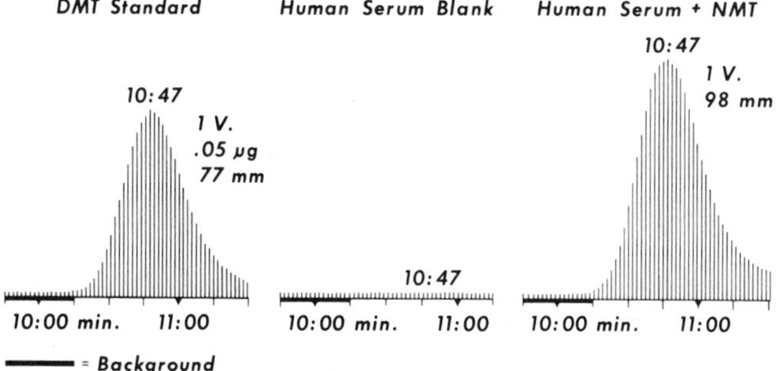

Figure 2 Single ion monitor (*m/e* 58) of standard DMT (0.1 µg), a blank without N-methyltryptamine (NMT) and a serum sample incubated with *S*-adenosylmethionine and NMT. The quantity of DMT in the sample can be calculated from the peak heights of the standard and sample.

early infantile autism and of normal controls (see Narasimhachari *et al.* (9) Strahilevitz *et al.* in preparation).

In study 3, a double-blind study of the group comprised of 23 children with a diagnosis of autism and 13 normal subjects 9 of 23 subjects in the patient group and 1 of 13 subjects in the control group were positive for bufotenin. The one positive subject in the conrol group had previously reported the occurrence of mental illness in the family.

In the case of the 18 children diagnosed as autistic by family physicians or psychiatrists whose urines were screened for bufotenin in order to select at least 10 patients for a later study to be carried out at the Galesburg Hospital under controlled conditions and where the diagnosis could be evaluated under identical conditions, 6 were positive for bufotenin.

In the earlier investigation when the 12 subjects, six normal children and six children who had been diagnosed as early infantile autism, were first studied, we did not have a sensitive test for DMT on TLC, nor did we use the GC-MS technique of monitoring a selected ion as a routine procedure. When these methods began to be used routinely (Narasimhachari and Himwich, (7)), we detected DMT in a few of the urine samples (Table 1).

DISCUSSION

The data obtained so far demonstrate that children with a diagnosis of infantile autism do excrete DMT and bufotenin in their urines. Of a total of 59 normals, including those serving as controls in earlier studies on schizophrenia, bufotenin has been detected in the urine samples of 14 subjects. One was the subject in the control group in Study 3 in whose family there was a history of mental illness; the other 13 subjects positive for bufotenin were the parents and grandparents of children diagnosed as autistic. It must be mentioned here that during the course of these studies most of the families of these children expressed an eager desire to understand the theory of the etiology of the illness and evinced an interest so great that many of the children's relatives--parents and grandparents--agreed to make available 24-hour urinary collections. Whether this finding of 13 of these 27 'normals' positive for bufotenin indicates a genetic origin of the illness and that these normals free of actual clinical symptoms are carriers of a metabolic defect or whether the presence of the metabolites, DMT and bufotenin, in the urine does not reflect a disease condition requires further investigation of a large clearly-defined control population in which a history of mental illness in the family can be definitely excluded.

A study of 10 children with a diagnosis of infantile autism and of 10 normal controls matched for age, sex, height and weight is now in progress. The use of specific methods, TLC, GC-MS and selected ion monitoring to determine whether or not there are quantitative and qualitative differences between the two groups should provide some clarification of this challenging problem.

REFERENCES

1. Bender, L. *Hosp. Community Psychiat. 20*, 230 (1969).

2. Bender, L. *J. Autism Child. Schiz. 1*, 115 (1971).

3. Himwich, H. E., Jenkins, R. L., Fujimori, M., Narasimhachari, N. and Ebersole, M. *J. Autism Child. Schiz. 2*, 114 (1972).

4. Kanner, L. *Nervous Child. 2*, 217 (1943).

5. Narasimhachari, N. and Himwich, H. E. *J. Psychiat. Res. 9*, 113 (1972).

6. Narasimhachari, N. and Himwich, H. E. *Biochem. Biophys. Res. Commun. 55*, 1064 (1973).

7. Narasimhachari, N. and Himwich, H. E. *Life Sci. 12*, 475 (1973).

8. Narasimhachari, N., Heller, B., Spaide, J., Haskovec, L., Fujumori, M., Tabushi, K. and Himwich, H. E. *Biol. Psychiatry 3*, 9 (1971).

9. Narasimhachari, N., Lin, R.-L., Plaut, J. and Leiner, K. *J. Chromatogr. 86*, 123 (1973).

10. Narasimhachari, N., Plaut, J. M. and Leiner, K. Y. *Biochem. Med. 5,* 304 (1971).

11. Narasimhachari, N., Avalos, J., Fujimori, M. and Himwich, H. E. *Biol. Psychiat. 5,* 311 (1972).

12. Narasimhachari, N., Baumann, P., Pak, H. S., Carpenter, W. T., Zocchi, A. F., Hokanson, L., Fujimori, M. and Himwich, H. E. Gas chromatographicmass spectrometric identification of urinary bufotenin and dimethyltryptamine in drug-free chronic schizophrenic patients. *Biol. psychiat. 8,* 293 (1974).

13. Ornitz, E. M. In *The Schizophrenic Syndrome.* Edited by Cancro, R. Brunner/Mazel, New York, pp. 652-671, (1971).

14. Ornitz, E. M. and Ritvo, E. R. *Arch. Gen. Psychiat. 18,* 76 (1968).

15. Rimland, B. *J. Autism Child. Schiz. 1,* 161 (1971).

16. Rutter, M. In *Early Childhood Autism.* Edited by Wing, J. K. Pergamon, New York, pp. 51-75, (1966).

17. Strahilevitz, M., Narasimhachari, N., Fischer, G. W., Meltzer, H. Y. and Himwich, H. E. *Biol. Psychiat. 10,* 287, (1975).

18. Wing, J. K. In *Early Childhood Autism.* Edited by Wing, J. K. Pergamon, New York, pp. 3-50, (1966).

MENTAL HEALTH IN CHILDREN, Volume III
Edited By D. V. Siva Sankar

LANGUAGE DISORDERS OF NEUROLOGICALLY IMPAIRED AND EMOTIONALLY DISTURBED CHILDREN

Marie E. Brittin

Ohio State University
Columbus, Ohio

INTRODUCTION

Communication disorders provide significant clinical information in differential diagnosis. Disturbed processes may be noted which impede perception, comprehension, formulation and expression of thoughts. Conceptual deficits, communication strategy or negation of communication are different for neurologically impaired and emotionally disturbed children. These children interact differently in their language environments. Sensory-motor development and perceptual cognitive functions are requisite to achievement of language competence.

Speech production and language use are dynamic functions which reflect mental, physical, and emotional status. Language reflects cognitive and affective development. Evaluation of language behavior provides insight as to the functional deficits and potential of a child. The intent in using oral language to influence other persons or convey thoughts evidences a high level of social interaction.

Communication skills essential for human relationships are crucial to learning and social maturation. Defective speech and language of children brings many parents to specialists.

One of the primary questions asked by parents bringing young children for evaluation to medical centers is, "Will he or she talk?"

Speech is not a simple performance. The miracle of speech and language, particularly the amazing rapidity of development of this ability in normal children, continues to challenge researchers. Research is being pursued on development and remediation by speech and language pathologists, psycholinguists, linguists, neurologists, and ethologists. Extensive advancements in understanding are being made although complete answers have yet to be found.

These papers consider language development from the point of view of the linguist, the range of speech and language problems shown by neurologically impaired and emotionally disturbed children, research efforts by psychiatrists to study language, a planning approach for language training of mentally retarded, and rehabilitation theory and procedures for training children with speech and language problems.

The speech and language problems of neurologically impaired and emotionally disturbed children present a special challenge in differential diagnosis. This is due to the severity of the presenting problems and individual variations. The etiology of communication problems may not be easily discerned. Specialists may hold different concepts about children with language learning disorders or parents may be confronted by what seem to be differences of opinion among professionals regarding their child. Teachers and therapists urgently desire direction in order to plan effective educational and remedial procedures for these children. As the interests of psychiatrists, psychologists, and speech and language pathologists converge in evaluation and understanding, we shall better discern differences in the speech and language of these children and be more successul in our specialized efforts to help such children.

Consideration of the language a child uses is significant for: (a) Language reveals the interaction of the child's endownment, maturation, and language stimulating environment. (b) Clinical descriptions of personality disorders include or may be based on language behavior. (c) A child's verbal skills are requisite to social and educational experiences and therefore become goals in remediation.

Language may be considered to be a system of labels for our concepts. Language as defined by Carroll (1) is a "structured system of arbitrary vocal sounds and sequences of sounds . . . used in interpersonal communication . . . which catalogues things, events, and processes in the human environment." Carroll considers "speech" in contrast to language as "the actual behavior of individuals in using language." "Speech" may be considered the production and articulation of sound--audible behavior. Language encompasses a system of sounds in words and grammatical patterns. Language codes include four aspects: (a) phonology or sound phonemes, (b) morphology or sound combining systems which form words, (c) syntax or grammatical patterns in which words are arranged and (d) semantics--the meanings of words and syntactical patterns in relation to human experience. Speech conveys thought by recognizable sequence of sounds. Language involves choices of words and structures of word combinations to convey meaning which permit us to represent experience, organize ideas, and relate cause and effect to achieve solutions. We are concerned with the mental processes of coding, association, and decoding. Language involves reception and expression.

The processes required for language acquisition are: (i) cognition or the capacity to recognize, discriminate, and manipulate experience, (ii) audio-linguistic or psychoacoustic discrimination which permits comprehension of speech and language, and (iii) motor patterning or the ability to approximate the articulatory positions by tongue, lip and palatal movements which permit production of sound sequences conforming to adult speech and language patterns. According to Chomsky (2), "Each language can be regarded as a particular relationship between sound and meaning."

The study of language disorders in children is not new. Gall, a forerunner in neurology, described the faulty memory of children for speech in 1825. Freud in publications in 1897 and 1953 sought to differentiate disturbances in the language of children from faulty acquisition of language. We continue to seek a learning theory which accounts for all aspects of language acquisition. Condon and Sander report (3) that neonate movement is synchronized with adult speech. These researchers found that as early as the first day of life, the neonate moves in precise and sustained segments of movement in response to adult speech. Conditioning of infant vocalizations to social responses of an adult has been shown to be possible as early as three months of age by Schiefelbusch (4). The child's alertness and use of sensory, perceptual abilities can be stimulated through auditory and visual experiences as well as by physical touch.

We recognize the need for a nurturing type of model with whom the child interacts to motivate development of communication. It is interesting, however, that we find children who are extremely shy and generally fearful who also present an accompanying lack of audio-linguistic skills. The relationship between prolonged anxiety and language delay has yet to be thoroughly studied. Audio-linguistic skills of children reflect learning experiences. A child makes a perceptual-motor-auditory match in imitation of language models. Children's audio-linguistic skills explode between two to three years of age and basic language function is rather well established by five years. Research supports vocabulary development of three hundred words at twenty-four months which increases to nine hundred words at thirty-six months and to fiften hundred words at forty-eight months. A five year old responds with sentences having a mean length of 5.7 words and soon approaches a comprehension vocabulary of 15,000 words according to Templin (5).

The steps of perception, imagery, symbolization and conceptualization lead to normal language. Craik (6) has found in research on levels of encoding in memory that the depth of processing or extent of coded analyses performed on perceptual experience determines learning and recall. Although much of our language acquisition is unconscious, language is systematically developed. Comprehension or receptive language precedes expressive language. We develop auditory comprehension before visual comprehension of printed symbols. We progress from concrete to abstract language and from simple to complex verbalizations. The child's ability to manipulate language is shown by the structure of syntax.

SPEECH AND LANGUAGE OF NEUROLOGICALLY IMPAIRED CHILDREN

Children with neurological involvements present motor, sensory, and perceptual developmental profiles that deviate from normal. Neurological evidence and encephalogram findings usually support this syndrome of organicity. Piaget's developmental concepts do not apply or are different for these children. If perception is disturbed, the imagery of experience is distorted. Defective perception of auditory experience interferes with comprehension and acquisition of meanings. If the defect is in relating or recalling appropriate symbols to represent experience then concept development seems defeated. Defective verbal learning prevents memory, integration of experience, and finally oral language.

The language disorder of the neurologically impaired child may occur at the level of auditory perception. Audition may not function normally although the ear mechanism permits hearing which is adequate for speech. The child receives, but cannot decode the input. There is inability to organize auditory events by keeping these in mind for scanning, comparison and classifying. Classification and organization for thought is therefore defective. Some of these children seem to ignore auditory signals, but respond to visual or comprehend better if both auditory and visual symbols are presented. Environmental sounds may be perceived as meaningful while speech sounds seem too confusing. Such children can match isolated auditory speech sounds, yet not discriminate these in connected speech. Speech for these children may be composed of sounds without meaning. Normal speaking rates may be too rapid for these children to comprehend. If a speaker reduces the rate of speaking, separates words, and speaks distinctly the child's understanding improves.

A smaller number of these children understand language, but cannot express language. Their production of speech lags excessively behind their understanding. Such children present diverse language profiles and may be (i) retarded in onset of speech; (ii) use only a limited vocabulary typical of a younger child; and (iii) show delay in developing syntactic proficiency. When such children begin speaking their language is often grammatically incorrect due to omission of functional words.

Motor patterning for speech may be unsatisfactory. Certain of these children are delayed in phoneme production or accurate articulation of sounds. This may be due to defective motor control of articulators for the synchronized movements of speech. These children often have developmental histories of response to sounds and playing baby games. They may have cried often, but did not use early vocal play or babbling. Echolalia or the approximate imitation of environmental speech sounds expected during the pre-speech development stage at nine to twelve months may not be observed. Parents of such children may report that their child was a feeding problem due to preference for liquids or soft foods. Motor control for chewing and swallowing solid food was difficult for them.

We can generalize that neurologically impaired children show perceptual dysfunctions in one or more sensory modalities, but *not* in all modalities. Language function is usually below that expected for their mental age. Optimal conditions are required for auditory comprehension. These conditions are: slower rate of speech, absence of distracting noise, fatigue, frustration or any awareness that they may have made an error. Perseveration, hyperactivity, emotional lability, and even catastropic behavior are cited as characteristic of neurologically damaged children. Their frustration in failure to comprehend or express themselves has been mistakenly considered emotional disturbance. These children often vary in learning performance from day to day. They may be observed to lose the grasp of a principle necessary for completion of a task or fail to generalize by applying a principle learned in one task to another. If we accept the best performance these children give as indicating their intellectual potential, they approximate norms on non-verbal standardized test inventories.

The neurologically impaired child attempts to relate to people. These children look at you to observe your facial expression and gestures. They enjoy watching other children. They are capable of genuine affection. We may observe that such children have rather effective gesture language. They may use single words with meaningful inflections. Although such children may be hyperactive this is not necessarily related to emotional reactions, but may follow a sense of inadequacy in performance, short attention span, or inability to assume the appropriate mental set. The drawings of such a child are often poor. Their drawings reveal confused or incomplete concepts as well as poor eye hand coordination. Gross motor behavior may not be obviously defective. The fine motor control of articulators may be less than satisfactory to support accurate speech. Figure ground confusion is shown in auditory as well as visual perception. The language behavior of such children, although inadequate, reveals an attempt to communicate with persons and relate to events within the environment. Although plateaus may break expected language progress and day to day performance is somewhat inconsistent, we observe progress in language remediation.

SPEECH AND LANGUAGE OF EMOTIONALLY DISTURBED CHILDREN

The speech and language disorders shown by emotionally disturbed children are so diverse as to seem almost unique to a child, but assessment of oral behavior merits attention. These children are different in language usage from normal children and from hard of hearing as well as mentally retarded or neurologically impaired children. We notice differences in the following areas: (a) developmental history of speech onset and language development, (b) the purposes for which speech seems to be used, (c) the consistency with which speech and language skills are or are not maintained, and (d) the non-verbal behavior which may or may not support the oral language.

Autistic and schizophrenic children form a rather heterogeneous group and the diagnosis of autism may disguise or discourage evaluation of the language which would permit differentiation of primary neurological etiology. There are differences in the (i) quantity or mean length of oral responses, (ii) the quality of these responses or language level, and (iii) the intent or meaning.

The range of language performance in autistic children varies from elective silence or mutism to almost constant sound production with varying degrees of appropriateness and meaning. Autistic children are often reported to have been almost silent as babies. Babbling and sound play of baby games may not have been attempted. This absence of sound gives the impression of a profound hearing loss. Their failure to react to the human voice may be noticeably different from the hard of hearing or deaf child due to lack of eye contact, and absence of physical response to touch which accompanies the familiar voice. A month old normal child has been known to show alertness and physical movement in response to a father's voice on radio or television. Severely hard of hearing children reveal responsiveness when the vibration of a heavy step or engine noise cues the child that a parent is approaching. Rimland poses that 50% of autistic children are mute (7), although Stark and Giddan (8) believe that language at some level can be evoked from many of these children.

If a child chooses to be silent, speech once initiated may be abruptly interrupted for a period of time or may develop late. The absence of speech by the age of three is a discouraging prognostic sign. Regressive, infantile behavior may be accompanied by similar speech signs as the sound omissions, substitutions, and distortions of "baby talk." Excessive fantasy, day dreaming, and introversion reduce the amount of oral communication. Unusual fears and chronic anxiety may reduce meaningful speech to crude jargon and screams. Exaggerated emotional reactions produce excessive talking in a quarrelsome, argumentative manner, lacking in reason and defective in grammatical construction. The speech of these children can be a reflection of the verbalizations of emotionally disturbed peers or adults in the environment rather than indicative of the true state of mind of the child.

The child who stops speaking without having sustained a sudden severe loss of hearing due to catastrophic illness, is capable of understanding and using language. This child often begins speaking again as suddenly as speech stopped. The speech and language level at which communication is re-initiated is usually at the same level as before speech was interrupted. There is a lag in language development due to this interruption. Experience in speaking and trial and error language performances seem essential to progressive development. Voice quality may be unusual also after a period of silence.

The autistic child's language does not always convey meaning to the listener. Such children seem to use language as a means of isolation or to conceal themselves rather than for communication. Speaking is sporadic, inappropriate and includes only a few understandable words, phrases or snatches of song. These children often whisper, but their whispered speech is usually non-communicative and unintelligible. Such speech appears to have meaning to the child, but not to the listener. Their repetition of phrases or delayed duplication of something said in their presence termed automatisms are considered significant symptoms of autism by Rimland (7).

Imitiative speech is exhibited late by the autistic child. The normal child may present echolalia as early as nine months or at the latest from eighteen to thirty months. The normal child uses echolalia temporarily as a stage of vocal play. This normal language learning experience is displaced to a much later deveopmental period for the autistic child, who may use echolalia at six years or later. Piaget (9) indicated that a self-world of confusion accounts for the limited imitative language. Echolalia varies in quality and may be used for self-talk, to prevent verbal interaction or to reflect obsession. Personal pronouns repeated as heard are cited as language errors. Answers to questions become repetitions of questions. Echolalia is considered by Risley and Wolf (10) to be a predictor for training speech. Imitative speech may be evidence of an effort at identification with other persons.

Idiosyncratic speech, invented words or unusual application of words is shown by autistic children. This unique speech results from rearrangement of phonemes and morphemes or the stringing of phonemes together which only approximate words. This may be due to disordered auditory memory span for speech sounds or inconsistent use of hearing potential. Myklebust (11) writes of the autistic child as not using audition and refers to psychic deafness. Impaired ability to relate to stimuli or defective memory for experiences basic to cognition may explain the retardation in mental development of such children.

Autistic children as a group or category are inconsistent in language behavior. Some children have large, impressive vocabularies for their chronological age. Verbal intelligence scores may be high. Recall of detailed information may be surprising, yet the recitation may be self-talk or to an imaginary person and unrelated to a speaking situation. The speech and language of the autistic child may change or noticeably deteriorate. This may at first seem to be related to certain situations or to be in the presence of a particular person.

The non-verbal behavior of such a child is often disturbed or inconsistent with oral language. An expressionless face or grimace unrelated to the tone of voice, inflection or word choice is startling. Bodily movements such as distracting arm swinging, head shaking, covering of the face, or bizarre mannerisms are unrelated to clarifying communication. The normal child reinforces language by eye contact, facial expressions of smiles or frowns, comes closer to the listener, and uses descriptive gestures which would be almost meaningful even without words.

Emotionally disturbed children often disregard sounds, while neurologically impaired children are highly distractible or seem unable to shut out auditory or visual stimuli. These children respond to people, look at a speaker, gesture meaningfully and reveal genuine affection in their smiles and responses. Even if language is limited to single word responses, these are spoken with revealing inflection. Conceptual development may be delayed, but concepts which are learned are usually consistently applied. Erratic behavior can be moderated as attention span is lengthened and behavior comes to be self-controlled. Motor control, although defective, improves with training. Language progress can be charted. The child himself may show initiative in innovating ways to learn or overcome a perceptual problem and control his own behavior. The sensory impaired child attempts communication in some form.

CONCLUSION

Speech and language behavior reveals organic and functional problems, sensory-motor or neural interaction, and the psychodynamics of interpersonal relations. Language behavior tells us much. There are discretely different explanations or "why" answers to the language or non-language performances of a child. Acceptance, love and secure relationships, as important as these are to life, are not enough to explain these differences. We would be wrong to assume that language disorders result from psychological factors alone or not to differentiate other etiologies. There seems to be a direct relation between the severity of the speech and language disorder and the sensory-perceptual dysfunction or the severity of the emotional disturbance. The child with the sensory impairment usually attempts communication in some form while the emotionally disturbed child may not speak or manipulates communicative strategies. As our multi-disciplinary viewpoints converge we should improve the accuracy of our insight and effectiveness of our efforts in helping these children.

REFERENCES

1. Carroll, J. B., In *Methods in Special Education.* Edited by Haring, N. G. and Schiefelbusch, R. L. McGraw-Hill Book Co., New York, p. 50, (1967).

2. Chomsky, N. *Language and Mind.* Harcourt Brace and World, New York, p. 15, (1968).

3. Condon, W. S. and Sander, L. W. Neonate movement is synchronized with adult speech: Interactional Participation and Language Acquisition. *Science, 183,* No. 4120, January 11, 1974, pp. 99.

4. Schiefelbusch, R. L., "Language Development and Language Modification," In N. G. Haring and R. L. Schiefelbusch, (Eds.), *Methods in Special Education,* McGraw-Hill Book Co., New York, 1967, p. 55.

5. Templin, M., *Certain Language Skills in Children: Their Development and Interrelationship,* University of Minnesota Press, Minneapolis, 1957, p.111.

6. Craik, R., "Levels of Analysis: View and Memory," In P. Pliner, L. Krames, T. Alloway, (Eds.), *Communication and Affect: Language and Thought*, Academic Press, New York, 1973.

7. Rimland, B., *Infantile Autism,* Appleton-Century Crofts, New York, 1964.

8. Stark, J., J. J. Giddan, and J. Meisel, "Increasing Verbal Behavior in an Autistic Child," *Journal of Speech and Hearing Disorders,* v. 33, no. 1, 1968, pp. 42-47.

9. Piaget, Jean, *Language and Thought of the Child,* World Publishing Co., New York, 1971.

10. Risley, T. and M. Wold, "Establishing Functional Speech in Echolalic Children," In H. N. Sloane and B. D. Macaulay, (Eds.), *Operant Procedures in Remedial Speech and Language Training,* Houghton Mifflin Co., Boston, 1968, pp. 157-184.

11. Johnson, D.J. and H. Myklebust, *Learning Disabilities,* Grune and Stratton, New York, 1967.

MENTAL HEALTH IN CHILDREN, Volume III
Edited by D. V. Siva Sankar

PJD Publications Ltd., Westbury, N. Y.

CHANGING PATTERNS IN HABILITATION OF CHILDREN WITH COMMUNICATION DISORDERS

Don A. Olson

Northwestern University Medical School
Chicago, Illinois

The acquisition of speech and language is an unique human phenomenon. When the child suffers an emotional, physical, mental, or social insult to normal speech and language development processes, a co-ordinated team approach to the management of the resulting disabilities is indicated. Professionals interested in the communication problems of childhood can no longer work in isolation but must comprehend and use the skills of professionals in both medical and paramedical areas in order to meet the needs of children with communication handicaps. The interrelationship of language development that is, listening, speaking, reading, and writing, are dependent on the physical, social, and emotional growth of the child and the degree of actualization of language skills depends on a specific time table of development. If the child veers greatly from expected language acquisition at critical stages in his development, language limitations and learning disability appear in adolescence and adulthood. The early intervention and management of the child with communication problems is imperative if actualization of a child's true potential is to be realized.

Normal speech and language development are part of a normal learning process. Man must have adequate hearing for normal speech and language, he needs to comprehend the language of others and to be able to formulate thoughts. There must be adequate movement of the oral mechanism in coordination of the muscles used in speech. Further, intellectual abilities must be within normal limits for normal speech and language development. The personal and social growth must be satisfactory for normal language learning.

The impact of personal, emotional, and psychological growth has been greatly neglected by the field of speech pathology. The review of the literature and the work in this field shows few research findings and an examination of the work force reveals few therapists functioning in clinics for the emotionally disturbed. In spite of this, the speech pathologist could be a major person functioning on the psychiatrist's team as he and others would understand the personal relations of the child and his communication abilities.

It is difficult to maintain a real perspective of children's needs. The biases of professionals engaged in work with children are greatly affected by their training, education, and the limitations of their individual practices. Thus they tend to see different things in the child according to the way they have been trained.

The psychiatrist looks at the child predominantly from the psychiatric view point, the physician looks at the child predominantly from the physical view point, the speech pathologist looks at the child predominantly from the speech view point, the occcupational therapist looks at the child primarily as regards his ability to dress and function in living situations, the therapeutic recreation specialist looks at the child's play habits. If we are truly to understand the child, all of these professionals must see the total child and the implications of each of these areas to that functioning individual.

Whenever children are involved in a field of study, the atmosphere becomes emotionally loaded. Unfortunately, professionals who work with children and diagnose their speech and language problems are at best primitive in their approach. The field of Speech Pathology and Communicative Disorders is one of the youngest professions interested in changing the behavior of the human being. Although speech pathologists have been active since 1928, it was not until 1950 that a separate professional organization was developed. Research in this area is too frequently limited and in a sense the "experts" are just finding their way in understanding the speech and language development of the young child.

The profession of Speech Pathology had initially as its major emphasis a type of research concerned with counting the words of youngsters, the volume of their speech and language, the types of sounds they made and in general the output that they could produce. Later the emphasis switched more to concern over the child's language, the linguistic factors and the rules of language. The past few years have seen a shift into research which is concerned with interaction of the child with the mother or with the family and more stress is placed on how other members of the child's environment talk to him. Research is focusing on the mother's response to the child, the way the mother handles the child, the way the mother talks to the child. Consideration of person-to-person reactions in the development of speech and language is gaining increased importance in research and clinical approaches. This new thrust in research makes even more important interdisciplinary approaches to understanding the child. In considering a comprehensive evaluation of the child, many factors are involved and speech and behavior can only be understood in relation to these various factors, which are Social, Physical, Psychological, Vocational, Communicative, Intellectual. It is important to "put the whole patient together", and consider his problems as one, not merely concentrate on one major area of one's interest. The main goal for all patients is to make them functioning social beings and this can only be done by the integration of all these major diagnostic areas.

It is clear that one profession alone cannot handle a comprehensive evaluation. A team approach is indicated and has been shown through the years to be the most effective method of patient management. The basic primary team can be made up of speech pathologists and psychiatrists along with the family physician, child development specialist or educator, social worker, psychologist, physical therapist, therapeutic recreation specialist, play therapist, and others as needed. The more that is learned about the youngsters, the more it becomes evident that the total approach to evaluation is necessary in order to truly understand their needs and to encourage speech and language development.

Several factors have impeded the comprehensive evaluation of youngsters. First is the tremendous growth of professionalism and the interest in one's own profession over the interest of the patients in the past few years. The professions have been threatened by government control, lack of appropriate funding, manpower shortages, and other obstacles. These problems have frequently made people loyal to the profession rather than to the individuals they were supposed to serve.

Second is the lack of good test measures in all of the areas. Recently, at Northwestern University, a three-year comprehensive study of children's language and learning potential was completed. This study involved some three days of testing of over 500 children and group testing of some 2,000 children. A group composed of supposedly learning disability youngsters and a group of learning disability and language deficient children and a normal group were subjected to this test which purported to discriminate between problem children and non-problem children. The test included such recognized measures as the Wexler Intelligence Scale, social motor, psychological, visual perceptual, and as comprehensive a battery of tests as can typically be given to youngsters with language and learning problems. In addition, a complete medical examination, including electroencephalogram, neurological, ophthalmological and other medical examinations, was given. The age level of these children was from 6-10 primarily as it was felt that the child has reached some stability by that time and also that the test measures were more reliable by that age; the lack of reliability and validity of measures below 5 years of age is well known. The results of the psychological, physical and neurological battery were very disappointing in discriminating differences between the groups of children. The most significant test to come out of the evaluation was a rating scale which classroom teachers developed. This pointed up the need for observation and functional indices of the behavior of the child as being more important than formal and standardized testing. A critical factor revealed in this study was poor attention and concentration in relation to children's inability to learn language and school work. The reason was not revealed. This factor was more discriminating than others in evaluating the children.

Third is the frequency of one's haste to "do something to" the child. Thoreau once said that he would rather have his boy not learn to read until age 12 and grow up loving books than have him be the first child on the block to grow up hating books. One of the greatest problems of the present day is that this freedom cannot be allowed for the children. There is considerable evidence that most of the speech and learning problems which are organic or physical in nature disappear with the passage of time. Society, as reflected in the schools, is particularly against allowing the passage of time to be the healer. The great myth of total equality of ability is perpetuated and as a result, parents are under pressure to have their child be like every other child, and teachers are under pressure to have everyone in the room read up to grade level. If the child does not mature by age 12, there are few teachers or therapists or schools interested in him. However, if the parents watch their child struggle through special programs, and expensive treatment with little or no observal progress, they should not despair. The important thing is to have some remedial education available whenever the child is ready, and not to cease protecting him as much as possible from pressure. Time may very likely solve the problem.

Professionals have the tendency to "attack" the children with tests. The most popular approach in clinics and schools can be termed a frontal *attack* on presumed developmental or neurological weakness. If the child has visual perceptual problems, individual perceptual tests are ordered. Activities most frequently connected with this approach are use of balance beams, crawling tunnels, jumping boards, trampolines, extensive practice and eye-hand coordination activities with the blackboard and with mimeographed handouts, as well as with visual practice such as following swinging balls with the eyes and matching similar and dissimilar patterns. The emphasis on these programs is on developing motor skills and visual perception. Some programs also emphasize auditory discrimination, having the child spend a significant amount of time listening to and discriminating among sounds. The theoretical approach which underlines these activities appears to be sound. Early pioneers in learning speech, language and learning problems were neurologists and optometrists and the approach is consistent with the developmental theories held in these fields and by some modern educational theorists. However, if the parents, educator or physician would look at the independent scientific research done on programs of this nature, they would discover that there is really a very small amount of valid research done showing that the improvement in motor skills, vision skills or perceptual skills is a direct result of the therapeutic process. Some of the direct approaches make use of the machines, flashcards, letters, symbol words, word phrases. There is a large amount of well done research on the effectiveness of this type of training. It one were to believe this research the child would be better off walking on balance beams, an unprofitable task in itself. Machines have great motivational value but this is fleeting; even with better students the tachistoscopes are the poorest possible means of increasing reading speed.

Chemical therapy also comes under the heading of directed *attack* on a child. It is unfortunate that the word "drug" has negative connotations in today's world and also that there have been so many sensational articles written about the use of drugs to treat learning disabilities and language problems. It appears that for every child who might have been helped with some concentration difficulties through chemical therapy, there are more children for whom the approach has caused difficulties in attention problems as a result of chemical inbalance. The long term results of chemical therapy are not known and most of the short term results of chemical therapy are not known and most of the short term results are not very effective.

Another factor which has contributed to poor understanding of children in trouble has been the lack of trust and information sharing between agencies. A community may have excellent diagnostic clinics, visiting nurse associations, mental health clinics, but frequently these agencies do not share information with each other nor do they work with each other in a way to truly work out the child's problems. All too often the child is shifted from one agency to another with little follow-through or carry-over from the initial to the secondary agency. The establishment of interagency cooperation in order to assure a good diagnosis of youngsters would be one of the first steps in helping children with problems.

In spite of some lack of sound research, isolated approaches to evaluation and too much therapeutic pressure in some instances, certain factors have been found to be significant and consistently related to speech and language growth. One, a study of work done on the subject to the present date reveals general agreement that there are definite developmental patterns for social, motor, speech and language growth, that is, many of the limitations that have been revealed at early stages in childhood development are permanent. Two, much has been heard about the importance of early diagnosis so that changes can be achieved in the auditory memory span of the relationship of many children, even with therapy. Therapy should more importantly be directed toward helping the child to compensate for the deficiencies rather than actually improving on the deficiencies. This is true of very young children as well as older children. Three, it is also agreed that the earlier the referral the better the opportunity for significant comprehensive evaluation therapy. Early referral in retraining has been found to be a significant factor in making progress with youngsters with speech and language problems. Four, there is a shift in thinking from isolating the child in special classes and special training programs to integrating him into regular classrooms and having him share the experiences of normal children in order to encourage speech and language development. Special classes and special programs are being made a part of regular classes and regular programs and it appears that only through this approach can one be successful with children. Finally, research has pointed up the importance of auditory attention span and auditory comprehension as a significant area of diagnosis. We have not paid enough attention to this particular area in our work with children and it seems highly related to not only speech and language growth but to the total emotional integration of the child. The child's ability to concentrate, to pay attention and to comprehend language about him appears to be very important to emotional integration. Therapy with the child should frequently include training and exercises in the area of auditory tension span, auditory comprehension, auditory memory and concentration in order to achieve maximum communication, skill development and maximum psychological integration.

A growing factor in all professions and one which will affect much of the work of the coming years will be the demand of parents and children for accountability. One of Webster's definitions of accountability is "the act of time of rendering or reckoning"; "responsibility" is an appropriate synonym. Accountability demands a broad view of communication disorders and a broader view then many professionals are accustomed to. The broad view includes the concept of many disciplines working together in a comprehensive evaluation of children with communication problems. It is only through a coordinated approach of many specialists that the complicated phenomenon of speech, language and learning development in young children can be understood.

MENTAL HEALTH IN CHILDREN, Volume III
Edited by D. V. Siva Sankar

LANGUAGE TRAINING STRATEGIES FOR RETARDED CHILDREN

R.L. Schiefelbusch

University of Kansas
Lawrence, Kansas 66044

Abstract

In this paper language is regarded as a complex, generative system that can be taught. It is proposed that the same transactional system used by adults (usually parents) in the natural environment be adapted for clinical interventions. Much of the functional bases for language acquisitions have been described by Premack (1) and Bloom (2).

The adult should help the child "map out" the relationships between symbols and environmental events. Probably the child is able to affix labels to events that he has learned to conceptualize. The teaching process then is limited at all times to the range of the child's semantic functions. The language curriculum of the professional instructor should be geared to this development.

Although semantic functions have not been as well catalogued as linguistic events, they often can be inferred from the child's play and from informal language tests administered as part of the *initial evaluations.* The *language program* then should be designed to lead to both intermediate and long term objectives. A *maintenance program* also should be devised to serve the management and motivational purposes of the program and a system for *continuing evaluation* should be employed to serve the purposes of task selection and refinement as the program continues.

In the strategic instructional design the child should be taught that language enables him to *control* the environment. He should also be taught how to *extend* his language functions and how to *integrate* language into his daily activities in all situations.

Any overview of language problems suggests that we must allow for a wide range of differences in the level of language already acquired. Some children have language with near normal syntax and phonology while others are virtually lacking all linguistic structures. Some are relatively adequate in receptive language, but are extremely limited in expressive features. Since language instruction programs frequently include such a wide range of differences among their clients, it seems appropriate that the technology for language intervention should be developed which will take into account these wide divergencies and still represent a procedure that is appropriate for individual instruction.

A language program must be extremely functional to span across such a wide range of language delays and dysfunctions. It is the purpose of this paper to suggest strategies for accomplishing this functionality. Let us begin by considering Premack's functional analysis of language.

A Functional Analysis of Language

Premack's (1) basic analysis of the functions of language involve four issues: 1) discrimination of symbols, 2) discrimination among symbols, 3) discrimination among environmental events, and 4) discriminations among sequential arrangements of the symbols. If these indeed are four basic essentials of a functional language system we should consider them carefully.

Please note that each of the four functions is a *discrimination.* Premack (1), has demonstrated that each of these discriminations can be effectively made by chimpanzees.

However, he clearly demonstrates that the functions must be separated from the training procedures used to teach the functions. The first list is a set of functions to be trained; the other is a set of procedures used to teach the functions (essentially the discriminations).

Let us first discuss the discriminations and then the procedures. The first, discrimination of symbols, is essentially a concept. For example, a symbol of some kind stands for, or represents, an object. Premack used metal backed pieces of plastics of varying shapes, sizes, textures and colors to represent words. Each piece was placed before the chimp on a magnetized slate beside an apple or a banana. Thus the symbol, or word, was carefully associated with the object. The chimp was trained to put the plastic form on the board, after which he was given the fruit.

After several such associations were learned the chimp was able to express preference by discriminating between two symbols (two forms and one type of fruit). The chimp's task was to select the language form which designated the fruit. After the chimp learned to discriminate among symbols the language program was expanded to include other meaning classes--for example, an agent (a person or another chimp) or an event (such as "give"). These functions represented the third discrimination class, that is, the discrimination among different environmental events. Finally, when the plastic strings (arrayed vertically from top to bottom) were extended to include "Mary give apple Sarah," it was clearly apparent that the chimp had learned to discriminate among sequential arrangements.

The foregoing reference to Premack's analysis of language is sufficient to make an important point: namely, language can be analyzed apart from phonology and, indeed, independent of auditory process. However, the point is made that a careful analysis of the human condition shows phonology to be an indispensible part of the complex symbol system. It does not seem conceivable that a sufficient number of different visual or audible word units can be devised or remembered in order to accommodate to the complexity of human society without using a phonemic system. Such a system reduces word parts to about fifty different phonemes with which an inexaustible number of different words can be created. Consequently, human language systems are overwhelmingly audible and are strategically phonemic in nature. These facts then predict that the job of analyzing human language is greatly more complicated than is the job of mapping the potential language of chimps.

Premack points out that the same comparative complexity (between human and chimp language) holds for the experimental task of teaching the two language systems. Let us then turn our attention to the operational task of teaching. He established a simple social transaction in teaching the chimp. The first transaction series was undertaken at feeding time. He placed a piece of fruit on the table and watched the young chimp eat it. In the second step he placed a plastic piece (symbol) beside the piece of fruit. The third step required the chimp to place the plastic on the table prior to receiving the fruit. Following this step a number of transactions were possible. Each was essentially a manipulation of some aspect of the transaction (involving a donor, an action, an object and a recipient). The donor gives the object. The recipient recieves it. The action is the act performed in the transaction of giving. The object, of course, is the specific piece of fruit.

This transaction, incidentally, is much like the agent-action-object in the context learning reported by Bloom (2) in her recent work at Columbia University. She reports on the events involving a small child and the mother during the child's early language learning phases.

Perhaps the important feature of the language transaction reported by both Bloom and Premack is that language functions are devised to fit the concrete transaction events and to give the learner an active part in the transaction. Premack observes that "this can be an advantage in training young subjects, since the control of attention is more certain when the subject is required to respond rather than merely to observe."

An example of the donor-action-object-recipient reported by Premack involved the sentence "Mary give apple Jim." This transaction and the accompanying language functions were difficult to complete because Mary was reluctant to give up the apple. The experimenter solved this problem by giving

Mary a tidbit more preferred than the fruit. Mary then completed the action.

In addition to simple sentences, Premack also demonstrated that chimps can perform correct functions with compound sentences, interrogative sentences, and correct associations on metalinguistic tasks such as "name of" and "not-name of," and "yes" and "no".

Spradlin (3) points out the importance of Premack's work as a model for training. Its primary importance is that it treats language as a system. This aspect of Premack's work comes across clearly in the many probes he made to test the chimps performance on untrained tasks. Premack taught the chimp the word for food in one context and then probed to determine if that word was used appropriately in another linguistic context. Secondly, Premack presented a complex language function, then laid out an operational procedure for testing or for establishing this function. Thirdly, Premack made it clear that language is semantic or marks a conceptual base, that is, words referred to significant classes of events in the environment. Furthermore, he has demonstrated explicit procedures for determining if the subject had the concept prior to starting language training. Finally, Premack has begun to conduct research which will resolve many of the current conflicts between psycholinguistic theory and behavioristic theory. Such a resolution is important. Linguists have much to say about structures that exist as language, and behaviorism has a technology for developing or teaching functional behavior.

Bloom's work with 19-20 month old normal children in home environments also provides provocative information about language intervention. Although her work is not experimental in the sense that she manipulated variables in the child's environment, nevertheless, she does describe functions that are similar to Premack's experimental functions. For instance, she found that children learn notions of agent-action-object as concepts which are prelinguistic. Children interact in a world of objects, events, and relations; and their perceptual-cognitive strategies suggest that their understanding of this experience includes these relational notions. Their subsequent learning of linguistic structure may depend on the prior development of certain conceptual structures.

She finds that the status of the referent (object) and the child's actions with the referent were important to the child's learning language. There seems to be a congruence between the naming, stating, asking, etc. and the actions performed with the physical referents. Of especial importance were: a) existence of the referent, b) reoccurence of the referent, c) action upon the referent, and d) non-existence where expected.

The child seems to develop understanding of the relational features of language by perceiving the context in which it is spoken. It follows that the child's comprehension (receptive language) is aided by the cues in the situation. It also follows that since he is a co-participant in an action sense he selects, names, and acts reciprocally to these same responses as performed by the adult agent. Perhaps the child becomes a mirrored facsimile of the response system of the adult performed in the physical context with him. Although the child's response unit is initially a one word unit, he soon is able to use agent-action-object functions in a response string (similar to the strings reported by Premack). The primary difference, of course, is that Bloom reports about language learned in human child response modes--using the auditory channel and audible word units. The point to point comparison of the contextual symbolization of agent-action-object, however, is striking. Premack, of course, refers to two different agents in his functions--donor and recipient. The child and the adult can function as either agent depending on the action performed on any object.

Guess, Sailor and Baer (4) use the same situational strategy in teaching language to severely retarded children. Their program involves *persons* and *things* and *actions* with persons and things in concrete operations before going to descriptions of actions with persons and things in a more abstract set of functions. In the latter the functions can be performed in the absence of the objects and physical actions. In the more advanced phases of their program, they systematically add a range of conceptual training utilizing possession, color, size, and relation. Their program is sequenced and developed to include important operational features required for evaluation and maintenance.

An important part of their strategy is their use of reference (symbolization) training, control training, self-extended control training, and intergration training. These strategic training operations are combined in a continuous series of steps (61 in all). The *reference* training involves both responding *to* and responding *with* objects and also involves the agent and action. Also it includes the productive form (spoken) and the receptive form (stimuli spoken by the *other* person).

The *control* training involves functions that lead to the child's control of environment. The assumption is that labels are powerful. The child is taught to request or to respond verbally.

Observations of natural environments (2, 5, 6, 7) imply that language is an important controlling feature within the child's environment. One way to observe the control function is to observe the subsequent event following a language response. If the request or the question results in a prompt subsequent event the control function is apparent.

Sailor, Guess and Baer (8) speculate that the function of control can be taught. That is, the child can learn that labels are powerful. Request forms can become productive events which are reinforcing to the child. For this reason the transaction should generate control behavior. The labels for objects and actions should be learned at signals for control functions that the child can imitate. His learning that productive speech has consequences that control events may be a critical part of the language acquisition process.

Marshall, Hegrenes and Goldstein (6) observed that mothers of retarded children use a larger percentage of mand (command) behavior than do mothers of normal children. It may be that these mands result in motor performance by the child which reinforces the mother's manding behavior. The child may comply to the mother's commands by acting rather than talking. The possible result of this type of control may be a talking parent and a non-verbal, acting child. Clearly, the instructions in such cases should be changed to provide additional opportunities for the child to experience control through verbal behavior. This objective might be accomplished by teaching mands to the child during the early transaction events. In this way the demonstration of child-agent control might be accelerated.

Extension

Sailor, Guess and Baer (8) also suggest that an important strategy in language learning is *self-extended control.* They point out that, even after the child learns the importance of speech for control, he is bound to find that he cannot control his environment extensively because he does not know the labels for all the necessary things, actions and actions-with-things. Thus, it is necessary for the child to extend his referents. This may be done by teaching him to request further information. The productive strategy for extension, then, may be self initiated as soon as the child learns a new class of behavior--question asking. The question forms should be simple--probably not a complete interrogative string such as, "What is that?" or "What are you doing?" Perhaps a simple "What that?" or "What doing?" would serve for the child with a limited, functional grammar.

Integration

The term *integration* implies that language is or becomes an integral part of the child's behavior. Stated simply, language that is learned is used. New forms become active forms. Information gained through questions is stored and used. A new speech form that is correctly articulated in the clinic is also correctly used in the home or in the play activities at school.

Instructional procedures should contribute to integrations. Indeed, strategies for integration are among the most important in language teaching. Terms such as *carry-over, generalization,* and *transfer of training* are frequently used to identify techniques developed by different clinicians. Frequently, the techniques serve to generalize the usage from one context to another within the formal teaching environment.

Perhaps the control, extension, and integration strategies can be developed for use in a range of natural environments. These and similar procedures may greatly reduce the time required by teacher and clinicians in teaching language to special children.

Let us conclude this functional summary by saying that language is a complex system of rules and symbolic representations (meanings) which are presented and received as speech events. The speech events take place in an interpersonal arrangement in which performance is influenced by the feedback from the other person. The child in a remarkably short time is expected to learn the complex language system, the complex topography of motor events (speech), and the skills that enable him to cope effectively with the complex, contingent events in which he must communicate his language functions. If the child has failed to learn any part of this complex set of features, the teacher's task is to help him to learn the missing parts and to put it all together.

In the next section we will discuss procedures that may be used to plan and carry out a language teaching program.

A General Analysis of a Language Teaching Program

This section is designed to show how a clinician might proceed to develop a functional language program. The main emphasis is upon the procedures and the technology used in planning and maintaining the program. The strategy is divided into four parts: 1) Initial Evaluation, 2) Language Program, 3) Program Maintenance, and 4) Program Evaluation. The *initial evaluation* part discusses ways to determine the child's current level of language functioning and suggests a point of departure for language training. In a behavioral sense the initial evaluation should provide a baseline for planning, for comparison with subsequent stages of development, and for making decisions about the design of the language program, the maintenance strategies, and the subsequent evaluations. In a functional sense the initial evaluation should map out the child's concepts which serve as a basis for word acquisitions and linguistic relationships.

The *language program* refers to the language curriculum that the instructor will attempt to teach. It includes a sequential series of phases that will be used to reach the projected goal for this child. The curriculum includes both the structures and the functions of language that the instructor determines to be necessary for the child to reach the projected level of language functioning.

The *program maintenance* part includes the scheduling, the selecting and arranging of stimulus materials and the training environment, the criteria levels used for each sequential phase, the incentives to be used for this child, and the extensions to be used as part of the long term program. The chief purpose of the maintenance program is to assure that the effectiveness of the program is continued throughout its full range.

The *program evaluation* model includes probe evaluations and periodic long term evaluations. Both are formative evaluations but each is intended to provide strategically different information, nevertheless. The probe evaluations provide frequent checks upon the effectiveness of the instructional sequences and strategies. The periodic evaluations help the instructor evaluate the general progress of the child and guides the redesigning of the program if the data indicates that the planning and the maintenance strategies are inappropriate.

The four part strategy is intended as a covenience for the instructor in preparing programs for individual children and for preparing general strategies for language instruction. The author has also found the system to be useful in organizing the mounting volume of good work that is available to the language teacher. The parts are interrelated and should not be regarded as discrete. Nevertheless each serves to emphasize an important and natural aspect of the total program.

Initial Evaluation and Planning

The evaluation recommended here is not intended to be a diagnosis of the child's etiological problem. Rather the intent is to provide the instructor with information that can be used directly in planning for the language training program.

Auditory testing may provide information that is especially important to language instruction. There is an obvious connection between poor hearing and poor language acquisition. The reduced input of the hearing impaired child may result in an impoverishment in language stimulation. Improvements in hearing testing techniques have brought accurate evaluations to all age children with whatever reduced level of functioning (9, 10). Early detection and diagnosis also may lead to a special preschool language program for deaf and hard of hearing children. Programs of training are also available now for multiply handicapped deaf children (11). Since receptive processes are obviously involved in the child's communication, the teacher should give careful attention to auditory data in the child's case report. Hearing losses may also indicate the need for a special program of auditory training prior to or as a part of corrective speech activities for children throughout the school years.

Sensory impairments, both auditory and visual, may prolong the child's sensory-motor period and require more stimulation in order for the child to acquire conceptual orientations that are later mapped as functions of language. Bricker and Bricker (12) describe the developmental bridging that can be devised to give the young handicapped child a better set of motor and vocal imitation skills. These skills can assist the handicapped child to develop early language functions.

Initial Behavioral Evaluation

In addition to physical and sensory examinations the clinician or teacher should look carefully at several behavioral functions. Prominent among the important "entry" behaviors are attending, motor control, and motor and vocal imitation (for very young or severely impaired children) and inappropriate or disruptive behavior for older children. The selection of functional reinforcers are likely to be important for subsequent effectiveness with all children.

The time required subsequently to train appropriate entry behaviors for children with limited development may cover several sessions. Other children may respond more quickly while still other children may have appropriate behaviors at the beginning session. Gross behaviors may be easily controlled with appropriate contingencies, usually positive attention or other positive reinforcers. A number of effective

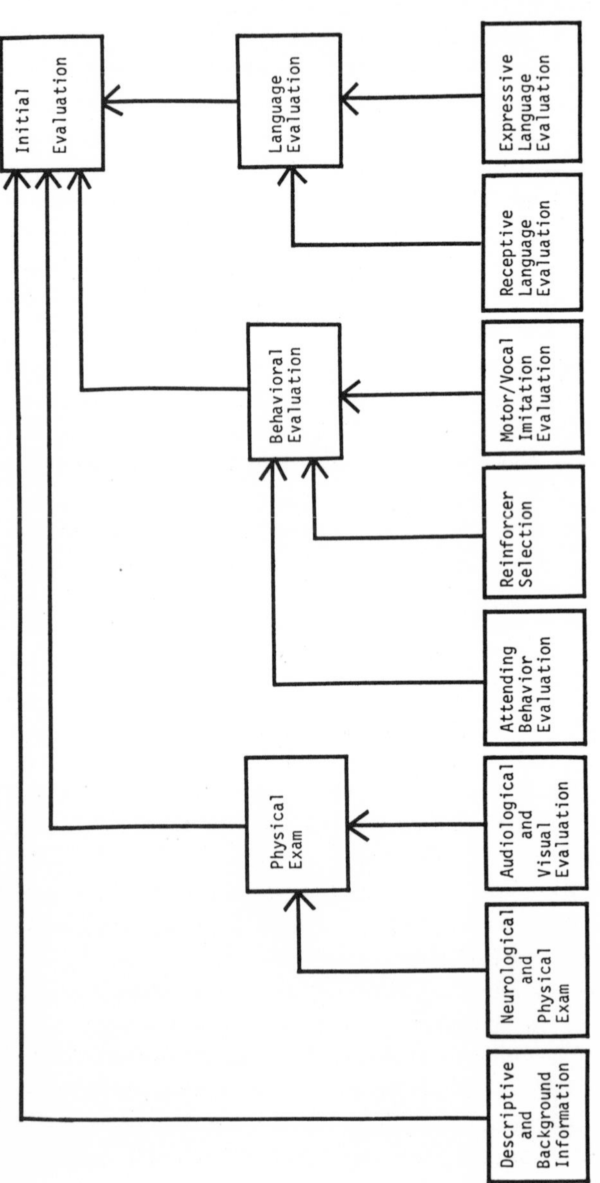

INITIAL EVALUATION AND PLANNING

Figure 1

Reproduced from ,"*Teaching Special Children*" by Haring and Philips. Used with permission of McGraw-Hill Book Company.

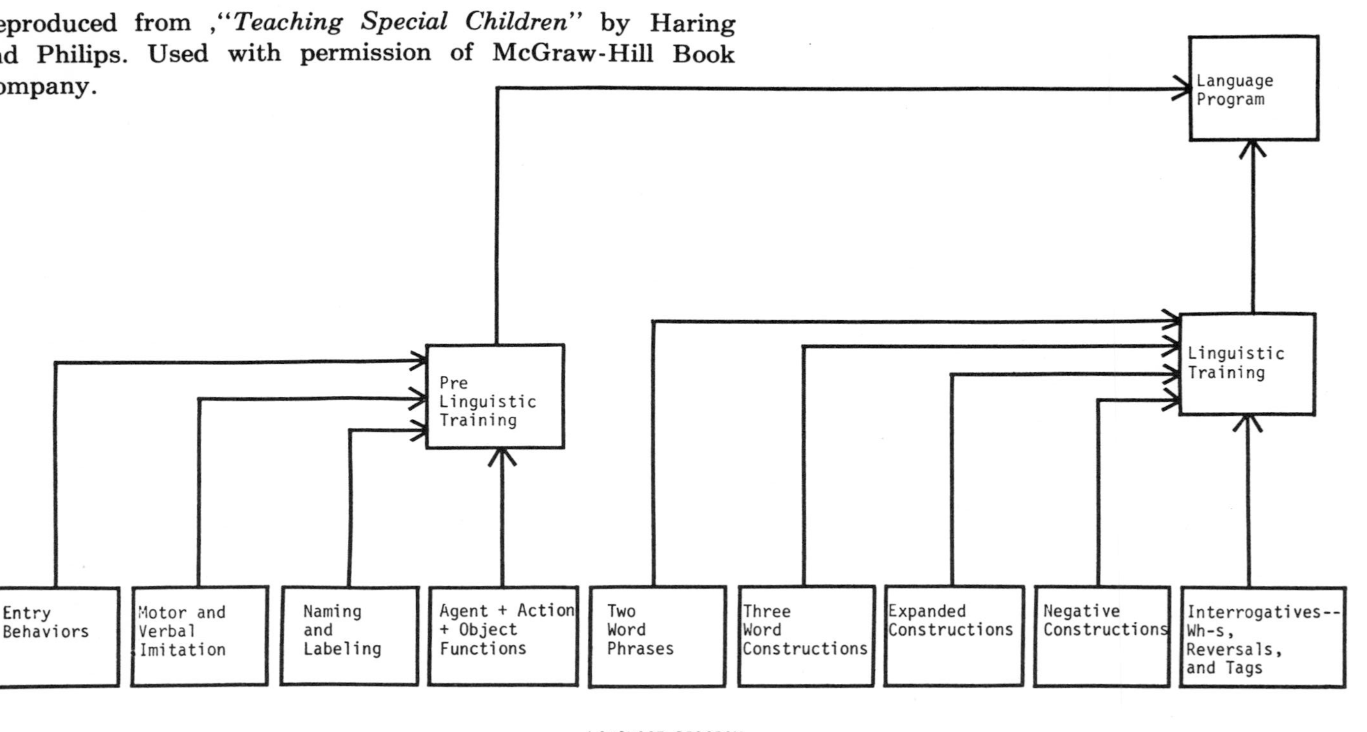

LANGUAGE PROGRAM

Figure 2

procedures have been devised for increasing desired behavior and extinguishing inappropriate behavior.

Evaluations of motor and vocal imitation may play an important part in the behavioral evaluations of severely limited children. Sailor, Guess and Baer (8) discuss the importance of generalized imitation skills. They also offer three procedures for training motor and vocal imitations prior to the initiation of language training. Striefel (13) has developed a manual for detailed programming of motor imitation.

Procedures for selecting functional reinforcers have also been discussed in several sources.

Ultimately the effectiveness of a reinforcer is determined by the function it plays. The functionality is determined by the response data. If the response increases in frequency of correct response, the reinforcer is considered to be functionally effective. Otherwise, as Lindsley (14) has pointed out, a response is simply a *movement* and a consequent event is simply an *arrangement* with no apparent contingency effects.

Initial Language Evaluation

An initial language evaluation can be as simple as listening appropriately to a child and making informal assessments of his language performance. More often the instructor should use more careful or more systematic efforts to sample language behavior and to record data that can be used as a baseline for subsequent comparisons. The recorded information can be used as a basis for planning, for indications of progress, or as a means of comparison with the reports given by others who talk with the child in other settings. There are often considerable variations in the way a child may use language in different settings with different people. For this reason, one strategy to use in sampling is to set up a variety of arrangements and different tasks as a means of evoking language.

A prominent aim of a performance baseline is to determine a functional range of variability for the child under different stimulus arrangements. Thus the baseline should not be a product of one observation, but rather should be based upon a continuous assessment of behavior over a period of time until a functional range has been obtained. Thus the initial evaluation is extended to later phases of the program and serves only as a first sampling in a series of samples that guide the language training program and provide the information that is used to evaluate progress.

The Language Program

The language program is built upon the information developed in the initial language evaluation. However, there are several assumptions used in designing the program to be followed. The first is that language is acquired, learned, in a series of phases or stages. Thus, the instructor can set down a predicted sequential design of language units. The design is a practical curriculum which includes a goal, in addition to the sequential series of phases. In the instance shown, the goal is a level of language use comparable to a normal preschool child. The child who might fit into this hypothetical program may not be a child in the 3 to 4 age range but, regardless, the language curriculum is generally the sequential program that we think happens to a small child in a natural environment with the informal assistance of parents, other children and friends of the family.

The assumptions about the ways in which language should be taught to the over-age child are also important. But first let us look at the program. There are two sub-goals: prelinguistic training and linguistic training. The former designation implies that there are no linguistic rules or no strings of words learned during this phase for which syntactic rules imply.

The prelinguistic training, as shown, includes *entry behaviors, motor* and *verbal imitation, naming* and *labeling,* and the *symbolic functions* of *agent, action* and *object.* All of these activities have usually been acquired by a normal child by 18-19 months. In this illustrative statement we will discuss each of the four phases only briefly. Each phase can be comprehensively programmed by adding small steps leading up to the completion of the behavioral unit.

It is important to say here that the suggested are very likely antecedent to other more complex language learning phases and should be carefully built into the developmental plan by instructors of early language learning problems.

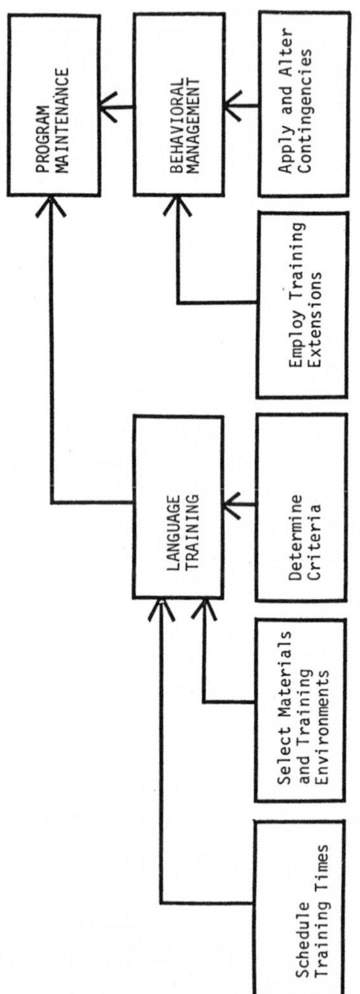

MAINTENANCE STRATEGIES

Figure 3

Quickly, the rationale for these four phases are in order:

1) To prepare the child attentionally (to watch carefully the actions of the instructor and to listen to the verbal events), to assume appropriate sitting posture during instruction, and to handle the objects used in instruction in an appropriate functional way;

2) To learn to imitate gestures and vocal signs and to demonstrate a generalized imitative skill;

3) To learn the symbolic relationship between a spoken word and an object and the naming of several such objects; and

4) To learn the words for the agent who participates with the child, the actions that are performed interpersonally and the objects that are physically present.

The functional words learned at this stage are individual words that are presumably combined later into word strings of two, three or more units. The individual (holophrastic) word phase is thought to be important to the child's mapping of the orientating relationships between people (agents), objects (physical world), and actions (functional movements) in which he participates. Piaget (15) speculates that the child develops a conceptual (representational) system during these early motoric and symbolic experiences that serve as the basis for subsequent language learning.

The second subheading, *linguistic training,* includes two word phrases, three word constructions, expanded constructions, negative constructions, and interrogatives. Again, each of these phases can be broken down into subprograms with as many operational steps as the instructor should decide to use. For instance, Sailor, Guess and Baer (8) have worked out a program of 61 phases leading up to language performances required for pre-reading activities. Each phase in the sequence can be further subdivided. In the following section the instruction program for the five phases is detailed programmatically.

In order, the five linguistic phases suggest that:

1) *Two word phrases* are extensions of the naming and the one-word agent, action, object phases, (usually, agent + object, agent + action, or action + object;

2) *Three word phrases* represent further expansions to include, usually, agent + action + object strings;

3) *Expansions* that include adjectives, adverbs and prepositions;

4) *Negative constructions* including "Wh" questions, who, what, etc.; and

5) *Interrogatives* including alternative "Wh" forms, reversals (Is he running?) and tag questions (He is running, right?).

Each of these phases of language acquisition can be functionally taught as receptive or expressive processes. The format as shown by the work of Bricker and Bricker (16) is to present the linguistic form first as an imitative operation, next as a receptive operation and finally as an expressive operation. These are assumed to represent the order of difficulty and also the sequence which allows the teacher to use antecedent operations most effectively.

Maintenance Strategies

The term "maintenance strategies" suggests that there are instructional procedures that aid the teacher-clinician to continue the program effectively from start to finish. This literally is the design of the maintenance program. The program has two subparts. One part relates to behavioral management and the other to language training. There are two principal features of behavioral management that are treated here--the application and alteration of contingencies and the use of training extensions and environments. The maintenance features under language training are scheduling, materials selection, and criteria.

Contingencies. In simple terms the contingency is applied by the clinician-teacher to increase desired behaviors and to decrease undesired ones. A useful discussion of contingencies is provided by McReynolds (17) under the heading of Contingencies and Consequences in Speech Therapy. In her discussion a contingency is a consequent event. She is interested in the kinds of consequent events that can be used with antecedent events (stimuli) to increase the efficiency of training.

The consequence most frequently used by clinicians is positive reinforcement. The reinforcer is a subsequent event to the response of the child. The purpose of the subsequent event, of course, is to increase the child's rate of responding. It is combined as a teaching strategy with carefully programmed antecedent events (stimuli) which also have shaping properties for the child's speech topography. For instance, when the clinician monitors a word or a phonemic unit to the child, he also may have a direct subsequent effect upon the child's speech. The skillful utilization of antecedent and subsequent events comprises the primary basis of face-to-face language instruction.

In language training sessions the use of teacher attention and the selective use of social approval form the primary bases for contingency management. However, the use of tokens which allows the child to select a desired tangible reinforcer (after the session or periodically during the training sessions), also may stimulate greater rates of responding. The teacher should study the child and use both antecedent and subsequent events in relation to the child's already acquired interests and his social history. The above suggestion sounds extremely familiar to all good teachers. The only point really in emphasizing contingency management as a part of the maintenance system is to point out the systematic and precise way the system may be used, as well as the utility it may have for any teacher-clinician in analyzing the response events of a non-responding child.

An interesting issue on response contingencies has been suggested by Spradin (3). He suggests that a single rein-

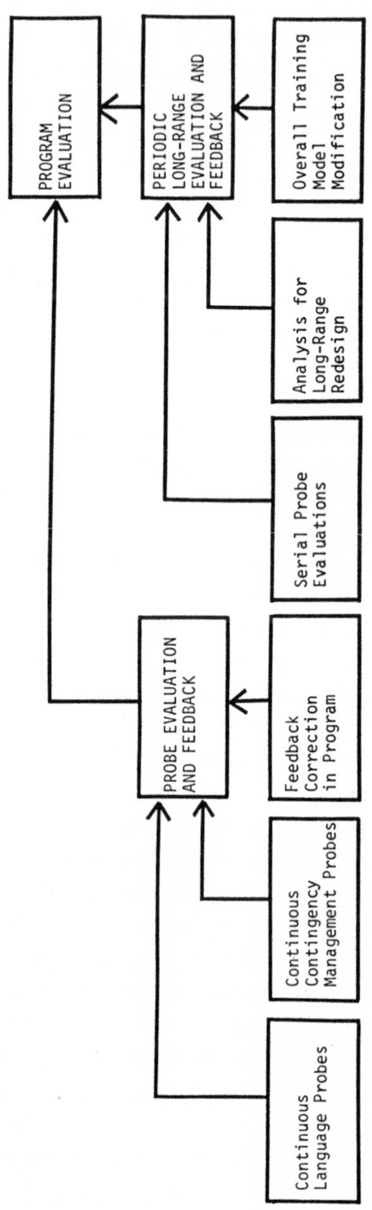

PROGRAM EVALUATION MODEL

Figure 4

forcer applied to many different kinds of linguistic responses may be inefficient. He points out that if one looks at the learning of children's language in the natural environment, there is a congruence between verbal response and reinforcer. For example, if a child says "ice cream," "milk," "toast," or "kitty" as a request, there is likely to be a different reinforcer associated with each of those responses. Spradlin speculates that this congruence or uniqueness of reinforcer associated with each response helps keep the child from confusing responses.

It seems probably that both the stimulus features of antecedent events and the response supporting features of subsequent events become part of the child's semantic orientations in learning language. This possibility is already suggested by the work of Bloom (2), Broen (5), Farwell (7) in studying children in natural environments. Perhaps the cue to the child's semantic acquisitions is the close, intimate way in which the child and adult respond to each other (the agents) and to the objects and actions in their shared environment. In the naturally occuring, reciprocal chain of events, the participants serve as each other's antecedent and reciprocal events. In responding to the adult's visual and vocal acts the child receives double exposure to his own receptive and expressive language functions. That is, he receives language events, initiates language events, and receives reinforcing confirmations to both. The child's awareness is that the mother's speech is important to him; and, in turn, his is important to mother. Both events in the chain have orienting and reinforcing effects.

Training Extensions and Environments. A training extension may be any effective carry-over or transfer (in time or location) beyond the extent of the training session.

Sailor, Guess, and Baer (8) have developed an interesting procedure for effecting self-extended control. They reason that, as the child with limited language learned to control his immediate environment with the word units at his command, he finds great need for other units he does not know. He does not know the necessary labels for the things, actions, and actions-with-things he wishes to use. Thus it is important to extend the child's referents, mainly by teaching him to request further instruction in specific contexts. This is taught in the form of questions, such as "What that?" in response to unknown things and "What (are) you doing?" in response to unknown actions. "In effect the child learns to request further, specific training outputs, based on his discrimination of what he does not know from what he already knows. This can be conceptualized as two simple chains controlled by two complex discriminative stimulus classes: previously trained events produce labels, whereas not-previously-trained-events produce questions" (8).

Two operational issues apply to this strategy. First, the child must be taught question asking as a response class or he must already have this behavior prior to the instruction series. The other issue is the possibility of teaching broad classes of behavior as strategies for the development of still other classes. Instead of reinforcing individual units (only) as a strategy of instruction, perhaps the instructor should select and reinforce broad classes that can become a functional part of the child's learning history.

Language Maintenance. The maintenance features which support the ongoing language program are in many respects like those which have just been discussed. As a further point of emphasis, however, a number of conductive issues can be served by effective scheduling, selection of materials, and use of criteria. Each of these features play an important part in the programmatic effectiveness of language training.

It is unnecessary to tell any parent or teacher that a child is variable. However, the actual method of recording systematic variations in the child's daily cycles may not have been tried. If the child's behavior is stable and appropriate in the language training session, this issue may seem unimportant. However, if the child is unresponsive or hyperactive, there may be better scheduling strategies that can be used. Simple charting procedures (discussed in the next section) might be used in altering the time for training sessions.

Materials selection is a functional part of the total stimulus program for any child. The teacher should be urged to plan individual programs for each child using available materials and rationales as they fit into the programs. Often the unique patterns of interest for children suggest homespun strategies that teachers can uniquely employ. An issue of special value is for the teacher to have a wide range of materials and arrange contexts for training. In such arrangements the child is likely to gain added dimensions of meaning and usage. A characteristic noted in some badly planned language programs is a uni-dimensional use of stimulus materials. The interest level of both child and teacher are usually not maintained when the language "games" become limited and esthetically bleak.

The use of performance criteria can be effectively used to plan and maintain a schedule of events over an extended period of time. Language training is maintained through a number of phases. These phases must be identified and performance levels attained by the child before the program is moved along to the next phase. In the reports on language training the term "criterion" means simply that the child attained the required number of, or correct percentage of, responses during the session. The use of prescribed criteria is thus a strategy that is reflected in the data record on each child and is used as the bases for moving the child along through the program.

Evaluation Program

An evaluation program is planned and maintained for a number of important purposes. In addition to the evaluation used to determine initial baseline levels of functioning and initial language planning, there are other short and long term uses of evaluation programs (or procedures). For instance, the clinician needs feedback on the short term progress of the child, on the effectiveness of contingencies, and on the rate of the correct responding (relative to criteria). Subtle changes in strategy are dependent upon immediate data feedback. Clinical hunches are useful, but cannot substitute for objective, direct information about the effects of antecedent and subsequent events.

Simple reliable procedures have been developed for charting and graphing behavior and for maintaining a cumulative record. The latter shows a record of progress and reveals differences in performance dimensions under various "experimental" conditions. Along with procedures for recording behavior, strategies for using a variety of recorders have emerged. Parents, teaching aides, older children and even children themselves have been trained to record events critical to the program.

Continuous language probes are used with great frequency in language maintenance. Probes are used to sample a child's level of performance in specific parameters of the program. Usually the clinician will sample the child's performance on a phase before the training for that unit is begun. In that case the probe provides a specific baseline to use in proceeding with the unit. Also a probe can be used to check on performance maintenance for phases that have already been completed. In some instances probes show the need to recycle back to an earlier training phase to reestablish a performance unit that has been lost. At other times there may need to be a probe of the effects of a contingency system to see if it is functional.

A typical probe might involve the sampling of several words or phonemic units in a class of responses that have been taught or are soon to be taught. The responses can be charted and reviewed in relation to criteria or to anticipated baselines. Probes usually are mini-replications of the same stimulus-response (antecedent-subsequent event) units that have been or will be taught.

Frequent use of feedback derived from data descriptive of short-term effects qualifies the clinician-teacher as an experimental agent because the information aids in refining and improving the procedures. Perhaps it is not enough to develop a set of procedures that result in progress. The aim should be to develop an optimal system that results in maximum progress within a given period of time. Efficiencies developed in this way also can be described and built into subsequent programming.

In such efforts data developed for long-term evaluation also is extremely useful. This data may include tabulations of short-term data, serial probe evaluations, and periodic broader samplings of performance that compares back to data derived in the initial evaluation. These data, in aggregate, enable the clinician to develop major changes in the program and/or to substantiate the long range design.

Summary

Language can be taught, and indeed *is* taught, in both natural and planned environments. The mother and/or teacher-clinician uses a simple transaction system. This system, whether it is informally employed or carefully designed, involves improvisional features that enable the adult to teach language functions. In this context, *to teach* means that the adult helps the child map out the relationships between symbols and environmental events, that is, agent + action + object relationships. Probably the child is able to affix labels to events that he has learned to conceptualize. The teaching process then is limited at all times to the range of the child's semantic functions. The language curriculum of the professional instructor should be geared to this development. However, in all probability the range of experience in language training contributes to the range of semantic functions while at the same time mapping the symbolic features that eventually become a linguistic code. Although semantic functions have not been as well catalogued as linguistic events, they often can be inferred from the child's play, from sensorimotor tests, and from informal language tests.

Important sources of information for planning language programs include functional analysis of behavior, psycholinguistics, and cognitive structure. The last may be especially important in determining the relationships between the cognitive and the linguistic structures in language development.

Language is viewed as a complex, generative system. Instructions in key units of language may generate other units. Instructions in key strategies also may stimulate new language acquisition. Perhaps the ultimate knowledge about teaching language to children will lead to selected interventions that will key other desired changes.

Ideally, too, the transactions that are maintained will involve both planned and natural environments, the latter figuring actively in the control, extension, and integration phases of language acquisition.

References

1. Premack, E. A functional analysis of behavior. *J. Exp. Anal. Behav. 14,* 107, (1970).

2. Bloom, L. Semantic features in language development. In *Language of the Mentally Retarded.* Edited by Schiefelbusch, R. L. University Park Press, Baltimore, (1972).

3. Spradlin, J. E. Psycholinguistic training with retarded children. Speech given at a symposium "Psycholinguistic Development in Children: Implications for Children with Developmental Disabilities." Sponsored by the Department of Health Rehabilitation Services, Division of Retardation, Tampa, Florida, (1973).

4. Guess, D., Sailor, W., and Baer, D. M. To teach language to retarded children. Unpublished manuscript. University of Kansas, (1973).

5. Broen, P. A. The verbal environment of the language-learning child. *ASHA Monograph No. 17,* (1972).

6. Marshall, N.R., Hegrenes, J.R. and Goldstein, S. Verbal interactions: Mothers and their retarded children versus mothers and their nonretarded children. *Amer. J. Ment. Defic. 77,* 418, (1973).

7. Farwell, C.B. The language spoken to children. In *Committee on Linguistics, Papers and Reports on Child Language Development,* Vols. 5 and 6. Stanford University, Palo Alto, (1973).

8. Sailor, W., Guess, D., and Baer, D. M. An experimental program for teaching functional language to verbally deficient children. *Mental Retardation, 11,* 27, (1973).

9. Lloyd, L.L., and Fulton, R.T. Audiology's contribution to communications programming with the retarded. *Language Intervention with the Retarded.* Edited by McLean, J.E., Yoder, D.E. and Schiefelbusch, R.L., University Park Press, Baltimore, (1972).

10. Fulton, R.T. A program of developmental research in audiologic procedures. In *Language of the Mentally*

Retarded. Edited by Schiefelbusch, R.L. University Park Press, Baltimore, (1972).

11. Berger, S.L. A clinical program for developing multimodal language responses with atypical deaf children. In *Language Intervention with the Retarded.* Edited by McLean, J. E. Yoder, D. E., and Schiefelbusch, R. L. University Park Press, Baltimore, p.212, (1972).

12. Bricker, D. D., and Bricker, W. A. Early childhood intervention. Unpublished manuscript. George Peabody College, (1973).

13. Striefel, S. *A Motor Imitation Program.* Managing Behavior. Behavior Modification: Teaching a Child to Imitate. H & H Enterprises, Inc. Lawrence, Kansas, (1974).

14. Lindsley, O.R. Direct measurement and prosthesis of retarded behavior. *J. Educ. 147,* 68, (1964).

15. Piaget, J. Piaget's theory. In *Carmichal's Manual of Child Psychology.* Vol. I. Edited by Mussen, P. John Wiley, New York, p. 703, (1973).

16. Bricker, W. A. and Bricker, D. D. An early language training strategy. *Language Perspectives - Acquisitions, Retardation and Intervention.* Edited by Schiefelbusch, R. L. and Lloyd, L. L. University Park Press, (1974).

17. McReynolds, L. V. Contingencies and consequences in speech therapy. *J. Speech Hearing Disorders 35,* (1970).

MENTAL HEALTH IN CHILDREN, Volume III
Edited By D. V. Siva Sankar

DIFFERENCES IN THE CONTENT OF SPEECH OF GIRLS AND BOYS AGES 6 TO 16

Louis A. Gottschalk

University of California at Irvine
Irvine, California 92717

SUMMARY

Five minute speech samples were obtained, in response to purposely ambiguous and non-directive standardized instructions, from 109 Caucasian children, stratified for sex and grade, in a public school system in Southern California. These speech samples were scored for thematic content according to content categories included in a group of (Gottschalk-Gleser) content analysis scales for the measurement of psychological states. All those content categories in which the mean difference between sexes was significant at the 0.10 level (two-tailed test) or better were noted. These sex differences are compared to content differences observed in the language of adults.

* From the Communications and Measurement Laboratory, Department of Psychiatry and Human Behavior, College of Medicine, University of California at Irvine, Irvine, California (92717).

The technical assistance of Daniel Bates, B. A., and Claire A. Cable and the statistical assistance of Herman Birch, Ph.D., are acknowledged with appreciation.

The measurement of transient psychological states, sensitively and with specificity, precision, and objectivity, has always posed serious and unsolved obstacles. Many of these measurement problems have been recently solved for the assessment of such states in adults by Gottschalk and his collaborators through the content analysis of speech (1, 2). Since it is our intention to use these studies with adults as a paradigm and as guidelines for the development of a similar measurement method with children, a survey of the content analysis approach of Gottschalk is appropriate. After summarizing key aspects of this content analysis method, an illustration of the usefulness of this procedure will be provided through reporting sex differences found in the content of speech of a sample of children (N=109) ranging in age from six to 16 years.

The approach of Gottschalk and his co-workers uses a function that is uniquely human, namely, verbal behavior and its content or semantic aspect. Small samples of speech, as brief as two to five minutes, have been found sufficient to provide objective measures of various psychological states such as anxiety, hostility outward, hostility inward, social alienation-personal disorganization (schizophrenic syndrome), human relations, hope, achievement strivings, and so forth.

The development of this method has involved a long series of steps. It has required that the psychological dimension to be measured (for example, anxiety or hostility) be carefully defined; that a unit of communication, the grammatical clause, be specified; that the content, i.e., the lexical cues, be spelled out from which a receiver of the verbal message infers the occurence of the psychological state; that the linguistic, principally syntactical, cues conveying intensity also be specified; that differential weights, signifying relative intensity, be assigned for semantic and linguistic cues whenever appropriate; and that a systematic means be arrived at of correcting for the number of words spoken per unit time so that one individual can be compared to others or to himself on different occasions with respect to the magnitude of a particular psychological state as derived from the content of verbal behavior. The method requires also that a formal scale of weighted content categories be specified for each psychological dimension to be measured; that content analysis technicians be trained to apply these to typescripts of human speech (much as biochemical technicians are trained to run various complex chemical determinations by following prescribed procedures); that the interscorer reliability of two trained content technicians using the same scale be 0.85 or above (a modest but respectable level of consensus in the psychological sciences for these kinds of measurements). Moreover, a set of construct validation studies have had to be carried out to establish exactly what this content analysis procedure is measuring, and these validation studies have included the use of four kinds of criterion measures: psychological, psychophysiological, psychopharmocological, and psychobiochemical. On the basis of these construct validation studies, changes have been made in the content categories and their associated weights of each specific scale in the direction of maximizing the correlations between the content analysis scores with these various criterion measures.

Construct validation is a step-by-step process that requires repeated re-examination and re-testing, in new situations, of the constructs being evaluated. After initial validation studies were completed in adults (ages 17 through 70) for verbal behavior measures of the psychological constructs of anxiety, hostility out, hostility in, ambivalent hostility, social alienation-personal disorganization (the schizophrenic syndrome), a large variety of additional investigations were carried out using these verbal behavior measures. These have provided considerable data on the ways in which such verbal behavior scores relate to other relevant measurable phenomena. These data have afforded evidence as to how the constructs measured by these verbal behavior measures "fit" with other empirical data (3, 4, 5, 6, 7, 8).

The formulation of these psychological states has been deeply influenced by the position that they have biological roots. Both the definition of each separate state and the selection of the specific verbal content items used as cues for inferring each state were influenced by the decision that whatever psychological state was measured by this content analysis approach should, whenever possible, be associated with some biological characteristic of the individual in addition to some psychological aspect of some social situation. Hence, not only psychological but also physiological, biochemical, and pharmacological criterion measures have all provided further construct validation.

These long term studies with adults have provided empirically derived steps for measuring the magnitude of psychological states in adults.

Methods and Procedures

Several steps were involved in extending the content analysis of speech, now available as a measurement method for psychological states in adults, to a method equally applicable to children. These steps may be enumerated:

1. Obtaining speech samples from children under such circumstances that there are minimal effects of the means, context, or person eliciting the speech and so that the major variance in the psychological scores derived from the content analyses of the speech originates from the speaker.

2. Establishing a satisfactory level of scoring reliability from the content analysis technicians.

3. Obtaining a cross-sectional set of speech samples from a stratified sample of normative children in terms of sex and educational level (grades one through twelve).

4. Scoring all speech samples according to the scales previously developed for adults and calculating preliminary norms, including percentile scores, for sex and grade level for each psychological dimension.

5. Determining to what extent, if any, there are quantitative differences in affect and other psychological scores according to sex and age.

6. Initiating new validation studies for each of the content analysis scales.

Procedure for Eliciting Speech Samples from Children

Our goal with children was, as it was with adults, to develop a measurement procedure for psychological states that was both highly sensitive to rapid phasic fluctuations in emotions as well as to the more gradual and slow changes in the magnitude of psychological responses customarily called traits. Obviously, the means and personal characteristics of the individual evoking speech, as well as the situational context in which the speech is brought forth, are all quite capable of influencing the kind and quantity of the psychological responses, especially of a very sensitive psychological measure. But since the major goal of such a measurement tool is that it reflects primarily a process going on in the speaker, namely a psychobiological process, either innate or acquired and, in any event, internalized, we try to standardize or otherwise control these external variables and stimuli so that the major portion of the variance in the content abnalysis scores originates in the speaker. Once a reliable and validated psychological measure has been developed, the effect of varying these external factors one at a time (the means of eliciting the speech, the interviewer, and the situational context) can be investigated; in fact, such studies can provide further construct validation of the measure.

Laguna Beach School District Study

This was our initial cross-sectional study of 109 Caucasian children, stratified for sex and grade, in the Laguna Beach School District. In this study, as was done in our adult studies (1, 2, 9), standardized procedures were used in eliciting verbal behavior. These instructions, it can be seen, are purposely ambiguous and non-directive, so that they aim, like projective test stimuli, to catalyze the speaker to reveal the self without being aware of so doing.

Borrowing directly from our procedure with adults (2) research team members eliciting speech samples from children first repeated the standardized instructions used with adults.

"I have a tape recorder here and here is a microphone. I would like you to speak into this microphone, please."

"This is a study of speaking and conversational habits. Upon a signal from me, I would like you to speak for five minutes about any interesting or dramatic life experiences you may have had. Once you have started I will be here listening to you, but I would prefer not to reply to any questions you may feel like asking me until the five minute period is over. Do you have any questions you would like to ask me now before we start? Well, then you may begin."

If the child was unable to respond, the following instructions were tried: "I'll tell you what to do; try telling me any stories you like about yourself."

If the child did not respond after about one minute, the instructions were further modified, "Try telling me any stories about any one you know." (Pause) "Or try telling me about any television program you have recently seen."

Following these speech samples, other data were obtained on these children: (1) demographic data; (2) school grades; (3) I.Q. and other test scores from school records; (4) Minnesota Percepto-Diagnostic Test (10); (5) psychological questionnaire battery.

In this preliminary report, only the differences in the content of speech of the girls and boys will be detailed.

Content analysis technicians, not informed of the purpose of this study, scored the speech samples obtained from these children on the following scales: anxiety, hostility outward, hostility inward, ambivalent hostility, social alienation-personal disorganization, achievement strivings, human relations, and hope.*

Statistical comparisons were made of the frequency of use by girls and boys of each content category of each scale, using a special program (11) on the PDP 10 computer. All those content categories in which the mean difference between sexes was significant at the 0.10 level (two-tailed test) or better are listed below. The scale from which the content category was taken is identified in this listing.

Results

The sexual differences in thematic content of the speech of the children are summarized in Table 1 and are listed below.

Girls used significantly ($p<.05$) *used more of the following speech content categories than boys:*

1. References to the self expressing concern for other people; references to missing others when they are away (HRSA3A).

2. References in which people are alienated, drawn apart, kept at a distance from one another (HRSC3B).

3. Interpersonal references involving the self having thoughts, feelings, or reported actions of avoidance, leaving,

TABLE I

Differences in the content of Speech of Boys and Girls Ages 6 to 16

Speech Content Category	Mean Use (per 100 words)		P (two tailed, Mann Whitney U tests)
	Boys	Girls	
1. HRSA3A	.000	.028	.05
2. HRSC3B	.006	.040	.01
3. SA-PDIA1	.002	.058	.05
4. SA-PDID2	.567	.602	.05
5. HOS1C2	.098	.117	.05
6. ANX2B2	.192	.335	.05
7. HRSH1A	.031	.076	.10
8. HRSA3B	.000	.018	.10
9. HRSB3	.197	.379	.10
10. ANX6A3	.048	.131	.10
11. SA-PDIIIB1	1.094	.845	.05
12. ANX5D1	.024	.001	.05

* All of the content categories that were examined in the speech samples of the children are given in the appendix to this paper, and these are listed according to the content analysis scale in which these content categories originated. The lettered and numbered notations below and in Table 1 are a short-hand way of specifying the content analysis scale and content category, e.g. (HRSA3A) refers to Human Relations Scale and content category A3A.

deserting, spurning, not understanding of others (SA-PDIAI).

4. Interpersonal references to others being intact, satisfied, healthy, well (SA-PDID2).

5. References to overt hostility outward, specifically, self criticizing or depreciating others in a vague or mild manner (HOSIC2).

6. References to injury, tissue or physical damage or anxiety about injury or threat of such experienced by or occurring to others (ANX2B2).

Girls used more ($p < 0.10$) of the following speech categories than boys:

7. References to the self giving to, supporting, helping or protecting others (HRSAIA).

8. References to others expressing concern about the self; references to others missing the self when one is away (HRSA3B).

9. References of a non-evaluative sort to any kinds of human relations which are generalized or ambiguous as to person(s) interacted with and impersonal (HRSB3).

10. References, by word or phrase, to anxiety and/or fear involving the self, without distinguishing the type of source of anxiety (ANX6A3).

Boys used significantly more ($p < .05$) of the following speech content cagegories than girls.

11. Repetition of ideas in a sequence: words separated only by a word (SA-PDIIIB1).

12. Denial of shame anxiety. References to denial of ridicule, inadequacy, shame, embarrassment, humiliation, overexposure of deficiencies or private details, or threat of such (ANX5D1).

Discussion

The findings of this study of the speech content of children, evoked in response to standardized instructions, point to differences in the speech content of boys and girls ages 6 to 16. Our sample of children is not large enough (109) to permit us to break down meaningfully the sample for each grade to explore at what ages between 6 and 16 these sex differences in children's speech make their appearance; only 10 children or less from each school grade were available for this study. Future studies will have to pursue this goal.

In the meantime, let us try to summarize the sex differences and contrast them to sex differences we have found in the content of speech of adults. The findings show that girls, ages 6 to 16, are more preoccupied than boys with relating to, giving to, being with, concern for, and being alienated from or avoiding other people. Girls speak more than boys of their interest in other people being healthy and well. In summary, in the area of interpersonal relations, girls are more people-oriented, more affiliative, than boys. Studies of the speech patterns of adults suggest that women have significantly higher average scores than men on the Human Relations Scale, the Scale from which many of the content categories come that are referred to above (2, 12). Also, women tend to have higher average scores than men on the Hope Scale, a content analysis scale which focuses on measuring the relative magnitude of an optimistic attitude about human relationships, existential, and cosmic matters (13).

With respect to the expression of overt hostility outward, the present finding that girls tend to criticize or depreciate others more than boys ($p<.10$) is somewhat unexpected, although this thematic category is only one of ten of the Overt Hostility Outward Scale. There were no significant other differences between scores of girls and boys in the Overt Hostility Outward, Covert Hostility Outward, Hostility Inward, and Ambivalent Hostility Scale. Our studies with adults, involving a larger total sample ($N=322$), indicate opposite trends for adults. The average score on hostility outward for a sample of employed men (0.92) was higher than that for a group of employed women (0.79) at the 0.03 level of significance. The mean hostility outward score for male college students was slightly higher than that for female students, and likewise for male and female patients, although these differences did not reach statistically significant levels. The average hostility outward scores for all men was higher than that for women at the 0.05 level of probability. There were no significant differences between the sexes in the mean or medians for hostility inward or ambivalent hostility in any of these studies (14). The Overt Hostility Outward Scale consists of ten thematic categories and the category of self criticizing or depreciating others in a vague or mild manner is only one of these ten. The Covert

Hostility Outward Scale consists of fifteen thematic categories. The Total Hostility Outward Scale combines the scores of the Overt and Covert Hostility Outward Scales, comprised altogether of 25 thematic content categories. We do not know which of all these content categories account for the male-female differences among adults. Increasing use of computer analysis has enabled us to examine these details with children; whereas, with adults we did not in these earlier studies look at differences in these subscale scores.

In the area of anxiety, girls expressed more diffuse anxiety than boys; that is, anxiety without specifying the type of source. With adults, sex differences in the anxiety subscales were examined in samples of 107 psychiatric outpatients. For outpatients, the women had significantly higher average scores on diffuse, separation, and shame anxiety. Since anxiety subscale scores are highly skewed, despite using a square root transformation, the distribution of scores for each subscale was obtained separately for men and women. In comparing the median scores, the sexes differed significantly only on diffuse and shame anxiety; there were no significant differences between the sexes in the inpatient sample. In a normative sample of 173 men and 109 women, women as compared to men had significantly higher average scores *on separation* and *shame* anxiety and significantly lower scores on *death* anxiety. Comparing median scores, the differences between these adult subscale scores become more marked, and there was a tendency for men to have higher *mutilation* anxiety scores (2) than women.

To account for the variation between children and adults with respect to sex differences in speech content, it is suggested that children--at least pre-adolescents--are less exposed to death, dying, illness, or injury on the average than adults and, hence, the spector of these stresses has not had the opportunity to mobilize so much anxiety or fear. Adolescence usually presents youth occasions to become exposed to the risks of life, certainly in some subcultures of our society more than others, and males more than females. One might expect that a study of a larger sample of adolescent children than we have available in the present sample would reveal a trend to higher death and mutilation anxiety subscale scores in adolescent boys than girls. The finding that our sample of boys use more denial of shame anxiety than girls may indicate a beginning, among our sample of male children, of the adoption of the masculine stereotype of pride or stoicism and the covering up feelings of inadequacy, although the adult male's greater preoccupation than women with death or mutilation has not yet manifested itself.

The fact that the boys as compared to girls, in our sample of subjects, used more repetition of words and asked more questions of the interviewer is interesting from two points of view. Many educators have stated that boys develop slower than girls and, as a group, are less articulate during early childhood and puberty. These differences do not distinguish adult men and women. Whether these youthful differences with respect to word repetition indicate a primary difference in brain organization or a derivative of the less people-oriented and less social preoccupation of boys or is completely acquired and learned no one can say with certainty. Probably before one tries to explain the cause of this finding, it should first be replicated.

There is evidence that female sex hormones are associated with nuturing, affiliative, and active interpersonal relationships. Female mice and rats become receptive to mating with injections of female sex hormones and with removal of the female gonads mating and nursing activity is stopped. Injection of male sex hormones block female mating and nursing behavior. Cats, dogs, and primates react similarly to these hormones (15).

However, gender roles are also thought to be learned, especially those involved in interpersonal relations, child and doll care, food preparation, and so forth.

Girls are encouraged by their parents to participate in nuturing roles and considerable emphasis is made on teaching them to be docile and tractable (in spite of the women's liberation movement). Boys are encouraged to acquire skills in competitive aggressive sports and to learn boxing or wrestling; the expression of affection and tenderness by boys after a certain age, unfortunately, is often discouraged as being sissified or effeminate. In any event, the learning of somewhat different roles for males and females is characteristic of every society; and these roles tend, for the most part, to fit the biological make-up and special features of the sex of the human organism.

The present study is not designed to determine what the origins are of differences in content of language of boys and girls. Rather, differences in speech content have been located and identified, and both nature and/or nuture could account for or be said to account for them.

BIBLIOGRAPHY

1. Gottschalk, L. A. and Hambidge, G., Jr. *J. Prof. Tech. 19,* 387, (1955).

2. Gottschalk, L. A. and Gleser, G. C. In *The Measurement of Psychological States Through the Content Analysis of Verbal Behavior.* Univ. Calif. Press, Los Angeles, Berkeley, (1969).

3. Gottschalk, L. A., Gleser, G. C., Daniels, R. S., and Block, S. L. *J. Nerv. Ment. Dis. 127,* 153, (1958).

4. Gottschalk, L. A., Gleser, G. C., Springer, K. J., Kaplan, S. M., Shanon, V. and Ross, W. D. *Arch. Gen. Psychiat. 2,* 632, (1960).

5. Gottschalk, L. A., Gleser, G. C., Magliocco, E. B., and D'Zmura, T. L. *J. Nerv. Ment. Dis. 132,* 101, (1961).

6. Gottschalk, L. A., Gleser, G. C., and Springer, K. J. *Arch. Gen. Psychiat. 9,* 254, (1963).

7. Gottschalk, L. A. and Gleser, G. C. Distinguishing characteristics of the verbal communication of schizophrenic patients. In *Disorders of Communication A.R.N.M.D. 42,* 400. William and Wilkins, Baltimore, (1964).

8. Gleser, G. C., Gottschalk, L. A., and Springer, K. J. *Arch. Gen. Psychiat. 5,* 593, (1961).

9. Gottschalk, L. A. and Kaplan, S. M. *Amer. Med. Ass. Arch. Neurol. Psychiat. 79,* 688, (1958).

10. Fuller, G. B. *J. Clin. Psychol.* Supplement #28, 1, (1969). (revised). *J. of Clin. Psychology.* Monograph Supplrmrny #28, 1, (1969).

11. Nie, N. H., Bent, D. H., and Hull, C. H. In *Statistical Package for the Social Sciences.* McGraw Hill, New York, (1970).

12. Gottschalk, L. A. *Brit. J. Med. Psychol. 44,* 131, (1971).

13. Gottschalk, L. A. *Arch. Gen. Psychiat. 30,*779(1974).

14. Gottschalk, L. A., Winget, C. N., and Gleser, G. C. In *Manual of Instructions for Using the Gottschalk-Gleser Content Analysis Scales: Anxiety, Hostility, and Social Alienation-Personal Disorganization.* Univ. Calif. Press, Los Angeles, Berkeley, (1969).

15. Garattini, S. and Sigg, E. B. In *Biology of Aggressive Behavior.* Edited by Garattini, S. and Sigg, E. B. Excerpta Medica Foundation, Amsterdam, (1968).

APPENDIX I
Anxiety Scale*

1. Death anxiety--references to death, dying, threat of death, or anxiety about death experienced by or occurring to :
   a. self (3).
   b. animate others (2).
   c. inanimate objects (1).
   d. denial of death anxiety (1).

2. Mutilation (castration) anxiety--references to injury, tissue or physical damage, or anxiety about injury of threat of such experienced by or occurring to:
   a. self (3).
   b. animate others (2).
   c. inanimate objects destroyed (1).
   d. denial (1).

3. Separation anxiety--references to desertion, abandonment, ostracism, loss of support, falling, loss of love or object, or threat of such experienced by or occurring to:

    a. self (3).
    b. animate others (2).
    c. inanimate objects (1).
    d. denial (1).

4. Guilt anxiety--references to adverse criticism, abuse, condemnation, moral disapproval, guilt, or threat of such experienced by:

    a. self (3).
    b. animate others (2).
    d. denial (1).

5. Shame anxiety--references to ridicule, inadequacy, shame, embarrassment, humiliation, overexposure of deficiencies or private details, or threat of such experienced by:

6. Diffuse or nonspecific anxiety--references by word or phrase to anxiety and/or fear without distinguishing type or source of anxiety:

    a. self (3).
    b. animate others (2).
    d. denial (1).

NOTES:

1. In the above scale, the reference is not scored if the speaker is the agent and the injury, criticism, etc. is directed to another.

2. When "we" is used, score as "I."

3. Death, injury, abandonment, etc. may come from an external source or situation.

4. In any of above, the weight should be increased by 1 if the statement of anxiety or fear is modified to indicate that the condition is extreme or marked.

APPENDIX II

Hostility Directed Outward Scale: Destructive, Injurious, Critical Thoughts and Actions Directed to Others

(I). Hostility Outward--Overt

Thematic Categories

a 3* Self killing, fighting, injuring other individuals or threatening to do so.

b 3 Self robbing or abandoning other individuals, causing suffering or anguish to others, or threatening to do so.

c 3 Self adversely criticizing, depreciating, blaming, expressing anger, dislike of other human beings.

a 2 Self killing, injuring or destroying domestic animals, pets, or threatening to do so.

(II) Hostility Outward--Covert.

Thematic Categories

a 3* Others (human) killing, fighting, injuring other individuals or threatening to do so

b 3 Others (human) robbing, abandoning, causing suffering or anguish to other individuals, or threatening to do so.

c 3 Others adversely criticizing, depreciating, blaming expressing anger, dislike of other human beings.

a 2 Others (human) killing, injuring, or destroying domestic animals, pets, or threatening to do so.

b 2 Self abandoning, robbing, domestic animals, pets, or threatening to do so.

b 2 Others (human) abandoning, robbing, domestic animals, pets, or threatening to do so.

c 2 Self criticizing or depreciating others in a vague or mild manner.

c 2 Others (human) criticizing or depreciating other individuals in a vague or mild manner.

d 2 Self depriving or disappointing other human-beings.

d 2 Others (human) depriving or disappointing other human beings.

e 2 Others (human or domestic animals) dying or killed violently in death-dealing situation or threatened with such.

f 2 Bodies (human or domestic animals) mutilated, depreciated, defiled.

a 1 Self killing, injuring, destroying, robbing wildlife, flora, inanimate objects or threatening to do so.

a 1 Wildlife, flora, inanimate objects, injured, broken, robbed, destroyed or threatened with such (with or without mention of agent).

b 1 Self adversely criticizing, depreciating, blaming, expressing anger or dislike of subhuman, inanimate objects places, situations.

b 1 Others (human) adversely criticizing, depreciating, expressing anger or dislike of subhuman, inanimate objects places, situations.

Thematic Categories

c 1 Self using hostile words, cursing, mention of anger or rage without referent.

Thematic Categories

c 1 Others angry, cursing without reference to cause or direction of anger; also instruments of destruction not used threateningly.

d 1 Others (human, domestic animals) injured, robbed dead, abandoned or threatened with such from any source including subhuman and inanimate objects, situations (storms, floods, etc).

e 1 Subhumans killing, fighting, injuring, robbing, destroying each other or threatening to do so.

APPENDIX III

Hostility Directed Inward Scale: Self-Destructive, Self-Critical Thoughts and Actions

I. Hostility Inward

Thematic Categories

a 4* References to self (speaker) attempting or threatening to kill itself, with or without conscious intent.

b 4 References to self wanting to die, needing or deserving to die.

a 3 References to self injuring, mutilating, disfiguring self or threats to do so, with or without conscious intent.

b 3 Self blaming, expressing anger or hatred to self, considering self worthless or of no value, causing oneself grief or trouble, or threatening to do so.

c 3 References to feelings of discouragement, giving up hope, despairing, feeling grieved or depressed, having no purpose in life.

a 2 References to self needing or deserving punishment, paying for one's sins, needing to atone or do penance.

b 2 Self adversely criticizing, depreciating self; references to regretting, being sorry or ashamed for what one says or does; references to self mistaken or in error.

c 2 Referenes to feelings of deprivation, disappointment, lonesomeness.

a 1 References to feeling disappointed in self; unable to meet expectations of self or others.

b 1 Denial of anger, dislike, hatred, blame, destructive impulses from self to self.

c 1 References to feeling painfully driven or obliged to meet one's own expectations and standards.

APPENDIX IV

Ambivalent Hostility Scale: Destructive, Injurious Critical Thoughts and Actions of Others to Self

II. Ambivalent Hostility

Thematic Categories

a 3* Others (human) killing or threatening to kill self.

b 3 Others (human) physically injuring, mutilating, disfiguring self or threatening to do so.

c 3 Others (human) adversely criticizing, blaming, expressing anger or dislike toward self or threatening to do so.

d 3 Others (human) abandoning, robbing self, causing suffering, anguish, or threatening to do so.

a 2 Others (human) depriving, disappointing, misunderstanding self or threatening to do so.

b 2 Self threatened with death from subhuman or inanimate object, or death-dealing situation.

a 1 Others (subhuman, inanimate, or situation), injuring, abandoning, robbing self, causing suffering, anguish.

b 1 Denial of blame.

APPENDIX V

Content Analysis Scale of (Schizophrenic) Social Alienation and Personal Disorganization

Categories and Scoring Symbols#

	Scores (Weights)	
	Modified*	Original†
I. Interpersonal references (including fauna and and flora).		
A. To thoughts, feelings or reported actions of avoidance, leaving, deserting, spurning, not understanding of others.		
1. Self avoiding others.	0	+1
2. Others avoiding self.	+1	+1
B. To unfriendly, hostile, destructive thoughts, feelings, or actions.		
1. Self unfriendly to others.	+1	+1
2. Others unfriendly to self.	+⅓	+1
C. To congenial and constructive thoughts, feelings, or actions.		
1. Others helping, being friendly towards others.	−2	−1
2. Self helping, being friendly towards others.	−2	−1

3. Others helping, being friendly towards self.	−2	−1
D. To others (including fauna, flora, things and places).		
1. Bad, dangerous, low value or worth, strange, ill, malfunctioning.	0	+1
2. Intact, satisfied, healthy, well.	−1	−½
II. Intrapersonal references.		
A. To disorientation-orientation, past, present, or future. (Do not include all references to time, place, or person, but only those in which it is reasonably clear the subject is trying to orient himself or is expressing disorientation with respect to these. Also, do not score more than one item per clause under this category.)		
1. Indicating disorientation for time, place, or person or other distortion of reality.	+2	+1
2. Indicating orientation in time, place, person.	0	−½
3. Indicating attempts to identify time, place, or person without clearly revealing orientation or distorientation.	0	+½
B. To self.		
1a. Physical illness, malfunctioning (references to illness or symptoms due primarily to cellular or tissue damage).	0	+1
1b. Psychological malfunctioning (references to illness or symptoms due primarily to emotions or psychological reactions *not secondary* to cellular or tissue damage).	+1	+1
1c. Malfunctioning of indeterminate origin (references to illness or symptoms not definitely attributable either to emotions or cellular damage).	0	+1
2. Getting better.	−2	−½

3a. Intact, satisfied, healthy, well; definite positive affect or valence indicated.	−1	−1
3b. Intact, satisfied, healthy, well; flat, factual, or neutral attitudes expressed.	−1	−1
4. Not being prepared or able to produce perform, act, not knowing, not sure.	+½	+½
5. To being controlled, feeling controlled, wanting control, asking for control or permission, being obliged or having to do, think, or experience something.	+½	+1
C. Denial of feelings, attitudes, or mental state of the self.	+3	+½
D. To food.		
1. Bad, dangerous, unpleasant or otherwise negative; interferences or delays in eating; too much and wish to have less; too little and wish to have more.	0	+1
2. Good or neutral.	0	−½
E. To weather.		
1. Bad, dangerous, unpleasant or otherwise negative (not sunny, not clear, uncomfortable, etc.).	0	−½
2. Good, pleasant or neutral.	−1	−1
F. To sleep.		
1. Bad, dangerous, unpleasant or otherwise negative; too much, too little.	0	+1
2. Good, pleasant or neutral.	0	−½
III. Miscellaneous.		
A. Signs of disorganization.		
1. Remarks or words that are not understandable or inaudible.	+1	+1
2. Incomplete sentences, clauses, phrases; blocking.	0	+1
3. Obviously erroneous or fallacious remarks or conclusions; illogical or bizarre statements.	+2	+1

B. Repetition of ideas in sequence.		
1. Words separated only by a word (excluding instances due to grammatical and syntactical convention, where words are repeated, e.g., "as far as," "by and by" and so forth. Also, excluding instances where such words as "I" and "the" are separated by a word).	0	+½
2. Phrases, clauses (separated only by a phrase or clause).	+1	+1

New Items

IV. A. Questions directed to the interviewer.	+1	0
B. Other references to the interviewer.	+½	0
V. Religious and biblical references.	+1	0

APPENDIX VI
Human Relations Scale (Revision 4-7-67)

Score each clause of the verbal sample with one of the code symbols preceding the following thematic categories whenever the content of the clause denotes similar or equivalent content to any of these thematic categories. Many clauses may not contain themes that are similar to these categories and hence can be left unscored.

Scoring weights are given in the left-hand margin beside each category. Total words of the verbal sample should be counted and used as a correction factor to arrive at a final score. Where it is possible to score a clause under two different categories, choose scoring which is weighted minus rather than plus and give the lowest rating toward the nagative pole, i.e., give priority to pathology. Give only one score per clause.

Content Categories and Scoring Symbols	Weights
A1. References to giving to, supporting, helping or protecting others.	
a. Self to others--specific.	+2

a'. Self to others--references in which the giving etc. is inferential or the object is unspecified. +1
b. Others giving to others or others receiving from and being taken care of by others. +1

A2. References to warm, loving, congenial human relations or human relations in which a desire to be closer is expressed. The reference should be specific rather than inferred. Do not score such key words as marriage or friends in this category unless there is additional evidence of congeniality. Rather, score in B2, below.
a. Involving self or self and others. +2
b. Involving others. +1

A3. Concern for other people; references to missing others when they are away. References should be to specific others only.
a. Self about others. +1
b. Others about self. +1
c. Others about others. +½

A4. Praise or approval of others, indicating more than neutral relations(see B2, below) but not conveying as much positive feeling or warmth as A2, above.
a. Self to others. +1
b. Others to self. +1
c. Others to others. +½

B1. References to manipulative relationships with other human beings. The reference should involve demanding someone do something largely in the service of one's own needs (exploitive) or deliberately making someone feel shame or guilt, e.g., by putting emphasis on how one is made to suffer.
a. Self manipulating others. —½
b. Others manuplating self. —1
c. Others manipulating others. —½

B2. Neutral: nonevaluative references to any kinds of human relations which specify the person(s) interacted with, but which do not specify the nature of the deeper involvement and which are not classified elsewhere. All references to self and others (e.g., we drove, we reached, we thought, etc.) not scorable elsewhere and coded B2a.
- a. Self or self and others. +¼
- b. Others. +¼

B3. Neutral: nonevaluative references to any kinds of human relations, which are generalized, ambiguous as to person(s) interacted with and impersonal. —½

C1. Expulsive: references to competitive, hostile, depreciating, and smearing attitudes, impulses, actions.
- a. Self to others. —½
- b. Others to self. —1
- c. Others to others. —½

C2. Retentive: references to witholding affection, approval or attention from people: references to disapproval.
- a. Self from others. —1
- b. Others from self —1
- c. Others from others. —½

C3. Distancing: references in which people are alienated drawn apart, kept at a distance from one another.
- a. Focus on self. —1
- b. Focus on others. —½

D1. Optimism: references to self receiving from, getting from, being taken care of by other people in gratifying and positive ways; interest in other people in gratifying and positive ways; interest in other people based on what they can do for

oneself; asking others for help; emphasis on the self as the recipient of nurturance and sustenance.
a. Self receiving from others. +2

D2. Pessimism: references to frustration in being taken care of or to poor or inadequate protection, support or care.
a. Self. −½
b. Others. −½

D3. Separation: any reference to separation, loss,death death, not scored elsewhere.
a. Self. −1
b. Others. −½

D4. References to eating or to food in connection with others.
(1) Positive valence. +½
a. Self.
b. Others.
(2) Neutral valence. +½
a. Self.
b. Others.
(3) Negative valence.
a. Self. −1
b. Others. −½

D5. References to difficulty talking, to not knowing to say, to being at a loss for words with interviewer or others. 0

D6. Direct interaction with interviewer.
a. Asking questions of interviewer when standardized verbal sample instructions have been used. +½
b. Other direct references: "you know," or statements addressing interviewer directly by name or as "you." +½

E1. References to lack of humans or subhumans in the environment. The references must contain evidence of lack of interest in or need for human or subhuman objects. —2

E2. References to eating, food, drinking, meals, etc. out of the context of other people. Code both self and others. —1

E3. References to bathing alone (no other people in view) or to undifferentiated or amorphous substances or surroundings involving no discernible human beings. —1

APPENDIX VII

Achievement Strivings Scale

Score all codable clauses. Distinguish between references to the self or others by adding the following notation: (a) self or self and others; (b) others.

I. Vocational, occupational, educational references, including naming and identification.

II. Other constructive activities where emphasis is on work or labor rather than play. Emphasis may be in form of overcoming hardships, obstacles, problems, toward reaching a goal. Exclude all sports and entertainment activities.

A. Domestic activities: moving; buying or selling major items; decorating, painting, cleaning, cooking, doing chores.

B. Activities that require some effort or perseverance to carry out or activities done with speed or accuracy, activities involving trying new experiences as in eating new food or traveling to new places (score no more than three in succession of references to traveling to new places). Score references to learning new information or habits, needing to satisy curiosity, or attempting to unlearn undesirable attitudes or behavior.

III. References to commitment or sense of obligation to responsible or constructive social and personal behavior; to obligation to perform well or succeed in a task; to commitment to a task and to carrying it out or completing it. References to inculcation by others or self of sense of responsibility for one's actions or for welfare of others; responsibility for leadership; evidence of positive superego or ego ideal; evidence of high standards or standards that are hard to live up to (score these even when reference is to fears of not achieving, e.g., "I felt terrible about doing so badly on the test").

IV. Deterrents

A. External dangers or problems or fear of loss of control or limit setting on part of others. References to lack of control by others; references to errors or misjudgments by others that might injure the self.

B. Internal obstacles: references to difficulties in setting limits on oneself or problems in disciplining the self; references to errors or misjudgments by self that might harm the self.

C. Interpersonal: arguments or troubles getting along with others; problems in interpersonal relations, such as inability to make friends.

V. Sports (note that some sports, such as swimming, may be A, B, or C, depending on context).

A. Spectator.

B. Team or organized.

C. Solitary or small group.

VI. Entertainment.

A. Spectator.

B. Amateur.

C. Professsional.

APPENDIX VIII

"Hope" Scale

Content Categories and Coding Symbols	Weights
H 1. References to self or others getting or receiving help, advice, support, sustenance, confidence, esteem (a) from others; (b) from self.	+1
H 2. References to feelings of optimism about the present or future (a) others; (b) self.	+1
H 3. References to being or wanting to be or seeking to be the recipient of good fortune, good luck, God's favor or blessing (a) others; (b) self.	+1
H 4. References to any kinds of hopes that lead to a constructive outcome, to survival, to longevity, to smooth-going interpersonal relationships (this category can be scored only if the word "hope" or "wish" or a close synonym is used.)	+1
H 5. References to not being or not wanting to be or not seeking to be the recipient of good fortune, good luck, God's favor or blessing.	−1
H 6. References to self or others not getting or receiving help, advice, support, sustenance, confidence, esteem (a) from others; (b) from seld.	−1
H 7. References to feelings of hopelessness, losing hope, despair, lack of confidence, lack of ambition, lack of interest; feelings of pessimism, discouragement (a) others; (b) self.	−1

MENTAL HEALTH IN CHILDREN, Volume III
Edited By D. V. Siva Sankar

QUANTITATIVE LINGUISTICS AND PSYCHIATRIC RESEARCH

Gerald Silverman

St. Bernard's Hospital
Southall, Middlesex UB1 3EU
England

Prologue and Exposition

Most papers that have been written on the subject of speech and language studies in psychiatric research begin with the usual platitudinous remarks about speech being unique to the human species; inextricably intertwined with "thought"; the means of interpersonal communication (whether in psychotherapy, diagnosis, intrafamilial dynamics, etc.) and go on to stress that in some psychiatric disorders at least, "abnormalities of speech" are grossly evident and are treated as crucial diagnostic symptomatology. Thus, psychiatrists have been interested in speech (and language) for a long time, often without being explicit about it: in fact it is hard to see how this could have been otherwise. There are however, at least two somewhat different ways in which this "interest" may be defined and develop. A Psychiatrist may rightly claim that he is most concerned with what a patient has to say to him, i.e. the messages that are spontaneously offered to him and the responses to questions directed to him. Since these are conveyed almost entirely in the spoken mode the psychiatrist rightly assures himself that speech is of great interest and importance. Speech is regarded as virtually indispensible but is also, somehow or other, taken for granted. The fact that speech usually does perform efficiently in conveying messages from patient to psychiatrist and vice versa can easily be disregarded as unremarkable. On occasions speech not only carries the messages of pathology but exhibits a degree of abnormality in itself which may assume importance as the major pathologcal symptom of the illness. Such a situation may provoke a second type of interest in speech. A psychiatrist may then begin to ask questions about the very nature of speech itself. Seeing speech for the amazing complex, ubiquitous and versatile behaviour that it is, he may then, far from taking it for granted, wonder at the remarkable fact that it exists at all. He may even ponder the question of how one distinguishes speech from non-speech or mere sound. It is this second type of "interest" in speech about which this article concerns itself, and in so doing it further restricts itself to only a small area of that field of interest, for the field is staggeringly large, complicated and still only lightly tilled.

Because of the complexities of speech and language research it is necessary in an article such as this to provide some introduction to certain very basic notions without which any real discussion cannot proceed. These basic notions are also simple and as such might be easily overlooked. It is because they are occasionally overlooked and ignored that the aims and underlying rationale of Quantitative Linguistic research is sometimes seriously misunderstood. At the onset objection is sometimes raised to the whole notion of the two types of "interest" alluded to above: it is argued that what speech conveys as a message is so much speech itself that the two, the message and the medium are indivisible, and to think of speech at all without considering "what it has to say" can only be fruitless and absurd. This is a faulty objection however, resulting from a casual but serious logical error, an error of the kind that occurs just because speech and language are such tricky things. It is *not* "speech" that has something to say; it is some person who speaks. Speech is a means of conveying the message; it is *not* itself, the message. Some simple analogies may be helpful here in clarifying this point. All sorts of messages may be required to be sent to and from the captains of various ships at sea. This may be accomplished in a number of ways. A mariner may shout from the bows of one ship to another. He may amplify his voice with a megaphone or a loud-hailer. Still using his voice he can transmit a spoken message by radio. He can, however, dispense with the voice altogether and use the radio to transmit a message in Morse-code; here we can think of him first *transcribing* the *un*spoken message into the code. In all these examples the message is received in the auditory mode. A Morse-signal might instead be transmitted as long and short pulses of light. Under these conditions the message is sent out by the rapid action of a finger on a switch and is received in the visual mode. Thus any *one* message may be carried from one person to another in a number of very different ways, and by the same coin, an *infinite* number of messages may be carried by any *one* means of communication. Speech is thus only one variety of a family of means of communication; speech is obviously not the same thing as the message which is communicated and can therefore be studied independently of the message.

It is now appropriate to look more closely at the term "means of communication". At its simplest, a means of communication presupposes the following: (a) some form of *physical link* between a message-sender and a message-receiver across which (b) some form of *physical stimulus* can be imposed by the former upon the latter and (c) an *expectancy* on the part of the receiver for the incoming stimulus to be a message or part of one: finally (d) the receiver must be able to *interpret* the stimuli or rather their patterns in terms of the intentions of the sender. A great deal of work has been done in the area of message sending and means of communication which is now subsumed under the title of an important new discipline "Information Theory". For those already conversant with the bases, even, of Information Theory this introductory part of the present article will already have proved tedious, but it is necessary for those who are strangers to the field as a whole that I continue this section so that enough conceptual framework is provided to make the discussion to follow meaningful. The theoretical and experimental science of Information Theory which largely stems from the classical work (1) has now become highly sophisticated and somewhat daunting to many psychiatrists because of its mathematical side. Fortunately the fundamental principles underlying it are really very simple. What I shall provide here is an exposition of some of these principles with what I can only call certain personal and slightly heterodox modifications to suit the specific purpose of this article. Let us return to messages and means of communication. It is axiomatic that at least *two* physical states can be *chosen* by the message-sender to make a physical stimulus "informative". Obviously if a stimulus is, *of necessity*, always present then it is no longer a "stimulus" in communication terms, since no intention on the part of the sender can be inferred by the receiver. A simple example will illustrate this. A burglar-alarm bell may, hopefully, never ring from the day it is installed until the day a store is demolished, but provided it is known to be correctly installed then the *possibility* of its ringing gives its silence considerable informative value; i.e. that the store isn't being burgled. Note that the *possibility* of the alarm being sounded turns the continued silence into an informative stimulus. *Theoretically* any one of an infinite number of messages may be transmitted allowing that the sender has a choice of operating at least *three* different physical states. Let us call these states "ON", "OFF Type I" and "OFF Type II". "ON" does not require further explanation but the other states do. "OFF Type I" is the absence of the state "ON" for a time interval that has a defined upper limit of duration, "t", and thereby can *group* the preceding "ON" with the succeeding "ON". "OFF Type II" is the absence of the "ON" state for *any* duration which exceeds that of "OFF Type I", or "t". For convenience these states will be denoted respectively as "ON"s, "OFF" and "SPACE" or symbolically as 1, 0 and -. Clearly, if the receiver knows that a group of 'ON's (or 1's) of a particular specified number "N" (e.g. -101010- ; N=3) implies a *specific* message *uniquely* associated with that "N", then, extending this concept, since the possible unique values of "N" is the set of all positive integers, an infinite set of messages could *theoretically* be sent in this way. By now the "means of communication" should have become a clearer concept in terms of its four parts previously mentioned as (a), (b), (c) and (d). It is quite obviously *not* in any way the same as the "message" since its "design" and "feasibility" are *not* dependent on the actual content of the messages, i.e. their import on the receiver about the intentions of the receiver. The *design* is, however, greatly determined by a knowledge of the total number of messages that might even be sent and the relative frequency with which each message is likely to be selected. What I call here "design" is part of the general area of "coding" which is a central part of Information Theory. The "feasibility" is largely determined by the actual properties of the sender, the receiver and the intermediary physical system in terms of the physical stimuli involved and the design chosen; reciprocally the design, or choice of code, will be influenced by these aspects of feasibility. Again a simple example will be of help here. Given that there are only *three* possible messages that might ever be sent, then, as we have seen, each of these can be defined uniquely by a *group* of "ON"s of number "N" provided all "N"s are different. Now we might choose for our three messages (M1, M2 and M3) the groups N=1, N=2 and N=3; more technically the messages are "encoded" as the three groups N1, N2 and N3 (here the numbers are subscripts). On the other hand we might have chosen "N"s equalling 23, 24 and 25 respectively. If the physical system assumes a receiver listening to a pitch of 0.25 secs. (the "ON" stimulus) grouped by "OFF"s of 0.5 secs. then he is quite likely to confuse the sequences N=23, 24 and 25 but much less likely the sequences 1, 2 and 3. Similarly the sender of the message is more likely to make a mistake in the number of pulses he actual transmits. That is, the former situation is much more prone to error in *decoding* and *encoding* respectively. It may be that error is even less with "N"s equalling 2, 4 and 7. It is clear that the feasibility of a communications system has a lot to do with the neurophysiological or psychological idiosyncrasies of the persons in communication and puts constraints on the choice of the physical aspects of the system and the choice of coding design. Let us pursue this idea further with a situation where there are *six* possible messages in total that might be sent. We could choose a code so that messages, "M" 1 to 6, are represented by groups of "N"s equalling 1, 2, 3, 4, 5 and 6. It is easy to see that confusion is very likely with this system. Using larger "N"s with greater relative differences is not a very satisfactory solution either because of fatigue and/or the limitations of short-term memory, especially if different messages are to be sent quite frequently. The "design", or "coding" can be improved markedly if we introduce a *fourth* physical state available to the message-sender or encoder. This we can call "OFF Type III" or symbolically ",". This state is defined as a duration of *absence* of "ON" which is longer than that of "OFF Type I" and shorter than that of "OFF Type II". The value of "," is that it can *group* the simpler groups already available into higher-order groups, thus two groups where "N"=1 and 2 can be grouped as -1, 2- (or in full -10, 1010-). For messages 1 to 6 then we could have a code such as (-1-), (-1, 2-), (-2, 1-), (1, 3-), (-3, 1-) and (-3-). This will lead to less errors than the previous code, particularly if the durations of "o" and "," have some fixed values which are further in a fixed ratio to each other. It just happens to be that for the human only a limited number of elements can be perceived as a *pattern.* When each "N" is sufficiently small, and each *group* of "N"s similarly small, then we have two orders of elementary combinations that allow the whole to be perceived as a *pattern.* We do not have to *count* a display ensemble of three or four elements, auditory or visual, to tell them apart; we *do* have to count when deciding between an ensemble of seventeen and nineteen (I am disregarding here the occasional "genius" and *idiot savant*). Information Theory has always been intricately concerned with the problem of *errors* which occur in communication systems. I choose to say "which occur" rather than "which might occur" since the notion of an entirely error-free system is as purely *theoretical* an abstraction as that of a frictionless system in mechanics. Two of the sources of "error" that can distort a message in the interpersonal situation have been touched on already; these are the neurophysiological and psychological limitations of the human animal, first as sender and second as receiver. The other unavoidable source of error is due to the imperfections that exist in any physical channel for transmitting informative stimuli. Physical changes may get lost *en route,* or be distorted, and additional physical activity is superimposed on the stimulus train as it is transmitted. In more technical parlance, "noise" is an inevitable aspect of any real "communication channel". The way one designs coding is often determined by the nature of potential *error*; in fact coding as a whole can be reduced to a strategy to deal with error.

Let us return to the example of the *six* possible messages and the vessel at sea. Even with the higher ordering of elements there can still be error and erroneous inferences made by the receiver. Some errors are, however, considerably more costly than others; it may be that mistaking message "4" for any other could be very serious indeed. Message "4" might imply that the ship is on fire and that help is urgently required. Normally there are serious disadvantages to long trains of stimuli, as we have seen; they are cumbersome and costly. However it is a fair assumption that message "4" is not only deserving of high reliability in reception but also that it is hopefully very rare. Message "4" then might be represented by (-3, 3, 3, 3, 3, 3, -) or even (-3, 3, ... ad infinitum or until the ship is rescued or sinks). If we forget all about ships and fires and just say that one of the messages is "vital and rare" we enable the coder to do his task that much better. We have *not* told him *what* the message is but we have disclosed something of its nature in terms of frequency and costliness if in error. By now the reader should have some intuition for the fact that *completely* "optimal" coding for any particular communications system *would* require total knowledge of the nature and import of all messages, their respective values for the individual sender and receiver (not always equivalent), as also a total knowledge of the neurophysiological performance of the two persons and the precise physical characteristics of the communication channel which will set "feasibility" constraints. Such a coding design would unfortunately be as *restricted* in usefulness as it would be optimal to that particular situation; outside a particular context it could be considerably *sub*-optimal. Human beings communicate during their lifetime with many other human beings, under very varied circumstances and about innumerable different matters. Some messages may change from important to trivial, or the reverse, through either the passage of time or change of environment, etc. Obviously what is required is an optimal code *in general* for human speech. Such coding not only *need not* but *must not* be based on prior knowledge of all messages and their detailed content. For this reason we should expect to find, in the design of human speech, much that reflects *coding* but which cannot easily be related to the *meaning* of the messages which speech helps to transmit. It should be no surprise to find aspects of speech which are relatively invariant regardless of the speaker, what is being spoken, and about what; these aspects will be a reflection of the optimal coding of natural speech. We shall see later that there are such features and the constancy which they show has so impressed some workers in the past as to lead them to talk about universal linguistic *laws.* Before embarking on the next section it need only be said that "quantitative linguistics" is much concerned with just these constancies, or *apparent* constancies, for it is also concerned with the *subtle* differences in coding that can and do occur. To the experimenter in this field then, quite small changes mean a lot; large changes are momentous. Very large changes, *a priori,* suggest a cautious interpretation and a scrutinous appraisal of methodology.

The Type-Token Ratio

Historically the "type-token ratio", or TTR, is amongst the oldest quantitative linguistic measures; it is also probably the one that has most been used in psychological and psychiatric work. For any discrete language sample the TTR is the proportion of *different* words to the *total* number of words in that sample; this is usually expressed as a decimal fraction. In 1944 there were published four, now classical, papers dealing with the TTR (2, 3, 4, 5). It is interesting to see how many of the hopes and cautions about this measure that are equally applicable today were expressed at that time by these workers; sadly not all the cautions have been registered by subsequent workers and there is still much to be explored using this measure. The TTR has probably commended itself so much because it appears, at least superficially, to be a very simple measure. Also with relatively small samples of language text it is not too arduous to compute with fair accuracy. For written material, (5), the growth of the number of different words against the total number of words was a logarithmic function. Chotlos worked with very large samples in terms of numbers of words, 3000, and his subjects were children who wrote about whatever they liked for a while each day until the appropriate number of words had been collected from each subject. Three curves illustrating the growth of different words against total words is most illuminating, showing as they do curves for three different I.Q. groups. There is no doubt that the TTR is significantly greater for the high I.Q. group than the normal I.Q. group, which itself is significantly greater than for the low I.Q. group, but this differentiation does not really begin to show itself until the size of the samples reaches about 500 words. It is worth mentioning that the I. Q. groups really were *very* different with means of 116, 102 and 84 respectively and also that the really dramatic difference in the TTRs was between the normal and low I. Q. groups: that between the normal and high was far less impressive. As far as I know there has been no study which has attempted anything similar to this "normative" venture by Chotlos using 108 Iowa schoolchildren. This is a serious matter when one considers the use of the type-token ratio applied to the language of adults and not merely to written material but to transcripts of speech. The lapse is understandable however in terms of the difficulties that arise in manual computation of the ratio for texts longer than 100 words; just as the TTR declines exponentially with length of word sample the effort in computing it rises exponentially as does the likelihood of numerical error. This fact is no longer an excuse; the advent of high-speed digital computers allows such computations to be performed in a matter, literally, of seconds. It is a prerequisite of working in quantitative linguistics today that one comes to terms with the computer, not merely to calculate TTRs but many other and more complex statistical properties of texts. There are two quite distinct forms of type-token ratio and an understanding of their difference is essential if one is not to be mislead when reading literature on the TTR. One form is the *overall* TTR and the other the *mean segmental* TTR. For a text, say, of 500 words the overall TTR is the proportion of *all* the different types in the whole sample to the total number of tokens (i.e. different words to total words). Another value that might be computed however is the TTR for the first 100 words, then *quite independently*, that for the second 100 words and so on giving *five* 100 word TTRs or *segmental* TTRs; the arithmetic mean of these five values gives the mean 100 word segmental TTR for the whole sample. Unfortunately the function relating mean segmental TTRs and overall TTRs is not a constant one and there is no real way of mathematically evaluating, even with remote certitude, the one from the other or vice versa. Indeed my own work confirms largely what was hinted at by some very early workers; the two values are measures of different aspects of verbal organization. The crucial importance for stressing this distinction lies in the fact that workers have been tempted to use the mean segmental value for a text as a substitute for the overall value because of its considerably greater ease in manual computation. For these reasons the TTR is only applicable in comparative studies when the sample-size in number of words is kept constant and if segmental values are used these are also kept strictly comparable numerically. Thus a table is given (6) showing very diverse type-token ratios (collected from a number of studies by various workers) with no information about sample-size. Resort to the original reports shows that the large diversity in values reflects, by and large, the differences of sample-sizes rather than the psychopathological information which is provided in the table.

This brings one to the psychiatrist's interest in the TTR in the first place. Logically, the TTR must, in some sense, be a function of actual expressive vocabulary diversity, and possibly of overall vocabulary store or knowledge, though these are *not* synonymous with each other. A number of workers have reported lower TTRs in the written or spoken texts of schizophrenic subjects compared with normal control subjects. Fairbanks (3) compared ten schizophrenics and ten college freshmen. Though admittedly the "control group" could well be objected to, not so her statistical methodology. 3000 word samples were used to provide for each subject a mean segmental TTR based on 30 separate 100 word TTRs. Although there was one overlap between the groups in raw values the confidence intervals at 1% did not overlap for the group means.

TABLE I

Schizophrenics	Controls
0.62	0.67
0.61	0.66
0.60	0.66
0.58	0.64
0.57	0.64
0.56	0.64
0.56	0.64
0.55	0.63
0.53	0.63
0.49	0.61

Mean Segmental 100 word TTRs for texts of 3000 words each for ten schizophrenic patients and ten college freshman (adapted from Fairbanks (3)).

Fairbanks' TTRs are reproduced in Table I and Maher's in Table II to underline two points: the absolute need for standardizing sample-size, and the very small true variation to be found in the TTR. This very small variation, or inflexibility, is just the kind of feature which we have been looking for in view of the previous discussion of optimal coding in speech. Work of my own (7) has shown statistically lower values for the TTR in the speech of schizophrenics than in control subjects - though again this work is far from free from methodological criticism. Undoubtedly one way of improving the experimental design is to take recorded samples of speech from subjects who are actively schizophrenic and later when they are improved or

TABLE II

SUBJECTS	TTR	SOURCE
Schizophrenics (S)	0.57	Fairbanks
Freshman (S)	0.64	
Schizophrenics (W)	0.66	Mann
Freshmen (W)	0.71	
Chronic Schizophrenics (W)	0.39-0.57	Pavy *et al.*
Chronic Schizophrenics with medication (W)	0.58	
Acute Schizophrenics (W)	0.66-0.70	
Acute Schizophrenics with medication (W)	0.69	
Schizophrenic (W)	0.26	Critchley
Schizophrenic (W)	0.65	
Schizophrenics, thought-disordered (W)	0.71	Maher *et al.*
Schizophrenics, non-thought disordered (W)	0.74	

(S)=spoken (W)=written material. Some values are means, some ranges and two (Critchley's) are individual values. Detailed references to the original sources are to be found in Maher's original paper. (Adapted from Maher (6)).

in remission. There are, however, many experimental contaminants that might operate and a convincing study will require very thorough design and is at present being initiated by the author. Viewed from the angle of a decreased diversity of words available, or in any event *used*, a number of constructions have been placed upon the relevance of this for the schizophrenic. One of these, "egocentricity" of speech stems largely from the pioneer work of Zipf (8, 9), who is in some senses the founding father of quantitative linguistics (though not its earliest practitioner). Zipf conjectured that the vocabulary of speech was a compromise between repetition and diversity. The more diverse the expressive vocabulary, he argued, the more clearly and unambiguously could a person convey meaning to another person but that this was payed for by a loss of an economy that could be bought with a more restricted verbal range. In the schizophrenic, it is argued, there is an autistic attitude, a lack of motivation to communicate with others, a disinterest in precision of speech and this is reflected in the restricted or *egocentric* vocabulary. Zipf himself did not use the TTR as his measure but rather the characteristics of the curve produced by plotting the logarithmic rank frequency against the actual logarithmic frequency of words in a text. Essentially, however, he was looking at the same thing. There is not room here to discuss further Zipf's contributions and his "famous" *law* which has latterly fallen into some disrepute as have many of his other *laws*. The rank-frequency curve has been studied by other workers since; more recently others (10), for example, tried to measure "rigidity" or a shift from "sociocentricity" to "ego-centricity" in subjects under *stress* conditions using this tool (with ambiguous results). The roots of the idea of "egocentricity" are essentially *psychodynamic* and more *neurophysiologically* congruent models might be proposed. Schizophrenics with low TTRs also show abnormalities in other aspects of their speech. The latter is usually much lower in overall verbal output rate (i.e. words per unit time) and pause time is increased considerably in some subjects. Now if we think of speech as being generated somewhere in the brain in *the simplest possible model* then we can imagine a *word store* which feeds words into an *organiser* i.e. a mechanism for arranging words in appropriate syntactic and linear relationships for the semantic purpose at hand. If, for some reason, the availability of words from the word store is impaired, or merely the *rate* of availability, then we might expect the retarded psychomotor features of speech in schizophrenia. With a little more conjecture we could also suggest that the *organiser* continues to emit and handle words while it has them, so to speak, and that it discards words when new words are eventually supplied from the word store on "command". This is not quite as fanciful as it sounds. Only moderate acquaintance with computers impresses one with the importance of complete synchrony in a complex information handling device comprising networks, organizers and stores, etc. If a computer became asynchronic, so that passage of data from one step to the next slowed up, then the output would contain *inappropriate repetition* of elements in its content; there would be *perseveration*, to put it clinically. Now perseveration alone will lead, in linguistic terms, to a diminished type-token ratio. These concepts of what we might call *low word-store arousal* and *organisational asynchrony* are of course grossly crude and simplistic hints at what might be occuring in the most complex and subtle of all information-processing systems known, the human brain, but I believe them to be heuristically more helpful than psychodynamic concepts. There is however a little more in the way of empirical support for this notion. Normal spoken language (and written) is to a great extent "redundant". This simply means that part of it may be omitted without true loss of information. This redundancy is part of *coding* and is a device to counteract error in encoding, decoding and transmission due to "noise" (*vide supra*). This redundancy can be measured by a technique known as Cloze Procedure where words in a text are omitted and the mutilated text is reconstructed by guesswork without previous knowledge of the complete text. The degree to which missing words can be restored accurately gives an indication of the redundancy of the text at the lexical level. The standard technique is to omit every *fifth* word systematically. Using this method a number of workers (11, 12, 13) have shown transcripts of schizophrenic speech to be *less* redundant than normal speech. This is difficult to account for purely in terms of a restricted vocabulary; indeed the reverse might be expected. Inappropriate repetition of words could explain this well however. On this basis one should expect to find some positive correlation between decreased TTR and low redundancy. Salzinger *et al.* (11) failed to demonstrate such a significant correlation. In a study of my own (7) such a correlation was found. The apparent conflict between Salzinger's results (11) and my own can be explained purely methodologically. Salzinger and his co-workers used 100 word TTRs while I used overall 200 word TTRs. This in itself could be crucial. In terms of detecting *repetition* the TTR will be insensitive if it is based on too large a sample size, or too small; its sensitivity will depend upon the *size* of the linguistic units that are repeated (repetition of chunks of words must also be considered), and the *periodicity* of the repetition. Further, in my own study I also used a modified Cloze Procedure, alongside the traditional one, involving deletion of every *fourth* word. This showed up as much more sensitive as described more fully (13). There is thus still a great deal more to be explored with such a deceptively simple measure as the type-token ratio.

Yule's Characteristic K

Unlike the type-token ratio, this measure has been given scant attention by workers in "pathopsycholinguistics" (a word I find useful despite its sesquipedentialism) and I know of only one reference to its use in the study of schizophrenic speech, or rather, the speech of schizophrenics (outside of my own studies). The reason for its neglect is probably largely due to two factors; it is unlikely that a psychiatrist or psychologist would read the field of linguistics in a fashion where it might be encountered, and further its computation is mathematically *very* tedious assuming one is not on talking terms with a digital computer. George Udney Yule was an emiment Cambridge statistician who in the 1940's whiled away the war years with a problem which he admitted was hardly important or even very interesting in itself. The problem was simply, who was the author of the "*De Imitatione Christi*"? Was it Thomas à Kempis or Gerson. This led, eventually, to the publication of a volume, "*The Statistical Study of Literary Vocabulary*" (14) in which is described the evolution, rationale, and usefulness of the measure which is now known as Yule's Characteristic K and which I will abbreviate for ease as Yule's K. Yule was very much aware of the effect that varying sample sizes had upon measures such as simple ratios and sought to find a measure of linguistic organization that was relatively invariant with respect to text length. The statistical reasoning behind the measure is beyond the scope of this article but should *not* be omitted by anyone who employs it (vide infra). If "X" is the frequency which a word, or number of different words, may have in a text (i.e. it is a frequency category) then "f_X" is the numbers of different words that occur with that frequency. Plotting the value of "f_X" for all possible values of "X" gives a frequency distribution with a first moment, S1 of $\sum f_X .X$ and a second moment, S2, of $\sum f_X .X^2$. The formula 10,000 (S2 - S1)/S1 gives that value of Yule's K. It has been argued convincingly (15) that Yule's K is a measure of the *repeat rate* of words in a text. In a very important and sophisticated study of schizophrenic speech (16) 900 word texts were used and the values of Yule's K were found to discriminate more clearly between schizophrenic subjects and matched controls than TTR measures; also Yule's K seemed much less affected by ethnic and other "background" variables than the TTR. As it happens the sample sizes were kept constant in this study but it is important to note that what Yule would call *small* samples are gargantuan compared to those used in speech studies, especially employing monologue material. Studies of my own have shown that though the order of magnitude of Yule's K is remarkably constant for speech samples of sample-size ranging from 500 down to 100 words this can be dangerously deceptive when inferences are being drawn; the actual values of Yule's K *do* vary and there is not *always* a close correlation between the values for the first 300 words of a monologue and the first 500 words of the same monologue. Two further points need stressing. Yule's original work was carried out on the counts of *nouns* only; the importance of this will be referred to later. Further it has been shown (15) how Yule's K is properly applicable in theoretical terms to the middle-frequency range of words only. In one of my own pilot experiments four student nurses, all female native English speakers with comparable verbal I.

Q.'s and ages, were asked to produce monologues on three separate days. At each session they were asked to talk on three topics, the order being changed for each session. Two of the topics were kept *fixed* and chosen by myself (religion and women's rights). The third topic was left to the subject's own choice at each session. Further the subjects rated, before and after each monologue, the knowledge they felt they had for the topic, their interest in it and their ability to talk about it; these ratings were combined as a composite score (see Table III). Table IV shows the values of Yule's K for all these (300 word) monologues and also values for the measure Yule's K Decap; this is Yule's K computed in a fashion to exclude all words occurring more than 10 times in frequency. A two-way analysis of variance (see Table V) shows that the simple Yule's K distinguishes between neither subjects nor topics but that Yule's K Decap (I had to invent some name for it!) though still not distinguishing between subjects clearly *does* significantly distinguish between *topics*; further statistical analysis shows that this difference is solely due the difference between the "own choice" situation and the "supplied choice" situation. Obviously the latter may have engendered more frustration and anxiety in the subjects than the former which would in its turn have allowed greater motivation and possibly a greater vocabulary for the topic. By setting the upper limit for frequency category in this way as 10 for a 300 word sample the sacrifice in number of *types* for each text was never greater than *five*; that is, over all something less than 3% since the *mode* value was *four* types sacrificed. Table VI also gives the values for the overall 300 word TTRs and Table V shows the analysis of variance applied to these. This again distinguishes topics in the predicted direction but less so than the Yule's K Decap; it is my hope that this measure will prove to be a powerful tool in the analysis of texts by quantitative linguistic methods and it is now being used by the author to study the effects of anxiolytics in subjects under stress, as well as the differences between schizophrenic and other speech. One factor that emerges from this pilot experiment very clearly is that the actual potentially influential variables in speech experiments are numerous and must be adequately controlled for in one way or another.

TABLE III

TOPICS	SUBJECTS			
	J.H.	S.J.	S.M.	S.S.
Own Choice (1)	25	18	16	19
Own Choice (2)	24	19	19	17
Own Choice (3)	23	22	21	23
Religion (1)	13	9	12	17
Religion (2)	11	11	12	17
Religion (3)	11	17	14	14
Women's Rights (1)	19	10	10	18
Women's Rights (2)	16	10	12	12
Women's Rights (3)	19	15	12	12

Composite scores for self-ratings by four subjects before and after talking on topics at sessions (1), (2) and (3) for knowledge of, interest in and ability to talk on the topic.

Epilogue

I hope that by now the reader will have gained some idea of the goals and techniques of quantitative linguistics as used in the framework of abnormal psychology. It has not been possible to be anywhere nearly comprehensive of the subject; this was not the intention. Many areas have been entirely omitted - the development of methodology is rapidly changing and improving. It would be foolish to claim that we understand very much about the very *real* differences in the measures that we make, but they *are* measures of the most complex, probably,

TABLE IV

TOPICS	J.H.		S.J.		S.M.		S.S.	
	Y	YD	Y	YD	Y	YD	Y	YD
Own Choice (1)	115	72	138	68	144	101	86	63
Own Choice (2)	168	81	159	62	176	72	158	78
Own Choice (3)	137	107	158	73	97	68	153	84
Religion (1)	138	99	139	106	152	89	158	103
Religion (2)	137	88	150	86	174	116	144	85
Religion (3)	167	91	156	83	117	85	127	76
Women's Rights (1)	144	106	176	103	149	82	106	90
Women's Rights (2)	169	92	118	110	153	93	129	101
Women's Rights (3)	126	106	187	91	146	108	139	93

Values of Yule's K (Y) and Yule's K Decap (YD) for four subjects talking on topics at sessions (1), (2) and (3).

of all aspects of human behaviour. The eventual understanding of the mechanism of speech will probably come beyond my own or the next generation's lifetime (and I'm not even autumnal yet). The whole field of psycholinguistics is expanding at great pace but the answers to most of the problems still seem astronomically distant. We talk vaguely of a *word-store*, a *lexicon*, for instance, yet the neurophysiological substrate of such a store is still *totally* unknown; it shares the obscurity that shrouds most of the neurophysiology of memory in general. Throughout this article I have so far avoided the issue of defining just what is a *word* and I have said nothing about the

TABLE V

SOURCE OF VARIATION	S.S.	D.F.	M.S.	F ratio ratio	
	for Yule's K				
Topics	222.1667	2	111.0833	0.18	n.s.
Subjects	1844.5556	3	614.8519	0.97	n.s.
Interactions	796.2778	6	132.7130	0.21	n.s.
Error	15232.0000	24	634.6667		
Total	18095.0000	35			
	for Yule's K Decap				
Topics	2689.5556	2	1344.7778	8.85	$\ll 0.01$
Subjects	331.4167	3	110.4722	0.73	n.s.
Interactions	508.0000	6	84.6667	0.56	n.s.
Error	3648.6667	24	152.0278	0.56	
Total	7177.6389	35			
	for Overall TTRs (300)				
Topics	7690.7223	2	3845.3611	5.31	< 0.05
Subjects	4192.0833	3	1397.3611	1.93	n.s.
Interactions	1888.1666	6	314.6944	0.43	n.s.
Error	17374.6667	24	723.9444	0.43	
Total	31145.6389	35			

Two-way analyses of variances for the values of Yule's K, Yule's K Decap and overall 300 word TTRs as illustrated in Tables IV and VI.

TABLE VI

TOPICS	SUBJECTS			
	J.H.	S.J.	S.M.	S.S.
Own Choice (1)	.467	.510	.443	.530
Own Choice (2)	.450	.470	.483	.457
Own Choice (3)	.460	.467	.527	.487
Religion (1)	.433	.430	.443	.420
Religion (2)	.463	.443	.427	.480
Religion (3)	.463	.443	.510	.487
Women's Rights (1)	.437	.417	.477	.487
Women's Rights (2)	.450	.440	.440	.460
Women's Rights (3)	.420	.420	.427	.463

Overall 300 word TTRs for the four subjects talking on the three topics in sessions (1), (2) and (3).

enumerations and statistical procedures that can be applied to elements of speech larger than the word (clauses, sentences, etc.) or smaller than the word (phonemes, syllables, etc.). With this respect some explanation must be given. Words occupy a very special place in the study of speech in that they are universally those elements in the continuous stream of speech which are heard intuitively as separate and bounded elements which can recur and be recombined in a variety of ways. The word is a psychological reality for everyone. To quote the footnote to an article "Sapir pointed out, after long experience of reducing American Indian languages to writing, that untrained native speakers generally have no difficulty in deciding what portions of connected speech constitute words" (17). The higher and lower order elements of speech are in some sense the creations of literacy and later, linguistics. One of the problems with psycholinguistics is that it has grown out of the common interest of workers trained in very diverse disciplines. To the linguist it might be more reasonable, for instance, to count all singular all plural inflections of words as the same word; thus the pairs *leg* and *legs*, *mouse* and *mice,* would each be treated in a text as the occurrence of the *same* word. From my own, more psychological orientation the question only seems to make sense in whether for instance, *leg* and *legs* occupy similar but separate loci in some hypothetical word-store, or whether only *leg* is stored and the plural is generated after its retrieval by a later operation. Obviously any study should have a consistent *operational* definition of "word" but it is to be hoped that flexible studies in quantitative linguistics will shed light on the true distinctions between *different* words and the *same* words in different *forms.* This will complement the rather unreal language which has provided so much material for the development of *transformational grammars.* Meanwhile quantitative linguistic measures are rather like the electrocardiogram when it first entered cardiology. The patterns were extraordinarily constant in many ways and certain gross deviations of pattern were known to be related to pathologies of various types but the link between the pathology and the pattern was obscure. The EKG has advanced far and was useful long before it was at all understood in fundamental terms. The electroencephalogram likewise is useful but *its* underlying genesis is at least as obscure as that of the patterns of words and their statistical attributes; quantitative linguistics deserves at least as much research and exploitation as the electroencephalogram. I hope this article will have induced in some readers an inclination to share this view.

REFERENCES

1. Shannon, C. "A Mathematical Theory of Information" 27: 379-423 1948.
2. Johnson, W. "Studies in Language Behaviour: a program for research" 56: 1-15 1944.

3. Fairbanks, H. *Psychol. Monogr. 56,* 19 (1944).
4. Mann, M. *Psychol. Monogr. 56,* 41, (1944).
5. Chotlos, J. *Psychol. Monogr. 56,* 77, (1944).
6. Maher, B. *Brit. J. Psychiat. 120,* 3, (1972).
7. Silverman, G. *Brit. J. Psychiat. 122,* 407, (1973).
8. Zipf, G. In *The Psycho-Biology of Speech,* Houghton Miffin Co., (1935).
9. Whitehorn, J. and Zipf, G. *Arch. Neurol. 49,* 831, (1943).
10. Sunshine, N. and Horowitz, M. *Language Speech 11,* 160, (1968).
11. Salzinger, K., Portnoy, S. and Feldman, R. *Ann. N. Y. Acad. Sci. 105,* 845, (1964).
12. Moroz, M. and Fosmire, F. *Dis. Nerv. Syst. 27,* 408, (1966).
13. Silverman, G. *Psychol. Med. 2,* 254, (1972).
14. Yule, G. In *The Statistical Study of Literary Vocabulary.* Cambridge University Press, (1944).
15. Herdan, G. In *Quantitative Linguistics.* Butterworths, London, (1964).
16. Hammer, M. and Salzinger, K. *Ann. N. Y. Acad. Sci. 105,* 861, (1964).
17. Jones, D. *The History and Meaning of the Phoneme,* Le Maitre Phonetique, (suppl.) (1957).

MENTAL HEALTH IN CHILDREN, Volume III
Edited By D. V. Siva Sankar

PJD Publications Ltd., Westbury, N.Y.

ELECTIVE MUTISM IN CHILDREN: A FOLLOW-UP STUDY

Michael Koch

University of Minnesota
Minneapolis, Minnesota 55455

Elective mutism is a decriptive term first used by Tramer (1) to describe children who are silent among all of their interpersonal contacts with the exception of a small circle of intimate friends and relatives. He distinguished these children from those with language retardation, schizophrenic mutism and other forms of mutism including hysteria. The subject has recently been comprehensively reviewed by Halpern (2). He summarized the conditions commonly implicated in the etiology of this disorder. They are: (1) a predisposing constitutional shyness, for example, manifested by social reticence; (2) a traumatically experienced event during critical periods of language development, for example, mouth injury or belittling the child's speech attempts; (3) an insecure environment, for example, family psychopathology; (4) psychological fixation; and (5) neurotic symptoms arising out of familial conflicts. According to Halpern, mutism has also been associated with a variety of difficulties such as school phobia, speech defects, obstinancy, enuresis, withdrawal, compulsivity and separation difficulty.

Generally, children with this disorder are regarded as making only slow response to treatment. Recommended therapies vary from outpatient individual psychotherapy and family therapy to changing the home environment and in-patient milieu treatment. The few studies subject to outcome review usually involve less than a half dozen children (3-6). Better results in a larger number of children was reported by Wright (7) who evaluated 24 children ages 5 to 9 years with elective mutism. Three of these were admitted to an inpatient service. Nineteen cases were available for follow-up, the interval being from six months to seven years. Eleven of the children and parents were personally interviewed, the remainder contacted by telephone. Four children showed no signs of a previous problem and there were no signs of maladjustment. Eleven children were adjusting well at home and in school but had indications of shyness of controlling behavior. Three children are marginally adjusted in school and were uncomfortable in social relations. One child was unable to adjust at home and school. He found that younger children generally responded well to short-term treatment and that the prognosis for the later adjustment of young children presenting the symptom of refusal to talk in school was positive.

More recently, desensitization techniques have been effectively used in selected cases of elective mutism. Reid *et al.* (8) described a marathon behavior modification of a selectively mute child and Straughan *et al.* (9) utilized peer reinforcement in treating a 14 year old mildly retarded electively mute boy. Halpern (2) placed three electively mute subjects in a situation where speech was required in school. Long-term follow-up was not reported for any of these behavior modification studies.

Method

The present study re-examines those children who were considered electively mute while hospitalized on the child psychiatry service at the University of Minnesota. All of them spoke normally with at least one parent at home but refused to talk outside the home and at school. Seventeen children had been discharged with this diagnosis. However, only fifteen of them could be located at the time of follow-up. They (10 boys and 5 girls) and their families are the basis of this report. Both the subjects and parents were interviewed in private and conjointly; interviews consisted of a non-structured discussion and the administration of a modified M-B history record (10). The Minnesota Multiphasic Personality Inventory was administered to subjects and they were either tested with the Shipley-Hartford Intelligence Test or individually tested by a psychologist. School reports and data from social agencies and mental health facilities were obtained.

At the time of the follow-up evaluation all of the subjects were living at home. The youngest, age 8 years, had a four year follow-up. The remainder ranged from ages 14 to 21 and the average follow-up interval for the total group was 9 years.

The age of onset of mutism was from 3 to 6 years. There were three sets of twins. With nine of the children there was a discernable event which seemed to precipitate the onset of mutism. Two became mute when their mothers were hospitalized and another when instructed to be quiet at his mother's employer's house. Seven children became mute upon entry to school. None of the children in the study had a history of notable mouth injury or trauma at the time language developed.

Hospital Course

Most of the children were seen individually in psychotherapy sessions and parental counseling was done when indicated and possible. All attended school and occupational therapy when in hospital. The average length of stay was 14 weeks and the usual hospital course was that of gradual use of speech with peers and ward staff. Along with this they became less shy and began to make friends in the hospital. Eleven of the children had no pressure put on them to stimulate speech. There seemed to be a reluctance to do this because of the concern about getting a power struggle over speech production. At discharge three of these children still demonstrated elective mutism with the doctor or some of the hospital staff, but only one of them refused to talk to anyone outside of family members.

In contrast with the aforementioned approach, four of the children had rewards systems established for speaking and had withdrawal of some of the usual privileges unless they were requested by the child. This was effective whereas the previous approach of ignoring the mutism had failed with these four children.

Follow-up Results

An attempt is made to compare the presenting symptoms and the characteristics with the state of those symptoms at the time of follow-up.

School Functioning

Two of the three mentally retarded children had been in classes for the educable mentally retarded. Both were introverted and friendless. There was little spontaneity and speech consisted of simple replies to questions. The remaining twelve children attended regular school classes. Only two achieved age appropriate grade levels. Eleven children were of normal intelligence initially and at follow-up and were behind one to two years in their grade levels. Usually this was because of earlier school decisions made when they were mute. Another child was initially tested as mildly mentally retarded and at follow-up was in the borderline range. Although a high school graduate, she functioned far below high school level in academic performance. Eight out of the nine children still in school were currently having school problems, e.g., truancy or extreme shyness.

Psychological Testing

With the exception of a child whose full scale IQ went from 59 to 76 at the time of follow-up there was little shift in intelligence determinations. MMPI's were not done during hospitalization. At follow-up two retarded children had invalid MMPI profiles. Five subjects had MMPI profiles or projective testing indicating either schizoid functioning or being socially reserved with low energy or activity levels. Clinically, they all fit these descriptions. Two others had indications of poor impulse control and were on probation for delinquency and truancy. Only one child showed psychometric evidence of considerable anxiety. Six children had normal profiles.

Personality Traits and Peer Relationships

A symptom list based on chart review at the time of admission indicated that the most commonly reported symptom at that time was shyness (61%). Next in order were rebelliousness (54%) and fear of father (23%). At the time of follow-up, behavioral traits most commonly reported by parents were shyness (85%) and stubbornness (45%). These traits were apparent and important when considering peer relations. Only three subjects at follow-up appeared to have satisfactory interpersonal relationships outside the home. The others were shy, introverted and had few or no friends. Frequently they preferred to associate with children three to four years younger than themselves.

Speech

At the time of discharge from University Hospital only one child refused to speak to anyone except family members. Ten years later she was one of the nine subjects who spoke spontaneously and clearly to strangers including the examiner. Two other children demonstrated mutism to a lesser extent when originally discharged. One had worsened over the years and was currently hospitalized and being unsuccessfully treated for mutism. Fourteen years old, she communicated surprisingly well with her peers by means of gestures. Another child refused to talk to his therapist at discharge and spoke only reluctantly to those outside his family when seen at follow-up. Although the remaining twelve children were speaking spontaneously when discharged, nine of them subsequently had or were receiving speech therapy because of shyness and reluctance to talk. One, a rather stubborn girl, was mute with her current speech teacher but not with other people (a good reason to question continuing this kind of help for her and an indication of the concern about mutism shown by some of the school personnel). Five were still very reluctant to speak with strangers but would answer questions with terse, soft-spoken replies.

Family Adjustment

All of the subjects were living at home. Eight had what was regarded by themselves, their parents and the author as a satisfactory relationship with parents and other siblings. One of the subjects was still mute outside the family setting. Four subjects had notably competitive relationships with other siblings. With two of these the involved sibling was a twin.

Fear of father was noted in five of the children initially hospitalized. At follow-up two of the subjects, ages 22 and 16 years, still indicated being afraid of their fathers and in frequent conflict with them. Parents of the other three had divorced but when the fathers returned home, the 16, 17 and 22 year old subjects still had notable conflicts with them. With one exception, the subjects' mothers tended to speak for them during the interview and to dominate the session. They tended to blame either the child's father or a teacher as being the reason for the mutism.

Psychological Treatment

Five subjects had not had any psychiatric, psychological or social work evaluation or treatment following discharge. The parents were not particularly concerned about their shyness. The other ten subjects had these contacts. Four had been admitted to residential facilities. One had recently been discharged from an adolescent treatment facility where he had been diagnosed as schizophrenic. At the time of discharge from this center and at the time of follow-up interview and testing, he did not show any clinical or psychometric evidence of schizophrenic thinking or behavior. Another child at follow-up was hospitalized in an adolescent psychiatric hospital because of mutism and school problems. She was in the process of having a trial of various medications and hypnotic sessions to see if there would be any benefit from this. Another had attended a state school for the retarded and had had repeated contacts with counselors and school psychologists because of regressive and disruptive behavior. The other child admitted to a residential facility had recently been discharged from a juvenile correction center.

Seven of the children had had outpatient involvement of various types. Two had been seen because of mutism, two for delinquency and three for schizoid and overly withdrawn behavior. The majority of the children did not know why they had originally been in the hospital. One child had repeated outpatient contacts but could not recall any of this and claimed his speech had returned after his father left home and after he had a religious conversion at age 10 years.

Subjects were rated on a 5-point scale developed by Quast and Hafner for their following study adolescents.* Factors considered in determining the degree of incapacitation were: (1) school or vocational adjustment; (2) social relationships with parents, peers and siblings; (3) autonomous functioning; (4) self-concept. The frequency, intensity and pervasity of problem behavior was considered and psychological test data was used in conjunction with other data sources.

Results

	No. of subjects
1. Positive mental health, above average in total life adjustment.	0
2. Problem behavior, not incapacitating: problem behavior not apparent or interfering with life adjustment factors to any significant degree. Behavior within normal limits.	4
3. Problem behavior mildly incapacitating: some evidence of problems: behaviors interfering with life adjustment factors.	3

*Unpublished data. University of Minnesota, Division of Child and Adolescent Psychiatry.

4. Problem behavior moderately incapacitating: significant impairment of functioning and life adjustment factors. 5

5. Problem behavior severely incapacitating: impairment in life adjustment factors to the degree that the individual is essentially unable to function autonomously and requires institutionalization and/or primary support and protection by others. 3

Problem behaviors in children rated 4 and 5 were seldom mutism. Major difficulties were with socialization, family conflicts, school adjustment and appropriate independence and work history.

Discussion

Because the subjects were referred for hospital study, the sample is probably skewed in the direction of more severely disturbed individuals. A review of the major findings indicate that children who are electively mute are a heterogenous group of individuals. Milder cases responded to separation from the home and to an inpatient psychiatric ward program. Elective mutism decreased during hospitalization and was accompanied by increased socialization and autonomy; those children who did not begin to speak did respond to an operant conditioning approach using a reward system. The seven children who did well at outcome (ratings of 2 or 3) had the following findings: average or better intelligence, a history of precipitating events which brought on the mute behavior, and a stable family structure with parental interactions being satisfactory with each other and with their children. Personality testing was normal in five of these seven subjects. These children were isolated and shy but tended to be happy and content. Speech was satisfactory in all except one who did not speak to individuals she disliked. Two children had graduated from high school and one was at an age appropriate level in school. Three were one to three years behind and the one that dropped out was failing.

The eight subjects with poor outcome (ratings 4 or 5) were a less homogenous group than those who did better. Three of them had subnormal intelligence. The family interactions were regarded as inadequate in five and there was a history of schizophrenia in first degree relatives of four cases. Three had an aggressive and frightening father who was still an adversive influence on them. Only one child had normal results in personality testing. In contrast to the group which did well at outcome, these children were not only introverted and shy but were friendless in seven of eight cases. Only a girl with a recent history of delinquent behavior had overtly satisfactory social relationships. Speech was satisfactory in only three of these children, whereas another four were very reluctant to speak to strangers and one was mute. School performance was good in only one case; in two cases the children were truant. One had been expelled for mutism and behavior problems, one was still mute and two were one to two years behind in class placement. Another had graduated from high school but was failing academically at the time.

Because of the small number of subjects, the results do not lend themselves to statistical evaluation. The age of onset of mutism, age of initial treatment and duration of mutism before hospitalization did not differ between the two groups. Only the mean difference between good and poor outcome groups for admission and follow-up IQ are statistically significant. Means for the scales of the MMPI are uniformly more pathological for the poor outcome group but the results do not approach statistical significance for any scale. The significant difference in variance for length of hospitalization is due to a long hospital stay for one subject in the good outcome group.

Conclusion

Recent treatment reports using behavior modification techniques indicated success with small numbers of electively mute children. It would seem advisable to try these techniques, and if possible keep children in school classes appropriate for their age and intelligence. Even those children in our study who were speaking spontaneously at follow-up were behind in school

Table I

	Age at F.U.	Age Initial Treatment	Age Onset	Adm. I.Q.	F.U. I.Q.	Hosp. Weeks
Good Outcome (Mean)	16.9	7.2	4.7	105	104	17.4
Poor Outcome (Mean)	17.1	7.9	5.1	83	83	11.0
Difference between means	NS	NS	NS	.05	.05	NS
Difference between variables	NS	NS	NS	NS	.05	.05

grade levels because of school decisions. Because of the cost of hospitalization it is advisable to work with the child as an outpatient in the formulation of a plan for getting the child to speak in school. Cooperation of the parents, school administrators and teachers is needed for this. Only if this approach fails is hospitalization warranted.

In our series hospitalization was excessively long for many of the children and it would seem that a structured behavior modification program was also indicated in the hospital setting. Subsequently, however, there must be continual follow-through by teachers and parents until the new pattern of responding verbally is established. Because of the lack of such follow-up, one child in this series became much more mute over the years and subsequently would not even respond to a structured inpatient approach.

References

1. Tramer, M. *A. Kinder. Psychiat. 1,* 30, (1934).

2. Halpern, W.I. and Hammond, J.R. *J. Amer. Acad. Child Psychiat. 10,* 94, (1971).

3. Reed, G.F. *J. Child Psychol. Psychiat. 4,* 99, (1963).

4. Pustrom, E. and Speers, R.W. *J. Amer. Acad. Child Psychiat. 3,* 387, (1964).

5. Mora, G., DeVault, D., and Schopler, B. *J. Child Psychol. Psychiat. 3,* 41, (1962).

6. Elson, A., Pierson, C., Jones, C.D., and Schumacher, E. *Arch. Gen. Psychiat. 13,* 182, (1965).

7. Wright, H.L., Jr. *J. Amer. Acad. Child Psychiat. 7,* 603, (1968).

8. Reid, J.B., Hawkins, W., Keutzer, C., McNeal, S.A., Phelps, R.E., Reid, K.M., and Mees, H.L. *Child Psychol. Psychiat. 8,* 27, (1967).

9. Straughan, J.H., Potter, W.K., and Hamilton, S.H. *J. Child Psychol. Psychiat. 6,* 125, (1971).

10. Briggs, In *M-B History Record.* Clinical Psychology Publishing, Brandon, Vermont, (1969).

MENTAL HEALTH IN CHILDREN, Volume III
Edited By D. V. Siva Sankar

COMMUNICATION THERAPY: A REEXAMINATION

L.A. Buck

N. Freshley, J.K.Y. Lee and L. Shapiro

Suffolk Hearing and Speech Center

I. Autonomy as a Primary Goal

The purpose of the present paper is to extend the evaluation of the "Communication Therapy Program" at the "Suffolk Hearing and Speech Center." As previously discussed (1), this Program is founded upon the conception that language and hearing deficits are best viewed as part-processes of the total personality and of the family and social communication networks within which the individual functions: stuttering, articulation defects, and hearing impairments cannot be worked with as isolated events.

If the focus is upon the total human being, language learning must be integrated with general social, emotional and cognitive growth. The primary issue which arises from this orientation, then, is the promotion of autonomy and independence. Previously it has been argued that the development of language and cognition are inextricably interwoven with the individual's autonomy (1, 2). This position is also consistent with developmental theory (3, 4).

A valuable analysis of autonomy (5, 6) has been provided which is relevant to the primary goal of the "Communication

Therapy Program." First of all ego autonomy is *relative,* and is crucially related to intellectual and linguistic functions. Autonomy of the ego, however, can be undermined from two directions: the intensification of powerful drives and the coercion of environmental forces. The primary guarantee against the impairment of autonomy rests upon inborn ego apparatuses i.e., functions such as perception and thought which provide for adaptation to external reality. A balance between external and internal forces promotes relative ego autonomy and, consequently, optimal growth of language and speech. If drives or external stimuli are increased excessively or severely blocked (e.g., hearing impairment, organic damage, emotional conflict, overdependence), autonomy will be undermined, and the linguistic functions intertwined with it will deteriorate or be delayed. The initial task, therefore, when deafness, severe deprivation, etc. stifle growth and interfere with communication processes is to provide an atmosphere which leads the individual in the direction of greater autonomy and independence.

A variety of writers have recommended the use of psychotherapeutic techniques with communication problems (7, 8, 9, 10, 11), but others (12, 13) have provided a more extensive integration of dynamic principles with the traditional roles of the speech therapist. The "Communication Therapy Program" at the Suffolk Hearing and Speech Center (1) has developed a therapeutic approach toward language and speech problems which permit the client to take the initiative in his own therapy in order to experience progress as part of a process of self-mastery.

The roots of this approach are derived from both psychoanalytic and client-centered psychotherapy. The centrality of the goal of individual autonomy in classical psychoanalysis (14) has been indicated. It was proposed that Freud's primary purpose was to strengthen the individuality of the person relative to society. This emphasis upon autonomy has also been espoused in (15) psychoanalytically-oriented psychotherapy. Attention has also been given to the need for the promotion of independent functioning in client-centered psychotherapy (16, 17): techniques which emphasize the therapist's refusal to be drawn into an advice - or information-giving role are based upon this premise. However, a crucial element of any therapeutic approach which hopes to cultivate autonomy rests upon the type of atmosphere created. Such an environment (18) has been described as non-authoritarian, non-manipulative and respecting. This is analogous to the caring, genuine, accepting conditions described by others (17, 19).

In the case of the "Communication Therapy Program" the goal of facilitating individual growth and autonomy has been applied to a group approach which makes use of the dynamics of the group itself. Play therapy is chosen because it begins with a level of behavior which is characteristic of the young child's own means of communication -- play (20, 21). In addition, these non-directive approaches emphasize a non-authoritarian orientation. The group dynamic focus (i.e., concern with the relationships between members of the group rather than just perceiving separate individuals in the same setting) is more clearly represented in the psychoanalytic literature (22, 23). However, both sources place great emphasis upon permitting the individual (i.e., in this case, the child) to take the primary initiative in his own growth. This can lead to the sense of achievement and mastery (3) rather than a continuation of external and authoritarian control, and can culminate in the state of "we-ness" (24) which is the context from which language grows.

II. Play Group Referral and Structure

The "Communication Therapy Program" involves an attempt to integrate the total family (by means of parent and child groups) within the therapeutic process (1), but the present assessment focuses its principal concern upon the child play groups. Children referred to the communication therapy groups are those who, after observation during the initial evaluation session or during a period of individual speech therapy, exhibit characteristics that lead to the expectation of difficulty in gaining maximum benefit from a conventional program of speech therapy. These are children who might show extreme dependence; lack of motivation, self-confidence or initiative; inhibition in regard to interpersonal communication; hyper-activity; excessive distractibility; withdrawal; or disruptive aggressiveness. Decisions for placement in play groups are made, therefore, relative to the child's capacity for self-directed, independent functioning; classical diagnostic categories are deemphasized (thus, the children included in these groups range from normal adaptation problems to psychotic adjustments). The rationale for this system of referral is based upon the need for, at least, minimal initiative, motivation and self-control (i.e., relative autonomy) in order to utilize the materials available within the traditional speech therapy setting. Building upon self-directed activity, language growth becomes incorporated as the child's own accomplishment, and therefore, helps cultivate a sense of competence which becomes a foundation for further reaching out for language.

Children are placed in groups of five to eight with two adults who serve as a group leader and an assistant. The adults are speech therapists and selected college students under the supervision of the consulting psychologist. Groups are homogeneous in terms of chronological age and quality of language functioning, and are heterogeneous in terms of behavioral styles and types of communication impairment. Consequently, a group might consist of active and passive children three to four years of age whose communications deficits might be attributed to maturational delay, mental retardation, emotional disturbance, or hearing loss. While variation of personal style fosters group dynamics, a limited range of maturational levels is essential in terms of permitting the cultivation of the social interaction which provides the crucial context for the communicative significance of language. The ideal maximum for maturational differences (typically, but not entirely, decided by chronological age) is approximately two years.

An example of the selection process involved in the child play therapy is represented by a group of 6-8 year old boys who are all attending school (two require special placement). Prior diagnosis, for this particular group, includes delayed language, autism, deafness, and articulatory problems. The activity level is generally high, although there is a numerical balance of three passive and three active children. The dynamic common denominator is a communicative problem with its roots in the childs dependence upon adult direction. The goal in referring each child to this group is based upon his achieving autonomy within a peer situation that would permit the child to develop at his own pace. Therefore, a four year old child would not be likely to be able to learn the age-appropriate social and emotional behavior of the average child in this group even if there were good progress toward autonomy. Furthermore, additional active-aggressive or passive children, who fit into the desirable age category, are likely to upset the balance of the existing group either overwhelming the passive-withdrawn members or leading to such quiescence that active children would be unable to promote a dynamic atomsphere. It is particularly important during the early stages of a group to select children who will complement the age levels present and who will fit in with the current equilibrium of behavioral styles. As the group becomes established, it may be better able to incorporate new participants who would have interfered with progress at an earlier time: the movement toward increased activity by this group of 6-8 year old boys suggests that it may be able to handle another passive or withdrawn child at this time.

The diversity of children dealt with by The Center in the "Communication Therapy Program" is illustrated by the case of a young boy who was four and one half years of age at intake. MN's initial evaluation reported inconsistent responsiveness to verbal and gestural directions and expressive language which was characterized by unintelligible jargon and echolalia. A few isolated words were available, but the remainder of his verbal communication was limited to stereotyped, ritualistic speech forms such as TV commercials. Behavioral and gestural communication had a similar repetitive, compulsive quality (e.g., humming, rocking, covering his ears). Eye contact was present, but passivity and withdrawal had resulted in an independent, psychiatric diagnosis of autism (no neurological findings were elicited). While language was ineffective as a basis for socialization, early motor development was relatively adequate. The family context involved a highly overprotective orientation on the part of both parents (most exaggerated in the father), and a communicative network had been established which assigned to MN and his younger brother (the two youngest of five children) roles of passivity, dependence and helplessness. The recommendation for the "Communication Therapy Program," therefore, was based upon the necessity of helping the total family break out of this established pattern of communication, but MN's placement in a play group was specifically oriented toward promoting his own individual growth toward greater independence. His stereotyped use of language indicated that he had the capacity for well articul-lated speech, but he was not able to use language for the purpose of interpersonal interaction. A situation which did not confirm his existing expectations (i.e., excessive protectiveness or mothering in response to his helplessness) would permit new communicative patterns to develop. Growth of autonomy required an environment which permitted free response and self-initiated activity.

The initial and perhaps most critical problem faced by this approach is introduced by the referral of a child to a play group and the parents to an adult group. This immediately confronts one of the basic assumptions of the "Program": communication therapy deals with the total child rather than a single aspect of this growth such as stuttering or defective articulation. The necessity for total involvement as a family unit attacks tightly held preconceptions regarding the nature of speech therapy on the part of both clients and staff. The parents participation and cooperation is required on several levels. On the most basic level, it is the parent who must bring the child to therapy. A breakdown in this primary parent responsibility has often occurred mostly due to the necessity of their participation in the parent group. (The 40% cancellation rate of the first three years of the program's existence has been reduced to 20% in the last year, but this still reflects a range, for particular groups, from 10% to 80%) A variety of methods has been used to express their resistance: cancellation of appointments, lateness, inability to schedule meetings, anger, denying their problems exist, bringing other children that have to be cared for so that they cannot participate in parent meetings, bringing the child for play therapy and then going shopping and, ultimately, termination of therapy. Parental feedback has indicated that they are seeking advice and direction from the professional staff. They are used to the medical model which prescribes pills and solutions with equal facility. Since experts are supposed to possess all of the answers, they anticipate being told what is "right" and "wrong" for their children. Since the "problem" (e.g., delayed speech, poor articulation) is viewed as taking place in the child rather than in themselves, parents do not have the initial self-motivation that is typical of a mental health center. In addition, the average client at the Center comes from a low socio-economic and socio-educational background which is not prepared for a psychotherapeutic orientation. (Educational levels of the parents currently participating in the "Program" include: 16% who did not go beyond the 8th grade, 24% with some high school attendance, 46% who graduated from high school and 14% with some college study.) Therefore, the initial focus of resistance relates to the experience of responsibility for the child's past difficulties and future progress, and this leads to the need for ongoing clarification of the purposes of the group program. In view of the decrease in cancellation rates, it appears that progress is being made in terms of more effective incorporation of parents into the "Program," but it is necessary to maintain these reductions or continue to improve on them in order to substantiate this trend.

Additional problems arise from practical questions of group placement. Group selection seeks to assign each child in a fashion that maintains homogeneity with respect to age (maturational level) and heterogeneity according to sex, communication deficit and behavioral style. This framework has often met with difficulty based upon the population of children which is available. There are substantially fewer girls than boys in the "Program," but this ratio is consistent with that of boys and girls receiving speech therapy generally. No girls are participating in the older groups (6-8 and 8-10 year olds), and only five of the fourteen children in the 3-5 year group are females. (These figures are consistent with long range trends at the Center. Of the last 96 children admitted, only 20 were girls. In addition, girls are even less representative of older groups: only 4 of these girls were involved in any groups beyond the 3-5 year level). In the same fashion, it has been impossible to maintain optimum age limits within some groups. This can arise from the lack of an opening in a group with the appropriate age-range, or from the nonexistence of such a group. Finally, independence and personal style may take priority over chronological age patterns. Where an overly passive child has been unable to deal with his highly aggressive peers, placement in a younger group may be the only practical choice. Adequate numbers of active and passive or aggressive and inhibited children have been too limited to provide optimum balance for all age groupings. This means that the ideal blending of behavioral styles and age levels must be sacrificed, at times, in order to meet the individual needs of specific children. Nevertheless, even where an ideal balance cannot be achieved minimally satisfactory group compositions can be attained by including at least two children who could become isolates if they were alone (e.g., two withdrawn children in an active group or two girls in a male group).

This need for consideration of individual dynamics in regard to group placement arose for MN in his third year of participation in communication therapy. While considerable progress had taken place in regard to his ability to utilize language for the purpose of interacting with peers and the adults in the group, and greater autonomy was evident in terms of his aggressiveness and ability to initiate activities with others, the group that he was placed in was becoming hyperactive and highly competitive. Even though this group was age appropriate, it became evident that MN was being scapegoated and isolated so effectively that he was withdrawing again into passive helplessness. However, since no other group was available at his own age level, he was placed in a younger group which did not meet the ideal age requirements. This group permitted MN to practice at leadership roles and to return to his efforts toward interacting with others.

III. Technique

Since the primary goal of communication therapy is to offer "an environment within which a child can grow in a self-directed, autonomous, creative fashion", the adults (i.e., leader and assistant) in the situation approach therapy with an active listening attitude and attempt to minimize direction of the children's behavior. Instead, it is expected that the children can originate and coordinate their own play and resolve their own interpersonal conflicts. The adults became involved only to curb extreme aggressiveness or to arrange the situation in ways that make it possible for associations among children to begin. It is experience with the process of decision making which promotes autonomy and gives rise to self-initiated, self-confident action (20, 21).

The group leader's communications emphasize descriptions of on-going activities in language that is appropriate to each age-group. For the younger age levels (3-5-year olds), non-verbal communications such as approaching the child, nodding or smiling are most suitable for their limited linguistic capacity. For example, a child who is new to a group typically will not become an active participant at first, but will sit on the outskirts of the group while observing the other children or while playing quietly by himself. By exchanging eye contact or smiles the group leader can acknowledge the child's presence and begin to include him as a member of the group. Nevertheless, while this is an invitation to participate, it is not a demand. Similar, active response is directed toward a child who has been in the group for awhile, but who still plays as an isolate. As children demonstrate increased responsiveness to language by their spontaneous vocal activity (either speech or non-meaningful soundmaking), speech is used more frequently by the leader. Thus, the initiative is left to the child in terms of communicative activity. Underlying all such techniques is the expectation that each child, given the appropriate conditions, is capable of becoming self-directed. The leader's verbalizations, while being maintained at a non-interpretive level, are intended to provide stimulation for verbal or behavioral responses from the child. A child who is just sitting and not playing with toys might react to comments such as "I wonder why Mark isn't playing with any of the toys" or "Everyone's playing with something and Mark is just sitting." The child's responses might take the form of squirming in his chair, approaching a toy, or saying "Don't want to." Or, other children might react by looking at the child and inviting him to join their play. The leader's intention here, however, is only to stimulate movement in communication; no particular response is demanded.

In addition to responding to the comments of each child individually, the group leader attempts to point out interactive behavior or group activities: "Frank and John are playing with the garage," "Chris and Barbie both want the teapot," "Everyone is doing something different," or "David gave Richard some marbles, and now everyone can play." Communications which focus on the interchange between two or more children are more apt to promote awareness of the total network of interpersonal relationships. This awareness facilitates the group's ability to find its own solutions. For example, the group is capable (frequently by itself) of controlling a bully or encourageing the participation of an isolate. Whether spontaneously developed or stimulated by communications of the leader, the main point is that the group is usually capable of resolving its own crises. If a child continues to bother others by kicking over toys, the other children can collaborate to prevent further disruptions by barricading the toys or pushing the child away until his behavior is more acceptable. If a child is playing alone, crying softly or just watching, other children tend to approach him to tug at his arm, to offer a toy or to remark to the adult that the child is crying.

Little effort is made to provide information, or to give advice or help -- especially with older, more integrated groups -- in order to permit cooperation and self-help in dealing with problems that arise. For example, if a child comes to the adult for assistance in making a simple repair on a toy, the therapist's response might be a modified imitation of the child's request: "You want me to fix the truck's wheels?" Such a remark might invite help from one of the other children, or might lead the child to fix the toy himself. But regardless of these possibilities, this type of communication rests upon the assumption that the child can do it himself. This example also demonstrates the use of a questioning form of response which not only reflects the active listening and observing orientation of the therapist by overtly pointing to the child help-seeking behavior but directly invites a response (i.e., cultivates but does not require social participation). It is critical that questioning is not turned into an interrogation--no particular response is required.

Within the framework of each group setting, the specific goals of therapy are different for each child. Because each child's personality is unique, the behaviors and characteristics to be developed in therapy will relate to the particular individual. With an extremely passive child, for instance, a major accomplishment might be an increase in aggressiveness; with a highly aggressive child, improvement might involve a reduction in combativeness.

Change in the passive, withdrawn child occurs as a result of the group leader's communications and the behavior of the active members of the group. The therapist can sit beside the child while commenting about activities: "You're watching Jimmy put the train tracks together." Smiles from the child are returned. Play with nearby toys could be initiated in an attempt to draw the child into activity. However, these communicative behaviors must not become commands: the child must feel free to respond in an openended fashion or remain mute and uninvolved. Often the ones to bring the more passive child into play are the aggressive and active children who, in their exploration of objects and people in the environment, inevitably come upon the child playing quietly. Interactions between children may be sporadic at first, and may result in domination by the active child. Yet if having toys taken from him becomes meaningful, the passive child will begin to defend himself and the toys he has, and may start to develop more aggressiveness, initiative, and self-assurance. At any rate, the motion of the active children inevitably encompasses the whole environment, and the passive or even withdrawn child becomes a de facto (even if non-voluntary) participant.

The aggressiveness of some children can be so severe as to cause panic and regression in others. Such extreme behavior sometimes cannot be managed by the spontaneous activity of the children, but must be controlled by consistent behavioral responses from the adults who then assume a more active, but nonpunishing, role (25, 26). The child is held by the group leader briefly and calmly as soon as an inappropriate action occurs and every time it occurs. No verbal commands or direct interpretations of behavior are made since remarks such as "no" may contain other connotations fostered by parents (words like "no" have been used too inconsistently by most parents). In addition, non-verbal communication is simpler, more direct and more consistent with the linguistic capacities of these children. Even the oldest group (8-10) is still within the age range (4) considered to be preconceptual (i.e., not capable of full abstraction). However, while non-verbal limit setting is preferable, descriptive (but noninterpretive) statements may be made by the group leader in order to foster communicative movement. A child's striking of another or his throwing of articles can be managed by the adult stepping between the children to make it difficult for the aggressive one to reach his target or by taking hold of his throwing hand or the object to be thrown. By receiving a consistent response from the group leader the child comes to know the limits of behavior in the situation, and learns to substitute other behaviors until more adaptive methods are achieved. The reduction of extreme aggressiveness permits relative autonomy from such internal enslavement and encourages the growth of more effective self-control--as a result adaptive communication becomes possible.

Since it is desirable to restrict therapist initiated limit-setting to the minimum required by the situation (the children should be allowed to solve all issues that they are capable of handling), the environment and the play material can be managed in order to reduce the need for such involvment. The general conditions of the playroom should be arranged, ideally, so that there are no dangerous pieces of furniture or equipment present, and the walls should be made of durable, easily cleaned material. With aggressive children soft, inexpensive toys preclude the necessity of attempting to prevent the destruction of throwing of materials. In the same way the space of the playroom can be managed in order to reduce the need for limit setting. For example, open spaces communicate the opportunity for vigorous running, fighting, etc., but an object like a table (which calls for sitting behavior) placed in the middle of such an area breaks up the potential runway. Finally, time can be managed in order to reduce therapist intervention. Toys and games will draw the attention and interest of a particular group of children for a specific period of time; beyond this point a highly distractible, active group will convert the toys to aggressive purposes requiring limit setting by the group leader. New material, introduced before group contagion has taken over, can attract the interest which will maintain constructive play. Play during the initial minutes of a session may involve cooperative games such as checkers or a set of trains. As interest fades some children begin to wander over to other sub-groups. If their attempts to join in play are rejected, retaliation may take the form of disruptive behavior-pushing checkers off the table or scattering train tracks around the floor. Before the number of such children increases to an unmanageable level, a change in materials can restimulate interest and foster a return to cooperative play.

The limits of behavior prescribed for each group will vary with the particular group leader since personality differences will give rise to diverse levels of tolerance for aggressiveness. One leader will be more accepting than another of such behaviors as climbing onto furniture or throwing toys even when these actions will not endanger anyone. The important factor is that these limits must be consistently implemented within the boundaries established by each group leader. However, while individual differences in leadership style must be acknowledged, the primary goal remains one of preventing physical injury and avoiding the trauma of a passive child being overwhelmed by the aggression of another. Constant vigilance needs to be directed toward the meaning of the child's behavior and the leader's feelings regarding the need for a protective response. Taking over for the child when he is capable of handling the situation himself communicates an expectation of helplessness on the part of the adult. Nevertheless, no growth in independence is going to occur where "real" terror and panic is permitted. Sometimes when a child throws objects into a corner, sweeps toys off a table or stands on furniture, he is only attempting to gain attention or to manipulate the therapist in ways similar to those employed with his parents. When those actions are not physically dangerous, the therapist should recognize the behaviors in an undisturbed manner and with simple statements such as "You're pushing the dishes off the table," or "You kicked the playhouse over." Such comments are usually not the response expected by the child--i.e., punishment, angry words, or other inappropriate forms of attention. Failure to receive these anticipated responses permits some other alternative communication which is more adapted to achieving attention and affection.

It is evident from the previous discussion that techniques and therapeutic expectations are relative to the particular phase of group development and to different maturational levels. This also relates to the degree of cooperative play which is established. Free play groups are used as the therapeutic context because play is the natural environment within which children attain much of their overall growth and gain much of their experience with inter-personal communication. Newly established and younger groups are likely to emphasize solitary play (i.e., each child playing at unrelated tasks with little social or linguistic interaction). This is expected for all young children and is likely, at least initially, for older age groups (even 6-8 and 8-10 year old groups) which are characterized by communication deficits. While older groups may rapidly move on to parallel play (i.e., children playing at similar tasks, but with little interpersonal exchange), younger children may remain for considerable periods of time at the solitary level. Maturational gain as well as therapeutic advance is required for progress at the earlier ages. Full cooperative play (i.e., play which integrates the whole group's activity relative to a single game and involves sufficient rules and regulations as to require high levels of inter-personal contact and linguistic exchange) cannot be expected at all in younger groups. Such play activity is also highly unlikely in newly established groups; cooperative play is the result of a long process of maturational development and therapeutic progress. However, since it is an achievement which results from considerable experience, preliminary stages of cooperative play will appear early in the process of development of the older groups. Therefore, several children may initiate cooperative play activity which does not include the total group or breaks down before it becomes a highly organized game (isolated and parallel play are also preparatory forms). These are expectations regarding the maturational relativity of socialization, play and the growth of language (27, 28).

These phase changes are relevant to technique in terms of the therapist's expectations and the type of play materials which are utilized. The toys used are selected according to appropriate age and interest levels of the children, but also in terms of the extent to which they permit or encourage cooperative play. For example, extremely open-ended toys like undifferentiated sets of blocks are particularly useful for younger children; they permit isolated, parallel or cooperative play. In contrast, specialized block type material which can be integrated into a single fort or farm grouping or a set of cars with a single track tends to invite cooperative play. While cooperative play and mature social communication can be considered desirable goals, the means of achieving these skills is crucial. Within this program it is essential that these skills are the result of the growth of autonomy -- that is, the therapist's role is to let the child move toward cooperative play as a result of his own self-initiated activity rather than as a consequence of external directives or authoritarian control (3). The therapist must have the expectation that the child can grow in these directions or he is likely to be drawn into organizing and controlling activity. However, appropriate play material, active listening and therapist communications related to cooperative interaction are necessary.

MN's therapeutic progress provides a good example of a shift from isolated play through parallel and cooperative forms. Initially he was highly withdrawn using his unintelligible or stereotyped TV commercial speech to make it difficult for others to communicate with him. This was followed by some progress in being able to respond to others, even if inconsistently, and the use of the names of other group members. Nevertheless contact was primarily limited to the adults or was a response to the initiatives of other children. Play remained highly solitary or parallel to other children's activity. During the second year of group participation, cooperative interaction with one or two children at a time was noted along with more active assertive behavior. By his fourth year in the program, he was initiating considerable activity, competing for a leadership role and sometimes joining in group cooperative play. This progression was characterized by alternating periods of sociability and withdrawal depending upon the challenge provided by the group. While cooperative, social interaction is not yet completely stabilized, as it is not in any child of this age, the overall progression continues in the direction of autonomy.

A variety of problems have been isolated in the attempt to implement the "Communication Therapy Program." Since the free play situation confronts each child with a novel environment which requires a new mode of adaptation, some initial crying, withdrawal, anxiety, etc. is anticipated. The child's habitual techniques for dealing with difficult situations will be the first communicative avenue utilized, and this is likely to be followed by an intensification of the initial mode of response in the same fashion that we are likely to raise our voices when another person seems not to have heard what we have said. For example, a passive-dependent child may communicate his helplessness and need to be taken care of by whimpering and tears. If this message does not lead to an appropriate response by the adults, intense, tantrum-like screaming may eventually result. When this behavior doesn't succeed, alternative forms of communication, which may be better adapted to cooperative exchange, will be attempted. During this time, however, the child's discomfort may compound the parent's feelings of resistance to the "Program" leading to termination.

Responsiveness to the child's discomfort can also lead to rigidification of habitual parental behavioral patterns which have prevented the growth of autonomy. For example, if a child is having difficulty joining in the play of other children, the parent may, even more than usual, attempt to solve the situation for him. Even more frustrating for the staff, is the situation where the child is attempting to experiment with a new approach (e.g., a passive child attempting some assertive aggressiveness) which is part of the therapeutic process, when the parents remove the child from the program. This is exemplified by the growth in assertive behavior in a young boy, TN. As this mode of response became more apparent at home and in school, the parents, after two semesters, withdrew him from the "Program" denying that their son had any problems other than an articulation disorder. The parents' expectations of a "good" boy required passivity (while, at the same time, desiring autonomy). The parent group had insufficient time to open up new alternatives for them. However, any behavioral change in the child throws the total family network off balance, and requires new adjustments from the other family members. All of these examples are indicative of the crucial importance of gaining the parents' trust in order to secure a working relationship with the total family unit.

The child's previously established patterns of behavior also provide difficulties for the group leader and the assistant. At the outset of this form of therapy, it is not unusual for the child to remain either close to the adult or off by himself until he becomes more comfortable within this "new" situation. This dependence may continue for extended periods, the child seemingly waiting for the adult to participate in some authoritarian or protective fashion. The patience which must be demonstrated by the group leader tests his capacity for active listening. There is no clear line between withdrawal (or even panic) and subtle manipulation, and the therapist must be prepared to deal with a fluid situation which requires spontaneity. Techniques applied in a mechanical fashion can become more destructive than helpful, and, therefore, a compromise must be developed by the group leader between the use of his own feelings as a clue to the meaning of the child's message and the technical rules which are intended to promote autonomy. This type of conflict requires continuing reassessment on the part of the group leader and extensive supervision. The meaning of a communication can be confirmed by its behavioral consequences, but this requires adequate time for repeated corroboration. Hypotheses regarding the meaning of a communication should be held tentatively until they are confirmed over a sufficient period of time in a variety of different contexts.

An additional aspect of this same issue involves the coordination between group leader and assistant. The timing for communication, limit setting, exchange of toys, etc. is established by the group leader. The primary role of the assistant is to attempt to fit into the style of the leader even when the assistant feels that aggressive behavior should be limited sooner or that a particular communication should not be made at a certain time. A group leader and an assistant who function together for long periods of time may develop considerable consistency in their timing, but even then they are vulnerable to manipulations which set one against the other. A child who cannot obtain help from one adult may seek it from the other. For example, D.L. liked to climb on the group leader and the assistant. If one did not respond as he wished, he went to the other, and then back-and-forth between the two. Eventually he learned that neither could be manipulated into an exclusive relationship, and the frequency of this behavior decreased. After this, other more appropriate social maneuvers were tried. Many difficulties can be avoided by the assistant taking his cues from the group leader, but frequent discussion between leader and assistant is desirable.

While difficulties can arise from having two adults in the playroom, the assistant provides considerable flexibility in dealing with the play materials and for limit-setting with more than one child at a time in highly active or aggressive groups. The need for assistants, however, raises the problem of recruitment. The group leaders are certified speech pathologists who have been specifically trained for "Communication Therapy Groups," but assistants have been obtained as volunteers from local colleges. While the use of undergraduate psychology students as assistant group leaders provides one of the innovative contributions of the program, the time and training required has not always made it possible to supply adequate personnel. The Center has expanded its vistas to include all colleges in the area, but the in-service training requires a substantial number of sessions which often is not commensurate with the longevity of a volunteer's involvement. The value of this aspect of the "Program" must be viewed, then, in terms of the preliminary training of people for future professional roles as well as immediate service to the Center. The difficulty of providing adequate supervision is related to the model of communication which underlies the whole approach. The understanding and exploration of the meaning of the children's communication requires some self-exploration on the part of the assistant, and this can lead to sufficient discomfort to drop out of the group.

The same issue (i.e., self-exploration) applies to the group leaders. Constant reassessment of how the leader affects others becomes part of the preparation for effective functioning in the child group. With this in mind the group leaders (actually the entire staff of the Center) have established a weekly group meeting -- "We Meetings" -- which are oriented toward the dynamic exploration of the group leader role. The "We" group, by means of the experience of participating in a therapeutic atmosphere, provides the staff with an opportunity to understand the situation that is offered to their clients. In addition, it gives rise to the opportunity for sharpening skills of active listening and observing; for working through one's own acceptance of the hostility, dependence or withdrawal exhibited by the children; or for the expression of frustration regarding absenteeism of the children which disrupts the essential continuity of group sessions. A typical "We" meeting may include discussion of how a particular child's behavior causes a therapist to react. For instance, R.F. tended to harass a therapist by pulling out his shirt, tugging at his jacket and throwing toys in his direction. The therapist talked about his angry feelings toward this child, and how this affected his methods of setting limits and of relating to him in a positive manner. Other "We" meeting members were invited to compare similar situations. Information which helped to explain R.F.'s behavior was offered thereby providing the therapist with new alternatives for understanding R.F.'s provocative actions.

IV. Goals and Termination

The goal of the "Communication Therapy Program" is to allow each client to achieve maximum autonomy. In psychoanalytic terms this means extending the control of the ego over internal factors such as primitive drives and other outside forces which are aimed toward the enforcement of authoritarian control. This means the augmentation of the client's capacity for self-determination and freedom of choice. While any conception of "absolute freedom" leads to a philosophical impasse or even absurdity, the conception of relative autonomy (5, 6) provides a viable foundation for a therapeutic ethic.

The major focus in terms of the evaluation of treatment programs should be directed, at this time, toward the exploration of the basic values (i.e., implicit or explicit assumptions) which underlie therapeutic attitudes and technique. Psychotherapy becomes a "meaningless" endeavor without an explicit formulation of its value base (14). This conclusion rests upon the political, moral and human consequences which result from any form of diagnosis of treatment (14, 29). While there is a growing awareness that the fundamental values of any model of therapy have ramifications for the total system (17, 24, 30, 31, 32, 33, 34, 35, 36), the direct relationships between the therapist's philosophy of man and technical maneuvers have just begun to be explored. Until these issues are fully examined little progress can be anticipated in dealing with questions regarding the effectiveness of one system of therapy versus another; the "meaning" of words like "cure" or "improvement" must be explored within the context of each model. Finally, the problem cannot be dismissed by resort to experimental verification. Each research technique is limited by its own value structure. The contradictions and inconsistent claims in the area of psychotherapy research are largely dependent upon a failure to explore the values implicit in the terminology of different approaches.

While the "Communication Therapy Program" cannot claim to have explored or understood all of the value implications of promoting autonomy, the techniques, environment and therapeutic attitudes which are currently being used have been selected in terms of their consistency with this goal. The emphasis upon self-initiated activity on the part of the client (child and parent) which has been assessed in detail in the previous section is a result of this analysis. In addition, part of the supervisory process involves a continuing examination of the therapist's attitudes and feelings. Technique cannot be prescribed in a mechanical fashion. For example, holding a child in an effort to set limits for aggressive behavior can be a calm but consistent attempt to prevent destructiveness, and the group leader's attitudes can continue to be respect and acceptance of the child. On the other hand the same form of restraint can communicate suppression or forced conformity. This is likely where the group leader feels that he is in a battle to subdue undesirable behavior in the child. The therapist's response in both situations may appear to be highly similar, but the values implicit in these divergent orientations toward people will lead to critically different meanings for the child.

An additional value in this approach is the assumption that autonomy and free-choice are the preconditions for self-actualization (18). This means that movement in terms of characteristics such as more effective interaction with peers, improvement in the use of speech and language and increased adequacy in coping with conditions at home and at school is considered to be indicative of progress toward greater autonomy. Our hope is that when a child and his parents leave the group program, they will be better equipped to handle the problems which are a part of the process of living. However, this means the self-confidence and willingness to choose for one-self, and a sense that one is capable of influencing one's own future. Maslow's conception implies the gratification which results from going beyond simple deficiency needs, but even self-actualization as a model of health should not be imposed as a standard. If autonomy is the primary goal, termination is relevant when people experience themselves as being capable of solving their problems in living; termination is a decision that parents must be intimately involved with.

Since living is part of a continuing process, termination cannot wait upon an attempt to prevent all future problems. Life guarantees that crises will arise, but individuals who have made progress in solving their own problems have greater capacity for meeting new demands. For instance, J.C., released from a play group six months ago, continues to encounter academic problems in school because of a moderately severe hearing loss. Both parents and child can now cope with these difficulties in an adaptive fashion. The parents call upon members of the staff at the center to participate in conferences with school personnel in order to enable J.C. to continue attending regular public school classes. Mr. and Mrs. C. are able to provide the teacher with support when needed, and can deal with J.C.'s decreasing incidents of tantrum behavior. Obviously the process is not finished -- nor can it be -- but these parents have a greater sense of making their own decisions. Although they may still lean upon the help of the staff at the Center, they are moving away from this form of dependence.

While examples are easy to provide in terms of the value of "Communication Therapy," it is difficult to estimate the total effect. Many terminations are not based upon therapeutic merit, but are related to practical requirements: the shift of hearing impaired children to schools for the deaf, the necessity of parents moving to another location, a change of the treatment responsibility from the Center to the public school, etc. An adequate criterion for movement toward autonomy which can be utilized for statistical review has not yet been established. However, 29% of a sample of 90 children have remained with the "Communication Therapy Program" for a sufficient period of time (more than a year) to provide an analysis of behavioral change. An additional 36.6% have been retained for more than four months and can be explored in terms of movement toward autonomy. While an examination of these cases in terms of improvement has not been completed, it is evident that most terminations take place by five years of age (76.7%). This relates to the shift from preschool to regular school placement. In addition, when termination is analyzed in terms of disability (some subgroups are too small at the present time to provide reliable analysis), diagnostic categories (i.e., hearing loss, delayed speech, stuttering, emotional problems, brain injury, cleft palate, and mental retardation) do not appear to contribute differentially to termination rates. Obviously this data (as additional cases become available) needs to be explored in terms of alternative interpretations of termination rates and estimates of therapeutic change.

V. Conclusions

This paper represents an attempt to extend the description and evaluation of the "Communication Therapy Program" at the "Suffolk Hearing and Speech Center." The present analysis is intended to provide an exploration which helps to open up problem areas and raise questions for future research. In addition, the discussion is designed to describe child play therapy as a means of dealing with the total child rather than focusing upon isolated behaviors (e.g., articulation defects and hearing impairments).

When the emphasis is upon the total human being, language learning must be integrated with social, emotional and cognitive growth. The essential issue, then, is the promotion of autonomy and independence, but this can be understood only within the context of the family and social communication networks within which the individual functions. Finally, this paper has attempted to begin to explore the relationship between the therapy technique utilized and the values implicit in the stated goal of autonomy. It is obvious that most of the questions raised here wait upon the results of future investigation for their resolution.

REFERENCES

1. Buck, L.A., Gallant, R.V., and Freshley, N. *J. Commun. Disorders 6,* 53, (1973).

2. Buck, L.A. *J. Crit. Anal. 1,* 40, (1969).

3. Erikson, E.H. In: *Childhood and society.* 2nd ed. Norton, New York, (1963).

4. Piaget, J. In: *Six psychological studies.* Random House, New York, (1967).

5. Rapaport, D. The autonomy of the ego. In *The collected papers of David Rapaport.* Basic Books, New York, (1967).

6. Rapaport, D. The theory of ego autonomy: a generalization. In *The collected papers of David Rapaport.* Basic Books, New York, (1967).

7. Barbara, D.A. Stuttering. In *American handbook of psychiatry, Vol. 1.* Edited by Arieti S. Basic Books, New York, (1959).

8. Laffal, J. In Pathological and normal language. Atherton, New York, (1965).

9. Ostwald, P. F. In *Soundmaking*. Thomas, Springfield, Ill., (1963).

10. Ruesch, J. In *Therapeutic communication.* Norton, New York, (1961).

11. Watzlawick, P., Beavin, J. H., and Jackson, D.D. In *Pragmatics of human communication.* Norton, New York, (1967).

12. Wyatt, G.L. In *Language learning and communication disorders in children.* Free Press, New York, (1961).

13. Goldman-Eisler, F. *Language Speech 1,* 59, (1958).

14. Szasz, T.S. In *The ethics of psychoanalysis.* Basic Books, New York, (1965).

15. Paul, I.H. In *Letters to Simon.* Inter. Univ. Press, New York, (1973).

16. Rogers, C.R. In *Client-centered therapy.* Houghton-Mifflin, Boston, (1951).

17. Rogers, C.R. In *On becoming a person.* Houghton-Mifflin, Boston, (1961).

18. Maslow, A.H. In *Toward a psychology of being.* Second edition. Van Nostrand Reinhold, New York, (1968).

19. Jourard, S.M. In *The transparent self.* Rev. Ed. Van Nostrand, New York, (1971).

20. Axline, V.M. In *Play therapy.* Ballantine, New York, (1969).

21. Dorfman, E. Play therapy. In *Client-centered therapy.* Edited by Rogers, C.R. Houghton-Mifflin, Boston, (1951).

22. Bion, W.R. In *Experiences in groups.* Basic Books, New York, (1961).

23. Foulkes, S.H., and Anthony, E.J. In *Group psychotherapy.* 2nd ed. Penguin, Baltimore, (1965).

24. May, R. In *Power and innocence.* Norton, New York, (1972).

25. Redl, F. In *When we deal with children.* Free Press, New York, (1966).

26. Redl, F., and Wineman, D. In *The aggressive child. Children who hate: Controls from within.* Free Press, Glencoe, Ill., (1957).

27. Piaget, J. In *The language and thought of the child.* Meridian, New York, (1957).

28. Piaget, J. In *Play, dreams and imitation in childhood.* Norton, New York, (1962).

29. Szasz, T.S. In *Ideology and insanity.* Anchor, Garden City, New York, (1970).

30. Argyris, C. *Harvard Educ. Rev. 41,* 550, (1971).

31. Chomsky, N. In *For reasons of state.* Pantheon, New York, (1973).

32. Frankl, V.E. In *The doctor and the soul.* Bantam, New York, (1967).

33. Lowe, C. M. Value orientations -- an ethical dilemma. In *Human values and abnormal behavior.* Edited by Nunokawa, W. D. Scott, Foresman, Fair Lawn, N. J., (1965).

34. Patterson, C.H. The place of values in counseling and psychotherapy. In *Human values and abnormal behavior.* Edited by Nunokawa, W.D. Scott, Foresman, Fair Lawn, N.J., (1965).

35. Smith, M.B. "Mental health" reconsidered: a special case of the problem of values in psychology. In *Human values and abnormal behavior.* Edited by Nunokawa, W.D. Scott, Foresman, Fair Lawn, N.J., (1965).

36. Tomlinson, T.M. and Whitney, R.E. Values and strategy in client-centered therapy: a means to an end. In *New directions in client-centered therapy.* Edited by Hart, J.T. and Tomlinson, T.M. Houghton-Mifflin, Boston, (1970).

MENTAL HEALTH IN CHILDREN, Volume III
Edited By D. V. Siva Sankar

THE ANALYSIS OF SKILL AND ITS IMPLICATIONS FOR TRAINING THE HANDICAPPED*

Kevin Connolly and Ann Harrison

University of Sheffield, U.K.

The accomplishment of an action designed to achieve a goal involves the recognition and analysis of a problem, the choice of appropriate responses and the execution of selected movements. Each of these stages can be carried out with varying degrees of efficiency. However, the evaluation of improvement in motor performance is often restricted to the measurement of the speed and accuracy of the total process. Such criteria ignore the possibility that strategies which in the long term are more effective may in the short term offer no benefit and may indeed take longer to execute. The instruction to perform a task as quickly and accurately as possible implies that these parameters are the only important ones. However,

* The work reported in this paper was supported by a research grant from the Spastics Society, London which the authors gratefully acknowledge.

various factors contribute to the time used. The care demanded of the individual in specifying task input, the time required to select the response, the precision with which the component movements are programmed, the time involved in monitoring the movement and in error correction and the decision to terminate the action all contribute to the overall time taken.

Training a person to select a better balance between the speed and accuracy parameters of a response requires that he can be provided with the necessary information to rank the attempts that he makes. Even then the experimenter cannot be sure that the subject is employing the time used to optimum effect. If a subject adopts a new time sharing strategy which does not change the accuracy of his performance then it is arguable that this is of no significance. Any extra time which does not bring with it improved precision will be considered wasted. The problems here are many. How do we know what time sharing strategy is being employed? Is it possible to distinguish the strategies which underlie optimum performance and to what extent can these be generalised across individuals? Is it possible to instruct an individual to alter his strategy in particular ways, for example asking him to give less processing time to the ongoing monitoring of task components? How do we know when to terminate training; when can we say that an individual will not refine his performance further? Indeed we cannot be sure that the strategies we choose to reinforce (which may be effective in the short term) will not in the long term be sub-optimal solutions to a motor problem.

The dimensions of speed and accuracy can be measured and on these parameters an individual given accurate feedback. A further dimension which may be applied in evaluating an action is that of economy. It is logically conceivable that two different motor programmes will give rise to identical speed and precision characteristics, but that one will involve greater energy consumption. In this context it is interesting to consider whether persons can judge with any degree of accuracy the energy consumption involved in an action, possibly in terms of how many times a movement can be repeated before a rest is necessary. It may be that the above example of motor programmes which differ only in the energy they require is rare and that to some extent energy consumption offers a single index of the precision and speed achieved. If this is so the desire to be more economic could underlie the search for more skillful strategies by already competent performers.

The accuracy of a movement depends in part on the extent to which its programming and progress are monitored. Festinger and Cannon (1) have shown that central impulses for movement can be monitored. Visual information and afferent messages from muscle spindles, joint and tendon receptors can be used to gauge the congruity between the movement planned and that which is achieved. Phillips (2) has suggested that a correct pairing of alpha and gamma efferent activity could ensure an automatic correction for movement errors. The accuracy of the final movement depends upon the extent to which feedback is used and the extent to which errors are diagnosed and corrected.

However, skill does not always lie in safeguarding maximum performance for this may entail an unwarranted expenditure of processing capacity. More important is the ability to distinguish between those movements which require only a rough approximation and those which demand the subject's greatest accuracy. Skill also involves relating the level of monitoring to the probability that mistakes will occur, and to the importance of error detection. In some instances the absence of any monitoring of the output will be less wasteful than the incursion of an occasional mistake. In this instance skill is far removed from maximising speed and accuracy on all occasions; it devolves around a keen appreciation of the importance of the various task components which have to be completed.

Improvements can and do occur in the analysis which an individual makes of the problem he faces. More rapid decisions about the movement required will occur if a subject learns to isolate the cues most relevant to that task and ignore irrelevant changes which would waste processing capacity. In these ways the execution of an already appropriate response will be speeded (3). The movement may be further improved if an individual is able to distinguish important new cues or reanalyse old stimuli in some more appropriate manner.

So far we have been concerned with improvements in an individual's ability to tackle a contemporary task. Long term improvements may occur if the person can generalise from specific situations in such a manner as to improve his overall appreciation of motor control. An improved general understanding may promote a fruitful reappraisal of old strategies and an increased flexibility of approach. It should also enable him to solve new motor problems more quickly than he would have otherwise done. Overall improvement may be a reflection of changes in the subject's appreciation of environmental cues, available to him.

Improved control can in principle be achieved in a number of ways. The situation can be simplified such that external cues are more clearly defined and highlighted. The subject may be provided with augmented feedback against which to isolate, and perhaps recode, intrinsic feedback (4). Performance can be improved by the provision of ongoing unambiguous information which enables the subject to gauge his performance as it proceeds, or knowledge of results which helps by providing terminal information.

PROBLEMS IN TRAINING THE CEREBRAL PALSIED

The functional complexity of the spastic neuromusculature presents a major problem. The retention of 'primitive' reflexes and the presence of 'abnormal' reflex patterns (5) are both aspects of the spastic syndrome and represent patterns of movement which must be suppressed, avoided or incorporated if good and reliable motor control is to be achieved. The hyperactivity of alpha motoneurons in the spastic neuromusculature creates a situation in which contraction of a muscle can be triggered by sensory stimuli and by activity in related muscle groups. In comparison with the normal neuromuscular system the range of stimuli which can cause a muscle group to contract is wide. The spastic person thus faces an extremely complex task in mapping the various pathways available and in defining the interactions between the forces present. In terms of motor control he faces special problems in planning movements in order to avoid unwanted concomitant activity. And also problems of isolating the particular combination of forces which will most effectively realise the movements required in the execution of a given action.

Movements can be monitored in a number of ways. Attention the the efference copy and interpretation of exafferent and reafferent messages are used by normal subjects and may exist within the capabilities of many spastic subjects. The efference copy allows the subject to examine how accurately a movement is programmed, but it does not allow the progress of the movement to be monitored and any interference detected. Use of the efference copy requires that the subject has experienced conditions in which he has learned the correlation between efferent firing and the resultant movements. However, given the presence of induced contractions it is difficult to imagine how the spastic subject could distinguish between directly and indirectly triggered contractions and so achieve the necessary correlation. Further, it is questionable whether the spastic individual could avoid the incursion of excess activity and so produce the efference copy alone on enough occasions for the learning to occur. Similar problems exist for the spastic who is using visual feedback to monitor movements. What the subject sees is the end product of a potentially complicated interaction of forces. Whether he is able to assess the forces which are operative is questionable - for very different patterns may result in indistinguishable movements. Gamma efferent hyperactivity is thought to underlie some spastic syndromes (6), and Harrison and Connolly (7) argue that this hyperactivity may render reafferent messages difficult to interpret. Without some training in deciphering the messages available, the spastic may lack the capacity to accurately monitor and define ongoing activity and thus efficiently diagnose errors*.

The complexity also presents difficulties for any therapeutic procedure aimed or training aimed at providing feedback as a means of elucidating the functioning of the motor system. Recording from a large number of sites is required to 'track' the origins of contractions and to detect possible errors in a trained response, but practical considerations limit the

* Unless otherwise stated, when monitoring is referred to in later passages, it is taken to include all of the above monitoring systems.

number of muscle sites which can be monitored. The possibility therefore always exists that consistent isolated contractions are triggered by different patterns of forces, and that errors will go undetected. Errors may occur through interference from other muscle groups even though the programming of relevant muscles has been perfectly executed. Harrison (8) showed that in the particular muscle groups she tested, induced activity was triggered with reliable force. This finding exemplifies a major problem facing the spastic subject, for he has to distinguish from the reliable package of contractions which occur, those triggered directly and those triggered by peripheral routes. Such a distinction is essential if he is to define interference forces and correlate central programmes with the muscle contractions they produce.

The lack of an adequate general model of good motor control restricts training to instruction on particular tasks. It can be argued that this is the manner in which motor control is normally developed, the child gauging and gradually acquiring improved control under specific task conditions. However, skills are generalised in terms of operational subroutines (9) as well as task analysis and strategies for monitoring feedback. If we knew which subroutines were essential, or indeed most useful, we could give priority to tasks which aided their modularisation through practice (10). Given that such information were available we could perhaps devise more effective training schemes, isolating the vital subroutines from less important aspects of a task and giving training in their execution. It is important to recognise that if models of the optimally functioning normal and spastic neuromuscular systems were available, they might differ radically. Therefore, the subroutines and the tasks which the spastic subject should be taught might not be identical with those which the neurologically normal child chronologically tackles. Whilst acknowledging such possibilities it would seem that until further information is available the best tactic is to try and equip the cerebral palsied individual to tackle tasks in which competence is normally expected.

When consideration is given to normal movement a meaningful distinction can be drawn between the abilities to monitor movements and programme their execution. It is possible to conceive of poor control being exhibited because of inadequate monitoring of feedback information even though the subject is in possession of all the executional capacities required. Likewise, a subject whose ability to monitor his output is adequate will tackle a new task badly if he lacks suitable movement programmes. In these instances concentrating on refining the motor programme or on improving the monitoring of feedback information should bring about some improvement. In situations where the subject is able to utilise information acquired from previous experience he has only to master some components of the new task. However, the situation in which the subject has no relevant previous experience, that is situations in which his motor control is so impoverished that he has to discover all the perceptual and executional requirements of the task, presents a very different problem. For many spastic children this appears to be the reality. Here the usefulness of manipulating the monitoring process carried out by an individual in the hope of improving precision breaks down. Harrison (8) examined the ability of spastic and normal subjects to repeat tension levels in a single muscle group and found that the spastics were significantly less accurate. And in later scaling studies, some spastic subjects were incapable of producing a set of six significantly ranked tension levels. Both of these studies showed that spastic subjects lacked the very crude control required to reproduce already executed responses and to produce a small number of contractions of increasing strength. These point to a dual impairment, to deficits in both motor programming and monitoring ongoing activity. The acquisition of monitoring ability depends upon the subject being able to replicate movements and so isolate and analyse the feedback messages involved. Good execution in turn depends on the ability to monitor movements and so diagnose errors that occur. Tasks, therefore, need to be devised in such a way that the spastic subject is able to isolate the programming required, to decipher the inherent feedback messages, and to define sources of interference and suppress them.

The use of augmented feedback offers a general technique for improving task performance. In a number of studies in our laboratory, spastic subjects were given an index of muscular contraction on a voltmeter. This feedback provided an unambiguous measure of ongoing activity and made clear the operational definition of error and improvement. Such augmented feedback is likely to be especially beneficial to the spastic subject, for it has been argued that he lacks a 'normally' sensitive system to monitor intrinsic feedback from his movements.

Initially the speed with which spastic and normal subjects relax from various tension levels was compared and spastic subjects were found to take significantly longer. Given augmented feedback the performance of the spastic subjects improved significantly though they remained unable to achieve normal relaxation speeds, Figure 1. The augmented feedback in the shape of the meter display provided the spastic cerebral palsied subjects with a means of gauging the success of attempts to suppress residual activity. Whether extended practice with such a display would give rise to normal performance is not known. It is possible that the difficulties of suppressing hyperactivity and identifying which of the many possible sources of residual activity is responsible for residual unwanted activity will preclude the attainment of normal performance in this respect.

Normal and spastic subjects have also been set the task of maintaining prescribed levels of contraction as accurately as possible over a 10 second period. Again, the control shown by the group of spastic subjects was significantly impoverished - both in terms of the appropriatness of the level held and the greater uncorrected drifts away from the target response, Figures 2 and 3. When the meter was introduced, the spastic subjects' conception of the target response improved, Figure 2. Some curbing of the drifts away from the prescribed level was also observed (Figure 3) but the improvement was too small to achieve significance. We do not yet know whether spastic subjects would eventually learn to diagnose errors and correct them with anything like normal precision were training continued.

It has been shown that normal subjects can learn to control the firing of a single motor unit, the smallest functional unit of muscular contraction (11,12). Simard and Ladd (13) have also demonstrated that pre-school age thalidomide children can develop similar control provided that they possess the intelligence to interpret the augmented feedback provided. Using an oscilloscope display of muscular activity, Harrison and Connolly (7) demonstrated that spastic subjects were able to isolate and control the lowest level of activity to which the recording apparatus was sensitive. Spastics took significantly longer to complete the task. However, they were able to suppress hyperactivity and to control this very fine level of neuromuscular activity with 'normal' accuracy.

In later investigations ongoing augmented feedback was abandoned in favour of a knowledge of results paradigm which provides a *post hoc* or terminal assessment of task performance. The subject was thus able to assess his attempts in terms of the operational definition of improvement. This approach was employed because we believe that giving the subjects augmented feedback may well inhibit their making a full analysis of inherent cues and further it is likely to promote a dependence upon information which is not normally available.

In the first of these studies, spastic subjects were taught to control three discrete levels of activity in the forearm flexor muscle group, these being referred to as the Black, Red and White targets. Each time the subject made an attempt at a given target, he was simply told whether it was correct, too high or too low. The precision demanded was stringent and was finer than the 'working' accuracy displayed by normal subjects in earlier studies. Given such information, spastic subjects learned to control high, low and intermediate contractile strengths. They learned to produce these when demanded from randomised lists and after prescribed delays, Figures 4 and 5.

Later studies were concerned with teaching spastic subjects to control activity in two muscle groups, again targets were referred to by a colour code. The results of these experiments showed that spastic subjects were able to switch from muscle group to muscle group, producing high and low contractions with great accuracy, Figure 6. The final task set in this series of experiments required the subject to control simultaneous contractions of the biceps and forearm flexor muscle groups. An initial barrier to attaining such control was pre-

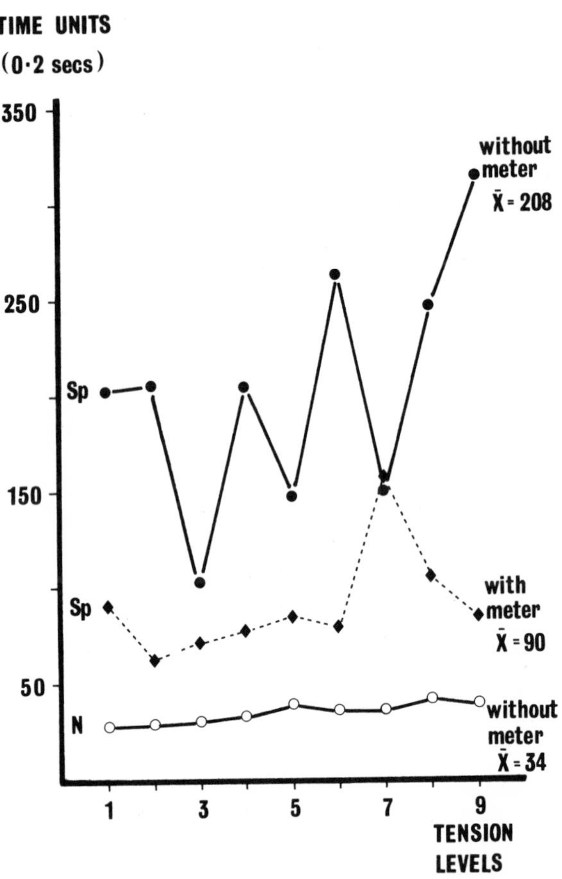

Figure 1. Time taken by spastic (Sp) subjects with and without augmented feedback and normal (N) subjects without augmented feedback to relax from nine tension levels.

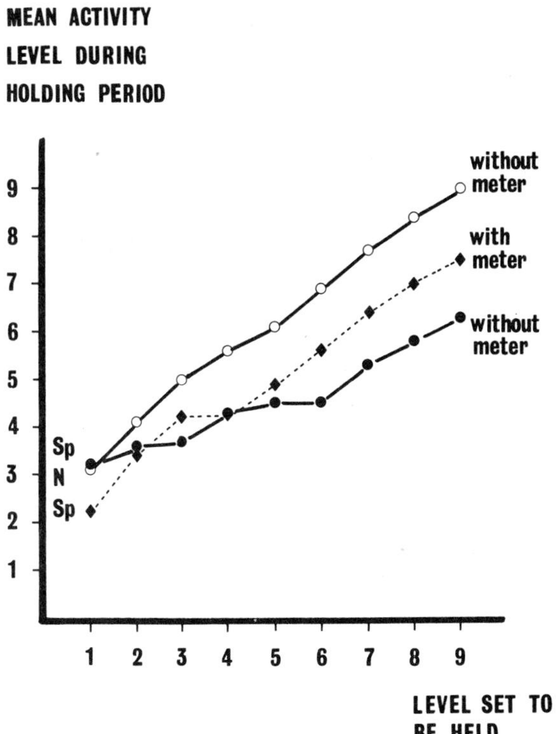

Figure 2. Mean activity level held by spastic (Sp) subjects with and without augmented feedback and normal (N) subjects without augmented feedback when instructed to hold constant the nine tension levels set.

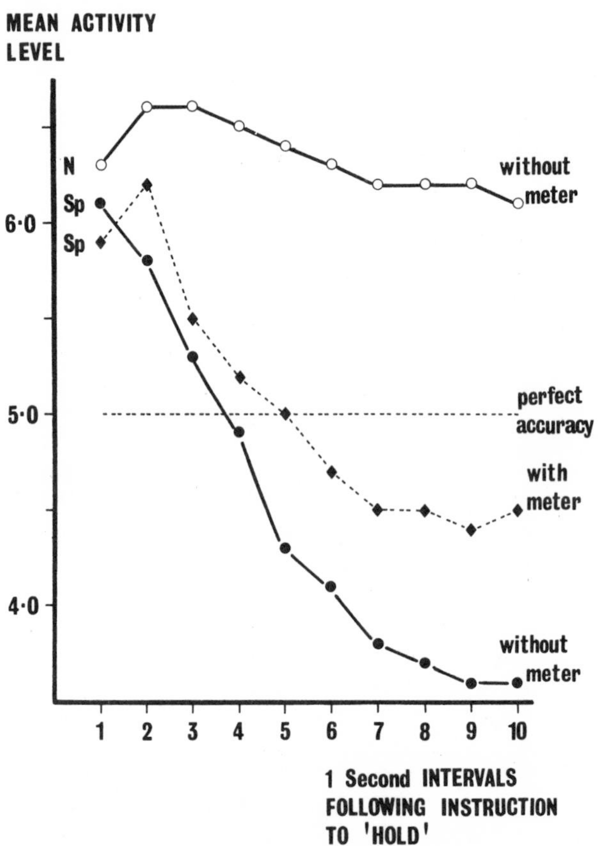

Figure 3. Change in activity observed across 10 sec holding period for spastic (Sp) subjects with and without augmented feedback and normal (N) subjects without augmented feedback.

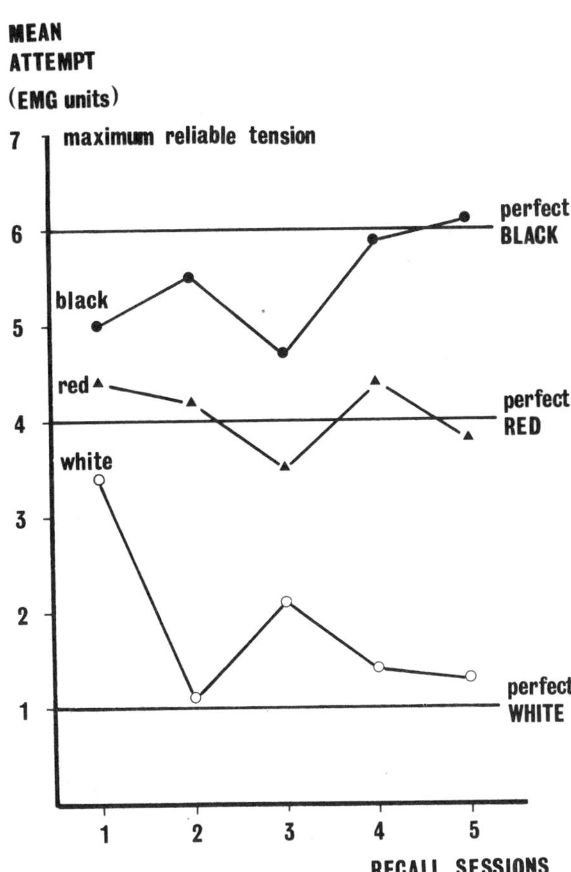

Figure 4. Recall accuracy achieved by spastic subjects at various stages during training for the three target levels of forearm flexor activity. Session: (1) pre-training; (2) recall for each target immediately after training on that target; (3) recall for random order of three targets before further training; (4) recall for random order of targets after practice; (5) as session 4 but with variable time delay prior to the start of a contraction.

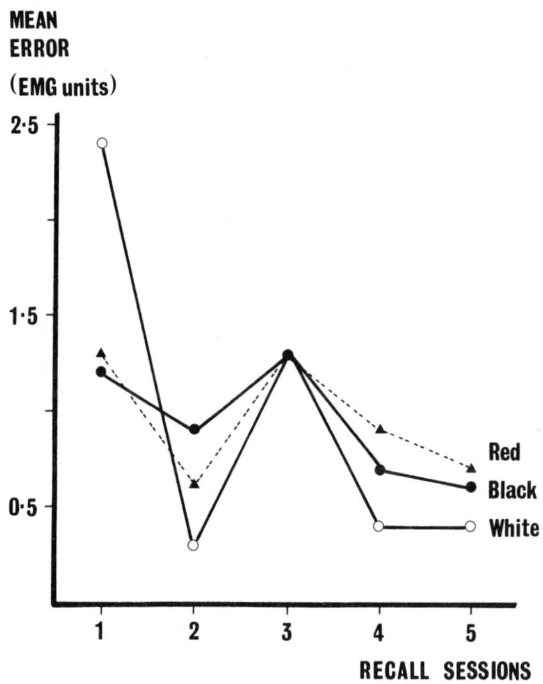

Figure 5. Recall error shown by spastic subjects for the various stages of training specified in figure 4.

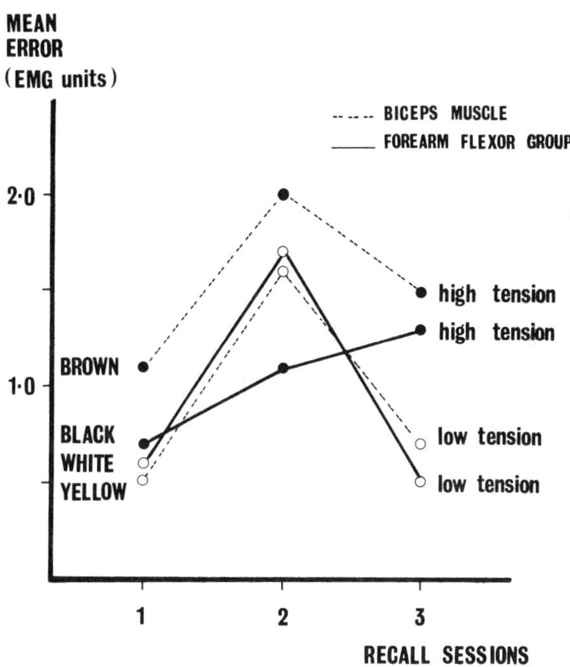

Figure 6. Recall accuracy of spastic subjects at various stages in training. Session: (1) recall for each target following training on that target; (2) recall for random order of four targets before further training; (4) recall for random order of targets after practice.

sented by the 'spreading phenomena' or 'reflex radiations' encountered in the spastic syndrome. Contraction of one muscle triggered the contraction of the other, and in some cases the activity induced exceeded the target response. The spastic subjects were able to use the Knowledge-of-Results (KOR) information provided to curb induced activity and to meet the criteria set. Given knowledge about this functional link in their neuromusculature, the spastic subjects were able to isolate and develop strategies for suppressing 'automatically' triggered responses. The results indicate that ignorance of this link was responsible for their inaccuracy in earlier trials, the subjects being unaware of (and therefore failing to control) an important source of error.

The tasks which the spastic subjects were taught to perform were relatively simple, the most complex involved the control of only two muscle groups. It is important to consider whether improvement under these conditions has any prognostic significance in regard to the potential for acquiring 'useful' control. Useful is here taken to refer to tasks which will increase the individual's independence, his ability to communicate and to interact effectively with the environment. An alternative approach would be to set specific tasks such as feeding, lifting or grasping and to provide feedback on these. This is the level of training chosen by occupational therapists and under such conditions improvements have been reported. We would argue that the spastic person's ability to improve under these conditions is limited by his incomplete appreciation of the functioning of his neuromusculature. Global feedback in terms of overall accuracy is unlikely to help except in those conditions were some understanding is already present or where the subject by chance stumbles on a more adequate motor programme. A global error score for a feeding task will not allow the individual to define interference sources, map functional links and isolate strategies for suppressing hyperactivity. The approach described above allowed such a definition to be acquired, albeit so far for the activity of only one or two muscle groups. Only when the individual has acquired some understanding at this level can he start to decipher more complex monitoring and programming problems, for he will take to new tasks some facility for control and analysis.

Control over these simple tasks should be relevant to other more complex ones. It seems likely that subjects will acquire both monitoring and executional abilities which will generalise, and further they will learn to avoid, and possibly suppress, movements which commonly disrupt planned actions. The expectation is thus that the spastic's ability to tackle more complicated tasks will be altered by his exposure to simpler ones. Improvement is therefore not dependent upon the chance isolation of a better approach but stems from the ability to utilise relevant information. Problems do exist in providing useful feedback for more complex tasks, but the improvement shown in the studies so far completed gives us the confidence that the attempt will be worthwhile.

References

1. Festinger, L. and Cannon, L. K. *Psychol. Rev.* *72,* 373, (1965).
2. Phillips, C. G. *Proc. Roy. Soc. B.* *173,* 141, (1969).
3. Connolly, K. Response speed, temporal sequencing and information processing in children. In *Mechanisms of motor skill development.* Edited by Connolly, K. Academic Press, London, (1970).
4. Connolly, K. *Develop. Med. Child Neurol.* *10,* 697, (1968).
5. Bobath, K. *The motor deficit in patients with cerebral palsy.* Heinemann, London, (1966).
6. Rushworth, G. *J. Neurol. Neurosurg. Psychiat.* *23,* 99, (1960).
7. Harrison, A. and Connolly, K. *Develop. Med. Child Neurol.* *13,* 762, (1971).
8. Harrison, A. Studies of neuromuscular control in spastic persons. Unpublished Ph. D. thesis. University of Sheffield, U. K., (1973).
9. Elliott, J. and Connolly, K. Hierarchical structure in skill development. In *The growth of competence.* Edited by Connolly, K. and Bruner, J. Academic Press, London, (1974).
10. Connolly, K. Factors influencing the learning of manual skills by young children. In *Constraints on learning.* Edited by Hinde, R. A. and Stevenson-Hinde, J. Academic Press, London, (1973).

11. Hefferline, R., Bruno, L. J. J. and Davidowitz, J. E. Feedback control of covert behaviour. In *Mechanisms of motor skill development.* Edited by Connolly, K. Academic Press, London, (1970).
12. Basmajian, J. V. *Science, 141,* 440, (1963).
13. Simard, T. G. and Ladd, H. W. *Develop. Med. Child Neurol. 11,* 743, (1969).

MENTAL HEALTH IN CHILDREN, Volume III
Edited by D. V. Siva Sankar

A BEHAVIOR MODIFICATION TRAINING PROGRAM IN SELF-CONTROL FOR HOSPITALIZED ACUTELY MENTALLY ILL YOUNG ADULTS

Frances E. Cheek, Anna Kline and Cintra Sander

New Jersey Neuropsychiatric Institute
Princeton, N.J. 08540

ABSTRACT

This paper describes a pilot training program in behavior modification techniques for hospitalized mentally ill young adults aimed at increasing their self-control in order to facilitate their social rehabilitation. Over a period of four months, twenty-four patients, 19 male and 5 female, were taught techniques for relaxation, desensitization, improved self-image, behavior analysis, behavior control, correct assertiveness and rational thinking. The training was given in eight one-and-one-half-hour group sessions with two sessions per week over a four-week period.

The effectiveness of the program was examined by pre- and post-program measures of anxiety, assertiveness, self-image degree of inner control and ability to image as well as subjective evaluations immediately following the training and three months later. Significant changes in level of anxiety and self-acceptance appeared. The subjective evaluations indicated that a majority of the patients understood the goals or aims of the program and how to use the techniques, and had made use of them while still hospitalized and after leaving the hospital.

These preliminary but encouraging findings suggest that this approach to facilitating the social rehabilitation of the mentally ill should be further pursued and rigorously evaluated.

This paper describes a pilot program conducted at the New Jersey Neuropsychiatric Institute during the summer of 1972 in which a group of acutely mentally ill young adult patients participated in a special four-week Behavior Modification Training Program emphasizing the development of self-control.

In most attempts to date to utilize behavioral techniques in the treatment of the mentally ill the model of external control has been utilized, as in the operation of token economies (1,2,3, 4,5,6,7), and in the development of training programs in which nurses, attendants (8-10) and family members (11-18) have been taught the systematic use of rewards and punishments in order that they may be able to modify disturbed behaviors of patients.

The idea of using behavioral techniques to enhance *self-control* patients developed as a consequence of the past research experiences of the present investigators. An observation regarding parental use of social control mechanisms in the family of young adult convalescent schizophrenics (19) led to the development in 1965, of an experimental program in which the parents of convalescent schizophrenics were taught to apply operant conditioning to modify aspects of the disturbed behavior of their offspring. Lindsely's method of pin-pointing recording and consequating (20) was the principal technique used.

The success of this program led to the development in 1970 of a similar program for the wives of alcoholics (21) aimed at training them to modify destructive aspects of their interaction with their treated alcoholic husbands. However, in this program it soon became evident that the hostilities and deep resentments felt by the wives toward their husbands seriously interfered with any attempt to train the wives in the use of reinforcement techniques. Before operant conditioning could be successfully introduced, it was first necessary to modify the destructive emotional and attitudinal aspects of the husbands' and wives' interaction. For this reason, then, it was decided to combine two procedures used in clinical practice -- relaxation and desensitization -- with the more traditional Skinnerian techniques.

The usefulness of this combined approach in treating the wives of alcoholics led to an expanded program for both the wives and their alcoholic husbands (22) in which two more clinical techniques were introduced -- self-image training, using Susskind's Idealized Self-Image Procedure (23) and assertive training. This revised program was subsequently adapted for use with heroin addicts (24) with the addition of an additional modality -- rational thinking (25).

The training program now consisted of eight one-and-one-half hour meetings, two per week over a four week period plus a preliminary orientation. The eight meetings covered relaxation, desensitization, self-image training, behavior analysis, behavior control, assertive training, rational thinking and, in a final meeting, a set of guidelines on when and how to use the techniques. The meetings included lectures, practice in the techniques, role playing and group discussions. Private sessions to work over the material were also offered. Workbooks, presenting all the material of each meeting as well as illustrative poetry and drawings were given to each participant.

In the course of working with the alcoholics and their families, we had begun, without realizing, to shift our attention from control of the *other,* using a Skinnerian approach, to techniques for controlling the *self,* using the methods of clinical practitioners. This combination appeared remarkably useful in altering the interaction styles of the alcoholics and their wives and in facilitating in adjustments of the addicts on methadone maintenance.

Several factors suggested to us that this kind of training program emphasizing self-control might also be useful in the treatment of young adult mentally ill patients, most of whom would be diagnosed as schizophrenics. It has frequently been pointed out that one of the major problems in the treatment of the mentally ill person lies in helping him to bridge the gap from the close supervision of life in a hospital ward to an independent life in the community. It has been demonstrated, for example, that 40% to 60% of discharged schizophrenic patients require readmission within two years of discharge. Furthermore, only 15% to 35% of all ex-patients ever achieve what can be described as an "average" level of community adjustment (26).

It was felt that the behavior modification program would be useful in facilitating a more successful community adjustment for these patients in several ways. In the first place, a number of researchers have demonstrated the existence of an internal state of hyperstimulation in some schizophrenic patients (27). The relaxation procedure appeared appropriate for treating this problem. Moreover, it was felt that desensitization would be potentially useful in helping the patient cope with different situations he might face upon his discharge, such as job interviews, problems with family members, adjustments at school or social situations with friends. Prior to leaving the hospital, this technique could also be useful to him in handling difficult situations on the ward, with staff members and other patients.

In view of the low self-image characteristics of mentally ill patients generally, as well as the disturbed self-image of schizophrenics, it was felt that the Idealized Image training would be useful in helping them develop a more stable, positive and realistic self-image.

Furthermore, assertive training should be useful because of the tendency of many of the mentally ill, again, schizophrenics in particular, to inhibit their needs and their emotions and then to release them explosively in an aggressive, often dangerous, manner. If the patients could be taught to assert their feelings at the appropriate time and in an acceptable fashion, later outbursts of aggressive behavior would be less likely to occur. A recent study (28) suggests the usefulness of this approach with older schizophrenics though the results with a younger group similar to age to those in our own study, have been favorable.

Again, training in "Rational Thinking" would be strategic in view of the stereotypes of "mental illness' and the "mentally ill" with which the convalescent patient would have to deal, in his own thinking as well as that of others.

These considerations led to a decision to adapt the behavior modification program previously used with alcoholics and drug addicts for use with adolescent mentally ill patients, and to conduct a pilot program in order to see how mental patients would react to the techniques and also, to measure in a preliminary way, changes that might occur.

METHOD OF PROCEDURE

The Research Setting

The pilot behavior modification training program for mentally ill patients was conducted at a Regional Mental Health Center on the grounds of a state mental institution. The Regional Center is a 73 bed unit with a staff of 40, including 1 medical director, 2 physicians, 2 psychologists, 4 social workers, 2 supervisor nurses, 5 head nurses, 6 practical nurses, and 18 attendants and technicians. The Center also services an average of 120 patients per month on an outpatient basis.

The Regional Center draws on patients from Somerset County which immediately surrounds it. The patient population is varied as to age, socio-economic background, diagnostic category, length of stay and type of commitment. Of the average of 45 in-patients per month serviced by the Regional Center, the usual age in range is between 16 and 90, although patients as young as 12 years old have been admitted on occasion. Of this group, about 50% are geriatric patients.

The modalities of in-patient therapy at the Regional Center include drug, ECT, one-to-one and group psychotherapy, recreational, music, occupational and Erg therapy.

PROGRAM PERSONNEL

The program was conducted by members of the Experimental Sociology Section of the Bureau of Research in Neurology and Psychiatry with the cooperation of the staff psychologist at the Regional Center.

The senior author was responsible for the planning and design of the program, acted as group leader in the first training session and supervised the data analysis. The second author prepared the write-up of the study, acted as group leader in most of the subsequent sessions and assisted, with the other authors, in the program planning and data analysis. The psychologist assisted in the program planning and in the coordination of the program with the on-going clinical program of the Regional Center.

SELECTION OF SUBJECTS

It was decided to work with young adult male and female patients as there already existed an on-going group therapy program for these patients at the Regional Center which could be converted into a pilot behavior modification program.

Patients were chosen for the group by a team of staff members (including nurses, psychologists and psychiatrists) involved in the patients' care at the Regional Center.

Patients were selected who were between the ages of 17 and 30, who were expected to remain hospitalized for the full four weeks that the program would be in progress and who were judged well enough to participate in a group program.

Twenty-four young adult mentally ill patients, (five females, nineteen males) participated in the program. The relatively small proportion of females reflected, in part, the smaller population in the appropriate age group at the Regional Center at the time the program was in progress (an average hospitalized population in the seventeen to thirty age group of 5 females as compared to 10 males). Of that population, the females generally were hospitalized for a shorter length of time, so that it was difficult to find suitable females who would be hospitalized for the full 4 weeks of the program.

CHARACTERISTICS OF THE SUBJECTS

Research data was obtained on 5 females and 12 males. It proved difficult to get the questionnaires filled in, particularly on those who dropped out after one or two sessions.

Table 1 shows the background information for male and female patients.

All except one of the patients were Caucasian with predominantly middle class families (occupying levels II, III and

IV on the Hollingshead Index of Social Position). All of the patients were living at home with their parents prior to entering the hospital. Six patients, 4 males and 2 females, reported a history of mental illness in their immediate families. Other family mental health programs mentioned were alcoholism (mentioned by 3 males and 3 females) and mental retardation (mentioned by 1 male).

ILLNESS HISTORY

Table 2 provides information regarding the diagnosis and illness history of the patients.

A majority of the patients (a total of 14) were diagnosed as schizophrenic.

DESCRIPTION OF THE PROGRAM

Schedule

Four consecutive programs, each running for four weeks with two one-and-one-half-hour sessions per week, were conducted in which both male and female patients participated. Sessions were held two afternoons a week from 1:00 to 2:30 p.m. Attendance was encouraged, though the program was technically voluntary.

Size of the Groups

The number of participants attending the meetings ranged from 2 to 6, and depended largely on the number of eligible patients available at the Regional Center at the time of the programs. The first group had a larger population to draw on and maintained a consistent number of 6 participants (3 male and 3 female) at each session. The second group began with 9 males, although only 4 attended regularly beyond the first meeting. The third group began with only 2 members (1 male and 1 female). After the fourth meeting of the third group, however, the female was discharged and 3 more patients

Table 1

BACKGROUND INFORMATION

	MALE	*FEMALE*
AGE		
Range	17-24	17-25
Median	20	21
MARITAL STATUS		
Never Married	12	4
Common-law	0	1
Married	0	0
Separated	0	0
Divorced	0	0
Other	1	0
Total	13	5
RELIGION		
Catholic	4	3
Protestant	6	1
Jewish	1	0
Atheist, Agnostic	1	1
Other (Cath. & Prot.)	1	0
Total	13	5
ETHNIC BACKGROUND		
Caucasian	12	5
Puerto Rican	1	0
Total	13	5
LAST SCHOOL GRADE		
8th. grade or less	2	0
Up to 3 years H.S.	3	2
High School Graduate	4	3
Up to 3 years college	4	0
Total	13	5
OCCUPATION OF PATIENT (In terms of Hollingshead Occupation Scale)		
Higher Executives	0	0
Business Managers, etc.	0	0
Administrative Personnel, etc.	0	0
Clerical and sales workers, etc.	0	2
Skilled manual employees	3	0
Machine Operators and		

Semi-skilled employees	3	0
Unskilled Employees	2	1
Student	2	0
None	1	0
M.D.	2	2
Total	15	5
EMPLOYMENT STATUS IMMEDIATELY PRIOR TO ENTERING HOSPITAL		
Full time	6	1
Part time	1	1
Student	1	0
Unemployed	5	3
Total	13	5
SOCIAL CLASS OF FAMILY (Hollingshead)		
I	0	0
II	5	1
III	0	1
IV	6	1
V	1	1
M.D.	1	1
Total	13	5
LIVING ARRANGEMENTS		
Alone	0	0
Spouse or friend of opposite sex	0	0
Friend or friends, same sex	0	0
Parents or relatives	13	5
Total	13	5
HISTORY OF MENTAL HEALTH PROBLEMS IN FAMILY		
Mental Illness	4	2
Alcoholism	3	3
Drug Addiction	0	0
Mental retardation	1	0
Epilepsy	0	0
None	0	0
M.D.	7	1
Total	15	6

TABLE 2

ILLNESS HISTORY

DIAGNOSIS	
Schizophrenic, Chronic Undifferentiated type	6
Schizophrenic, Paranoid type	4
Schizophrenic, Schizophrenic-affective	2
Schizophrenic, Simple type, Chronic	1
Schizophrenic, Acute spisode	1
Psychosis with Epilepsy	2
Epilepsy	1
Psychosis with Drugs	1
Drug Dependency	2
Psychosis with Drug Intoxification	1
Adjustment Reaction of Adolescence	2
Total	23
COMMITMENT	
Voluntary	17
Class B	5
Class C	1
Total	23
NUMBER OF PREVIOUS ADMISSIONS	
None	13
One	5
Two	3
Three	1
Four	1
Total	23

TABLE 3

Attendance (All 4 Programs Combined)

Number of Meetings	*Number Attending*
8	7
	4
6	2
5	1
4	1
3	2
2	1
1	3
Orientation only	2
1 Special Session	1

TABLE 4

Changes in Psychological Measures from Pre- to Post-Program

	+	0	-	Level of Sig.
Level of Anxiety	1	0	10	.01
Self-Acceptance	10	0	1	.01
Positiveness of Self-Image	9	0	2	.05
Disparity between Present and Ideal Self-Image	2	0	9	.01
Level of Assertiveness	7	0	3	N.S.
Susceptibility to External Control	3	1	6	N.S.
Ability to Image	4	2	2	N.S.

CHART 1

Outline of the Behavior Modification Program

Meeting 1

Lecture - Introduction to the Program
Group Discussion
Lecture - Introduction to Relaxation
Lecture - The Calm Scene
Discussion - Selection of Calm Scenes
Training Session - The Muscle-Relaxant Method
Group Discussion

Meeting 2

Training in Relaxation, "Lightness" and "Heaviness"
Group Discussion
Lecture - Introduction to Desensitization
Discussion - Selection of Up-Tight Scenes
Training Session - Desensitization
Group Discussion

Meeting 3

Practice - Relaxation and Desensitization
Group Discussion
Lecture - Behavior Modification is a Head Trip
Lecture - Idealized Self-Image

Discussion - Selection of Self-Image
Practice Session - Idealized Self-Image
Group Discussion

Meeting 4

Practice - Relaxation, Desensitization and Self-Image
Group Discussion
Lecture - Introduction to Behavior Analysis and Behavior Rehearsal
Behavior Rehearsal - Playlets
Group Discussion

Meeting 5

Practice - Relaxation, Desensitization and Self-Image
Group Discussion
Lecture - Making the Scene - And Writing Your Own Script
Lecture - How to Modify Undesirable Behaviors
Behavior Rehearsal - Playlets
Group Discussion

Meeting 6

Practice - Relaxation, Desensitization and Self-Image
Group Discussion
Lecture - Self-Assertion
Identification of Responses as Under-, Over- or Appropriate Assertion
Case Studies in Assertive Training
Playlets
Group Discussion

(1 female, 2 males) joined the group, bringing the total of Group 3 up to 4 patients. Group 4 included two of the 3 patients who joined midway through the third group as well as 3 more patients, making a total of 5 males.

Location

Sessions were held in the conference room of a building next to the Regional Center which was used to house officers of the psychology staff. It was a pleasant room with comfortable chairs and offered freedom from noise and other disruptions, factors which were particularly important in conducting the relaxation exercises.

Program Content

The content and format of each meeting, as shown in Chart 1, was planned in advance. Lectures, demonstrations and practice in behavior modification techniques, role-playing by staff and patients, and group discussions were included.

The first 3 meetings focussed on inner experience. Meeting 1 introduced the program, offered a rationale for the training in relaxation, described the use of "calm scenes" to facilitate relaxation, and offered instruction and practice in the "Muscle Relaxant" method. Meeting 2 began with the introduction of two additional methods of relaxation. "Lightness" and "Heaviness". This was followed by a lecture introducing desensitization and then practice in desensitization, moving from less anxiety-arousing to more anxiety-arousing scenes. In Meeting 3, a rationale for self-image training was presented and Susskind's Idealized Self-Image techniques described, images were selected, and practice begun. At every subsequent meeting, practice in relaxation, using the Muscle Relaxant and Heaviness methods in sequence, desensitization and self-image training was continued.

In the following 3 meetings, external experience was emphasized. Meeting 4 dealt with the shaping and maintenance of social behavior through rewards and punishments, and Meeting 5 described specific techniques for bringing about behavior change in others. Material in the lectures was illustrated by playlets prepared by the staff and enacted by the staff and the patients. Meeting 6 introduced assertive training, with a lecture followed by examples of over-assertive, under-assertive, and correctly assertive behavior which the group was asked to classify, playlets illustrating the technique, and brief summaries of case histories from Wolpe and Lazarus. Meeting 7 presented a lecture on rational thinking based on Albert Ellis' Book, *Rational Thinking*. Some common errors in thinking were presented, along with suggestions for correcting these errors. The four errors discussed were dichotomous reasoning, over-generalization, excessive reliance on other people's judgement, and enculturation and over-socialization. Albert Ellis' "Rational points of Emphasis" were also presented. The final meeting was devoted to a review of the program with suggestions in the lecture, "Guide Lines," describing how the various parts of the program might be used by the patient when he left the hospital.

At each meeting group discussions followed presentation of the material to insure that it was understood, and assignments were given to be undertaken before the next meeting.

The Workbook

Prior to the beginning of the program, a workbook was prepared. This included outlines of the meetings, lectures delivered, techniques introduced, illustrative playlets, worksheets for assignments and practice in techniques, as well as a list of useful reference works. The workbook also contained poetry collected by the staff and later contributed by some of the patients which illustrated points made in the meetings. In addition, illustrative drawings by staff and patients were included throughout the book.

The workbook was handed out at the first meeting and the patients brought them to each of the subsequent meetings.

Evaluation of the Program

Pre- and post-program measures of anxiety level, kinds of reinforcement (external versus internal) to which the patient was susceptible, nature of self-image and degree of assertiveness were obtained. Reactions to and evaluations of the program were also elicited immediately following the program and 3 months later.

The following batteries of instruments were used:

Pre-Treatment:

1. Data sheet - demographic data, information on past history of drug use, etc.
2. Taylor Manifest Anxiety Scale (29).
3. Rotter I-E Scale (30).
4. An adaptation of the Gough Adj. Check List (31).
5. Level of Assertiveness (developed from a series of questions regarding assertiveness in *Behavior Therapy Techniques* (32).
6. Imagery Scale (Specially developed for the study)

Post-Treatment:

1. Taylor Manifest Anxiety Scale
2. Rotter I-E Scale
3. An adaptation of Gough Adj. Check List
4. Level of Assertiveness
5. Imagery Scale
6. Program Evaluation Questionnaire - Examining reactions to the program and the techniques.

Three Months After the Program was Completed:

Program Evaluation Questionnaire - Examining continuing use of the techniques and reactions to the program.

The standardized tests were scored and frequency counts on the items of the evaluation questionnaire performed so that comparisons between pre-, post- and three month performance might be made.

RESULTS

Attendance

Because the program was voluntary, attendance at meetings may be viewed as one indication of its success. The attendance of the males and females at each of the four programs is presented in Table 3.

Of the 24 patients, a total of 4 females and 11 males attended 4 or more meetings, one male and one female were discharged after attending fewer than 3 meetings and 1 male escaped from the hospital after attending only 3 meetings. One male in the second program was deeply interested in attending the group, but it was felt by the regional center staff that he would not be suitable for participation in a group setting. He was permitted, however, to meet privately on one occasion with the group leader at which time she explained some of the ideas and techniques of the program. Of the 8 patients that attended fewer than 4 meetings, then, only 5 can be considered drop-outs in that they were available on the unit but refused to attend the meetings. Of these 5, however, one of the males was still quite disturbed at the time of his entrance into the group. After 3 weeks had elapsed and his condition had improved he repeatedly expressed a strong interest in rejoining a subsequent group, though he was discharged before this could be made possible.

The Test Battery

As noted earlier, though a comparison group was not used, some measures of the effectiveness of the program was attempted by the administration of a battery of relevant tests before and after the program. The Wilcoxon Matched Pairs Signed Ranks test was used as a test of significance of changes.

Table 4 shows the changes which occurred on the various measures from pre- to post-program as well as the significance levels.

Level of anxiety, self-acceptance, ideal self-image, disparity between present and ideal self-image showed significant and positive changes, though level of assertiveness and susceptibility to external control, both decreased for a majority of patients and ability to image increased.

SUBJECTIVE EVALUATION OF THE PROGRAM

In addition to the measures obtained with the standardized tests, evaluation questionnaires measuring the patients' subjective reactions to the program were obtained immediately following the program and three months after. Post-program evaluation questionnaires were obtained from 11 patients, all of whom had attended 4 or more meetings.

1. *Communication of aims and techniques of the program*

Nine of the 11 patients reported that they understood the goals or aims of the program while 2 of the patients reported that they were not sure. Eight patients reported that they understood how the techniques were related to aims of the program, 2 reported that they were not sure, and 1 did not respond. Seven patients reported that they understood how to use the techniques, 1 patient reported that he did not, 2 were not sure, and 1 patient did not respond.

2. *Reactions to various parts of the program*

Patients were asked to indicate the meetings which they preferred, their preference for the various techniques taught in the program and the degree of success they experienced in using the different techniques.

A. *Meetings*

When asked to indicate which meetings they preferred those dealing with inner experience or those dealing with outer experience, 6 of the 11 patients who responded preferred the sessions dealing with inner experience. Two patients reported that they enjoyed both equally, while 1 patient did not respond.

Because of the techniques taught in the sessions dealing with inner experience depended upon the ability of the patient to get and hold images in her or his mind, it was decided to examine how well the patients were able to do this. It was found that while only 3 patients reported trouble getting vivid, detailed images in their minds initially, 8 reported that they had trouble holding the images in their mind. All 8 reported that this became easier getting vivid images initially as they went through the program, while 2 reported that it did not.

It is possible that the difficulty experienced by 8 of the patients in holding images in their minds might account for the fact that most of the patients preferred the sessions dealing with outer experience, which didn't depend upon the patients' imagery ability.

The patients were also asked to indicate on a five-point scale the degree to which they enjoyed each of the eight meetings. A rank ordering of the results appears in Table 5.

As can be seen, the meetings dealing with muscle relaxation and how to change behavior were most preferred, followed by the meeting dealing with how behavior is influenced.

B. *The Techniques*

When asked which forms of *relaxation* they preferred, 5 reported that they preferred the Lightness Technique, 3 the Muscle Relaxant Method, 1 both the Muscle-Relaxant and Lightness Techniques equally, and only 1 preferred the Heaviness Technique. Averaged ratings on a 5-point scale of the effectiveness of the various methods suggested that lightness was the best (3.9) followed by muscle-relaxant (3.6) and heaviness (3.0). Interestingly, however, just thinking of the calm scene alone was judged equally as effective as the lightness method in reducing tension, receiving an average rating, like the lightness technique, of 3.9.

Only two of the 11 patients reported that they were unable to reduce tension just by thinking of the calm scene. Most of the calm scenes described (8 out of 10) were solitary scenes, and involved such situations as being at the beach, sitting on a rock in the woods, relaxing by a lake, and so forth. Of the 2 patients who described scenes involving other people, one imagined himself falling asleep in his girlfriend's arms and the other thought of a dream he had had in which he saw himself with a family, happily married to a girl he had once known while in school.

Only 5 of the 11 patients responded to the question dealing with the extent to which *desensitization* decreased their tension while they were imagining their tense scenes. Of the 5, 4 reported a decrease in tension. Seven patients, however, reported that they went through an actual tense situation while in the program to which they had previously desensitized themselves. Of these 7, 2 reported little or no decrease in tension (a rating of 1 or 2 on a 5-point scale), 2 reported marked tension decrease (a rating of 4 and 5), while 3 patients rated the amount of their tension decrease as 3. Most of the tense scenes chosen to work with involved difficult situations encountered in the hospital, such as being put in confinement, talking with the doctor, or trying to get in touch with the doctor, being "made

TABLE 5

EVALUATION QUESTIONNAIRE (POST-PROGRAM)

Enjoyment of Meetings

Meeting (In order of preference)	Averaged Rating (On a one-to five Scale)	Rank Order
Introduction, Muscle Relaxation, Meeting 1	4.2	1.5
How to Change Behavior-Practice, Meeting 5	4.2	1.5
How Behavior is Influenced-Theory, Meeting 4	4.1	3
Lightness, Heaviness-Desensitization, Meeting 2	3.9	4
Idealized Self-Image, Meeting 3	3.8	5
Assertive Training, Meeting 6	3.6	6.5
Guidelines for the Future, Meeting 8	3.6	6.5
Rational Thinking, Meeting 7	3.5	8

TABLE 6

Ratings of Helpfulness of Various Parts of the Program at 3-Month Follow-up

Parts of Program (in order of Helpfulness)	Number Responding	Average Rating	Rank Order
1. Workbook	10	3.5	1
2. Guidelines for Future Lectures	9	3.4	3
3. Rational Thinking	9	3.4	3
4. Group Discussions	10	3.4	3
5. Playlets	10	3.3	5.5
6. Assertive Training	10	3.3	5.5
7. Relaxation	12	3.2	8.5
8. Idealized Self-Image	11	3.2	8.5
9. Training in how to change behavior	11	3.2	8.5
10. Lectures	9	3.2	8.5
11. Private talks with group leaders	9	3.1	11
12. Training in how behavior is influenced	11	3.0	12
13. Poetry	10	2.9	13
14. Desensitization	11	2.5	14

TABLE 7

AMOUNT OF PRACTICE OF TECHNIQUES DURING 3-MONTHS AFTER FINISHING PROGRAM

	Have Not Practiced	Practiced Infrequently	Practiced Regularly
Relaxation	3	8	1
Relaxation & Desensitization	4	6	1
Improvement of Self-Image by Imaging the Future	4	4	3
Noticing How Behavior is Influenced	4	5	2
Rewarding of Others to Change their Behavior	3	4	3
Appropriate Assertiveness	5	3	2
Rational Thinking	1	6	2

anxious" by a nurse, and having to wait through the week-end without any visitors. Other scenes mentioned were being stuck in a crowded elevator, "loss of senses", and arguing with one's stepmother.

Most of the patients reacted favorably to the *Idealized Self-Image.* Seven patients reported that they felt their attitudes or behavior change to become closer to their ISI, while 3 reported that they were not sure. None reported no change. Most of the self-images chosen to work with included such personal characteristics as being more confident, independent, able to stand pressure and tension, relaxed and worry-free. Four reflected concern about having satisfactory employment and only two mentioned characteristics having to do with personal appearance. It's interesting that none of the patients' self-images reflected a concern with family or social relationships. This is in sharp contrast to the self-images mentioned in our behavior modification program for drug addicts, in which the affection and respect of family members and friends were repeatedly expressed as an important concern.

We also looked whether the patients has used the program to change the behaviors of others. Five of the 11 patients reported that they had. Staff members, other patients, and, in one case, the patient himself, were the targets. Behaviors to be changed included insensitivity to the patient's presence, depression, resentment, arguments and fighting. Rewards used were, "a helping hand", friendliness and concern, kind words, respect, and help in solving the other's problems. Four patients reported that they were successful, and one that he was "somewhat" successful.

Five of the patients reported that both their ideas and behavior about *assertiveness* had changed while one reported that only his ideas had changed. One reported no change and four were not sure.

3. *Use of the Techniques*

Seven patients reported that they had applied some of the techniques they learned in the program in a particular situation. Most frequently mentioned were relaxation and use of the calm scene (3), followed by rewarding of others (2) and changing assertiveness (1).

4. *Continued Use of Techniques*

When asked which of the techniques they planned to practice in the future, 5 of the patients checked "improvement of self-image by your own effort," 4 checked "relaxation," 3 checked each "rewarding of others," "Self-assertiveness" and "rational thinking." Only 1 checked that he would continue to practice "desensitization".

5. *Expectations of the Helpfulness of the Program*

The patients generally seemed to feel that the program would be helpful to them both during and after their hospitalization. When asked to express this on a 5-point scale, the patients rated the expected helpfulness of the program highest for after they leave the hospital (4.3), giving a rating of 4.1 to the expected helpfulness of the program while they were still hospitalized.

THE THREE MONTH EVALUATION QUESTIONNAIRE

This questionnaire was filled in by 12 of the program participants, 8 males and 4 females. All of this group had attended 4 or more meetings.

1. *Characteristics of the Respondents*

Of the 12 respondents, 10 had been discharged from the hospital since their participation in the Behavior Modification Program, while 2 were still hospitalized. Of the 10, 4 had been readmitted to the hospital once since their discharge and 5 had had contact with the hospital out-patient clinic.

Of those who were discharged, 6 lived with their families and 2 lived at an aftercare home. 4 of the respondents received complete support from their families during their discharge, 2 were partly self-supporting, 1 received some help from his family, and 1 received assistance from the Bureau of Child Services & Rehabilitation.

Four reported that they saw their families more frequently since the behavior modification program, 5 reported no change and 1 reported that he saw his family less frequently.

Seven reported that they were better able to get along with their families since the behavior modification, 2 reported no difference and one that he was not as able to get along.

Three reported improved relations with the hospital staff, 3 reported no difference, and 1 reported worsened relations. Of those who were discharged, 5 reported improved relations with friends and 1 reported no difference, 4 reported improved relations with their supervisors and colleagues at work, 1 no difference, and 1 worsened relations. Two reported improved relations with teachers and 1 no difference.

2. *General Effects of the Program*

Asked to what extent the behavior modification program made a difference in their lives during the last 3 months, 2 checked 5 (5 indicating "very much" on a 1-5 scale), 1 checked 4, 4 checked 3, 2 checked 2, and only 1 checked 1, "not at all". The average rating was 2.9. Asked to comment on how the program had made a difference, one stated that he had gotten a job through using the idealized self-image technique, while others stated that they felt happier and better about themselves generally.

3. *Helpfulness of the Various Part of the Program*

Patients' ratings of the helpfulness of the various parts of the program are presented in Table 6.

The workbook was rated as being most helpful to the patients during the 3 months following the program, with the Guidelines for the Future lectures which dealt with the kinds of situations that patients could expect to be faced with after their discharge with tips on how to apply behavioral techniques to better manage them, rated second. Of the techniques alone, rational thinking, assertive training and relaxation were rated most helpful in that order although in respect to the program as a whole, they received a rank order of 3, 5.5, and 8.5 respectively.

4. *Practice of Techniques*

Table 7 shows the number who practiced the various techniques during the 3 months following the program.

Rational thinking and relaxation were practiced most regularly. Assertiveness was least regularly practiced.

5. *Use of Workbooks*

Asked if they had reread their books, 4 replied once or twice only, while 8 had not read them at all. This contrasted sharply with the reports of the drug addicts, most of whom tended to re-read their workbooks several times.

6. *Effectiveness of Specific Techniques*

Eight reported that they went through an actual tense situation to which they had *desensitized* themselves, while 4 had not. Asked to rate on a 1-5 scale the extent to which their tension decreased in the situation as a result of desensitization, 6 checked 3, and 2 checked 4.

When asked whether their attitude or behavior had changed over the past 3 months to become closer to their *Idealized Self-Image*, 5 replied yes, 4 no, and 3 were not. One patient commented that he now felt more comfortable and was better able to realize his mistakes.

Asked if they had attempted to *modify* anyone's *behavior* using rewards during the past 3 months, 4 stated that they had while 5 had not. Mentioned as targets were a fellow employee, patients and staff of an aftercare home, a girlfriend and a younger brother. Rewards used were compliments, favors, love and, in the case of the younger brother, reading him a story. Two reported that they were successful and two somewhat successful.

Five felt the program had changed both their ideas and behavior with regard to *assertiveness*, 1 felt his ideas had changed only, 2 felt there was no change and 4 were not sure.

Asked whether they had applied the techniques they learned in a *particular situation*, 6 said yes and 6 said no. The most frequent technique mentioned was relaxation, with proper assertiveness and idealized self-image also mentioned.

7. *Helpfulness of the Program in General*

Asked to rate on a 1-5 scale how helpful in general they felt the program had been in the past 3 months, 1 checked 5 (very helpful), 3 checked 4, 2 checked 3, 3 checked 2, and 2 checked 1. The average rating was 2.8.

8. *Particular Ways in Which it was Helpful*

Asked to rate on a 5-point scale the extent to which the program was helpful in specific ways, feeling better about yourself was rated first (3.3), followed by job adjustment (3.2), family adjustment (2.7), school adjustment (2.6), social adjustment (2.4), and adjustment with hospital staff and patients (2.3).

DISCUSSION

Although an adequate evaluation was not possible in the absence of a comparison group, the pre- and post-program test data nevertheless provide some indication that the behavior modification program produced some favorable changes in the mentally ill young adults who participated in it. Post-program test data show that the patients experienced a significant decrease in tension as well as a significant improvement in their self-images after taking part in the program.

Perhaps more importantly, however, the study suggests that such a program is not only possible with patients hospitalized for mental illness, but potentially a very useful aspect of their rehabilitation. Prior to the beginning of the study, it was questioned whether patients hospitalized for mental illness would be able to successfully participate in a program as highly structured as the behavior modification program. It soon became evident, however, that the patients not only were able to attentively sit through eight 1 1/2 hour highly structured sessions, but that they generally remained interested and actively participated in the meetings, understood the subject matter and the techniques, and were able to independently apply the techniques appropriately both during and after their hospitalization.

The subjective test data lend further support to these conclusions. As reported above, most of the patients claimed that they understood the aims of the program, how the techniques were related to the aims of the program and how to apply the techniques. Their descriptions of how they had applied the techniques in actual situations seem to suggest that this was, in fact, the case. The relaxation techniques and use of the calm scene as well as techniques relating to behavior analysis and control were most preferred and used most frequently.

Even more persuasive than the questionnaire data, however, was our observation of the enthusiasm with which the program was received by many of the patients. This is illustrated by one incident in which one of the patients in the program ran away from the hospital, taking his behavior modification workbook with him. He was apprehended by the police several hours later in a bar, diligently explaining behavior modification techniques to the interested customers.

It was also successfully found that the awarding of diplomas to anyone who had successfully completed six or more meetings became a very important aspect of the program for many patients. One patient said that he planned to use the diploma to remind him of the things he was taught in the course, so that if, for example, he felt that he was going to lose his temper, the diploma would serve as a reminder to him to control his emotions and behave more rationally. Indeed, he reported that he had already used the expectation of receiving the diploma to control violent behavior while he was still hospitalized.

Although the majority of patients responded well to the program, a few patients, these in particular, presented difficulties. One, a paranoid schizophrenic, was highly suspicious and hostile, indicating on a number of occasions that there was no way in which the program could be of benefit to him. Another patient, diagnosed as schizophrenic, chronic undifferentiated type, exhibited highly suspicious behavior initially, although after two or three meetings, he began to enjoy the group and take an active part in discussions. Despite his attitude change, however, he remained consistently unwilling to relate the program to his own problems, evading them by either shifting the discussion to the problems of other group members or by "intellectualizing," discussing his problems in such abstract and general terms that the real issues were avoided. Finally at the last meeting, however, he began to discuss his family situation realistically and to begin to look for the first time at how his problems might better be handled. It was felt with both of these patients that more positive results could have been obtained had the program extended for a longer period of time, and, since that time, we have frequently had patients request to participate twice in the program.

The third patient, however, also diagnosed as schizophrenic, chronic undifferentiated type, presented more serious difficulties. This patient talked excessively, often about topics that were irrelevant to the program content, and as a result often seriously disrupted the group discussions. He also had difficulty concentrating and was unable to comprehend much of the material presented in either the workbook or lectures. He did, however, respond well to the relaxation and the use of the calm scene. This suggested to us the possible value of adapting the section of the program dealing with relaxation separately for patients such as this who are unable to benefit from the program in its entirety.

The present study made very clear to us the importance of extending the program to include others dealing directly with patients while they were hospitalized and afterward. For instance, the techniques would be made significantly more powerful if they were known to and utilized by staff members working with the patients daily on the ward. Also, the psychiatrists of patients undergoing the training might utilize in individual therapy sessions a more intensive application of those particular techniques best suited to the needs of their patients. The importance of following up the hospital program with a program directed at patients' families and staff working with them as out-patients was also suggested by comments from the patients during the period of aftercare.

Perhaps the greatest significance, however, is our observation that hospitalized acutely mentally ill patients, most of whom were schizophrenics, are able to respond to behavioral techniques emphasizing self-control. This is especially important insofar as the majority of behavioral techniques utilized with mentally ill to date have stressed external control. Our study suggests, in a preliminary way, that these patients are interested in such techniques, understand them and are able to utilize them in an appropriate and profitable fashion.

REFERENCES

1. Allyon, T. Intensive treatment of psychotic behavior by stimulus satiation and food reinforcement. In *Experiments in Behavior Therapy.* Edited by Eysenck, H. J. MacMillan, New York, (1964).
2. Allyon, T. Some behavioral problems associated with eating in chronic schizophrenic patients. In *Case Studies in Behavior Modification.* Edited by Ullman, L. P. and Krasner, L. Holt, Rinehart and Winston, New York, (1965).
3. Allyon, T., and Azrin, N. H. *J. Exp. Anal. Behav. 7,* 327, (1964).
4. Allyon, T. and Haughton, E. *J. Exp. Anal. Behav. 5,* 343, (1962).
5. Allyon, T. and Haughton, E. *Behav. Res. Therapy 2,* 87, (1964).
6. Krasner, L. *Res. Psychother. 2,* 61, (1963).
7. Krasner, L., and Ullman, L. *Case Studies in Behavior Modification.* Holt, Rinehart and Winston, New York, (1965).
8. Atthowe, J. and Krasner, L. The systematic application of contingent reinforcement procedures (token economy) in a large social setting in a psychiatric ward. Paper read at American Psychological Association Meeting, Chicago, Illinois, (1965).
9. Allyon, T. and Michael, T. *J. Exp. Anal. Behav. 2,* 323, (1959).

10. Lee, D. and Zenachko, G. *J. Psychiat. Nurs. Ment. Health Serv. 6,* (1968).
11. Allen, K. and Harris, F. R. *Behav. Res. Therapy 4,* 79, (1966).
12. Ferster, C. B. *Child Develop. 32,* 437, (1961).
13. Ferster, C. B. and Simons, J. *Psychol. Rec. 32,* 437, (1966).
14. Holzschuk, R. D. Teaching teachers, parents, children and self in the use of behavior management principles. Paper read at the American Psychological Association, September, (1967).
15. Huakes, R. P., Pettsan, R. T., Schweid, E., and Bijou, S. W. *J. Exp. Child Psychol. 4,* 99, (1966).
16. Walder, L., Breiter, D. *et al.* Teaching parents to modify the behavior of their autistic chidren. Paper read at the american Psychological Association Meeting, New York, September, (1960).
17. Walder, L., Cohen, S. *et al.* Teaching behavioral principles to parents of disturbed children. Paper read at the Eastern Psychological Association, Boston, (1967).
18. Walder, L., Cohen, S. *et al.* Behavior therapy of children through their parents. Paper read at American Psychological Association, Washington, D. C., (1967).
19. Cheek, F. E. *J. Schizophrenia 1,* 18, (1967).
20. Lindsley, O. R. Speech on behavior modification with families. Delivered at Temple University, Department of Behavioral Science, Philadelphia, (1968).
21. Cheek, F. E., Franks, C. M., Laucius, J., and Burtle, V. *Quart. J. Stud. Alc. 32,* 456, (1971).
22. Cheek, F. E., Burtle, V., Laucius, J., Powell, D., Franks, C. M., and Albahary, R. A behavior modification training program for alcoholics and their wives. Paper presented at the Association for the Advancement of Behavior Therapy, Washington, D. C., (1971).
23. Susskind, D. *Behav. Therapy 1,* 538, (1970).
24. Cheek, F. E., Tomarchio, T., Standen, J., Franks, C. M., and Albahary, R. Methadone Plus - a behavior modification training program for male and female addicts on methadone maintenance. In press, 1972.

25. Ellis, A., and Harper, R. *A guide to rational thinking.* Prentice Hall, Englewood Cliffs, (1961).
26. Mosher, L. R. New treatment systems for schizophrenics. *Schizophrenia,* (1971).
27. Mirsky, A. T. *Annu. Rev. Psychol. 20,* 321, (1969).
28. Weinman, B., Gellart, P., Wallace, M. and Post, M. *J. Consult. Clin. Psychol. 39,* 246, (1972).
29. Taylor, J. A. *J. Abnormal Soc. Psychol,* (1953).
30. Rotter, J. E. *Psychol. Monogr. 80,* 609, (1966).
31. Gough, H. G. *Reference Handbook for the Gough Adjective Check List.* Consulting Psychologists Press, Palo Alto, (1965).
32. Wolpe, J. and Lazarus, A. *Behavior Therapy Techniques.* Pergamon Press, London, (1966).

MENTAL HEALTH IN CHILDREN, Volume III
Edited By D. V. Siva Sankar

BEHAVIOR THERAPY WITH CHILDREN: A REVIEW OF UNDERLYING ASSUMPTIONS, TREATMENT TECHNIQUES AND RESEARCH FINDINGS

Walter vom Saal

Millersville State College
Millersville, Pa. 17551

ABSTRACT

An overview of the theory, principles and practice of behavior therapy and behavior modification with children. The paper begins with a discussion of the basic approaches and underlying assumptions of behavior therapy and behavior modification. The special relevance of this approach both to normal children and to children with emotional and behavioral problems is noted. There follows an overview of the major principles of behavior change, including principles for increasing specific behaviors, decreasing specific behaviors, developing stimulus control, and modifying emotional responses.

The major portion of the paper is devoted to illustrative research and clinical material indicating current behavioral approaches to treatment of children. The areas covered include phobias and anxiety responses, antisocial behaviors, delinquency, hyperactivity, tantrums and self-injurious behavior, muteness, toilet training, and mental retardation. Implications for the rearing of "normal" children are also considered. Finally, an attempt is made to evaluate both the possible weaknesses and limitations of the behavioral approach, and the strengths and contributions that the behavioral approach has provided in the understanding and treatment of disordered behavior in children.

CONTENTS

4. Modifying emotional responses (classical conditioning)
   a. Establishing fear or anxiety
   b. Eliminating fear or anxiety

E. *Illustrative research and case studies*
   1. Phobias and anxiety responses
   2. Antisocial behaviors: fire setting
   3. Delinquency
   4. Hyperactivity, tantrums, and self-injurious behavior
   5. Muteness
   6. Toilet training; enuresis and encopresis
   7. Mental retardation: self-help skills, social skills, language training

F. *Implications for the rearing of normal children*

G. *Strengths and weaknesses of the behavioral approach*
   1. Strengths
   2. Weaknesses
   3. Conclusions

A. BASIC ORIENTATION AND UNDERLYING ASSUMPTIONS OF BEHAVIOR MODIFICATION AND BEHAVIOR THERAPY

Behavior modification is an approach which emphasizes defining the problem in terms of behavior, and treating the behavior directly, making use of a set of learning principles derived from laboratory experiments. It may be contrasted with psychodynamic or 'insight' approaches which assume that behavior problems are necessarily 'symptoms' of some underlying disorder, and which assume that direct treatment of the 'symptom' will be ineffective or possibly harmful in the absence of more general (and less observable) changes in 'personality,' 'adjustment,' and 'basic, underlying problems.'

A complete understanding of the approach described as behavior modification would require three things. First, an understanding of a number of *basic underlying assumptions* that characterize this approach. Second, an understanding of the major *laboratory-derived priniciples* of behavior change on which specific therapeutic strategies and techniques are based. And third, a knowledge of some of the *specific techniques* used by behavior therapists in attempting to treat specific classes of behavior problems. Some attempt will be made to communicate each of these in the present article: basic assumptions will be described in this section, principles of behavior change will be briefly described in a subsequent section, and specific techniques

The purpose of this article is to review some of the work that has been done on behavior modification in children. The article is directed to the reader who is interested in psychiatric and psychological problems of children and who, while not committed to a behavioral approach, is open to the possibility that behavioral analysis and treatment may have something to offer in dealing with childhood problems. The article begins with an attempt to specify more precisely what is meant by 'behavior modification' or 'behavior therapy.'* This is done by describing the major underlying assumptions which, taken together, constitute the essence of behavior modification or behavior therapy. The argument is then made that this approach has special relevance to children, both 'normal' and 'abnormal.' A brief overview of the major laboratory-derived principles of behavior change is presented. This is followed by illustrative research and case studies in a number of areas, including phobias, antisocial behaviors and delinquency, self-destructive behaviors, muteness, toilet training, and mental retardation. There is no attempt to thoroughly review the literature in these areas, but rather in each area material is presented that illustrates some of the behavioral attempts at treatment that have been reported. As will become apparent, a behavioral approach does not dictate some single rigid treatment procedure, but rather suggests a variety of possible strategies. The material below has been chosen to illustrate some of these possible strategies. Finally, the article concludes with the attempt to summarize both the advantages and disadvantages of a behavioral approach.

*The terms 'behavior modification' and 'behavior therapy' will be used here interchangeably. Distinctions that have sometimes been made between these terms are discussed in a separate section below.

will be illustrated in the case material presented in later sections.

It is important to realize at the outset that these three areas (underlying assumptions, learning principles, therapeutic techniques) are not identical. For example, some authors have argued that the essence of behavior therapy is its reliance on experimental method (1-3). If this is so, then even if some of the major learning principles now employed as a basis for therapy were shown to be invalid or irrelevant, the value of behavior therapy could still be defended. As another example, it is important to realize the distinction between *theory* and *technique* in behavior therapy. If a particular technique is shown not to be effective, that would not necessarily disprove the theoretical structure behind it. Or on the other hand, if a particular technique *is* shown to be effective, that would not necessarily support the theoretical structure in which that technique was originally derived. Wolpe's technique of systematic desensitization is an illustration of this. Although the technique was originally explained in terms of learning theory, it has been pointed out that when one considers what actually occurs in a systematic desensitization session, the major components are that the therapists and patient interact verbally, the therapist instructs the patient to relax, and the patient attempts to 'imagine' certain scenes. This has led others to question whether systematic desensitization works for the reasons Wolpe said it does, and to argue that the procedure is more properly classed a cognitive therapy than a behavioral therapy (5-10). Therefore the finding that systematic desensitization seems to be an extremely effective treatment technique does not necessarily support the theoretical structure on which this treatment was originally based.

The distinction between theory and technique has implications for both researchers and clinicians. For the researcher, it emphasizes the importance of empirically validating each treatment technique in its own right, and suggests the value of research examing whether a treatment technique works for the reasons it was expected to work. One illustration of such research is the Valins and Ray study examining a cognitive component in desensitization (5). Another illustration is the finding that, (consistent with implications of learning theory) an 'anxiety relief' procedure employing shock offset to reinforce coping self-statements reduced phobic behavior, but, (inconsistent with learning theory) the shock procedure was still effective even when the particular contingencies were reversed. This finding undermines the 'conditioning' explanation for the effectiveness of the anxiety relief procedure (11, pp 423-425).

For the clinician, the distinction between theory and technique suggests that clinicians of a particular theoretical inclination should be open to the possible value of techniques originally presented within a different theoretical framework. Behaviorally oriented therapists might be willing to admit that a treatment prodecure such as Rogers' client-centered therapy is called for in some instances, but might wish to interpret that procedure in terms of extinction of anxiety instead of self-actualization. On the other hand of the coin, the reader who disagrees with every one of the underlying assumptions of behavior modification described below, might still find treatment techniques he considers valuable described later in the paper.

We turn now to a description of some of the basic orientations and underlying assumptions of behavior modification. It has been argued that these basic assumptions, rather than any specific set of procedures or techniques, are the essence of behavior modification. Specific procedures may change, but the basic orientation that behaviors may be treated directly rather than indirectly, that laboratory-derived principles of learning may be used to derive explicit treatment strategies, and that continual experimental verification and evaluation of treatment is essential, are likely to remain lasting contributions whether or not any particular treatment strategy survives.

Of the underlying assumptions listed below, the ones just mentioned have usually been regarded as defining characteristics of behavior modification. The remaining assumptions may be regarded as corrolaries or derivatives of these, and include the belief that there is no necessary distinction between 'normal' and 'abnormal' behavior (or at least that the same learning principles apply to both); the belief that symptom substitution need not necessarily occur; the hesitation to apply traditional diagnostic labels; the belief that problems can be treated without historical insight; the emphasis on variables maintaining behavior in the natural environment; and the use of nonprofessional agents of change.

1. Defining the problem in terms of behavior

The behavioral approach emphasizes defining the problem in terms of behavior -- either the presence of a specific behavior or behaviors that is undesirable, or the lack of a behavior or behaviors that is desirable. Ullmann (12) has emphasized that behavior therapists must 'shift from the traditional *why* questions to *what* questions. He must ask: *What* is the person doing? Under *what* conditions are these behaviors emitted? *What* are the effects of these acts?' In a 21-step interview quide for behavioral counselling with parents, Holland begins with the reduction of a general complaint to a list of specific problem behaviors, followed by specification of the precise behaviors the parents desire to increase in frequency and the precise behaviors they desire to decrease in frequency (13).

A rigorous attempt is made to avoid terms that are only loosely descriptive and that depend on a particular (usually psychodynamic) theory. Such terms include ego strength, unconscious attraction, passive aggressive, transference, unresolved guilt, negative attitude, feelings of insecurity, immature behavior, bizarre behavior, low self-esteem, overprotective parent, regression, internalized hosility, rapport, and self-actualization. Terms and phrases of this sort are carefully avoided because they do not point out specific behaviors, and are extremely difficult to define objectively.

It should be pointed out that in one sense, behavioral description is just objective description, and is therefore theory-less. It would be perfectly possible to give a careful, precise, behavioral description of a problem behavior, and then go on to give a psychodynamic interpretation of that behavior and suggest a psychodynamic cure. In actual fact, however, it turns out that behaviorally oriented therapists give much greater attention to careful and specific definitions of the problem behavior, and the stimulus situation in which it occurs, than do therapists of other persuasions. Stuart gives an excellent example of this in presenting a detailed case history of a ten-year old boy seen for reading and eating problems (14, ch 6). Stuart presents the complete psychiatric report, reading evaluation, staff conference report, and final summary prepared by a social worker. He then points out numerous specific examples of terms and phrases in the reports which served to confuse rather than clarify the boy's problems. In this case, after eighteen months of unsuccessful psychotherapy, careful specification of the problem behaviors and their direct treatment led to rapid cure.

2. Treating the behavior directly

The behavioral approach may be contrasted with what has been termed the 'medical model.' According to the medical model, problem behaviors are symptoms of some underlying deficit or disease, and treatment of the 'symptom' directly will be ineffective. The behavioral approach begins with the more parsimonious assumption that the problem behavior has arisen out of the conditions of learning that the child has experienced, and that correction of the behavior can be achieved by subjecting the child to new learning experiences. If the child sets fires, teach him not to set fires. If he has a school phobia, expose him to a set of experiences directly designed to eliminate the anxiety he may experience, and reinforce him for attending school. If he engages in bizarre self-destructive behavior, apply principles of reward and punishment to directly modify that behavior. If he is mute, train him to speak. If he cannot control bowels, train him to do so.

The above statements may seem offensively simplistic. If one could simply 'teach' the child to stop setting fires or engaging in tantrums, why would he ever be brought to a clinic? Why would not parents or teachers have 'taught' the desired behaviors long ago? The answer is two-fold. First, although the principles of conditioning and learning may seem simple, in actual practice they are not. Several of the clinical examples described below will illustrate cases where the parents were able to modify the child's behavior fairly rapidly following careful professional analysis of the variables that were maintaining the deviant behavior, even after having unsuccessfully tried for some time to change the behavior by ineffective means. Second, even the professional with wide experience and knowledge in the application of behavior principles may have to experiment. Without knowing all the details of what is maintaining the deviant behavior, it may be necessary to try several tactics before finding one that works. Often the professional begins with some of this background before him, since he knows what things the parents have tried that haven't worked, and can form hypotheses about what may be maintaining the behavior.

Two additional points may be made about treating the behavior directly. First, specifying a specific problem behavior may be beneficial because it specifies a clear goal for both the therapist and the client. Second, there seems to be increased willingness among behavior modifiers to consider not just overt behavior, but also cognitions and sentences people say to themselves, as legitimate behaviors to be dealt with by behavioral techniques. For example, Susskind (15) views her technique of self-image training and confidence training as a behavioral approach, Meichenbaum (11) has described behavioral approaches to 'modifying what clients say to themselves,' and Lazarus (16) has argued for a concept of 'broad-spectrum behavior therapy' which draws upon a variety of techniques without insisting on dealing only with overt behavior.

Finally, whenever it is proposed that problem behavior should be dealt with directly, the question arises whether symptom substitution will occur. This question will be treated in a separate section below.

3. Use of learning principles derived from the laboratory

The basic approach to treatment employed by the behavior therapist makes use of a set of learning principles, or principles of behavior change, based on laboratory experiments with humans or animals. Ullmann and Krasner have pointed out that at present only the broadest, most thoroughly established concepts are used in the clinical setting (17). Although there are a number of controversies and discrepencies within the experimental literature, most theorists agree on a basic framework of learning principles, and behavior therapy makes use of these.

A later section of this paper will present an overview of these major principles of behavior change. For now it is sufficient to point out that they are the basic principles of classical conditioning and operant conditioning, such as reinforcement, secondary reinforcement, extinction, discrimination learning, and punishment. The classical conditioning principles have their greatest application in the treatment of phobias and anxiety responses by systematic desensitization and counterconditioning procedures. It is probably fair to say that, in treating children's behavior, the operant conditioning principles have been more widely employed. These principles are particularly appropriate when some new behavior is to be trained, such as in toilet training or in teaching self-help skills to retardates.

Two examples illustrate the systematic employment of operant principles for the modification of children's behavior. In his 21-step interview guide for behavioral counseling with parents, Holland presents a systematic and detailed procedure for helping parents deal with problem behavior (13). The steps cited include specifying the precise target behaviors desired; discussing how the parents may proceed to the terminal behavior in a step-by-step manner; listing what positive and negative reinforcements are possible; discussing stimulus situations that affect the present likelihood of the target behavior; and discussing various tactics for increasing or decreasing the target behavior with rewards, witholding or removal of reward, timeout from positive reinforcement, and modifications of the stimulus situation. As another example, the excellent book *Changing Children's Behavior* by Krumboltz and Krumboltz is organized around sets of principles for strengthening existing behavior, developing new behavior, maintaining new behavior, and stopping inappropriate behavior, plus a final section on modifying emotional responses (18).

These principles of directly influencing behavior by manipulating the environment, by changing the stimuli that control the behavior and by arranging the positive and negative consequences of the behavior, constitute the theoretical framework for behavior therapy. This theoretical framework excludes many traditional psychoanalytic assumptions such as infantile sexuality, fixations, the unconscious, and defense mechanisms. And the framework has a number of additional implications, including the view that there is no necessary distinction between 'normal' and 'abnormal' behavior, the belief that symptom substitution need not necessarily occur, and the belief that problems can be treated without historical insight. Each of these implications will be described separately below.

4. Experimental approach to treatment and its evaluation

Behavior therapy developed historically largely out of research-oriented settings, and behavior therapists continue to be heavily interested in and involved in research. Franks has noted that one of the characteristics of behavior therapy is its 'emphasis upon the systematic, rigorous and controlled methodology which has become the hallmark of the good behavioral scientist' (19). Writers in the field of behavior therapy continue to emphasize the importance of good experimental evaluation of their treatment procedures, including concern with proper control procedures to insure that their claimed treatment effects do not result from such nonspecific effects as experimenter bias (20) or demand characteristics (21).

Behavior therapists are not only concerned with evaluation of their procedures in controlled laboratory or group studies, but make wide use of experimental evaluation within individual subjects. In fact Yates (1,2) has argued that the essential characteristic of behavior therapy is its 'treating the patient as the object of a rigorous experimental investigation' and its use of 'controlled experimental studies carried out on the individual patient' (1, p.96). Yates views this experimental approach not simply as a procedure to satisfy scientific curiosity, but as essential to the treatment of the individual patient.

While Yates' view is more extreme than that of many behavior therapists, it is fair to say that within the behavioral approach there is a strong emphasis on careful and systematic evaluation of objectively defined progress within the individual patient. Unlike the more traditional counselor, the behavior therapist is likely to keep, or assign the patient to keep, charts and records of progress. The very act of keeping such charts may be an aid to treatment in that it forces the client to attend to and carefully define his behavior. For example, a mother who is instructed to give her child a gold star on a special chart each time he engages in certain behavior may find herself attending to that behavior, and reinforcing it with praise, attention, and approval, in ways she had previously been unable to do. The token system in this case may have its important effect not in the way it directly influences the child's behavior, but in the way it changes the mother's behavior. Another virtue of charts and records is that they may serve as a motivational device to keep the parent (and counselor!) going when improvement occurs slowly and might not otherwise be noticed.

Experimental evaluation of treatment effectiveness in an individual case can also be extremely important in maintaining subsequent treatment. For example, a nine-year-old retarded girl who vomited in class an average of almost twice a day, and sometimes as often as 21 times a day, was put on an extinction procedure where the vomiting was no longer reinforced by being sent to her dormitory (22). Over a period of six weeks the vomiting dropped out, and no vomiting occurred in the final 42 class days. However, this change could have been attributed to other changes in the environment besides the explicit extinction procedure. In the class the next year, the initial conditions were re-introduced, with the child returned to her dormitory each time she vomited for a three month period. Vomiting increased until its occurred in over one-third of the class sessions. Following a return to the extinction procedure vomiting declined again in an orderly manner until there was only one case of vomiting in class during the last two months of the school year. In this case a simple extinction procedure, which one initially might have viewed with skepticism as an effective treatment for vomiting, was shown to be effective. Such a demonstration that the teacher's reaction to the vomiting was in fact maintaining and increasing such behavior could be important in convincing the teacher not to reinforce vomiting.

5. *No distinction between 'normal' and 'abnormal' behavior*

Writers within the behavioral approach have sometimes argued that there is no distinction between normal and abnormal behavior except in terms of arbitrary criteria set by society. Perhaps this view is too extreme, since there are clear cases of physical deficits, such as in brain damage and mongolism, in which behavior is certainly different in major respects from that classified as 'normal.' Even granted this, however, the behavior therapist would point out that in many cases of abnormal behavior, it is quite possible that the abnormal behavior is a result of learning which obeyed the same principles that govern learning in normals. As Jehu has noted, 'abnormal behavior is a result of the same determinants as normal behavior. In particular, the same *processes* of learning are common to both normal and abnormal behavior, but in the case of the latter the *conditions* of learning have been such as to produce deviant rather than normal stimulus-response relationships' (23, p. 18).

There are three reasons for at least beginning with the assumption that even severely abnormal behavior is susceptible to influence by general rules of learning. First, it is possible that a large amount of abnormal behavior in which there is no clear physical deficit may not result from any 'hidden' physical deficit, such as 'minimal brain damage' or some subtle and undiscovered biochemical deficiency. Such behavior may be simply a product of learning under unusual conditions which generated behavior appropriate to those conditions, but subsequently labeled 'abnormal.' Second, even in cases of clear physical deficit, principles of conditioning may be employed to achieve optimimum development of the individual given his deficits. Third, and most important, premature assumption of physical limitations, or of serious, deep psychological problems, may remove the individual from a normal feedback process and produce further degeneration. Once a child is labeled 'retarded,' for example, adults begin to expect deficits and no longer require from him behaviors he may well be capable of performing. We will return to this point in the section on the behavior therapist's hesitation to apply traditional diagnostic labels.

6. Symptom substitution need not occur

According to the 'medical model,' behavior problems are symptoms of some underlying illness. This view has two implications: The first is that direct treatment of the behavioral problem is less likely to be successful than treating the 'underlying problem.' The second is that even if the 'symptom' is removed from direct treatment, the basic underlying pathology has not been resolved and will reveal itself in some new problem behavior. This 'symptom substitution' hypothesis is possibly the major reason that many clinicians hesitate to employ behavior modification techniques.

Behavior therapists point out that whether symptom substitution occurs is not a theoretical question, but an empirical one. There is no way to answer it except by trying to treat the problem behavior directly and observing the results. Yates notes that 'considering the significant role such a distinction has played in clinical psychology, experimental demonstration of its existence is singularly lacking' (24, p.372). Many writers have discussed symptom substitution as a discredited hypothesis (e.g. 25-29), and a large number of studies have reported nothing resembling symptom substitution following successful behavior treatment (e.g. 30-38). Baker conducted a study explicitly designed to examine whether symptom substitution would occur following treatment of enuresis in thirty elementary school children using a conditioning treatment or other control treatments (30). No evidence was found for symptom substitution, but rather the opposite. Children treated with conditioning techniques were reported to be happier, less anxious, and more grown-up, assuming new responsibility and venturing into new activities.

This latter finding, that specific treatment of a single problem behavior is followed by general improvement or beneficial side-effects, has frequently been noted. Several reports have noted that treatment of children's phobias has been followed by beneficial side-effects such as reduction in fears beyond the specifically treated phobias (29, p.187), increased ability to engage in recreational activities (29, p. 189), improvement in school work (34), increased sociability with other children (39), and more general improvements such as a decrease in moodiness, increased willingness to participate in household chores, and more congenial relationships with peers (40). Wetzel reports a case in which use of behavioral techniques to eliminate compulsive stealing in a ten-year-old boy seemed to result in improved relationships with peers (41). Patterson and his co-workers have emphasized that modification of a specific behavior will probably change the feedback from the child's environment, and this in turn will produce additional changes in behavior (42,43). For example, if specific treatment reduces the rate of some aversive behavior, positive behaviors may occur which are reinforced by the teacher or peer group, leading to additional positive behaviors, additional reinforcement and so on.

The second main point with regard to 'symptom substitution' is that, when such an effect appears to occur, it may be possible to describe it within the behavioral framework and to deal with the new problem behaviors within that framework. Not all behavior therapists take the extreme position that there is no such thing as symptom substitution. For example, Goldiamond has pointed out that even though 'there is a danger in premature assignment of behavioral deficits as symptomatic, there is also a danger in premature assumption that the alteration of the presenting problem is the final solution' (44, p.852). And Wolpe (45) has argued that 'even when aversion therapy succeeds in removing a compulsion, deconditioning of anxiety is still likely to be needed [because] the continued presence of the neurotic anxiety can provide a basis for 'symptom substitution' (p.200), and 'symptom substitution is only found when therapy is carried out without attention to the autonomic core of neurotic reactions' (p.277). Treatment of a specific behavioral symptom may be ineffective because more general anxiety exists, but in this case, Wolpe would argue, the more general anxiety can still be behaviorally defined and behaviorally treated.

That the successful treatment of a specific problem behavior may be followed by the occurrence of new problem behaviors can be readily understood with a learning theory framework. Among the possible causes for this are (a) the patient has been subjected to new stresses or new learning experiences following treatment, giving rise to new problem behaviors; (b) only one of several original problem behaviors have been treated, and complete treatment must involve dealing with each of the problem behaviors in turn; (c) the problem behavior has been modified only in the presence of limited stimuli (for example tantrums have stopped at school but not at home); and (d) if the original problem behavior was the top item in a hierarchy (for example a hierarchy of attention-getting behaviors), eliminating the top item may reveal other members of the hierarchy which were not previously seen in strength.

A careful program of behavioral treatment can take many of these possibilities into account in the initial treatment procedure. For example, (a) attempts can be made to treat the behavior in a variety of stimulus situations so the new behavior will generalize; (b) the initial evaluation can carefully examine whether there may be sets of problem behaviors rather than just one; (c) the therapist can be on the lookout for new ways of getting attention that may arise and arrange in advance that they not be reinforced. Finally, it may sometimes be necessary to deal sequentially with a number a problem behaviors. For example, Ullmann and Krasner (27, p. 14) describe a series of behaviors by a child at a camp for handicapped children. At first the child was self-punishing, engaging in behaviors such as hitting, slapping, and biting himself. When this was not reinforced by the counselors' attention, he went through a series of other behaviors including throwing tantrums, taking off his clothes in public, stealing food, defecating and smearing feces, and piling up all the other children's shoes. None of these behaviors was reinforced, and none became permanent. For the remainder of the camp session the child engaged in adaptive responses.

As a final point on symptom substitution, it may be noted that even those who believe in symptom substitution might find that direct treatment of the problem behavior is often indicated. Since we cannot be sure in advance that symptom substitution will occur, the most parsimonious approach might be to begin by directly treating the problem behavior and seeing if this works. And even if 'symptom substitution' occurs, it is clear that some 'symptoms' are more disruptive to both the individual and society than other 'symptoms.' Better to have an individual 'take out his aggressions' as a hard-working businessman than by burning down buildings.

The behavioral point of view on the question of 'symptom substitution' may be summarized as follows. First, it is untrue that direct treatment of the problem behavior will inevitably lead to symptom substitution, and careful experimental studies in such areas as conditioning treatment of enuresis have failed to show such an effect. Second, the behavior therapist is well aware that there is often a constellation of behavioral problems, and that successful treatment of one problem behavior may sometimes by followed by increases in other problem behaviors. However, he insists that this is not profitably viewed as 'symptom substitution' because of some deep underlying problem, but rather an effect that can be both described and treated within the behavioral framework.

7. *Hesitation to apply traditional diagnostic labels*

The first characteristic of behavior therapy described above was the emphasis on defining the problem directly in terms of behavior. One implication of this is a hesitation on the part of behavior therapists to apply traditional diagnostic labels to patients. The basic problem with such diagnostic labels is that they are simply not objective. Instead of describing an observable phenomenon on which all observers could agree, they contain a mixture of vague references to observable behavior along with theoretical conceptualizations of that behavior.

Diagnosis has been described in a recent book by Stuart as having the five major functions (14, p.67):

1. To identify the presenting problem;
2. To identify conditions associated with its occurence;
3. To suggest a plan for therapeutically removing the problem;
4. To predict the probable outcome of this treatment; and
5. To predict the salient post-therapy behavior of the patient.

The first two of these involve *description*; the remaining three involve *prediction* of the probable course of events both without treatment and with treatment of various sorts. Stuart argues that traditional psychiatric diagnosis has failed on both counts (14). In terms of description, studies have shown disappointingly low 'reliability' or agreement among different individuals in terms of classifying patients. Stuart cites many studies and concludes that it is 'common for studies to show that very coarse categories such as 'neurotic' or 'psychotic' may be reliably applied, but reliability breaks down markedly when the finer categories are employed' (14, p.69). In terms of prediction, Stuart cites studies showing that traditional psychiatric diagnostic systems do not predict which treatment will be undertaken, that the terms of diagnosis may be essentially irrelevant to treatment, and that diagnosis predicts neither the success of treatment nor the probable outcome following hospitalization (14, pp.80-91).

An often-cited illustration of the irrelevance of much tradition diagnosis is a study by Haughton and Ayllon (46). Using cigarettes as reinforcers, these authors established stereotyped broom-holding behavior in a hospitalized 54-year-old female schizophrenic. Two psychiatrists who were asked to observe and evaluate the patient gave the following evaluation. Dr. A: 'The broom represents to this patient some essential preceptual element in her field of consciousness. How it should have become so is uncertain: on Freudian grounds it could be interpreted symbolically, on behavioral grounds it could perhaps be interpreted as a habit which has become essential to her peace of mind. Whatever may be the case, it is certainly a stereotyped form of behavior such as is commonly seen in rather regressed schizophrenics and is rather analogous to the way small children or infants refuse to be parted from some favorite toy, piece of rag, etc.' Dr. B: 'Her constant and compulsive pacing holding a broom in the manner she does could be seen as a ritualistic procedure, a magical action. When regression conquers the associative process, primitive and archiac forms of thinking control the behavior. Symbolism is a predominant mode of expression of deep seated unfulfilled desired and instinctual impulses. By magic, she controls others, cosmic powers are at her disposal and inanimate objects become living creatures. Her broom could be then: (1) a child that gives her love and she gives him in return her devotion; (2) a phallic symbol; (3) the sceptre of an omnipotent queen. Her rhythmic and prearranged pacing in a certain space are not similar to the compulsions of a neurotic, but because this is a far more irrational, far more controlled behavior from a primitive thinking, this is a magical procedure in which the patient carries out her wishes, expressed in a way that is far beyond our solid, rational and conventional way of thinking and acting' (46, pp. 97-98).

Although this is perhaps an extreme example, it illustrates some of the problem with the traditional psychodiagnostic approach. In particular, it offers no hint as to a treatment procedure. In this case, for instance, removal of the reinforcement for broom-holding rapidly eliminated the behavior.

The first three reasons for hesitating to apply traditional diagnostic labels, then, are that they are not objective descriptions of behavior, they are demonstrably low in both reliability and validity, and they assume a psychodynamic theoretical structure at variance with the behavioral approach. A fourth reason is that such labels may be not just useless, but actively harmful. Stuart (14, ch.5) points out that diagnostic labels are almost always negative, and may negatively affect not only the patient himself but also his social interactions and opportunities for jobs. Such labels may encourage the patient to play the 'sick role' and to assume that the responsibility for behavior change has passed from him to his doctor. And such labels may remove normal expectations and contingencies that were beneficial. For example, Pascal (47) taught the parents of a nine-year-old brain-damaged child to apply behavior modification techniques in teaching the child to produce intelligible speech. Part of the problem was that the parents, and others in the child's environment, had not called for any more adept verbal behavior on the part of the child because he had been labeled 'retarded.' A memo was sent to the adults involved that pointed this out, emphasized that the child *could* learn to speak, and described procedures for requiring and reinforcing new words. After nine weeks the child's verbal repertoire had expanded from almost no intelligible words to 183 intelligible words. The author notes that the child's teachers at school still operate under the assumption that he is untrainable, and that the influence of these differing sets of expectations at home and at school is quite profound.

8. Problems can be treated without historical insight

An implication of the learning principles that underly behavior therapy is that treatment can be carried out without necessarily understanding the historical development of the behavior problem. Since it is assumed that problem behaviors are learned, they can be 'unlearned' without the absolute requirement that the patient obtain insight - especially psychodynamic 'insight' - into the origin of the symptom. In many cases the behavior therapist will focus more on the present, emphasizing those factors which are maintaining the problem behavior in the patient's present environment. This was the case, for example, in the treatment of vomiting cited above, where careful removal of possible reinforcement of the vomiting behavior led to its disappearance (22).

Such a focus on the present may be contrasted with a psychodynamic view that an historical understanding of the symptom is a central goal of treatment, and that such understanding may automatically lead to remission of the symptom. The behavioral view, on the other hand, is that even if the patient fully understands the conditioning background that led to the symptom, that symptom may remain unless a new conditioning experience occurs. This would be the case, for example, in a patient who required desensitization training for anxiety following an automobile accident.

The author has illustrated this point to groups of students by asking each student to imagine that he has carefully removed the fuse to a particular electrical outlet, and has convinced himself that the electricity is off by trying out a lamp. He is then asked to imagine that he carefully licks his two fingers and places them in the socket. Most persons cannot hear this described, let alone actually do it, without a noticeable increase in tension. The point is that cognitively 'knowing' there is no electricity does not eliminate the conditioned anxiety response, neither does 'knowing' that you are anxious only because of your past history. The anxiety response can only be eliminated by some new conditioning procedure, such as systematic desensitization training, that counters the original conditioning. Many cases of extreme anxiety gradually extinguishing with continued exposure probably occur in the natural environment, without the individual ever obtaining 'insight' into the origin of the anxiety. Consider the young college professor who gradually loses his fear of speaking in public, the teenager whose anxiety about urinating in public lavatories with others present gradually extinguishes, or the wife whose anxiety about being seen nude by her husband gradually diminishes.

In much of therapy with children, 'insight' would be meaningless because the child's level of verbal sophisticaion is too low. This would be the case with the mute child being taught to speak, the enuretic child being taught bladder control, the school-phobic being gradually exposed to a set of positive school experiences, and the self-destructive child whose injurious behaviors were being extinguished. In each case attempts to produce 'insight' offer little hope for success, while direct behavioral treatment is likely to produce beneficial effects.

It should be noted that behavior therapists' statements on the lack of necessity for historical knowledge about the symptom have sometimes been too extreme. For example, Goldiamond describes a session in which a patient being seen for marriage problems 'started to talk about his childhood and was summarily cut off.'

'Shouldn't I talk about this with a psychologist?' he asked. 'Isn't this one of the things that interests you? Doesn't it affect me now?'

'Look,' I said. 'A bridge with a load limit of three tons opens in 1903. The next day, a farmer drives eighteen tons over it; it cracks. The bridge collapses in 1963. What caused the collapse?'

'The farmer in 1903,' he said.

'Wrong,' I said. 'The bridge collapses in 1963 because of the cracks that day. Had they been filled in the preceding day it would not have collapsed. Let's discuss the cracks in your marriage.' (44, p. 859)

Such a view seems ridiculously extreme. Wouldn't the people in 1963 like to have known what happened in 1903? Might not that knowledge have suggested that cracks might be there, and even given hints where the cracks might be? Although the behavior therapist would argue that historical knowledge is not *essential* for treatment, he would certainly think some kinds of historical knowledge can be *valuable* to treatment. The kinds of knowledge he would want, however, would not be what is meant by psychodynamic 'insight' but rather specific information about the origin of the problem behavior, the previous occurrence of similar behaviors, and details of the circumstances in which each of these behaviors occured and what consequences followed them.

9. Attention to variables maintaining behavior in the natural environment

The behavior therapist views problem behavior as behavior which has been developed and maintained as a consequence of the patient's interaction with his environment. An implication of this is that treatment must take the patient's natural environment into account, and that the optimum way for the benefits of treatment to be maintained is through modification of the patient's environment.

A systematic attempt to make use of the natural environment in treating children has been described by Tharp and Wetzel (48). These authors point out that a persistent theme in any account of mental health work is the failure of treatment techniques in the face of an adverse environment. They describe a mental health services project in Arizona whose main emphasis is on directing the forces of the patient's natural environment toward therapeutically effective ends. For example, a case might be brought to the clinic involving a young child who was a 'consistent trouble-maker' at home and at school. Assessment procedures would involve precisely specifying the problem behaviors, and conditions under which they occured, present reinforcers for those behaviors, potential reinforcers that could be employed in treatment, and potentials for mediation in the natural environment (such as parents and teachers). Treatment would involve the development of a program for eliminating the problem behavior and instigating and maintaining more socially acceptable behavior, through the use of shaping, prompting, and modeling new behavior, reinforcing these new behaviors, and eliminating problem behaviors through extinction and punishment. These procedures were employed by members of the child's natural environment, such as parents and teachers, following consultation with agency personnel. In many cases contracts were written that explicitly specified these contingencies for both the child and the adults involved. The important element of this program is that the 'treatment' involves explicit changes in the child's natural environment designed to eliminate maladaptive behavior and encourage adaptive behavior.

A similar emphasis on the child's environment has been noted by other workers. For example, Patterson used a 'magic teaching machine' with a nine-year-old hyperactive boy (49). The machine was used with the child in the classroom, and had a light that could be flashed when the child was sitting still and attending to his work. The critical point is that the light flashing indicated money or candy earned which would subsequently be shared among all the children in the class. This arrangement led to the peer group becoming a source of social reinforcement that probably had a strong influence on the observed improvement in the child's behavior. A similar procedure was used successfully with an eight-year-old child who was inattentive and physically aggressive in school (50). Patterson has repeatedly pointed out that the success of a treatment procedure will be critically affected by the effect that the changed behavior produces in the natural environment. If a decrement in the number of aggressive behaviors is immediately followed by approval of parents, teachers, and the peer group, such a reduction is likely to be maintained or improved. On the other hand if negative consequences occur, as might happen with a delinquent peer group, the changes are unlikely to be maintained (42). It has been argued that 'the major focus of the behavior modifier should be upon the task of directly manipulating the reinforcement, programmes being provided by the social environment rather than upon the behavior of the individual subject. In effect, we are accusing the behavior modifier or following too closely the medical model. In the medical model, the behavior modifier would remove the 'tumor' (change the deviant behavior) and then terminate his treatment program. It is reasonable to believe that changing the deviant behavior is simply not good enough; the goals for the behavior modifier must also be that of re-programming the social environment in which the subject finds himself' (43, p. 293).

10. Use of nonprofessional agents of change

The final aspect of behavior therapy that deserves mention is the frequent use of nonprofessional agents of change. In the last section it was noted that behavior therapists emphasize maintenance of behavior in the natural environment. It follows from this that behavior therapists often explicitly train parents, teachers, and other adults in contact with disturbed children to carry out the therapy. Nonprofessional agents of change have also been used in traditional institutional settings.

Gelfand and Hartmann have pointed out that parental 'sabotage' has been reported less often in behavior therapy than in the more traditional play-therapy interventions (51). This may be related to the historical progression from the view that parents should be eliminated from the child's treatment, to the view that the family must be considered as a unit and the disturbed child invariably has a disturbed parent (so that effective treatment of the child necessitates treatment of the parent), to the view that the parent is a possible co-therapist, a potentially powerful ally and a major component in the child's treatment (52). Similarly Tharp and Wetzel have argued that perhaps the major disadvantage of the medical model is that it disqualifies societies greatest potentials for help, the adults who have daily contact with the child in his natural environment (48).

If one grants the value of engaging parents, teachers, and other nonprofessional agents of change in the therapeutic process, there are several reasons why a behavior modification approach is especially attractive for use with these people. Behavior modification procedures are often relatively simple, possible to specify precisely, and therefore easier for the nonprofessional to use. In addition, their rationale may 'make more sense' to the parent or teacher of the disturbed child, and so be more readily accepted and employed by them.

The behavior therapy literature gives many examples of the use of nonprofessional agents of change. Parents have been taught procedures to eliminate hand-slapping and develop intelligible speech in a brain-damaged child (47), increase social responsiveness and decrease hyperactivity in a two-year-old child (53), reduce 'commanding' behavior of a six-year-old boy who dominated his parents (54), reduce 'dependent' and increase 'independent' behavior in a four-year-old boy (54), reduce 'stubbornness' and oppositional behavior (54), eliminate the self-destructive behavior of a five-year-old girl who scratched herself repeatedly until she bled (55), and eliminate psychogenic seizures in a ten-year-old girl (56). Nonprofessional employees and volunteers have also been employed in a variety of treatment settings. One of the earliest reports of explicit use of nurses and ward personnel in treatment of mental patients was Ayllon and Michael's report of 'the psychiatric nurse as a behavioral engineer' (57). Undergraduates have been taught to reinforce appropriate behaviors in autistic children in a private day care center (58). Volunteer adults and high school seniors have been used in the treatment of retarded and emotionally disturbed junior high school students (59).

Tharp and Wetzel have described an ambitious community treatment program making systematic and widespread use of nonprofessionals (48). This program employed a hierarchical organization that included four levels for the treatment of any individual case: 'superior,' 'Behavior Analyst,' 'mediator,' and client or 'target.' The supervisor was a psychologist whose only contact with the case was through the behavior analyst. The Behavior Analyst was a person selected for intelligence, energy, and flexibility, but specifically without any previous training in the helping professions, and was responsible for direct handling of the case and all case contacts. Mediators were selected for a particular case by the Behavior Analyst assigned to it, and included members of the target's community, such as teachers and parents, that might be able to directly modify the target's behavior. Finally, the target was a child referred for treatment for misbehaviors at school and/or home. The authors report considerable success in treatment of a wide range of problem behaviors including theft, mischief, runaways, property destruction, classroom disruption, defiance, and physical aggression.

Finally, a major use of nonprofessional agents of change involves training teachers to deal effectively with problem behaviors at school. For example, teachers have been taught to explicitly observe behavior and to make positive events such as teacher attention, tokens, or opportunity for free play contingent on appropriate behavior. Several books have described the application of conditioning techniques in the classroom (60-63, 124-125).

B. COMMENT ON 'BEHAVIOR THERAPY' VERSUS 'BEHAVIOR MODIFICATION'

In concluding the discussion of defining characteristics of behavior therapy, some mention should be made of the possible distinction between 'behavior therapy' and 'behavior modification.' Although no distinction is implied in the present paper, distinctions have sometimes been made between these terms. For instance, Ashem and Poser reserve the term 'behavior modification' for attempts to modify behaviors that are 'self-limiting and well within the normal range', while using the term 'behavior therapy' for attempts to counteract forms of 'maladaptive behavior' (64). This distinction is unsatisfactory since it is almost impossible to specify clearly what is meant by 'self-limiting and within the normal range.' Indeed, as has been pointed out above, one implication of the behavioral view is that the distinction between 'normal' and 'abnormal' behavior may be difficult to specify or defend.

A second distinction implied in some writing is that 'behavior modification' is a broader term that would encompass a variety of procedures, including token economies in prisons, shock treatment of homosexuals, conditioning a severely brain damaged human to move one arm for food reinforcement, teaching children to behave well in a classroom, ward management procedures for chronic psychotics, and so on. 'Behavior therapy' would then be reserved as shorthand for 'behavioral approaches to psychotherapy,' with the implication that it typically involved a psychologist or psychiatrist seeing clients in an office on a regular basis. Although a definition of 'behavior therapy' as being a specific system of psychotherapy seems appropriate in some instances, it is less satisfactory in others. It is especially awkward in discussing the treatment of children, since the standard weekly meeting in the therapist's office may be particularly inappropriate in dealing with children's behavior.

This second distinction, like the first, seems difficult to maintain upon close inspection. Since there seems to be no generally accepted distinction between the terms 'behavior therapy' and 'behavior modification,' they will be used interchangeably in this paper.

C. SPECIAL RELEVANCE OF BEHAVIOR THERAPY FOR THE TREATMENT OF CHILDREN

There is by this time a great body of literature arguing the pros and cons of behavior therapy as a treatment approach. Without getting into that debate, it is possible to point out that several of the characteristics of behavior therapy described in the preceding sections suggest that a behavioral approach may be especially relevant with children. Several points may be made.

First, children seen in treatment are often nonverbal or minimally verbal. This is clearly the case in children whose treatment problem includes muteness, autism, or mental retardation. Even in other children, however, insight therapies or highly verbal methods may prove ineffective. Since behavior therapy makes explicit use of largely nonverbal procedures, such as arrangements of appropriate reinforcement contingencies, such methods may be especially appropriate with children.

Second, to the extent that behavior modification approaches emphasize control of the natural environment, such control may be easier and more common with children than with adults. The behavioral approach employs agents of change in the school and home where the child is spending most of his time anyway. Therefore the therapist can effectively manipulate the child's social experiences by instructing a fairly small group of people, the teacher and parents. These people have considerable control over the child. Manipulation of the social environment would be considerably more difficult in the case of the adult, both because that environment is less localized, and because its members would be less willing to impose clear contingencies and constraints on behavior.

Third, children unlike adults seldom come to the clinic of their own volition. It is often someone else (parents or school officials) who want to change their behavior rather than they themselves. Thus control over reinforcement contingencies may be indicated and necessary. Another implication is that usually it is specific behavior that we want to change: the child wets his bed, has tantrums, won't speak, is disruptive in school, and so on. This is the situation in which analysis of variables currently maintaining behavior, and application of principles explicitly derived for modifying behavior, would be expected to be most beneficial.

Fourth, as has been pointed out above, behavior therapy treatment is often relatively simple and direct, and therefore more readily accepted by parents. A therapy which the parents understand, agree with, and contribute to is more likely to be successful than treatment which the parents fail to understand either in theory or practice, make no contribution to, and may view with some suspicion.

Finally, in attempting to deal with maladaptive behavior, behavior therapists make explicit efforts to identify, encourage, and reinforce adaptive behavior. A behavioral assessment not only points to maladaptive behaviors to be reduced, but also to positive behaviors that can be strengthened. Explicit attempts are made to produce adaptive responses that will be maintained by natural feedback from the child's environment. This may change the child's interaction with his environment from a largely negative one to a more positive one, and contribute to the development of a happy child who will continue to develop new skills and achievements as he grows up.

D. OVERVIEW OF MAJOR PRINCIPLES OF BEHAVIOR CHANGE

Space prevents giving a thorough review of the major principles of behavior change, and such reviews are available elsewhere both in texts specifically concerned with behavior modification (29,65) and in more general learning texts (66-69). It will be useful, however, to have a brief outline of the basic principles used by behavior therapists to develop and describe treatment techniques. One value in such an outline is that it will make clear, when specific treatment procedures for particular behavior problems are described later, that many specific treatments draw on a combination of these principles rather than a single isolated principle. The first two major sections describe principles of operant conditioning, since they concern methods where a positive or negative reinforcer is contingent on a particular *response*. A third major section describes principles of classical conditioning since it concerns the pairing of positive or negative reinforcers with a particular *stimulus*.

1. *Principles for increasing specific behaviors* [*operant conditioning*]

These methods may be used to strengthen existing behavior, to develop new behavior, or to maintain new behavior which has been developed.

a. Modeling. Individuals often tend to imitate what others do around them. This principle is not typically listed in the learning literature derived from animal experiments, but Bandura has been emphasizing its importance in changing the behavior of children for many years (29). Modeling is an important method of initiating new behavior that may then be maintained by positive reinforcement.

b. Positive reinforcement. A response followed by a positive reinforcer will be more likely to occur in the future. Positive reinforcers may be categorized into 3 classes: physical reinforcers such as food, social reinforcers such as praise, and activity reinforcers such as the opportunity to play with toys.

c. Shaping. Shaping is the gradual improvement in behavior that occurs when reinforcement is made contingent on behaviors that more and more closely approximate the desired goal. Shaping may be used to develop a new behavior that occurs seldom or not at all in the patient's present repertoire. An important feature of many behavior treatment programs is arranging to approach the target behavior gradually in a step by step fashion.

d. Secondary reinforcement. Signals paired with primary reinforcers come to act as reinforcers in their own right. Mother's smile or mother's praise may come to be reinforcers if in the past they were paired with being held, being comforted, and other positive events. If in the past they were paired with aversive events, they would not be expected to be reinforcers now. The principle of secondary reinforcement (also called 'conditioned reinforcement') is often explicitly employed in treatment programs, especially when 'token' reinforcers are used.

e. Escape learning. A response followed by the termination of a negative reinforcer will be more likely to occur in the future. The child whose mother nags until he cleans his room may clean the room to terminate the nagging. This principle is seldom explicitly employed in behavioral treatments. One problem is that often an undesirable response can also terminate the stimulus (the child may escape the nagging by leaving the house). A second problem is that the use of aversive stimuli may have a variety of negative emotional responses (the child becomes anxious near the mother).

f. Avoidance learning. If a response prevents the occurrence of a negative reinforcer which might otherwise occur, that response may become learned. There is some debate in the theoretical literature about how avoidance learning should be characterized, though it undoubtedly occurs. Avoidance learning usually involves a cue that signals impending negative events if the response does not occur. Mother's arrival home is a cue that unless Johnny gets off the counter he will be spanked. Avoidance learning and punishment often go hand in hand; getting on the counter is punished, getting down is an avoidance response. Like escape learning, avoidance learning is seldom explicitly used because of possible negative side effects.

2. *Principles for decreasing specific behaviors* [*operant conditioning*]

a. Extinction. If inappropriate behavior is maintained by reinforcement then eliminating the reinforcement will eliminate the behavior. This may often by quite striking, such as in the case described above where the child's classroom vomiting was eliminated when it no longer resulted in her return to the dormitory, and in many other cases where teacher attention has been shown to be maintaining undesired behavior. However, two precautions should be made when using extinction alone. First, extinction is often followed by a temporary increase in response rate, and this should be prepared for. Second, extinction should be sudden and complete. If some reinforcement is still available, the response will now be on a schedule of 'partial reinforcement' or 'intermittent reinforcement' and will be even more difficult to eliminate. (This suggests, for instance, that extinction of delinquent behavior would be a poor choice if that behavior continued to receive occasional reinforcement from the peer group.)

b. Drive satiation. The term 'satiation' has been used in the literature in three separate ways, which here will be separately labeled drive satiation, stimulus satiation, and response satiation. The traditional use of the term drive satiation refers to eliminating a drive - for example, feeding a hungry subject. Drive satiation is useful because, if the maladaptive response is maintained by reinforcement with respect to a particular drive, eliminating the drive may eliminate the behavior. For example, if a delinquent child steals food because he is hungry, feeding him will stop the stealing. This principle is not often reported in the behavior therapy literature because the responses are seldom specifically related to such a single clear drive.

c. Stimulus satiation. Aylon eliminated the towel-hoarding behavior of a hospitalized 47-year-old schizophrenic by having the nurses gradually fill her room with towels (70). Prior to this treatment she had an average of approximately 20 towels in her room at any time, but after the room was gradually filled to 625 towels, she began removing them and subsequently did not hoard them. The effectiveness of this procedure may be related to its aversive components.

d. Response satiation or negative practice. An inappropriate behavior may be eliminated by requiring that it be repeated over and over until it becomes aversive. This procedure has been used unsystematically by a teacher to eliminate classroom horseplay and by a mother to eliminate smoking in a young child (18), and more systematically to treat juvenile fire-setting behavior (71). Again, its effectiveness probably depends on its aversive components.

e. Rewarding alternative behavior. A major method of eliminating maladaptive behavior is to establish more adaptive behavior in its place. Any of the principles in the previous section may be employed. Often a negative consequence for the maladaptive behavior is combined with positive consequences for adaptive behavior and explicit attempts to initiate and maintain adaptive behavior. This is facilitated if the maladaptive behavior presently occurs under fairly specific stimulus conditions.

f. Punishment. Behavior followed by aversive events will diminish in frequency. If punishment is used, it is often combined with an escape or avoidance contingency so that a specific positive response will terminate the aversive situation. For example, tantrum behavior might be treated by placing the child in a 'quiet room' from which he is let out only following five minutes of quiet behavior. As with escape training and avoidance training, punishment is often avoided as a treatment procedure because of possible negative side effects.

3. The development of stimulus control

Most of the principles above describe contingencies for behavior: if a certain behavior occurs, a certain consequence will follow. It is usually the case that these contingencies are not constant, but depend on the stimulus situation. Stimulus control over responding is therefore likely to develop. Such stimulus control, or discrimination learning, is desirable in some cases and not in others. We do want the child to learn that sometimes he should speak up and sometimes not, that coloring paper is good but coloring walls is not, that eating cookies is legal in the playroom but not the living room, that playing roughly with older brother is allowed but not with the baby. In such cases explicit discrimination training may be useful. In many cases, however, we do not want discriminations to form. We do not want the child to learn climbing on the counter will be punished only if Mommy is home, neatness is rewarded only when company is coming, aggressiveness is reinforced in the peer group but not at home. Especially, we do not want the child being treated for a behavior problem to discriminate the conditions of treatment for more 'normal' conditions. In these cases explicit steps must be taken to encourage not only initiation of the appropriate behavior, but generalization of that behavior across a variety of situations.

4. Modifying emotional responses [classical conditioning]

If certain stimuli are consistently paired with positive or negative reinforcers, classical conditioning may occur. In application of principles of classical conditioning to children's behavior, the response most often discussed is 'fear' or 'anxiety.'

a. Establishing fear or anxiety. A stimulus paired with an aversive event may come to produce fear or anxiety. This may be desired, as in teaching a child to keep his fingers out of electric outlets, to refrain from leaning out the window, to look before crossing the street or to avoid danger in a variety of other situations. Explicit treatments designed to produce this effect employ an aversive counterconditioning procedure. For example, alcoholics have been treated by pairing alcohol with electric shock or drugs that induce illness, and male homosexuals have been similarly treated by pairing pictures that were previously sexually stimulating with aversive events.

The establishment of fear or anxiety may also be deleterious. This may occur when aversive stimuli are used in escape, avoidance, or punishment paradigms. If the parent is consistently paired with the aversive stimulus, anxiety and fear may develop to the parent. A variety of deleterious fears may also develop in the child as a result of accidental or unplanned experiences. The child who almost drowns may fear the water, the child teased in school may refuse to go to class, the child who falls in a race may refuse to compete in games.

b. Eliminating fear or anxiety. Inappropriate or deleterious fears may be reduced or eliminated by pairing the stimulus involved with positive events. This is most effectively done by gradually increasing the exposure to the feared situation while the child is otherwise comfortable or secure. Parents frequently do this without special instruction, as in encouraging a reluctant child to come into the water by advancing a bit at a time. This general approach, termed 'desenitization,' is the most frequent behavioral technique for treating children's phobias. Two kinds of desensitization may be distinguished. Desensitization *in vivo* is when the actual feared object is gradually approached. Wolpe's systematic desensitization refers to a procedure that employs hierarchy of verbal description of the most feared situation. The subject is then put into a state of relaxation and asked to imagine successively more fearful items in the hierarchy, over a number of sessions, without exposure to the actual feared situation. Cases illustrating desensitization procedures in dealing with children's phobias will be described in a later section.

E. ILLUSTRATIVE RESEARCH AND CASE STUDIES

Selected research and case studies will now be described to illustrate behavior therapy approaches to treatment of a number of childhood problems. The problem areas covered will include phobias and anxiety responses; fire-setting as an illustration of antisocial behaviors; delinquency; self-destructive behaviors and tantrums; muteness; toilet training; and mental retardation. Within each area, no attempt will be made to systematically review the literature. Rather, the goal will be to illustrate behavioral approaches to treatment by describing a few selected studies in sufficient detail for the reader to get a reasonably clear picture of what was done. One of the conclusions to be drawn from the material below is that 'behavior therapy' neither offers nor demands a single 'treatment of choice' for any of the problem behaviors described, but rather suggests a variety of specific tactics that might be employed. Choice of a specific procedure requires detailed analysis of the specific behavior involved, evaluation of the potential behaviors of the individual subject and the potential reinforcers and agents of change in that particular child's environment, and sometimes, simple trial and error.

Many of the individual studies described below have been reprinted in one of several collections of papers on behavior therapy (27, 72, 73).

1. Phobias and anxiety responses

The behavior therapist views phobias and anxiety responses as learned responses which can be eliminated by new learning. One of the earliest demonstrations of the learning of a phobia was reported by Watson and Raynor in 1920 (74). An eleven-month old boy was tested and found to show no fear responses to a variety of suddenly-presented stimuli including a white rat, rabbit, dog, monkey, cotton wool, and so on. He was then given conditioning experience in which the white rat was suddenly taken from a basket and presented to him, followed by a loud sound made by striking a four-foot long suspended steel bar with a hammer. After seven such conditioning trials over two training sessions, presentation of the rat caused the infant to cry, turn sharply to the left and fall over on the left side, and crawl away from the rat. Tests carried out five days later showed negative reactions (withdrawal, whimpering) to the rat and also to a rabbit, similar but less pronounced reactions to a dog and to cotton wool, and no negative reaction to playing with blocks. Watson and Raynor emphasized that they had observed the development of a phobia without reference to unconscious mechanisms or displacement, and argued that successful treatment would not involve psychodynamic understanding, but new learning experiences. They suggested habituation or extinction of the response by repeated presentation, or 'reconditioning' by pairing the feared object with positive events such as the presentation of food or (a lingering Freudian influence?) tactual stimulation of the erogenous zones.

Watson and Raynor did not attempt to experimentally eliminate the anxiety response they had established because the child was withdrawn from the hospital. However, in 1924 Mary Cover Jones reported a variety of techniques in the elimination of children's fears (75,76). The methods of disuse (the idea that fears would disappear with time if the stimuli were avoided), repression (ridicule or teasing), and verbal appeal were ineffective. Repeated presentation of the feared object (termed habituation or extinction) was more effective, and most effective was direct reconditioning by pairing the feared object with positive events. Similar findings were reported a decade later by Jersild and Holmes in a study of methods used by parents to eliminate children's fears (77). They pointed out that parents frequently help their children overcome fears, such as fears of the dark, fears of water, fears of the dentist, and fears of animals, by presenting the feared object in graduated steps, and by pairing such presentation with comfort and support.

A major new input in the years since these early reports was Wolpe's method of systematic desensitization. The essential elements of this technique are: (a) training the client in relaxation; (b) the construction of a hierarchy of feared items or situations; and (c) graduated presentation of the imagined items while the subject is relaxed (45). Although this procedure has produced wide success with adults, it may be less effective with children. First, it may be difficult to teach children to relax (although there are few direct studies of this and at least one author (78) has reported successfully teaching psychotic children to relax). Second, it may be difficult to get children to clearly imagine the feared situations. Tasto has reported a case of failure in the use of systematic desensitization with a four-year-old boy who had developed extreme psychophysiological and motor reactions to loud sounds (39). Although the boy appeared to relax well, he never reported any anxiety when instructed to imagine the feared events. Indeed, he specifically asked whether he would only have to imagine the stimuli or whether the therapist would actually produce the stimuli, such as popping a balloon. As long as he was told that he would only have to imagine the stimuli, he did not display any noticeable signs of anxiety.

In this case subsequent treatment with 'in vivo' (or 'direct' or 'real life') desensitization proved effective. Relaxation training was continued and real life stimuli, such as dropping a board or popping a balloon, were presented systematically in the office. The parents also employed systematic presentation at home. For example, the boy was brought target practicing with the father and gradually moved closer and closer to the gun until he was shooting it himself. The father also played a game where he inserted a dime in a balloon and the boy could get in by popping the balloon. The balloons were gradually blown larger until the boy could pop a full-size balloon without noticeable signs of fear. Prior to treatment, he would become extremely frightened at just the sight of a balloon. One-month and four-month follow-ups after treatment showed no relapses and increased sociability with other children.

A similar treatment by gradual exposure to the feared situation was employed in treating the water phobia of a one-year-old girl (79). The girl first became afraid of water following a fall in the bathtub. She refused further bathing with violent screams, and during the next few days reacted with violent emotion not only to the bathtub, faucet, and water in the tub, but also to being washed in the handbasin, faucets or water at any part of the house, and the wading pool. Treatment involved systematic attempts, over a one-month period, to get the child exposed more and more closely to water. These involved tactics such as placing toys in the dry tub so she had to reach into the tub to get them; moving her toys gradually closer to the kitchen sink and finally having them float in it; requiring her to move through a basin to get her toys, and so on. After a month of systematic treatment the child played normally in the tub and happily initiated approach responses to water. A 42-month follow-up indicated that recovery from the phobia was still complete and no 'symptom substitution' had been observed.

There were several reports of treating school phobias and separation anxiety with real-life systematic desensitization. For example, Montenagro describes a six-year old boy who became very agitated when separated from his mother even for few minutes (80). The boy had been removed from kindergarten by school officials because as soon as his mother left he began to cry and shout desperately. He was terrified of doctors. The treatment procedure involved first seeing the child with the mother and then, in subsequent sessions, having the mother wait outside in sight with the door open, out of sight with the door closed, and so on, until after ten sessions the boy would go off on a tour around the hospital with the therapist. After completing this hierarchy in ten sessions, the parents were given a number of instructions to carry out at home. For instance, they were instructed to leave the child at home with a baby sitter for successively longer periods. He then was placed in a summer nursery school, and finally entered first grade with no adjustment problems.

Two articles have described more complex and sophisticated treatment procedures for school phobia and separation anxiety using a combination of classical and operant procedures. In each case desensitization procedures for separation from the parents were combined with operant reinforcement of more appropriate behavior. The specific details of procedure were quite different in the two articles however. In one case real-life systematic desensitization was the major treatment procedure (40). The patient was a nine-year-old boy who avoided attending class when school began at the end of the summer vacation. When referred for treatment he had been absent for three weeks and could be induced to return with neither threats, bribes, nor punishment. Treatment began with the therapist accompanying the boy on a walk to school when it was not in session. On the next two days the boy and therapist walked to school, played briefly in the schoolyard, and returned home. Then the therapist and boy entered the classroom with no one else present after school was over for the day. For three days, the boy and therapist entered school at the normal time, chatted briefly with the teacher, and left after opening exercises. This gradual exposure procedure continued until the boy would spend the morning at school with the therapist in class, then with the therapist in the library, and finally with the therapist leaving school entirely at successively earlier times. At this point a specific token reward system was instituted for attendance at the school without the therapist. Over a period of three weeks, the boy accumlated enough tokens to buy an agreed-upon baseball glove. He then agreed with his parents that rewards of this kind were no longer necessary.

The second report in which treatment combined operant and classical procedures employed real-life desensitization only after ten sessions in which the boy and therapist engaged in doll play (81). During this period, the seven-year-old boy was reinforced with M & M candies and social approval for doll play in which the boy doll said he wasn't afraid or would stay in the situation. Structed doll play centered on three themes: separation from the mother, school attendance, and anxiety about physical injury while playing with peers. In each case the boy was reinforced for describing the doll behaving appropriately, such as not being afraid, continuing on to school, playing outside without thinking about Mamma, and so on. After ten sessions like this, real-life desensitization procedures for school attendance were begun. Over the course of 13 sessions, he gradually attended school for longer and longer periods of time by himself. On a follow-up three months after termination of treatment, the school reported dramatic improvement in his general adjustment as well as no further evidence of fearfulness.

It might be argued that the above treatments of school phobias involve excessive time and effort for the simple goal of getting the child to attend school. However, given the possibility of further and serious deterioration if no systematic treatment program had been begun, the effort involved seems minimal. And even though treatment outside the office was called for, it is likely that such treatment could be successfully carried out by graduate students, paraprofessionals, or parents. It is an empirical question whether similar results could be obtained with the therapist remaining in the office.

One promising office treatment approach is the 'emotive imagery' desensitization technique of Lazarus and Abramovitz (34). Noting that reciprocal inhibition using feeding or relaxation may not be feasible in certain situations, Lazarus and Abramovitz employed a systematic desensitization procedure with children in which relaxation instructions were replaced with 'emotive imagery.' This phrase describes imagery designed to evoke positive affective reactions, such as feelings of self-assertion, pride, affection, or humor, which are assumed to be anxiety-inhibiting. For example, a fourteen-year-old boy suffered from an intense fear of dogs, two and a half to three years in duration. He took two buses on a roundabout route to school rather than risk exposure to dogs on a direct 300-yard walk. Questioning revealed a burning ambition to own a sports car and race it at the Indianapolis 500 event. The technique involved asking the subject to close his eyes and imagine himself driving in his sports car. 'Notice the beautiful sleek lines. You decide to go for a drive with your friends. You sit down at the wheel...You start up and listen to the wonderful roar of the exhaust...the speedometer is climbing into the nineties...you look at the trees whizzing by and you see a little dog standing next to one of them--if you feel any anxiety, just raise your finger,' and so on, presenting items higher and higher on the hierarchy of fear of dogs.

After three sessions using this technique, the boy reported marked improvement in his reaction to dogs. Therapy was terminated after two additional sessions in which field assignments were given. Reports from the patient and relatives twelve months later indicated no trace of the former phobia. Other cases reported in the same article are a ten-year-old boy treated for excessive fear of the darkness over three sessions, and an eight-year-old girl treated for school phobia over four sessions. The brevity and apparent success of this treatment should encourage further exploration of it.

To summarize, behavioral approaches to the treatment of phobias in children are typically based on the model of systematic desensitization or systematic reconditioning. The essential component is the careful structuring of new experiences for the child in which the feared situation is gradually and systematically approached, over a number of sessions, while other conditions ensure comfort and support. Both real-life desensitization and desensitization using imagery in the office have been used. In cases where a specific response (such as attending school) is desired, it may be useful to also incorporate in the treatment program the explicit reinforcement of the desired appropriate behavior.

2. *Antisocial behaviors: fire setting*

The variety of possible behavioral approaches to treating antisocial behaviors will be illustrated with one particular antisocial behavior, setting fires. As with other antisocial behaviors, this behavior is one that has serious consequences for the community and cannot be simply allowed to extinguish over time. Three articles will be described that illustrate a broad range of possible treatment approaches, from aversion training, to stimulus satiation, to positive reinforcement of incompatible behavior.

Denholtz has reported an aversion treatment of compulsive fire-setting in a 17-year-old boy (82). The boy was known to have set three fires, and suspected of setting a fourth fire that destroyed the home in which he lived. A series of color slides was taken of the boy standing over a newspaper fire, lighting matches near curtains, lighting matches near furniture, sitting beside burning tissues in an ashtray, and so on. Another series of slides showed him with members of this family and with the family car, which evoked extremely positive feelings in him. These slides were placed in a slide tray, with fire slides alternating with family and automobile slides.

During treatment sessions the boy presented slides with a remote control device. Shock was presented to the subject's hand whenever a fire slide appeared, and remained on until the boy activated the remote button that changed the scene to a non-fire scene. Fire scenes were therefore paired with shock onset, and removal of fire scenes (and presentation of non-fire scenes) was paired with shock offset. After observing treatment in the office, the parents continued treatment at home for 45 daily sessions of at least 15-min length. Sessions were reduced to three times a week, and subsequently to one every two months, with treatment stopped after 24 months. After five weeks of treatment the patient reported he would no longer light a fire if told to do so by voices in his head. He had developed such an aversion to fire and the whole concept of lighting matches that he avoided unlighted matches. He reported that should he try to light a match, even without the shock apparatus attached, he felt a shock in his right arm. Increased sociability and better schoolwork were also reported and a 3½ year follow-up showed no further fire lighting incidents.

Use of stimulus satiation to eliminate fire-setting behavior in two young boys has been described by Welsh (71). For example, a seven-year-old was seen for repeated incidents of deliberate fire-setting in addition to other discipline problems at home. For the first satiation session twenty boxes of small wooden matches were on hand and the patient was told he would be learning how to light matches properly. Four rules were put into operation: (a) the match must be held over the ashtray at all times; (b) after taking the match out of the box the cover must be closed before striking; (c) only one match at a time would be lit; and (d) the burning match must be held until heat is felt on the fingertips, then blown out. The patient followed this procedure happily for 40 minutes in the first session. In the second session, he soon became restless and asked to something else. He was asked to light a few more matches, then allowed to play with the toys in the room. In the third session he did not want to practice lighting matches, but was forced to light ten matches before being allowed to play with toys. In a second patient, a similar procedure was employed except that satiation took seven sessions and many more trials than with the first client. In both cases six-month follow-ups showed the fire-setting behavior had not returned.

Although this procedure is labeled 'stimulus satiation,' it is likely that the aversive components of the procedure played an important role. The procedure was specifically designed to make match-lighting aversive. Another aspect of the procedure that may have been important was the emphasis on positive reinforcement for non-lighting behavior. Once the subject stopped lighting matches, strong reinforcers for other behavior were available in terms of toys in the playroom.

The explicit use of positive reinforcement, coupled with the threat of serious punishment, was used by parents to eliminate fire-setting behavior in a seven-year-old boy (83). The boy was setting fires in the home once or twice weekly, usually on mornings of weekends whenever matches were available and the parents were still in bed or out of the house. Punishments such as being slapped, locked in his room, or touched with a smoldering object were effective for only short periods. Both parents, but especially the mother, felt helpless and enraged. The mother seldom expressed anything positive toward the child and her attempts to control his behavior employed almost exclusively aversion. The treatment program was carried out by the father since the mother saw little hope of change. The first strategy was to temporarily suppress fire-setting with the threat of strong punishment. The father told the boy that if further fires were set he would take back a new baseball glove which the boy had just received and valued highly. The second strategy was to reinforce the behavior of bringing matches to the presence of the parents, a behavior that would be incompatible with fire-setting.

To begin shaping match-bringing behavior, the boy was told by his father that if matches or match covers were found, they were to be brought to the father immediately. An empty packet was left conspicuously on the table on the assumption that if would be of little value to the boy and so he might readily obey the father's command. He did so, and was rewarded by being given five cents and being told he could now go and spend it at the store if he wished. During the same evening and the next few evenings, the father left packets of matches around the house, and the boy brought these to the father and was reinforced. He was also reinforced for bringing in matches he found outside the home. The father was told to combine monetary rewards with social reinforcement, approval, and so on.

A second procedure was used to strengthen non-striking behavior. The boy was given a full pack of 20 matches and told that he could light them all under his father's supervision. The father also placed 20 pennies beside the pack and said for every match unstruck he would receive one penny, but for each match struck one penny would be removed. The first time the boy lit ten matches and received ten pennies. The following evening the boy earned 17 pennies, and the third time, 20 pennies. Subsequently the boy was told he would not know how much money he would receive for not lighting a match and the reward was varied from no money to ten cents.

This program took three weeks to develop and implement, after which it was carried out be the father with little guidance from the therapist. Fire-setting behavior was ended and no reoccurrence had been observed at an eight-month follow-up. An interesting side effect was that the mother began to become involved in the program and to employ similar techniques in other problems involving disobedience. The mother began to relax her aversive control and was able to express affection for the boy, which had rarely occurred prior to that time.

These three reported treatments of fire-setting behavior illustrate that a variety of approaches to the treatment of such behavior is possible within a behavioral framework. The treatment ranged from aversion training to operant reinforcement, from office to home, from classical conditioning to operant conditioning, from punishment of inappropriate behavior to reinforcement of incompatible appropriate behavior. Moreover, since each of these is a case report, in none of the cases can we be absolutely certain of the factors responsible for change. However, the cases do illustrate possible treatment approaches derived from a behavior framework. And they suggest that treatment aimed at directly modifying inappropriate behavior, by carefully specifying the consequences of that behavior, can be successful.

3. *Delinquency*

Patterson has reviewed a number of studies in which delinquent and pre-delinquent behaviors have been modified by parents in the home (84). Several procedures are common in these studies. Often the parents are first instructed in basic principles of behavior change such as those described in the previous section of this paper. Several simple texts have been written specifically for this purpose (85-87), and one of these may be assigned to the parents to read before treatment begins. Then an attempt is made to specify a program whereby deviant behavior is nonreinforced or punished, and appropriate behavior is reinforced. Explicit procedures to encourage reinforcement of appropriate behavior may be used, such as contracts in which the contingencies are carefully spelled out, or token systems in which appropriate behaviors earn tokens which may later be turned in for 'backup' reinforcers such as priveleges or material rewards.

In many cases parents have in the past unwittingly reinforced inappropriate behavior, and the therapist may make careful efforts to ensure that such behavior is no longer reinforced. In some cases inappropriate behavior may be punished, ment procedure that has proven effective with younger children in the home is a 'time-out.' Following inappropriate behavior (which has been carefully and consistently defined) the child is placed on a chair or in a room for a brief period of time such as five minutes. The parent is instructed to remain calm, to refrain from engaging in lengthy explanations or speeches, and to child is not allowed to resume normal play until he has been quiet on the chair for a brief period.

Most of the studies reviewed by Patterson (84) involved preschool children, and none involved adolescents. Three studies will be described here to illustrate application of behavioral principles with older delinquent and pre-delinquent children.

Wetzel has described the use of behavioral procedures in a case of compulsive stealing in a ten-year-old boy (41). The boy's history had included varied disciplinary problems in his home (including setting fire to his bed), expulsion from first grade, expulsion from a special education class, and eventual placement in a foster home at age eight. In the first half of his eighth year he lived alternatively under juvenile detention and in foster homes, where complaints were received about his stealing and destruction (he chopped up a dining room chair with an ax). He was subsequently placed in a residential treatment center for mildly disturbed children. At the center some of his behaviors improved, but a problem of central concern remained his 'compulsive stealing.' He stole in school, in the home, and from other children.

Because of improvements in other behaviors, the boy was placed again in a foster home, but after five months was re-admitted to the residential treatment center at the age of almost ten. His stealing appeared to occur even more frequently than before, and at this point a treatment program was begun. The staff of the center was instructed to carefully record all stealing behavior. To establish a positive reinforcer, a cook, Maria, was asked to spend considerable time with him, inviting him into the kitchen, taking him to her home for visits, taking him shopping, and so on. His relation with the cook had originally been better than that with the other staff members, although not particularly strong. After several days of this special treatment, he appeared to look forward to his visits with her.

At this point a contingency was imposed. Maria was told that whenever she was informed by other staff members that the boy had stolen, she should say 'I'm sorry you took (so-and-so's blank) because now I can't let you come home with me tonight.' She was to say nothing else, and to listen to no explanations or excuses, but just turn and walk away. The next day she should again be warm and friendly.

The results showed a marked decline in stealing behavior. A setback occurred during a period when several stealing incidents considered too minor by the staff were not reported; this was followed by renewed increases in stealing. After strict and careful recording and consequences were again imposed, the stealing again diminished to a very low level. After a period of time incidents of positive nonstealing behavior began to occur which were heavily reinforced. The boy periodically reminded the staff that he had not stolen or lied, for which he was reinforced. During the last recorded month, he began to lose some interest in his visits with Maria, his visits with her dropped to two or three times a week. He began to spend more time with his peers, and anecdotal evidence indicated his relations with his peers were improving. During the 170 days for which records were kept, stealing dropped from an average of one every two days prior to treatment, to none in the last 50 days of treatment.

Phillips and his co-workers have described the use of a token economy to modify a number of behaviors of pre-delinquent boys at Achievement Place, a community based family style behavior modification center (88,89). The boys committed to Achievement Place were judged by court officials to be in danger of becoming habitual law breakers and described by terms such as 'aggressive,' 'inferior attitude,' 'dangerous to other children,' 'poor motivation,' and so on.

The token economy involved having each boy carry with him an index card on which points earned or lost were recorded. The difference between points earned and lost was used by the boy to buy rewards or priveleges such as use of tools, telephone and radio; snacks; television; and permission to leave the grounds to go home or downtown. The results of several experiments with residents of the center showed that a number of behaviors could be reliably modified by making tokens contingent on their occurrence. The results obtained with different groups of boys included reduction in poor grammar, increased tidiness, increased amount of homework completed, increased promptness at school, at bedtime and on errands, and increased watching of television news shows (88, 89). Additional results showed that a high level of room-cleaning behavior could be maintained even when point consequences were delivered on only 8% of the days. Another finding worth noting was that threats and demands, while they might initially produce changes in behavior, had at best only temporary effects when not backed up by point consequences (89).

The results at Achievement Place indicate that a variety of behaviors of 'pre-delinquent' boys are amenable to modification and that a token reinforcement system provides a practical means of modifying these behaviors. An important question, however, concerns the degree to which these changes will transfer back to the 'real world' where such contrived contingencies do not exist. Indeed, it could even be argued that the unusual specificity of the contingencies at Achievement Place would be detrimental to transfer back to the natural environment. In preparation for this transfer, youths at Achievement Place who had behaved well on the point system over a period of time were placed on a merit system where all privileges were free and only social consequences were applied to their behavior. Successful performance on this system was followed by the homeward bound system which involved additional preparation to return to the natural home (89). Further research seems necessary on procedures for fading from an artificial token economy back into the 'natural' environment in which consequences of behavior are often much different, almost always much less consistent, and frequently much less positive.

Tharp and Wetzel's community based treatment program for pre-delinquent behaviors has already been described (48). That program involved intervention in the home or school to arrange explicit reinforcement of appropriate behavior and nonreinforcement of inappropriate behavior. The kinds of behaviors treated included (in order of frequency) failure to carry out home chores, poor academic work, disruptive behaviors, defiance, fighting, truancy and tardiness, property disruption, bed wetting and soiling and stealing. The authors describe many case reports illustrating a number of treatment tactics. In all cases, however, the treatment involved explicit statements of behaviors and their consequences, and in all cases the treatment was carried out in the field by members of the child's natural environment.

One technique for improving school behavior was effective with older students as well as younger children (though unfortunately the case reports frequently neglect to specify the age of the patient). This was to have the teacher specify the behavior required and send home a note with the child each day that the behavior was satisfactory. The parents would make no comment and impose no penalty when no note was brought, but would dispense positive consequences when the child did bring home a note. Positive consequences might include material rewards such as money, or social rewards such as playing with the father.

4. Hyperactivity, tantrums, and self-injurious behavior

These three classes of behavior problem are considered together for several reasons. First, it is possible that they form a continuum, with one behavior blending into the other. Second, the behaviors have in common that they are aversive to adults, and therefore normally receive negative feedback, but they continue despite this feedback. This has led to the view that they must reflect some basic, underlying pathology. While that may be so in some cases, examples of each of these behaviors have been shown to be sensitive to normal learning principles and capable of modification by reinforcement and punishment. It is possible that each of these behaviors is frequently maintained by the same form of reinforcement, parental attention. Finally, similar techniques have been used to treat each of these behaviors.

Hyperactivity has often been thought to derive from neurological impairment and be unamenable to psychological manipulation, being treated largely with tranquilizing drugs. However, several investigators have reported modifying hyperactivity with behavioral treatment. Patterson's use of a 'magic teaching machine' to control the behavior of a hyperactive boy was described earlier in the section on variables maintaining behavior in the natural environment (49, 50). Other techniques for controlling hyperactivity in a school setting include using the opportunity for noisy play to reinforce sitting quietly and attending, and guiding the teacher to make social reinforcers contingent on the occurrence of socially acceptable behavior (60-63).

Another technique which may prove useful with the hyperactive child is training in relaxation. Graziano and Kean have presented a brief but intriguing account of the use of daily relaxation training with four autistic children aged seven to eleven (78). Since the children did not understand the concept 'relax,' they were given brief daily training periods, averaging 4 minutes in length at the beginning of training and 13 minutes after 105 training sessions. Instructions to be comfortable, breathe easily, be calm and settled were given along with gentle manipulations of the arms, legs, and necks by the therapist. The children gradually met behavioral criteria of relaxation, and were able to report when relaxed. Of greatest interest was the author's report of a marked decrement of generalized excitement and high-activity responses through the day.

Turning to tantrum behaviors, several studies have shown that tantrums can be increased or decreased in frequency by modifying their social consequences. One interesting illustration of this was the finding that the tantrum behaviors of a nine-year-old retarded child during an experimental verbal training program would increase in frequency if the tantrums were systematically followed by easier training trials, but would decrease in frequency if the tantrums were systematically followed by more difficult training trials (90). The tantrum behaviors include lashing out with one arm, clutching at her groin with the other, jerking her legs wildly, sometimes falling to the floor, crying and screaming. They had been described by observers as 'extreme pain,' 'excessive anger,' or 'masturbating excessively to orgasm.' However, the authors felt the behaviors might be highly functional since they frequently produced the effects of terminating contact with other individuals who were making some demand on her. During verbal training, systematic procedures were employed whereby tantrums were followed by trials with easier words (in some sessions) or trials with more difficult words (in other sessions). When tantrums led to easier trials they were maintained at a high level, but in the conditions where tantrums led to more difficult trials tantrum behavior dropped systematically over sessions to a low level. Tantrum behavior was clearly influenced by operant contingencies.

Two behavioral procedures for the treatment of tantrum behavior are extinction and mild punishment (time-outs). In a relatively early study, Williams supported the successful treatment of tantrum behavior in a 21-month-old child by extinction (91). The boy had been seriously ill for much of his first 18 months and much special care and attention had been given to him. He gained considerable control over his parents' behavior by crying and tantrums. For instance if the parent left the bedroom after putting him to bed, he would scream and fuss until the parents returned. As a result the parents were unable to leave until the child went to sleep, which usually took from half an hour to two hours. The parents were instructed to extinguish the crying and tantrum behavior by putting him to bed in a leisurely and relaxed fashion, then leaving and closing the door. The parent was not to re-enter the room despite the child's screaming and raging. Screaming lasted 45 minutes the first night, but gradually diminished to zero over 10 sessions. Then an aunt put the child to bed and some screaming occurred, which was reinforced by the aunt returning to the room and remaining with the child. A second extinction series was again effective in ten sessions, and no further tantrums at bedtime were reported during the next two years.

Temper tantrums have been treated in an autistic preschool child with the use of a time-out procedure (92). The tantrum behavior included head-banging, hair-pulling, face-scratching, face-slapping, whining and crying. The time-out procedure involved placing the child in his room contingent on each tantrum. The door of the room was opened only after tantrum behavior ceased, thus reinforcing non-tantrum behavior. Similar procedures were adopted for handling the behavior both on the ward and at home, and the data showed reduction in tantrum behavior to a very low level during 180 days of treatment.

The tantrum behavior in the above case included mild forms of self-destructive behavior. Another behavior which is not normally classified self-destructive but which would seem to be aversive to the normal child is vomiting. Two studies have demonstrated that vomiting can be controlled by its consequences. In one such case which has already been mentioned a nine-year-old retarded girl who vomited in class an average of twice a day was put on an extinction procedure where the vomiting was no longer reinforced by being sent to her dormitory (22). This simple extinction was shown to be effective in eliminating the vomiting. Another study involved a sixteen-year-old mute patient in a home for the retarded (93). Following a meal the patient almost invariably went to one side of the room, vomited several times, and then consumed the vomitus. The treatment program, initiated after about six months during which the vomiting behavior was consistent, involved punishing the vomiting with a 2 to 5-minute timeout, making the vomitus aversive by sprinkling it with pepper, and strengthening incompatible behaviors by reinforcing them with candy. Over a 60-day treatment period, the vomiting response was completely eliminated. However, when treatment was turned over to nontrained attendants after 19 days with no vomiting, the response returned in full strength. A third example of treatment of vomiting behavior employed aversive conditioning with an electric stimulator belt to control vomiting in a severely retarded six-year-old boy (94). The authors reported rapid elimination of the behavior and no recurrence over a 93-day follow-up period.

Successful treatment of behavior more closely resembling serious self-destructive behavior has been reported for a child who engaged in scratching (95). The parents sought help for a five-year-old girl who was alert, friendly, and well-mannered, but who for a year had been scratching herself until she bled. The scratching had resulted in large scores and scabs on her forehead, nose, cheeks, chin, and one arm and leg. Neither pediatric nor psychiatric consultation had eliminated the scratching, and the last recommendation made to the mother had been to fit the child with pneumatic arm splints in order to restrain the activity. The parents had employed punishment and aversive controls in attempting to control the scratching, but unsuccessfully. The mother reported she had come to dislike the child and was repelled by her appearance, and the marriage itself was threatened by constant quarrels over disciplinary procedures.

Observation of the mother and child at the clinic showed that the child was a highly capable and competent girl with many social, intellectual and physical skills. However, the mother spoke to the child only to criticize, direct, or explain why the child should behave differently. The mother kept records at home which revealed periods in the day when the child engaged in constructive activity and did not scratch herself. The records also revealed once again that the mother's interaction with the child, although not involving physical punishment, was almost entirely negative in terms of criticism and verbal punishment.

The treatment procedure was carried out in the home. First, all scratching was to be ignored, no matter how bloody the result. Second, if the child played for 20 or 30 minutes without scratching this was to be rewarded by playing warmly with the child and giving her a gold star to paste in a little booklet. This seemed to somewhat diminish scratching during the day, but additional procedures were added to reduce scratching at night. Each afternoon of a scratch-free day the mother and daughter went shopping and bought an item for her Barbie doll that the daughter had picked out. This was placed in sight at home, and if there was no evidence of fresh scratching the next morning, the child was praised and given the item.

The authors report some instances of backsliding due to problems with the treatment program, but these were worked out and there was a consistent reduction in scratching behavior. As the child's appearance improved, the mother became more able to give social reinforcement and interact positively with the child. Near the end of the program, external rewards were gradually faded out. After six weeks of the program, all sores had healed completely, and at a four-month follow-up there was no evidence of renewed scratching.

Results of this study indicate that direct treatment of self-destructive behavior may be effective. The self-destructive behavior in this case was not as severe as behavior sometimes seen in retarded or autistic children, and occurred in a child who appeared healthy in other respects. However, the behavior was clearly injurious, had continued for a year prior to treatment, had led the mother to seriously consider having the child removed from the home, and had led at least one professional to suggest the use of pneumatic splints. It is frightening to contemplate what might have happened if the behavior had not been treated directly at the time that it was.

Both positive reinforcement of other behavior and punishment of self-descructive behavior have been used in treating severe cases of self-destructive behavior. Peterson and Peterson treated an eight-year-old retarded boy who engaged in behaviors such as slapping his head or leg, hitting his hand against his teeth, banging his head and hands against chairs, tables and walls (96). His face, arms and legs were covered with bruises, scabs, abrasions and occasionally open wounds. The treatment procedure involved reinforcement in the form of food and the word 'good' contingent on very brief (initially three- to five-second) periods with no self-injurious responses. Such procedures reduced the self-injurious behavior, although there was no evidence that the reduction was retained following treatment. Other authors have described a procedure in which reinforcement of an incompatible behavior successfully reduced the severe self-injurious behavior of a nine-year-old schizophrenic girl who had displayed such behaviors dating back to three years of age (97). Again, however, there was no evidence that the reduction was permanent.

Other reports have indicated lasting effects of treatment. In one case a severely retarded adolescent girl beat her head against the wall a total of 35,906 times in four six-hour observation periods. A time-out contingency was then put into effect, where she was physically confined to a chair in a time-out area following the occurrence of injurious behavior. Head banging dropped sharply to a level of 7, 2, 0, 1, and 0 for five successive weeks and never reappeared during nine months of follow-up study (98).

Several authors have treated severe self-injurious behavior by punishment with electric shock (99-101). Once the self-injurious behaviors were diminished, more appropriate behaviors were more likely to occur and could be positively reinforced. Moral and ethical questions surround the use of electric shock punishment, but when the self-injurious behavior is so serious as to produce permanent physical damage, and when electric shock can be shown to eliminate that behavior where other techniques are ineffective, then to use shock may be more ethical than to withhold its use (cf. 102). A case that seems to fit these circumstances has been described by Tate and Baroff (100). A nine-year-old blind male had engaged in self-injurious behavior from the age of four. His behavior included banging his head forcefully against floors, walls, and other hard objects, punching his face and head with his fists, hitting his shoulder with his chin, and kicking himself. At age eight, bilateral cateracts, complete detachment of the left retina, and partial detachment of the right retina were discovered. Observation showed self-injurious behavior at the time of treatment averaged over one per minute throughout the day.

Observation indicated that physical contact with others was strongly reinforcing, and being left alone was aversive. A study was then conducted that showed self-injurious behavior could be sharply curtailed by withdrawing physical contact when such behaviors occurred and reinstating contact following a brief period with no such behavior. The behavior was not completely eliminated however, and there was some danger that the right retina would become completely destroyed. A procedure was then begun in which a cattle prod was used to apply painful electric shock to the right leg following each self-injurious response. The child was restrained except during treatment, but treatment periods gradually became longer and longer until he was out of bed 9 hours a day, with few or no self-injurious behaviors emitted. At the time this procedure was reported it had remained effective over a six month period.

The hyperactive behaviors, tantrum behaviors, and self-destructive behaviors described in this section illustrate a broad range with respect to severety of the problem behavior and sensitivity to treatment. At one extreme, some hyperactive or tantrum behaviors seemed to be maintained by teacher or parent attention and are readily eliminated by removing such attention and providing reinforcement for alternative behaviors. At the other extreme, violent self-destructive behaviors may sometimes be impervious to all but the most extreme forms of treatment, and one suspects that such behaviors do indeed reflect some serious underlying disorder. Even where such underlying pathology is suspected, however, there may be several reasons to employ a carefully structured behavioral approach as the initial attempt at treatment. For one thing, the view that the problem behavior was developed and maintained because of reinforcement contingencies in the environment, and is amenable to treatment by changing those contingencies, is perhaps the view that is simplest and most readily tested. For another, behaviors that on the surface seem unlikely to be maintained by their consequences - such as the child who vomited repeatedly in class or the child who scratched herself at home until she bled - may turn out to be so maintained, and to be suspectible to straightforward treatment. In such cases relatively simple procedures, but procedures carefully and systematically applied, may prevent further and serious deterioration to the point where such procedures would no longer be effective.

5. *Muteness*

As with hyperactivity, tantrums, and self-destructive behavior, muteness covers a range of degrees of defecit and amenability to treatment. Behavioral techniques have been employed to develop vocal imitation and speech behavior in autistic and echolalic children (103-105), in remedial speech and language training of retarded or speech deficient children (106), in treating stuttering (107-109) and in other areas. One of the areas in which behavioral treatment may be most dramatically effective is in treatment of selective muteness, and three case studies illustrating such treatment will be described in this section.

One example is the treatment of a five-year-old selectively mute girl (110). For about a year she had refused to speak to anyone, then she resumed talking to her family while remaining mute to anyone else both inside and outside her home. The child was reinforced first for whispering a line of a book to her mother in the remote presence of a social worker, then for reading longer segments, reading more loudly, and reading with the social worker closer and closer. Finally she was reinforced for reading to the social worker with the mother absent. The reinforcers used were candy, colored stars, and social attention and approval. The patient began speaking to other adults and children again, and follow-up a year later showed her to be behaving normally at home and school with no muteness and no symptom substitution.

A somewhat less structured procedure was used by a first grade teacher to generate talking in a child who never spoke at school (111). The child did not speak to either teacher or peers throughout either his first year in kindergarten or a repeat year in kindergarten. He did talk at home, however. In his last few weeks in school the end of the second year he was moved into the first grade class. The teacher was instructed to make no reference to his speech and create no demands for him to talk. The other students in the class also cooperated in this. In addition, the teacher attempted to reinforce any nonverbal communication with attention and approval. This course of action was continued at the start of the next school year. However, the teacher gradually began to stop reinforcing nonverbal behavior to the point where she would not respond when he tugged her skirt or raised his hand to show her a picture. Four weeks after school started the boy began to speak, initially on the bus and in the playground. His first speech in the classroom was a loud whisper, followed shortly with direct communication with the teacher. The teacher had been instructed that when he spoke she should attend a smile, but make no special fuss. No further problems were reported during the year, and follow-up after three years showed that the boy was not viewed by teachers as a special problem.

The final example is a marathon one-day treatment of a six-year-old girl (112). She would speak to no one but her immediate family, and not even to a family member when a stranger was present. Many attempts to get her to talk by parents, nursery school and kindergarten teachers, and playmates had failed.

On the treatment day the child was brought to the clinic without breakfast at 8 a.m. Every thirty seconds the mother, alone in the room with the girl, would offer her a bite of food if she requested it. The child responded appropriately on every trial with verbalizations such as "orange juice" or "I'd like some cereal please, Mummie." Then a therapist was gradually faded into the room, pretending to read a book but moving gradually closer on each trial. The therapist gradually faded into the interaction, first asking the mother to ask the child if she wanted something to eat, then asking the child directly, then sitting opposite the child. At this point the child was, for the first time, conversing with a stranger although in a limited and structured manner.

After a rest period this process was continued, and another therapist was gradually faded into the room until she was also sitting at the table. Following another break, a third therapist was introduced along with the mother and the first two therapists, and the new therapist initiated conversation with the girl about a puzzle piece. After several minutes the girl responded, and this was followed by other questions, delayed responses, and finally more rapid and less structured verbal interaction. At noon the child went to the home of another team member for lunch. Other children were present and she spoke freely with a three and a half year old child. After lunch all seven therapists, the mother, child, and playmate gathered in the therapy room and activities included games, naming colors, asking questions and offering M & M candies.

The child and mother returned to the clinic two weeks later for a similar procedure, but at that time the child began speaking freely in the presence of others within minutes. On this visit the child's behavior was qualitatively different. She was free and spontaneous, initiating topics and showing almost none of her previous fearfulness. The mother subsequently reported that the child had begun to speak to other people outside the family, such as her Sunday school teacher and friends of the family.

6. *Toilet training*: *enuresis and encopresis*

Enuresis is lack of bladder control or incontinence of urine. It may be diurnal (pants wetting), nocturnal (bed wetting) or both. Encopresis is incontinence of feces, or soiling pants. Both enuresis and encopresis have been treated with behavioral procedures.

A common behavioral treatment of bedwetting involves arranging a device consisting of a sensitive electric circuit arranged to activate a buzzer or bell when a small amount of urine is present in the bed. This device will awaken the child when he wets the bed. The assumption is that, through conditioning, the internal cues present prior to micturation will awaken the child so that he is able to use the bathroom. The other possible result is that the conditioning procedure will improve nighttime bladder control so that the child remains dry until the morning. This buzzer procedure was first proposed by Mowrer and Mowrer in 1938 (113), and a number of articles describing its use up to 1960 have been reviewed by Jones (114). Two important questions are: is the procedure more effective in eliminating bedwetting than traditional psychotherapy or than the spontaneous remission that would be expected in an untreated control group? And even if it is effective will symptom remission or symptom substitution occur? The question of symptom substitution is particularly interesting since many authors have made statements such as "the removal of the symptom of enuresis, without providing other outlets for the child, leads to a replacement by other symptoms..." (115). It is an empirical question whether such a statement is correct.

A comparison of the conditioning procedure, traditional psychotherapy-counseling (of unspecified type), and a no treatment control group was made by DeLeon and Mandell (116). The subjects were 87 children, ages 5½ to 14, referred to a community mental health center with the diagnosis of functional enuresis. A criterion of cure was reached by 86% of the conditioning subjects, but only 18% of the psychotherapy subjects and 11% of the control subjects. A mean bedwetting measure over twelve weeks of treatment showed little change in the latter two groups but dropped markedly in the group that received conditioning treatment. Relapse rates were high in the conditioning group, but this measure is difficult to interpret because the definition of relapse was quite strict (a single wet night following treatment). The severity of enuresis in relapse was significantly lower than in the pretreatment period.

A study explicity designed to examine the possibility of symptom substitution using the conditioning procedure found no evidence for such an effect (117). Thirty enuretic children ranged in age from six to twelve years. All but four of the children had been wetting since birth, and more than half were wet seven nights a week. Subjects in the conditioning group were kept on the device until there were 14 consecutive dry days. Subjects in a comparison "wake-up" group were awakened regularly each night by parents in a procedure similar to the routine prescibed by many pediatricians. A waiting list control received no immediate treatment.

Treatment results showed a decrease in wetness in both groups in the first few weeks of treatment, but continued improvement from that point was significantly greater in the conditioning group than the wake-up group, and after 10 weeks there was significantly less wetting in the conditioning group. Eleven of fourteen subjects in the conditioning group obtained initial arrest, but only two of fourteen subjects in the wake-up group.

A number of measures of adjustment were taken before and after treatment. These showed no worsening in adjustment following treatment; rather, other improvements were found. The most frequently reported observation of parents was the child's happiness at becoming dry. Many children were able for the first time to sleep overnight with friends and relatives or go to a summer camp; three boys immediately joined the Boy Scouts. Children were reported to be taking on more responsibility and becoming more autonomous. Independent measures of adjustment showed improvement in the cured subjects relative to controls. The author concludes that "it is possible that new symptoms did not arise because bedwetting is simply a habit deficiency rather than an expression of, and outlet for, internal conflict. In any case, the dangers of a direct treatment of enuresis seem to have been overstated, and similar research on other classical disorders might be of considerable value in further understanding the symptom-substitution issue and the more basic question of symptom formation" (117, p. 49).

In describing a behavioral treatment of encopresis, Neale pointed out that the problems of incontinence of urine and incontinence of feces are physiologically and behaviorally quite different (118). The first requires inhibiting the tendency to empty the bladder and the development of the ability to store urine. The second requires encouragement of the act of defecation and restoration of the physiologically normal state of emptiness of the rectum. The subject must be taught to become aware of the sensation of fullness when a fecal mass moves into the rectum, and to proceed to the lavatory and defecate there following this sensation. Neale argues that children who soil their pants typically inhibit normal elimination and that this inhibition is a result of fear. The treatment program he describes therefore has two components: creating cirsumstances where the conditioned anxiety response can decay, and encouraging the normal defecation response in the lavatory by reinforcement with candy, stars in a book, pennies, and approval. The procedure was to bring the child to the lavatory four times daily, after each main meal and at bedtime. The child was provided with candy and a comic book, measures designed to reduce the anxiety associated with sitting on the toilet. If elimination occurred the child was reinforced. No punishment or rebuke was administered for soiled pants. This procedure was successful in treating encopresis in three hospitalized children who had been encopretic for several years, but unsuccessful with a fouth child.

Peterson and London have reported the use of similar procedures with a child at home, but with greater emphasis on verbal encouragement and instructions (119). A three-year-old child had had several experiences in which defecation failed to occur for several days, so that when defecation did occur it was painful. At the time of treatment the interval between eliminations was typically about five days, and elimination usually occurred either under a bed (if indoors) or behind a bush (if outdoors). Treatment involved verbal suggestions that it would not hurt if he went to the potty and that Mommy and Daddy would be very happy. This was followed by defecation on the toilet for the first time in three months, which was reinforced by the parents with praise and a popsicle. Continued encouragement, suggestion, and reinforcement led to continued success, and normal toilet behavior followed. A somewhat similar procedure has been described for the rapid toilet training of a normal nineteen-month old child whose parents were about to leave on a trip (120). A book describing a much more thorough and systematic method for training bowel and bladder control in psychotic and retarded hospital inpatients has recently appeared by Foxx and Azrin (121).

7. *Mental retardation: self-help skills, social skills, language training*

No studies in mental retardation will be reviewed in detail here since several illustrations of behavioral treatment with mentally retarded patients have already been described. A review of research on behavior modification techniques with the retarded has been presented by Gardner (122). He notes that applied behavior change (behavior modification and programmed instruction) is the largest area in learning research with the retarded, and behavior modification is the largest category within applied behavior change. An analysis of research articles published from 1963 to 1968 showed a relatively steady number of articles on teaching self-help and self-care skills, such as toileting and eating, but a dramatic rise (from two in 1963 to over 30 in 1968) in articles on learning social skills.

Behavior modification techniques with the retarded may be applied in three areas: self-help skills, social skills, and language skills. Self-help skills include toilet training, feeding, dressing, tooth brushing, and so on. Social skills include classroom training (especially elimination of undesirable classroom behavior), elimination of undesirable behaviors such as self-destructiveness, abusiveness to others, "brat syndrome," attention-seeking, and hyperactivity, and increasing various desirable activities such as interaction with others and outdoor play. Language training includes procedures ranging from shaping the production of vocalizations and imitation, through remedial training in more advanced language skills as vocabulary and grammar. Gardner has reviewed research in many of these areas (122).

F. IMPLICATIONS FOR THE REARING OF NORMAL CHILDREN

One of the underlying assumptions of the behavioral approach is that there is no clear distinction between "normal" and "abnormal" behavior. And an important characteristic of behavioral treatment procedures is that the same treatment techniques used to eliminate "abnormal" behavior may also be used to deal with "normal" behavior problems in "normal" children. One of the exciting potentials of behavior therapy is that it may help us to deal more effectively with minor behavior problems before they become major. One can look forward to the day when there is a sufficient technology of behavior change, and sufficient mechanisms for making this technology available to parents, teachers and members of the helping professions, so that many of the behavior problems of today can be regularly and readily dealt with before they become seriously disruptive and possibly more resistant to treatment.

Many examples have already been presented of "abnormal" behavior that was readily treated with behavioral techniques but which, if untreated, might conceivably have degenerated to the point where treatment would be considerably more difficult. Three such examples were the cases of selective muteness in young children, the case of the child who scratched herself, and the case of the child whose vomiting in class was reinforced by being returned to her dormitory. A further example is a psychogenic seizure case (56). A ten-year-old girl was brought to the hospital for a "seizure" which included rhythmical head rolling accompanied by hair pulling. Hospital tests revealed no obvious physical cause. For several weeks prior to the seizure the girl had manifested increasingly frequent somatic complaints, and several temper tantrums including one that the mother said "looked sort of like a convulsion." It seemed possible that the somatic complaints had been maintained at least in part by parental attention. Moreover, the child had inadvertently been presented a "model" for psychosomatic behavior several months earlier when the mother was taken to the hospital for a headache of such intensity that she "rocked and banged."

Therefore in three counseling sessions the parents were given instructions to ignore unjustified somatic complaints, tantrums, and seizure behavior, and reward other appropriate behavior with attention and approval. Following discharge from the hospital, the frequency of seizure behavior dropped to zero, and both tantrum behavior and somatic complaints stabilized at levels considerably below the pretreatment level estimated by the parents.

In the 26th week of follow-up, the parents were instructed to deliberately reinstate attention for somatic complaints and tantrums. Within 24 hours of this deliberate reinstatement of attention to somatic complaints, such complaints showed a dramatic increase to about one per hour. Then the girl manifested a seizure. When these behaviors were again ignored they again dropped to lower levels. Follow-up interviews after a year revealed that no further seizures had occurred.

This case again illustrates "abnormal" behavior that was amenable to treatment by relatively direct manipulation of consequences maintaining that behavior. Once again, the apparent inadvertent shaping of deviant behavior by the parents seemed well within the bounds of the type of situation that could occur readily in many homes.

Another situation in which the kinds of treatment described in this paper have been applied to more "normal" behavior is the control of classroom behavior. Procedures such as careful manipulation of teacher attention, rewarding appropriate behavior with free time, and the use of token systems have been used in special cases of hyperactive, retarded, and emotionally disturbed children. However, identical procedures have also been employed in classrooms of entirely "normal" children (60-63, 124, 125).

It was pointed out above that two of the characteristics of behavior therapy are that attention is paid to variables maintaining behavior in the natural environment, and that considerable use is made of nonprofessional agents of change. Many behavioral intervention programs involve training parents in principles of behavior change, and guiding the parents in the application of those principles. This can be done productively with parents of "normal" children as well as children with behavior problems. The methods of teaching self-help skills to the retarded are similar to methods for effectively teaching those same skills to young children. (Indeed, it has been argued that by having to work harder to teach such skills to the retarded child, we learn more about what the most effective teaching procedures are which are applicable to any child.) The kinds of approaches used in helping parents deal with delinquent and pre-delinquent children (48,84) are effective in dealing with the minor behavior problems that arise in any family. Holland's 21-step interview guide for behavioral counseling with parents (13) may be used to deal with serious and "abnormal" behaviors or with simpler problems like getting a child to keep his room clean, encouraging more positive interaction with playmates, or reducing family squabbles.

Because the behavior change principles that underly behavior therapy strike many people as simple-minded, there is sometimes a tendency to assume parents employ such procedures "naturally" and correctly. This is a wrong assumption and a dangerous one. Even parents who are aware of behavioral principles frequently find that their application is neither simple nor obvious. For example, I have been teaching behavior principles for several years. Some time ago both my wife and I realized, at about the same time, that when I arrived home in the evening and sat down to read or watch TV, there was a noticeable and consistent increase in unruly behavior in our young children. After further thought, we realized there was a simple "rule" that was in effect. When I arrived home I was tired and didn't want to be bothered by the children for a while. The rule was, "if you want Daddy's attention, be bad." That rule was very clear, very simple, and consistently applied by me. The point is that the children had detected this "rule" long before the parents, and it had strikingly affected their behavior.

Although it may seem simple to say that behaviors that are reinforced will occur more frequently, and those punished or non-rewarded will occur less frequently, the elaboration and application of these principles is complex. An awareness of the contingencies or "rules" that explicitly or inadvertentaly exist in a family situation is a major contribution to be made by proponents of behavior therapy. It is disturbing to note how seldom are behavioral principles discussed in texts of child development. For example, one text notes that abnormal behavior "is the child's way of showing that for some reason his growth is being blocked or hampered" (123, p. 19). Throughout this text problems of childhood are discussed in terms of frustrations, blocked or inhibited growth, "the tensions of the atomic age," vaguely defined "parental support," "poor self-image," underlying anxieties, and so on. There is little or no reference to the fact that disturbed behaviors can be generated, maintained, and potentially treated by the consequences that follow those behaviors.

To summarize, one of the important characteristics of behavior therapy is that the basic approach to treatment is relevant not only to modification of "deviant" behavior in "abnormal" children, but also to the day-to-day process of rearing normal children. This is particularly important if one believes that there is no sharp dichotomy between "normal" and "abnormal," but rather a continuum of behaviors that vary with respect to their probability of occurrence, their social acceptability, and possibly their amenability to treatment. It is likely that over the next few years we will see an increase in articles and texts describing the applicability of the behavioral approach to the process of rearing normal children. An excellent book on this topic which has recently appeared is *Changing Children's Behavior,* by Krumboltz and Krumboltz (18).

G. STRENGTHS AND WEAKNESSES OF THE BEHAVIORAL APPROACH

The number of books and articles on behavior therapy continues to increase at an ever accelerating rate. It seems clear that the behavioral approach to therapy now stands as a viable approach, with its own coherent theoretical structure, its own set of therapeutic procedures and techniques, its own group of ardent proponents and enthusiasts, and its own professional organizations devoted to the furtherance of its cause.*

Although it is certain that behavior therapy as a discipline is growing, there is some debate as to the direction its growth should take. On the one hand there are those who argue that behavioral psychologists are beginning to expand beyond their original narrow framework, beginning to accept thoughts and cognitions as important variables, and that this broadening of scope is good. On the other hand there are those who argue that such "broadening" of the behavioral approach is unfortunate and dangerous because it loses the essence of the behavioral approach. Two recent sets of papers dealing with such issues are illustrative. One debate concerned the movement toward a broader definition of "behavior" to include cognitions as well as externally observable overt behavior (126-128). Another debate concerned whether an eventual integration of behavior therapy with dynamic psychiatry is possible and, if so, whether it is desirable. One author in this group of papers said such integration is highly desirable since behavior therapy and dynamic psychiatry "tend to have reciprocal advantages and shortcomings" (129). In reply another author argued that such integration is undesirable because it would obscure fundamental and important differences between the two approaches, and that an attempt at integration would merely result in weakening and diluting the behavioral approach (130). A third author agrees that the techniques and theories of dynamic psychiatry have been rejected too hastily by behavior therapists, but argues that the preferred approach is to expand the behavioral approach by incorporating reference to internal events and covert cues, rather than prematurely encouraging a "marriage with a high probability of ending in divorce" (131).

Such debates are likely to continue for some time, and no one can predict with certainty the direction that "behavior therapy" as a discipline may take over the coming years. It may be useful, however, to at least list some of the strengths and weaknesses that the behavioral approach seems to have. If we can agree on some of these, we might begin to chart the kinds of changes we would hope behavior therapy as a discipline might make as it continues to grow.

1. Strengths

Most of the strengths of the behavioral approach have been previously described in this paper, and many have been discussed in some detail. They will be briefly listed again here.

a. Comparative brevity of treatment.

b. Explicitness of treatment. The patient (or parent) is told what to *do*. In addition, it may be more possible for a successful therapist to communicate to other therapists what he has done.

c. Breaking the symptom-cause-symptom cycle. For example, bedwetting causes anxiety causes more bedwetting. Or aggressiveness in the child produces a situation where social feedback from peers produces more aggressiveness, and so on. Directly treating the behavior may interrupt such negative cycles.

d. Applicability to certain classes of patient. Behavior therapy may be effective with classes of patient difficult to help with traditional psychotherapy, including less verbal and less well educated patients, severely retarded or psychotic patients, and very young children.

e. Widening the resources of change. Behavior therapists employ parents, teachers and others in the social environment as agents of change. One advantage of this with children is the relative ease with which their social environments may be controlled by dealing with a relatively small number of people.

f. Relevance to "normal" as well as "abnormal" behavior. This is a strength if one believes there is a continuum from "normal" to "abnormal" rather than a sharp dichotomy, and that "abnormal" behavior may often develop out of "normal" behavior as a consequence of rules of learning common to all behavior.

g. Acceptability to parents. The behavioral approach may seem more reasonable and practical to patients and to parents than traditional therapy, leading them to accept it more readily and have more confidence in the possibility of change.

h. Experimental approach, and reliance on objective measures of change. With individual patients, behavior therapists are more likely to be aware of the multiplicity of possible approaches to treatment, and to view any one treatment of a particular problem as a treatment to be tried, evaluated, and if necessary modified. More generally, the behavior therapist hopes to be able to employ treatment procedures that have been experimentally evaluated and verified. If the behavioral approach has any lasting effect a generation from now, it may not be the specific procedures in use today, but the basic orientation of carefully and explicitly defining whatever procedures one uses, and experimentally testing those procedures to evaluate their effectiveness.

i. Effectiveness of treatment. The final strength of the behavioral approach, and the criteria against which its value must ultimately be tested, is the effectiveness of treatment. The kinds of applications described in this article are an indication of areas where behavioral treatment has seemed to be quite successful.

2. Weaknesses.

a. Symptom versus behavior. The controversy over whether certain forms of behavior should be treated directly as behaviors, or instead as symptoms of an underlying problem, is likely to be with us for some time. If underlying problems are present but the behavior therapist ignores them in favor of surface problems that may be more obvious and more amenable to treatment, this would be a weakness.

b. Difficulty in dealing with certain general problems. Jehu has noted that "it is difficult to see at present how to apply behavior therapy to certain types of problems, which are hard to analyze into particular dysfunctional behavior, however broadly defined" (23). Such problems might include general depression, unhappiness, lack of meaning or purpose in life. Behavioral treatment of such general dissatisfactions has not been much explored as yet.

c. Danger of becoming committed to a given list of techniques. The behavior therapist must not lose sight of the distinction between the basic approaches and underlying assumptions of behavior therapy, which are likely to be a permanent contribution, and the specific techniques currently employed by behavior therapists. He must be open to change as new techniques are tried and old ones discarded as not living up to their original promise.

d. Treatment techniques not based on stated theory. One of the criticisms leveled at behavior therapy is that the treatment techniques employed bear only a remote relationship to the learning theory on which they are supposedly based (e.g. 132-134). To the degree that this is true one's satisfaction with behavior therapy as a coherent discipline must be lessened.

e. Overenthusiasm may cause too quick rejection of alternatives. This danger, like the previous one, is not limited to behavior therapists. Nevertheless, behavior therapists have not been immune to overstating their case. For example, one wonders whether the sometimes emotional and violent rejection of the "medical model" of mental illness has not caused rejection of certain insights that model might offer.

f. Observation and data gathering a mixed blessing. Patterson has pointed out that although behavior therapists emphasize careful observation and problem behaviors as an alternative to traditional assessment, such observation may be a mixed blessing (84, pp 761-763). Many would argue that systematic observation of deviant children's behavior in classroom or home situations if far more useful than traditional assessment. However, such observation involves serious methodological problems such as the presence of significant bias in parental reports, and the fact that an observer's presence may strongly influence behavior.

g. Unjustified use of behavioral terminology. To the extent that behavior therapy becomes popular, many traditional therapies may begin to adopt some of the terminology of behavior therapy without really following its basic principles. But one does not become a behavior therapist simply by sprinkling conversation with the word "reinforcement." If behavior therapy continues to increase in popularity it may face weakening and diffusion of what is has to offer as others adopt its surface attributes without adopting - or perhaps without even understanding - its more important underlying assumptions.

h. Danger of the misuse of control. A serious issue that concerns many therapists - those in favor of behavior therapy as well as those opposed to it - is the degree to which the therapist "controls" the patient's behavior. This issue seems to be of particular concern for behavior therapy since goals of treatment are often so explicit, and procedures so direct. It is not clear that the danger of the misuse of control should be classified as a weakness, however, since we only become concerned about the ability to exert control when we begin to learn how to produce results. It can be argued that *any* effective procedure for modifying disordered behavior must raise the problem of exerting control, whether that procedure is behavioral or not. Perhaps the problem of exerting undue control should be classified as a *danger* but not necessarily a *disadvantage.* It is, however, a danger that must be considered and discussed.

3. Conclusions.

Behavior therapy is many things. It is a set of underlying assumptions about the nature of problem behavior; it is a theoretical framework that views behavior change in terms of principles of reinforcement and conditioning; it is a group of specific techniques used by behavior therapists to treat specific behavior disorders. An attempt has been made in this paper to communicate each of these aspects of behavior therapy as it applies to the treatment of behavior problems in children. It is clear that behavior therapy is not a single, unified approach to treatment that clearly specifies one treatment of choice for each particular childhood problem. Rather there are a variety of treatment techniques suggested, some clearly demonstrated as effective, some not yet proven. But the studies cited in this paper show that behavior therapy has had considerable impact on the treatment of childhood disorders and has had many successes. The behavioral approach offers great promise of further increasing both our understanding of problem behaviors and our ability to treat them.

FOOTNOTES

This article was written while the author was on a leave of absence from Princeton University, serving as Assistant Director of Behavior Modification Programs at New Jersey Neuropsychiatric Institute, Princeton, New Jersey. The author thanks Dr. Frances E. Cheek of New Jersey Neuropsychiatric Instritute for administrative support during the writing of this article. Reprints may be obtained from the author at the Department of Psychology, Millersville State College, Millersville, Pa 17551.

The terms "behavior modification" and "behavior therapy" will be used here interchangeably. Distinctions that have sometimes been made between these terms are discussed in a separate section below.

The American Association for Advancement of Behavior Therapy (AABT), 475 Park Avenue South, New York, New York 10016. This is an organization of "professional persons interested in the possibilities for application for learning principles to assessment and modification of behavior in a clinical setting" (bylaws). AABT had 1500 members as of June 1, 1974. Over 85 papers and 36 3-hour workshops were presented at its seventh annual convention in December 1973.

REFERENCES

1. Yates, A. J. *Behav. Ther. 1,* 92, (1970).
2. Yates, A. J. *Behav. Ther. 1,* 113, (1970).
3. Mikulas, W. L. *Behavior Modification: An Overview.* New York, Harper and Row, (1972).
4. Wolpe, J. *Psychotherapy by Reciprocal Inhibition.* Stanford University Press, Stanford, California, (1958).
5. Valins, S. and Ray, A. A. *J. Personal. Soc. Psychol. 7,* 345, (1967).
6. Beck, A. T. *Behav. Ther. 1,* 184, (1970).
7. Bergin, A. E. *Behav. Ther. 1,* 205, (1970).
8. Locke, E. A. *Psychol. Bull. 76,* 318, (1971).
9. Wilkins, W. *Psychol. Bull. 76,* 311, (1971).
10. Davison, G. C. and Wilson, G. T. *Behav. Ther. 4,* 1, (1973).
11. Meichenbaum, D. H. Cognitive factors in behavior modification: modifying what clients say to themselves. In *Annual Review of Behavior Therapy, Theory and Practice, 1973.* Edited by Franks, C. M. and Wilson, G. T. Bruner/Mazel, New York, p 416, (1973).
12. Ullmann, L. P. The major concepts taught to behavior therapy trainees. Paper presented at the American Psychological Association, Washington, D. C., September, 1967. In *Behavior Therapy with Children.* Edited by Graziano, A. M. Aldine-Atherton, Chicago, p 367, (1971).
13. Holland, C. J. *Behav. Ther. 1,* 70, (1970).
14. Stuart, R. B. *Trick or Treatment: How and When Psychotherapy Fails.* Research Press, Champaign, Illinois, (1970).
15. Susskind, D. J. *Behav. Ther. 1,* 538, (1970).
16. Lazarus, A. A. *Behavior Therapy and Beyond.* McGraw-Hill, New York, (1971).
17. Ullmann, L. P. and Krasner, L. *Case Studies in Behavior Modification.* Holt, Rinehart and Winston, New York, p 15 (1965).
18. Krumboltz, J. D. and Krumboltz, H. B. *Changing Children's Behavior.* Prentice-Hall, Englewood Cliffs, New Jersey, (1972).

19. Franks, C. M. Implications of behavior therapy for the future of clinical psychology. Paper presented at the American Psychological Association, Washington, D. C., September, 1967. In *Behavior Therapy with Children.* Edited by Graziano, A. M. Aldine-Atherton, Chicago, p 17, (1971).
20. Rosenthal, R. *Experimenter Effects in Behavioral Research.* Appleton-Century-Crofts, New York, (1966).
21. Orne, M. T. *Amer. Psychol. 17,* 776, (1962).
22. Wolf, M. M., Birnbrauer, J. S., Williams, T., and Lawler, J. A note on apparent extinction of the vomiting behavior of a retarded child. In *Case Studies in Behavior Modification.* Edited by Ullmann, L. P. and Krasner, L. Holt, Rinehart and Winston, New York, p 364, (1965).
23. Jehu, D. *J. Behav. Ther. Exp. Psychiat. 1,* 17, (1970).
24. Yates, A. J. *Psychol. Rev. 65,* 371, (1958).
25. Eysenck, H. J. *J. Ment. Sci. 105,* 61, (1959).
26. Eysenck, H. J. *Psychiat. Dig. 27,* 45, (1966).
27. Ullmann, L. P. and Krasner, L. *Case Studies in Behavior Modification.* New York, Holt, Rinehart and Winston, (1965).
28. Ullmann, L. P. and Krasner, L. *A Psychological Approach to Abnormal Behavior.* Prentice-Hall, Englewood Cliffs, New Jersey, (1969).
29. Bandura, A. *Principles of Behavior Modification.* Holt, Rinehart and Winston, New York, (1969).
30. Baker, B. L. *J. Abnormal Psychol. 74,* 42, (1969).
31. Kahn, M., Baker, B. L., and Weiss, J. M. *J. Abnormal Psychol. 73,* 556, (1968).
32. Lazarus, A. A. *J. Abnormal Soc. Psychol. 63,* 504, (1961).
33. Lazarus, A. A. *Behav. Res. Ther. 1,* 69, (1963).
34. Lazarus, A. A. and Abramovitz, A. *J. Ment. Sci. 108,* 191, (1962).
35. Nolan, J. D., Mattis, P. R. and Holliday, W. C. *J. Abnormal Psychol. 76,* 88, (1970).
36. Paul, G. L. *J. Consult. Psychol. 31,* 333, (1967).
37. Paul, G. L. *J. Abnormal Psychol. 73,* 119, (1968).
38. Wolpe, J. *J. Nerv. Ment. Dis. 132,* 189, (1961).
39. Tasto, D. L. *Behav. Res. Ther. 7,* 409, (1969).

40. Lazarus, A. A., Davison, G. C. and Polefka, D. A. *J. Abnormal Psychol. 70,* 225, (1965).
41. Wetzel, R. *J. Consult. Psychol. 30,* 367, (1966).
42. Patterson, G. R., Jones, R., Whittier, J. and Wright, M. A. *Behav. Res. Ther. 2,* 217, (1965).
43. Patterson, G. R. and Brodsky, G. A. *J. Child Psychol. Psychiat. 7,* 277, (1966).
44. Goldiamond, I. *Psychol. Rep. 17,* 851, (1965).
45. Wolpe, J. *The Practice of Behavior Therapy.* Pergammon Press, Elmsford, N.Y., (1969).
46. Haughton, E. and Ayllon, T. Production and elimination of symptomatic behavior. In *Case Studies in Behavior Modification.* Edited by Ullmann, L. P. and Krasner, L. Holt, Rinehart and Winston, New York, p 94, (1965).
47. Pascal, C. E. Application of behavior modification by parents for treatment of a brain damaged child. In *Adaptive Learning: Behavior Modification with Children.* Edited by Ashem, B. A. and Poser, E. G. Pergamon Press, New York, p 299, (1973).
48. Tharp, R. G. and Wetzel, R. J. *Behavior Modification in the Natural Environment.* Academic Press, New York, (1969).
49. Patterson, G. R. An application of conditioning techniques to the control of a hyperactive child. In *Case Studies in Behavior Modification.* Edited by Ullmann, L. P. and Krasner, L. Holt, Rinehart, and Winston, New York, p 370, (1965).
50. Patterson, G. R., Ray, R. and Shaw, D. Direct Intervention in Families of Deviant Children. In *New Tools for Changing Behavior.* Edited by Diebert, A. N. and Harmon, A. J. Research Press, Champaign, Illinois, pp 127-129, (1970).
51. Gelfand, D. M. and Hartmann, D. P. *Psychol. Bull. 69,* 204, (1968).
52. Graziano, A. M. *Behavior Therapy with Children.* Aldine-Atherton, Chicago, p. 364, (1971).
53. Johnson, S. M. and Brown, R. A. *J. Child Psychol. Psychiat. 10,* 107, (1969).
54. Wahler, R. G., Winkel, G. H., Peterson, R. F. and Morrison, D. C. *Behav. Res. Ther. 3,* 113, (1965).

55. Allen, K. E. and Harris, F. R. *Behav. Res. Ther. 4,* 79, (1966).
56. Gardner, J. E. *J. Consult. Psychol. 31,* 209, (1967).
57. Ayllon, T. and Michael, J. *J. Exp. Anal. Behav. 2,* 323, (1959).
58. Davison, G. C. The training of undergraduates as social reinforcers for autistic children. In *Case Studies in Behavior Modification.* Edited by Ullmann, L. P. and Krasner, L. Holt, Rinehart and Winston, New York, p 146, (1965).
59. Staats, A. W., Minke, K. A., Goodwin, W. and Landeen, J. *Behav. Res. Ther. 5,* 283, (1967).
60. Ulrich, R., Stachnik, T. and Mabry, J. *Control of Human Behavior, Volume 3: Behavior Modification in Education.* Scott, Foresman, Glenview, Illinois, (1974).
61. Klein, R. D., Hapkiewicz, W. G. and Roden, A. H. *Behavior Modification in Educational Settings.* Charles C. Thomas, Springfield, Illinois, (1973).
62. Ackerman, J. M. *Operant Conditioning Techniques for the Classroom Teacher.* Scott, Foresman, Glenview, Illinois, (1972).
63. Meacham, M. L. and Wiesen, A. E. *Changing Classroom Behavior: A Manual for Precision Teaching.* International Textbook Co., Scranton, Pa. (1969).
64. Ashem, B. A. and Poser, E. G. *Adaptive Learning: Behavior Modification with Children.* Pergamon Press, New York, (1973).
65. Kanfer, F. H. and Phillips, J. S. *Learning Foundations of Behavior Therapy.* Wiley, New York, (1970).
66. Deese, J. and Hulse, S. H. *The Psychology of Learning.* McGraw Hill, New York, (1967).
67. Hilgard, E. R. and Bower, G. H. *Theories of Learning.* Appleton-Century-Crofts, New York, (1966).
68. Kimble, G. A. *Hilgard and Marquis' Conditioning and Learning.* Appleton-Century-Crofts, New York, (1961).
69. Reynolds, G. S. *A Primer of Operant Conditioning.* Scott, Foresman, Glenville, Illinois, (1968).
70. Ayllon, T. *Behav. Res. Ther. 1,* 53, (1963).
71. Welsh, R. S. The use of stimulus satiation in the elimination of juvenile fire-setting behavior. In *Behavior Thera-*

py with Children. Edited by Graziano, A. M. Aldine-Atherton, Chicago, p 283, (1971).

72. Graziano, A. *Behavior Therapy with Children.* Aldine-Atherton, Chicago, (1971).
73. Ashem, B. A. and Poser, E. G. *Adaptive Learning: Behavior Modification with Children.* Pergamon Press, Elmsford, N.Y., (1973).
74. Watson, J. B. and Rayner, R. *J. Exp. Psychol. 3,* 1, (1920).
75. Jones, M. C. *J. Exp. Psychol. 7,* 382, (1924).
76. Jones, M. C. *Pediat. Sem. 31,* 308, (1924).
77. Jersild, A. T. and Holmes, F. B. *J. Psychol. 1,* 75, (1935).
78. Graziano, A. M. and Kean, J. E. Programmed relaxation and reciprocal inhibition with psychotic children. In *Behavior Therapy with Children.* Edited by Graziano, A. M. Aldine-Atherton, Chicago, p 215, (1971).
79. Bentler, P. M. *J. Child Psychol. Psychiat. 3,* 185, (1962).
80. Montenegro, H. *J. Child Psychol. Psychiat. 9,* 93, (1968).
81. Patterson, G. R. A learning theory approach to the treatment of the school phobic child. In *Case Studies in Behavior Modification.* Edited by Ullmann, L. P. and Krasner, L. Holt, Rinehart and Winston, New York, p 279, (1965).
82. Denholtz, M. S. "At home" aversion treatment of compulsive fire-setting behavior: case report. In *Advances in Behavior Therapy: Proceedings of the Fourth Conference of the Association for Advancement of Behavior Therapy.* Edited by Rubin, R. D. Fersterheim, H., Henderson, J. D. and Ullmann, L. P. Academic Press, New York, p 81, (1972).
83. Holland, C. J. *Behav. Res. Ther. 7,* 135, (1969).
84. Patterson, G. R. Behavioral intervention procedures in the classroom and in the home. In *Handbook of Psychotherapy and Behavior Change.* Edited by Bergin, A. E. and Garfield, S. L. Wiley, New York, p 751, (1971).
85. Patterson, G. R. *Families: Applications of Social Learning to Family Life.* Research Press, Champaign, Illinois, (1971).
86. Patterson, G. R. and Gullion, M. E. *Living With Children: New Methods for Parents and Teachers.* Research Press,

Champaign, Illinois, (1971).
87. Watson, L. S. In *Child Behavior Modification: A Manual for Teachers, Nurses, and Parents.* Pergamon Press, New York, (1973).
88. Philips, E. L. *J. Appl. Behav. Anal. 1,* 213, (1968).
89. Phillips, E. L., Phillips, E. A., Fixsen, D. L. and Wolf, M. M. *J. Appl. Behav. Anal. 4,* 45, (1971).
90. Sailor, W., Guess, D., Rutherford, G. and Baer, D. M. *J. Appl. Behav. Anal. 1,* 237, (1968).
91. Williams, C. D. *J. Abnormal Soc. Psychol. 59,* 269, (1959).
92. Wolf, M., Risley, T. and Mees, H. *Behav. Res. Ther. 1,* 305, (1964).
93. Blackwood, R. O., Horrocks, J. E., Keele, T. F., Hundziak, M. and Rettig, J. H. Operant Conditioning of social behaviors in severely retarded patients. In *Behavior Therapy with Children.* Edited by Graziano, A. M. Aldine-Atherton, Chicago, p 83, (1971).
94. Luckey, R. E., Watson, C. M. and Musick, J. K. *Amer. J. Ment. Def. 73,* 139, (1968).
95. Allen, K. E. and Harris, F. R. *Behav. Res. Ther. 4,* 79, (1966).
96. Peterson, R. F. and Peterson, L. R. *J. Exp. Child Psychol. 6,* 351, (1968).
97. Lovaas, O. I., Freitag, G., Gold, V. J. and Kassorla, I. C. *J. Exp. Child Psychol. 2,* 67, (1965).
98. Hamilton, J., Stephens, L. and Allen, P. *Amer. J. Ment. Def. 71,* 852, (1967).
99. Lovaas, O. I., Freitag, G., Kinder, M. I., Rubenstein, D. B., Schaeffer, B. and Simons, J. B. Experimental studies in childhood schizophrenia: Developing social behaviors using electric shock. Paper presented at American Psychological Association, Los Angeles, (1964).
100. Tate, B. G. and Baroff, G. S. *Behav. Res. Ther. 4,* 281, (1966).
101. Lovaas, O. I. and Simmons, J. Q. *J. Appl. Behav. Anal. 2,* 143, (1969).
102. Bachman, J. A. *J. Abnormal Psychol. 80,* 211, (1972).
103. Lovaas, O. I. A behavior therapy approach to the treatment of childhood schizophrenia. In *Minnesota Symposia*

on Child Psychology. Vol. 1. Edited by Hill, J. P. University of Minnesota Press, Minneapolis, p 108, (1967).

104. Lovaas, O. I., Berberich, J. P., Perloff, B. F. and Schaeffer, B. *Science 151,* 705, (1966).
105. Risley, T. and Wolf, M. *Behav. Res. Ther. 5,* 73, (1967).
106. Sloane, H. N. and MacAulay, B. A. *Operant Procedures in Remedial Speech and Language Training.* Houghton Mifflin, Boston, (1968).
107. Browning, R. M. *Behav. Res. Ther. 5,* 27, (1967).
108. Kondas, O. *Behav. Res. Ther. 5,* 325, (1967).
109. Gregory, H. H. *Learning Theory and Stuttering Therapy.* Northwestern University Press, Evanston, Ill., (1968).
110. Sluckin, A. and Jehu, D. *Brit. J. Psychiat. Soc. Work 10,* 70, (1969).
111. Brison, D. W. *J. Sch. Psychol. 4,* 65, (1966).
112. Reid, J. B., Hawkins, N., Keutzer, C., McNeal, S. A., Phelps, R. E., Reid, K. M. and Mees, H. L. *J. Child Psychol. Psychiat. 8,* 27, (1967).
113. Mowrer, O. H. and Mowrer, W. M. *Amer. J. Orthopsychiat. 8,* 436, (1928).
114. Jones, H. G. The behavioral treatment of enuresis nocturna. In *Behavior therapy and the Neuroses.* Edited by Eysenck, H. J. Pergamon Press, New York, p 377, (1960).
115. Sperling, M. *J. Amer. Acad. Child Psychiat. 4,* 19, (1965).
116. DeLeon, G. and Mandell, W. *J. Clin. Psychol. 22,* 326, (1966).
117. Baker, B. L. *J. Abnormal Psychol. 74,* 42, (1969).
118. Neale, D. H. *Behav. Res. Ther. 1,* 139, (1963).
119. Peterson, D. R. and London, P. A role for cognition in the behavioral treatment of a child's eliminative distrubance. In *Case Studies in Behavior Modification.* Edited by Ullmann, L. P. and Krasner, L. Holt, Rinehart and Winston, New York, p 289, (1965).
120. Madsen, C. H. Positive reinforcement in the toilet training of a normal child: a case report. In *Case Studies in Behavior Modification.* Edited by Ullmann, L. P. and Krasner, L. Holt, Rinehart and Winston, New York, p 305, (1965).

121. Foxx, R. M., and Azrin, N. H. *Toilet Training the Retarded: A Rapid Program for Day and Nighttime Independent Toileting.* Research Press, Champaign, Illinois, (1973).
122. Gardner, J. M. Behavior modification in mental retardation: a review of research and analysis of trends. In *Advances in Behavior Therapy: Proceedings of the Third Conference of the Association for Advancement of Behavior Therapy.* Edited by Rubin, R. D., Fensterheim, H., Lazarus, A. A. and Franks, C. M. Academic Press, New York, p 37, (1971).
123. Jenkins, G. G., Shacter, H. S. and Bauer, W. W. *These are Your Children.* (Third Edition), Scott, Foresman, Glenview, Illinois, (1966).
124. Becker, W. C. *An Empirical Basis for Change in Education: Selections on Behavioral Psychology for Teachers.* Science Research Associates, Chicago, (1971).
125. O'Leary, K. D. and O'Leary, S. G. *Classroom Management: The Successful Use of Behavior Modification.* Pergamon Press, New York, (1972).
126. Beck, A. T. *Behav. Ther. 1,* 184, (1970).
127. Ullmann, L. P. *Behav. Ther. 1,* 201, (1970).
128. Bergin, A. E. *Behav. Ther. 1,* 205, (1970).
129. Birk, L. *Behav. Ther. 1,* 522, (1970).
130. Rachman, S. *Behav. Ther. 1,* 527, (1970).
131. Levis, D. J. *Behav. Ther. 1,* 531, (1970).
132. Breger, L. and McGaugh, J. L. *Psychol. Bull. 63,* 338, (1965).
133. Rachman, S. and Eysenck, H. J. *Psychol. Bull. 65.* 165, (1966).
134. Breger, L. and McGaugh, J. L. *Psychol. Bull. 65,* 170, (1966).

MENTAL HEALTH IN CHILDREN, Volume III
Edited By D. V. Siva Sankar

THE RELATIONSHIP OF MATERNAL ATTITUDES AND CHILD BEHAVIOR TO SELECTION OF DAY SCHOOL OR RESIDENTIAL TREATMENT

Arthur Wolpert, Leonard White, Jon Neiditch and Joseph Currier

Central Islip State Hospital
Central Islip, New York 11722

Precis

Parental ratings of child behavior and evaluations of maternal attitudes toward child rearing were conducted in consecutive admissions to a day-care treatment program (N = 21) and a residential treatment center (N = 17) serving children in the same catchment area.

The results suggest that behavioral variables rather than maternal attitudes are considered in placement. There may be inadequate consideration given to parental attitudes during the referral process and in the determination of treatment setting.

The current shift in emphasis from residential treatment to community based mental health programs has created many questions regarding the relative merits of the programs and the factors leading to the choice of the particular treatment modality. Parental child rearing attitudes have been considered as factors in the etiology of child behavior disorders and in the determination and maintenance of therapeutic gains (1,2,3). However, there has been little written concerning the importance of family attitudes and the mother-child relationship in determining the choice of residential or day-care treatment of children.

The purpose of this study was to evaluate the relationship between parental attitudes and child behavior in the selection of day care or residential treatment for the disordered child.

Suffolk County is a catchment area containing approximately half a million children in the age range of 3 to 16. Within ten miles of each other there are a 192 bed children's psychiatric hospital and a day school with a capacity to serve 175 emotionally disturbed children. These centers serve the entire catchment area; both service the same age groups and both are supported in such a manner as to make family finances an unimportant variable in the selection of programs.

Method

Referrals are made to either center via community agencies, schools, professionals, or the parents themselves, the latter being the most infrequent source of referral. In the present study none of the cases studied were self-referrals.

A copy of the Devereaux Child Behavior Rating Scales (4) was mailed to the parents at the time of application. They were requested to complete the form and to provide other developmental and background information on the child. These materials were either returned by mail or brought by the parents at the time of the initial intake screening. As an alternative, the forms could be completed at the center while awaiting the screening interview. The parents were asked not to consult each other when completing the forms.

The Devereaux scale was selected because it covers a wide range of behaviors represented by psychiatric populations of children. Generally, these behaviors can be readily observed and the scale has been found to require little training for reliable use. The scale consists of 97 items which are scored in terms of frequency of occurrence or degree to which they are characteristic of a child's recent behaviors. The behaviors are scaled on a five to eight point continuum. Seventeen factors are derived from the scale which cover the areas of language-communication, emotional responses, coordination, socialization, and various specific symptoms.

Mothers' child rearing practices were evaluated at the time of screening via a semi-structured interview using a scale devised by Dielman *et al.* (5). We have found, as have other investigators (6), that parental responses regarding their own feelings and attitudes are more likely to be honest and spontaneous during an interview than with a questionnaire. The scale consisted of 103 items divided into 16 factors covering the areas of use of punishment, parental involvement, affection toward child, permissiveness, and so forth. During our early experiences, two raters were present during the semi-structured interview. When we were satisfied that reliability between raters was adequate (Pearson r = .82 for 15 interviews) interviews were conducted by a single rater.

We studied 38 cases, 17 from the residential center and 21 from the day center. In 34 of these cases only the mothers ratings were obtained. Although more families were seen, only those cases which were admitted to either the residential center or the day school were included since many of the other screenings were considered to be inappropriate referrals to an intensive clinical program or to present primarily organically based disorders.

Results

The mean reliability of mothers and fathers in concurring on their children's behavior over all factors on the Devereaux scale was .74. This suggests that the ratings accurately reflected the child's behavior.

In order to evaluate differences between centers, students t tests were calculated on the various factors derived from the Devereaux Scale and the Parental Attitude form. The behavioral ratings of the children from the two centers were found to yield statistically significant differences on several factors (see Table 1). Seven of the 17 behavioral factors were significantly higher (worse behavior) at the residential school than in the day school children. In addition, language useage, which was rated but not included in the factors, was at a higher level among the residential children and the mean age of these children was also greater.

TABLE 1

COMPARISON OF PARENTAL RATINGS OF CHILD BEHAVIOR ON DEVEREAUX RATING SCALE BY TREATMENT SETTING

Behavior Factors	*Residential*		*Day School*		
	Mean	*S.D.*	*Mean*	*S.D.*	*P*
Age	127.8	25.7	84.8	5.0	.01
Social Aggression	12.8	4.6	8.4	4.1	.001
Unethical Behavior	11.7	5.1	6.8	3.5	.001
Emotional Detachment	15.9	4.2	13.0	3.6	.02
Proneness to Emotional Upset	28.8	7.5	22.7	6.5	.01
Anxious-Fearful Ideation	22.3	6.4	16.6	6.5	.01
Impulse Ideation	11.3	4.2	8.3	3.8	.02
Inability to Delay	28.0	5.3	24.1	6.8	.05
Poor Language	1.6	1.2	2.8	1.8	.05

Only one of the factors from the Mother's Parental Attitude Scale, promotion of independence, was found to differentiate the two centers ($t = 2.3$, $df = 36$, $p < .05$), with higher scores occuring in the day school group. This may have represented a random rather than a true difference, since it is the only one of 16 factors to show a significant difference.

We went further to examine the relationship between parental child-rearing attitudes and child behavior since it was reasonable to hypothesize that the attitudes of parents would influence the ratings of their own childs' behavior. In effect, we attempt to demonstrate a correlation across the two scales.

Six major factors were derived by varimax factor analysis using the 17 factors of the behavior scale and 16 factors of the parental attitude scale, and the additional factors: mothers age; childs age; language useage; and treatment center (see Table 2).

TABLE 2

FACTOR ANALYSIS OF PARENTAL ATTITUDE AND CHILD BEHAVIOR SCALES

Factor I - Anxious/Acting Out	*Loading*
Center - Residential	.73
Poor self-care	-.54
Inadequate need for independence	-.66
Proneness to emotional upset	.82
Anxious-fearful ideation	.64
Impulse ideation	.74
Inability to delay	.50
Social aggression	.85
Unethical behavior	.89
Language useage	-.73
Factor II - Organic Features	
Distractability	.74
Emotional detachment	. 65
Poor coordination and body tonus	.59
Incontinence	.66
Messiness - sloppiness	.72
Unresponsiveness to stimulation	.70
Inability to delay	.64
Factor III - Use of Reinforcement	
High use of physical punishment	-.51
Low use of reward	-.85
Lack of affection	.66
Low use of praise	.74
Factor IV - Low Positive Expectation	
Low involvement	.72
Strict discipline	.55
Permissiveness	.77
Early socialization training	-.88

Table 2

Factor V - Socially Oriented Child/ High Parental Discipline	
Social Isolation	-.86
Anxious-fearful ideation	-.57
Low use of discipline	-.63
Factor VI - Insecure Mother	
Mother's age	-.77
Mother's lack of self-confidence	.74
Low child orientation	.51

The first factor, composed of treatment center and behavioral variables, appears to be associated mainly with anxious, acting out children who were referred for residential treatment. This is the only factor in which the treatment center variable had a significant loading.

The second factor was a cluster of features which we interpreted as measuring the degree of organic involvement in the child's disorder.

Of the next four factors, Factors III, IV and VI indicate clusters of parental attitudes towards the disordered child, which we have labeled Use of Reinforcement, Low Positive Expectation, and Insecure Mothers, respectively.

Factor V was the only factor in which both behavioral and attitudinal variables appeared. The socially oriented child and a parental belief in strict discipline appears to be correlated here.

An analysis of trend between attitudes and behavior ratings was also conducted to examine any curvilinear relationships between these factors. There were no significant quadratic or cubic trends in the data. Barring any complex interractions among parental attitudes, a child's "true" behavior, and ratings of behavior, these findings suggest that the attitudes did not unduly bias the behavior ratings.

Discussion

In regard to the major question posed in this study, we found that parental attitudes played little role in the selection of treatment centers. Rather, it was shown that the child's behavior, unrelated to the parental attitudes, was a major factor in determining whether the child was referred to the day school or residential school.

Our findings suggest that the more aggressive, acting out, higher functioning, older child is more likely to be referred to a residential program, while the younger child with lower social functioning and with symptoms more suggestive of apparent organic involvement, is generally referred to a day program. We cannot say with certainty that the settings in which this study was conducted were representative. It does appear, however, that the children's behavior, as presented to the referring sources, determined the particular treatment program selected. Since we did not find that parental attitudes were different between residential and day care centers it may well be that they were inadequately considered in the referral process. If parental attitudes were taken into consideration during the referral and admission process, it may be that some cases currently being treated in an inpatient facility may be better served on an outpatient basis. Conversely, it may at times be found that some of the lower functioning children may be better served via a residential placement.

Another question that remaines to be explored is the possibility that the older children may have already had a wider exposure to different treatment procedures and their referral to inpatient settings signified that all other appropriate outpatient resources had been ineffective. It was our general impression, however, that these children had not had the opportunity to utilize a total day care program, and in effect, skipped over this intermediate approach between outpatient therapy and residential care.

References

1. Goldfarb, W. *Psycho-social Prog.* *1,* 9, (1970).
2. Furer, M. *Psycho-social Prog.* *1,* 65, (1970).
3. Lovaas, O. I., Koegel, R., Simmons, J. Q. *et al.* *J. Appl. Behav. Anal.* *6,* 131, (1973).
4. Spivack, G. and Spotts, J. Devereaux Child Behavior Rating Scale Manual. The Devereaux Foundation, Devon Penn, (1966).
5. Dielman, T.E., Cattell, R.B. and Lepper, C. *Child Develop.* *42,* 893, (1971).
6. Becker, W.C. and Krug, R.S. *Child Develop.* *36,* 329, (1965).
7. Dixon, W. J. (Ed) BMD: Biomedical Computer Programs X-Series Supplement Univ. of California, Los Angles, (1970).

The authors wish to thank Dr. S. Rosenberg, Mrs. M. Bollar, Mrs. E. Zaffuto and Mrs. M. Pardini for their assistance.

A. Wolpert, M.D., Ph.D. is Director of Research and Training at the Sagamore Children's Center, Melville, N.Y. L. White is a Senior Research Scientist and J. Neiditch is a Research Psychologist at the Long Island Research Institute, Central Islip, N.Y. J. Currier, Ph.D. was Executive Director at the Suffolk Child Department Center, Bay Shore, N.Y.

MENTAL HEALTH IN CHILDREN, Volume III
Edited By D. V. Siva Sankar

A COMPARISON OF TWO RESIDENTIAL TREATMENT UNITS FOR CHILDREN

Harvey R. Alderton

Thistletown Regional Centre
Rexdale, Ontario, Canada

This study compares the length of admission on two residential units in a children's psychiatric centre. The aims were; 1) to determine if there were significant differences in length of stay; and 2) if there were such differences, to attempt to identify possible reasons.

Method

(a)*Units*: The two units (Unit I and Unit II) were structurally mirror images, each providing facilities for 20 six to twelve year old children. Identical proportions of boys and girls were treated on the units, each of which included five groups of four children. Each group had its own bedroom but shared the other unit facilities such as a living room for reading, playing games

or watching television. Both units provided an intensive milieu therapy program based on psychodynamic principles with strong emphasis on the importance of interpersonal relationships. Both units were multi-disciplinary and under psychiatric direction with identical staffing. Each group of four children had its own child care staff who worked intensively with them.
(b)*Subjects*: Children were randomly admitted to the units from a waiting list of latency aged children requiring residential treatment. Prior to 1967 the decision to accept a child was made by an Admissions Committee on the basis of clinical records provided by the referring source. After that date an Outpatient Clinic was established, where referrals were screened and if accepted, placed on the waiting list with admission to either unit as a bed became available.

To eliminate the influence of diagnosis and sex on the comparison only boys were included in whom a diagnosis was made of either primary childhood behaviour disorder (1) or an equivalent term was used (such as neurotic behaviour disorder or character disorder). Using the diagnostic classification proposed by the Group for the Advancement of Psychiatry these would have fallen into the category of personality disorder, tension-discharge disorders (2). The diagnosis was made at an assessment conference conducted six to eight weeks after admission following a multi-disciplinary study. The presence of significant organic factors, psychosis or mental retardation were excluding factors. These were seriously disturbed youngsters for whom intensive residential treatment was necessary.

Wards of Children's Aid Societies (wards) were examined separately from children living with their own parents before and after admission (non-wards) in view of previous evidence of differences in treatment response of these two groups (3, 4).
(c)*Time Periods*: Two four-year periods were examined, 1961-64 and 1965-68 inclusive. All subjects who met the above criteria and who were admitted during these periods were included, a total of 113. Prior to 1961, one unit had included only boys and the unit would not have been comparable. After 1972 the units were discontinued and the children treated in

eight or ten bed houses. By that time all subjects admitted during 1965-1968 had been discharged.

(d) *Measures*

i) Length of admission was calculated in months; additional days of 16 or more counted as one month, 15 days or less disregarded. Eight a priori comparisons (5) were made: 1 and 2 - lengths of stay of wards on Unit I with that of wards on Unit II for each time period; 3 and 4 - length of stay of non-wards on Unit I with that of non-wards on Unit II for each time period; 5 to 8 - length of stay of wards on Unit I and Unit II for 1961-1964 compared with that for 1965-1968, and of non-wards on Unit I and Unit II for these time periods. Dunn's Multiple Comparison Procedure (6) was used.

ii) The relationship between age at admission and length of stay was examined by eight a priori correlation coefficients to determine whether a significant association existed. If so, the comparability of the units with regard to subject age at admission would be determined.

iii) Ratings of child adjustment at admission and discharge were routinely introduced during the second time period and were available for 43 of the 56 subjects. The instrument used was the Children's Pathology Index (C.P.I.) (7,8). Values for Factor I (disturbed behaviour towards adults) are shown in the tables since of the four factors, this has been found to provide the most useful measure of treatment response and to best predict follow-up adjustment (7,9). Possible values range from 40 to 200, a higher score indicating better adjustment. To ensure that subjects were rated at comparable times it was decided a priori to include only ratings made within six weeks of admission and within six weeks before or 10 days after discharge. Ratings were sought shortly before discharge but were occasionally omitted because of child care workers absence or illness. It was decided to include ratings made up to 10 days after discharge in view of staff's intense knowledge of these children with whom they had worked closely. C. P. I. ratings were used to confirm that the random admission procedure had resulted in children of comparable severity of disturbance on the two units. (Staff at no time had access to rating results since the C. P. I.'s predictive validity had not been established and was in fact being studied so that this might be determined.) In order to further confirm the comparability of the subjects, separate comparisons between units were also made for the remaining three factors.

iv) Ratings of family functioning on admission and discharge were first introduced in 1970 and used as an indirect measure that the adjustment of the families of non-wards were comparable on the two units. The Giesmar and Ayres Scale (10, 11, 12) was used by the social worker seeing the family. Such family involvement was a mandatory part of the total treatment program. This scale measures family adjustment in nine main and 26 sub-categories on seven point scales. The average scale for each main category was computed and the total adjustment score derived. The possible range extended from nine to 63, a higher value indicating better adjustment. Satisfactory reliability for this instrument and the C. P. I had previously been established in this setting. The results of family ratings were not available to staff.

Throughout the study, a significance level of .05 was selected as necessary to reject the null hypothesis.

Results

The mean length of stay ($\overline{X}$) and sample standard deviations (s) for ward and non-wards are shown in Table I. It can be seen that for both wards and non-wards, and for each time period, admission was longer on Unit I than on Unit II. Two of the a priori comparisons reached statistical significance (Dunn's Multiple Comparison Procedure (6)). These were the length of stay of non-wards on Unit I in 1961-1964 compared with 1965-1968 ($p= < .01$), and their length of stay in 1965-1968 compared with non-wards on Unit II for the same time period ($p= < .05$). The increase from first to second time period for non-wards was 71.33% on Unit I compared with 32.61% on Unit II.

Table II presents the correlation coefficients between age at admission and length of stay. Seven of the eight values were negative, three exceeding the .05 level of significance. Age at admission was therefore examined (Table III) but there were no inter-unit significant differences for either wards or non-wards.

Figures I and II show the cumulative frequency discharge curves for wards and non-wards for each time period. These

TABLE I

MEAN LENGTH OF STAY IN MONTHS AND SAMPLE STANDARD DEVIATIONS

UNITS I AND II, 1961-1964 AND 1965-1968

	Wards						Nonwards					
Unit	I			II			I			II		
	N	$\overline{X}$	s	N	$\overline{X}$	s	N	$\overline{X}$	s	N	$\overline{X}$	s
1961-4	9	25.89	6.67	14	18.71	6.25	19	18.94	9.67	15	15.27	6.81
1965-8	12	25.75	10.78	17	17.35	7.61	11	32.45	8.50	16	20.25	6.50

reveal the close approximation of ward and non-ward discharge curves for Unit II and how little these changed for the two time periods. While the curve for Unit I wards also shifted little over time (although clearly separable from the curves for Unit II throughout) the considerable shift to the right for non-wards on Unit I during 1965-1968 is apparent. This data shows that it was not only the mean length of stay which increased for Unit I non-wards but that the proportion of children discharged after brief admission had fallen. For example, on Unit I some 30% of non-wards had been discharged within a year in 1961-1964 while in 1965-1968 the comparable period had risen to almost 28 months, equivalent figures for Unit II were 12 and 17 months respectively.

The mean Factor I C.P.I. ratings at admission and discharge appear in Table IV, together with the mean admission age and length of stay. No significant unit age differences were found for wards or non-wards. It can also be seen that no significant differences in severity of disturbance were present at admission between comparable groups on the two units. As expected, length of stay for wards and non-wards was significantly longer on Unit I than on Unit II. In spite of this, subjects at discharge did not show higher C. P. I. ratings on Unit I. For wards and non-wards all correlation coefficients were non-significant between age at admission and C. P. I ratings at admission and discharge. No significant differences were found between unit ratings on Factors II, III or IV at admission or discharge.

Table V shows the family adjustment for 24 non-ward boys admitted between 1970 and 1972 who met the same diagnostic criteria as the subjects of the study. No significant differences were present thus providing indirect confirmation that the random admission procedure had resulted in comparably adjusted families on the two units. Ages at admission of these boys were also very similar on both units (Table VI) and did not differ significantly from those of the study subjects for the second time period shown in Table III. Family adjustment at discharge was available for 13 boys meeting the same diagnostic criteria (Table VII) and no significant inter-unit differences were found. (Levels of significance in Table V and VII were all two-tailed.) Note that family adjustment at

TABLE II

CORRELATIONS (r) BETWEEN AGE AT ADMISSION AND LENGTH OF STAY
UNITS I AND II, 1961-1964 AND 1965-1968

	Wards		Nonwards	
Unit	I	II	I	II
1961-1964	-0.3186	-0.2346	-0.5190	-0.5888
p	>.2	>.5	*<.05	*<.05
1965-1968	-0.5016	-0.6916	-0.5751	0.3164
p	>.05	*<.01	>.05	>.2

Levels of significance are two-tailed throughout

TABLE III

AGE AT ADMISSION, WARDS AND NONWARDS UNITS I AND II, 1961-1964 AND 1965-1968

Unit	Wards						Nonwards					
	I			II			I			II		
	N	$\overline{X}$	s	N	$\overline{X}$	s	N	$\overline{X}$	s	N	$\overline{X}$	s
1961-1964	9	109.22	19.06	14	102.79	9.93	19	108.32	18.90	15	112.00	21.29
	t = .8841 p = >.2						t = 0.5098 p = >.5					
1965-1968	12	102.58	21.07	17	113.53	17.52	11	111.82	13.35	16	106.19	18.77
	t = 1.4185 p = >.1						t = 0.8759 p = >.2					

TABLE IV

MEAN C. P. I. FACTOR I ADMISSION AND DISCHARGE RATINGS

UNITS I AND II, 1965-1968

		N	Mean Age (months)	Mean Length of Stay (months)	Mean Admission C. P. I. Factor I	Mean Discharge C. P. I. Factor I
Wards	I	8	104.50	26.75	125.88	164.38
	II	14	114.14	17.36	127.43	164.35
		t = 1.0833 ns		t = 2.5205 p = < .025*	t = 0.1480 ns	t = 0.0015 ns
Nonwards	I	7	116.57	30.43	123.71	153.28
	II	12	109.08	22.17	121.08	160.58
		t = 1.1832 ns		t = 2.3229 < .025*	t = 0.1345 ns	t = 0.4650 ns

* 1 tailed

Figure I

CUMULATIVE DISCHARGE FREQUENCY CURVES, WARDS AND NONWARDS 1961-1964

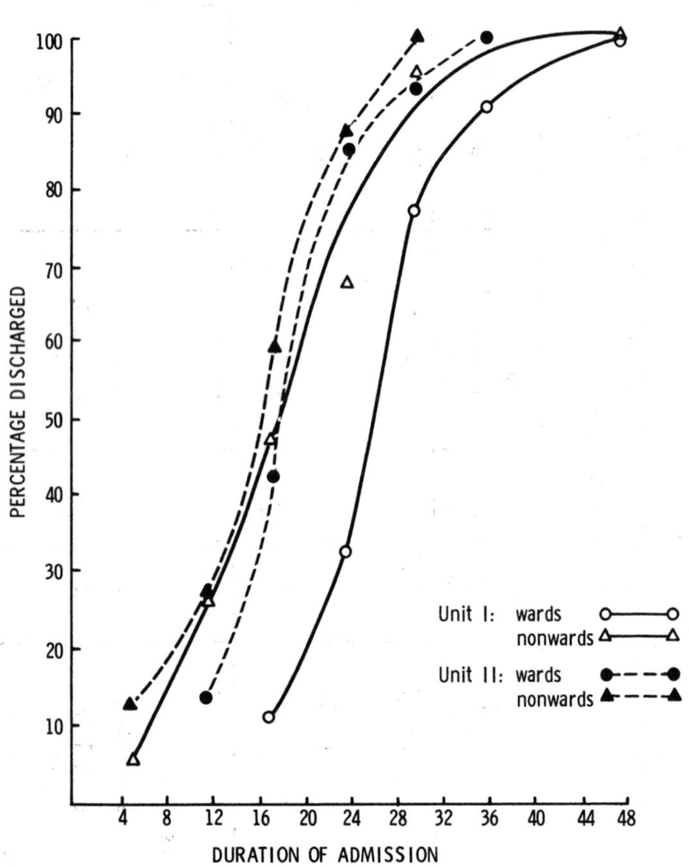

Figure II

CUMULATIVE DISCHARGE FREQUENCY CURVES, WARDS AND NONWARDS 1965-1968

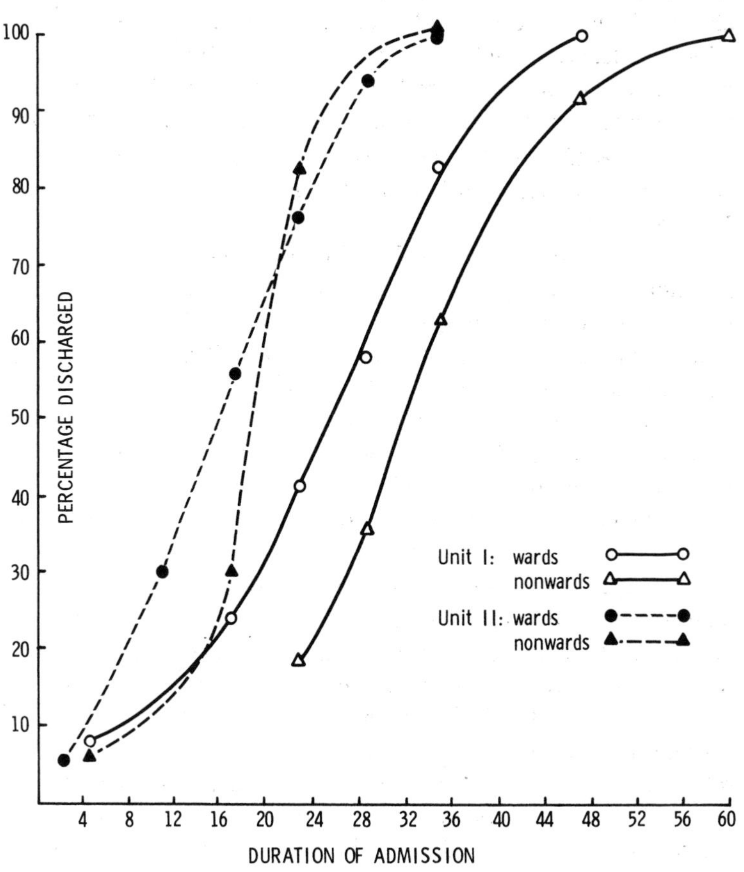

admission and discharge (Table V and VII respectively) cannot be compared since the samples were different.

Discussion

In spite of a random admission procedure to two identically staffed residential units employing the same treatment modality, very considerable differences in length of stay were demonstrated, particularly for non-wards, over an eight year time span. Prior to the study it had been believed by unit staff that difficulty in obtaining foster homes was most often responsible for delayed discharge. Duration of admission of wards remained, in fact, remarkably constant over the two time periods although longer on Unit I for 1961-1964 and 1965-1968 (7.18 and 8.40 months, respectively, Table I). There was a considerable increase in length of stay for non-wards in 1965-1968 on Unit I.

These results showed that the longer admission of wards and non-wards on Unit I could not be explained by their being more disturbed at admission. The random admission procedure made this very unlikely. Furthermore the C. P. I. ratings on sub-samples which included most subjects in the second time period demonstrated, as expected, that the boys were comparably disturbed. A second possible explanation, that children were not discharged from Unit I until they had achieved a higher level of adjustment was not supported by the discharge C. P. I. ratings.

Age at admission was shown to influence length of stay. These programs were designed for latency aged children although maturity was more important than age in determining when a child's needs could no longer be met. It is apparent that the older a child at admission the more probable his early discharge. The results showed that this was due not to a relationship between age at admission and degree of disturbance but rather attributable to the arrival of adolescence after a briefer stay in those children who were older when admitted. The absence of a significant correlation between age at admission and discharge adjustment is particularly interesting and suggests that younger children were maintained on the units longer after reaching their maximum level of adjustment than were older subjects, whose discharge was precipitated by adolescence.

A third possibility was that the longer admission of non-wards on Unit I was due to their families being more disturbed, and requiring more prolonged casework or family therapy. Once again, the random admission procedure made this highly improbable. The availability of family ratings for a comparably sized sample admitted between 1970 and 1972 showed no evidence that the social workers on Unit I regarded these families as more disturbed than those on Unit II.

The total findings of this study indicated that children were maintained longer on Unit I, having reached their maximum level of adjustment, than on Unit II. Additional data made it possible to test this hypothesis. Six-weekly C. P. I. raings were available throughout admission for 12 of the subjects admitted to Units I and II between 1963 and 1967 who responded satisfactorily to treatment. The criterion for such a response was a discharge Factor I score of 157 or over, this being the cut-off value best predicting follow-up status (7, 9). The years of admission were comparable for the six subjects admitted to each unit. It was not possible to exactly match numbers of wards and non-wards on each unit; there were two wards and four non-wards on Unit I, four wards and two non-wards on Unit II.

It was decided a priori to determine the earliest that sustained improvement occurred for each subject, characterised by at least three of four consecutive Factor I ratings reaching 157 or more. This would represent a period of at least three consecutive months of high level functioning.

From the findings of this study, it was predicted that on Unit II the interval between the end of such a period and discharge (post-plateau interval) would be less than on Unit I. The interval between admission and the end of this stable period of improvement (pre-plateau interval) permitted a comparison of the rapidity of treatment response on the two units. It was predicted that there would be no significant differences between the units with regard to the pre-plateau interval on the basis of the findings of this study. Results are shown in Table VIII together with the length of stay in weeks, admission and discharge Factor I ratings, t-test values and levels of significance. It is apparent that although admission and discharge ratings were comparable on the two units, there

TABLE V

FAMILY ADJUSTMENT NONWARDS AT ADMISSION
UNITS I AND II 1970-1972

UNIT	I	II
N	13	11
$\bar{X}$	50.41	54.09
s	5.13	5.24
t	1.65 p = >.1	

TABLE VI

AGE AT ADMISSION IN MONTHS FOR SUBJECTS
WITH FAMILY ADJUSTMENT RATINGS
UNITS I AND II 1970-1972

UNIT	I	II
N	13	11
$\bar{X}$	108.77	111.09
s	11.29	18.19
t	0.35 p= >.5	

TABLE VII

FAMILY ADJUSTMENT NONWARDS AT DISCHARGE UNITS I AND II 1970-1972

UNIT	I	II
N	7	6
$\overline{X}$	52.42	53.54
s	4.35	5.04
t	0.94 p = >.2	

was a highly significant difference in mean length of stay which was 23 weeks longer on Unit. I. The findings show that this resulted from a significantly longer post-plateau interval on Unit I and not from a difference in the pre-plateau interval which was almost identical on the two units. Both hypotheses were supported. The two aims of the study were therefore realised: significant unit differences in length of stay were identified, and a number of possible explanations sustained or refuted, by the use of relatively simple rating scales.

These unit differences may have resulted from a number of factors, including a more rapid perception of sustained improvement on Unit II, or greater confidence in the child's continuing capacity to adjust following discharge.

The earliest discharge of children from residential treatment compatible with satisfactory family, school and community adjustment is clearly desirable. There currently exists a lack of data by which to determine the optimum time for discharge. Obvious variables to be considered include the child's level of function, that of his family, and the nature and intensity of available post-discharge services.

TABLE VIII

PRE-PLATEAU AND POST-PLATEAU INTERVALS LENGTH OF STAY AND ADMISSION AND DISCHARGE RATINGS UNITS I AND II

Unit		Length of Admission	Admission Factor I	Pre-Plateau Interval	Post-Plateau Interval	Discharge Factor I
I	$\bar{x}$	106.17	135.00	74.50	31.67	176.67
	s	10.90	10.18	15.28	18.32	10.93
II	$\bar{x}$	83.00	133.17	71.67	11.33	182.17
	s	20.31	10.12	28.81	9.93	9.39
	t	2.2484	0.2855	0.1942	2.1822	0.8533
	p	*<.025	<.40	>.40	*<.05	<.25

levels of significance one-tailed throughout

If residential services are to be used wisely two vital requirements must be met. First, a variety of reliable and valid measures of child and family function must be available to the clinician to provide objective and comparable data to assist in decision making. These must at the same time, be sufficiently simple to be completed and processed as part of the routine operation of a clinical program. Together with length of stay, they would permit a centre to effectively monitor its clinical function. Second, the predictive value of the measures used most be known and whether the length of time that satisfactory functioning is maintained prior to discharge is a significant variable. Follow-up studies are essential relating child and family adjustment to subsequent status.

Finally, a note of caution is in order. While the psychological hazards of prolonged institutionalization are well known, it should not be assumed that brief admission is always preferable to one that is longer. As public money is increasingly devoted to mental health services for children, it is natural and proper that the use of expensive residential facilities should come under intensive scrutiny. In the absence of the necessary measuring instruments and follow-up findings, policy making tends to be based on theoretical assumptions rather than hard data. However appealing the theoretical basis for reducing the length of stay, it is crucial that continuing research be conducted to provide this data. Only then will it be possible to ensure that the duration of residential treatment, which constitutes only one part of a child's total therapeutic program, is as brief as possible.

REFERENCES

1. Manual for the classification of psychiatric diagnoses. The Queen's Printer, Ottawa, 7th revision. (The current revision I. C. D. A. - 8 was not published until after 1961 - 1968 , in 1969.)
2. Group for the Advancement of Psychiatry: Vol. VI, Report #62. Psychopathological disorders in childhood: Theoretical considerations and a proposed classification. pp. 245-249, 1966.
3. Alderton, H. R. *Can. Med. Ass. J.* *100*, 1035, (1969).
4. Alderton, H. R. *Can. Psychiat. Ass. J.* *17*, 291, (1972).
5. Kirk, R. E. Multiple comparison tests. In *Experimental Design: Procedures for the Behavioural Sciences.* Wadsworth Pub. Co. Inc., (1968).
6. Dunn, O. M. *J. Amer. Statist. Ass.* *56*, 52, (1961).
7. Alderton, H. R. and Hoddinott, B. A. *Can. Psychiat. Ass. J.* *13*, 353, (1968).
8. Alderton, H. R. and Hoddinott, B. A. *The Children's Pathology Index.* (Copyright 1971, H. R. Alderton)
9. Alderton, H. R. *Can. Psychiat. Ass. J.* *15*, 289, (1970).
10. Geismar, L. and Ayres, B. Measuring family functioning. A manual on a method of evaluating the social functioning of disorganised families. Family Centred Project. St. Paul, Minn., (1960).
11. Geismar, L., LaSorte, M. and Ayres, B. *Marr. Fam. Liv.* *24*, 51, (1962).
12. Geismar, L. *Fam. Process* *3*, 91, (1964).

MENTAL HEALTH IN CHILDREN, Volume III
Edited by D. V. Siva Sankar

COMPARISON OF PSYCHIATRIC INPATIENT ADOLESCENT DRUG AND NON-DRUG ABUSERS

Valerie Klinge, Habib Vaziri, and Kathleen Lennox

Lafayette Clinic
Detroit, Michigan 48207

Literature in the area of drug abuse has focused primarily on younger, non-institutionalized adults. More recently, however, there have been a number of studies concerned with the adolescent drug abuser (e.g., Klinge and Vaziri (1); Braucht, Brakarsh, Follingstad, and Berry (2)) and with particular subgroups of these adolescents (e. g., Klinge and Vaziri (3); Klinge, Vaziri, and Lennox (4)). To date, however, there have been very few studies comparing those adolescent psychiatric inpatients who have abused drugs with those who have not.

The purpose of the present study was to define those variables which would delineate the drug abusing adolescent inpatient from the inpatient adolescent who did not use drugs. The comparison of these two groups is extremely important at this time since within the last several years the drug abuse statistics, even within our own institution, have implicated not only increasingly younger populations but also increasing numbers of admissions to psychiatric treatment centers for adolescents with drug-related psychopathology. For example, between the years 1966 and 1968 inclusive, we admitted a total of 22 drug-abusing patients whose mean chronological age at admission was 15.73 years; in 1966 only two were admitted, in 1967 six, and in 1968, fourteen. In 1969 alone, however, we admitted 29 drug-abusing patients whose mean age at admission was 15.69 years; in 1970, 45 were admitted with a mean age of 15.58 years, and in 1971, the average age of the 47 abusers admitted was 15.36. These findings, which illustrate both the increasing number of admissions and a concomitant decrease in chronological age, plus the general paucity of literature comparing psychiatrically disturbed adolescents who have and have not abused drugs, have emphasized the need for further research in this area.

The objectives of the current study were threefold:

1. To delineate those variables which might differentiate the abuser from the non-user;
2. To investigate the relationship of abuse to psychopathology;
3. To attempt to determine differential strengths and weaknesses of these two groups which might affect not only prognosis but which might also shed light on defining those particular psychiatrically disturbed adolescents who would abuse drugs.

To reach these objectives, the present research examined psychosocial correlates of drug abuse and compared abusers with non-users who had been institutionalized on a psychiatric inpatient adolescent service.

METHOD

Patient Population:

The adolescent studied in the present research had all been inpatients on the Adolescent Service at the Lafayette Clinic, a State-supported psychiatric facility in downtown Detroit, Michigan. This ward contains at any one time 40 (20 male and 20 female) patients whose average length of stay, at the present time, is approximately two months. The service accommodates patients between the ages of 12 and 18 years from various geographic areas in lower Michigan. (A comprehensive description of the Adolescent Service at Lafayette Clinic is provided by Beckett (5)).

The adolescents reported upon in the present study consisted of 71 drug abusers and 71 non-users, admitted to the Clinic as inpatients between 1966 and 1971, inclusive. The 71 drug-abusers we studied were drawn from the total number (143) of drug-abusers we had admitted between 1966 and 1971 inclusive; this entire population has been described in an earlier paper (1). This group of 143 was divided in half*, leaving 71 drug-abusers in each group. These two groups of 71 abusers each were then matched on a group basis for each of 107 variables (reported on below) in such a way that there was no significant difference between the two groups on any of the variables. The 71 abusers had had major involvement in drugs at the time of their admission here, but in no case was the primary diagnosis drug abuse. In the present study, drug involvement or abuse has been defined as the non-medical use of psycho-toxic drugs for more than 40 times during the year immediately prior to inpatient evaluation at the Clinic. Verification of drug abuse was obtained for each of the 71 abusers by one or more of the following criteria:

1. All patients admitted that they had abused drugs for at least 40 times in the year immediately prior to their evaluation at the clinic.
2. Their urines, when taken, confirmed abuse.
3. The source of referral, i.e., police, social agency, Juvenile Court, etc., confirmed abuse.
4. Many of the drug abuse patients were observed both prior to and at admission onto the service ward to demonstrate many clinical behaviors associated with drug abuse.

Conversely, for none of the 71 non-users were any of the above mentioned criteria met. The 71 abusers were paired with

* During the six months that the study was in progress, we learned that one of the 143 abusers had committed suicide and since we are currently planning a follow-up of our abusers, it seemed most reasonable to omit the data on the patient who suicided.

the 71 non-users, using a matched-subject design on the following variables:

1. Age at admission within three months.
2. Date of admission within three months.
3. Annual family income per dependent within $600 per dependent per year.
4. Sex.
5. Race.
6. Primary diagnosis at admission*

Table I and II below present demographic and diagnostic characteristics of the 142 patients.

Procedure:

The procedure used for defining the psychosocial characteristics of these two groups was to obtain information on their status at admission to the Clinic using a questionnaire format. For patients admitted during the years 1966 through 1970, inclusive, the questionnaires were completed by two trained psychological raters who obtained the data from the medical and psychological case records. For drug abusing adolescents admitted during 1971, the questionnaires were completed by the patient's psychiatric resident(s) on the basis of information obtained directly from the patient, his parents, private physician, and/or psychiatrist(s), and outside agencies. For non-abusing adolescents admitted during 1971, the questionnaires were completed by one of the two psychology raters mentioned above and the information was obtained from the medical and psychological case records.

Reliability between the two psychology raters on each of the 107-item questionnaire yielded phi coefficients indicating a median of 100% agreement with a range from 100% agreement on 74% of the items to 18% agreement on 1 of the items. Reliability between the psychologist and the psychiatric resident was determined by having both raters complete the question-

*Patients were matched on the basis of diagnostic nomenclature and code numbers presented in the *Diagnostic and Statistical Manual of Mental Disorders* (DSM-II), 3rd Edition. See Table II.

TABLE I

DEMOGRAPHIC CHARACTERISTICS OF PATIENTS STUDIED

	ABUSERS N=71	NON-USERS N=71	t VALUE
Chronological age at admission	15 years, 6 months	15 years, 4 months	<1
Sex and Race	40 Male (20 Black) (20 White)	40 Male (20 Black) (20 White)	<1
	31 Female (16 Black) (15 White)	31 Female (16 Black) (15 White)	<1
Annual Income per Dependent	$3,030.	$2,383.	<1
I.Q. Scores*			
Verbal I.Q.	106.1	101.6	t=1.78, n.s.
Performance I.Q.	107.8	98.5	t=3.97, p<.01
Full Scale I.Q.	107.6	99.3	t=3.42, p<.01

* Wechsler Adult Intelligence Scale or Wechsler Intelligence Scale for Children administered, as age appropriate.

TABLE II

REFERRAL AND DIAGNOSTIC DATA

		Abusers N=71	Non-Users N=71
Source of Referral to Clinic:			
Court/Juvenile Authorities		25.3%	4.2%
School		5.6	11.2
Private Doctor/ Psychiatrist		32.3	50.7
Police		4.2	0.0
Parents		19.7	8.4
Community Agency		5.6	9.8
Self		2.8	2.8
Other		4.2	12.6
Diagnosis at Admission:			
Personality Disorders	N=	38	38
Adjustment Reaction to Adolescence	N=	14	14
Neuroses	N=	7	7
Psychoses	N=	4	4
Behavior Disorders of Childhood	N=	3	3
Chronic Brain Syndrome (Mental Retardation)	N=	3	3
Specific Learning Disability	N=	1	1
Feeding Disturbance	N=	1	1

TABLE III

FACTORS 1 - 4

FACTOR 1 - INTELLECTUAL PERFORMANCE

Variables	Beta Loading
Good academic performance in hospital	.780
High verbal I.Q.	.709
High performance I.Q.	.645
Good capacity for organizing, and planning	.619
High motivation for attending school	.569
High academic performance prior to hospitalization	.455
High energy level	.437
Many acting-out behaviors	.382
Relatively good overall personality adjustment prior to hospitalization	.356

FACTOR 2 - OVERT PSYCHOTIC SYMPTOMATOLOGY AT ADMISSION

Variables	Beta Loading
Poor oriented place	.860
Poor oriented time	.847
Poor oriented person	.611
Relatively long duration of (Non-drug related) psychopathology	.400
Auditory hallucinations	.384
Thinking disorder at time of hospitalization	.361

FACTOR 3 - LIVING SITUATION

Variables	Beta Loading
Residing in commune, institution, etc.	.842
Not residing with biological parent(s)	.750
Use of drugs and/or alcohol by father	.480
Lack of contact with true parent(s)	.454
Use of drugs and/or alcohol by mother	.444
Relatively good school attendance prior to hospitalization	.393

FACTOR 4 - PRIOR PATIENT ANXIETY--DEPRESSION AND MATERNAL INSTABILITY

Variables	Beta Loading
High depression prior to hospitalization	.572
Absence of acting-out behavior(s)	.548
Evidence mother is emotionally disturbed	.543
High anxiety prior to hospitalization	.528
Negative maternal relationship with patient	.526
Relatively poor overall personality adjustment prior to hospitalization	.494

naires on a group of 20 patients, 10 abusers and 10 non-users. Their ratings were correlated. The present study includes data on only 73 of the original 107 items. The 34 questions dealing directly with drug abuse (e.g., type of drugs used, frequency, and duration of abuse, method of procurement, etc.) were omitted from the current analysis since these questions were obviously not applicable to the non-users.

All information concerning past and present school-related material such as grades, involvement in school activities, etc., was completed by school personnel at Lafayette Clinic on the basis of the patient's prior school records and current in-hospitalization academic performance. A more detailed description of the questionnaire can be found in Klinge and Vaziri (1).

RESULTS

Data Analysis:

The date were initially analyzed by computing 2 x 2 (male-female x abusers-non-users) analyses of variance on each of the 73 variables. Sex was included as a variable because recent factor analyses (4) computed comparing male and female drug abusing patients had suggested that for females, drug abuse and psychopathology in general were associated with family-related variables; for males, comparable factor analyses had indicated that patient drug abuse and patient pathology emerged as orthogonal to family drug abuse and family psychopathology. These findings had raised the hypothesis that the female abuser's pathology was more reactive to the family situation and hence suggested that when the female separates from the family her pathology will decrease more so than that of the male who separates. Thus, with knowledge of these findings, the factor of sex was included in the analyses of variance comparing abusers with non-users.

In the current study, however, only one significant abuse x sex interaction out of 73 variables obtained ($F=4.823$, $df=1/104$, $p<.05$); this variable indicated that female non-users were significantly more hyperactive behaviorally than were any of the other groups ($p<.05$ in each comparison).

There were, however, several significant main effects for

sex, regardless of abuse of non-use of drugs. Females presented themselves as significantly ($F=10.469$, $df=1/129$, $p < .01$) more depressed at admission than males, and also acted out more sexually than did males ($F=6.630$, $df=1/131$, $p < .01$). Females also tended ($F=3.432$, $df=1/119$, $p < .10$) to perform better academically in the hospital and tended ($F=3.226$, $df=1/119$, $p < .10$) to have mothers who were more emotionally unstable than mothers of males. No other main effects of sex or interactions of sex with drug abuse were statistically significant. On the basis of these findings, male-female data were combined, and all further data analyses compared only drug abusers with non-users.

Factor Analysis:

Next, 49 variables derived from the original 73 were factored by principal axis solution (6). Variables which had shown no variability within either of the two groups and/or which correlated highly ($r > +.85$) with other variables were deleted. Using principal axis solution the number of factors which accounted for no more than 98% of the total variance were retained and orthogonally rotated to terminal solution. From the 49 variables, nine factors emerged, accounting for 94.22% of the total variance. On each of these nine factors, factor scores for each patient were computed using the beta weights for all 49 variables. These nine factors were then named using variables with beta weights greater than .350 (see Tables III and IV).

Intellectual Performance:

Note (from Table III) that Factor I, labeled 'Intellectual performance', accounts for 21.15% of the total variance. Individual factor scores for abusers and non-users were then derived separately on this factor, and an analysis of variance was computed which indicated no significant difference between abusers and non-users on 'Intellectual performance'. Although it is of statistical legitimacy to compare the groups on individual variables when the factor as a whole does not significantly differentiate the groups, it can be of clinical interest to inspect

TABLE IV

FACTORS 5 - 9

FACTOR 5 - PATIENT ANXIETY - DEPRESSION AT HOSPITALIZATION

Variables	Beta Loading
Depression at hospitalization	.579
Anxiety at hospitalization	.546
No significant record of undesirable (illegal) activities	.525
Poor school attendance prior to hospitalization	.389
Relatively little use of drugs and/or alcohol by mother	.376
Seclusive behavior at time of hospitalization	.359

FACTOR 6 - SIBLING/PATERNAL PATHOLOGY

Variables	Beta Loading
Sibling use of drugs and/or alcohol	.739
Sibling record of undesirable (illegal) activities	.573
Sibling psychiatric symptomatology	.514
Number of siblings	.475
Paternal negative relationship with patient	.374

FACTOR 7 - DEVELOPMENTAL PATHOLOGY

Variables	Beta Loading
Evidence of thinking disorder prior to hospitalization	.678
Previous psychiatric care	.599
Developmental retardation (i.e., not reaching developmental milestones within appropriate time ranges).	.512
Thinking disorder at time of hospitalization	.398
Not living with parents during childhood	.396

FACTOR 8 - SOCIAL INTERACTION

Variables	Beta Loading
Poor peer relationships	.836
Poor involvement in age-appropriate social activities	.826
Lethargy	.574
Negative relationship of father with patient	.409

FACTOR 9 - COVERT PSYCHOPATHOLOGY AT ADMISSION

Variables	Beta Loading
Visual hallucinations	.696
Auditory hallucinations	.653
Negative relationship of father with patient	.531
Thinking disorder at time of hospitalization	.379

more closely those variables which do separate the two patient groups, especially since these are the variables with high beta weights. For example, looking at the variable of the Wechsler score, abusers had significantly higher ($F=11.687$, $df=1/120$, $p < .01$) Full Scale I.Q.s than did non-users. (Table I presented above gives exact Verbal, Performance, and Full Scale I.Q.s for both groups.) Again on academic performance within the hospital, there is a significant difference between abusers and non-users ($F=24.079$, $df=1/119$, $p<.001$). The Clinic school teachers rated the non-users as "average" in academic performance while the abusers were rated as "above average". (At the time of the teachers' ratings of the youngsters' hospital academic achievement, they were naive as to the patient I.Q. scores and past academic records.) Correlations computed between Full Scale I.Q. and academic performance in the hospital were $r = +.558$ for abusers and $r = +.549$ for non-users, correlations of almost identical magnitude, suggesting that both patient groups were performing academically within the hospital on levels commensurate with their I.Q. scores, also obtained in the hospital.

Another variable which loaded on the Intellectual performance factor was 'capacity for organizing, planning and assuming leadership'; on this variable, too, the abusers were rated as being significantly better ($F=7.001$, $df=1/108$, $p<.01$). The correlations between this variable, I.Q., and academic performance were of almost identical positive and significant magnitudes for both abusers and non-users. These findings add support to the validity of the questionnaire since these three particular variables were obtained from three independent sources: the psychology rater(s), the school teacher(s), and the psychology I.Q. examiner(s). Nonetheless, despite the significant differences between the two patient groups on the individual variables of I.Q., hospital academic achievement, and capacity for organizing and planning, the factor 'Intellectual performance', taken as a whole, did not significantly differentiate the abusers from the non-users.

Overt Psychotic Symptomatology:

Factor 2 which emerged from the analysis accounts for 14.56% of the total variance and has been labeled 'Overt psychotic symptomatology at admission'. Individual factor scores computed for abusers and non-abusers were compared using an analysis of variance which proved to be statistically significant ($F=6.075$, $df=1/140$, $p<.01$). The significant difference on this factor between the two groups confirmed that at admission the drug abusers were significantly better oriented for person, place and time than the non-users. Further, the duration of non-drug-related psychotic symptomatology was less for the abusers than the non-users. Thus, from this factor we can conclude that at admission the non-user displayed significantly more overt psychotic and psychotic-like symptomatology than did the drug abuser. In spite of this finding the non-users were given *better* prognoses than the abusers. Thirty-eight percent of the abusers were given 'poor' prognoses, 36% were given 'fair' prognoses, and 26% were given 'good' prognoses. For the non-users, 27% were given 'poor', 25% 'fair' and 48% were given 'good' prognoses. This finding is particularly interesting in view of the patients' having been matched on primary diagnosis, a factor which should certainly have implications for prognosis.

Living Situations:

Factor 3, which has been labeled "Living situation", accounts for 12.94% of the entire variance (see Table III). Individual factor scores computed for abusers and non-users on this factor, when compared by analysis of variance, indicated a significant difference between the two groups ($F=15.559$, $df=1/140$, $p<.01$). Analysis of the individual variables with high beta loadings on this factor indicated that a significantly greater number of non-users lived with their biological families than did drug abusers. Drug abusers reported to have lived in many more and varied situations, such as with relatives, in communes, with roommates, etc. than had the non-users. Further, with increasing chronological age of the patient significantly more drug abusers had left the family home than had non-users. Of all those patients who had remained in the home situation, a significantly higher percentage of non-users had both true (biological) parents present than had the drug abusers ($t=65.354$, $df=71$, $p < .001$). Also loading on the Living situation factor with significant beta weights are the variables of use of drugs and/or alcohol by mothers and fathers of drug abusers to a greater extent than substance abuse by the parents of non-users. Thus, this factor, when broken down, reveals that it is not only the physical presence of parental figures which plays an important part in whether or not the psychiatrically disturbed adolescent abuses drugs, but also whether or not the parental figures themselves abuse drugs and/or alcohol.

Prior Patient Anxiety-Depression and Maternal Instability:

Factor 4, accounting for 11.21% of the total variance has been labeled 'Prior patient anxiety-depression and maternal instability.' Factor scores were computed for abusers and non-users and compared by analysis of variance. This analysis showed a significant ($F=6.325$, $df=1/140$, $p<.01$) between the two patient groups. Closer analysis of those individual variables with highest beta loadings on this factor suggests that it is the non-users who, prior to hospitalization, were more depressed, had demonstrated fewer acting-out behaviors, had had more mothers who had evidenced mild to moderate emotional disorders than the abusers, show more anxiety and, generally, have reported to have had a poorer overall personality adjustment prior to hospitalization. Relatively speaking, then, again on this factor, the abusers appear to have suffered less anxiety, less depression and less maternal emotional instability than had the non-users.

Patient Anxiety-Depression and Seclusive Behavior at Hospitalization:

Factor 5, which accounts for 8.60% of the variance, has been labeled 'Patient anxiety-depression and seclusive behavior at hospitalization'. This factor did not significantly differentiate the two patient groups ($F < 1$). Again, however, we more closely inspected the variables with high beta weights loading on this factor. Analyses of variance computed on these individual variables indicated that at the time of hospital admission the non-users were significantly more depressed($F=5.204, df=1/129$ $p<.05$), more anxious ($F=43.471, df=1/133, p<.001$) and more withdrawn and seclusive ($F=45.939$, $df=1/126, p<.001$) than the abusers. The non-users also had a tendency ($F=2.773$, $df=1/84$, $p < .10$) to have had poorer school attendance immediately prior to hospitalization, had a tendency ($F=3.249$, $df=1/70$, $p < .10$) to have fewer mothers who used drugs and/or alcohol and had significantly fewer records of undesirable (illegal) behaviors ($F=5.905$, $df=1/130$, $p < .05$). Thus again, the non-users at hospitalization appear to be in considerably more internal distress than the drug abusers. This internal distress is associated with avoiding school and, perhaps, avoiding social activities which might have led them to acquire records (e.g., police, court, etc.) of undesirable, i.e., illegal, behaviors.

Sibling/Parental Pathology:

Factor 6, accounting for 7.49% of the variance, describes the pathology within the families of both groups of patients. Individual factor scores computed on both groups were subjected to an analysis of variance which proved that the two groups were significantly different ($F=21.146$, $df=1/140$, $p < .01$). The drug abusers had had more experience with siblings who had more records of undesirable activities (e.g., from the courts, juvenile correctional facilities, police records, etc.). Further, the abusers themselves showed more psychiatric symptomatology than the non-users' sibs and more often had fathers who had had negative relationships with them. However, this factor must be looked upon with some suspicion because the drug abusers had significantly more siblings than had the non-users. The average number of siblings in the drug abuse group was 4.13, while the average number of sibs in the non-users was 2.39 ($F=24.610$, $df=1/117$, $p<.001$). The very fact that the abusers had more sibs than the non-users could well explain why there was more pathology, acting-out, drug abuse, etc., among siblings in the drug abuse group than in the non-use group. We cannot account for the fact that abusers came from larger families than the non-users.

Developmental Pathology:

'Developmental pathology', Factor 7, accounts for 7.13% of the variance. An analysis of variance computed on the individual variable scores on this factor yielded an insignificant F value, indicating that the two patient groups were not significantly different in their historical-developmental pathology. When the variable of developmental retardation was analyzed separately for male and female abusers and non-users, the means indicated no significant differences among any of these four groups. Group means were all in the 'normal' range. Thus it appears that developmental factors, at least as measured by the variables we considered, do not contribute to a later differentiation of abusers from non-users.

Patient's Social Interaction:

This factor, Factor 8, entitled 'Patient's Social Interaction', while accounting for only 5.64% of the total variance, is perhaps one of the clearest factors to emerge from the analysis. This social interaction factor did distinguish the drug abusers from the non-users significantly ($F=7.900$, $df=1/140$, $p < .01$) and indicated that generally the non-users have had fewer peer relationships both prior to and at hospitalization, lesser involvement in age-appropriate social activities, more seclusive behaviors at hospitalization, less energy for socialization, and had, relatively speaking, more negative relationships with their fathers. The abusers' relatively superior social interactional skills were not, however, always socially acceptable, in that it was this group, the drug abusers, who had significantly more records of undesirable, e.g., illegal, activities than had the non-users ($F=5.905$, $df=1/130$, $p < .05$). The abusers' high record of illegal activities has been discussed in two earlier papers (1, 4) and might best be accounted for by the abusers' needs to steal money and/or merchandise to pay for their drugs. As Table II indicates, a greater percentage of the drug abusers' sources of referral were from agencies such as the courts, police, juvenile authorities, etc.

Covert Psychopathology at Admission:

The last factor to emerge, accounting for 5.50% of the variance, appears to be the least clearly interpretable of any of the 9 factors. Only four variables load with beta weights above .350 on this factor and they are: visual hallucinations, auditory hallucinations, negative father-patient relationships and thinking disorders at the time of hospitalization. Looking at each of these four variables individually, the tendency in each case is that the non-users are the ones with more frequent visual and auditory hallucinations, a higher percentage of thinking disorders at hospitalization, and more negative relationships with their fathers. This factor, despite the fact that only four variables load on it with high beta weights does significantly differentiate the abusers from the non-users ($F=43.722$, $df=1/140$, $p<.001$).

In summary, our results have indicated that of the 9 independent factors which emerged from the factor analysis, 6 did statistically differentiate the psychiatrically disturbed adolescent abusers from the non-users. Those factors concerned with symptomatologies prior to and present at admission (factors 2, 4, 8, and 9) suggest that while both groups are psychiatrically disturbed, it is the non-users who are in more internal distress and have fewer adaptive social interactions than the abusers. The other two factors which differentiated these two groups of psychiatric adolescents (factors 3 and 6) indicate that it is family-related pathology and not only internalized psychiatric symptomatology which is associated with drug abuse.

DISCUSSION

The patients we studied in the present research were paired on primary diagnosis, using a matched-subject design. The diagnostic nomenclature we employed considered only type or quality of the disorder, but no effort was made to match the patients on severity or intensity of the problem(s). Possibly it was because of this that the non-users, at least on the variables considered, presented worse psychiatric symptomatological pictures than did the abusers. It could be that the drug abusers we studied had less severe non-drug related psychiatric symptomatology than the non-users, even though the patients were matched on the type of disorder, e.g., primary diagnosis.

It is also possible that our staff, in admitting the abusers, were more responsive to the patient's abuse of drugs than to their psychiatric symptomatologies. This hypothesis seems particularly plausible in view of our finding that prior to hospitalization it was the abusers who had a better overall personality adjustment. If it is the case, i.e., that our staff was more reactive to abuse than to psychiatric symptomatology per se, then it is not so ironic that despite the fact that the two groups were matched on a subject-by subject basis for primary diagnosis, and despite the fact that the non-users appeared more psychiatrically disturbed than the abusers, that it was the non-users who were given *better* prognoses than the abusers.

A second possible explanation for our finding that the abusers appeared to be in less internal distress is that drug abuse might mask psychopathology. In other words, it is possible that our abusers did suffer the same severity of psychopathology as did the non-users but that it was masked by drug abuse. For example, while the drug abusers appeared to be more socially oriented (e.g., being involved in more school and social activities, having more friends, etc.), it is possible that this apparent independence represented a pseudo-sophistication or maturation rather than a productive, adaptive development. Our results indicated that the abusers had a more unstable living and family situation that the non-users and it is possible that the abusers' social interaction and involvement with peers suffered the same lack of insensity and stability (although we did not measure this dimension).

A third possibility for the drug abusers appearing to be in less internal distress is that the staff, in observing and rating these patients attributed pathology to the use of drugs rather than to non-drug related psychiatric symptomatology, and dismissed the pathology as being primarily drug reactive.

It is our hope that our current follow-up study on both these groups of disturbed adolescents will clarify these possible explanations and provide us with a more comprehensive method of admitting, diagnosing, and treating the psychiatrically disturbed adolescent.

ACKNOWLEDGEMENT

The authors gratefully acknowledge the assistance of Dr. Phillip M. Rennick, Chief Psychologist, Lafayette Clinic, for his assistance in preparation of this manuscript.

REFERENCES

1. Klinge, V. and Vaziri, H. Characteristics of drug abusers in an adolescent in-patient psychiatric facility. In press. *Dis. Nerv. Syst.,* (1973).
2. Braucht, G. N., Brakarsh, D., Follingstad, D.andBerry, K.L. Deviant drug use in adolescence.*Psych.Bull. 79,* 92,(1973).
3. Klinge, V. and Vaziri, H. EEG abnormalities in adolescent drug abusers. In press. *Adolescence,* (1973).
4. Klinge, V., Vaziri, H. and Lennox, K. Comparison of psychiatric in-patient male and female adolescent drug abusers. *Intern. J. of Addictions. 11* (2), 309, (1976).
5. Beckett, P. G. *Adolescents out of step: Their treatment in a psychiatric hospital.* Wayne State University Press, Detroit, Mich., (1965).
6. Wilt, H. S. and Ralston, A. *Mathematical methods for digital computers.* John Wiley and Sons, New York pp. 204, (1960).

MENTAL HEALTH IN CHILDREN, Volume III
Edited By D. V. Siva Sankar

CHILDHOOD AND ADOLESCENT REMISSIONS AND ADULT ADJUSTMENT IN SHOCK TREATED SCHIZOPHRENIC CHILDREN

Lauretta Bender

New York State Psychiatric Institute
New York, N.Y. 10032

Between 1935 and 1952 over 600 children were diagnosed schizophrenic at Bellevue Psychiatric Hospital of New York City (1). Several follow-up studies have been reported on these children (2-6). Between 1938 and 1942, 43 children age six to 14 years, received Metrazol convulsive therapy (MeCT) (7,8). After 1942 electric convulsive therapy (ECT) was used. Over 500 children received ECT between 1942 and 1956.

PREVIOUS FOLLOW-UP STUDIES

In 1947 a five year evaluation (9) of 98 children who had received ECT showed that about half were home and half were in institutions but that there was considerable movement between home and institutions, especially for the middle third. It was concluded that the essential schizophrenic process did not appear to be modified, but the child appeared to be better able to cope with anxiety and secondary behavior disorder. The IQ remained remarkably stable, the EEG showed no lasting effects and tended to maturate normally and in some cases even better than would be anticipated from age alone. Children appeared to be better able to tolerate convulsive therapy than adults, with minimal complications and a positive post-shock modification of behavior and clinical course.

Many of the children were in adolescence at the time of follow-up, and, as we will see later, this a time of difficult evaluation of treatment since many untreated cases remit spontaneously at this time.

In 1950-51 a five to 15 year follow-up study (6) was made on 313 children including 43 treated with MeCT, 100 treated with ECT, 50 schizophrenic children without convulsive therapy and 120 children on the Bellevue children's ward at the same time who were not diagnosed schizophrenic. The diagnosis was confirmed in 89% of the schizophrenic patients, and the anticipated one-third chronic-hospital-adjusted, one-third community-adjusted and one-third in between, was also confirmed for the schizophrenic patients who received convulsive therapy. Only two of the 50 untreated schizophrenic patients could be located in the community, probably due in part to the uncooperative families who in some cases refused treatment for the patient in the hospital. However, one fourth of the children observed at Bellevue at the same time but not diagnosed schizophrenic, were subsequently diagnosed schizophrenic after they left Bellevue for other agency of hospital care.

A 25-year follow-up (10) on 25 boys who had received MeCT showed that a symptomatic relief of behavior disorders was obtained in chronic autistic children, a good remission which often persisted was obtained by prepubescent boys with an acute schizophrenic psychosis and a relapsing remission was obtained by boys treated shortly after an onset of a puberty episode.

In 1968 (11) I reviewed the world literature on follow-up studies of childhood schizophrenia and allied conditions and found 12 reports with a total of 759 cases of which 229 or 31.5%

---

* Dr. Bender is Professor of Clinical Psychiatry, College of Physicians and Surgeons, Columbia University, and Clinical Professor, University of Maryland School of Medicine, 423 Ben Oaks Drive West, Severna Park MD 21146

were reported to be making an adequate or normal adult social adjustment. This is a little less than one third.

In 1969 before the Society of Biological Psychiatry, I reported (4) on the life course of 100 individuals recognized as schizophrenic in childhood at Bellevue hospital from 1935 to 1952. They were 2½ to 13 years of age on their first admission to the hospital and were 22 to 46 years of age, if alive, on follow-up in 1968. The diagnosis of schizophrenia was confirmed in 94 in adulthood. It was shown that childhood schizophrenia was an early onset of a life time of schizophrenia of every possible type. Thirty-six or a little better than one third have been able to make some kind of social adjustment as adults in the community while 64 have made a chronic institutional adjustment, of whom eight have died.

CASE MATERIAL FOR THIS REPORT

In 1971 before the Society of Biological Psychiatry a preliminary report was made of the adult adjustment of the shock treated children in this series. (Unpublished). Since these 100 cases included only 18 who had no convulsive treatment (NoCT) six more cases from the same period who had NoCT and had recent follow ups were added, making 106 cases.

The presently discussed 106 cases consists of 84 boys and 22 girls, a ratio of one to four. Of this total group 40 or 37.7% have been in social adjustment in the community since adulthood at least and 66 or 62.3% have been chronically institutionalized.

It should be emphasized that these patients had all been subjected to very intensive treatment programs at Bellevue in addition to the convulsive therapy. Since then many of them have had every treatment modality that has been developed in the last 30 years whether in an institution or in the community. In some cases this included courses of convulsive therapy in adolescence and adulthood and pharmacotherapy in the last 20 years.

Kalinowsky (12) reported that convulsive therapy in adult patients increased the remission rate from the spontaneous rate of 20% to 25% to that of 40% to 50%, or doubled it. Chronicity was found to be the most important unfavorable

TABLE I

Remissions associated with No Convulsive Treatment (NoCT), Metrazol Convulsive Treatment (MeCT) and Electric Convulsive Treatment (ECT) given in childhood to 106 schizophrenic patients.

TREAT-MENT	*BOYS*			*GIRLS*			*TOTAL*		
	N	R	P	N	R	P	N	R	P
NoCT	16	8	.500	6	5	.833	22	13	.590
MeCT	24	21	.875	1	1	1.000	25	22	.880
ECT	44	28	.636	15	9	.600	59	37	.627
Total	84	57	.679	22	15	.682	106	72	.679

N - number of patients
R - number of remissions
P - proportion of remissions to number of patients

Tests for statistical significance:
NoCT versus MeCT Boys t = 2.60
NoCT versus MeCT Total t = 2.47
ECT versus MeCT Total t = 2.32

The remainder of the comparisons failed to exceed the t value of 1.96 required for significance beyond the .05 level.

TABLE II

Number of adults who achieved Social Adjustment in comparison to Chronic Institutional Adjustment after having had No Convulsive Treatment (NoCT), Metrazol Convulsive Treatment (MeCT) or Electric Convulsive Treatment (ECT) in childhood.

TREAT-MENT	*BOYS*			*GIRLS*			*TOTAL*		
	N	SA	P	N	SA	P	N	SA	P
NoCT	16	6	.375	6	2	.333	22	8	.364
MeCT	24	13	.540	1	0	0.0	25	13	.520
ECT	44	18	.409	15	1	.667	59	19	.322
Total	84	37	.443	22	3	.136	106	40	.377

N - number of patients
SA - social adjustment
P - proportion of patients that achieved social adjustment

None of the tests done between proportions relieved a significant difference.

factor. If treatment was given within 1½ years of onset of symptoms or psychotic episode, the remission rate was higher even to 80%. So far, however, relapses were reported to occur so that the final outcome was not better in treated than untreated adults, although it was emphasized that the treated patients spent more of their life out of hospitals in remissions than the untreated.

DIFFERENCES BETWEEN BOYS AND GIRLS

There is a difference in the incidence of childhood schizophrenia between boys and girls which has been well documented (13,14,15,16). It is generally reported that there are two to four times as many boys as girls who decompensate with schizophrenia before puberty. This relationship is reversed after puberty. In this series the ratio is four boys to one girl. There is also a difference in the course of schizophrenia between the two sexes which I have discussed elsewhere (17). There is also a difference in the outcome as seen in this study where 37 or 44% of the 84 boys made an adult social adjustment while only three or 13% of the 22 girls made an adult social adjustment (Table II). Two of these girls had NoCT and the third girl was one of 13 girls who received ECT. One girl had MeCT followed by a good remission from eight to 17 years of age but has been chronically ill in a hospital since then. Kalinowsky (12) claims no difference between the sexes of adults in their response to shock treatment. This does not seem to have been true of the children treated at Bellevue.

It was one of the unexpected observations made in our follow-up studies of prepuberty children with schizophrenia that remissions occurred in some of the boys at pubery (from 10¼ years) and in girls earlier in latency (from eight or even six years). (See Table I). The remissions in both often lasted well into adolescence followed by recurrences with pseudoneurotic or pseudopsychopathic features (2, 18) or typical schizophrenic psychotic episodes in early adulthood. In some cases the remissions continued with ambulatory states or social adjustment into adulthood.

BOYS

In this series of 106 children of whom 84 were boys, 16 boys had no convulsive treatment (NoCT) of whom eight or one-half had spontaneous remissions on leaving Bellevue, four staying out of the hospital in social adjustment to the present, and four remaining in remission six months to seven years but returning to a hospital in a recurrence at 15 to 18 years of age. Two of these remained in chronic care making a total of ten of 16 NoCT boys who became chronic. Two left the hospital again in their twenties for community adjustment following pharmacotherapy making six of the ten who are socially adjusted.

Twenty-four boys received MeCT at ages 6-2 to 14-3 years. Twenty-one of these or 87.5% had remissions in puberty following treatment in or near puberty (Table I). But 11 of these had an insufficient remission to make satisfactory adjustment at home or school and returned soon to a hospital for chronic care. Ten had good remissions following MeCT at ages 9-11 to 13-9 years lasting from four months to six years and two continued into adult social adjustment.

Five boys who received MeCT after the onset of puberty (12-7 to 14-3 years) did not remit and were subsequently given insulin coma treatment and still did not respond and have been chronically incapacitated since.

Four boys who received MeCT from age 8-1 to 13-6 years all with a childhood onset (not autistic from infancy) had remissions delayed two to four years after treatment. All four developed pseudopsychopathic defenses and remained in social adjustment, but with considerable turmoil in the community. Their mean IQ was 84. Of course the treatment may not have been the effective agent for the remission in these cases.

Finally 13 or 54% of the 24 boys who received MeCT became socially adjusted as adults (Table II) while 21 or 87.5% had remissions in puberty following the MeCT. This is better than the social adjustment and puberty remission rate of non-shock treated children. It also shows that nine or 46% of the boys who remitted following MeCT subsequently relapsed. The number of the NoCT boys is not enough for statistical validation. The MeCT seems to have facilitated remissions in cases where the onset was not with early autistic development, where the intelligence was adequate and when the treatment was given near to or early in puberty and within a year or so of onset of symptoms or of an acute episode.

Forty-four boys had ECT but at a younger age (2-10 to 11-10 years mean age 7-10 years) than the boys who received MeCT (mean age 10-7 years). Twenty-eight or 63.6% responded directly to treatment, or seemed to, with remissions (Table I). This is compared to 50% remissions in the NoCT boys and 87.5% in the MeCT boys. All of the boys who remitted with ECT had a normal or better intelligence. All but one subsequently obtained an adult social adjustment. Finally a total of 18 or 41% of the boys treated with ECT have attained adult social adjustment (Table II). Ten or 35.7% of the 28 ECT boys who remitted subsequently relapsed. Sixteen or 36% did not respond sufficiently to leave the hospital nor did they have a later puberty or adolescent remission which had occurred in about half the boys with NoCT or MeCT. The majority of these unresponsive ECT boys were autistic in infancy and were untestable on standard psychometric tests or had very low IQ's. Six as adults were able to leave the hospital and become socially adjusted at a dependent level mostly after treatment with the tranquilizing drugs. These six also had higher IQ's.

GIRLS

Three of the 22 girls attained a social adjustment after 20 years of age apparently as a result of the program of tranquilizing pharmacotherapy and socialization available in the New York State Hospitals in the 1950's. Two had received NoCT and one MeCT. Fifteen girls, or 68.2% of the total of 22 girls had remissions starting eight to 11 years of age and lasting four to eight years. Five of the six girls with NoCT and one of the two with MeCT and nine of the 15 girls with ECT had remissions. All relapsed and returned to a hospital at 14 to 17 years of age. Failure to respond to treatment or to remit spontaneously in these girls as in the boys was associated with chronic autism, organicity and low IQ's.

DISCUSSION

Children diagnosed as schizophrenic at Bellevue, 1935 to 1952, tended to run the following courses. Many who were autistic from infancy and also had organic factors and did not develop adequate language or intellectual functioning tended to run a chronic course. Secondary behavior disorders such as inadequate eating habits, poor sleeping patterns, denuding, compulsive masturbation and failure in toilet training usually responded to varying degrees to a comprehensive treatment program including convulsive therapy making them more manageable in the institution. The chronic course was not changed, however. A few who evolved from their autism early with some speech and better intelligence had a somewhat better prognosis but this did not appear to have been affected by convulsive therapy.

Other children who had a more acute onset of schizophrenia following a more or less normal early development and with a childhood or puberty psychosis showed a more varied developmental course and response to a comprehensive treatment program which included convulsive therapy.

Spontaneous remissions with NoCT occurred in 50% of the boys at puberty or early adolescence (10¼ to 14 years) and in five of the six girls in latency through early adolescence (8½ to 14 years). Relapses occurred, however, in late adolescence or early adulthood so that only 37.7% of the total 106 cases attained an adult social adjustment.

Convulsive treatment as a part of a total treatment program appears to have facilitated remissions at least in the boys, of whom 87½% responded with remissions after MeCT and 63½% after ECT. Of the 15 girls who had ECT, 60% responded with a remission. Convulsive therapy appeared to be more effective if given within a year of onset of symptoms or recurring episodes and if given about the time of puberty in boys and in latency in girls. Delayed remissions which occur in puberty or adolescence when the treatment was given earlier may not have been the result of the convulsive therapy since there is a natural history of such remissions in a considerable number of patients.

Relapses occurred. The final figure for adult social adjustment in boys was 54% following MeCT and 41% following ECT which was better than the 37½ following NoCT or the 31½% predicted in the literature (11).

Estimation for statistical validity (Table I) shows that MeCT was better than NoCT or ECT in boys and since boys comprise 80% of the total cases, the same holds true for the total number.

There was a positive trend for MeCT to be better than NoCT in terms of social adjustment in adulthood of males and ECT to be better in terms of both remissions and adult social adjustment for both males and females, but the trend was not statistically significant (Table I and II).

CONCLUSIONS

It was the impression of the staff on the children's service at Bellevue from 1935 to 1952, that there was an improvement in many of the children receiving convulsive therapy both electric and Metrazol and that the remission rate in both girls and boys was greater so that more children could be out of the hospital receiving education and socializing experiences during latency (in girls) and adolescence in both boys and girls. The final outcome in terms of an adult social adjustment shows a positive trend towards a greater number of such adjustments from the convulsive treated children but this proved not to be statistically significant.

MeCT seems to have been more effective in producing remissions especially in boys during puberty and early adolescence.

Poor results were obtained in children, especially girls, where the onset of schizophrenia was with autism in infancy, associated with organic features and with a low or untestable IQ and where language development was inadequate.

I wish to give credit to Peter Schilder, Ph.D. M.D. for the statistical analysis and preparation of the two tables.

References

1. Bender, L. *Psychiat. Quart.* *27,* 663, (1953).
2. Bender, L. *Amer. J. Orthopsychiat.* *29,* 491, (1959).
3. Bender, L. *Hosp. Community Psychiat.* *20,* 230, (1969).
4. Bender, L. *Biol. Psychiat.* *2,* 165, (1970).
5. Bender, L. *Amer. J. Psychiat.* *30,* 783, (1973).
6. Bender, L., Freedman, A. M., Grugett, A. E. and Helme, W. *Trans. Amer. Neurol. Ass.* *77,* 67, (1952).
7. Cottington, F. *Amer. J. Psychiat.* *98,* 397, (1941).
8. Cottington, F. *Nerv. Child* *1,* 172, (1942).
9. Bender, L. *Trans. Amer. Neurol. Ass.* *72,* 165, (1947).
10. Bender, L. A twenty-five year view of therapeutic results. In *Evaluation of Psychiatric Treatment.* Edited by Hoch, P. and Zubin, J. Grune and Stratton, New York, pp. 129, (1964).
11. Bender, L. Discussion of "Prognosis of infantile psychosis and neurosis." In *Proceedings of the Fourth World Congress of Psychiatry, Madrid,* Edited by Lopez Ibor, J.J. Excerpta Medica Foundation, Amsterdam, pp. 124, (1967).
12. Kalinowsky, L. B. Effects of somatic treatment on the clinical course, psychopathological and pathophysiological research in schizophrenia. In *Psychopathology of Schizophrenia.* Edited by Hoch, P. and Zubin, J. Grune and Stratton, New York, pp. 412-424.
13. Kallman, F. J. and Roth, B. *Amer. J. Psychiat.* *112,* 599, (1956).
14. Kanner, L. and Eisenberg, L. *Amer. J. Orthopsychiat.* *26,* 55, (1956).
15. Kanner, L. Child Psychosis; Initial Studies and New Insights, V. H. Winston and Sons, Washington, D. C., (1973).
16. Szurek, S. A. and Berlin, I. N. *Clinical Studies in Childhood Psychoses.* Brunner/Mazel, New York, (1973).
17. Bender, L. *Amer. J. Orthopsychiat.* *26,* 499, (1956).
18. Bender, L. *Biol. Psychiat.* *3,* 304, (1971).

MENTAL HEALTH IN CHILDREN, Volume III
Edited By D. V. Siva Sankar

A COMPARISON OF FIFTEEN AND FIVE YEAR FOLLOW-UP STUDIES OF CHILDHOOD PSYCHOSIS

Leonard R. Piggott and Clyde B. Simson
Wayne State University

Robert W. Amidon
Northeastern Child Guidance Clinic
Detroit, Michigan

Alexander Lucas
Rochester, Minnesota

This is a comparison of two follow-up studies of children diagnosed as psychotic, who were hospitalized at Lafayette Clinic during the years 1956-1958, (Group A), and during the years 1966-1968, (Group B). The studies were conducted in the years 1971 through 1973. There was a total of twenty patients diagnosed as psychotic during 1956 through 1958. Current information was obtained on sixteen of the twenty patients (80%) in Group A. Information up to 1969 and 1970 respectively was obtained on two other patients. Current information was obtained on fourteen of the fifteen patients (93%) in Group B. Information up to 1971 was obtained on the remaining patient. Thus information was obtained on 90% of the patients in Group A and 100% of the patients in Group B. Total number of followed-up patients was 18 and 15 for Group A and B respectively.

The mean time interval since discharge from Lafayette Clinic for Group A was thirteen years ten months and for

Group B was five years eight months. The average duration of hospitalization for Group A was 11.2 months for Group B was 5.7 months.

The average ages at follow-up were twenty-three and fifteen years for Group A and B respectively. See Table I.

TABLE I

Time Comparisons

	1956-58 group	*1966-68 group*
Mean time from adm.	14 yr. 8 mo.	6 yr. 1 mo.
Mean time from disc.	13 yr. 10 mo.	5 yr. 8 mo.
Mean dur. hosp.	11.2 mo.	5.7 mo.
Mean age at admission	8 yr. 9 mo.	9 yr. 8 mo.
Mean age at follow-up	23 yr. 5 mo.	15 yr. 9 mo.

The two groups were divided on the basis of admission I. Q. scores (untestable, less than 80, more than 80) for the purposes of comparison. See Table II.

The charts of all the patients were reviewed for the presence or absence of the British Working Party Criteria of the Schizophrenic Syndrome. See Table III and IV.

There was a significant difference (p .01) for I. Q. between Group A and Group B in the children with I. Q.'s below 80. See Table II. There were no significant differences between the children with I. Q.'s over 79 for either I. Q. or presence of British Working Party Criteria of the Schizophrenic Syndrome.

TABLE II

Distribution of Study Samples within
Three I.Q. Levels

Admission I.Q. Score	*Group A*		*Group B*	
	N	*Mean I.Q.*	*N*	*Mean I.Q.*
I.Q. greater than 79	8	96.2	9 *	95.6 +
I.Q. less than 80	6	57.6	4	72.5 ++
Untestable	4	----	1	----

+ t = 0.09 p = .92 n.s.

++ t = 4.02 p = .01

* The tenth child in this category was not tested. He was discharged A.M.A. before testing was completed. Records indicate that he was functioning at average levels though there was no formal testing accomplished.

Results: On follow-up, all the Group A untestable children were living in institutions--three in institutions for the mentally retarded and one in an institution for the mentally ill. Their overall adjustment was rated as very poor. The one Group B untestable child was living at home after recent release from an institution for the mentally retarded. She was being enrolled in a trainable school program.

Though there was marked differences between the two groups of children with testable I. Q.'s below 80, they cannot be compared in that the average I. Q. for Group A is 14.9 points below that of Group B, (p < .01). See Table V.

TABLE III

Mean Number of British Working Party Criteria Present Per Patient

I.Q.	Mean Number Criteria Present Per Patient	
	Group A	*Group B*
Mean I.Q. greater than 79	3.4	3.6
Mean I.Q. less than 80	4.3	4.2
Untestable	6.2	5.

p = 0.96

p = 0.79

The children in Group A were hospitalized at Lafayette Clinic approximately twice as long as the children in Group B (13.8 and 6.2 months respectively). The children in Group A were all in state institutions five years following discharge and five of the six were still in state institutions at the time of follow-up, whereas only one of the children in Group B was in an institution five years post discharge. None of the children in Group A had attained more than a sixth grade education, only two of the Group B children were functioning below the seventh grade level and it is likely that they will attain at least seventh grade level before adulthood.

Those children who tested over 79 on admission demonstrated follow-up findings as in Table VI.

These children were comparable for tested I. Q. (averages 96.2 and 95.6 ranges 82-117 and 83-125 respectively) and British Working Party Criteria of the Schizophrenic Syndrome. The children in Group A were hospitalized at Lafayette Clinic significantly longer than the children in Group B (9.9 and 4.9 months respectively, p = .051). At follow-up only three (37.5%) of Group A were living in situations that might be termed

TABLE IV

NUMBER OF PATIENTS EXHIBITING EACH OF BRITISH WORKING PARTY CRITERIA OF SCHIZOPHRENIC SYNDROME

	Group A	N = 18		Group B	N = 15	
	N = 8 above 79	N = 6 below 80	N = 4 untestable	N = 10 above 79	N = 4 below 80	N = 1 untestable
1. Gross & sustained impairment of emotional relationships with people.	8=100%	6=100%	4=100%	9=90%	4=100%	
2. Apparent unawareness of his own personal identity to a degree inappropriate to his age - posturing or exploration, or scruting of parts of his body. Repeated self directed aggression. Confusion of personal pronouns.	1=12.5%	3=50%	3=75%	2=20%		
3. Pathological preoccupation with particular objects.	2=25%	1=16%	4=100%	1=10%	1=25%	
4. Sustained resistance to change. Strives to maintain sameness.			1=25%			
5. Abnormal perceptual experience. Excessive diminished or unpredictable response to sensory stimuli.	5=62.5%	3=50%	2=50%	8=80%	3=75%	1
6. Acute, excessive & seemingly illogical anxiety. Often precipitated by change.	1=12.5%	3=50%	1=25%	6=60%	1=25%	1
7. Speech may have been lost or never acquired or may have failed to develop beyond a level appropriate to an earlier stage.	2=25%	1=16.6%	4=100%	1=10%	1=25%	1
8. Distortion in motility patterns, hyperkinesis, immobility, bizarre postures, ritualistic mannerisms, such as rocking and spinning.	8=100%	4=75%	4=100%	6=60%	3=75%	1
9. Background of serious retardation with islets of normal, near normal or exceptional intellectual function or skill.		5=83.3%	2=50%		3=75%	1

TABLE V

Children with Testable Admission I.Q.'s Below 80

Item	Group A	Group B
Number	6	4
Mean I.Q.	57.6	72.5
I.Q. Range	47-65	69-78
Mean Dur. of Hospitalization at Lafayette Clinic (mo.)	13.8	6.2
Residence		
At present		
Institution for Mentally Retarded	2 (33.3%)	0
Institution for Mentally Ill	2 (33.3%)	1 (25%)
Family Care Setting	1 (16.6%)	0
Home	1*(16.6%)	3 (75%)
Five Years Post Discharge		
Institution for Mentally Retarded	3 (50%)	
Institution for Mentally Ill	3 (50%)	
Home	0	
Educational Attainment		
Preschool Levels	2	0
Below 3rd. Gr. Levels	3	0
3rd. to 6th. Gr. Levels	1	2**
7th. to 9th. Gr. Levels	0	0
9th. to Completion of High School	0	2

* This child was discharged from an institution for the mentally ill in 1969. He is presumably with his parents but we were unable to trace him after his discharge.

** Both children are still in school one at the sixth grade level (age 15), the other at third grade level (age 13).

TABLE VI

Children with Admission I.Q.'s Over 79

Item	Group A Follow-Up		Group B Follow-Up	
Number	8		10	
Mean I.Q.	96.2		95.6	
Range of I.Q.	82-117		83-125	
Duration of Hospitalization at Lafayette Clinic (mo.)	9.9		4.9	p = .051+++
Residence				
At present				
Institutions for Mentally Ill	2		1	p = .411
Home with Legal Guardians (parents, etc.)	2*		7	p = .076
On Own	3		1+	p = .206
Unknown	1**		1***	
Age-appropriate living situation	3		8	p = .088
Psychiatric Hospitalizations within 5 yr. of Discharge	4	(50%)	3 (30%)	p = .352
In State Hospital, 5 yr. Post-discharge	3		1	p = .205
Educational Attainment on Completion of Formal Education:				
3rd. to 6th. Gr.	2	(25%)	0	p = .183
7th. to 9th. Gr.	1	(12.5%)	2 (20%)	p = .588
Completed High School	5++	(62.5%)		
Completed High School prior to age 20 or presently at age grade level	2	(25%)	8 (80%)	p = .031

* Ages 23 and 27 yrs.
** Left home 1970 - not heard of since.
*** Discharged from a residential placement to parents in 1971 because of anti-social behavior. Unable to trace further.
\+ In the armed forces.
++ Two received post high education, one of whom was in college at time of fp;;pw-up.
+++ Represents probability from t test of means. Rest of probabilities evaluated by Fisher Exact Test of Probability.

appropriate for their age. Of these three, one was living alone and also working regularly and productively. One was living alone and was unemployed. He had been recently divorced after four years of marriage; one was living with his second wife, he had a work history of numerous unskilled jobs held for a few months at a time. The two former patients in Group A, ages twenty-three and twenty-seven who were living with their parents were both isolative individuals. The older person attended college but she had almost no social life. The twenty-three year old lived with his mother and sister and had worked productively and regularly for the six years prior to follow-up. He was described as shy and did not date girls. Seven of the Group B members were living at home which for their ages (12-20, average 15.3) can be considered appropriate. One was in the Navy. Thus, eight of the ten (80%) could be said to be living in age appropriate situations at time of follow-up. Whether this will be true fifteen years post discharge is problematic. Their overall social adjustment seems to be somewhat better than Group A but still is not good. Five of the eight are reported to be relatively isolative with only a few if any friends. Two are reported as being quite outgoing and active. One was a member of his school's student council. The fellow in the Navy has shown considerable antisocial behavior including lying, fighting and being A.W.O.L.

Educationally, Group B is showing better function than Group A. Two (I. Q.'s = 109 and 82) of Group A never reached beyond sixth grade. All of Group B reached beyond sixth grade level. One of Group A (I.Q. 95) left school in the eighth grade to get a job because of family instability. Two of group B left junior high school. The other five (62.5%) in Group A are: (a) still in school at college level--(n=1), (b) have attained post high training though no longer in school--(n=1), (c) completed high school--(n=1) or (d) completed high school equivalency during young adulthood--(n=2). The girl still in college did not complete her high school equivalency until she was twenty-three. Only two (25%) of Group A completed high school before age twenty. In Group B eight (80%) of the ten are still in high school placed in grades appropriate to their age and thus conceivably could complete high school when age appropriate ($p = .031$).

Discussion: During the years 1956 through 1958 there were four children admitted who were untestable and on discharge had psychotic diagnoses as compared to only one during the years 1966-68. All four of the Group A untestable children were functioning at severely retarded levels on follow-up fifteen years later. All four resided in institutions and were markedly dependent on the support of others. Three of these four had been diagnosed as infantile autism. Two of these three are presently in institutions for the mentally retarded and have present diagnoses including mental retardation and psychosis. The third is in an institution for the mentally ill and has a diagnosis of schizophrenia. The fourth of the untestable children had an initial diagnosis of childhood schizophrenia and mental retardation. He presently resides in an institution for the mentally retarded where he continues with the same diagnosis (mental retardation and schizophrenia). The prognosis for this group of untestable children by follow-up was very poor. Their level of function had not appreciably changed from that at the time of their initial evaluation.

The one Group B child, who was diagnosed as psychotic and was untestable on admission, at follow-up was living at home functioning at markedly retarded levels. She had been released from an institution for the mentally retarded just two months prior to follow-up and was being enrolled in school classes for the trainable.

Comparison of the two groups of children who tested below 80 at the time of admission to our Children's Unit is not valid, as the intellectual capacities of the two groups is significantly different ($p < .01$). The group admitted in the years 1966-1968 is presently showing a markedly better adjustment than the group admitted in the years 1956-1958. This may be due to a variety of factors but the basic difference in functioning intellectual capacity is probably of major importance. A number of follow-up studies (1, 2) have demonstrated that functional I.Q. is one of the better predictors of future outcome for childhood psychotics.

Meaningful comparisons of outcome can be made on the two groups of children with measured I. Q.'s above 79 at time of admission. Their I. Q.'s and clinical pictures on hospitalization were comparable. Their differences in outcome though not so marked as in the children testing below 80 are still appreciable. In addition the duration of hospitalization for the group admitted in the years 1966-1968 was only half that of the group admitted in the years 1956-1958 ($p = 0.51$). We feel that a considerable portion of the differences are due to a greater effectiveness of our hospital program in the years 1966-1968 as compared to the years 1956-1958. Another factor we believe to be significant is a greater community supportive capactiy, particularly that of school settings.

During the ten years between 1956-1966 we had become increasingly aware of the variability of the child's ego capacities. A cognitive-perceptual-motor testing program was developed in which the child's abilities were evaluated in twelve areas. See Table VII. Once these areas were evaluated the child was placed in an individualized educational program. Each child initially was given work in the various areas at the levels at which he could function. Then by a combination of slow incremental increases in work expectation--keeping within his developing capacities--and concrete and verbal rewards for accomplishment, his self esteem and functioning abilities were enhanced. This educational approach was not limited to the school setting but was also included in the ward and O.T. settings so that by far a major portion of the child's day was spent in activities which were believed would assist in developing deficit capacities. He was grouped with other children of similar capacities in each of the school, O.T. and ward setting. He might be included in a different grouping of children in each of these areas because each area calls for the use of a different combination of abilities. As his abilities improved he was moved to different groupings. Within the various groups much emphasis was also placed on the development of social skills. Repeatedly we have been impressed by the parallel movement of improvement of cognitive-perceptual-motor abilities and the improvement of social skills.

At the time of discharge every effort was made to communicate the information we had obtained about the child's capacities to the receiving school setting, residence, etc. We attempted where possible to have our teachers in particular pass on their information not only in written form but also in face to face mettings with the child's new teachers. We feel that this has been quite valuable in helping the receiving school setting to understand and perpetuate a program more in tune with the child's capacities and needs.

TABLE VII

AREAS OF C. P. M. TESTING

1. Tactile - Kinesthetic - Proprioceptive - Perception
2. Gross Motor Coordination -- eye-hand, extremities, ------
3. Orientation -- space, size
4. Fine Motor Control
5. Visual Perception -- discrimination, constancy
6. Auditory Perception -- discrimination, constancy
7. Time Orientation
8. Linguistics Input
9. Memory -- immediate rote, immediate meaningful, delayed rote
10. Integration -- non-verbal, symbolic
11. Linguistics Output
12. Inferential Reasoning

From Rubin, Braun, Beck, and Lorens, 1972

In addition to the comprehensive educational program the child was included in individual and group therapies and given medication as felt to be indicated. His parents were consistenly involved whenever possible in counseling directed at helping them to better understand the child's problems and accept his limitations. These sessions were also directed at helping them to understand and work through some of their own problems so that they would be able to supply a more stable, structured and accepting environment for the child on his return home.

Since 1968 we have increasingly involved parents with our milieu staff when the child psychiatrist and social worker feel the parents can benefit. This includes having parents sit in on the classroom and ward activities with their children with concurrent or later discussions between the parents and the teachers and nursing staff, as indicated. Conjoint sessions involving parents, the child, social worker, child psychiatrist, and intermittently various members of the milieu staff have also become increasingly common. We feel, though we have no objective proof, that this increased parental - milieu involvement is quite valuable.

Medication has been used to treat target symptoms such as hyperkinesis, impulsivity, isolation, irritability or target affects such as anxiety or depression rather than being used as part of a program for a diagnosis, i.e. phenothiazines for schizophrenia. Hyperkinesis is seen as a symptom which may represent physiologic motor dyscontrol as well as a symptom which may be due to underlying anxiety. In many cases there are both physiologic and psychologic factors underlying this and other symptoms. We tend to use the amphetamines or ritalin when we feel that the hyperkinesis represents a physiologic motor disturbance or developmental lag and tend to use the phenothiazines when we think the hyperkinesis is primarily a manifestation of overwhelming anxiety, if we think medication is indicated. Phenothiazines are also used for other symptoms when we feel they represent underlying or manifest anxiety.

This combination of evaluation of the disturbed child in terms of ego strengths and deficits and in terms of degree and reasons for anxiety and depression, the development of an individualized educational milieu program with concomitant psychotherapeutic work with child and parents, the use of medication for target affects or symptoms, and the preparations of receiving school and community settings for the child on discharge, we think has been useful in shortening the duration of hospitalization and improving the prognosis of disturbed children. This study of the children admitted in 1966 thru 1968 as compared to those admitted in the years 1956 thru 1958 provides some substantiation to this assertion.

REFERENCES

1. DeMyer, M. K., Allen, J., Barton, S., DeMyer, W. E., Norton, J. A., and Steele, F. *J. Autism Child Schizo.* *3,* (1973).
2. Rutter, M., and Lockyear, L. *Brit. J. Psychiat.* *113,* 1183, (1967).

MENTAL HEALTH IN CHILDREN, Volume III
Edited By D. V. Siva Sankar

COMPARATIVE APPROACHES TO PROGRAM EVALUATION

Richard K. Eyman
Neuropsychiatric Institute
Pomona, California 91766

Charles D. Windle
National Institute of Mental Health
Bethesda, Maryland 20014

Introduction

There is much variation in the definition of program evaluation in the existing literature. Generally it is considered comparison among sets of program activities in terms of outcome or process characteristics which can readily be given valuation (1). It can also consist of an assessment of a given program along a value dimension. The most common such value dimension is a program goal. Numerous formats and models for program evaluation have been proposed. Shulberg *et al.* (2) distinguish two types: (1) the goal attainment model, and (2) the systems model. In contrast, James (3) suggested four classifications for the evaluation of health programs: effort, performance, adequacy of performance, and efficiency. Deniston (4) focused on program effectiveness and program efficiency as the primary components of program evaluation. More extensive is the classification by Schaefer (5), who identified types of program evaluation corresponding to various combinations of program development stages and product-service-outcome consequences.

As far as a given program's management is concerned, program evaluation can be used as a basis for management decisions to improve programs, a source of information to justify continued support for existing programs, or a procedure required by funding sources. From the perspective of a community or governmental or insurance reimbursers or a program, program evaluation is desirable to determine if benefits are consonant with costs and to be a process which will prevent improprieties or inefficiencies in the expenditure of resources. Program evaluation also has a number of fringe benefits, including increased prestige for institutions which conduct research and facilitated administration from increased attention to data.

A number of writers (6, 7, 8, 9, 10, 11, 12, 13) have discussed the methodological problems involved in evaluation. Campbell (10), in particular, provides an extensive analysis of threats to validity in program evaluation due to such factors as maturation, regression artifacts, selection, experimental mortality, etc. In other words, changes in outcome measures frequently occur as a result of the above rival explanations and thus in a specific investigation obscure whether there is any genuine effect of a program or treatment.

The purpose of this paper is to describe and briefly compare several approaches which can be taken to evaluate programs. Because purposes and threats to validity may differ, a fundamental distinction should be made between 'internal' and 'external' evaluation. Internal evaluation is initiated by the agency responsible for conducting the program and consists of research which program staff can use to improve the program or increase support for the program. External evaluation comes from groups outside the agency, and is likely to be used for monitoring or comparison among programs.

Internal Evaluation

Literature Review

For certain types of program questions a literature review is a minimum prerequisite. Neglect of previous findings and developed methods can lead to costly errors in evaluation design, unnecessary duplication of effort, inconclusive findings, and proliferation of many poorly developed measuring instruments. Since the literature contains mainly basic research which involves general theory and variables rather than specific programs, this literature is relevant mainly to evaluate the program hypothesis and not the operation of a specific program.

An example of the value of such reviews is Anthony *et al.*'s (14) survey of literature to determine the comparative effectiveness of various psychiatric rehabilitation procedures. Two outcome criteria were selected: recidivism and post-hospital employment. The percentage of psychiatric patients receiving the traditional hospital regimen of drug treatment and individual or group therapy, who were able to remain out of the hospital and/or find employment, was established as a baseline against which the specific effects of rehabilitation procedures could be evaluated.

Some conclusions of this review were: (a) Most all types of inpatient treatment innovations improve the patients' in-hospital behavior, but the research does not indicate that these approaches can singularly effect post-hospital adjustment. (b) Ex-patients who attend aftercare clinics have a lower rate of recidivism than non-attenders. (c) Transitional facilities reduce recidivism but demonstrate little effect on enabling patients to function independently, as measured by post-hospital employment, in the community. (d) There is a definite need for the continued use of specific outcome criteria so that the comparative effectiveness of various psychiatric rehabilitation procedures can be meaningfully evaluated.

Experimental and Quasi Experimental Design

A second approach, strongly favored by researchers, is the experiment. Historically, the experiment was considered the only way of verifying improvements and also the only way of establishing a cumulative tradition in which improvements can be introduced selectively without sacrificing existing competence (15, 16). More recently, Campbell and Stanley (6) have argued that although there are many natural social settings in which the investigator can introduce something like experimental design into his scheduling of data collection procedures, he usually lacks full control over the scheduling of experimental stimuli or treatment exposure which makes a true experiment possible. 'Collectively such situations can be regarded as quasi-experimental designs' (6).

Campbell (10) further states: 'The general ethic here advocated for public administrators as well as social scientists, is to use the very best method possible, aiming at 'true experiments' with random control groups. But where randomized treatments are not possible, a self critical use of quasi-experimental designs is advocated. We must do the best we can with what is availabe to us.'

Sometimes a random assignment of patients to treatment conditions is possible as in the study of Hogarty *et al.* (17) on day hospitals. Patients accepted for treatment at the day hospital and judged to be otherwise in need of inpatient care were assigned randomly to treatment in either a day hospital or an outpatient clinic. Patients were evaluated at the beginning and end of treatment and two and 12 months after treatment by a team of independent assessors not involved in the treatment programs. After this excellent 'experimental' start, however, as most investigators in field situations find, circumstances lessened the investigators' control. Part of the population which was to be included in the random assignment had to be excluded because some referral sources specifically requested day hospital treatment. Some patients were lost during the treatment and follow-up time periods. In fact, the major finding of this study was not a main effect from the experimental condition, but rather an interaction effect requiring analysis by diagnosis. Schizophrenic patients treated at the day hospital showed greater improvement in a constellation of symptoms reflecting increased accessibility than those given routine outpatient chemotherapy. 'Drug therapy alone on the other hand proved to be a significantly more rapid and equally efficacious form of treatment for non-schizophrenic patients.' This study suggests that it may not have been the experimental versus control comparative feature which was most critical, but rather the analytic comparisons.

Perhaps the crudest alternative to an experiment is to simply correlate the characteristics of individuals in a given group with outcome. While appropriate for exploration, such a gross examination suffers from many threats to validity. An example of a quasi-experimental design will be provided. In a study by Eyman *et al.* (8), individuals admitted to Pacific State Hospital between 1958 and 1962 were followed for a four year period. Two groups were studied: residents selected by admitting staff to be in school within three months after admission and individuals not selected to be in school. The two groups were roughly matched on background variables known to be important in selection for a school program, e.g., age, IQ, toilet training, etc. The status of each group was checked yearly. The three possible results of these yearly checks are shown below.

Status	*For School Sample*	*For Non-School Sample*
E_3 Most Preferable Outcome	Released on Indefinite Leave to Home, Foster Care, Work Placement, or Discharged.	Released on Indefinite Leave to Home, Foster Care, Work Placement, or Discharged.
E_2 Satisfactory Outcome	In Hospital, still in Day School, or no longer in Day School, but in Industrial Therapy or Night School	In Hospital; enrolled in Industrial Therapy.
E_1 Unsatisfactory Outcome	In Hospital; dropped from school for lack of progress or behavior problems and not in Industrial Therapy or Night School	In Hospital; not participating in Industrial Therapy

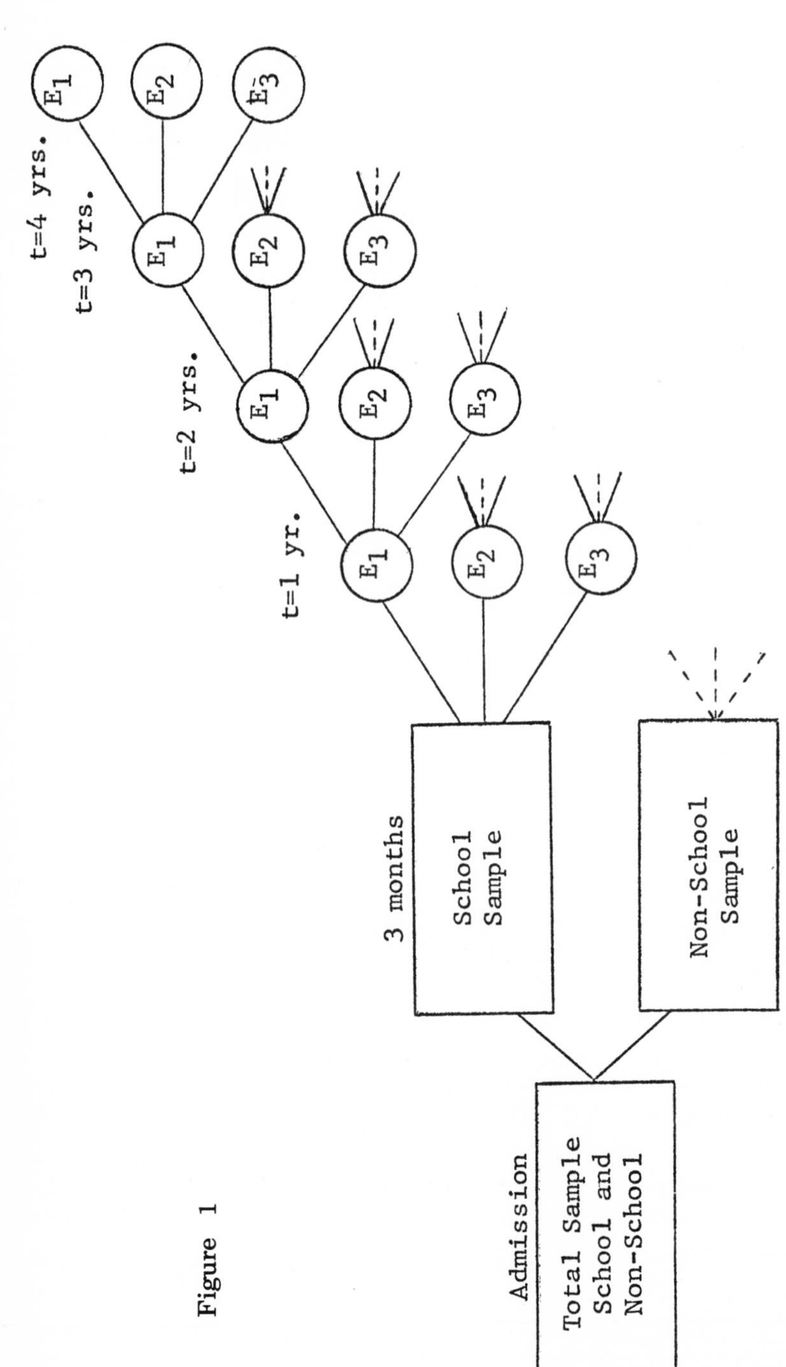
Admission
Total Sample
School and
Non-School
3 months
School
Sample
Non-School
Sample
t=1 yr.
t=2 yrs.
t=3 yrs.
t=4 yrs.
E_1
E_2
E_3

Figure 1

Effectiveness can be examined simply by comparing the number of residents released from the hospital by the end of the fourth year from the school participants and the non-school group. Significantly more residents were released from the school sample than the non-school sample. However, this comparison did not take initial status into account.

To do so, as well as provide more information, a simplified version of time dependent Markov chains were used to study change and to evaluate the school program. A cross tabulation of patients' status at one time against their status a year earlier (see Figure 1) yields a transition frequency matrix shown in Table 1.

TABLE I

Transition Frequency Matrix for Change in Status from One Year after Admission to Two Years After Admission

		Years (1, 2) t = time of determination of status, i.e. two years after admission			
		$E_1(t)$	$E_2(t)$	$E_3(t)$	Total
t-1 = yr.	$E_1(t-1)$	N_{11}	N_{12}	N_{13}	$N_1.$
after	$E_2(t-1)$	N_{21}	N_{22}	N_{23}	$N_2.$
admission	$E_3(t-1)$	N_{31}	N_{32}	N_{33}	$N_3.$

In Table 1 each capital N represents the number of patients falling in a designated cell. This type of tabulation gives a fairly good picture of the amount of change taking place. From this cross tabulation, a Markov probability matrix can be easily calculated.*

* The model equation for the Markov chain takes the form of

$$P[\text{an individual in } E_i(t-1) \text{----} E_j(t)] = P_{ij}(t-1, t)$$

$$ij = 1, 2, 3$$
$$t = 1, 2, 3, 4$$

and reads, "the probability of transition from E_i to E_j, given that the individual is in E_i at time t-1," is P_{ij} (t-1, t). The estimated probabilities are computed by

$$P_{ij}(t-1, t) = N_{ij}(t-1, t)/N_i(t-1, t)$$

and the sum of probabilities in each row equal to one

$$\sum_{J=1}^{3} P = 1$$

N_{ij} is the number of patients in cell_{ij}; N_i is the row total.

The probability matrix is simply the number of individuals in a cell, e.g., N_{11} divided by its row total, N_1. The result gives the 'odds' of an individual changing status in each time period. The probabilities are conditional and based on the assumption that the outcome of the third year depends on the outcome of the second year but not on that of the first.

This approach can test differences in probability of release for the school and non-school groups by assessing whether the two sets of transition matrices could come from a common universe. Similarly, the effect of schooling or non-schooling experience over time can be tested in change in transition rates over time.

The results from the Markov chain indicated no differences in conditional probabilities for change between the school vs. non-school groups, although some significant time trends appeared. Tests for time trends showed age to be the most significant factor.

A second example illustrates designs more suitable to control for several variables in the data analysis. To determine the relative effectiveness of five alternative ambulation and toilet training programs for retarded individuals admitted to Pacific State Hospital between 1966-1968, all admissions were followed for three years and their self-help skills assessed annually (18).

Five variables other than program were felt likely to affect outcome: age, IQ, diagnosis of motor or spinal dysfunction, and ambulation and toilet training status on admission. An analysis of covariance was used which treated final status on ambulation and toilet training as outcome variables, program placement as the independent variable, and age, IQ, etc., as covariates whose effect on outcome was removed for meaningful comparison between groups.

Children assigned to standard institutional care improved less than those receiving special habilitative programming on their ward. Community placement was appreciably better than standard institutional care, but significantly less effective than special programming.

These two examples of quasi-experimental designs illustrate the use of sophisticated statistical techniques in field situations where pure experimental designs were impossible to implement. Although valid descriptive and correlational conclusions are possible from such designs, cause-effect conclusions are usually impossible to infer without a pure 'experiment.' Lord (13, 19) provides an extensive and insightful discussion of common problems of statistical adjustments when comparing preexisting groups and measuring change. Basically, there is no way to completely control for the selection factor without random assignment to groups. No matter how many variables are statistically adjusted in analyzing preexisting groups, there is always the possibility that an unknown factor still exists which can influence the final outcome.

Clinical Approaches to Program Evaluation

Guttentag (11) has argued that most statistical models make assumptions which cannot be met in the natural setting and involve relatively superficial outcomes analogous to a single treatment. She concludes that often there is little relationship between the data which are compatible with t or F tests and the real aims of the program or courses of action open to decision makers.

Although Guttentag's (11) remarks appear exaggerated in terms of past accomplishments based on good experimental and quasi-experimental designs, she does represent some of the real concerns of clinicians and suggests an interesting subjective approach to program evaluation.

Glaser and Backer (20) also discussed several clinical approaches to program evaluation. These approaches attempt to incorporate the judgments of people involved with a program in the measurement process, rather than to use standardized tests of predefined program outcomes. This approach has several features described succinctly by Glaser and Backer. One issue concerns how to deal with the idiosyncratic goals appropriate for each patient in a way that permits comparisons. The best known solution is Kiresuk's Goal Attainment Scaling (21). Goals are set, in collaboration with the client, and objective outcome criteria are specified along five levels of success. By assuming these levels to be normally distributed, comparisons can be made.

Guttentag (11) has described another type of solution for measuring the social utilities of decision makers. A Decision-

Theoretic Evaluation method based on Bayesian statistics* is suggested in which judgments of utility of possible actions are combined with separately derived value dimensions encompassing these actions in order to arrive at an overall utility or cost effective function on a subjective but systematic and quantifiable basis. Once these value dimensions and utility judgments are specified and decisions reached, further objective methods of evaluation can validate the subjective estimates.

To some program evaluators the clinical models are more relevant and offer alternative inferential approaches which more closely fit the reality of programs in the field (22). Others (23) caution that it is premature to discount the classical experimental approach as most of the clinical models are really not available in a utilizable form or tested as to their practicality. Moreover, considerable controversy surrounds the use of subjective probabilities (24, 25). For example, Bargmann (25) and Mainland (26) warn of the unrelenting pressures by some groups who employ statisticians, to have their desires masqueraded as subjective probabilities, which when given the full Bayesian treatment, can be accepted as legitimate scientific research. Determining the basis for evaluation from the administrators and staff of a program is certainly important, but the investigators must not depend too heavily upon these goals. Unexpected results may be as important as outcomes on the goals of the program.

In summary, Campbell and Stanley (6) clearly enumerated sources of invalidity of some 16 possible experimental and quasi-experimental *designs* for applied research. The advantage of presenting these designs in connection with their sources of

---

* The Decision-Theoretic Evaluation method includes (a) subjective probabilities and (b) Bayesian statistics which provide a model for incorporating these probabilities into the data analysis as 'prior distributions.' Hence, it is possible to quantify opinions (subjective probabilities) on the 'odds' of an outcome and treat these numbers as objectively determined probabilities in the acceptance or rejection of a hypothesis on a program's worth.

invalidity is to encourage their *self-critical* use. The quasi-experimental designs illustrated in this paper were of the "Ex Post Facto Analyses" type where "selection" and "Mortality" are usually the major threats to validity. Hence, replication of findings from several different samples is essential before cause-effect relationships can be inferred. Still, these designs including the interrupted time series design (10) represent some of the more refined ways to do "the best we can with what is available to us."

Clinical methods of program evaluation certainly merit attention as ways to capture hard to define goals and increase acceptance by practitioners. Goal attainment scaling, for example, offers the client an ongoing report of his progress as well as a means of comparing clients with different problems. However, subjective evaluations should not replace objective experimental methods. The former methods need more testing of reliability and validity, and the latter methods can be increased in relevance to field problems with additional ingenuity and statistical sophistication. Both methods require insightful use with special attention to the possible sources of invalidity.

Cost Benefit Models

Considering the primitive state of our techniques for assessing program outcomes, social benefits, and program costs, it is not surprising that there are few examples of program evaluation using cost benefit or cost effective measures. An exception is a study done by Meredith (27). The Markov Chain model was used to predict probable time dependent developmental outcomes four years in the future of mentally retarded children placed in specified institutional programs. The expected progress of these children was then compared to long-range program costs and the estimated time the children would be in the program. A determination of the effective value of the programs was extrapolated from the resulting longitudinal data on outcome, cost, and stay times.

Cost benefit models reflect the current 'Zeitgeist' for total accountability. For an example of a cost benefit model suitable for clients of an employable age receiving services from mental health programs (28).

Client Satisfaction

An approach which is high in face validity, but vulnerable to misinterpretation is assessment of client satisfaction. Techniques for measuring client satisfaction are being surveyed by McPhee, Zusman, and Joss (29). While clients should be the most aware of their own problems, they are not free to express their true feelings to the providers of service and their perceptions may be distorted by their problems. Client satisfaction usually appears glowingly high, a fact which led Campbell (10) to advocate it for 'trapped administrators' who want evidence to support rather than evaluate their programs.

Aside from validity, client satisfaction may have a therapeutic benefit in making treatment more participatory. On the negative side, it may seriously compromise patients' rights to privacy.

External Evaluation

A preferred option for program evaluation which is not internally controlled is to orient procedures toward third party accountability systems. At present some promising mechanisms seem to be: utilization review procedures, PSRO procedures, professional accreditation standards, court imposed standards for 'active' treatment, Federal-State service monitoring systems using comparative norms for measures of process goals, citizen group evaluation and use of mass media.

Use of Standards

Changes are occurring in the way mental health services are financed. An increasing portion of the cost is being born by third party payors, a trend likely to culminate in National Health Insurance coverage. This change is reinforcing the establishment and use of standards, a type of program evaluation which has had little role in the field of mental health in the past. This form of evaluation seems relatively feasible as a way to obtain practical criteria which can be used to determine minimal eligibility for reimbursement. Professional groups also find such criteria helpful in regulating their own membership, at least to the extent that clearly non-credentialed persons can be excluded and gross violations of customary practice can be eliminated, and yet the freedom for most professionals is not greatly hampered.

There are, at present, established standards for different types of professional practice or facilities (30, 31), standards for accreditation of medical facilities (32, 33, 34), and ethical standards which apply to particular professional groups (35).

In addition to these standards, the Regulations for the Community Mental Health Centers Program specifiy that States, as a part of their plan for the construction of community mental health centers, should set forth standards for the maintenance and operation of community mental health centers, and (in a proposed revision promulgated for rule-making purposes in February 1972, but not approved over a year later) methods for their enforcement.

Another form that standards are taking is in the precedents which courts set by rulings in class-action suits and other judicial decisions concerning right to treatment and other patient rights. A major new legal thesis is that adequate treatment for the institutionalized mentally ill is a constitutional right (36). Cases have focused on the rights of persons involuntarily committed. For example, in a case in Alabama the court specified criteria for adequate treatment in the areas of a humane psychological and physical environment, qualified staff, and individualized treatment plans.

It is our feeling that the use of standards of any of the above types in appraising particular facilities qualifies as one form of program evaluation, although it is usually not so classified. Further, it is a type likely to have large impact on program decisions. When facilities fail to be accredited they become ineligible for third-party reimbursement. This may cost the facility a large amount of money. Thus, this form of program evaluation is highly consequential for program actions.

Peer Review of Utilization

The current shift in financing of mental health services toward increasing reliance upon third party payments is making another form of program evaluation increasingly important because it is being used as a requirement for eligibility for these third-party reimbursements. The legislation that established Medicare set the requirement that each hospital develop a systematic procedure for evaluating the quality of medical care on the basis of documented evidence to support diagnosis and treatment and to justify utilization of hospital facilities. Professionals have preferred to establish peer review systems for this surveillance. Many facilities have a utilization review committee to evaluate the appropriateness of the services rendered. The American Psychiatric Association's monograph, Psychiatric Utilization Review (37), describes general principles and objectives. It does not provide specific criteria for various types of problems. Foreseeing the desirability of developing such procedures which could be used by community mental health centers, NIMH gave a contract to Yale University which has supported the Psychiatric Utilization Review and Evaluation (PURE) project (38). This project has developed an evaluation procedure which provides criteria for evaluating the quality of written records of psychiatric patients. For utilization review, following the medical-surgical model, charts are selected for critical review for those patients who have deviated from norms developed by the facility. The PURE project's experience suggested that criteria of *appropriateness* of treatment could be more reliable if instead of diagnoses, measures of psycho-social, environmental and biological functioning in such broad treatment categories as inpatient, partial hospitalization, or outpatient care, were used. Criteria of *adequacy* focus on the treatment process to ensure at least minimal standards. The examples suggested for this were: parental involvement required in the treatment of adolescents, the need for neurological examinations if particular conditions exist, and diagnosis-specific guidelines for the use of psycho-tropic medications. Criteria of *effectiveness* should measure the success of particular treatment sequences. This may be examined either from a patient-specific or a program-specific perspective. But in either case criterion outcomes states need to be defined--and these may use techniques from other forms of program evaluation.

The most recent impetus to the use of peer review is the provision in the Social Security Amendments of 1972 for

Professional Standards Review Organizations consisting of physicians in designated geographic areas to review appropriateness and quality of medical services. What procedures can be used in such reviews are now under active development (39).

Use of the community for Program Evaluation

As the Zeitgeist of mental health services has favored a community location for services, the approach of using the community in program evaluation has increased in respectability and salience. There are several reasons why the community is a reasonable source of evaluations for public programs. One is that it is both the right and responsibility of taxpayers and the citizens for whom programs are designed, to make informed judgments and provide guidance about public programs. This guidance may be given simply by voting for officials, who represent people in supporting or changing programs. Guidance may also be given more directly in referendums for funds to support programs or by participation in the governance of facilities. The more direct the influence of the citizen on the service, the more closely that service can represent the wishers of the community. A second reason for involving the community in evaluating mental health services is that such involvement of the community makes community support of the services more likely. As decentralization of mental health service programs increases reliance on local government and/or community funds, the more program directors will feel the advantages of involving communities in governing the program.

A third reason that communities are appropriate in program evaluation is that their assessments may be more valid in some respects than the assessments of others. Insofar as mental health problems reflect social rather than medical conditions, community representatives may be better assessors than care providers. Further, the special interests of providers of service can be corrected by evaluation from the community perspective. Studies have documented differences between therapists and clients or families in the goals or outcomes of treatment (40).

There are at least five types of organizations which may do evaluations representing the community: (1) The National Association of Mental Health has produced a protocol which local associations can use for 'site visitations' to community mental health centers. These forms are designed to apply to persons on the street, caretaker groups, and community mental health centers. Using these forms local associations have identified a number of critical issues about service deficiencies in centers and found a number of benefits from this citizen evaluation program (41).

(2) The Center for the Study of Responsive Law, as an institution whose function is to serve as citizen advocate, has done an external, critical evaluation of the Community Mental Health Centers Program in a so-called 'Nader' Report (42). A main strength of such an approach is its deliberate stance of freedom from, if not opposition to, vested interests of professional providers and allied industries.

(3) Another approach to getting informed community-representative evaluators is the Programs Evaluation By Summer Interns (PEBSI) activity supported by HEW on a 1% evaluation contract. The contractor who carried out this test during the summer of 1970 on more than 100 projects of 15 different program types, including community mental health centers, concluded that: 'PEBSI was a success in spite of a myriad of problems, many of them directly attributable to its experimental nature, others due to opposition within HEW and elsewhere to what suddenly became a controversial project. PEBSI--showed that college students and community people can make excellent program evaluators.' (43).

(4) Citizen representatives may be included in evaluations by other groups. Recently NIMH and State site visit teams have begun to include citizen representatives in their site visits. One of the barriers against such inclusion has been the reluctance of agencies to reveal information about their operation to the public, and the reluctance of governments to subject these agencies to exposure of information simply because they are grant recipients. Recent interpretation of the Freedom of Information Act suggests that the evaluative information from site visits to grantees should be accessible (44). Thus a barrier to the inclusion of citizens on site visits is removed, and site visits

teams can benefit from the broader perspective which citizen-advocates bring.

(5) A team of researchers from Tufts University is developing techniques which citizen groups can use to evaluate mental health services. As part of this study an ad hoc group of citizens in Missouri has been formed to evaluate the delivery of mental health services at the Mid-Missouri CMHC. The team is currently completing an evaluation instrument and expects the actual evaluation to take about three months. This experience will be used as a base for developing a manual of evaluation procedures.

In addition to these five types of organizations there are at least two other sources of citizen representation in evaluation. One is the investigative and reporting activities of public media, the press, TV, and radio. The most usual form of this type of evaluation is exposure of unfavorable conditions in institutions.

The last type of evaluation is that which citizens do as clients and voters. In a free marketplace they can choose to patronize or avoid services, and a well informed electorate can make their evaluations at the ballot-box (45).

The Legal Model

An extension of external evaluation is a legal model proposed by Levine (22). A jury of experts can render a judgment based on an adversary model in which arguments and counter arguments are heard in connection with alternative interpretations of data on effectiveness of programs. 'Issues of evidence, the inferences which can be drawn from evidence, and methods for evaluating arguments and evidence constitute the process of ascertaining truth in the legal stystem....Evidence is classified according to whether it is direct or circumstantial. Assertions of fact are separated from direct evidence. The jury comes to a finding based on the preponderance of evidence' (22). In many ways, the legal model resembles a Peer Review System wherein a group of experts decides from 'observation' the quality and value of a program. Although less formalized, many of the arguments regarding available evidence are involved. Although the legal system offers an intuitively interesting approach to evaluation, it has yet to be tested in field situations. Like subjective evaluation as opposed to experimental approaches, evidence is needed as to what it can offer over other forms of external evaluation.

With the exception of the legal model, most of these other evaluation methods which are based on professional or lay judgment are a political reality.

Summary

A number of classical and new approaches to program evaluation have been discussed. Program evaluation can be seen as often experiencing a conflict between orientations toward TRUTH or toward immediate UTILIZATION. The academic training of social scientists makes a scientific orientation basic. Further, their specialized career ladder often involves publishing or perishing. This makes their work high on validity but low in immediate utility.

Persons with program concerns usually are mainly concerned either with enhancing the benefits or reducing the costs. The simplest way to enhance a program is by increasing its size, for which public relations advertising is helpful. The simplest way to reduce costs is to decrease the program, for which much-raking exposes are effective. Historically, internally controlled program evaluation often is used for the former and externally controlled program evaluation for the latter. These tend to be high in utility and low in truth.

Emil Bend (46) has suggested that many of the failings of evaluative research are well known, but unlikely to be changed by researchers until...'sponsors of such research translate their dissatisfaction...into economic acts by refusing to award and pay for poor quality or useless outputs, or...the subjects of evaluation refuse to cooperate or participate.' It may be necessary to change the reward system for professionals to lead them into new orientations. This should be considered by program managers if they too want to enhance the utilization of evaluation.

On the other hand, it should also be kept in mind that when all is said and done, the validity of all of these evaluation procedures is a very complex and elusive commodity. The threats of validity outlined by Campbell and Stanley (6) apply as much to the subjective and external methods of evaluation as they do to the experimental methods. Hence, it is still necessary to proceed cautiously with attention to replication of findings if good evaluation is to be accomplished.

References

1. Levey, S., and Loomba, N. P. In *Health care administration.* Lippincott, Philadelphia, (1973).
2. Schulberg, H. C., Sheldon, A., and Baker, F. In *Program evaluation in the health fields.* Behavioral Publications, New York, (1969).
3. James G. *Amer. J. Pub. Health 52,* 1145, (1962).
4. Deniston, O. L., Rosenstock, I. M., and Getting, V. A. Evaluation of program effectiveness. *Pub. Health Rep.* Public Health Service, US Dept. HEW, April 1968, *83*:4.
5. Shaefer, M. *Evaluation/decision-making in health planning administration.* The University of North Carolina Press, Chapel Hill, (1973).
6. Campbell, D. T., and Stanley, J. C. Experimental and quasi-experimental designs for research on teaching. In *Handbook of research on teaching.* Edited by Cage, N. L. Rand McNally, Chicago, p. 171, (1963).
7. Kirk, S. A. Research in education. In *Mental retardation.* Edited by Stevens, H. A. The University of Chicago Press, p. 57, (1964).
8. Eyman, R. K., Tarjan, G., and McGunigle, D. *Amer. J. Men. Def. 72,* 435, (1967).
9. Tarjan, G., Eyman, R. K., and Dingman, H. F. *Amer. J. Ment. Def. 70,* 529, (1966).
10. Campbell, D. T. *Amer. Psychol. 24,* 409 (1969).
11. Guttentag, M. *Evaluation 1,* 60, (1973).
12. Bereiter, C. Some persisting dilemmas in measurement. In *Problems in measuring change.* Edited by Harris, C. W. The University of Wisconsin Press, Madison, p. 3, (1963).
13. Lord, F. M. Elementary models for measuring change. In *Problems in measuring change.* Edited by Harris, C. W. The University of Wisconsin Press Madison p.21,(1963).

14. Anthony, W. A., Buell, G. J., Sharratt, S., and Althoff, M. E. *Psychol. Bull.* *78*, 447, (1972).
15. Fisher, R. A. In *The design of experiments.* Hafner Publishing Co. New York, (1935).
16. Fisher, R.A. In *Statistical methods and scientific inference.* Hafner Publishing Co. New York, (1956).
17. Hogarty, G. E., Guy, W., Gross, M., and Gross, G. *Med. Care.* *7*, 271 (1969).
18. Eyman, R. K., Silverstein, A. B., and McLain, R. The acquisition of self-help skills in community vs. institutional training. Paper presented at the meeting of the Psychological Association Convention, Montreal, Canada, (1973).
19. Lord, F. M. *Psychol. Bull.* *72*, 336, (1969).
20. Glaser, E. M., and Backer, T. E. *Evaluation* 54 (1972).
21. Kiresuk, T.J. *Evaluation* 12, (1973).
22. Guttentag, M. *J. Theory Soc. Behav.* *1*, 75, (1971).
23. Davis, H. R. The use of program evaluation in front line services. In *Planning for creative change in mental health services: Use of program evaluation.* U. S. Department of Health, Education, and Welfare, Rockville, Maryland, p. 3, (1971).
24. Good, I.J. *J. Amer. Statistical Ass.* *64,* 23, (1969).
25. Hartley, H. O., Bross, I. D. J., David, H. A., Zelen, M., Bargmann, R. E., Anscombe, F. J., Davis, M., and Anderson, R.L. *J. Amer. Statistical Ass.* *64,* 50, (1969).
26. Mainland, D. In *Notes on biometry in medical research.* U.S. Government Printing Office, Washington, D.C. Note 91, (1970).
27. Meredith, J. *Amer. J. Men. Def.* *78*, 471 (1974).
28. Halpern, J., and Binner, P.R. A model for an output value analysis of mental health programs. *Administration Ment. Health* 40, (1972).
29. McPhee, C., Zusman, J., and Joss, R. Use of client satisfaction: A survey of procedures and a discussion of problems. Paper presented at the National Rehabilitation Training Institute Conference, Miami Beach, Fla., (1973).
30. American Psychiatric Association. In *Standards for psychiatric facilities.* Washington, D. C., (1969).

31. American Psychological Association. *APA Monitor* 12, (1974).
32. Joint Commission on Accreditation of Hospitals. In *Standards for residential facilities for the mentallly retarded.* Chicago, Ill., (1971).
33. Joint Commission on Accreditation of Hospitals. In *Accreditation manual for psychiatric facilities, 1972.* Chicago, Ill, (1972).
34. Joint Commission on Accreditation of Hospitals. In *Standards for community agencies serving persons with mental retardation and other developmental disabilities.* Chicago, Ill., (1973).
35. American Psychological Association. In *Ethical standards for Psychologists.* Washington, D. C., (1967).
36. McGarry, A. L. and Kaplan, H. A. Overview; Current trends in Mental Health Law. *Amer. J. Psychiat. 130,* 621, (1973).
37. American Psychiatric Association. In *Psychiatric utilization review: Principles and objectives.* Washington, D. C., (1968).
38. Tischler, G.L., and Riedel, D.C. *Amer. J. Psychiat. 130,* 913, (1973).
39. Decker, B., and Bonner, P. In *PSRO: Organization for regional peer review.* Edited by Decker, B. and Bonner, P. Ballinger, Cambridge, Mass., (1973).
40. Wilson, N.D., and Swanson, R.M. Goal attainment ratings as measures of treatment effectiveness. Updated report of 1971 presentation at WICHE Conference on Mental Health, Newport Beach, Calif., (1972).
41. Voorhis, E. Evaluation of the community mental health centers program: The perspective of community citizens. Paper presented at the American Psychological Association Convention, Washington, D. C., (1971).
42. Chu, F. D., and Trotter, S. In *The mental health complex. Part I community mental health centers.* Center for the Study of Responsive Law, Washington, D. C., (1972).
43. BLK Group. Programs evaluation by summer interns. Final report of HEW Contract OS-70102, Washington, D. C., (1970).

MENTAL HEALTH IN CHILDREN, Volume III
Edited by D. V. Siva Sankar

PROGRAM ANALYSIS AND COMMUNITY MENTAL HEALTH SERVICES FOR CHILDREN

Solomon Cytrynbaum, David L. Snow, Elizabeth V. Phillips, Phillip B. Goldblatt and Gary L. Tischler

Yale University School of Medicine
New Haven, Connecticut

Introduction: The Scope of Mental Health Program Analysis

A variety of recent socio-economic, professional, consumer, third party carrier and funding pressures upon community mental health center delivery systems have generated much interest in management information and data systems, program analysis, peer review and consumer accountability. In order to maintain an acceptable level of functioning, administrators are faced with the periodic need to assess the extent to which service activities and resources support the achievement of program objectives, to review the quality of services, to reevaluate priorities and to make rational changes in support of the stability and survival of the organization. This kind of ongoing program analysis requires an information base to monitor service and management activities, procedures for evaluating the quality of care, and feedback mechanisms to insure that the information obtained is translated into both operational policies and changes in service delivery (1-3).

In response to these and other pressures, much effort has recently been expended to develop mechanisms and models for the systematic evaluation and analysis of mental health programs. These developments include: 1) conceptual models and procedures for the analysis of mental health service delivery from a systems perspective (4-7); 2) sophisticated and complex management information or data systems for monitoring community mental health service delivery (8-13); 3) standardized forms for recording data pertinent to the psychiatric evaluation and the assessment of mental status and social role performance (14-18); 4) alternative ways of structuring the medical record, particularly the problem-oriented format (19-23); 5) computer-based recording, storage and retrieval systems and methods for linking to additional data sources (24-26); 6) professional review and accountability systems in the form of psychiatric utilization and peer review of comprehensive direct patient care and indirect service delivery (27-33); and 7) numerous alternative evaluative strategies and critiques focussing upon diverse aspects of the process and outcome of service delivery including such specific procedures as goal attainment scaling, output value analysis and multi-dimensional outcome assessment (34-49).**

To date, the major portion of this work has been concerned with adults or delivery systems serving the general patient population. Although instruments for collecting data on children and families for clinical, classification or research purposes are plentiful (50), the evaluation of children's community mental health services has received far less attention and the development of a systematic and comprehensive data system for children's services is in it's infancy.**

This chapter will address the need for a comprehensive data system for children and reports on progress towards devel-

---

*For a more systematic and critical review of approaches to program evaluation in general, see the chapter by Drs. Eyman and Windle in this volume.

**For example, some work on the development of a comprehensive data system for community mental health services for children is currently being carried on by the MSIS group at Rockland State Hospital (9-12) by Henderson and associates

oping an information system for the review, analysis and evaluation of children's mental health services. We will begin by reviewing recent developments in this area and specify the administrative, service and research requirements that such a data system must meet. Then, we shall describe some of the more recent collaborative work carried out by staff at the Connecticut Mental Health Center, the Hill-West Haven Division and the Mental Health Service Department of the Hill Health Center* in developing a comprehensive, community-oriented data system for children's services. Finally, we shall explore several implications and potential applications of this data system for service delivery, quality assessment and future research.

---

(51), at the Pittsburgh Child Guidance Center and by the Hill-West Haven Division of the Connecticut Mental Health Center and Hill Health Center in New Haven. These developments will be described below. To our knowledge, no other comprehensive and systematic data system for children's community mental health center services is currently in place and operative although the issue of classification and various classification schemes have received much recent attention (52, 53).

*The Hill West Haven Division is a major component of the Connecticut Mental Health Center (CMHC), a cooperative endeavor of Yale University and the Connecticut Department of Mental Health. The Division serves a catchmented area of about 75,000, composed of the Hill section of New Haven, a low income ghetto area of about 25,000 and West Haven, an adjacent largely white working class suburb with a population of about 50,000 persons. In-patient, day care, drug detoxification, research, training and administrative services of the Division are located in or nearby the larger CMHC. Field stations, located in the Hill and West Haven provide direct services in the form of individual, child and/or family therapy and indirect services including community consultation and education programs. The Hill Health Center, sponsored by the Hill Neighborhood Corporation, provides total medical care and mental health services to low income residents of the Hill. Formal and informal collaboration between the Hill Health Center's Mental Health Service Department and the Hill Field Station (housed in the Health Center) occurs at various levels.

Assumptions Underlying Existing Data Systems for Children's Mental Health Services

The prevailing ideology within psychiatric, mental health and social service institutions focuses on individual psychopathology and maladjustment and is associated with the use of treatment strategies aimed at correcting individual problems or disturbance. This position reflects an exceptionalistic rather than universalistic world view. A universalistic position views many mental health problems as derivative of, or responsive to imperfect social and economic conditions or social systems and their resulting life crises (54-56). To the degree that one's professional world view influences the establishment of priorities, the structure and organization of service delivery systems and treatment orientations, the dominance of the individualistic perspective has resulted in a disproportionate allocation of resources to direct patient care as opposed to multi-level approaches emphasizing both individual clinical and social system interventions. This view is reflected in the allotment of community mental health center resources at the national level. Table 1, a selective summary of data from the 1972-1973 Annual NIMH Inventory survey of federally-funded community mental health centers, provides a rough operational index of the priority assigned indirect services nationally. These data indicate a huge discrepancy between the amount of time devoted to direct patient care as opposed to indirect mental health services. The median values for time allocated to direct versus extramural consultation service is 76.4% versus 4.8% of total staff hours. While comparable values differ for centers in a given region (73.7% versus 6.7% in DHEW Region I) or for specific centers within any given region (64.1% versus 12.2%), the trend consistently favors direct patient care as opposed to indirect service activities. Even within the context of the total time allocated to consultation, most effort is expended in case-oriented as opposed to staff-or program-oriented consultation, (44.6% versus 18.8% versus 29.6%), further indication of the domination of the individualistic as opposed to universalistic perspectives.

Examples of Some Child Focused Data Systems

A tangible manifestation of the prevailing ideology is seen in the data systems that have been developed for children's mental health services. Consider, for example, the most recent efforts of the Multi-State Information System (MSIS) group at Rockland State Hospital (9-12) and of Henderson and associates (51) at the Pittsburgh Child Guidance Center. The former is largely aimed at meeting administrative needs; the latter is concerned with monitoring clinical and treatment decision-making.

With respect to intake and outcome, the MSIS group has proposed separate Children's Admission and Termination forms. When combined with the Direct and Indirect Contact Forms, the package provides a means for indexing client background, socio-demographic characteristics (e.g., age, sex, race, family composition, education, census tract, etc.), presenting problems, sources of referral, service utilization patterns, disposition, subsequent referral and status upon termination. Recent versions of the Admissions and Termination forms seem appropriate for their administrative audiences, but appear to be of limited utility for service deliverers.

The work in progress at the Pittsburgh Child Guidance Center has focused on the development of a data system that serves as an aid in clinical decision-making. The intake and evaluation system developed by Henderson and associates called *Minimal Data System For Child Psychiatry* (51) is based on decision and systems theory. The system is designed to arrive at a treatment decision, not a diagnostic decision. Therefore, data collection is limited to that information felt necessary and sufficient for making treatment decisions.

As outlined by the authors, the clinical decision-making model consists of four components: 1) the dispositional treatment options available to a given clinic population (individual therapy, family therapy, etc.); 2) intervening variables necessary to differentiate among those options; 3) the theoretical assumptions determining the type and number of intervening variables; and 4) the items (series of questions) designed to capture information relative to the identifying variables and differentiate the treatment options.

In order to illustrate this data system in relation to one of the defined treatment options (individual child therapy), the authors first specify a variable ("the presence of specific, non-adaptive responses to generally facilitating environments"), and the underlying assumption ("a child's symptoms are indicators of the child's efforts to resolve individual conflict(s)--these may be resolved by a facilitating relationship with a clinician"). Informational items are then generated to provide the necessary data in relation to these defined variables. In this case, questions are developed to assess disturbances in affective behavior, impulse control, thought processes, cognitive functions, social behavior and bodily functions. Additional variables are included, to complete the data collection concerning this dispositional option. The overall questionnaire is generated by application of this model to each available treatment option. The rating or answer to each question is coded to indicate a weighting for or against particular intervention choices. Taken as a composite, the scales are designed to provide an aid in determining the appropriate, effective intervention, and contraindicate others.

We have reviewed the work by Henderson and associates, because it represents a major step in specifying clinical decision-making processes. The system provides clarity and efficiency. The emphasis on minimal data fosters a more rigorous determination of whether information adds predictive power and contributes to the accuracy of decisions. The operations can be applied to any set of treatment or intervention options and, therefore, are generalizable to many types of settings and programs. Inherent in the system are matters of standardization which enhance data processing and make possible storage and immediate retrieval of clinical data.

The basic validity of the model has yet to be fully tested. Pilot studies seem to establish reasonable reliability. Care must be taken not to presume knowledge of all relevant variables to be incorporated in the assessment process. In this regard, the development of the instruments may need to be more broadly empirically based. Also, the present instrument only includes direct interventions. The possibility of applying this model for differentiating system and community level interventions, as well as clinical interventions, seems promising.

Data systems of this type reflect the prevailing orientation to problem analysis concerning children's mental health issues. The orientation is primarily individualistic. Assessment and documentation procedures lead to solutions which emphasize changing the individual child. As a working assumption, we believe that the data collected and the assessment procedures utilized by a service delivery system reflect a basic way of thinking, and in turn these data systems and the information recorded reinforce a particular conceptualization of problems and affect the process of determining which solutions and program efforts are made available and/or are indicated. In the absence of sufficient data regarding social and system influences on the individual, documentation of individual psychopathology can only lead to a view of the individual as the problem, to a justification for major emphasis on the continued development of direct services, and to research studies that support this type of analysis and process (57-59).

Data Requirements for Children's Community Mental Health Services

It is our belief that there is a need to broaden the problem appraisal capacity of intake and recordkeeping systems for clients seeking mental health services from facilities committed to providing both direct and indirect services. Our rational is: 1) Clients seeking service represent a major resource for documenting those familial, social and cultural factors that promote or interfere with effective community functioning. If individuals seeking help are casualties of either particular life experiences or social, political and economic forces, then systematic attempts to assess and document these influences are necessary. While the impact of such socio-economic and systems factors (including correlated ethnic and cultural patterns) on the demand for children's mental health services is well documented, (60-65) the incorporation of such data into our fixed information systems is generally neglected. 2) The community mental health movement has also led to the establishment of community-based mental health centers mandated to provide both direct and indirect services. Consequently, an interdisciplinary conceptual framework is required that emphasizes clinical, public health and consultative and social action approaches. Given this broader task definition, there is a need for intake and evaluation processes that reflect an ecological perspective and for "the development of standardized, quantitative, ecologically oriented profiling systems for work with individual handicapped, disadvantaged, or delinquent children, and the development of models of intervention programs embracing ecological concepts" (66). This view is supported by the community mental health center legislation. The requirement to provide comprehensive services to all catchment residents enhances the need for the implementation of broader and more comprehensive efforts to affect family, system and community influences on individual functioning as well as direct intervention with individuals (67). Within this context, expanded and multi-leveled assessment procedures are needed to record family-level, social and sytem-level and community-level problems as well as individual-level problems. In this way, the multiple tasks of the organization receive tangible recognition. 3) Finally, we come to the question of interagency collaboration and sharing data for regional planning and evaluative research. Currently, most agencies collect demographic data for purposes of administrative accountability and for internal utilization studies. An obvious problem with these unique data collection and storage systems is that, inter-program linkage is impossible. The additional case-related data collected is usually embedded in narrative records and are, therefore, practically irretrievable. The data system required for evaluative studies, psycho-social studies and research on family climate and family interactional patterns exist in agency records in this manner. It is not transportable and does not facilitate an evaluation of aspects of the family and social system variables to determine how these factors contribute to maintaining or creating the child's difficulties. This type of problem appraisal would make more possible the development of broader treatment and program interventions.

The major difficulty with present assessment and data collection procedures, is that potential influences of a psychosocial and system nature are not assessed or they are recorded in such a form that the data are of limited utility to anyone in the agency except the clinician. Therefore, we maintain that the requirements for program analysis and criteria for the creation of a data system for children's services in a community mental health center context are: 1) The data system must call for problem appraisal reflecting the influence of multiple individual, family, social system, and ecological determinents of a child's behavior; 2) In social system terms, the data system must provide information on relevant input (intake), throughput (intervention) and output (outcome) parameters; 3) The data system must be retrievable for administrative, clinical, program planning and research purposes and translatable into specific parameters and/or criteria for quality assessment; 4) The data system must have some degree of generalizability for application in different service delivery systems in order to facilitate area-wide linkage; 5) Program analysis must take into account and record multi-leveled direct and indirect interventions as part of the service deliverer's options; 6) Multiple sources of information should, where possible, be used with respect to different domains of the child's life; 7) Feedback mechanisms guaranteeing the use of results must be clearly spelled out; and 8) Outcome data should enable one to identify changes in the child, family or the child's eco-system attributable to multi-leveled direct or indirect interventions.

Given an approach which emphasizes a multi-leveled systems orientation, the initial data to be included (as defined by a task force composed largely of service deliverer's) are: a) socio-demographic variables; b) physical health and development history variables; c) presenting problem and behavior parameters; d) family assessment dimensions; e) school/family relationships; f) census tract and ecological data on the neighborhood and the immediate community; and g) child's functioning as a student in school.*

---

*Work on the development of a comprehensive psychosocial data system for children's community mental health services began about two years ago when a Task Force chaired

The Children's Assessment Package As An Alternative Data System

The Children's Assessment Package (CAP) jointly being developed by staff of the Hill-West Haven Division of the Connecticut Mental Health Center and the Mental Health Service Department of the Hill Health Center is one response to the above requirements. As currently formulated, it is intended to supplement the proposed MSIS Children's Admissions and Termination Forms.** CAP records multi-leveled information on the individual child, family, school and other social factors as well as on interventions during the intake assessment (input), intervention (throughput) and intermediate or long-term outcome (output) phases. In what follows, we shall describe the major parameters and sources of information which make up the data system and the current status of our developmental work.

The assessment at the individual child level incorporates four sets of data. The proposed MSIS Children's Admissions Form completed by Intake staff, is utilized for recording the history of previous contacts and the child's presenting problems. Information is obtained in a checklist format on previous contacts with mental health, retardation or related services, problems having to do with physical functions,

---

by the senior author was constituted. In addition to Drs. Cytrynbaum and Snow and Mrs. Elizabeth Phillips, the following have participated as members of this Task Force and have contributed to the development of CAP: Hal Brunt, M.D., Human Services and Resource Center, Hill-West Haven Division and Yale Child Study Center; Jim Jekel, M.D., Hill Health Center, Research; Kirby Neill, Ph.D., formerly of the Hill Field Station, Hill-West Haven Division, and Joe Suarez, M.S.W., Mental Health Service Department, Hill Health Center. Dick Granger, M.D., Yale Child Study Center, contributed to several of the early meetings and Robert Washington, Ph.D., Hill Field Station, Hill-West Haven Division, has recently joined the Task Force.

**The Task Force is currently pretesting the non-MSIS components of CAP.

retarded developmental progress, school functioning, school relations, child abuse, problem duration and others.

This form is supplemented by a developmental history completed by the child's parents (See Appendix A). Emphasis is on developmental landmarks, the emotional climate for mother, father and child during the pre- and post-natal period, and on father's involvement with both mother and child during the neonatal period.

Standardized information on the child's behavior* and academic performance in the school setting is obtained from the teacher or an appropriate school representative (Appendix B). Additional developmental and medical information is obtained from the pediatrician/family physician or appropriate medical clinic (Appendix C). These two sources of data broaden the evaluation of physical, behavioral or psychological difficulties present. Thus, the evaluation of the individual child, includes the perspectives of a number of important figures in the child's life--clinician, parents, teacher and physician.

Next, major attention is given to assessing family functioning and identifying recent life events that may have stressed the family system and precipitated family dysfunction. This includes an evaluation of the primary interactional patterns within the family to determine the nature and basic character of family dynamics as well as of the marital, parent-child, and child-child relationships.** The data is obtained from an assessment by intake or clinical staff of the family unit (Appendix D). Examples of items included are:

(1) *Family Dynamics*: patterns of parential dominance; alliances within the family; communication networks; problem-solving; mutuality and identifications; family affective or feeling tone; role differentiation; scapegoating; and intergenerational or religious conflict.

---

*The rating format and several of the items for assessing the child's behavior in school were derived from the work of Borgatta and Fanshel (68).

**Several items in this section were derived in a modified format from the Beavers-Timberlawn Family Evaluation Scale (69). We were also influenced by personal correspondence with the Philadelphia Child Guidance Clinic.

(2) *Marital Relationship*: level of open and unresolved conflict between husband and wife; degree of dissatisfaction with the sexual relationship by husband or wife; level of conflict between husband and wife regarding child rearing, financial matters and husband's and/or wife's work; degree of mutual satisfaction in the marital relationship.
(3) *Parent-Child Relationship*: extent to which husband or wife carries excessive amount of responsibility for parenting; husband or wife is hostile or seductive toward the child and husband or wife is rejecting or overprotective of child.
(4) *Child-Child Relationships*: level of fighting, competition or scapegoating among children; extent to which children are divided into hostile camps and child is often left in charge of his/her siblings. These data, reduced statistically to an appropriate output format, will allow staff to characterize in quantifiable clusters or patterns basic dynamics operative within the family.

In addition to the evaluation of family interactional patterns, information is obtained from the family regarding the possible occurrence of significant life crises during the year prior to agency contact (Appendix E).

These events are presented in relation to the family: (e.g., death of an important person, serious money problems, birth of a child, family moved to another home, etc.); the mother and father (e.g., emotional, physical health or work-related problems); and the child (e.g., child left home to live elsewhere, child had serious physical health problems, child injured by physical abuse, child became pregnant, etc.). Together with the interactional data the information concerning recent significant life events will provide a reasonable understanding of current family functioning and the type and degree of stress affecting the family.

Finally, the analysis of social and community factors includes a broad assessment of socio-psychological factors which may influence the functioning of the family. Included here are:

(1) *Basic Background and Demographic Information*

The MSIS Children's Admission form completed by Intake staff will serve as the basis for obtaining certain demographic data including race, age, family composition, marital status, education of child and family income. This material will be supplemented by the parents on the Family Information Form (Appendix F) in order to obtain information on the family's religion, the language spoken in the home, and the type of employment and level of education for both mother and father.

(2) *Social Stress Indices*

Several factors are assessed which are viewed as potentially contributing to the amount of stress impacting on the family or certain of its members. Information is obtained from the Family Information Form regarding movement history (number of times the family has moved in the past five years, extent of family disruption resulting from move to new residence, etc.), the type and quality of present housing, the degree of job satisfaction for mother and father, and the degree of satisfaction with level of education for mother and father.

(3) *Social Support Network*

This portion of the assessment is aimed at determining to what extent various social supports are available to the family. The special focus on this aspect of the evaluation is based on the view that deficiences in the support structure contribute to the degree of family isolation and, therefore, are sources of stress for the family. Several variables are utilized in evaluating the social support network including: the extent to which the family (including extended family) or supports outside the family are present in relation to child care needs; the availability of various family, friend and/or community resources when special problems arise (i.e., concerning family, health, financial, or child-related difficulties); the availability of extended family or friends as general sources of support; the degree of accessibility to means of transportation; the extent to which the family is in conflict with predominant neighborhood culture or values; the extent of intergenerational conflict; and, estimated from the above items, the level of overall physical or psychological isolation for the family.

(4) *Family-School Relationship*

The school setting is a primary system involving and affecting, the child, and one to which the family must relate. In addition to the clinician's assessment of school-related difficulties and the assessment of the child by school personnel, the Child's School Experiences Form (Appendix G) is included to obtain the family's view of the school program and of their child in relation to the school setting. This focus allows some determination of the parents' attitudes toward school and whether these are areas of conflict and tension between family and school. The parents' perspective on their child's school and educational program can be indicative of matters in the child's school experience, or in the relationship between school and family, that require intervention. Parents are asked to rate a series of questions that include items such as: my child likes to go to school; the difficulty my child is having is the fault of the teacher; the school authorities blame the family for my child's difficulties; my child has friends at school; my child trusts adults at school; my child is hard to control at school; no one in the school system cares what happens to my child and whether he/she learns anything; and my child needs a special class or teacher.

With the inclusion of this information from the family, a comparison of school-related data provided by clinician, teacher and the child's parents forms a broad basis for understanding the multiple dimensions of the child's school experience and the nature of the relationship between school and family.

CAP is intended as a comprehensive psycho-social data system for children and families. The entire set of instruments will serve as the intake assessment procedure. It should be noted that many of the component instruments such as the family assessment and school forms, as well as the proposed MSIS Children's Termination Form, can be used as measures of intermediate and long-term outcome or effectiveness. This creates the possibility of pre- and post evaluation of service studies as well as of comparative impact studies across different settings or client populations.

In order to complete the data system, it is necessary to record direct and indirect service interventions over time. Currently, direct and indirect service contacts with children, their families and relevant human service agencies or facilities such as schools are recorded continuously using modified versions of the MSIS Direct and Indirect Service Contact

Forms. These forms provide basic identification information on the service deliverer's involved, the direct or indirect service project, consultee, service recipient, the date, type, time and manner of contact, the type of service delivered and the service recipients present during the contact. The data are keypunched and stored on a monthly basis. Periodic reports relating client characteristics such as age, race, sex, diagnosis, etc. to types of service, length of stay, etc. are presented to the appropriate administrators and staff on a regular basis, and we now have the capacity to retrieve data pertaining to specific questions raised by administrators, clinicians or researchers within a reasonably short turn-over time.

Some Applications of the CAP Data System

The availability of a data system such as that described provides community mental health center administrators, program planners and evaluators with a powerful tool for program analysis. This can be illustrated in four major areas of administrative functioning: 1) needs assessment and the establishment of priorities; 2) monitoring the implementation of program objectives; 3) evaluating the concordance between stated goals and performance; and 4) evaluating the quality of care.

Administrative Establishment of Program Priorities

A catchmented community mental health center has responsibility for planning programs and making available service appropriate to the needs of its catchmented residents. In other words, entry boundaries must remain permeable. The intake portion of CAP can serve to identify needs of catchment residents. This kind of information is of value in the planning of new programs and in reassessing existing program priorities. For example, preliminary and impressionistic data from the staff of the Hill Field Station and Mental Health Service Department of the Hill Health Center suggest that in the Hill community about 40% of the children in the catchment area change schools within the school year, and that as many as 50%

Table 1

*ALLOCATION OF COMMUNITY MENTAL HEALTH CENTER STAFF TIME**

STAFF TIME BY SERVICE	Median Value all Centers in DHEW Region I	Median: All Centers in U.S.A. 50%ile
Total direct care hours as a percent of total hours	73.7	76.4
Extramural consultation hours as a percent of total hours	6.7	4.8
CONSULTATION ACTIVITIES		
Percent of total staff hours devoted to consultation	7.1	4.9
Percent of total consultation hours devoted to		
case-oriented consultation	41.0	44.6
staff development consultation	18.7	18.8
program-oriented consultation	37.4	29.6
law enforcement agencies	4.3	6.5
alcohol agencies	3.0	3.3
drug agencies	2.5	3.0
mental health facilities	1.6	2.6
health facilities	1.6	2.6
welfare agencies	2.6	3.3
agencies for aged	2.3	3.3
schools	40.1	30.0
Percent of school consultation devoted to		
pre-school	21.8	9.6
public primary schools	59.5	42.8
public secondary schools	17.7	37.4

*Source is NIMH Inventory results (1972-73)

Table 2

WEST HAVEN FIELD STATION SERVICES AS A FUNCTION OF AGE OF RECIPIENT: 1973-74

		DIRECT CLINICAL SERVICES			*INDIRECT SERVICES*		
		Number of contacts Annually	Percent*	Rate Per 1,000 Pop.*	Number of contacts Annually	Percent	Rate Per 1,000 Pop.*
Pre-School:	5	243	4.6	45.3	620	13.4	115.7
Elementary:	6-12	520	9.8	82.5	597	12.9	94.7
Adolescent:	13-17	496	9.4	113.2	771	16.6	176.0
Adult:	18-54	2,329	43.9	88.3	193	4.2	7.3
Senior Citizens:	55	127	2.4	12.2	482	10.4	46.2
Age not specified and/or contact with mixed ages		1,589	30.0	---	1,977	42.6	---
TOTAL		5,304	100.1**	---	4,640	100.1**	---

*Based on 1970 census.
**Rounding error.

have had three or more school moves by the end of the second grade. In addition, school problems are a frequent presenting problem at intake, a significant number of children are reading at least two years below grade level and parents frequently report a sense of powerlessness in dealing with a particular school or the school system.

CAP or a similar data system can be used by administrators to identify such clusters of needs and problems. In response, consultation and preventive programs can be designed with this client population as the ultimate target group. These services could be carried out in conjunction with or independent of existing individual and group treatment programs for children. Similarly, CAP could serve to substantiate impressions that housing quality and termination of heating and other utility services have become a major problem for a significant number of residents in our catchment. In response to this preliminary information, a systematic survey of a random sample of Hill catchment residents covering housing violations and utility payments is currently being proposed. The results of this survey will be used in an advocacy manner in relation to the Welfare Department and other appropriate city or state agencies.

Monitoring Utilization Patterns and the Achievement of Program Objectives

The CAP data system can provide administrators with systematic information on the socio-demographic and personal characteristics of the user population as well as current utilization patterns. The data below will serve to illustrate how the MSIS components of the data system are currently employed for this purpose.

Table 2 contains the distribution of direct and indirect services by age of recipient provided by the West Haven Field Station during 1973-74. These data indicate that during this period about 25% of direct service contacts and over 40% of indirect service contacts involved clients 17 years of age or under.

Table 3 presents the distribution of registered clients for the Hill and West Haven Field Stations by social class area. Here we note that the Hill Field Station services primarily residents of low income areas (78.2% of contacts with clients residing in social class area 4) while the West Haven Field Station served a much more heterogeneous population.

Table 3

DISTRIBUTION OF REGISTERED CLIENTS BY SES AREA FOR THE HILL AND WEST HAVEN FIELD STATIONS, 1973-74

	Hill Field Station	West Haven Field Station
Social class area	Percent	Percent
1	0.0	37.0
2	10.7	27.8
3	21.0	25.8
4	78.2	9.2
TOTAL	100.0	99.8

Tables 4 and 5 provide a breakdown for a similar time period of primary types of direct and indirect service contacts made by the two field stations. These kind of data can be used to monitor the achievement of several previous administrative priorities. For example, a decision was taken to have the West Haven Field Station serve as a direct portal of entry (in addition to the Emergency Room service at the Yale New Haven Hospital and the walk-in, triage and intake services located in the larger Connecticut Mental Health Center) for the West Haven catchment residents. Table 4 reveals that this objective was largely implemented in that over a third of all direct service contacts in the West Haven Field Station involved intake or evaluation services. In another instance, the Director and staff of the West Haven Field Station established a priority on

Table 4

DIRECT SERVICE CONTACTS BY PRIMARY TYPE OF SERVICE BY UNIT RENDERING SERVICE

	Hill Field Station		West Haven Field Station	
TYPE OF SERVICE	No.	%	No.	%
Intake (Screening)	41	1.2	123	2.6
Evaluation (1st or 2nd)	108	3.3	1,210	25.6
Evaluation (beyond 2nd)	116	3.6	184	3.9
Individual Treatment	1,064	33.2	745	15.8
Group Treatment	180	5.6	588	12.4
Family Treatment	166	5.1	852	18.0
Couple Treatment	67	2.0	169	3.5
Crisis Intervention	215	6.7	112	2.3
Concrete Service	142	4.4	114	2.4
Home Visit Service	144	4.4	54	1.1
Rehabilitation Services	8	0.2	----	---
Information Exchange	361	11.2	150	3.2
Client Planning & Review/Case Consultation	317	9.9	327	6.9
Expediting	200	6.2	42	0.9
Referral	39	1.2	30	0.6
Other	35	1.0	13	0.2
Missing	----	---	----	---
TOTAL	3,202	99.3	4,713	99.5

the delivery of group and family treatment services (as well as individual psychotherapy) for children and adolescents, whereas the Hill Field Station remained largely committed to individual treatment modalities. These priorities are reflected in the distribution of staff contacts. In the West Haven Field Station roughly 30% of direct service staff time was devoted to group and family treatment modalities compared to a little over 10% for the Hill Field Station staff. On the other hand, the Hill Field Station devoted a little over 10% of its direct service time to group and family treatment modalities, over a third to individual treatment and about 20% to other individually-oriented direct services including providing concrete services, home visit services and information exchange.

The indirect service contact data in Table 5 similarly reveal some intriguing differences. Reflecting the more individual orientation at the Hill Field Station 13% of indirect service staff contacts were devoted to case consultation, whereas an insignificant amount of West Haven Field Station staff time was devoted to this activity. The more social system orientation of the West Haven Field Station is reflected in the higher percentages of administrative and staff development consultation (7.8% and 4.0% respectively). The high percent of West Haven staff time devoted to preparation, planning and review (47.5%) primarily reflects student teaching and supervising time. Finally, it should be noted that the data system also allows for assessing whether program priorities have been implemented by monitoring the distribution of types of service rendered to particular clients over sequential time blocks.

Special Studies

Other potential studies with a program analysis focus can be identified. These include: 1) Comparative studies of patterns of utilization and drop-outs across catchment, delivery systems and social class; 2) Studies of the impact of various age, race and sex combinations of clinicians and patients on the quality of service and outcome; 3) Investigations of the validity of the criteria-oriented approach to the review of patient care by correlating expert reviewer ratings of the quality of care (in terms of the criteria of appropriateness, adequacy and effective-

Table 5
INDIRECT SERVICE CONTACTS BY PRIMARY TYPE OF SERVICE BY UNIT RENDERING SERVICE

Type of Indirect Service	Hill Field Station		West Haven Field Station	
	Number of Contacts	Percent	Number of Contacts	Percent
Case-oriented Consultation	183	13.0	29	.9
Program Consultation	82	5.8	153	4.9
Administrative Consultation	3	.2	243	7.8
Staff Development Consultation	21	1.5	125	4.0
Community Organizing	38	2.7	32	1.0
Other Consultation	77	5.5	19	.6
Ongoing Program Activity	350	24.8	620	19.8
Interagency Collaboration	84	6.0	248	7.9
Preparation, Planning and Review	193	13.7	1486	47.5
Group Work	67	4.7	46	1.5
Individual Work	137	9.7	16	.5
Expediting/ Advocacy/Concrete Service	81	5.7	72	2.3
Public Information/ Education	97	6.9	40	1.3
TOTAL	1413	100.2	3129	100.0

TABLE VI

*Appendices**

Appendix A	Child's Developmental History
Appendix B	School Report on Student's Behavior and Performance (Elementary, Junior High and Senior High)
Appendix C	Request for Medical Information
Appendix D	Family Assessment Form
Appendix E	Significant Life Events
Appendix F	Family Information Form
Appendix G	Child's School Experiences

*The instruments contained in Appendices A through G, supplemented by the proposed MSIS Children's Admission and Termination Forms and by the MSIS Direct and Indirect Service Contact Forms, comprise a comprehensive psychosocial data system for children's mental health services. The non-MSIS components of this data system were developed by a Task Force of Yale University faculty representing the Hill-West Haven Division of the Connecticut Mental Health Center, the Hill Health Center and the Yale Child Study Center. The following have participated as members of this Task Force: Solomon Cytrynbaum, Ph.D., Assistant Professor, Department of Psychiatry; Elizabeth Phillips, M.S.W., Assistant Clinical Professor of Psychiatry, Department of Psychiatry; David L. Snow, Ph.D., Assistant Professor, Department of Psychiatry; Hal Brunt, M.D., Assistant Professor, Department of Psychiatry and Yale Child Study Center; Dick Granger, M.D., Associate Professor of Clinical Pediatrics, Yale Child Study Center and Department of Pediatrics; Jim Jekel, M.D., Associate Professor of Public Health (Administration); Kirby Neill, Ph.D., formerly Assistant Professor, Department of Psychiatry; Joe Suarez, M.S.W., Assistant Professor of Social Work, Yale Child Study Center; Robert Washington, Ph.D., Assistant Professor, Department of Psychiatry.

ness) with CAP outcome information; and 4) Outcome studies focused on the impact of various combinations of multi-leveled direct and indirect interventions rendered to clients with different individual, family, school and community diagnostic profiles generated by CAP at intake.

Assessment of Quality of Care

A data system such as CAP also has implications for the assessment of the quality of direct and indirect services provided to children and adolescents. Next, we will briefly review the work of the Psychiatric Utilization Review and Evaluation Project at Yale, focusing our examples on the development of criteria in the area of direct services to adolescents. Finally, we will summarize a recent effort to extend this model into the review of indirect services.*

Utilization review has become a requirement for community mental health centers as well as for general psychiatric hospitals and extended care facilities. The Medicare Program, as a condition of participation, requires the institution make a commitment to a course of action in patient care surveillance and file a written description of their proposed utilization review program. In addition, public law mandates the formation of Professional Standard Review Organizations (PSRO's).

From 1969 to 1973 researchers at Yale (27, 28, 31, 70, 71) were independently at work to establish a model for performing peer review. They elaborated the basic requirements for: 1) an adequate data base to permit assessment of the quality of patient care; 2) selection mechanisms to choose cases or instances of abberrant care worthy of review; 3) the development of pre-determined criteria as to appropriate, adequate and effective treatment against which individual, selected cases can be compared; 4) the establishment of institutional processes to facilitate review, both of individual cases and programs.

---

*What follows is a shortened and highly abridged version of a previous presentation on utilization review for children's services (70). A more detailed presentation of the criteria-oriented approach to the review of patient care is available (31).

While the primary foci of the Psychiatric Utilization Review and Evaluation Project (PURE) was on the development of models for adult care, certain elements support the work described earlier in regard to child services. In this section we will briefly review these areas of overlap.

Basic Data System

Initially, the PURE project set up four panels to test alternative methods of developing criteria; the schizophrenia panel (a diagnosis); the suicide panel (a symptom); the intake panel (an institutional process); and the adolescent panel (a developmental epoch). Each panel was to elaborate appropriate care in its area and to test the emerging criteria empirically. To assist in these tasks a data group was established to provide relevant information as requested by the panels as well as to elaborate patterns of care which emerged from statistical analysis of the charts at participating mental health centers.

It quickly became obvious that the usual narrative, non-computerized record provided sketchy, unreliable, often non-useful information. Much effort was expended in collaboration with the Multi-State Information System to develop more rational records. The minimum information necessary to review treatment careers of individual patients and to examine patterns of care included: 1) Socio-demographic identifiers, such as age, race, sex, etc.; 2) Discharge data identifying information about sources of referral into the facility and places to which patients are subsequently referred; 3) Focus of care in the facility (e.g., OPD, Day Hospital, ER, etc); 4) Treatment data identifying types of treatment, care given, lengths of treatment, etc; 5) Patient movement data among units; 6) Categories such as diagnoses; 7) Description data about the presenting problems, prior history, mental status, problem inventories, etc.

All of the above information is included in CAP and the MSIS forms. These data can be organized in traditional narrative fashion or can be developed into a problem-oriented format suitable for computers.

Each of the panels in order to develop and to test criteria

had to generate data bases encompassing very similar variables as developed for CAP.

It is beyond the scope of this chapter to summarize each of the panel's results which are presented in detail elsewhere (31); however, a few examples will indicate the general approach. The work of the adolescent panel may be most relevant for our purposes. This panel developed a number of normative criteria about treatment parameters. For example, in regard to parents, the members agreed that parents should not be *required* to be involved in the treatment as long as the patient's life situation was not chaotic, if he was legally emancipated, or if the involvement of the parents during the initial phase of treatment would preclude the growth of a therapeutic alliance.

The panel felt that withdrawal without notification can often reflect poorer care than in the case of mutual agreement between clinician and patient as to termination and disposition. To test these criteria the panel studied in detail the chief complaints of adolescents coming to the center. The panel compared the congruence between the perceptions of the adolescent patient and the intake worker as to the nature and the severity of the chief complaint. The higher the congruence, the more likely the adolescent would enter treatment or arrive at a mutually satisfactory agreement as to disposition.

This panel, like the others, studied in detail the sociodemographic characteristics of the adolescent population and related their work in the area of chief complaints to these data. The panel found a subgroup of late adolescents, coming from working class backgrounds, who referred themselves for care primarily because of intra-psychic complaints of anxiety and depression. These were high school graduates, living away from home, struggling with the problem of defining an identity different from that of their families. They did not fit the familiar stereotype of the patient from the blue collar class, seeking psychiatric assistance for somatic and social complaints. These adolescents sought a relationship with a therapist who could deal with inner feelings and strivings. This was fed back to intake workers to alter some of the program foci by changing their stereotypes about this class of patients.

Such special studies are time consuming and expensive;

however, a by-product of such studies can be the development of indices (72) which can be presumed to infer something about the quality of care. These indices can use routinely collected items which would then have significance for utilization review, especially in the selection of units, patients, or clinicians who deviate from the normative or empirically derived norms for their class.

Further work of the PURE project developed a chart review checklist (71) to assist in individual case evaluation. In addition, a Utilization Review Committee was created to test the utility of the checklist and individual case selection mechanisms.

The information in the Children's Assessment Package can easily be converted to a format useful for reviewing quality of care and to meet utilization review requirements. A child services checklist is being developed to assist utilization review activities in a manner analogous to that used to review adult services.

In conclusion, the work of the PURE project demonstrated:

1. Upgrading of the record system to facilitate utilization review not only permits effective evaluation but assists the clinician in his daily work.
2. Standards or criteria can be developed which are valid and reliable at least for the work within a particular center.
3. Selection mechanisms can be employed to more easily identify aberrant cases, units or clinicians.
4. Formats such as the chart review checklist can be devised to apply the pre-established criteria of quality care.
5. The standards and formats for their use can themselves be subject to scientific criteria of effectiveness.

Most recently, the staff of the Hill-West Haven Division of the Connecticut Mental Health Center have invested considerable time and effort to develop a review process for center-sponsored indirect service or consultation activities for children and adults (73). For this purpose, consultation activities were limited to the general categories of case-oriented, staff-oriented and social sytem-oriented with either an organizational or community focus. Such a review procedure required: 1) an underlying rationale for ordering the complexity of the consultation process and for identifying benchmark parameters; 2) a data system and related data gathering instruments; 3) a set of criteria to be used as standards for assessing the appropriateness, adequacy and effectiveness of the consultation; 4) a mechanism for selecting consultation projects for indepth review; and 5) a procedure for providing feedback to administrators with program development or policy-making responsibilities.

In response to these requirements, the consultation process was conceptualized as a temporary social system which develops over time and involves three component phases: namely, Inception of Consultation, Events and Dynamics in the Consultation, Process and Termination and Review of Outcomes. Associated with each component phase were several benchmark parameters. A data system which incorporates these parameters was proposed. The data system included the following instruments: 1) The Project Registration Form; 2) The Indirect Contact Form; and 3) The Narrative Progress Record.*

The information in the data base was then translated into a checklist format. Criteria were developed for reviewing the appropriateness of the decision to enter a consultation relationship and of the intervention strategies, for assessing the adequacy of the consultant's performance and for judging the effectiveness of the consultation for different consultees. The Checklist for the Review of Consultation Activities was proposed as a first effort to make available a vehicle for the systematic and detailed review of the quality of consultation activities from the point of view of the criteria of appropriateness, adequacy and effectiveness. Procedures for selecting specific consultation projects for indepth review as well as other aspects of the proposed review process are still to be tested for feasibility.

---

*Copies of these instruments have been published (73) and are available from the senior author.

Some Implications For Service Deliverers

Finally, some implications of the CAP data system for service deliverer's should be noted. It is our belief that for clinicians, CAP would facilitate the formulation of diagnostic impressions, the arrival at a set of treatment objectives and the articulation of a treatment and management plan. This is expected because: 1) CAP would offer the clinician an extended range of data covering not only the individual client but information on the family system, the school system and the community social system; 2) CAP's retrievable format would provide the clinician with relatively immediate access to intake and outcome data; 3) The availability of multiple informants as sources of information would make possible independent confirmation of certain information or diagnostic impressions; 4) The involvement of parents in the data gathering process suggests the possibility of a role for parents as co-assessors with the clinician of social systems and other factors affecting the family; and 5) CAP's multi-level problem appraisal with its psycho-social focus would support the development of direct and indirect service options. The data system would also facilitate the identification and review of failures with respect to various treatments or interventions. Finally, we anticipate that the requirement for clinicians to gather information during the intake phase on various parameters of family, school and community functioning will serve to sharpen up the clinician's sensitivity to the contribution of various socio-cultural, social-psychological and ecological factors to the client's difficulties, particularly in the context of a community mental health-oriented service delivery system.

Summary

In this chapter we have attempted to summarize the current state of affairs and present some recent developments in the area of program analysis for children's community mental health services. At the heart of any system of program analysis for children's community mental health services is a feasible and operative data system for recording and monitoring the intake, intervention and outcome phases of such services. Developmental work with respect to such a data system is proceeding on several fronts. The Multi-State Information System (MSIS) group working out of Rockland State Hospital in New York has proposed a Children's Admissions Form and a Children's Termination Form to supplement existing direct and indirect contact forms as a data system for administrators as a primary audience. Henderson and associates at the Pittsburgh Child Guidance Center have focused their efforts on the development of a rather elaborate system, the primary task of which is to aid in the process of clinical decison-making with respect to treatment options. These data systems are representative of developmental work in the area. Because of their limited audiences (administrators and clinicians) and because of their highly individualistic focus, they are of limited utility as a comprehensive data system for children's community mental health services.

The Children's Assessment Package (CAP) is in the process of being developed by the staff of the Hill-West Haven Division of the Connecticut Mental Health Center and the Mental Health Service Department of the Hill Health Center in order to make available a more broadly focused psycho-social and community-oriented data system. The unique features of CAP are: 1) It calls for a broader, multi-leveled problem appraisal which reflects the influence of multiple, individual, family, social system, socio-demographic and ecological determinants of the child's behavior; 2) In combination with existing and operative MSIS Direct and Indirect Service Contact Forms, CAP will provide information on relevant intake, intervention and outcome parameters; 3) The total data system will be retrievable, making systematic information available to administrators for program planning, priority assessment and implementation, for utilization review and the evaluation of patient care, for clinical functioning and for several possible ongoing research projects; 4) CAP relies on multiple informants or sources of information with respect to various domains of the child's life; and 5) CAP provides essential information on relevant client socio-demographic and ecological variables, physical health and developmental health variables, presenting problem and behavior parameters, family assessment dimensions, school/family relationships, census tract and ecological characteristics of the immediate neighborhood and community, and data on the child's functioning as a student in school.

In order to illustrate the potential applications of the total data system composed of CAP, the MSIS Children's Admissions and Terminations Forms and the MSIS Direct and Indirect Service Contact Forms, some data on the socio-demographic characteristics of client populations, the distribution of staff time by type of service and age of client and patterns of service delivery were presented. These data were intended to illustrate how such a data base could be useful to administrators with respect to program planning, the realignment of priorities and the evaluation of the success or failure of program implementation. We also described selected aspects of the criteria-oriented approach to the assessment of the quality of patient care with respect to the delivery of adolescent services and we briefly introduced an adaptation of the criteria-oriented approach to the review and evaluation of indirect services, much of which focus on children as the ultimate target population. Several implications for the functioning of service deliverers and a number of potentially useful research questions were outlined.

Bibliography

1. Astrachan, B. M. MSIS input to administrative decision making. In *The Psychiatric Information System: Protection of Privacy and Confidentiality.* Edited by Laska, E. John Wiley and Sons, New York. In press.
2. Littlestone, R. Planning in mental health. In *The Administration of Mental Health Services.* Edited by Feldman, S. Charles C. Thomas, Springfield. pp. 3-28, (1973).
3. Hargreaves, W.A., Attkisson, C.C., McIntyre, M.H., Siegel, L.M. and Sorensen, J.E. *Resource Materials for Community Mental Health Program Evaluation: Part I Elements of Program Evaluation.* National Institute of Mental Health, San Francisco, (1974).
4. Dolgoff, T. Power, conflict and structure in mental health organizations: A general systems analysis. *Admin. Ment. Hlth.* 12-21, (1972).
5. Hutcheson, B.R. and Krause, E.A. *Community Ment. Health J. 5,* 29, (1969).
6. Holder, H. D. *Arch. Gen. Psychiat. 20,* 709, (1969).
7. Thomas, C.S. and Garrison, V. A general systems view of community mental health. In *Progress in Community Mental Health,* Vol. III. Edited by Bellak, L. and Barten, H.H. Brunner/Mazel, New York, pp. 265-332, (1975).
8. Wilder, J. F. and Miller, S. Management information. In *The Administration of Mental Health Services.* Edited by Feldman, S. Charles C. Thomas, Springfield, pp. 120-137, (1973).
9. Siegel, C. *Evaluating the Attainment of Process Objectives of Community Mental Health Centers Using An Automated Patient Data System (MSIS): Methodology and Application.* Orangeburg, New York: Information Sciences Division, Research Center, Rockland State Hospital, 1974.
10. National Institutes of Mental Health. *Community Mental Health Center Data Systems: A Description of Existing Programs.* U. S. Government Printing Office, Public Health Service Publication No. 1990, Series C-No. 2 Washington, D. C., (1969).

11. Laska, E., Logemann, G., Honigfeld, G., Weinstein, A. and Bank, R. *Evaluation, 1,* 66, (1972).
12. The Information Science Division, Research Center, Rockland State Hospital. *Multi-State Information System for Psychiatric Patients.* Orangeburg, New York: Research Foundation for Mental Hygiene, (1973).
13. Hargreaves, W. A., Attkisson, C. C., McIntyre, M. H., Siegel, L. M. and Sorensen, J. E. *Research Materials for Community Mental Health Program Evaluation: Part III Management Information Systems for Mental Health Centers.* National Institutes of Mental Health, San Francisco, (1974).
14. Spitzer, R. L., Fleiss, T. L. and Endicott, J. *Arch. Gen. Psychiat. 16,* 479, (1967).
15. Lorr, M. and Hamlim, R.M. *J. Consult. Clin. Psychol. 36,* 136, (1971).
16. Laska, E., Simpson, G.M. and Bank, R. *Comprehensive Psychiatry,* 10: 135-146, 1969.
17. Sletten, I. W., Ernhart, G. B. and Ulett, G. A. *Compr. Psychiat. 11,* 315, (1970).
18. Spitzer, R. L. and Endicott, J. *Arch. Gen. Psychiat. 24,* 540, (1974).
19. Hayes-Roth, R., Lonyabaugh, R. and Rybach, R. *Brit. J. Psychiat. 121,* 27, (1972).
20. Novello, L. R. *J. Nerv. Ment. Dis. 156,* 349, (1973).
21. Lipp, M. *Int. J. Psychiat. 11,* 355, (1973).
22. Rybach, R. S. and Gardner, J. S. *Amer. J. Psychiat. 130,* 312, (1973).
23. McLean, P. D. and Miles, L. E. *Arch. Gen. Psychiat. 31,* 622, (1974).
24. Evenson, R. C. *Hosp. Community Psychiat. 25,* 80, (1974).
25. Crawford, T. L., Morgan, D. W. and Giantunco, D. *Progress in Mental Health Information Systems: Computer Applications.* Ballingen Publishing Co., Cambridge Mass., (1974).
26. Laska, E. *The Psychiatric Information System: Protection of Privacy and Confidentiality.* John Wiley and Sons, New York. In press.

27. Riedel, D., Brenner, M. H., Brauer, L., Goldblatt, P. B., Klerman, G., Myers, J., Schwartz, C. and Tischler, G. L. *Amer. J. Public Health 62,* 1222, (1972).
28. Tischler, G. L. Psychiatric utilization review: An accountability technique. Paper presented at the Western Conference on Mental Health Program Management. San Mateo, California, (1972).
29. Brook, R. H. *Quality of Care Assessment: A Comparison of Five Methods of Peer Review.* U. S. Department of Health, Education and Welfare, (1973).
30. Etzioni, A. *Evaluation 1,* 55, (1973).
31. Riedel, D., Tischler, G. L. and Meyers, J. *Patient Care Evaluation in Mental Health Programs.* Ballinger, Cambridge, Mass., (1974).
32. Liptzin, B. *Amer. J. Psychiat. 131,* 1374, (1974).
33. Newman, D., Luft, L. L. *Amer. J. Psychiat. 131,* 1363, (1974).
34. Bell, E. C. and Holland, W. E. Evaluation of human service organizations. Paper presented at the American Psychological Association, Annual Conventionl Montreal, Quebec, (1973).
35. Wolfensberger, W. and Glenn, L. *Program Analysis of Service Systems.* National Institute on Mental Retardation, Toronto, Canada, (1973).
36. MacMahon, B., Pugh, T. F. and Hutchison, G. B. Principles in the evaluation of community mental health programs. In *Program Evaluation in the Health Fields.* Edited by Schulberg, H. C., Sheldon, A. and Baker, F. Behavioral Publications, New York, pp. 51-58, (1969).
37. Donabedian, A. Evaluating the quality of medical care. In *Program Evaluation in the Health Fields.* Edited by Schulberg, H. C., Sheldon, A. and Baker, F. Behavioral Publications, New York, pps. 186-218, (1969).
38. Deniston, O. L. and Rosenstock, I. M. Evaluating health programs. *Public Health Reports* Public Health Service, U. S. Department of Health, Education and Welfare, *85,* pps. 835-840, (1970).
39. Murphy, H. B. M. *Can. Psychiat. Ass. J. 16,* 525, (1971).
40. Walker, R. A. *Evaluation, 1,* 45, (1972).
41. Zusman, J. and Slawson, M. R. *Arch. Gen. Psychiat. 27,* 692, (1972).

42. Binner, P. R., Halpern, J. and Potter, A. Output value analysis: A method for the evaluation of mental health programs. Paper presented at the American Psychological Association, Annual Convention. Honolulu, Hawaii, (1972).
43. Fox, P. D. and Rappaport, M. *Arch. Gen. Psychiat. 26,* 172, (1972).
44. Mullen, E. J., Dumpson, J. R., *et al. Evaluation of Social Intervention.* Jossey-Bass, San Francisco, (1972).
45. Ciarlo, J. A., Lin, S., Bigelow, D. and Biggerstaff, M. A multi-dimensional outcome measure for evaluating community mental health programs. Paper presented at the American Psychological Association, Annual Convention. Honolulu, Hawaii, (1972).
46. Davis, H. R. *Evaluation 1,* 43, (1973).
47. Mushkin, S. J. *Evaluation, 1,* 30, (1973).
48. Binner, P. Program Evaluation. In *The Administration of Mental Health Services.* Edited by Feldman, S. Charles C. Thomas, Springfield pp. 342-383, (1973).
49. Ellis, R. H. and Wilson, N. C. Z. *Evaluation, 1,* 6, (1973).
50. Comrey, A. L., Backer, T. E. and Glaser, E. M. *A Source Book for Mental Health Measures.* Human Interaction Research Institute, California, (1973).
51. Henderson, P. B., Homann, J., Khachaturian, Z., Magnussen, M. G. and Synderman, B. A. *Minimal Data System for Child Psychiatry.* Unpublished manuscript. Pittsburgh Child Guidance Center, Pittsburgh, Pennsylvania, (1972).
52. Hobbs, N. *The Future of Children.* Jossey-Bass, San Francisco, (1975).
53. Hobbs, N. *Issues in the Classification of Children.* Jossey-Bass, San Francisco, (1975).
54. Ryan, W. *Blaming the Victim.* Vintage Books, New York, (1971).
55. Arthur, R. J. *Amer. J. Psychiat. 130,* 841, (1973).
56. Dokecki, P. R., Strain, B. A., Bernal, T. J., Brown, C. S. and Robinson, M. E. Low-income and minority groups. In *Issues in the Classification of Children.* Volume I. Edited by Hobbs, N. Jossey-Bass, San Francisco pp. 318-348, (1975).

57. Hobbs, N. Proposed model for classifying children. In *The Futures of Children.* Hobbs, N. Jossey-Bass, San Francisco, pp. 98-122, (1975).

58. Rhodes, W. C. and Sagor, M. Community perspectives. In *Issues in the Classification of Children.* Edited by Hobbs, N. Jossey-Bass, San Francisco, pp. 101-129, (1975).

59. Cohen, D. J., Granger, R. H., Provence, S. A. and Solnit, A. J. Mental health services. In *Issues in the Classification of Children.* Volume II. Edited by Hobbs, N. Jossey-Bass, San Francisco pp. 88-122, (1975).

60. Ryan, W. *Distress in the City.* Cleveland Press of Case Western Reserve University, (1969).

61. Joint commission on mental health in children. *Crisis in Child Mental Health, Challenge for the 1970's,* Harper and Row, New York, (1969).

62. Hersch, C. *J. Amer. Acad. Child Psychiat. 7,* 223, (1968).

63. Malone, C. A. *J. Amer. Acad. Child Psychiat. 6,* 332, (1967).

64. Chess, S. and Lyman, M. *Amer. J. Orthopsychiat. 39,* 77, (1969).

65. Fine, P. *J. Amer. Acad. Child Psychiat. 11,* 279, (1972).

66. Hobbs, N. *The Futures of Children.* Jossey-Bass, San Francisco, pp. 235, (1975).

67. Tischler, G. L., Aries, E., Cytrynbaum, S. and Wellington, S. The catchment area concept. Edited by Bellak, L. and Barten, H.H. *Progress in Community Mental Health,* Vol. III. Brunner/Mazel, New York, pp. 59-83, (1975).

68. Borgatta, E. F. and Fanshel, D. *Behavioral Characteristics of Children Known to Psychiatric Outpatient Clinics.* Child Welfare League of America, Inc., New York, (1965).

69. Beavers, W. R. Family variables related to the development of a self. Timberlawn Foundation Report No. 68, Timberlawn Foundation, Dallas, Texas, (1973).

70. Goldblatt, P. B., Cytrynbaum, S. and Snow, D. Psychiatric utilization review: Development of a model. Paper

presented at the Conference on Psychiatric Problems of Childhood. New York, (1974).

71. Goldblatt, P. B., Brauer, L. D., Garrison, V. and Henisz, J. E. *Hosp. Community Psychiat. 24,* 753, (1973).
72. Astrachan, B. M., Adler, D., Brauer, L. *et al. Brit. J. Psychiat. 121,* 529, (1972).
73. Cytrynbaum, S. The application of the criteria-oriented approach to the review of indirect service activities in a community mental health center. In *Patient Care Evaluation in Mental Health Programs.* Edited by Riedel, D., Tischler, G. and Meyers, J. Ballinger Press, Cambridge, Mass., pp. 179-212, (1974).

Appendix A

For Staff Use Only	Unit Code ______
	Client No. ______
	Clinician/Rater Code ______
	Date Completed ______
	Form I.D. ______

CONFIDENTIAL

Part I

CHILD'S DEVELOPMENTAL HISTORY

Name of child for whom help is being sought ______

Name of parent (s) or other adult completing this form ______

If not parent, indicate relationship to child ______

Single parent family (that is, only one parent lives home) ____ Yes ____ No

If yes, complete information on your family and self and provide as much information as you can on parent not living at home.

Please answer to the best of your knowledge the following questions which concern your child's developmental history.

1. What was the physical health of the child's mother during pregnancy?

   ____ Excellent ____ Good ____ Fair ____ Poor

2. What was the emotional condition of the child's mother during pregnancy?

   ____ Excellent ____ Good ____ Fair ____ Poor

3. Was any medication or drug administered to the child's mother during the pregnancy?

   ____ Yes ____ No

4. Was birth control used before this pregnancy? ____ Yes ____ No

5. Was this pregnancy planned? ____ Yes ____ No

6. How frequently did the child's mother visit a doctor during the pregnancy?

   ____ No contact, only for delivery

   ____ Less than regular contact (2 to 7 visits)

   ____ Regular contact (8 to 12 visits)

   ____ More than regular contact (more than 12 visits)

7. How was the child born?

   ____ Head first

   ____ Feet first

   ____ Breech (buttocks first)

   ____ Caesarean Section

8. What was the child's birth weight?

   ____ 5 lbs. or less

   ____ More than 5 but less than 8 lbs.

   ____ More than 8 but less than 10 lbs.

   ____ 10 lbs. or more

9. Was the child kept in the hospital after delivery for more than 4 days (or after the mother went home) because of illness or prematurity?

____ Yes

____ No

10. What was the physical health of the mother during the first year of the child's life?

____ Excellent ____ Good ____ Fair ____ Poor

11. What was the physical health of the child during the first year of life?

____ Excellent ____ Good ____ Fair ____ Poor

12. What was the physical health of the father during the first year of the child's life?

____ Excellent ____ Good ____ Fair ____ Poor

13. Did the mother have any emotional problems during the first year of the child's life?

____ Never ____ Often

____ Sometimes ____ Very often

14. Did the father have any emotional problems during the first year of the child's life?

____ Never ____ Often

____ Sometimes ____ Very often

15. Did the child have any emotional problems during the first year of life?

____ Never ____ Often

____ Sometimes ____ Very often

16. How helpful was the father toward the mother during the pregnancy?

____ Not at all helpful ____ Fairly helpful

____ A little helpful ____ Very helpful

17. How helpful was the father toward the mother at the time of the child's birth?

____ Not at all helpful ____ Fairly helpful

____ A little helpful ____ Very helpful

18. How helpful was the father toward the mother during the first year of the child's life?

____ Not at all helpful ____ Fairly helpful

____ A little helpful ____ Very helpful

19. At what age did the child walk alone?

____ Less than 12 mo. ____ More than 16 but less than 24 mo.

____ More than 12 but less than 16 mo. ____ 24 mo. or more

20. At what age did the child say his/her first word?

____ Less than 8 mo. ____ 15 mo. or more

____ More than 8 but less than 15 mo.

21. At what age did the child begin to talk in sentences?

____ Less than 18 mo. ____ More than 24 mo. but less than 36 mo.

____ More than 18 mo. but less than 24 mo. ____ More than 36 mo.

22. At what age was toilet training begun?

____ Less than 1 yr.
____ More than 1 yr. but less than 2 yrs.
____ More than 2 yrs. but less than 3 yrs.
____ 3 yrs. of age or later

23. At what age was bowel training completed?

____ Less than 1 yr.
____ More than 1 yr. but less than 2 yrs.
____ More than 2 yrs. but less than 3 yrs.
____ 3 yrs. of age or later

24. At what age was urinary training completed?

____ Less than 1 yr.
____ More than 1 yr. but less than 2 yrs.
____ More than 2 yrs. but less than 3 yrs.
____ 3 yrs. of age or later

25. If your child is a girl, has her menstral period begun? ____ Yes ____ No

26. If yes, indicate when it began:

____ Less than 10 years of age
____ Between 10 and 13 years of age
____ Between 13 and 14 years of age
____ More than 14 and of age

27. Has the child experienced serious illness or injury? ____ Yes ____ No

28. If yes, indicate below age of child in years for each serious illness or injury, whether the child was hospitalized and if so, the length of hospitalization in days.

Nature of Serious Illness or Injury	Age of child in years at time of injury or illness	Hospitalized (check)		If hospitalized, length of hospitalization in days
		Yes	No	

29. Does the child have any physical handicaps?

____ Yes
____ No

30. Check any of the following which apply to the child during the first three years of his/her life:

____ Sleeping problems
____ Unusual fears
____ Speech problems
____ Eating problems
____ Bladder or bowel problems
____ Other problems (specify) ________________
____
____

Appendix B

For Staff Use Only	Unit Code ______
	Client No. ______
	Clinician/Rater Code ______
	Date Sent Out ______
	Date Received ______
	Form ID ______

School Report on Student's Behavior and Performance

Part A of this form asks for information on the student's behavior and this should be provided by the person (teacher, guidance counselor, etc.) most familiar with the student. Part B focuses on the student's performance.

A. School Report on Student's Behavior

1. Identification Information

Student's Name ______

Name of school ______

Student's classroom or current homeroom teacher (if applicable)

______

Student's grade ______

Name of person completing Part A of this form ______

Position, title or function ______

______

How well do you feel you know this student?

____ Very well

____ Moderately well

____ Only casually

____ Only from the record on file

2. Behavior Rating

Indicate the extent to which the following statements apply to this student. If the description, behavior or statement does not describe this student, does not apply, seldom occurs or is not a problem, check the space for Does Not Apply. If the statement applies somewhat, the student exhibits the behavior occasionally or is sometimes a problem, check Sometimes Applies. If the behavior is fairly characteristic and/or occurs fairly often, check Often Applies. And if the statement definitely describes this student, is certainly applicable or if the problem is a serious one which the student exhibits frequently, check Certainly Applies. If you have no basis for making a judgement, so indicate in the last column.

	Certainly Applies	Often Applies	Sometimes Applies	Does Not Apply	No Basis For Making Judgement
1. Is rational and logical.	____	____	____	____	____
2. Shows fear in hetero-sexual matters or boy-girl relations.	____	____	____	____	____

	Certainly Applies	Often Applies	Sometimes Applies	Does Not Apply	No Basis For Making Judgement
3. Is demanding of attention from others, exhibitionistic.					
4. Is rigid in habits, excessively neat.					
5. Is defiant, rebellious, disobedient.					
6. Bullies or attacks other students.					
7. Shows lack of or appears incapable of expressing affection.					
8. Is anxious, fearful of new things/situations.					
9. Is slow in getting things done.					
10. Is dangerously daring, reckless.					
11. Is friendly, pleasant.					
12. Gets upset easily, quick to fly off the handle.					
13. Is socially withdrawn, solitary; does things alone.					
14. Accepts responsibilities, is conscientious.					
15. Speaks disrespectfully of parents.					
16. Is rough or unruly.					
17. Is assertive, does most of the talking in a group.					
18. Witholds information, misleads adults or lies.					
19. Has difficulty in learning things.					
20. Physically hurts or mutilates self.					
21. Is inhibited in normal physical exposure (e.g., gym change, bathroom, showers).					
22. Is antagonistic or negativistic towards others.					
23. Is overly nervous, emotional.					
24. Is sloppy or careless in dress and with property.					

	Certainly Applies	Often Applies	Sometimes Applies	Does Not Apply	No Basis For Making Judgement
25. Gets distracted easily, poor concentration.	____	____	____	____	____
26. Takes revenge, retaliates, fights with other students.	____	____	____	____	____
27. Is authoritarian, bossy.	____	____	____	____	____
28. Risks self harm without apparent concern.	____	____	____	____	____
29. Is interested in getting things done.	____	____	____	____	____
30. Overreacts to minor illness, aches or pains.	____	____	____	____	____
31. Is very tense, restless, fidgety.	____	____	____	____	____
32. Clings to adults dependently.	____	____	____	____	____
33. Is liked by other students.	____	____	____	____	____
34. Has temper tantrums.	____	____	____	____	____
35. Is over-concerned with cleanliness.	____	____	____	____	____
36. Is resistant.	____	____	____	____	____
37. Talks of suicide or hurting self.	____	____	____	____	____
38. Commits vandalism, destroys property.	____	____	____	____	____
39. Is intelligent.	____	____	____	____	____
40. Steals.	____	____	____	____	____
41. Is sour, sullen or surly in social relations.	____	____	____	____	____
42. Acts babyish or juvenile.	____	____	____	____	____
43. Is apparently unmotivated to do anything.	____	____	____	____	____
44. Is prim, prissy or fussy.	____	____	____	____	____
45. Pays attention to the task at hand.	____	____	____	____	____
46. Does not show fear when it is appropriate.	____	____	____	____	____
47. Truants from school.	____	____	____	____	____
48. Appears unhappy, distressed.	____	____	____	____	____
49. Has twitches, mannerisms, tics of face or body.	____	____	____	____	____

	Certainly Applies	Often Applies	Sometimes Applies	Does Not Apply	No Basis For Making Judgement
50. Bites nails or fingers.	____	____	____	____	____
51. Has a speech difficulty, stutters, stammers.	____	____	____	____	____
52. Sucks thumb or finger.	____	____	____	____	____

Additional comments on the student's behavior:

For Staff Use Only	Unit Code ________ Client No. ________ Clinician/Rater Code ________ Form ID ________

B. School Report on Student Performance: Elementary School

Please provide the information on the student's performance requested below.

1. Has this student repeated any grades? ____ Yes ____ No
2. If yes, please state which grade (s) ____________
3. Has this student skipped any grades? ____ Yes ____ No
4. If yes, please state which grade (s) ____________
5. At what level is this student currently performing in the following areas:

	Failing	Below Average	Average	Above Average
Reading	____	____	____	____
Arithmetic	____	____	____	____

6. In your judgement, at what level should this student be performing in the following subjects:

Reading	____	____	____	____
Arithmetic	____	____	____	____

7. Indicate the student's current reading level:

____ Below grade level by ________ (how many) grades

____ At grade level

____ Above grade level by ________ (how many) grades

8. Source of information on current reading level:

____ Standardized test scores

____ Classroom performance

____ Both

9. Indicate the student's current arithmetic level:

____ Below grade level by ________ (how many) grades

____ At grade level

____ Above grade level by ________ (how many) grades

10. Source of information on current arithmetic level:

_____ Standardized test scores

_____ Classroom performance

_____ Both

11. Have any recent marked changes in this student's school performance been noted?

_____ Yes

_____ No

12. If yes, please describe: ____________________

____

____

____

13. Name of person completing Part B of this form (if different from Part A)

____

14. Position, title or function ____________________

For Staff Use Only	Unit Code _____ Client No. _____ Clinician/Rater Code _____ Form ID _____

B. School Report on Student Performance: Middle or Junior High School

Please provide the information on the student's performance requested below.

1. Has this student repeated any grades? _____ Yes _____ No

2. If yes, please state which grade (s) ____________________

3. Has this student skipped any grade (s) _____ Yes _____ No

4. If yes, please state which grade (s) ____________________

5. At what level is this student currently performing in the following areas:

	Failing	Below Average	Average	Above Average
English	_____	_____	_____	_____
Mathematics	_____	_____	_____	_____
Science	_____	_____	_____	_____

6. In your judgement, at what level should the student be performing in the following subjects:

	Failing	Below Average	Average	Above Average
English	_____	_____	_____	_____
Mathematics	_____	_____	_____	_____
Science	_____	_____	_____	_____

7. Has this student repeated any of the above subject areas?

_____ Yes

_____ No

8. If yes, please indicate which subject areas:

____

____

____

9. Have any recent marked changes in this student's school performance been noted?

_____ Yes

_____ No

10. If yes, please describe: ____

____

____

____

11. Name of person completing Part B of this form (if different from Part A)

____

12. Position, title or function ______________________________

For Staff Use Only	Unit Code ____________ Client No. ____________ Clinician/Rater Code ________ Form ID ____________

B. School Report on Student Performance: High School

Please provide the information on the student's performance requested below.

1. Has this student repeated any grades? _____ Yes _____ No

2. If yes, please state which grade (s) ______________________

3. Has this student skipped any grade (s) _____ Yes _____ No

4. If yes, please state which grade (s) ______________________

5. In which course of study is this student currently enrolled?

_____ College Preparatory

_____ Business Preparatory

_____ Vocational Preparatory

_____ General Studies or Equivalent

_____ Other (specify) ______________________________

6. Check the subject areas which this student is taking as part of his/her present school program:

_____ English
_____ Mathematics
_____ Science
_____ Language
_____ Social Studies
_____ Stenography
_____ Typing
_____ Industrial Trades
_____ Building Trades
_____ Food Trades
_____ Other (indicate) _______________

____

____

7. At what level is this student currently performing in the subject areas which he/she is taking as part of his/her present school program:

	Failing	Below Average	Average	Above Average
English	_____	_____	_____	_____
Mathematics	_____	_____	_____	_____
Science	_____	_____	_____	_____
Language	_____	_____	_____	_____
Social Studies	_____	_____	_____	_____
Stenography	_____	_____	_____	_____
Typing	_____	_____	_____	_____
Industrial Trades	_____	_____	_____	_____
Building Trades	_____	_____	_____	_____
Food Trades	_____	_____	_____	_____
(Write in other if appropriate)				
_______________	_____	_____	_____	_____
_______________	_____	_____	_____	_____

8. In your judgement, at what level should this student be performing in the following subject areas:

	Failing	Below Average	Average	Above Average
English	_____	_____	_____	_____
Mathematics	_____	_____	_____	_____
Science	_____	_____	_____	_____
Language	_____	_____	_____	_____
Social Studies	_____	_____	_____	_____
Stenography	_____	_____	_____	_____
Typing	_____	_____	_____	_____
Industrial Trades	_____	_____	_____	_____

	Failing	Below Average	Average	Above Average
Building Trades	______	______	______	______
Food Trades	______	______	______	______
(Write in other if appropriate)				
______________	______	______	______	______
______________	______	______	______	______

9. Has this student repeated any of the above subject areas _____ Yes _____ No

10. If yes, please indicate which subject areas: ______________________

____

11. Have any recent marked changes in this student's school performance been noted?

_____ Yes

_____ No

12. If yes, please describe: ______________________

____

____

____

13. Name of person completing Part B of this form (if different from Part A)

____

14. Position, title or function ______________________

Appendix C

For Staff Use Only	
	Unit Code ______
	Client No. ______
	Clinician/Rater Code ______
	Date Sent Out ______
	Date Received ______
	Form I.D. ______

Request For Medical Information

TO: Name and Address of physician or medical facility providing information.

______

______

______

______

FROM: HUMAN SERVICES RESOURCE CENTER
270 Center Street
West Haven, Connecticut 06516
934-8687

RE: Name of Patient ______

Patient's Birthdate ______

Patient's Address ______

______

______

______

Father's Name ______

Mother's Name ______

Please provide the following information on the child named above who is registered with our facility as a client. Attached you will find a statement of permission to release this information.

1. Reason (s) for referral to you or your facility? ______

______

______

2. How long has the patient been known to you or your facility?

____ Week ____ 2 years

____ Month ____ Over 2 years

____ 1 year ____ Since birth

3. How well do you feel you know the patient?

____ Very well ____ Only casually

____ Moderately well ____ Only from the record on file

4. Were you aware that the family would seek help at our agency?

____ Yes

____ No

5. What diagnostic procedures have been done?

____ General physical exam
____ X-rays
____ Blood tests
____ Urinalysis
____ Vision
____ Hearing
____ Neurological exam
____ EEG
____ Psychological testing
____ Psychiatric consultation
____ Other (please indicate) ____________________

6. What other diagnostic procedures (if any) are planned? ____________________

____

____

____

7. Please summarize pertinent diagnostic findings, treatment recommendations or current medication:

____

____

____

____

____

Pregnancy, Birth and New Born Period

1. What was the physical health of the child's mother during pregnancy?

____ Excellent ____ Good ____ Fair ____ Poor

2. What was the emotional condition of the child's mother during pregnancy?

____ Excellent ____ Good ____ Fair ____ Poor

3. Was any medication or drug administered to the child's mother during the pregnancy?

____ Yes

____ No

If yes, please indicate what kind: ____________________

4. How frequently did the child's mother visit a doctor during the pregnancy?

____ No contact, only for delivery

____ Less than regular or normal contact (2 to 7 visits)

____ Regular or normal contact (8 or 12 visits)

____ More than regular or normal contact (more than 12 visits)

5. How was the child born?

____ Head first
____ Feet first
____ Breech (buttocks first)
____ Caesarean Section

6. What did the child weigh at birth?

____ 5 lbs. or less

____ More than 5 lbs. but less than 8 lbs.

____ More than 8 lbs. but less than 10 lbs.

____ 10 lbs. or more

7. Was the child kept in the hospital after delivery for more than 4 days (or after the mother went home) because of illness or prematurity?

____ Yes

____ No

8. Please note any other significant abnormalities of pregnancy, labour or delivery, any unusual conditions of the infant at birth or findings in the first month:

____

____

____

Developmental History

1. At what age did the child walk alone?

____ Less than 12 mo.

____ More than 12 mo. but less than 16 mo.

____ More than 16 mo. but less than 24 mo.

____ 24 mo. or more

2. At what age did the child say his/her first word?

____ Less than 8 mo.

____ More than 8 mo. but less than 15 mo.

____ 15 mo. or more

3. At what age did the child begin to talk in sentences?

____ Less than 18 mo.

____ More than 18 mo. but less than 24 mo.

____ More than 24 mo. but less than 36 mo.

____ More than 36 mo.

4. At what age was bowel training completed?

____ Less than 1 yr.

____ More than 1 yr. but less than 2 yrs.

____ More than 2 yrs. but less than 3 yrs.

____ 3 yrs. of age or later

5. At what age was urinary training completed?

____ Less than 1 yr.

____ More than 1 yr. but less than 2 yrs.

____ More than 2 yrs. but less than 3 yrs.

____ 3 yrs. of age or later

6. Onset of menses? ____ Yes ____ No

7. If yes, at what age:

____ Less than 10 yrs.

____ Between 10 and 12 yrs.

____ Between 13 and 14 yrs.

____ More than 14 yrs.

Health History

1. Has the patient experienced serious illnesses, injuries, operations or hospitalizations?

____ Yes

____ No

2. Does the patient have any physical handicaps?

____ Yes

____ No

3. If yes to either of the above, list below any serious illnesses, operations, injuries or hospitalizations, with child's age and any residua or handicaps:

Type of Illness, Operation, Injury or Hospitalization	Age of Child	Residua (if any)

4. Any difficulties in managing the care of this child or other family members?

____ Yes

____ No

If yes, please describe: ____________________

5. Please describe any other significant physical or mental health problems for the child or parents:

____

Signature of Physician or Authorized Representative

____
Date

Since we regularly revise this form, we would appreciate any reactions or opinions regarding this as a procedure for requesting medical information. Thank you.

Appendix D

For Staff Use Only	Unit Code ________
	Client No. ________
	Clinician/Rater Code ________
	Date Completed ________
	Form I.D. ________

For Clinical Staff: Family Assessment Form

Clinician completing this form ____________________

The Family Assessment Form has five sections. The structure of the family and source of information will determine which sections are to be completed by clinical staff.

Indicate which of the following structural arrangements applies to this family:

____ 1. Intact family with married mother (stepmother) and father (stepfather) consistently present.

____ 2. Single parent family (only one parent consistently present).

____ 3. Single parent-substitute parent family (one parent present and another adult of opposite sex viewed as a stable part of family also present such as boyfriend, girlfriend, common-law wife or husband or other stable substitute parent).

____ 4. Other (specify) ____________________

Indicate the source of information upon which this form is to be completed.

____ 1. Family interview with all relevant members of an intact family, single parent family, or single parent-substitute parent family.

____ 2. Conjoint interview with husband and wife or parent substitute.

____ 3. Interview with one parent or one parent substitute.

____ 4. Other (specify) ____________________

For all items below, indicate the extent to which the statements characterize relationships within the family. If the statement definitely describes the relationship, is certainly applicable or if the problem is a serious one which occurs frequently, check the space for Certainly Applies. If the statement is characteristic and/or occurs fairly often in the family, check Often Applies. If the statement applies somewhat, occurs occasionally or is sometimes a problem, check Sometimes Applies. If the statement does not describe the relationship, seldom occurs or is not a problem, check the space for Rarely or Never Applies.

A. Marital Relationship:

This section is to be completed on the basis of family, conjoint or individual parent interviews for intact or single parent-substitute parent families. Do not complete this section if a single parent family.

	Certainly Applies	Often Applies	Sometimes Applies	Rarely or Never Applies
1. The marital relationship is one characterized by mutual satisfaction.	____	____	____	____
2. Wife feels isolated and alienated from husband.	____	____	____	____
3. Husband feels isolated and alienated from wife.	____	____	____	____

	Certainly Applies	Often Applies	Some-times Applies	Rarely or Never Applies
4. Wife is dissatisfied with sexual relationship.	____	____	____	____
5. Husband is dissatisfied with sexual relationship.	____	____	____	____
6. There is conflict between husband and wife about how the child should be raised.	____	____	____	____
7. There is conflict between husband and wife over who controls the money.	____	____	____	____
8. The husband's work is a source of conflict in the relationship.	____	____	____	____
9. The wife's work is a source of conflict in the relationship.	____	____	____	____
10. There is conflict between husband and wife over household responsibilities and chores.	____	____	____	____
11. There is conflict between husband and wife over how leisure time should be spent.	____	____	____	____
12. There is conflict in the relationship about the use of alcohol or drugs.	____	____	____	____
13. One or both parents have stronger emotional ties outside the family, (i.e., with work, friends, extended family, etc.) than within the family.	____	____	____	____

B. Parent-Child Relationship:

This section should be completed on the basis of all sources of information for intact, single parent-substitute parent and single parent families. In the case of single parent families (where mother only present), answer only those items which are starred (*).

	Certainly Applies	Often Applies	Some-times Applies	Rarely or Never Applies
14. The father carries an excessive amount of responsibility for parenting and child care.	____	____	____	____
* 15. The mother carries an excessive amount of responsibility for parenting and child care.	____	____	____	____
* 16. No one can control one or more of the children.	____	____	____	____
* 17. Punishment of the child is often excessive or cruel.	____	____	____	____
The father:				
18. Often plays the child off against the mother.	____	____	____	____
19. Is rejecting of the child.	____	____	____	____
20. Withdraws from the child.	____	____	____	____
21. Is seductive towards the child.	____	____	____	____

		Certainly Applies	Often Applies	Sometimes Applies	Rarely or Never Applies
	22. Is overprotective of the child.	____	____	____	____
	The mother:				
*	23. Often plays the child off against the father.	____	____	____	____
*	24. Is rejecting of the child.	____	____	____	____
*	25. Withdraws from the child.	____	____	____	____
*	26. Is seductive towards the child.	____	____	____	____
*	27. Is overprotective of the child.	____	____	____	____
	The child:				
	28. Successfully plays one parent off against the other.	____	____	____	____
	29. Is rejecting of the father.	____	____	____	____
*	30. Is rejecting of the mother.	____	____	____	____
	31. Withdraws from the father.	____	____	____	____
*	32. Withdraws from the mother.	____	____	____	____
	33. Clings to or is dependent on father.	____	____	____	____
*	34. Clings to or is dependent on mother.	____	____	____	____
	35. Behaves seductively towards father.	____	____	____	____
*	36. Behaves seductively towards mother.	____	____	____	____

C. Relationships Among Children In The Family:

If child identified as client is an only child, omit this section.

	Certainly Applies	Often Applies	Sometimes Applies	Rarely or Never Applies
37. There is much general fighting among the siblings.	____	____	____	____
38. The child is often picked on by other siblings.	____	____	____	____
39. The children are divided into hostile camps.	____	____	____	____
40. The child often tags along with his/her siblings.	____	____	____	____
41. There is much generalized competition among the children.	____	____	____	____
42. The child is often left alone in charge of his/her siblings.	____	____	____	____

D. Family Dynamics:

This section should be completed on the basis of a family interview with all members of an intact family, single parent family, or a single parent-substitute parent family., begin with item 45.

	Certainly Applies	Often Applies	Sometimes Applies	Rarely or Never Applies
43. There is a pattern of marked dominance by one parent in the family.	____	____	____	____

	Certainly Applies	Often Applies	Sometimes Applies	Rarely or Never Applies
44. The parental coalition is stronger than any parent-child coalition in this family.	____	____	____	____
45. Individuals in the family are close but with distinct boundaries among members.	____	____	____	____
46. Individuals in the family are open and receptive to statements of other family members.	____	____	____	____
47. Family members are able to express clearly individual thoughts and feelings.	____	____	____	____
48. Family members demonstrate ability to negotiate and problem-solve.	____	____	____	____
49. Family members frequently speak up for one another or make "mind reading" statements.	____	____	____	____
The feeling tone of the family's interaction can be characterized as:				
50. Unusually warm, affectionate and optimistic.	____	____	____	____
51. Polite without impressive warmth or affection.	____	____	____	____
52. Overtly hostile.	____	____	____	____
53. Depressed.	____	____	____	____
54. Cynical, hopeless and pessimistic.	____	____	____	____
55. Family role divisions are clear and complementary.	____	____	____	____
56. The child, identified as client, is commonly scapegoated in the family.	____	____	____	____
57. There is much intergenerational conflict in the family.	____	____	____	____
58. There is much conflict around religion in the family.	____	____	____	____

E. Family Isolation:

59. Check all that apply for this family:

____ No relatives or family in the area.

____ No or little contact with extended family in the area.

____ No car or other private transportation.

____ Few or no close friends in nearby area.

____ No access to public transportation.

____ No telephone.

____ Other indicies of isolation (specify) ________________________

60. Assess the level of overall family physical and/or psychological isolation:

____ Not isolated, well integrated into neighborhood.

____ Moderate isolation, not seriously problematic.

____ Very isolated, few neighborhood relationships, limited use of community resources, problematic.

61. Rate the extent to which this family is in conflict with the predominant neighborhood culture or values:

____ Minimal conflict, well integrated.

____ Moderate conflict, not serious problem.

____ High level of conflict, serious problem, contributes to isolation.

Appendix E

For Staff Use Only	
	Unit Code ____________
	Client No. ____________
	Clinician/Rater Code ____________
	Date Completed ____________
	Form I.D. ____________

CONFIDENTIAL

Part III

SIGNIFICANT LIFE EVENTS -- FAMILY

Check in the space to the left of the item any of the following problems or events which have occurred to your family during the past year. For only those items which are checked, circle the time period on the right which best indicates when this problem began or event happened.

			When did this event happen or problem begin? (Circle)
1.	____	Death of an important person (spouse, close relative or friend).	1 2-3 4-6 7-9 10-12 months ago
2.	____	Serious money problems (rent, food, clothing, heat).	1 2-3 4-6 7-9 10-12 months ago
3.	____	Worry because of trouble with relatives.	1 2-3 4-6 7-9 10-12 months ago
4.	____	Worry because of trouble with friends or neighbors.	1 2-3 4-6 7-9 10-12 months ago
5.	____	Important family member left home.	1 2-3 4-6 7-9 10-12 months ago
6.	____	New person (friend or relative) moved into home.	1 2-3 4-6 7-9 10-12 months ago
7.	____	Marriage, divorce or separation of parents.	1 2-3 4-6 7-9 10-12 months ago
8.	____	Birth of a child.	1 2-3 4-6 7-9 10-12 months ago
9.	____	Family moved to another home.	1 2-3 4-6 7-9 10-12 months ago

10. List anything else important which happened during the past year which markedly changed the family's way of living: ____________________

____

____

____

SIGNIFICANT LIFE EVENTS -- MOTHER

Check in the space to the left of the item any of the following which have occurred to the mother during the last year. For only those items that are checked, circle the time period on the right which best indicates when this problem began.

			When did this problem begin? (Circle)
11.	____	Problems with work.	1 2-3 4-6 7-9 10-12 months ago

12. ____ Physical health problems. 1 2-3 4-6 7-9 10-12 months ago

13. ____ Emotional problems (includes problems with nerves, drugs, alcohol, sex, etc.). 1 2-3 4-6 7-9 10-12 months ago

List any other events during the past year which seriously affected the mother's life:

____

____

____

SIGNIFICANT LIFE EVENTS -- FATHER

Check in the space to the left of the item any of the following which have occurred to the father during the last year. For only those items that are checked, circle the time period on the right which best indicates when this problem began.

When did this problem begin? (Circle)

14. ____ Problems with work. 1 2-3 4-6 7-9 10-12 months ago

15. ____ Physical health problems. 1 2-3 4-6 7-9 10-12 months ago

16. ____ Emotional problems (includes problems with nerves, drugs, alcohol, sex, etc.). 1 2-3 4-6 7-9 10-12 months ago

List any other events during the past year which seriously affected the father's life:

____

____

____

SIGNIFICANT LIFE EVENTS -- CHILD

Check in the space to the left of the item theproblem or events which have occurred to your child during the last year. For only those items which are checked, circle the time period on the right which best indicates when this problem began or event happened.

When did this event happen or problem begin? (Circle)

17. ____ Child left home to live elsewhere. 1 2-3 4-6 7-9 10-12 months ago

18. ____ Child returned home from living elsewhere. 1 2-3 4-6 7-9 10-12 months ago

19. ____ Child had serious physical health problem (s). 1 2-3 4-6 7-9 10-12 months ago

20. ____ Child injured by physical abuse. 1 2-3 4-6 7-9 10-12 months ago

21. ____ Child injured by fire or accident. 1 2-3 4-6 7-9 10-12 months ago

22. ____ Child experienced death, loss or separation from a parent. 1 2-3 4-6 7-9 10-12 months ago

23. ____ Child talked about or tried to kill himself (herself). 1 2-3 4-6 7-9 10-12 months ago

24. ____ Child married, divorced or separated. 1 2-3 4-6 7-9 10-12 months ago

25. ____ Child was pregnant. 1 2-3 4-6 7-9 10-12 months ago

26. ____ Child was very upset by a frightening experience. 1 2-3 4-6 7-9 10-12 months ago

27. ____ Child failed in school and was held back. 1 2-3 4-6 7-9 10-12 months ago

28. List any other important events during the past year which seriously affected the child's life: ____

____

____

____

FAMILY SUPPORTS

29. When your family members have serious difficulty getting along with each other to whom would you turn for help? Check all that apply.

____ Parents or other close relatives

____ Neighbors or friends

____ Family doctor, health center or hospital

____ Local family, mental health or counselling service

____ Minister or other religious leader or group

____ Nobody

____ Other (specify) ____

30. When you or your spouse have a serious physical illness to whom would you turn for help? Check all that apply.

____ Parents or other close relatives

____ Neighbors or friends

____ Family doctor, health center or hospital

____ Local family, mental health or counselling service

____ Minister or other religious leader or group

____ Nobody

____ Other (specify) ____

31. When you have a serious money or job problem to whom would you turn for help? Check all that apply.

____ Parents or other close relatives

____ Neighbors or friends

____ Family doctor, health center or hospital

____ Local family, mental health or counselling service

____ Minister or other religious leader or group

____ Nobody

____ Other (specify) ____

32. When you have a serious problem with your child to whom would you turn for help? Check all that apply.

____ Parents or other close relatives

____ Neighbors or friends

____ Family doctor, health center or hospital

____ Local family, mental health or counselling service

____ Minister or other religious leader or group

____ Nobody

____ Other (specify) ______________________________

Appendix F

For Staff Use Only	Unit Code ______
	Client No. ______
	Clinician/Rater Code ______
	Date Completed ______
	Form I.D. ______

CONFIDENTIAL

Part IV

FAMILY INFORMATION

Please answer to the best of your knowledge the following questions which concern your family's background. Your family includes all members of your current household.

Name of person completing this section of form ______

Relationship to child ______

Family Background

1. What is your family's religion? (Check)

____ Protestant
____ Catholic
____ Jewish
____ Pentecostal
____ Jevhovah's Witness
____ Baptist
____ Muslim
____ No religion
____ Other (indicate) ______

2. Do any family members practice a different religion?

____ Yes
____ No

3. How important is religion to your family?

____ Very important to family life
____ Fairly important to family life
____ Not very important to family life
____ Not important at all to family life

4. Where did your child grow up?

____ West Haven
____ Hill area of New Haven
____ Other parts of New Haven city (indicate area ______)
____ New Haven County, but not City (indicate area ______)
____ State of Connecticut, but not New Haven County (indicate town ______)
____ Out of State of Connecticut, but inside U.S.A. (indicate city, state and country

______ ______ ______)
City State Country

____ Outside U.S.A. (indicate country ________________________)

5. Do you feel that your real home is where you live now?

____ Yes

____ No

If no, where do you consider your real home to be? ____________________
City

____
State Country

6. How many times has your family moved in the past 5 years? ____________

7. Was your last move:

____ Within the Hill

____ Within West Haven

____ From another part of New Haven City (indicate area ____________)

____ From somewhere else in the State of Connecticut (indicate town

________________)

____ From outside of Connecticut, but in U.S.A. (specify ____________
City

________________)
State

____ From outside the U.S.A.(specify ________________________)

8. Check the language (s) usually spoken at home by parents: (Check all that apply.)

____ English

____ Spanish

____ Italian

____ Portuguese

____ Polish

____ Other (specify) ____________

9. Do any other members of your family speak a different language?

____ Yes

____ No

10. Type of family home or residence:

____ Single family home

____ More than one family home

____ Apartment

____ Private housing project

____ Public housing project

____ Other (specify) ____________

____

11. Our family:

____ Owns our home (mortgage or paid off)

____ Rents our home

12. Number of rooms in house ________

13. Number of rooms used for sleeping ________

14. Check any of the following that are true for your house:

____ Share toilet with another apartment

____ Peeling paint

____ Broken windows

____ Not enough heat

____ Rats or other rodents

____ Fire hazard

____ Other housing violations (specify)

____

____

____

15. Indicate which of these adults are also important in raising the child: (Check all that apply.)

____ Grandmother
____ Grandfather
____ Boyfriend
____ Aunt
____ Uncle
____ Brother or sister
____ Other (specify) ____________________

16. Who takes care of your child during the day or after school? (Check all that apply.)

____ Child's mother
____ Child's father
____ Child's grandmother
____ Day Care
____ Child takes care of self
____ Paid sitter
____ Friend or neighbor
____ Other relatives
____ Child's brother or sister
____ Other (specify) ____________________

17. If you are separated or divorced, does the child have regular face-to-face contact with the parent who does not live at home?

____ Yes
____ No

18. If yes, how often does the child see the absent parent:

____ Once a week or more
____ Once a month
____ Every few months
____ Once a year or less

Mother's Background

This section is to be completed by the child's mother. If the mother is not in the home, the responsible female adult who cares for the child should complete this section. If such a female person is not living at home or is not available, the father or another adult should complete as much of this section as possible.

Name of person completing this section of form ____________________

Relationship to child ____________________

19. Where did you grow up? (Check)

____ West Haven
____ Hill area of New Haven
____ Other parts of New Haven City (indicate area ____________________)
____ New Haven County, but not City (indicate area ____________________)
____ State of Connecticut, but not New Haven County (indicate town ____________________)
____ Out of State of Connecticut, but inside U.S.A. (indicate city, state and country ____________________)
City State Country
____ Outside U.S.A. (indicate country ____________________)

20. Check the one which applies to the kind of work you currently do:

____ Unemployed
____ Private household workers
____ Armed Forces (Army, Navy, Air Force, etc.)

____ Service Workers (cleaning and food services, police, guards, firemen, personal and health service workers)

____ Farm workers

____ Unskilled Laborers, except farm

____ Semi-skilled workers (apprentices, attendants, factory workers, etc.)

____ Craftsman, foreman, construction, mechanics and repairman, other skilled workers

____ Clerical, secretary, stenographer, typist

____ Sales workers, retail trade (e.g., retail clerks, salesmen, insurance, etc.)

____ Managers and administrators, salaried or self-employed in government or retail trade (buyers, managers, etc.)

____ Professional, technical (including engineers, health workers, lawyers, teachers, etc.)

____ Other (specify) ______________________________

21. Current number of jobs held ________

22. Number of hours per day worked ________

23. Number of jobs held in past 5 years ______

24. What is your occupation? ______________________________

____

____

25. Are you generally satisfied with your present job?

____ Very satisfied

____ Job is OK -- not bad, not great

____ Very dissatisfied

26. If dissatisfied, why are you dissatisfied with your job? (Check all that apply.)

____ I am qualified for a much better job

____ My job demands more skills than I have

____ I have a lousy boss

____ I deserve higher pay for the work I do

____ The working conditions are very poor

____ There are a lot of hassles at work

____ I feel discriminated against at work

____ Other (specify) ______________________________

____

27. Check last grade of school you completed:

____ Completed 1-4 years

____ Completed 5-7 years

____ Completed 8 years

____ Completed 1-3 years of High School

____ Completed 4 years of High School

____ Attended 1-3 years of college

____ Completed 4 years of college

_____ Attended some Graduate School

_____ Completed Graduate or Professional School

28. Do you feel you have enough education?

_____ Yes

_____ No

29. If no, indicate which of the following apply:

_____ I want more education, but I am unable to go back to school

_____ I want more education, and I am planning to go back to school

_____ I want more education, and I am currently in school

Father's Background

This section is to be completed by the child's father. If the father is not in the home, the responsible male adult who cares for the child should complete this section. If such a male person is not living at home or is not available, the mother or another adult should complete as much of this section as possible.

Name of person completing this section of form ______________________________

Relationship to child ______________________________

30. Where did you grow up? (Check)

_____ West Haven

_____ Hill Area of New Haven

_____ Other parts of New Haven City (indicate area ______________________)

_____ New Haven County, but not City (indicate area ______________________)

_____ State of Connecticut, but not New Haven County (indicate town ______________________)

_____ Out of State of Connecticut, but inside U.S.A. (indicate city, state and country ______________________)
City State Country

_____ Outside U.S.A. (indicate country ______________________)

31. Check the one which applies to the kind of work you currently do:

_____ Unemployed

_____ Private household workers

_____ Armed Forced (Army, Navy, Air Force, etc.)

_____ Service Workers (cleaning and food services, police, guards, firemen, personal and health service workers)

_____ Farm workers

_____ Unskilled laborers, except farm

_____ Semi-skilled workers (apprentices, attendants, factory workers, etc.)

_____ Craftsman, foreman, construction, mechanics and repairman, other skilled workers

_____ Clerical, secretary, stenographer, typist

_____ Sales workers, retail trade (e.g., retail clerks, salesmen, insurance, etc.,

_____ Managers and administrators, salaried or self-empoyed in government or retail trade (buyers, managers, etc.)

____ Professional, technical (including engineers, health workers, lawyers, teachers, etc.)

____ Other (specify) ____________________

32. Current number of jobs held ____________

33. Number of hours per day worked ____________

34. Number of jobs held in past 5 years ____________

35. What is your occupation? ____________________

____

____

36. Are you generally satisfied with your present job?

____ Very satisfied

____ Job is OK -- not bad, not great

____ Very dissatisfied

37. If dissatisfied, why are you dissatisfied with your job? (Check all that apply.)

____ I am qualified for a much better job

____ My job demands more skills than I have

____ I have a lousy boss

____ I deserve higher pay for the work I do

____ The working conditions are very poor

____ There are a lot of hassles at work

____ I feel discriminated against at work

____ Other (specify) ____________________

____

38. Check last grade of school you completed:

____ Completed 1-4 years

____ Completed 5-7 years

____ Completed 8 years

____ Completed 1-3 years of High School

____ Completed 4 years of High School

____ Attended 1-3 years of college

____ Completed 4 years of college

____ Attended some Graduate School

____ Completed Graduate or Professional School

39. Do you feel you have enough education?

____ Yes

____ No

40. If no, indicate which of the following apply:

____ I want more education, but I am unable to go back to school

____ I want more education, and I am planning to go back to school

____ I want more education, and I am currently in school

Appendix G

For Staff Use Only	
	Unit Code ________
	Client No. ________
	Clinician/Rater Code ________
	Date Completed ________
	Form I.D. ________

CONFIDENTIAL

Part II

CHILD'S SCHOOL EXPERIENCES

Please complete this form if your child attends day care, nursery school or is of school age. Indicate the extent to which each of the following statements apply to your son's or daughter's experiences at school. If the statement is basically true for your child, check Always Applies. If it is true most of the time, check Often Applies. If it applies to your child every once in a while, check Sometimes Applies, and if it is not true at all for your child, check Never Applies.

Child's name ________________

Child's school ________________

	Always Applies	Often Applies	Sometimes Applies	Never Applies
1. My child likes to go to school.	____	____	____	____
2. I think my child's school is good.	____	____	____	____
3. The principal or teacher in my child's school sees him/her as a problem.	____	____	____	____
4. The difficulty my child is having is the fault of the teacher.	____	____	____	____
5. The school authorities blame the family for my child's difficulties.	____	____	____	____
6. My child likes his/her teacher.	____	____	____	____
7. My child has friends at school.	____	____	____	____
8. My child gets along with his/her classmates.	____	____	____	____
9. The school gives my child the special attention or support he/she needs.	____	____	____	____
10. My child is at ease around adults at school.	____	____	____	____
11. My child trusts adults at school.	____	____	____	____
12. My child is hard to control at school.	____	____	____	____
13. My child hangs around with kids who like to study.	____	____	____	____
14. My child hangs around with kids who like to play hookey.	____	____	____	____

	Always Applies	Often Applies	Some-times Applies	Never Applies
15. My child hangs around with kids who like to play sports.	_____	_____	_____	_____
16. My child has to be forced to go to school.	_____	_____	_____	_____
17. No one in the school system really cares about what happens to my child and whether he/she learns anything.	_____	_____	_____	_____
18. Because of his/her different background my child has trouble learning English.	_____	_____	_____	_____
19. My child listens more to his/her classmates and friends than to me.	_____	_____	_____	_____
20. My child listens more to his/her teacher than to me.	_____	_____	_____	_____

21. My child needs a special kind of class or teacher.

_____ Yes

_____ No

22. My child is in his/her right grade.

_____ Yes

_____ No

23. If no, he/she should be in (check)

_____ A higher grade

_____ A lower grade

MENTAL HEALTH IN CHILDREN, Volume III
Edited By D. V. Siva Sankar

THE ROLE OF A HOSPITAL BASED ADOLESCENT UNIT

Peter Bruggen
Hill End Hospital, St. Albans, Herts. U.K.

Mini Summary

The resources of an in-patient Adolescent Unit are used in the community to help families and professional referrers in crisis situations.

Admission is used only when community resources cannot cope with the adolescent or need time to reconstruct their support framework.

Introduction

Between the Coroner's Court and the family, somewhere, lies the resource of a hospital based Adolescent Unit. Less has been thought about the clinical functioning of such units than has there been pressure for *more* of them.

The thinking of a new unit for younger adolescents opened in Hill End Hospital, St. Albans, England, in 1969, has been in the light of considerable public pressure from the Government's Department of Health and Social Security for psychiatrists to work more closely with professional workers in the community and the Department's prediction that more such work would prevent the carrying through of many proposed admissions. The formation of policy has also had, as background, the increasing literature on family interaction and crisis intervention.

The Unit at Hill End Hospital, which is a specialist facility with an area commitment, decided that its aim should be to *support* referrers working in the community. This is in line with ideas expressed by Caplan (1), who pointed out that if cases are taken over from referrers, the specialist's caseload is rapidly filled and only a place on a waiting list can be offered. Nevertheless, an in-patient unit is inevitably involved in the crisis situation of admitting patients to a hospital ward and is involved in separating family members from each other. What should the criteria for admission be? And what should the benefits be?

Langsley (2) has reviewed the literature on in-patient and out-patient treatment, and writes in his book "Treatment of Families in Crisis," that "brief psychiatric hospitalisation can hope to accomplish:

1. Recompensation and remission of symptoms in the patient.
2. Protection of the patient and others during periods of crisis and exacerbation.
3. The provision of a period of rest for a patient and family when they have reached the point of exhaustion, frustration and confusion."

He studied, at six months' follow-up, 300 cases aged 16-60, who had families, and who had been diagnosed by a psychiatrist as needing admission to a psychiatric hospital. Of the 150 cases offered family crisis therapy, (an average of 5.8 sessions), none was admitted to psychiatric hospital during the period of treatment which, compared with the in-patient treatment of the control group, was one-third as long, led to one-fifth as long loss of social functioning, one-half as many subsequent admissions at one-third the length, and cost one-sixth as much.

He concludes that the benefits of admission to hospital can often be achieved by other means. Treatment, per se, is after all available both in hospital, and outside it. Other writers (3, 4, 5) have emphasised even more the negative sides of mental hospital life and the dangers of institutionalism.

Hansell (6) has demonstrated how the skillful use of relatively few beds can, with other resource methods, provide an area service.

Brandon (7) in his appraisal of crisis theory supports the view that a critical evaluation of the use of hospital admission in psychiatry is long overdue and little has in fact been written of the reasons behind the change in status from out-patient to in-patient and back. Jones and Pollack (8) in the British

Journal of Psychiatry, emphasised that one of their patients was admitted to hospital, not because of his schizophrenic illness, which had been basically unaltered for years, but because of a crisis in the group with whom he lived created by his brother having an operation. Similarly, Milner (9) in her book 'The Hands of the Living God' described how her patient, during a long illness, was once admitted to hospital "to give Mrs. Brown a rest." The crisis was in the "holders" and the Balint (10) type of "overall diagnosis" could be said to apply - in these cases "that the community cannot cope."

PROCEDURE OF THE ADOLESCENT UNIT

First stage: Telephone call

When a referral is made, a telephone call is held with the referrer, who is asked details of the overall situation - who is legally in charge of the adolescent, where he lives now and where he will live on discharge, who will continue his professional care, who wants him to be admitted to hospital and why. Emphasis is placed on the availability of a bed, should the person in authority find a crisis which he or she can no longer cope with by using community resources. This "backing" of the professional worker with the availability of a bed may continue throughout the younger adolescence of his or her client. With this backing, the referring agent may decide against admission being necessary at this stage.

Second stage: Professionals' meeting

If the referrer wishes, a multidisciplinary team (psychiatrist, psychiatric nurse, and social worker), goes to the referrer's place of work to meet him or her, together with any other significantly involved professionals. At this meeting, similar in many ways to the "screening-linking-planning conference" described by Hansell, a plan may emerge for the adolescent to remain in the community as the professional responsibility of the referrer, with the knowledge of the backing of an available bed should a crisis occur.

Third stage: First family meeting

At this stage the Unit team sees the case, together with the referrer, again somewhere other than at the Unit in order not to imply pressure towards, or assumption of, admission. As the Unit's task is not to make a medical diagnosis nor to formulate an individual therapeutic strategy, the adolescent is not seen separately and historical data is not sought. Rather, in order to investigate the crisis in the family and clarify the situation, the whole family, including siblings, are given a leaflet about how the Unit works, are told about it in terms which emphasises its position in a mental hospital and its structured regime and are then seen together for an hour. (A type of situation which often arises is that the parents describe some of the symptoms of the designated patient and say that they want him or her to be admitted for they think that this would be the best treatment. The concern expressed in these remarks is acknowledged by the staff, although they point out that treatment in itself may well be available elsewhere. The family is reminded that admission means separation and that this would affect all of them. They are asked about difficulties in the *family* and are asked what the symptoms mean to them all).

Bringing together the family in this way and disclosing their whole plight often enables the usual family therapy techniques to be particularly effective in producing positive change. (Commonly, the passive father - without whose presence the meeting will not go on - may be given, or may regain, some traditional masculine authority, or pairing between the adolescent and parent of the opposite sex may be interpreted). In such ways, the family may gain some useful understanding or may change in such a way as to enable them to *cope* with the crisis while continuing to work with the referrer. A bed remains free.

On the other hand, if members of the family use phrases like "we cannot bear it any longer", "I am not prepared to put up with in any more", "I need a break", "I cannot cope", then this is accepted as an understandable reason for admission. And if both parents are in agreement, then a second meeting, at the Unit, is offered.

Fourth stage: Admission meeting

Before the second meeting, the client group is shown around the building and then given a few minutes alone to discuss things together. They are then joined by the Unit team and the situation is explored again, the staff aiming to ensure that all aspects of the present situation are discussed before the decision, which must be taken by those adults holding legal parental authority, is made. Again, some families may decide at this stage that they can now cope, so the reason for admission disappears.

Fifth stage: Admission

If the reason remains, further aspects of the present situation may be discussed with the family before the final decision is made. The Unit's insistence that those holding *legal parental authority* must make the decision, means that if both parents are in the family then they *both* have to support each other before the Unit will accept the decision. The Unit also insists that the reason is in language which can be understood by all at the meeting.

A verbal agreement is then made which includes the following:-

The reason for admission.

On whose authority the admission was made.

The changes needed for discharge.

An agreement not to alter the arrangements except at another meeting, which may be called by any member of the present group.

An example of an admission agreement is - "Ian is being admitted here because his parents cannot cope with him at home. He will remain until things have changed, so that they can cope with him again; and none of us will change this agreement except at another meeting."

Sixth stage: In-patient Treatment

The family may then enter the period of "rest" advocated by Brandon, and the admission can be used, in Langsley's words, "to sort out what has been going on and to permit all participants to renew their energies so that the problems of living can be taken up again by the family and patient". Conflicts underlying the crisis or leading to it may be unearthed and taboo subjects disclosed, enabling change in the family dynamics to hasten the progress towards reunion. Within structured, confronting, and group oriented ward situations (11,12,13) knowledge of the crisis reason for admission enables the staff, and sometimes helps the patients, to discuss with a particular patient his or her part in *that* crisis or a *new* crisis within the unit. Such material is brought by nursing staff to regular review meetings with the adolescent and the family. These meetings also discuss the original reason for admission and enquire into how the family is coping without the adolescent - they become family therapy sessions with a clear cut and urgent focus. We find it essential to have a team of co-therapists, (if possible the original team), at these sessions to deal with the intensity and wealth of material and to make observations or interpretations necessary for therapeutic momentum to be maintained. These meetings may be attended by the referring professionals.

Sixth stage: *Discharge*

At one of these review meetings, the people in authority will decide that they can cope again, or express a willingness to do so when faced with staff anxieties about institutionalisation. Discharge is then arranged. The family may be reassured that the unit will readmit the adolescent should there be another crisis with which they cannot cope. Readmission may be 'booked' for an inevitable crisis - for example, a school holiday - and a sharing arrangement will start.

RESULTS

Data about the length of stay, the variety of patients admitted and how far the work supports Langsley's findings and justifies the Department of Health and Social Security's prediction that some admissions will be prevented, are presented elsewhere (12). In this paper the various degrees of involvement of the unit are illustrated by 5 clinical examples.

CASE HISTORIES

Case 1

A suicidally depressed 14 year old girl, whose mother had herself been treated for endogenous depression, was referred to a psychiatrist who felt that in-patient treatment would be more appropriate. The psychiatrist contacted the Unit but on hearing of the policy, he decided to see the girl and her family himself, in the knowledge that he could call on the Unit when *he* wanted it and that admission could be arranged if there were a "holding crisis".

The psychiatrist continued to treat the girl as an outpatient.

Case 2

The Unit team attended a case conference at a Social Services Department on a 15 year old West Indian girl, with no parent, who was the subject of a *Care Order.* She had frequently become infected with V. D. and so was unacceptable at the hostel where a place had been found for her - but was no trouble in the single room of a reception centre. The Unit was encouraged to admit her on the grounds of her high intelligence and ability to make relationships. Instead they offered an alternative plan. They proposed that she should be given a date for going to the hostel and should go on that date if she was infection free. If the hostel could in the future no longer cope with her then she should be returned to the reception centre forthwith until she was again infection free and the hostel could cope. But if neither the hostel nor the reception centre was able to cope with her then the Unit could be contacted and would admit her until one of them would take her back.

Dissatisfaction was expressed by some of the professionals at this plan. It was clearly felt that the Unit was depriving this girl, who was in need of its therapeutic skills. It was pointed out by the Unit team that if they had accepted her for treatment, and behaved similarly in other cases, then their beds would be full and no offer of a "safety net" could be made to Social Services Departments. In fact, the girl spent a year at the hostel, without a break, and then started work.

Case 3

At a clinical interview, a psychiatrist had diagnosed as acutely schizophrenic a 14 year old girl who had become withdrawn, behaved bizarrely at school, and expressed ideas of persecution. He prescribed chlorpromazine and arranged to see her again in two weeks' time. Hearing from the general practitioner that an emergency had arisen he suggested in-patient treatment. The family meeting was attended by the girl, her 17 year old twin bothers, her parents, their general practitioner, a nurse and psychiatrist from the Unit.

At the meeting the staff confronted the mother with the irrelevances she was talking and one of the sons confronted the father with his violent threats towards his sister. There was a discussion of the father's difficulty in supporting his menopausal wife as they both faced their daughter's emerging sexuality. After the girl's anxiety that the doctors would decide to put her in a hospital was interpreted, and it was stated that any such decision must be her parents', she spoke. She said that she *had* felt peculiar and did feel that people were getting at her. She added that she did not like wearing her mother's clothes and made it quite plain that the parental anxiety, that she was pregnant or on drugs, was unfounded. This fear had been verbalised, for the first time, at the meeting.

The parents could cope, so did not ask for admission. But a second meeting was fixed in a few weeks' time. At that meeting they reported that the daughter had got over her difficulties and was attending school.

The following year, the family general practitioner, who had been impressed by how much more he had learned about the family in one hour than in the ten previous years, wrote a "follow-up" letter to the Unit. He reported that the girl was attending school regularly, going to dances and social clubs every week.

But there was an extra "pay-off" in his letter. He added that he had started to see several family groups at his surgery and appeared to have helped them.

Case 4

A 13 year old girl, who was diagnosed by the referring psychiatrist as having anorexia nervosa, was seen at a Children's Home, together with her parents, the general practitioner to the Home, and the social worker from the Social Services Department. The staff of the Home had been measuring every ounce of water which the girl took - she took no solids - but still her weight went down. They were anxious that she would die. The parents, too, felt this anxiety terribly and, although they expressed a wish for her to be at home with them, said that they could not cope. The Unit team emphasised that, as they came from a medical unit, their anxiety about someone dying was less; they offered to have the girl stay with them until either the parents or the Children's Home staff were no longer too anxious to have her back.

After a few weeks in the Unit, when the family and the professional group were less anxious about her possible death, some of the conflicts were able to be explored. The girl's anxiety that only her sick and aged father was the concern of her mother was interpreted by the staff. The possibility of her returning home and the ability of the social worker to support the parents' authority to get her back to school (traunting had been the symptom which had led to the social worker being involved) was explored. The girl was discharged back to her parents, returned to school, and the social worker continued to work with them knowing that she could call on the Unit in a crisis.

Case 5

The mother of a chronically psychotic boy who had been admitted to the Unit a year before was able to ask for his readmission for three weeks so that she could go on her honeymoon.

DISCUSSION

Caplan, in his elaboration of crisis theory, suggested that the period of crisis, which lasts for 4 - 6 weeks, ends by the individual or family finding a "solution." This solution may be adaptive or maladaptive, but it becomes part of a repertoire for dealing with future crisis.

From Caplan's observations and from the theoretical approach suggested by Heard (14), it can be predicted that a family, which deals with a crisis by extruding an adolescent to a mental hospital, may be predisposed to do so again. This is supported by Langsley's findings. Since a family in crisis is likely both to change and to use outsiders to help them find solutions, intervention should occur before the crisis subsides. The Unit aims to offer the first meeting within a few days of referral and to fix the date of that meeting at the first telephone call.

Other suggestions of Caplan are followed in the Unit's policy to avoid historical data or memories, lest they distract from problem-solving, and make dependency, regression and long-term therapeutic commitment more likely.

In those cases where there is an obvious chronic "patient", the Unit's intervention may throw the family into a state of *unexpected* crisis. The frustration of the carers who make the referral may cause the family to face the hitherto avoided question of "Where will it all end?". Confronting the family in a meeting with the parents' own ageing and inability to protect the adolescent indefinitely, may precipitate a decision to admit because "We are not prepared to let things go on any more". A collusive bond between parent and child may be broken by mobilising parental authority.

For an Adolescent Unit, a high proportion of staff resources and staff time is involved in pre-admission work. Langsley's use of, on average, nearly six meetings, suggests that an even greater shift in this direction would be more effective. Unfortunately, the effects of such a shift, although in one way obviously therapeutic, might exacerbate some of the difficulties and disadvantages already present in this way of working.

The resultant low bed occupancy, essential if beds are to be available when referrers need them, may be disappointing for the staff and causes massive problems when attempting to justify an essentially *community* orientated service when the Unit's financers are responsible for *hospitals* and *hospital beds* within the National Health Service. Within a fee paying system of hospital administration such difficulties must be even greater. Professional referrers who have prepared a careful medical history as a reason for admission may be infuriated by the Unit's approach and use of the Balint overal diagnosis in offering admission if coping in the community breaks down, and, worse, leaving the decision to the parents. While the resolution of some conflicts in family meetings, resulting in no admission to hospital, may satisfy the therapeutic zeal of multi-disciplinary teams and may, we argue, be advantageous to the clients - to professional referrers the Unit may appear as unhelpful and "choosey" about whom it admits.

Staff find frustration in not being involved in long-term care and may be anxious about the premature discharge of patients upon the parents' initiative. The Unit's approach has sometimes been seen as rigid, uncaring, unsympathetic, depriving and irresponsible.

Any greater therapeutic efficiency must go hand in hand with greater administrative skills in dealing with these problems.

CONCLUSION

We have concluded that the expensive and dangerous resource of a hospital based Adolescent Unit can be justified only if:-

i) the resources of the Unit are also available to help other professionals who deal with disturbed adolescents.

ii) the professional resources of the Unit (psychiatrist, psychiatric nurse, social worker) are thrown into the pre-admission work, when the family or institution is in a state of crisis.

iii) the difference between out-patient and in-patient treatment is seen in terms of coping and non-coping, so that admission occurs *only* in those cases when the family or other community resources cannot cope.

REFERENCES

1. Caplan, G. *Principles of Preventive Psychiatry.* Tavistock Publications, London, (1964).
2. Langsley, G. and Kaplan, D. M. *The Treatment of Families in Crisis.* Grune and Stratton, New York, (1968).
3. Barton, R. *Institutional Neurosis.* J. Wright, Bristol, (1961).
4. Goffman, E. *Asylum* Doubleday Anchor Books, New York, (1961).
5. Wing, J. K. *Brit. J. Soc. Clin. Psychol.* *1,* 38, (1962).
6. Hansell, N. *Arch. Gen. Psychiat.* *17,* 204, (1967).
7. Brandon, G. *Brit. J. Psychiat.* *117,* 627, (1970).
8. Jones, M. and Polak, P. *Brit. J. Psychiat.* *114,* 169, (1968).
9. Milner, M. *The Hands of the Living God.* Hogarth Press, London, (1969).
10. Balint, M. *Lancet, 1.* 1177, (1965).
11. Benson, S. "Brian - a boy of our times". *Nurs. Mirror* (1973).
12. Bruggen, P., Byng-Hall, J. and Pitt-Aikens, T. *Brit. J. Psychiat.* *122,* (1973).
13. Raven, F. "Admission and Discharge in an Adolescent Unit. *Soc. Work Today,* (1973).
14. Heard, O. H. *J. Child. Psychol. Psychiat.* *15,* 111, (1974).

MENTAL HEALTH IN CHILDREN, Volume III
Edited by D. V. Siva Sankar

PJD Publications Ltd., Westbury, N. Y.

DEMOGRAPHIC STUDIES IN CHILD PSYCHIATRY II-GENERAL DATA FROM SECOND STUDY

Robert Chuda and D. V. Siva Sankar

Queens Children's Psychiatric Center
Bellerose, New York, N. Y. 11426

ABSTRACT: Previous studies (Sankar, 1969) on many demographic characteristics of child patients admitted to the Children's Unit of the Creedmoor State Hospital from 1957 through 1967, have been published. The present paper studies the demographic characteristics of the present day (from October 1971 through January 1976) patients of the same institution which has become the Queens Child Psychiatric Center effective about 1969. Between 1967 and 1971, the aims and goals of Psychiatry have changed. The present paper reports only on the present situation.

As before, there is a significantly larger proportion of Black children than is warranted by the regional population. One important finding in this study is that the patient population is not as young at admission as before. Further, children from large families are over represented significantly both in the over-all population of the patients and also in terms of length of stay in the hospital. The male child patient is admitted at a younger age than the female, even though neither is admitted at statistically as young an age as in the previous study. More detailed comparative aspects of these two demographic studies will be reported elsewhere.

INTRODUCTION: In any overview of the theories and practical considerations of mental illness, a study of the demographic patterns is of crucial importance (Vance, 1952). Such studies were the basis of our observation (Sankar, 1969) of the deeper involvement of biological factors in the Caucasian children

---

The authors wish to thank Gloria Faretra M. D. for her interest and support in this work.

and of deeper involvement of sociological mechanisms in the psychiatric hospitalization of Black children. This was further elaborated into a "Theory of Multithemic Etiology of Mental Disease" and of "Comprehensive Profile Based Therapy" by Sankar (see volume 1 of this series).

Research relating month of birth and intelligence reports a higher IQ among summer and autumn births (Orme, 1962). Orme was so impressed with his findings that he suggested further research to identify the cause of this phenomenon. His research was supported by Jacobs and Alper (1970) who found that month of birth and IQ effects were supported in areas where the seasons vary in climate. This is in contrast to an earlier study which found that month, season, and period of birth have no relationship with IQ (Lewinsky, 1954).

Studies on intelligence and prognosis in mental deficiency have found that the more intelligent patients show less favorable sensitivity to treatment (Lab, 1960). Hotyat (1954) found that, in a hospital setting, patients with an IQ less than 80 had fewer hospital related problems than those patients with an IQ higher than 80. He hypothesized that the efforts of the high IQ patients to cope with life in the institution led to more frustration than their low IQ counterparts. However, other studies have demonstraed that child schizophrenics with a low IQ are more often discharged unimproved than patients with a higher IQ (Pollack, 1960).

Birth order has long been a topic of concern for demographers. Phillips (1956) found that firstborn children are more likely to have mental health problems than their later born siblings. Cohen (1951) found the second born child to be superior to the first in all asspects that he considered. Sundararaj and Sridhara (1966) also concluded that the early born siblings are more affected by mental health problems than their later born siblings. In contrast to these findings, Schooler (1964) found more later born schizophrenics in his sample than earlier born. Langlois (1972) confirmed this for males, but found no significant effects of birth order for females. A detailed demographic account of child psychiatry in India was given by Sethi and Lal in Volume I of this series. Granville-Grossman (1966) found that both female and male last borns and later borns were over represented in the mental health population he examined. Lilienfeld and Pasamanick (1956) found that in general, there was an increase in mental deficiency with an increase in birth order, and this was again confirmed by Hare and Price (1970), who found that the later birth ranks were significantly over represented in a population of schizophrenics. Hinshelwood (1972) further concluded that studies could not be counted on to retain their validity in cross-cultural applications.

Erlenmeyer *et al.*, (1969), Clum and Clum (1970), Birtchnell (1971), and Birtchnell (1972) concluded that birth order is not a factor in schizophrenia or in mental illness in general. Birtchnell attributed previous findings of a birth order effect to experimental error on the part of previous investigators in that they did not correct for seasonal variations in the number of births and the size of family increases. Glass *et al.*(1963) offered a possible explanation for these contradictory findings by pointing out that birth order is more an ecological variable than a psychological one.

Along with birth order, family size has been examined for effect on mental illness. Prakash and Srivastrava (1963) found that children in families of four or fewer are better adjusted psychologically than children from larger families. Four or more in a family result in the later born being more represented in their population of schizophrenics. Biles (1971) also found that large families have a greater number of delinquents and children who exhibit aberrant behavior. However, Kennet and Cropley (1970) found no relation between family size and intelligence.

Length of hospitilization and factors which mediate increased length of stay have also been of interest. Hamlin and Ward (1973) found that short-term gains in WISC-IQ was a better predictor of length of hospitalization than symptom improvement. Cheadle and Morgan (1972) made an interesting relationship between low IQ and long hospitalization because of lack of understanding of common English. The patients in their sample understood only 63 percent of the verbal information the hospital staff tried to tell them. In partial support of this, though not relating to verbal behavior, is a study by Garcia (1960) who stated that the degree of mental impairment is strongly related to length of hospitalization. Finally, Dudly *et al.* (1973) in an attempt to produce a regression equation relating demographic variables and length of stay, found that deviation from their regression analysis was a valid indicator of degree of acute functional impairment.

Greenwald (1971) in his discussion of the schizophrenic's family, stressed that demographic characteristics should not be ignored in establishing a total picture of the patient. Discussions of mental disorder have increasingly lent importance to the part played by social and cultural variables and their effects on mental disorders. The most important determinants of mental disorder may be discovered by proper analysis of these variables, either by demographic or other means (Hunt, 1959). Psychological reports (Delph, 1956) can only benefit the patient, if they clearly provide information useful in determining factors pertinent to his situation. Mental health and community demography studies are a good check on the mental health system (Lin, 1969).

Hare (1971) found that births in the early months of the year were over-represented in a population of hospitalized schizophrenics. Barker (1966) found an excess of subnormals in intelligence born in the month of May that he could not attribute to seasonal variations in amounts of births for each month. Sankar (1969) working on a large patient sample at the Children's Psychiatric Unit located in Creedmoor Hospital identified a high percentage of births in the months of March and April. It was hypothesized that the fetus conceived in the summer months may have an increased amount of neurological damage resulting from inner city heat spells early in the gestation period. In contrast to these studies, Pile (1951) found that previous studies which identified winter and early month of the year births to schizophrenia (dementia praecox) could not be substantiated by his sample, which had an even distribution of month of birth. As an item of interest, at the time he did his study, separate institutions existed for blacks (which he refered to as colored) and white patients. He also found no difference in month of birth distribution across races. Dalen (1974) further states that if the sample considered is large enough, seasonal variations disappear.

Hunt (1959) found mental deficiency more frequent among negroes, especially when they formed a minority within their respective residential locals. Schizophrenia was reported to be more common in the lower classes in general. Spalt (1975) found that in contrast to schizophrenia, race and sex were not related to affective disorders, while Hunt, in the previously mentioned study, found many more male mental defectives in general than female.

Studies on the relationship of religion to mental disorders tend to lean towards the philosophical aspects, and will not be discussed in detail. Hirshberg (1956) summed up the research well in stating that religion can only aid a child's development if they both grow up together.

Significant correlations with social status have been identified for the prevalence of mental illness (the number ill in a group), the type of disorder, and the type of therapy received (Redlich *et al.*, 1953). This related to race variables in that at the time of the study, social status correlated very well with race. This raised the question of differential diagnosis across races. Klein (1952) stated that childhood schizophrenia may closely resemble severe mental deficiency. In the early 1950's, psychiatrists were predominently white, and the question is raised if the findings of Redlich were affected by this. A more recent study finds that although the number of mentally ill patients has an over representation of minorities, the diagnoses are equal across races. Bender and Grugett (1956) concluded that in examining their sample, heredity and endogenous factors relate heavily with childhood schizophrenia, while the neuroses often result from distorted relationships and severe affectional deprivation. Sankar (1969) concluded that blacks may exhibit a larger amount of sociopathology.

Studies on the demography of intelligence have shown that IQ may correlate with life experiences (Richards, 1951), while Harris (1952) stated that although general life experiences do indeed affect intelligence, it cannot be taken for granted that traumatic experiences will adversely affect IQ. Heber (1956) found that children who deviate in IQ scores also deviate in social status in the the same direction. Relating this with mental health, Maloney and Steger (1972) stated that the problems of patients in urban clinics are more dependent on low IQ than mental health problems, and they suggested that special programs be developed to compensate for this. Johnson (1952) found that male patients had a higher IQ than the female patients (see also Sankar, 1969), and this was contested by Finley and Thompson (1959), who found that there was no sex difference in the IQ of their sample of mental defectives. Relating IQ to diagnosis, Binder (1956) could not support the hypothesis that a differential impairment of intelligence correlated with schizophrenia.

MATERIALS AND METHODS:

One thousand one hundred and four cases of first admissions to the Queens Child Psychiatric Center between October 1971 and January 1976 were the subjects for the investigation. Case histories were obtained from the medical records. This information was keypunched on IBM 029 keypunch onto 80 column IBM computer cards. Variables like length of stay, age at admission etc were computed. The diagnostic categories used followed those of the APA and are shown in Table I. In cases where more than one diagnosis was offered, the more consistent one was used.

The final analysis consisted of one way frequency distributions, cross tabulations, breakdowns etc., contained in the SPSS (Statistical Package for the Social Sciences) procedure routines available on-line in the Fordham University Computing center. All analyses were performed on an IBM 370/125 computer, executed in a 180K partition.

It should be noted that every variable was not available in every case. In such instances, the method of analysis used was pair-wise deletion in the computation of all test statistics. This is the default option in the SPSS procedure routines. The number of cases available in each case is shown in the Tables. It was assumed (perhaps incorrectly) that the missing of the data occurred by chance.

RESULTS AND DISCUSSION:

The distribution of the month of birth in the patient population was more or less consistent except for a few months, especially January and August. In Sankar's 1969 study, more births were found in the late winter months (March and early April) and in August. This study does not indicate high births in the winter season except in January. The differences may be due to variability of either set of studies or equally due to the fact that the age of admission of the present population is much higher than that was found in the earlier study. In other words, the difference in the results from the two studies may be due to the different type of proportionate involvement of biological

TABLE I

Categorized DSM II Diagnoses Used in Analyses

Diagnostic Classification	Diagnostic Group
310 through 315	Mental Retardation
290 through 294	OBS-Psychotic
309	OBS-Nonpsychotic
295	Schizophrenic
296 through 298	Other Psychotic
300	Psychotic
301 through 304	Personality Disorder
305	Physiological Psychotic
306	Special Symptoms
307	Transient Situanl. Disturbances
308	Behavior Disorder
316 through 318	Other, Non-Classifiable, etc.

TABLE II

Distribution of Month of Birth

Month	Birth Frequency (As % of Total)
January	10.0
February	7.5
March	8.3
April	8.6
May	7.4
June	8.5
July	7.6
August	9.5
September	8.9
October	7.8
November	6.8
December	9.1

Total No. of Subjects = 1,076

TABLE III

Distribution of Diagnotic Categories

DSM-IIDaignosis	Percentage
Mental Retardation	6.0
OBS-Psychotic	10.9
OBS-Nonpsychotic	
OBS-Nonpsychotic	7.7
Schizophrenic	47.0
Other Psychotic	1.2
Neurotic	0.8
Personality Disorder	2.8
Special Symptoms	0.1
Transient Situnl. Disturbances	5.1
Behavior Disorders	18.1
Other	0.2

Total No. of Subjects = 972

TABLE IV

Relationship of WISC IQ and Diagnosis

Diagnostic Category	Mean I. Q.
Mental Retardation	54.5
OBS-Psychotic	72.9
OBS-Nonpsychotic	78.3
Schizophrenia	81.2
Other Psychotic	84.0
Neurotic	87.7
Personality Disorder	81.7
Transient Situnl. Disturbances	90.1
Behavior Disorders	84.4

Total No. of Subjects = 460

and sociopathological factors in the pathological process of the two sets of patients.

As before, black children and children of Latin descent are over represented among the patients than in the general regional population of Queens. As before, this may be due to

TABLE V

Relationship of Diagnosis to Length of Hospitalization

Diagnosis	Mean Length of Stay (in days)
Mental Retardation	260.4
OBS-Psychotic	243.4
OBS-Nonpsychotic	297.4
Schizophrenic	227.5
Other Psychotic	167.0
Neurotic	133.6
Personality Disorder	109.6
Transient Situanl. Disturbance	153.9
Behavior Disorders	184.0

Total No. of Subjects = 725

TABLE VI

Expected (Queens County, NYC) and Observed Percentages of Family Size

Family Size No. of Siblings	Expected % In Queens, 1973	Observed % Hospital Patients
1	33	8.1
2	31	15.4
3	18	17.5
4	9	13.5
5 or More	9	45.6

No. of Hospital Subjects = 440

the less advantageous medical and mental health that the less affluent classes enjoy in any given culture. The same kind of observation may be extended to the fact that the blacks and Latin children stay longer in the Institutions. The median Length of Stay (*LS-50*) of these children is another clear illustration of this point.

However, the differences in the length of stay of the children of the different ethnic origins is not as pronounced in the present study as it was in the previous. Similarly, males

TABLE VII

Relationship of Family Size to Mean Length of Hospital Stay

No. of Siblings in Family	Mean Length in Days of Stay in Hospital
1	189.3
2	169.2
3	181.3
4	215.9
5	206.3
6	237.3
7	326.7
8	266.2
9 or More	267.3

Figure 1. Gaussian Distribution of the WISC IQ's of the Hospital Patients. The mean is shifted down about 16 IQ points from a normal population. Total number of subjects is 460.

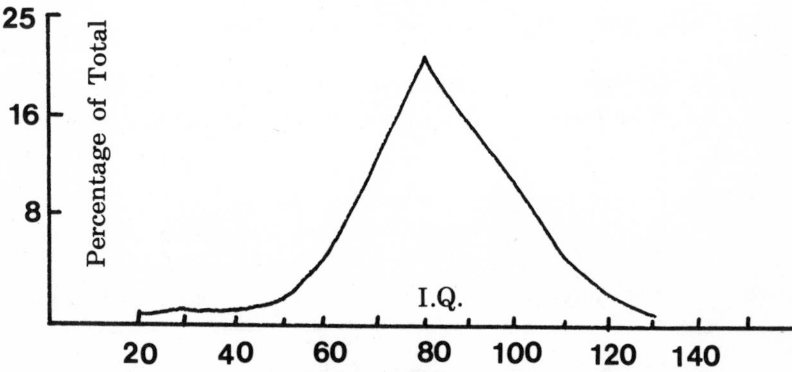

stayed an average of 222.9 days while the female child patients stayed almost the same mean length. The mean for the females was 222.8 days. As in our previous study, and that of many others, the males are more predominant in the patient population. In this study, the ratio of males to females is 68.8% to 31.2%.

The various religious groups were represented as follows: Catholics *20.6%*; Protestants *20.8%*; Jewish *2.5%* and no information of this nature was available on the remaining

Figure 2. Expected (from NYC Records) and Observed Race Distribution in the Hospitalized Children.

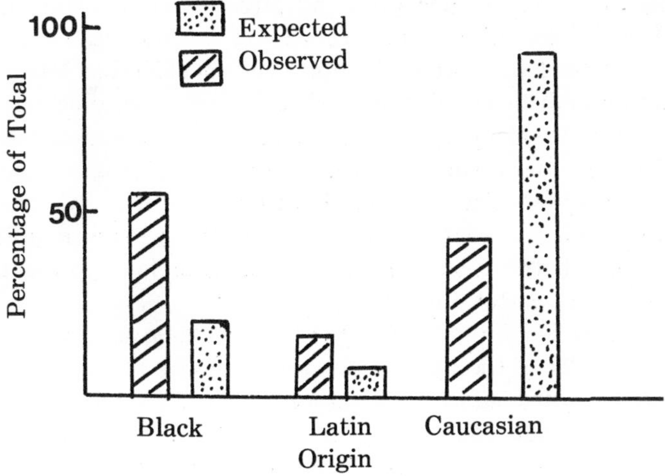

Figure 3. Distribution (as % of total subgroups) of patients with respect to length of stay in the hospital in years.

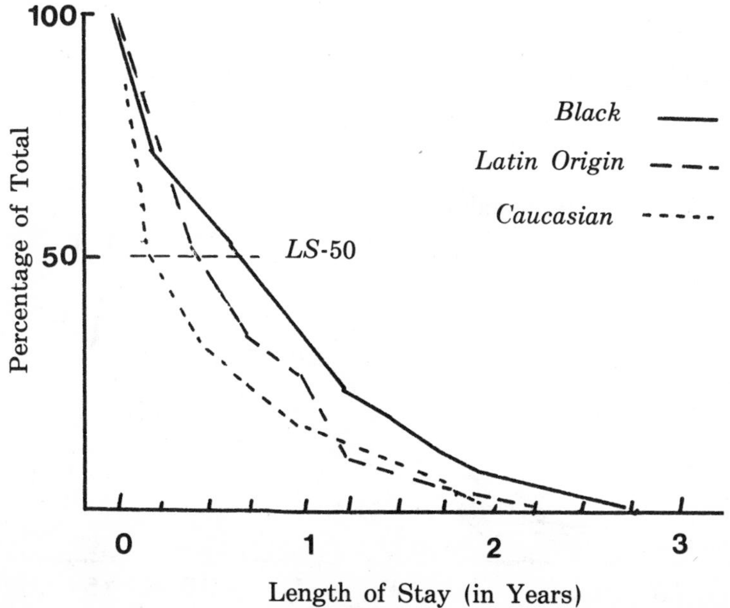

56.1% of the patients. No further studies on this aspect were undertaken at this time.

The variation of the diagnostic categories with relation to prevalence of diagnosis, IQ and Mean Length of Stay in the Hospital are presented in Tables III, IV and V.

The I.Q. of the patients is of considerable interest as our unpublished studies show that of all demographic variables involved, *I.Q.*, *Age at Admission* and *Sex* are the most relevant variables that seem to determine the average length of stay in the Hospital. The Gaussian distribution of the I.Q. in these subjects is shifted down by about 16 points, as shown in Figure 3. This distribution is based on the data for approximately 46.3% of the total cases.

While no significant differences could be attributed to the birth order of the patient, the total number of siblings in the family turned out to be a significant factor. The results in Table VI show that, compared to the local Queens family size, the families that these children came from, are much larger in size.

Figure 4. Relationship of Age at Admission and Sex of the Patient. The X-axis represents the distribution, as percentage, of the sex group. The Y-axis represents the Age of the patient at Admission.

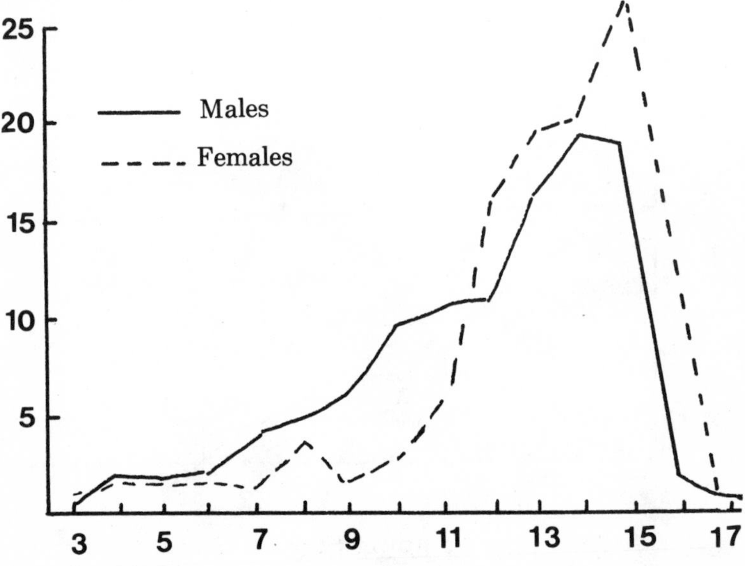

While only 9% of the local families contain five or more siblings 45.6% of the families of the children contain 5 or more siblings.

Similarly, the data in Table VII show that the larger the size of the family (up to about 7 siblings), the longer is the mean length of stay in the hospital.

One salient difference between this study and the last study is in the age of admissions. The average patient is admitted much later in this study. However, the age of admission of the males is still significantly lower than that of the female patients, as shown in Figure 4. The sharp decline at age 15½ is due to the cut off point in admissions into the Child Psychiatric Center.

References

Barry, Herbert, Jr.: *J. Nerv. Ment. Dis. 124,* 208 (1956).

Bender, L. and Grugett, Alvin E., Jr.: *Amer. J. Orthopsychiatry 26,* 131 (1956).

Bespal'ko, I.G.:*Zn. Nerv. Psychiat. 70,* 1837 (1970).

Biles, D.: *Aust. Psychologist 6,* 189 (1971).

Binder, Arnold: *J. Abnorm. Soc. Psychol. 52,* 11 (1956).

Birtchnell, John: *Nature 234,* 485 (1971).

Birtchnell, John: *Soc. Psychiat. 7,* 167 (1972).

Cheadle, J. and Morgan, R.: *Brit. J. Psychiat. 120,* 553 (1972).

Cleland, Charles C. and Phillips, B.N.: *Revista Interamer. psicol. 2,* 121 (1968).

Clum, G.A. and Clum, M. Judith: *J. Clin. Psychol. 26,* 271 (1970).

Cohen, F.: *Ind. J. Psychol. 26,* 79 (1951).

Dalen, Per: *Season of Birth in Schizophrenia and Other Mental Disorders.* Goteborg, Sweden (1974).

Delph, Harold A.: *Training Sch. Bull. 52,* 231 (1956).

Dudley, Harold K., Mason, Mark, and Rhoton, Gene: *J. Clin. Psychol. 29,* 197 (1973).

Erlenmeyer-Kimling, L, Van Dan Bosch, Elyse, and Denham, Bruch: *Brit. J. Psychiat. 115,* 659 (1969).

Farina, A., Barry, Herbert III, and Garmezy, Norman: *Arch. Gen. Psychol. 9,* 224 (1963).

Finley, Carmen and Thompson, Jack: *Calif. J. Educ. Res. 10,* 167 (1959).

Garcia de Onubia, Luis F. and Demselle de Maci, L.: *Acta Neuropsy. Argentina 6,* 458 (1960).

Glass, David C. Horwitz, Murray, Firestone, Ira and Grinker, J.: *J. Abnorm. Psychol. 66,* 192 (1963).

Golightly, Carole: *J. Consult. Clin. Psychol. 38,* 145 (1972).

Gorwitz, Kurt: *Health Serv. Rep. 89*, 186 (1974).

Granville-Grossman, K.L.: *Brit. J. Psychiat. 112*, 1119 (1966).

Greenwald, Shayna R.: *Comp. Psychiat. 12*, 423 (1971).

Hamlin, Roy M. and Ward, William D.: *J. Abnorm. Psychol. 8*, 11 (1973).

Hare, E.: *Vestnik Akad. Med. Naak SSSR 26*, 39 (1971).

Hare, E.H. and Price, J.S.: *Brit. J. Psychiat. 116*, 409 (1970).

Harris, Dale B.: In *Progress in Clinical Psychology*. Volume I. Edited by Bower, D. and Abt, L.E. Grune and Stratton, New York. pps. 26-45 (1956).

Havassey de Avila, Barbara: *Can. Psychol. 12*, 282 (1971).

Heber, Rick F.: *J. Educ. Psychol. 47*, 158 (1956).

Hinshelwood, R.D.: *Brit. J. Soc. Psychiat. Comm. Health 6*, 90 (1972).

Hirshberg, J. Cotter: *Menninger Quart. 10*, 22 (1956).

Holme, Richard: *Abnormal Psychology: Current Perspectives*. CRM Books. California (1972).

Hotyat, F.: *Enfance 1*, 131 (1954).

Hunt, Raymond g.: *Behav. Sci. 4*, 96 (1959).

Jacobs, John F. and Alper, Arthur E.: *Ment. Retard. 8*, 12 (1970).

Johnson, Elizabeth Z.: *J. Clin. Psychol. 8*, 298 (1952).

Kennet, K.F. and Cropley, A.J.: *J. Biosoc. Sci. 2*, 227 (1970).

Klein, Irwin Jay: *Nerv. Child 10*, 135 (1952).

Kramer, Morton: *Applications of Mental Health Statistics; Uses in Mental Health Programs of Statistics Derrived from Psychiatic Services and Selected Vital and Morbidity Records*. World Health Organization. Geneva, Switzerland (1969).

Lab. P.: *Encephale 49*, 544 (1960).

Langlois, Joseph E.: *Psychology 9*, 37 (1972).

Lewinsky, Robert J.: *J. Genet. Psychol. 55*, 281 (1954).

Lilienfeld, A.M. and Pasamanick, B.: *Amer. J. Ment. Defic. 60*, 557 (1956).

Lin, Tsung-yi: *J. Psychiat. Nurs. Ment. Health Serv. 1*, 42 (1969).

Maloney, Michael, P. and Steger, Herbert G.: *J. Consult. Clin. Psychol. 38*, 299 (1972).

Mason, Charles F.: *Dissertation Abstracts 15*, 2296 (1955).

Mendenhall, W. and Ramey, M.: *Statistics for Psychology*. Duxbury Press. Massachusetts (1973).

National Institute of Mental Health: *Mental Health Demographic Profile System Description.* DHEW Publication No. (ADM) 76-263. Superintendent of Documents, US Government Printing Office, Washington, D.C. (1975).

Nesbit, John D.: *Eugenics Rev. 49,* 201 (1958).

Nie, Norman H., Hull, C. Hadlai, Jenkins, Jean G., Steinbrenner, Karen, and Bent, Dale H.: *SPSS: Statistical Package for the Social Sciences.* Second edition. Mc Graw-Hill. New York (1975).

Nuttal, Ronald L. and Solomon, Leonard F.: *Behav. Sci. 15,* 255 (1970).

Orme, J.E.: *Brit. J. Med. Psychol. 35,* 233 (1962).

Peters, William S.: *Soc. Forces 35,* 62 (1956).

Phillips, E. Lakin: *J. Clin. Psychol. 12,* 400 (1956).

Pile, Wendel J.: *Va. Med. Mon. 78,* 438 (1951).

Pollack, Max: *Arch. Gen. Psychiat. 2,* 652 (1960).

Prakash, J. and Srivastava, P.K.: *Manas. 10,* 83 (1963).

Redlich, F.C., Hollingshead, A.B., Roberts, B.H., Robinson, H.A., Freedman, L.Z. and Meyers, J.K.: *Amer. J. Psychiat. 109,* 729 (1953).

Richards, T.W.: *Child Devel. 22,* 221 (1951).

Riess, Bernard F. and Safer, Jeanne: *J. Psychol. 85,* 61 (1973).

Rose, A. and Stub, H.R.: *Mental Health and Mental Disorder.* Norton. New York. pps. 87-103 (1955).

Sankar, D.V. Siva: In *Schizophrenia: Current Concepts and Research.* PJD Publications. New York. pps. 450-469 (1969).

Schooler, Carmi: *J. Abnorm. Soc. Psychol. 69,* 574 (1964).

Shinagawa, Fujiro: *Jap. J. Child Psychiat. 1,* 403 (1960).

Spalt, Lee: *Dis. Nerv. Sys. 36,* 209 (1975).

Stone, Leroy A. and Chambers, A., Jr.: *Psychology 2,* 27 (1965).

Sundararaj, J. and Sridhara Rana Rao, B.S.: *Brit. J. Psychiat. 112,* 1127 (1966).

U.S. Bureau of the Census. *Congressional District Data Book.* 93rd Congress. U.S. Government Printing Office. Washington, D.C. (1973).

U.S. Bureau of the Census. *Pocket Data Book: 1973.* U.S. Government Printing Office. Washington, D.C. (1973).

Vance, Ruppert B.: *Soc. Forces 31,* 9 (1952).

Subject Index